CAMBRIDGE STUDIES
IN ENGLISH LEGAL HISTORY

Edited by
D. E. C. YALE
Fellow of Christ's College
and Reader in English Legal History at the University of Cambridge

THE PUBLISHER WISHES TO THANK
THE ISOBEL THORNLEY BEQUEST FUND
THE MANAGERS OF THE MAITLAND MEMORIAL FUND AND
THE PUBLICATIONS FUND OF THE UNIVERSITY OF BIRMINGHAM
FOR THEIR GENEROUS SUBVENTIONS IN SUPPORT OF
THE PUBLICATION OF THIS BOOK

THE COMMON LAWYERS OF PRE-REFORMATION ENGLAND

THOMAS KEBELL: A CASE STUDY

BY

E. W. IVES

Senior Lecturer in Modern History in the University of Birmingham

CAMBRIDGE UNIVERSITY PRESS

CAMBRIDGE

LONDON NEW YORK NEW ROCHELLE

MELBOURNE SYDNEY

Published by the Press Syndicate of the University of Cambridge
The Pitt Building, Trumpington Street, Cambridge CB2 1RP
32 East 57th Street, New York, NY 10022, USA
296 Beaconsfield Parade, Middle Park, Melbourne 3206, Australia

First published 1983

Printed in Great Britain at
The University Printing House, Cambridge

Library of Congress catalogue card number: 82–1297

British Library Cataloguing in Publication Data

Ives, E.W.
The common lawyers of pre-Reformation
England: Thomas Kebell: a case study. –
(Cambridge studies in English legal history)
1. Kebell, Thomas 2. Lawyers – England – History
I. Title
344.2'0092'4 KD621.K/

ISBN 0 521 24011 5

CONTENTS

FIGURES AND TABLES

PREFACE

'Divinity, Law and Physick' are, in Joseph Addison's words, 'the three great Professions'. In this century, historians of England have paid much attention to the first but little by comparison to the second. We still have no history of the bar. The only comprehensive study of the judiciary is essentially biographical in interest and is well over a century old. We are still at the stage of exploration where we link a few charted features with plausible but unsurveyed invention. 'Here be dragons!'

This neglect is not explained by uncertainty about the common law as a profession. Defined either in terms of status and public esteem or in terms of professional structure and institutions, a legal profession has existed in England from at least the fourteenth century. Nor is there doubt about the importance and influence, perhaps baleful influence, of lawyers. What has held back research has been the nature of the subject – its diffuse documentation, the lack of basic groundwork, the need to wait upon related studies (especially in legal administration), the complexities of litigation and legal work. For the earlier centuries, too, there is the even greater problem of definition. When a cleric or a doctor acts professionally, his action is self-evident. A lawyer, once away from the identifiable contexts of the court-room and the conveyancing desk, may do what is indistinguishable from the help of a friend, an employee or a member of a client's family. Is the lawyer here no longer acting professionally, or are these competitors, in a sense, legal advisers? And if the answer is that legal practice is defined as the work of the legally qualified, who in the days before Edward Coke were the legally qualified?

Another deterrent at work, at least over the last twenty-five years, has been fashion. To study the legal profession is to study an elite, and elites are not in vogue. Here is neither the history of the common man, nor the study of class, nor the opportunity for large-scale statistical analysis. But in England, to the Civil War and beyond, the elite group did matter. As the fear and hatred of lawyers expressed by peasants and artisans and the reliance of the Commons on its lawyer-members demonstrate equally, contemporaries, widely separated, agreed in seeing the legal profession as a true catalyst, both of immediate events and of longer-term developments.

The purpose of this book is to go some way to remedying this neglect for the later fifteenth and earlier sixteenth centuries, the period from roughly the nadir of English government in the 1450s to the 1530s, the crisis decade of the Reformation. It covers the years when the first form of the common-law profession reached its peak of development and influence, before the rise of the barristers, law officers and king's counsel, and the drift of the serjeants-at-law ever further into a professional backwater. The first four chapters examine the role, social origins and the professional dimension of the common lawyers; Part II explores legal practice; the subject of the next section is the relation between the lawyers, society and the law, and the topic of the final chapters is the profession in society. The book thus sets out to bring within one compass social history and legal history, educational history and economic history, the courts, clients, the crown and the lawyers themselves.

This approach is open to the criticism that it is neither completely social history nor completely legal history. This is deliberate. No doubt a narrowly social study would have been able to examine a larger sample of the profession than the leaders of the Westminster bar who are the principal concern here – though there is little to suggest that the sources would have been adequate, or the chance great of reaching different or more sophisticated conclusions. Exclusive concern with legal development in the period would, in the same way, have had value, though this is a path I am not qualified to pursue in detail. But the design of this book expresses the conviction that study of a group such as the lawyers has value only if the totality of its role is considered. It is an attempt to open up the law, and especially the year books, to the concerns and approaches of social history and, at the same time, to look at social history from the point of view of professional interests and legal developments, and only in an effort of this kind is there hope of advancing, not merely multiplying, knowledge.[1]

At an early stage it became clear that there was no possibility of

1. Translation from the year books is more idiomatic than would be expected in a legal text book, and as much of the legal technicality has been omitted as is consistent with intelligibility.

investigating even a small sample of lawyers to the depth required, partly for lack of time and space and partly because there is adequate and uniform evidence only for the most obvious and unrevealing areas of the subject. There is little profit in the ability to establish the precise proportion of lawyers who were J.P.s, or who sat on commissions of gaol delivery! The solution adopted was to study in particular detail the life and career of one man, Thomas Kebell, and to weave around him a more general examination of the profession as a whole, as far as the sources allow. Kebell, a serjeant-at-law who died in 1500, chose himself by the unique level of documentation which has survived for him, but he must throughout be seen as an example of, never as a figure to be distinguished from, his fellows.[2] And this method had an added, humane, advantage; it presents the group in the person of an individual, not as a sociological print-out.

In the course of the time this study has taken I have incurred many debts. The Publications Fund of the University of Birmingham, the Maitland Memorial Fund and the Isobel Thornley Bequest have given the generous financial support so necessary in these days of economic stringency. I am grateful to the Masters of the Bench of Lincoln's Inn, the President and Fellows of Magdalen College, Oxford, and Capt. V. M. Wombwell for permission to consult material owned by them, and I acknowledge the kindness of the Marquess of Ailesbury in allowing me to publish the text of Appendix B. To S. T. Bindoff I owed the encouragement to enter what was then little-explored territory, where I found S. E. Thorne a generous pioneer. To Dr C. C. Dyer I owe not only material from the diocese of Worcester but valuable criticism of the social and economic chapters. I gratefully acknowledge the help of Mr J. C. Sainty, who made available to me his findings on the fifteenth-century exchequer. Dr J. H. Baker kindly read the full manuscript, and it was fortunate that, in the final revision, I was able to use his magisterial introduction to Selden Society Volume 94. Another publication which enabled me to avoid late pitfalls was Dr Marjorie Blatcher's study of the court of king's bench which now stands alongside Dr Margaret Hastings' work on common pleas. Although I sometimes differ from these scholars, my debt to them is plain. Miss Helen Miller generously found the time to scrutinise the final text and Mr R. J. Knecht to discuss the project on numerous occasions. Among other historians who have readily

2. The form Kebell has been adopted rather than the modern Keble, as reflecting the overwhelming usage of the period, although the serjeant used the spelling Kebeel.

helped me over the years I must single out Miss Margaret Condon and Dr J. A. Guy, not least because they introduced me to material in the Public Record Office which I would otherwise never have found. And as well as those named, there are the colleagues, friends and pupils who have not been too bored to talk about Kebell, nor too discouraged over the years to continue to bring me ideas and information. And my debt to my most patient critic, sub-editor and campaigner against technicalities will be appreciated only by other historians and their wives.

Warwick E.W.I.
Summer, 1980

ABBREVIATIONS

Abbott, *Law Reporting* L. W. Abbott, *Law Reporting in England, 1485–1585* (1973)

Account Rolls of Durham *Extracts from the Account Rolls of the Abbey of Durham,* ed. J. T. Fowler, Surtees Soc. 99, 100, 103 (1898–1901)

Admission Book *The Records of the Honourable Society of Lincoln's Inn: Admissions*, ed. W. P. Baildon (1896)

Ayscough, *Archaeologia* 16 S. Lyons, 'Copies of three remarkable petitions to King Henry VI', in *Archaeologia* 16 (1812), 3–4

Baker, *Camb. Law. Journ.* 27 J. H. Baker, 'Counsellors and barristers', in *Camb. Law Journ.* 27 (1969), 205–29

Baker, *Journ. Legal Hist.* 1 J. H. Baker, 'The attorneys and officers of the common law', in *Journal of Legal History* 1 (1980), 182–203

Bateson, *Leicester* *Records of the Borough of Leicester, 1103–1603*, ed. M. Bateson (Cambridge, 1899–1905)

Bayne, *Council of Henry VII* *Select Cases in the Council of Henry VII*, ed. C. G. Bayne, Selden Soc. 75 for 1956 (1958)

Bean, *Decline of Feudalism* J. M. W. Bean, *The Decline of English Feudalism* (Manchester, 1968)

Becon, *Prayers* Thomas Becon, 'The Flower of Godly Prayers', in *Primer of Private Prayer* (1553), reprinted in *Prayers and Other Pieces of Thomas Becon*, ed. J. Ayre, Parker Soc. 12 (1844)

Bennett, *The Pastons* H. S. Bennett, *The Pastons and their England* (Cambridge, 1932)

Black Book Lincoln's Inn Mss., Black Book

Black Books *The Records of the Honourable Society of Lincoln's Inn: the Black Books*, ed. W. P. Baildon (1897–1902)

Bland, *Furnival's Inn* D. S. Bland, *Early Records of Furnival's Inn* (Newcastle-upon-Tyne, 1957)

Bland, *J.S.P.T.L.* 10 'Henry VIII's royal commission on the inns of court', ed. D. S. Bland, in *J.S.P.T.L.* 10 (1969), 178–94

Blatcher, *Court of King's Bench* Marjorie Blatcher, *The Court of King's Bench, 1450–1550: a Study in Self-Help* (1978)

Blatcher, in *Elizabethan Government and Society* Marjorie Blatcher, 'Touching the writ of latitat: an act "of no great moment" ', in *Elizabethan Government and Society*, ed. S. T. Bindoff et al. (1961)

Blatcher, 'Working of king's bench' Marjorie Blatcher, 'The working of the court of king's bench in the fifteenth century', unpublished Ph.D. thesis, University of London (1936)

Brant, *Ship of Fools* Sebastian Brant, *Ship of Fools*, trans. Alexander Barclay (1509)

Bridgwater Borough Archives *Bridgwater Borough Archives, 1200–1485*, ed. T. B. Dilks et al., Somerset Record Soc. 48, 53, 58, 60, 70 (1933–71)

Bristol Wills *Notes or Abstracts of the Wills Contained in the Great Orphans' Book and Book of Wills at Bristol (1381–1605)*, ed. T. P. Wadley, Bristol and Gloucestershire Arch. Soc. (1886)

Brodie, *Trans. Royal Hist. Soc.*, 4 ser., 15 D. M. Brodie, 'Edmund Dudley: minister of Henry VII', in *Trans. Royal Hist. Soc.*, 4 ser., 15 (1932), 133–61

Bryson, *Equity Side* W. H. Bryson, *The Equity Side of the Exchequer* (Cambridge, 1975)

Bull. Institute of Hist. Research *Bulletin of the Institute of Historical Research*

Bull. John Rylands Lib. *Bulletin of the John Rylands Library*

Burton, *Leicestershire* William Burton, *Description of Leicestershire* (1622)

Cal. Ancient Deeds *A Descriptive Catalogue of Ancient Deeds in the Public Record Office* (1890–1915)

Cal. Close Rolls *Calendar of the Close Rolls preserved in the Public Record Office, Henry VI to Henry VII* (1933–63)

Cal. Fine Rolls *Calendar of the Fine Rolls preserved in the Public Record Office* (1911–63)

Cal. inquisitions post mortem *Calendar of Inquisitions Post Mortem and other Analogous Documents preserved in the Public Record Office: Henry VII* (1898–1955)

Cal. Patent Rolls *Calendar of the Patent Rolls preserved in the Public Record Office* (1891, in progress)

Camb. Law Journ. *Cambridge Law Journal*

Carpenters' Company *Records of the Worshipful Company of Carpenters*, ed. Bower Marsh (1913–39)

Cavendish, *Wolsey* George Cavendish, *The Life and Death of Cardinal Wolsey*, ed. R. S. Sylvester, Early English Text Soc. (1959)

Chambers, *More* R. W. Chambers, *Thomas More* (1938)

Chrimes, *Constitutional Ideas* S. B. Chrimes, *English Constitutional Ideas in the Fifteenth Century* (Cambridge, 1936)

Chrimes, *Henry VII* S. B. Chrimes, *Henry VII* (1972)

Christ Church Letters *Christ Church Letters*, ed. J. B. Sheppard, Camden Soc., n.s., 19 (1877)

Condon, 'Ruling elites' M. Condon, 'Ruling elites in the reign of Henry VII', in *Patronage, Pedigree and Power*, ed. C. Ross (1979), 109–42

Constable, *Prerogativa Regis* Robert Constable, *Tertia Lectura on Prerogativa Regis*, ed. S. E. Thorne (New Haven, 1949)

Cooper, *Cambridge* C. H. Cooper, *Annals of Cambridge* (Cambridge, 1842–1908)

Corner, *Archaeologia* 39 G. R. Corner, 'Observations on four illuminations representing the courts', in *Archaeologia* 39 (1863), 357–72

Cornwall, *Econ. H. R.* J. Cornwall, 'The early Tudor gentry', in *Economic History Review*, 2 ser., 17 (1965), 456–71

Coventry Leet Book *The Coventry Leet Book or Mayor's Register, 1420–1555*, ed. M. D. Harris, Early English Text Soc. (1907–13)

Dudley, *Tree of Commonwealth* Edmund Dudley, *The Tree of Commonwealth*, ed. D. M. Brodie (Cambridge, 1948)

Dugdale, *Origines* William Dugdale, *Origines Juridiciales* (1680)

Dunham, 'Indentured retainers' W. H. Dunham, 'Lord Hastings' indentured retainers, 1461–83', in *Trans. Connecticut Academy of Arts and Sciences* 39 (1955), 1–175

E.H.R. *English Historical Review*

Eliot, *The Gouernour* Thomas Eliot, *The Boke named the Gouernour*, ed. H. H. S. Croft (1883)

Elton, *Studies* G. R. Elton, *Studies in Tudor and Stuart Politics and* Government (Cambridge, 1974)

Emden, *Biographical Register of Oxford to 1500* A. B. Emden, *Biographical Register of the University of Oxford to 1500* (Oxford, 1957–9)

Farnham, *Medieval Pedigrees* G. F. Farnham, *Leicestershire Medieval Pedigrees* (Leicester, 1925)

Farnham, *Quorndon Records* G. F. Farnham, *Quorndon Records* (Leicester, 1912)

Farnham, *Village Notes* G. F. Farnham, *Leicestershire Medieval Village Notes* (Leicester, 1929–33)

Finch, *Northamptonshire Families* M. E. Finch, *The Wealth of Five Northamptonshire Families, 1540–1640*, Northamptonshire Record Soc. 19 (1956)

Fisher, *J.S.P.T.L.* 14 R. M. Fisher, 'Thomas Cromwell, dissolution of the monasteries and the inns of court, 1534–40', in *J.S.P.T.L.* 14 (1976–7), 111–17

Fortescue, *De Laudibus* John Fortescue, *De Laudibus Legum Anglie*, ed. S. B. Chrimes (Cambridge, 1949)

Foss, *Judges* E. Foss, *The Judges of England, with Sketches of their Lives*, 9 vols. (1848–64)

Fountains Abbey *Memorials of the Abbey of St Mary of Fountains*, ed. J. R. Walbran et al., Surtees Soc. 42, 67, 130 (1863–1918)

G.E.C., *Peerage* *Complete Peerage*, ed. G. E. Cockayne, revised V. Gibbs (1910–49)

Grey of Ruthin Valor *The Grey of Ruthin Valor*, ed. R. I. Jack (Sydney, 1965)

Guy, *Cardinal's Court* J. A. Guy, *The Cardinal's Court: the Impact of Thomas Wolsey in Star Chamber* (Hassocks, Sussex, 1977)

Guy, *Thought* 52 J. A. Guy, 'Thomas More as successor to Wolsey', in *Thought* 52 (1977), 275–92

Hall, *Chronicle* Edward Hall, *The Union of . . . York and Lancaster*, ed. H. Ellis (1809)

Hastings, *Common Pleas* Margaret Hastings, *The Court of Common Pleas in Fifteenth Century England* (Ithaca, New York, 1947)

Hastings Mss. H.M.C., *Report on the Mss. of the late R. R. Hastings* (1928–47)

Hemmant, *Exchequer Chamber* *Select Cases in the Exchequer Chamber before all the Justices of England*, ed. M. Hemmant, Selden Soc. 51, 64 (1933–48)

Henderson, *English Administrative Law* E. G. Henderson, *Foundations of English Administrative Law* (Cambridge, Mass., 1963)

H.M.C. Historical Manuscripts Commission

Holdsworth, *H.E.L.* W. S. Holdsworth, *A History of English Law* (1922–56)

Hoskins, *Age of Plunder* W. G. Hoskins, *The Age of Plunder: the England of Henry VIII, 1500–47* (1976)

Hoskins, *Essays* *Essays in Leicestershire History* (Liverpool, 1950)

Household Books of John (Howard) *Household Books of John (Howard), Duke of Norfolk*, ed. J. P. Collier, Roxburghe Club (1844)

Inner Temple Records *Calendar of Inner Temple Records*, ed. F. A. Inderwick (1896–1937)

Ives, *Bull. Institute of Hist. Research* 41 E. W. Ives, 'Andrew Dymmock and the papers of Antony, Earl Rivers, 1482–3', in *Bull. Institute of Hist. Research* 41 (1968), 216–29

Ives, *Bull. John Rylands Lib.* 52 E. W. Ives, 'Patronage at the court of Henry VIII: the case of Sir Ralph Egerton of Ridley', in *Bull. John Rylands Lib.* 52 (1970), 346–74

Ives, *E.H.R.* 82 E. W. Ives, 'The genesis of the statute of uses', in *E.H.R.* 82 (1967), 673–97

Ives, *L.Q.R.* 75 E. W. Ives, 'Promotion in the legal profession of Yorkist and early Tudor England', in *L.Q.R.* 75 (1959), 348–63

Ives, *L.Q.R.* 85 E. W. Ives, 'A lawyer's library in 1500', in *L.Q.R.* 85 (1969), 104–16

Ives, *L.Q.R.* 89 E. W. Ives, 'The purpose and making of the later year books', in *L.Q.R.* 89 (1973), 64–86

Ives, in *On the Laws and Customs of England* E. W. Ives, 'Crime, sanctuary and royal authority under Henry VIII: the exemplary sufferings of the

Savage family', in *On the Laws and Customs of England*, ed. M. S. Arnold et al. (Chapel Hill, North Carolina, 1981), 296–320

Ives, in *Profession, Vocation, etc.* E. W. Ives, 'The common lawyers', in *Profession, Vocation and Culture in Late Medieval England*, ed. C. H. Clough (Liverpool, 1982), 181–217

Ives, *Trans. Royal Hist. Soc.*, 5 ser., 18 E. W. Ives, 'The common lawyers in pre-Reformation England', in *Trans. Royal Hist. Soc.*, 5 ser., 18 (1968), 145–73

Ives, *Univ. Birmingham Hist. Journ.* E. W. Ives, 'The reputation of the common lawyer in English society, 1450–1550', in *University of Birmingham Historical Journal* 7 (1960), 130–61

Ives, in *Wealth and Power* E. W. Ives, 'Agaynst taking awaye of Women: the inception and operation of the abduction act of 1487', in *Wealth and Power in Tudor England*, ed. E. W. Ives, R. J. Knecht, J. J. Scarisbrick (1978), 21–44

Jacob, *Fifteenth Century* E. F. Jacob, *The Fifteenth Century, 1399–1485* (Oxford, 1961)

Jayne, *Catalogues* Sears Jayne, *Library Catalogues of the English Renaissance* (Berkeley, 1956)

Jones, *Chancery* W. J. Jones, *The Elizabethan Court of Chancery* (Oxford, 1967)

Journal of Prior More *Journal of Prior William More*, ed. E. S. Fegan, Worcestershire Historical Soc. (1914)

J.S.P.T.L. *Journal of the Society of Public Teachers of Law*

Keilwey, *Reports* *Relationes quorundam casuum selectorum ex libris Roberti Keilwey*, ed. J. Croke (1602). The second edition has been used, entitled *Reports d'ascuns Cases* (1688) (see below, p. 50 n. 77)

Kingsford, *E.H.R.* 35 C. L. Kingsford, 'Proceedings in the court of star chamber: *Stonor* v. *Dormer and others*, 1491', in *E.H.R.* 35 (1920), 421–32

L. and P. *Letters and Papers, Foreign and Domestic, of the Reign of Henry VIII*, ed. J. S. Brewer et al. (1862–1932)

Leadam, *Domesday* *The Domesday of Inclosures, 1517–18*, ed. I. S. Leadam (1897)

Lehmberg, *Sir Thomas Elyot* S. E. Lehmberg, *Sir Thomas Elyot: Tudor Humanist* (Austin, Texas, 1960)

'Le Strange', *Archaeologia* 25 D. Gurney, 'Extracts from the household and privy purse expenditure of Le Strange of Hunstanton, 1519–78', in *Archaeologia* 25 (1834), 411–569

Letters of Shillingford *Letters and Papers of John Shillingford, Mayor of Exeter, 1447–50*, ed. S. A. Moore, Camden Soc., n.s., 2 (1872)

Lewis, *L.Q.R.* T. E. Lewis, 'The history of judicial precedent', in *L.Q.R.* 46 (1930), 207–24, 341–60; 47 (1931), 411–27

Lincolnshire Pedigrees *Lincolnshire Pedigrees*, ed. A. R. Maddison, Harleian Soc. 50–2 (1902–4)

London, *Cal. Letter Books* *Calendar of Letter-Books of the City of London*, ed. R. R. Sharpe (1899–1912)

London City Church *Medieval Records of a London City Church*, ed. H. Littlehales, Early English Text Soc. (1905)

London, *Plea and Memoranda Rolls* *Calendar of Plea and Memoranda Rolls of the City of London, 1323–1482*, ed. A. H. Thomas and P. E. Jones (Cambridge, 1926–61)

L.Q.R. *Law Quarterly Review*

McFarlane, *Nobility* K. B. McFarlane, *The Nobility of Later Medieval England* (Oxford, 1973)

MacNamara, *Danvers Family* F. N. MacNamara, *Memorials of the Danvers Family* (1895)

Materials for the Reign of Henry VII *Materials for a History of the Reign of King Henry VII*, ed. W. Campbell, Rolls Ser. (1873)

Meekings, 'King's bench files', C. A. F. Meekings, 'King's bench files', in *Legal Records and the Historian*, ed. J. H. Baker (1978), 97–139

Miller, *Bull. Institute of Hist. Research* 28 H. Miller, 'Subsidy assessments of the peerage in the sixteenth century', in *Bull. Institute of Hist. Research* 28 (1955), 15–34

Milsom, *Historical Foundations* S.F.C. Milsom, *Historical Foundations of the Common Law* (1969)

Minutes of Parliament *Middle Temple Records: Minutes of Parliament*, ed. C. T. Martin (1904–5)

More, *Utopia* Thomas More, *Utopia*, trans. R. Robinson, 1551, ed. E. Arber (1869)

Myers, *Bull. John Rylands Lib.* 40 A. R. Myers, 'The household of Queen Margaret of Anjou, 1452–3', in *Bull. John Rylands Lib.* 40 (1957–8), 79–113, 391–431

Myers, *Bull. John Rylands Lib.* 50 A. R. Myers, 'The household of Queen Elizabeth Woodville, 1466–7', in *Bull. John Rylands Lib.* 50 (1967–8), 207–35, 443–81

Myers, *English Historical Documents, 1327–1485* *English Historical Documents, iv: 1327–1485*, ed. A. R. Myers (1969)

Nichols, *Leicestershire* John Nichols, *History and Antiquities of the county of Leicester* (1795–1815)

Nicolas, *Privy Purse Expenses* N. H. Nicolas, *Privy Purse Expenses of Elizabeth of York* (1830)

Ormerod, *History of Chester* G. Ormerod, *History of the County Palatine and City of Chester*, ed. T. Helsby (1875–82)

Oseney Abbey *Cartulary of Oseney Abbey*, ed. H. E. Salter, Oxford Historical Soc. 89, 90, 91, 97, 98, 101 (1929–36)

Paston Letters *The Paston Letters, 1422–1509*, ed. J. Gairdner (1910)

Paston Letters and Papers *Paston Letters and Papers of the Fifteenth Century*, ed. N. Davis (Oxford, 1971 and 1976)

Peterborough Monastery *Peterborough Local Administration: the last days of Peterborough Monastery*, ed. W. T. Mellows, Northamptonshire Record Soc. 12 (1947)

Plumpton Correspondence *Plumpton Correspondence*, ed. T. Stapleton, Camden Soc., o.s., 4 (1839)

Pronay, in *British Government and Administration* N. Pronay, 'The chancellor, the chancery, and the council at the end of the fifteenth century', in *British Government and Administration*, ed. H. Hearder and H. R. Loyn (Cardiff, 1974)

Putnam, *Early Treatises* B. Putnam, *Early Treatises on the Practice of the Justices of the Peace in the Fifteenth and Sixteenth Centuries* (Oxford, 1924)

Radford, *Trans. Devon Assoc.* 35 G. H. Radford, 'Nicholas Radford, 1385(?)–1455', in *Transactions of the Devonshire Association* 35 (1903), 251–78

Rawcliffe, 'Baronial councils' Carole Rawcliffe, 'Baronial councils in the later middle ages', in *Patronage, Pedigree and Power*, ed. C. Ross (1979), 87–108

Rawcliffe, *The Staffords* Carole Rawcliffe, *The Staffords, Earls of Stafford and Dukes of Buckingham, 1394–1521* (Cambridge, 1978)

Recorders of London *Recorders of the City of London, printed by direction of the Court of Aldermen* (1850)

Records of the Borough of Nottingham *Records of the Borough of Nottingham, 1155–1702*, ed. W. H. Stevenson (1882–1914)

'Records of Canterbury' H.M.C., 'Records of the City of Canterbury', in *Ninth Report* (1883–4), i. 129–77

Records of Oxford *Selections from the Records of Oxford*, ed. W. H. Turner, (Oxford, 1880)

Register of Archbishop Chichele *Register of Archbishop Chichele*, ed. E. F. Jacob, Canterbury and York Soc. 42, 45–7 (1937–47)

Roper, *Lyfe of Moore* William Roper, *The Lyfe of Sir Thomas Moore, knighte*, ed. E. V. Hitchcock, Early English Text Soc. (1935)

Roskell, *Bull. John Rylands Lib.* 42 J. S. Roskell, 'William Catesby, counsellor to Richard III', in *Bull. John Rylands Lib.* 42 (1959–60), 145–74

Rot. Parl. *Rotuli Parliamentorum* (1783–1832)

Rutland Papers H.M.C., *The Mss. of His Grace the Duke of Rutland* (1888–1905)

St Augustine's, Bristol *Two Compotus Rolls of St Augustine's, Bristol, for 1491–2 and 1511–12*, ed. G. Beachcroft and A. Sabin, Bristol Record Soc. 9 (1938)

St German, *Doctor and Student* Christopher St German, *Doctor and Student*, ed. T. F. T. Plucknett and J. L. Barton, Selden Soc. 91 (1974)

Simpson, *Camb. Law Journ.* 28 A. W. B. Simpson, 'The early constitution of the inns of court', in *Camb. Law Journ.* 28 (1970), 241–56

Simpson, *Camb. Law Journ.* 34 A. W. B. Simpson, 'The early constitution of Gray's Inn', in *Camb. Law Journ.* 34 (1975), 131–50

Simpson, *Land Law* A. W. B. Simpson, *An Introduction to the History of the Land Law* (Oxford, 1961)

Simpson, *L.Q.R.* 73 A. W. B. Simpson, 'Keilwey's Reports, temp. Henry VII and Henry VIII', in *L.Q.R.* 73 (1957), 89–105

Simpson, *L.Q.R.* 87 A. W. B. Simpson, 'The source and function of the later year books', in *L.Q.R.* 87 (1971), 94–118

Somerville, *Duchy of Lancaster* R. Somerville, *History of the Duchy of Lancaster, i.: 1265–1603* (1953)

Spelman, *Reports* John Spelman, *Reports*, ed. J. H. Baker, Selden Soc. 93, 94 (1977–8)

Star Chamber *Select Cases before the King's Council in the Star Chamber*, ed. I. S. Leadam, Selden Soc. 16, 25 (1903–11)

Starkey, *Dialogue* Thomas Starkey, *Dialogue between Pole and Lupset*, ed. K. M. Burton (1948)

Steer, *Inventories* F. W. Steer, *Farm and Cottage Inventories of Mid-Essex* (1950)

Stephenson, *Brasses* M. Stephenson, *List of Monumental Brasses* (1926)

Stonor Letters and Papers *The Stonor Letters and Papers, 1290–1483*, ed. C. L. Kingsford, Camden Soc., 3 ser., 29–30 (1919)

Testamenta Eboracensia *Testamenta Eboracensia: or wills registered at York*, ed. J. Raine et al., Surtees Soc. 4, 30, 45, 79, 106 (1836–1902)

Thompson, *Wyggeston Hospital* A. H. Thompson, *Calendar of Charters and Other Documents Belonging to the Hospital of Willliam Wyggeston at Leicester* (Leicester, 1933)

Thorne, *New York Law Review* S. E. Thorne, 'Tudor social transformation and legal change', in *New York University Law Review* 26 (1951), 10–23

Thorne, *Readings and Moots* S. E. Thorne, *Readings and Moots at the Inns of Court in the Fifteenth Century*, i, Selden Soc. 71 for 1952 (1954)

Thrupp, *Merchant Class* S. L. Thrupp, *The Merchant Class of Medieval London, 1300–1500* (Chicago, 1948)

Trans. Bristol and Gloucestershire Arch. Soc. 15 J. Maclean, 'Accounts of the churchwardens of St. Ewen's, Bristol', in *Transactions of the Bristol and Gloucestershire Archaeological Society* 15 (1890–1)

Trans. Leics. Arch. Soc. *Transactions of the Leicestershire Archaeological Society*

Trans. Royal Hist. Soc. *Transactions of the Royal Historical Society*

Tropenell Cartulary *The Tropenell Cartulary*, ed. J. S. Davies, Wiltshire Archaeological and Natural History Soc. (1908)

Tudor Men and Institutions *Tudor Men and Institutions*, ed. A. J. Slavin (Baton Rouge, 1972)

Valor Ecclesiasticus *Valor Ecclesiasticus temp. Henr. VIII, auctoritate regia institutus*, ed. J. Caley (1810–34)

V.C.H. Victoria History of the Counties of England (1900, in progress)

Visitation of Buckinghamshire, 1634 *Visitation of the County of Buckingham made in 1634*, ed. W. H. Rylands, Harleian Soc. 58 (1909)

Visitations of Essex, 1552 etc. *The Visitations of Essex, 1552, 1558, 1570, 1612, 1634*, ed. W. C. Metcalfe, Harleian Soc. 13, 14 (1878–9)

Visitations of Kent, 1530 etc. *Visitations of Kent, 1530–1, 1574*, ed. W. B. Bannerman, Harleian Soc. 74, 75 (1923–4)

Visitation of Kent, 1619–21 *Visitation of Kent, 1619–21*, ed. R Hovenden, Harleian Soc. 42 (1898)

Visitation of Norfolk, ed. Dashwood *Visitation of Norfolk in the year 1563*, ed. G. H. Dashwood et al. (Norwich, 1878–95)

Visitations of Northants., 1564 etc. *Visitations of Northamptonshire, 1564, 1618–19*, ed. W. C. Metcalfe (1887)

Visitations of Suffolk, 1561 etc. *Visitations of Suffolk, 1561, 1577, 1612*, ed. W. C. Metcalfe (Exeter, 1882)

Warwickshire Feet of Fines *Warwickshire Feet of Fines*, ed. Lucy Drucker, Dugdale Soc. 18 (1943)

Wedgwood, *Biographies* J. C. Wedgwood, *History of Parliament; Biographies of the Members of the Commons House, 1439–1509* (1936) (citations without page references are to the alphabetical list)

Weever, *Funeral Monuments* J. Weever, *Ancient Funerall Monuments* (1767)

Williams, *Early Holborn* E. Williams, *Early Holborn and the Legal Quarter of London* (1927)

Williams, *English Historical Documents, 1485–1558* *English Historical Documents, v: 1485–1558*, ed. C. H. Williams (1967)

'Wombwell Mss.' North Yorkshire Record Office, ZDV XI [unfoliated], printed in 'Wombwell Mss.', H.M.C., *Various Collections* (1901–14), ii. 28–56 (citations are by page number of the H.M.C. text)

Wood, *Medieval House* M. E. Wood, *The English Medieval House* (1965)

Y.B. *Les Reports des Cases*, ed. J. Maynard (1678–80) (citations are by term, regnal year, plea and folio)

York Civic Records *York Civic Records, 1475–1588*, ed. A. Raine, Yorkshire Archaeological Soc. Record Series, 98, 103, 106, 108, 110, 112, 115, 119 (1939–53)

York Memorandum Book *York Memorandum Book, 1376–1493*, ed. M. Sellers, Surtees Soc. 120, 125 (1912–15)

MANUSCRIPT SOURCES

PUBLIC RECORD OFFICE

Manuscripts at the Public Record Office, London, are quoted by the call number only, according to the following key:

C1	Early Chancery Proceedings
C3	Chancery Proceedings, Series II
C54	Close Rolls
C66	Patent Rolls
C67	Patent Rolls (Supplementary)
C82	Warrants for the Great Seal, Series II
C140	Inquisitions Post Mortem (Chancery), Series I (Edward IV)
C141	Inquisitions Post Mortem (Chancery), Series I (Richard III)
C142	Inquisitions Post Mortem (Chancery), Series II
CP25	Common Pleas, Feet of Fines
CP40	Common Pleas, *De Banco* Rolls
DL3	Duchy of Lancaster, Depositions and Examinations, Series I
DL5	Duchy of Lancaster, Entry Books of Decrees and Orders
E13	Exchequer of Pleas, Plea Rolls
E36	Exchequer, Treasury of Receipt, Books
E101	Exchequer, King's Remembrancer, Accounts
E150	Inquisitions Post Mortem (Exchequer), Series II
E159	Exchequer, King's Remembrancer, Memoranda Rolls
E163	Exchequer, King's Remembrancer, Miscellanea
E179	Exchequer, King's Remembrancer, Subsidy Rolls
E303	Exchequer, Augmentations, Conventual Leases
E315	Exchequer, Augmentations, Miscellaneous Books
E356	Exchequer, Pipe Office, Enrolled Accounts, Customs
E364	Exchequer, Pipe Office, Rolls of Foreign Accounts
E403	Exchequer of Receipt, Enrolments and Registers of Issues
E404	Exchequer of Receipt, Writs and Warrants for Issues
E405	Exchequer of Receipt, Rolls etc. of Receipts and Issues
IND 1324–38	King's Bench, Docket Rolls
IND 17180	Common Pleas, Recoveries
KB9	King's Bench, Ancient Indictments

KB27	King's Bench, *Coram Rege* Rolls
PROB11	Prerogative Court of Canterbury, Probate Registers
REQ3	Court of Requests, Miscellaneous Proceedings
SC6	Special Collections, Ministers' and Receivers' Accounts
SP1	State Papers, Henry VIII, General Series
SP12	State Papers Domestic, Elizabeth I
STAC1	Court of Star Chamber, Proceedings, Henry VII
STAC2	Court of Star Chamber, Proceedings, Henry VIII

OTHER REPOSITORIES

Althorp Park

Spencer Mss.	863–81, 889

Borthwick Institute

Diocese of York, Probate Registers iii, xiii (Prerogative and Exchequer Courts)

British Library

Additional Charters and Rolls	17209, 38757, 38758
Additional Mss.	16172, 19114, 20021, 21480, 28206, 41139
Hargrave Mss.	87, 388
Harleian Mss.	433, 1624
Harleian Rolls	K8
Lansdowne Mss.	127, 639

Canterbury Cathedral Library

City of Canterbury Corporation Archive	F8

Castle Ashby

Compton Muniments	995

Dorset Record Office

Weld of Chiddock Ms.	D16

Huntington Library

Ellesmere Mss.	EI2652
Hastings Mss.	HAI6250

Inner Temple Library

Mss. Additional	188

Leicestershire Record Office

Diocesan Mss. (Probate)	DE73, 170, 221
Farnham Mss.	5D33
Ferrers of Staunton Harold Mss.	26D53
Rothley Mss.	44' 28
Winstanley Mss.	DG5

Lincoln's Inn Library

Black Books	1, 2, 3
Hale Mss.	XII

Magdalen College

Fastolf Mss.	42, 71
Wanborough Deeds	

Norfolk and Norwich Record Office

Norwich City Records	Case 7.A–F

North Yorkshire Record Office

Wombwell Mss.	ZDV XI

Shakespeare Birthplace Trust

Baddesley Clinton Mss.	DR3
Stratford-upon-Avon Borough Collection	BRT1/1

Staffordshire Record Office

Lord Stafford's Mss.	D641

Warwickshire Record Office

Dormer Mss.	CR895

Wiltshire Record Office

Ailesbury Records	88:5

Worcestershire Record Office

Church Commissioners Archives	009:BA2636

Also Philipps Mss. sold at Sotheby's

TABLE OF CASES

Page numbers appear in italics, thus *295*

YEAR BOOKS (BLACK LETTER)

KEILWEY, REPORTS

INTRODUCTION

Among the minorities which have decisively influenced the civilisation of Western Europe, few have been more important – and none more persistent – than the lawyers. In Roman law, Justinian – in canon law, Gratian – in international law, Grotius – these are authorities who belong not simply to the history of European law, but to the wider history of Europe. In England, Glanvill and Bracton, Littleton and Coke profoundly affected not merely the development of the common law, but the development of English society as well.

Yet the influence of the lawyers has not been limited to the making of law. Because of the training which he received, the lawyer has been entrusted with a great deal of work which can only loosely be described as 'legal', and these 'extra-curricular' activities – both public and private – have given the profession an importance which its size and its strictly forensic activities did not warrant. In England, moreover, the lawyers have had a further significance. Never isolated from the rest of the community, as in some continental countries, disposing of the wealth, advancement and prestige which their skill won for them, they have been a catalyst in society, agents of social change.

In England, the influence of the legal profession was, in each of these ways, at its zenith between the middle of the fifteenth and the middle of the sixteenth centuries. These were the years during which the institutions of the English common law withstood the threat of the new legal machinery of the council and the prerogative courts, and years which saw the start of a legal reformation which shaped the law for centuries to come. Also in this hundred years, extra-curricular activities occupied the lawyers more than ever before or since. Employment today quite unconnected with the courts was then the rightful province of the profession, and the authority of the lawyers extended far and wide. In particular they established a dominant position in the administration of England, and the list of their names is a catalogue of the Yorkist and early Tudor civil service – Richard

Fowler, Thomas Lovell, John Mordaunt, Thomas Lucas, James Hobart, Thomas Audley. Names also bear witness to the influence of the common lawyers on the changing society of the times. In subsequent generations, peers as diverse as Thomas Fairfax, the victor of Naseby, 'Turnip' Townshend, Walpole's rival, and Thomas Brudenell, seventh earl of Cardigan and commander of the Light Brigade at Balaclava, could each trace the fortunes of his house to a successful lawyer of this period. The only lay profession, the law was one of the main avenues of social advancement, and as a means of acquiring that solvent of social barriers – hard cash – it had few rivals.

The legal profession of Yorkist and early Tudor England is known to historians very largely through the careers of its more distinguished members. Foremost among these is Thomas More, but with him stand John Fortescue, William Catesby, Edmund Dudley, Richard Empson and Thomas Cromwell. Yet, well known as these names are, it is characteristic that the claim of each to attention rests not on membership of the legal profession, but on political importance and misfortune. Of their fellows, only Antony Fitzherbert is at all well known, and that less for his legal treatise, the *Abridgement*, than for his supposed authorship of two farming manuals.[1] These men obviously had much in common with the rest of the profession, but to the extent to which they rose above their fellows, they ceased to be representative of them. Of the more typical common lawyers, we know little. In the mid-nineteenth century, Edward Foss prepared brief biographies of such men as reached the judicial bench, a task in part revised in the *Dictionary of National Biography*.[2] Studies of members of parliament have added to our knowledge, but not until the work of Professor S. E. Thorne has any extensive work been done on the common lawyers *per se*.[3] Particular enquiries have been even more limited. Two men, Thomas Frowyk and Thomas Marowe, were the subject of a monograph by Bertha Putnam.[4] John More and

1. 'Master' Fitzherbert, *The boke of husbandry* and *Boke of surveying* (both 1523). The author was almost certainly Antony's elder brother John, a man trained at an inn of court, possibly Gray's Inn: Ives, in *Profession, Vocation, etc.*, 210 n. 12.
2. E. Foss, *The Judges of England, with Sketches of their Lives*, 9 vols. (1848–64).
3. S. E. Thorne, *Readings and Moots at the Inns of Court in the Fifteenth Century*, i. Selden Soc. 71 for 1952 (1954). J. C. Wedgwood, *History of Parliament; Biographies of the Members of the Commons House, 1439–1509* (1936) contains valuable material, but is not always reliable and applies the label 'lawyer' too readily: *ibid.*, xiii–xiv.
4. B. Putnam, *Early Treatises on the Practice of the Justices of the Peace in the Fifteenth and Sixteenth Centuries* (Oxford, 1924).

Richard Eliot shine, reflectedly, in biographies of their offspring.[5] The majority, however, have little or no memorial.[6]

One of the most active members of the pre-Reformation legal profession, and one who has received little notice, is Thomas Kebell (*c.* 1439–1500), serjeant-at-law and squire of Humberstone in Leicestershire. Kebell left no *Tenures*, no *Abridgement*, to perpetuate his authority, but he was the most brilliant advocate of his generation; no-one ever cites *Kebell*, but from 1485 until his death, Thomas Kebell was the most frequently reported lawyer in the land. As Burton, the seventeenth-century antiquary concluded, he was:

> (as it appeareth by the book of Reports in King Henry the Seventh's time) one of the greatest practice in those days.[7]

Nor was Thomas Kebell confined to the court-room. He had his share of extra-curricular duties as a member of Lord Hastings' household, and ultimately as a royal adviser. In government service, he was heavily engaged in the judicial machine, both in the assize system and at Lancaster, and at one stage in his career he was active in royal administration, though less so than a specialist like Richard Empson. Upon society also, Kebell made his mark. With the wealth he accumulated, the serjeant was able to carve out a substantial stake in his own county – flocks, herds, acres and plate, all proclaiming that he had arrived.

The English common lawyers had, in the closing years of the middle ages, enormous influence as the interpreters of the law, as a professional monopoly and as aspiring and affluent members of society. Thomas Kebell stands as an exemplar of them all.

5. More: R. W. Chambers, *Thomas More* (1938); *Essential Articles for the Study of Thomas More*, ed. R. S. Sylvester and G. P. Marc'hadour (Hamden, Connecticut, 1977); R. W. Schoeck, 'Sir Thomas More, humanist and lawyer', in *University of Toronto Quarterly* 34 (1964), 1–14. Eliot: Thomas Eliot, *The Boke named the Gouernour*, ed. H. H. S. Croft (1883); S. E. Lehmberg, *Sir Thomas Elyot: Tudor Humanist* (1960).
6. But see also: Robert Constable, *Tertia Lectura on Prerogativa Regis*, ed. S. E. Thorne (New Haven, 1949); D. M. Brodie, 'Edmund Dudley: minister of Henry VII', in *Trans. Royal Hist. Soc.*, 4 ser., 15 (1932), 133–61; Edmund Dudley, *The Tree of Commonwealth*, ed. D. M. Brodie (Cambridge, 1948); S. E. Lehmberg, 'Sir Thomas Audley: a soul as black as marble?', in *Tudor Men and Institutions*, ed. A. J. Slavin (Baton Rouge, 1972); John Spelman, *Reports*, ed. J. H. Baker, Selden Soc. 93, 94 (1977–8).
7. W. Burton, *Description of Leicestershire* (1622), 128.

PART I

THE LEGAL PROFESSION

1

THE COMMON LAWYERS IN PRE-REFORMATION ENGLAND

The contrast between medieval and modern society has been variously described as an antithesis between faith and reason, scholasticism and classical learning, personal monarchy and state bureaucracy; in England it could equally well be considered as a contrast in attitudes to law. In the twentieth century it is a commonplace that personal freedom and the right to property depends upon the law of the land, but the overt importance of the law in everyday life is slight. Popular opinion regards it either as a body of statutes creating obligations and conferring benefits, or as a protection against crime, while certain political circles even see law as inappropriate to regulate important contractual relations. To consider the small print of an agreement is unusual, a lawsuit is a grave step only undertaken in the last resort, and administration – central and local – is the business of civil servants, government departments and quangos, not the police and the courts.

It was quite otherwise under the rule of the Yorkist and Tudor sovereigns; English society was intensely 'law-minded', obsessed with legal considerations, legal rights and legal remedies. Even the mutual obligations of the family were put into legal form. Husbands and wives tied each other to the terms of the marriage settlement as tightly as the law allowed. The profitable disposal of children in employment or wedlock called for bonds, indentures and obligations; one father even made his student son at Thavies Inn provide a mentor with an IOU to be called in should the boy slack![1] English men – and women – went to law with alacrity; with a population of just over two million, the main central courts alone handled in the order of three thousand new suits each year, to say nothing of those that never got beyond the opening stages.[2]

1. C1/94/14–16.
2. An accurate count of cases is impossible, but at the end of Edward IV's reign up to 700 common pleas cases were reaching exigent or the equivalent in a busy term. Chancery bills were running at 360 a year. No figure is available for king's bench, which had about 10% of the common pleas case load: Hastings, *Common Pleas*,

Critics at the time put the blame on human greed and weakness:

> For small occasion, for lytell greed and weakness,
> Unwyse men stryue, deuysynge falshode and gyle;
> Nowe every fole hath set his mynde and thought
> To seke the extreme of lawe.[3]

Later historians have dismissed this litigiousness as an instance of *autres temps, autres moeurs*, or else have regarded it as another unfortunate symptom of the evils of bastard feudalism.

Frenzied preoccupation with the law was, however, more than this. In part it was the consequence of the complexity and fluidity of property ownership in late medieval England. The breakdown in tenurial relationships symbolised by the statute *De Donis Conditionalibus*, the development of devices such as the entail and the use which made complicated and contingent family settlements possible, the confusions of forfeiture and restoration following treason and felony, the growth of a commercial land market, the interference of royal feudal claims and the wilful obfuscation designed to rebut them, all this combined to produce a situation where estate titles were all to a greater or lesser degree vulnerable. In those circumstances, a man's rightful estates were any which the law would gain for him; instead of a situation where the law guaranteed a man what was his by right, the situation prevailed where whatever he could secure by the law was his right. In the second place, the law was the arbiter of society. Of course bastard feudalism was manifested in legal abuses as well as in naked force, but litigiousness was not simply extortion under another name; indeed, since bastard feudalism offered what in many ways was the alternative justice of the retinue, it was essentially a rival to law.[4] Recourse to the courts was, therefore, a search for authority. Deficient though it may have been, the law was the only way to peaceful public settlement, given the ineffectiveness of administrative complaint or political query. Whereas today an anti-social development will be neutralised by parliamentary action, in Kebell's time it could be prevented by the law, or by force, and little else. And over all hung the possibility of sudden death – *timor mortis conturbat me*; court records have sufficient examples of litigation which arose from someone

190; Ives, *Trans. Royal Hist. Soc.*, 5 ser. 18. 166; Blatcher, *Court of King's Bench*, 21.

3. Brant, *Ship of Fools*, f.cxlix.
4. I. H. Jeayes, *Descriptive Catalogue of the Charters of the Gresley Family* (1895), 437.

falling mortally sick before he had time to formalise agreements he had made, to indicate the wisdom of putting even the friendliest arrangement in good legal language, and, death apart, complications of distance and communication always threatened. It is small wonder that men turned to the law, even though the law often failed them.

But the greatest single factor in making English men and women 'law-minded' was the way in which pre-Reformation society rested immediately upon the law as administered in the courts. Not only were property rights tested in the courts, but the routine buying and selling of land also was effected through a court, either by means of a final concord or, more riskily, a recovery. Contracts, agreements, liabilities to the monarch, all had to be expressed as obligations of debt. The government of the country was, at all levels, effected through the legal system. The chief financial organ of central government was the court of the exchequer; before a government department became fully organised it had to take on the character of a court, as the wards and the general surveyors did in the 1540s; the new machinery created during the Reformation was curial – the court of augmentations and the court of first fruits and tenths; parliament was a court. The conciliar rule of the Yorkist and Tudor kings produced more courts – star chamber, requests, the councils at York, Ludlow and in the west. Nor was it merely outward form; judicial procedure and administration were not clearly differentiated. Henry VII, for example, owed much of his fiscal and bureaucratic efficiency to the 'bye-courts' he set up. The most notable was 'the king's council learned in the law'. Staffed by lawyers of the calibre of Richard Empson and Edmund Dudley, the council learned was responsible for much of the financial extortion traditionally associated with the first Tudor.[5]

The same concurrence of law and administration is seen in county government. The most powerful officer was the justice of the peace and the most important organ the court of quarter sessions. Crime and county council business were dealt with side by side: a rogue might be bound over to keep the peace, or a householder to replace a ruinous public bridge on his property, while a respectable yeoman who forgot his share of road repairs might find himself prosecuted along with a pickpocket. Assisting the justices were juries which denounced malefactors and public nuisances with equal alacrity, and

5. R. Somerville, 'Henry VII's "council learned in the law" ', in *E.H.R.* 54 (1939), 427–42; Bayne, *Council of Henry VII*, xxv–xxviii; Condon, 'Ruling elites', 131–4.

other juries were empanelled and witnesses summoned on countless occasions to assist royal officials to collect information or investigate claims. The link between localities and the centre was again a judicial one. The justices of assize heard suits at *nisi prius* and tried serious criminal offences, but they also had to explain government policy to the justices of the peace, supervise their work and report to the monarch. Henry VII, on at least one occasion, assembled the assize justices at Windsor to give them instructions in person.[6] The private affairs of local communities, whether the management of the open fields, the destruction of a dangerous dog or the price of bread and beer, were likewise the concern of courts of law. The quality of manufactures, the rate of production, prices, wages, conditions of employment, all were under strict court regulation in corporate towns, and in the countryside were more and more coming under the surveillance of the justices of the peace.[7] Flood control and coastal protection was in the hands of commissions which functioned as courts under the supervision of king's bench.[8] The law dominated land management. Estate administration was not, primarily, a question of crop rotation, drainage or capital improvements, but of keeping the manorial court so as to produce a steady return from entry fines, heriots and the like. As for personal relations, a lawsuit could have the function of a 'final demand' and in the (admittedly extreme) cases of the third duke of Buckingham and the fifth earl of Northumberland, litigation was a deliberate 'management technique'.[9] In the England of Thomas Kebell, a court was no olympian tribunal; men went to law as part of everyday routine, and litigation was commonplace, almost instinctive.

With the law of such universal relevance, legal knowledge was at a premium and was widely diffused. Even the illiterate wife of a provincial gentleman, like Margaret Paston, needed to be familiar with writs, lawsuits and manorial courts.[10] In the first place, legal expertise was necessary for self-preservation. The advice which Agnes, the

6. *Plumpton Correspondence*, 161.
7. An excellent example of the penetration of society by legal concepts and methods is provided by the manor of Bromsgrove and King's Norton, Worcs. Enjoying the peculiar status of ancient demesne, the manor court dealt with a wide range of matters normally dispersed over a number of jurisdictions: A. F. C. Baber, *The Court Rolls of the Manor of Bromsgrove and King's Norton*, Worcestershire Historical Soc. (1963).
8. Henderson, *English Administrative Law*, 28–35.
9. Rawcliffe, *The Staffords*, 165–70, 174–6.
10. *Paston Letters and Papers*, i. xxxvii–xxxviii.

widow of Judge William Paston, gave her son Edmund is deservedly famous:

> to thynkke onis of the daie of yowre fadris counseyle to lerne the lawe, for he seyde manie tymis that ho so euer schuld dwelle at Paston schulde haue nede to conne defende hymselfe.[11]

Another reason for acquiring some legal skill was the increasing burden placed upon the gentry by the crown. Sir Humphrey Gilbert remarked in Elizabeth I's reign on their need:

> to be able to put their own Case in law and to haue some Iudgement in the office of *Iustice of peace and Sheriffe*,

and books to assist them were being produced from at least 1422.[12] But self-defence and public duty were not all. Keeping a manorial court demanded considerable legal ability, a point which Lord Chancellor Guilford was to emphasize as late as the end of the seventeenth century.[13] Here again manuals of instruction tell their own tale. At least eighteen printed editions of the treatise *Modus tenendi curiam baronis cum visu franci plegii* appeared between 1510 and 1550.[14] Those who assisted in the running of an estate required legal knowledge no less than the owner. Since the fourteenth century a steward had been expected to understand 'legal work and matters of high policy', and by the end of the fifteenth, a bailiff needed similar qualifications.[15] A government memorandum of 1484 spelled out the danger of using laymen:

> Where lords, knights and esquires, many of them not lettered, be made stewards of the king's livelihood in divers countries, they taking great fines and rewards of the king's tenants to their proper use, to the king's hurt and poverishing of his said tenants, and also wanting cunning and discretion to order and direct the said livelihood lawfully, with many more inconveniences, therefore it is thought that learned men in the law were most profitable to be stewards of the said livelihood for many causes concerning the king's profit and the weal of his tenants.[16]

Even the surveyor needed a sound grasp of law, for much of his work was concerned with questions of land tenure. It is no accident that the

11. *ibid.*, i. 27.
12. Humphrey Gilbert, *Quene Elizabethes Achademy*, Early English Text Soc., extra series (1869), 7; Putnam, *Early Treatises*, 237–86.
13. R. North, *Lives of the Norths*, ed. A. Jessop (1890), i. 29–31; iii. 106–8.
14. Wynkyn de Worde, *c.* 1510. Cf. F. Hearnshaw, *Leet Jurisdiction in England*, Southampton Record Soc. (1908), 35.
15. T. F. T. Plucknett, *The Medieval Bailiff* (Creighton Lecture, 1953), 5.
16. B. P. Wolffe, *The Crown Lands* (1970), 136.

earliest and one of the most influential works on surveying should have been written by a man trained at an inn of court.[17]

Naturally enough, such a pressure for legal expertise encouraged resort to professionals. Even in the minor courts where litigants could conduct their own cases, expert assistance was desirable. The complaint of John Wykys to the lord chancellor in the 1490s that the bishop of Winchester's steward refused to allow him counsel in the bishop's court – a not uncommon manoeuvre – tells its own tale.[18] In the royal courts an action could be pursued in person up to the stage of the hearing, although it was becoming usual to engage an attorney since few litigants could find the time to prosecute their concerns in person; but once a case reached the stage of pleading, then litigants had no choice but to engage professional help, and probably counsel. Indeed, a striking demonstration of the requirement for legal assistance is provided by the organisation of the profession itself. To deal with the mass of legal, especially chancery, business which did not fall naturally to either attorney or pleader, public demand called into existence an entirely new species of legal expert, the common solicitor.

Lawyers were in constant demand to assist landlords with manorial courts. Some even acquired a special reputation here; when Richard Roos was seeking to repair negligence on his Norfolk estates, he was advised:

> you had better let Geney keep the courts to peynne the tenants for the repair of their houses.[19]

Professional advice was sought in property deals, marriage settlements and inheritance arrangements. Lawyers regularly made up a large group on any magnate's council, while lesser men preferred to have some expert on whom they could rely. Nor did lawyers act only in legal matters. Whatever required a professional manager was opportunity for them. Wolsey's nephew, John Fairechild of Gray's Inn, applied to his uncle for the post of clerk of the works in the recently captured Tournai, and he set out his qualifications and experience in detail. He claimed to be qualified to act as a clerk in a common-law court, as an attorney or a solicitor, as a court-keeper, either in boroughs or on manorial estates, or as an auditor of both estate and household accounts, while as court-keeper and auditor he

17. See above, p. 2.
18. C1/231/27. Cf. *ibid.*, 38/240, 154/58; 'Wombwell Mss.', 32.
19. *Rutland Papers*, iv. 12. Cf. *Paston Letters and Papers*, i. 319–20; ii. 254, 271.

had had practical experience, part gained in the service of the duchess of Norfolk. His experience with her had, he claimed, also fitted him to act in household offices where financial skill and expert management went hand in hand – posts such as clerk of the kitchen or clerk controller (hence his suitability for a department of works) – and even as a nobleman's secretary.[20] 'Lawyer' was obviously synonymous with 'man of business'.

One such was Thomas Grice from Wakefield in the West Riding. His family had a tradition in management, and Thomas was certainly a lawyer, probably a member of one of the four inns of chancery clustered on each side of Holborn, where he had chambers.[21] He was employed by Sir Thomas, later Lord, Darcy of Templehurst, by at least 1492, and served as his 'learned steward and auditor' until the peer was executed after the Pilgrimage of Grace.[22] Over these more than forty years, Grice performed a multitude of services for the Darcys. He was regularly concerned with collecting rents as well as auditing accounts and redeeming plate pledged for cash.[23] Another duty was the purchase and transport of goods such as wine for Templehurst, or the sale and purchase of wood.[24] On the more strictly legal side, he kept courts for Darcy; a colleague attributed delay at one manor to Grice's absence 'for, Sir, I would not a given a pin for all our deeds if he had been away'.[25] He levied obligations, and organised the meeting of counsel or of any local commissions that concerned Darcy.[26] He was always expected to give advice; when, for example, Darcy left for France in 1492, he arranged that Grice should be consulted before any documents were sealed in his absence.[27] In 1521 Darcy ordered him to join with Thomas Fairfax in arbitrating between two of his tenants; in 1522, his friend Lord Monteagle asked Darcy for Grice 'to advise him on the drawing of his will'.[28] From 1526

20. SP1/10 f.52, printed in Ives, *Trans. Royal Hist. Soc.*, 5 ser., 18. 152.
21. Grice – of Wakefield and Medley, Yorks., and Holborn, gent.; J. P. West Riding from 1511; died 1546; there was another Thomas Grice, obviously a relative, who held the farm of Wakefield from 1500 to his death (before 1513): *Cal. Patent Rolls, 1494–1509*, 219, 242; *L. and P.*, i. 438 (3 m. 9), 1948 (77); R. B. Smith, *Land and Politics in the England of Henry VIII* (Oxford, 1970), 89, 157; Borthwick Institute, Probate Register xiii f.178; Dr J. H. Baker has discovered a Thomas Grice associated with the Middle Temple in 1530.
22. *Cal. Ancient Deeds*, v. A12116; *L. and P.*, Addenda i. 265.
23. *ibid.*, iii. 1261; Addenda i. 264, 280, 291, 295.
24. *ibid.*, Addenda i. 253, 282, 283, 370, 1233 (15).
25. *ibid.*, i. 186 (1); Addenda i. 277, 294; iv. 2527.
26. *ibid.*, i. 597; iv, 1285.
27. *Cal. Ancient Deeds*, v. A12116.
28. *L. and P.*, iii. 2664; Addenda i. 308.

to the mid-1530s, Grice was in the thick of Lord Darcy's long-drawn-out quarrel with his tenants at Rothwell, near Leeds. It was Grice who sent the first news that the tenants had complained to the duke of Richmond's council in 1526, who secured copies of their bills and who routed out details of a conspiracy to disturb his employer's title.[29] In 1529, when the matter was before the duchy of Lancaster, Grice wrote of weaknesses in the opposition pleas, and advised Darcy to 'remember Master Chancellor [Thomas More], and a little thing to Master Audelay, the attorney there, and that will help the matter to an end'.[30] When in 1531 Darcy's influence secured a duchy commission to arbitrate, he instructed his representative to keep Grice informed 'who in my right, I doubt not, is and will be cock sure', and at the same time to work with Grice in punishing the rebellious tenants.[31] The next year Grice was engineering the indictment of the ringleaders and advising Darcy how to get a special judicial commission from the crown in his favour, and in 1533 he was again reporting to Darcy, this time of the poor reception of the duchy decree at Rothwell and of a further conspiracy he was unravelling.[32]

Thomas Grice's activities are summed up in a memorandum which he and another of Darcy's servants, Richard Clerk, submitted to their employer, apparently in 1522.[33] They had pursued to a satisfactory conclusion the arbitration between Darcy and a local nunnery, and estimated the payments due to Darcy in consequence. The lordship of Torksey in Lincolnshire had been presenting difficulties. After some pressure the tenants had shown them the charters and the custumal, but much remained to be settled, and the farmer was determined to resign; a later letter shows Grice arranging for a replacement.[34] Throughout, Grice and Clerk note moneys owed and debts collected, to say nothing of recalcitrant tenants and disputatious neighbours. They also report on the condition of Darcy's estate, a house in decay, woods ripe for the felling, and the ferryboat over the Trent which was almost rotten.

Another side to Thomas Grice is revealed by the substantial docu-

29. *ibid.*, Addenda i. 491.
30. *ibid.*, xii(2). 186(41).
31. *ibid.*, Addenda i. 749,
32. *ibid.*, Addenda i. 782, 840, 841, 842.
33. *ibid.*, iv. 692. Clerk – of Lincoln, London and Kingston-on-Thames, gent.; Lincoln's Inn, admitted 1496, reader autumn 1515, treasurer 1514–15, 1517–18; recorder of Lincoln, M.P., J.P. Lindsey; died 1530: *ibid.*, i. 438 (4 m. 18), 1540; *Black Books*, i. 106, 175–6, 184; H.M.C., 'Mss. of Lincoln Corporation', in *Fourteenth Report*, viii (1895), 25, 32.
34. *L. and P.*, xii(2). 186(67).

mentation of Lord Darcy's part in the Pilgrimage of Grace – the lawyer as a political counsellor and personal representative. Grice was kept fully in touch with Darcy's actions, received information from him and fed him news in return, consulted with him on policy and accompanied him to the critical negotiations.[35] The royal lawyer, Richard Pollard, searching Darcy's correspondence for evidence of treason, commented 'it appeareth by divers letters sent by one Thomas Gryce unto the lord Darcy that he was a great doer among the commons in the insurrection'.[36] Thomas Grice was solicitor, bailiff, land-agent, accountant and confidant, all in one.

It is wrong to assume that professional lawyers necessarily engaged full-time in this wide-ranging calling. Humphrey Wingfield of Gray's Inn was an important and successful counsel.[37] In 1512 he became deputy chief steward for the north parts of the duchy of Lancaster, a notable prize.[38] He was a senior of his inn and in 1518 was listed amongst pleaders practising at Westminster.[39] In 1523 Wingfield was the only private lawyer selected, with nine judges, the attorney-general, the ex-solicitor-general and the attorney-general elect, to collect the 1524 subsidy in advance from members of the Westminster legal profession.[40] Humphrey himself was assessed at £130 in goods and stood twelfth of the seventy-seven members of the inns who were taxed. Other professional evidence can easily be added. He was the legal adviser of the king's brother-in-law, Charles Brandon, duke of Suffolk, and a member of the royal council, while in 1529 he was one of a score of lawyers who were appointed to hear cases in chancery.[41]

But there was another side to the life of this prominent but typical lawyer. From an important county family, J.P. for Suffolk in 1504 and for Essex in 1509, Wingfield was selected in 1516 to be *custos rotulorum* of Suffolk and in 1520 served as sheriff of Norfolk and Suffolk.[42] He sat for Ipswich in the parliament of 1523, was elected by

35. *ibid.*, xi. 678, 695 (ii), 706, 734, 899, 960, 997, 1042, 1112, 1113, 1123, 1127, 1155(4), 1182; xii(1). 171, 192, 392 (p. 191), 848, 849.
36. *ibid.*, xii (1). 379. Allegations against Grice suggest active involvement in violence: M. H. and R. Dodds, *The Pilgrimage of Grace* (Cambridge, 1915), 237, 295, 310–11.
37. Except where otherwise noted, this account of Wingfield relies on *D.N.B.*
38. Somerville, *Duchy of Lancaster*, i. 427.
39. Thorne, *Readings and Moots*, i. xiii; c82/474/36.
40. *Inner Temple Records*, i. 460.
41. 'Le Strange', *Archaeologia*, 25. 434, 443, 445 *et passim*; *L. and P.*, iv. 5666.
42. *Cal. Patent Rolls, 1494–1509*, 660; *L. and P.*, i. 1537; *ibid.*, ii. 2107; P.R.O., *List of Sheriffs*, List and Indexes ix (1898), 58.

Great Yarmouth to the Reformation Parliament, and became, in 1533, the first borough member to be chosen speaker. He sat again for Yarmouth in the 1542 parliament and had probably sat in the intervening sessions of 1536 and 1539. Humphrey was active in government work, notably in the dissolution of the monasteries, and he also took a large share of the routine administrative business of the county of Suffolk. Wingfield was something of a courtier as well. Chamberlain to Henry VIII's sister Mary, dowager queen of France, following her marriage to Charles Brandon, he acted years later as one of the knights welcoming to England another queen, Anne of Cleves. In the autumn of 1545 he died, full of years and honour, one of the leading figures in East Anglia. Was he lawyer or country gentleman? The question is impossible; quite clearly he was both.

Humphrey Wingfield was not exceptional. In the fifteenth century the lawyers of the Paston family had been equally at home at Caister as at the Inner Temple, while one of Wingfield's contemporaries, Sir Thomas Nevill, was just as prominent in society and the law.[43] Nor were lawyers with no estates to inherit any different; as soon as they were able, they acquired the lands and interest of the country gentleman. A similar situation is even to be seen lower in the professional scale. Amongst those included in the general pardon of 1509 was John Smith of Combe in Devon.[44] He combined tin-mining with some farming and was also clerk to the sheriff of the county and a professional holder of manorial courts. Another Devon man in the same pardon roll was John Herte of Bovey Tracey, tinner and tin-merchant; his legal interests embraced court-keeping and the post of clerk of the peace for Devon[45] The ancient rationale for the law terms was that everyone, litigant and lawyer alike, had a concern with land, and this remained true. It was one of the strengths of the English legal profession that, at all levels, it was integrated with the rest of society.

At the head of this far-flung profession were the eight or so judges of the ancient courts of king's bench and common pleas.[46] Although the inns of court and chancery were in direct control of legal education

43. Nevill heads the list of those practising at the bar in 1518 by virtue of his knighthood: c82/474/36. He was speaker of the commons in 1515.

44. *L. and P.*, i. 438 (2) m. 5.

45. *ibid.*, i. 438 (2) m. 6.

46. This was the usual number, but the total was not fixed. In the later years of Henry VI it was about eleven – four J.K.B., seven J.C.P.; after 1471 the total was reduced to seven, and sometimes six – two or three J.K.B., four J.C.P. To this should be added the C.B.Ex. when he was a serjeant (1483–6, 1522–9). The puisne barons of the exchequer ranked as apprentices: see below, pp. 18, 81–2.

and their own internal discipline, it seems probable that they were from an early date answerable to the judges; evidence of this is clear from 1466.[47] As for the professional conduct of lawyers, this was entirely for the court concerned; the inns had no say at all. The judges, however, were not distant autocrats; they themselves belonged to the dominant group within the common lawyers, the serjeants-at-law. The serjeants were selected by the crown from the most able and promising pleaders and withdrawn from the inns to act as assize judges and supply vacancies on the bench as required; in return they had certain privileges. Between the serjeants who were already full judges and the handful in reserve there were close ties, and their unity was visibly expressed by the distinctive white coifs they wore, from which judges and serjeants were known collectively as 'the order of the coif'. In cases of particular legal difficulty the whole order met as 'the court of exchequer chamber' to thrash the problem out, and this was the nearest England came to having any final court of appeal. Although the judges, therefore, were responsible for their courts and had responsibilities to the crown, the law was the construction of the whole order of the coif. As a result of these relationships, a judicial order regulating the profession was less likely to be a diktat than a consensus between judges, serjeants and the senior members of the inns of court, issued to each house on the authority of those judges and serjeants who had been members there, in conjunction with the current ruling body.[48] Historians of the inns may find precedents for self-government in the fifteenth and sixteenth centuries, but in fact the legal profession was ruled, in common with gilds and corporations of the time, by an oligarchy of senior members, backed by royal support and approval.

Below the eight judges and the half-dozen or so serjeants ranked the apprentices-at-law. On the origins of this misleading title it is unnecessary to dwell, and it is, in any case, probable that this suggestion of junior status was an archaism by the end of the fifteenth century. Instead, apprentices preferred the title 'gentleman', and so uniform was this that the very use of the term raises a presumption that the person concerned was a lawyer. The modern convention is to describe

47. See the case of Robert Hillersden, Black Book i. f. 148 [*Black Books*, i. 43–4].
48. Cf. the orders issued in 1510 regulating the keeping of vacations at Lincoln's Inn, promulgated by Rede C.J.K.B., Butler J.K.B., and Baron Allen, John More (serjeant), Newport and Newdigate (serjeants-elect), the governors and benchers: Black Book iii. f. 32 [*Black Books*, i. 161].

the apprentice as a barrister, the nearest equivalent term. In the fifteenth and early sixteenth centuries, however, 'barrister' was a rank within the inns and did not entitle the holder to practise in the central courts. It was the apprentices who (with the serjeants) were the pleaders at Westminster, and they were synonymous with the senior members of the inns of court. Apprentices had full audience in king's bench and exchequer, in chancery and the prerogative courts, all, indeed, except the common pleas, where the serjeants had a partial monopoly. Most advocacy at Westminster was, therefore, done by them. They also took, with the serjeants, the important legal work outside Westminster Hall, the senior recorderships, the retainers from the more prominent clients, lay and corporate, and the more notable cases at assize or *nisi prius*. These provincial opportunities included a number of judicial appointments, and there was also an opening for a few apprentices to sit as judges or 'barons' of the Westminster exchequer. The chief baron was a lawyer of the first rank; sometimes of the coif, it was not uncommon for him to double as a puisne in the common pleas, and he would go on assize whether or not he was a serjeant. Apprentices, however, could be puisne barons but they remained members of their inns and never took on the general judicial responsibilities of the coif or the chief baron.[49]

In all there were about fifty apprentices in practice at any one time.[50] In addition, there was probably an equivalent number in the Westminster legal machine. These were men such as the prothonotaries of the common pleas or the chief clerk of the king's bench. Although they did not normally plead at Westminster, they could give legal advice to clients and practise in the provinces. Indeed, some apprentices started as court clerks and later changed over to advocacy.[51] Other special openings for apprentices were in royal service. The king's attorney becomes a single identifiable figure early in the fifteenth century, replacing the group of legal representatives which the crown had relied on before, and a generation or so later the solicitor has, likewise, become established. Despite their titles, the law officers were always apprentices-at-law. The attorney derived his title from the use of 'attorney-general' to describe a magnate's principal legal executive, while the solicitor obtained his from the fifteenth-century meaning of the word – one who is in charge of, who solicits, his employer's suits, a general business agent, especially in

49. See below, pp. 81–2.
50. C82/474/36.
51. See below, p. 93.

legal affairs. In the pre-Elizabethan period the importance of the law officers grew. Where William Hussey A.G. resigned in 1478, took the coif and was promoted to the bench three years later, in the sixteenth century a number of law officers deliberately chose not to become serjeants and in 1519, for the first time, an attorney-general, John Erneley, was promoted to chief justice without first serving a term as a serjeant – promotion *per saltum*.[52] Nevertheless, this increasing importance was at first more in advising the crown than in leading the profession. There were no more promotions *per saltum* until 1592 (after which it became a usual practice), and where law officers were promoted it was to exchequer or, after the Reformation, to the post of master of the rolls.[53] Only in the middle of Elizabeth's reign did serjeants openly admit the superior professional opportunities of their juniors by resigning to become law officers.[54] Before the Reformation the offices of king's attorney and solicitor were significant, but they were not the certain passport to eminence in the courts that they became later.

The upper ranks of the profession, judges, serjeants and the leading apprentices, were tightly knit, homogeneous and wielded considerable influence. Compared with the rest of the profession, however, their number was minute, perhaps 120 at any one time; the great majority of the common lawyers were below this level. Every court needed a complement of attorneys, solicitors and miscellaneous clerks, whether the royal courts at Westminster, at Lancaster and elsewhere, municipal courts (varying from the complete judicial apparatus of London to the simplest borough franchise), quarter sessions and the

52. In the sixteenth century, the only examples of law officers resigning to become serjeants were John Fitzjames A.G., John Port, and Richard Weston S.G., serjeant 1559 and judge later that year. On refusals to take the coif, see Ives, *L.Q.R.* 75. 355–60. The procedure in promotion *per saltum* was for the candidate to be created serjeant the day before, or earlier on the day of his appointment to the bench; Dr J. H. Baker has discovered that Erneley was called to the coif on 26 Jan. and made C.J.C.P. on 27 Jan. 1519: Spelman, *Reports*, ii. *395*.
53. John Popham A.G., promoted C.J.K.B. in 1592. The patents of thirty-three law officers were terminated between 1461 and 1603 (19 A.G., 14 S.G.), five by death, eight by a change of sovereign, two by dismissal or resignation, and eighteen by promotion – one to lord keeper, two to chief justice, three to C.B.Ex., four to M.R., four to serjeant, one to puisne baron, one to chancellor of the duchy, one to chancellor of the augmentations, one to chancellor of first fruits and tenths. Richard Lyster A.G. was promoted C.J.K.B. in 1545 after serving as C.B.Ex. since 1529, taking the coif specially for that appointment.
54. To become S.G., Serjeant Popham resigned in 1579, Fleming in 1595 and Doderidge in 1604; Henry Hobart resigned in 1604 to become A.G.

older shire courts and lesser tribunals. Outside, lawyers supplied the demand for legal services at every level of society. At the bottom was a proletariat of local legal officials, land agents, professional court-keepers and *hommes d'affaires*, men miles away from and below Westminster Hall, but at once the most numerous and, for the mass of the population, the only lawyers who mattered.[55] Individuals can sometimes be identified by their descriptions – Richard Gurnay of Cory Mallet in Somerset, gentleman *alias* courtholder; Thomas Gunwyn of Glaston, also in Somerset, gentleman, *alias* yeoman, *alias* courtholder; John Fowler of Shackerstone in Leicestershire, gentleman, clerk of the peace.[56] Many appear in the *Valor Ecclesiasticus* of 1535. William At Mere, for example, was listed there as steward on the bishop of Norwich's estates and as receiver and steward to the college of St Mary in the Fields, Norwich, while letters to Thomas Cromwell suggest that Mere was, at the same time, one of the bishop's receivers.[57] He was probably also under-steward for the courts of Carrow Priory, a nunnery just outside the city; certainly he had held the post in 1530.[58] In addition to these posts, William was, as a chancery case shows, under-sheriff for Norwich.[59] And Mere was not unique – there were hundreds like him.

In popular terminology, lawyers below the sartorially distinct judges and serjeants were lumped together. They were all 'learned in the law', or more simply, 'learned men'; the French and Latin equivalents are *appris de la ley* and *legis peritus* or *juris peritus*. The wide gap between an apprentice who pleaded in Westminster Hall and a petty lawyer who kept a manorial court is obvious, yet in subsuming all common lawyers under one label, popular usage was recognising a vital fact about the profession, its unity. This was more than the implication of a common legal system or a similarity of interests; it was the direct consequence of education at the inns of court and chancery. Some minor lawyers and men in quasi-legal occupations must have learned what they knew by apprenticeship to an elder in the trade, or perhaps from books. However, it is clear that the dominant influence in providing trained men for all levels of legal work was

55. For another discussion of these minor lawyers and further examples, see Ives, *Trans. Royal Hist. Soc.*, 5 ser., 18. 147–9.
56. *L. and P.*, i. 438 (4 mm. 17, 19); (3 m. 18).
57. *Valor Ecclesiasticus*, iii. 282, 290; *L. and P.*, x. 79 (iii).
58. L. J. Redstone, 'Three Carrow account rolls', in *Norfolk Archaeology* 29 (1946), 71. The *Valor* for Carrow is mutilated: *Valor Ecclesiasticus*, iii. 306.
59. C1/390/42.

that of the inns. In the opening years of Henry VIII's reign, both deputy chief stewards of the duchy of Lancaster and the duchy receiver-general were all members of an inn of court.[60] The attorney-general of the bishop of Durham had been trained at Lincoln's Inn, the deputy at Lancaster to the chancellor of the duchy was a member of the Middle Temple, and the clerk of the common pleas there was a member of the Inner Temple.[61]

Even more of the lawyers practising locally seem to have been members of the junior inns. In 1509, James Grysy of Grysy in Cornwall and the Strand Inn was deputy receiver for the duchy of Cornwall; Jasper Filoll, probably of Furnival's Inn, had just completed a term as receiver of Melbury Sampford in Dorset. Thomas Strey of Clement's Inn was under-steward of Tickhill, clerk of assize for the northern circuit, deputy sheriff of Yorkshire, and in 1515 he became clerk of the common pleas at Lancaster.[62] Many lawyers with local practices also acted as attorneys for one of the Westminster courts. Andrew Pawe, clerk of the peace and clerk to the mayor of Norwich, was an attorney of the common pleas; his counterpart in Norfolk, Leonard Spencer, was likewise an attorney of the common pleas; another such was Thomas Sneth of Dalby who had a practice in Lincolnshire as a court-keeper.[63] These petty lawyers active in 1509 are no more than names, but a better-known example is James Gresham, the legal and business agent of the Paston family. Sometimes he is described as an early example of a solicitor, but this advances that branch of the profession by a century; actually he belonged to Staple Inn and was an attorney of the common pleas at Westminster.[64] He also had a local practice in Norfolk, pursuing Paston lawsuits, keeping their courts for them and supplying them with news and advice.[65] Another lesser lawyer who is well

60. Somerville, *Duchy of Lancaster*, i. 402, 426, 431.
61. See below p. 105; Somerville, *Duchy of Lancaster*, i. 479, 488.
62. Grysy: *L. and P.*, i. 438 (4 m. 16). Filoll: *ibid.*, i. 438 (4 m. 11); Bland, *Furnival's Inn*, 34. An alternative identification for Filoll of Furnival's Inn is Reginald, of Knygetstrete, Dorset, controller of the great roll of the exchequer: *L. and P.*, i. 438 (2 m. 22). Strey: Somerville, *Duchy of Lancaster*, i. 488, 529; *Cal. Patent Rolls, 1494–1509*, 209 *et passim*; *Yorkshire Star Chamber Proceedings*, ed. W. Brown etc., Yorkshire Archaeological Soc. 41, 45, 51, 70 (1909–27), i. 175; *Inner Temple Records*, i. 461. For other examples of minor lawyers trained at the inns, see Ives, *Trans. Royal Hist. Soc.*, 5 ser., 18. 150–1.
63. Pawe: C1/125/4; Blatcher, 'Working of king's bench', lix; *L. and P.*, i. 438 (2 m. 9). Spencer: *ibid.*, i. 438 (4 m. 2). Sneth: *ibid.*, i. 438 (4 m. 23).
64. CP40/802, roll of warrants mm. 2, 2d, 3d; of Staple Inn, *ex inf.* J. H. Baker.
65. M. Birks, *Gentlemen of the Law* (1960), 89.

documented is John Nethersole of Lincoln's Inn and Canterbury. A Westminster attorney with clients from a wide area, Nethersole was also deputy sheriff of Kent, on the pay-roll of the archbishop of Canterbury and deep in the counsels of the city.[66] In England, high and low, common lawyers were the products of the courts and the inns, in and around Westminster.

In the years before the Reformation, the English legal profession was both ubiquitous and cohesive. Neither quality won it affection, and sometimes not even toleration; the attack of the 1381 rebels on the inns of court is well known, as is also the 1404 prohibition on lawyers serving in parliament.[67] With the growth of a literature of social comment, the bad reputation of the lawyers became a cliché. The passion of a Latimer is to be expected, but even the judicious Thomas Starkey held the vulgar opinion of the lawyers that 'the covetous and greedy minds of them destroyeth all law and good policy'.[68] But vulgar error it was, for the place of the lawyers in English life was a symptom, not a cause, a symptom that legal procedures and legal ideas were integral to society. The profession which embraced individuals as far apart as the judge in scarlet and the tin-miner keeping a manor court was bound together by common service to one superior, the law, and that law provided the ligaments of the body politic.

66. Nethersole – of Canterbury; Lincoln's Inn, admitted 1465, left legacy of 40 marks for the inn library; attorney in king's bench and common pleas; agent for Thomas Tropenell, for the Pastons, for the city of Canterbury; attorney in common pleas for the archbishop of Canterbury; deputy sheriff of Kent, 1468; frequent commissions; J.P. 1493–7; died 1504–5: *Tropenell Cartulary*, i. 265–6; ii. 303–5, 308, 312–13, 348; Hastings, *Common Pleas*, 70–1; Blatcher, 'Workings of king's bench', lvi; *Admission Book*, i. 15; *Black Books*, i. 74, 135–6; *Paston Letters and Papers*, ii. 595; *Cal. Close Rolls, 1461–8*, 458; *Cal. Patent Rolls, 1485–94*, 490; *Year Books, 10 Edward IV and 49 Henry VI*, ed. N. Neilson, Selden Soc. 47 (1930), 22, 70; 'Records of Canterbury', 117b, 134b, 144a, 144b; PROB11/14 ff. 195v–196v.

67. Hostility to the lawyers in 1381 was both general and particular: J. P. Dawson, *The Oracles of the Law* (Ann Arbor, 1968), 36 n. 5; Myers, *English Historical Documents, 1327–1485*, 127–40.

68. Starkey, *Dialogue*, 113.

2

SOCIAL ORIGINS: THE KEBELLS OF REARSBY

In his panegyric on the English common law, Sir John Fortescue stressed that the law was a career for gentlemen.[1] Neither the poor nor the common people could afford the expense of the training, while merchants, who could, needed to keep their capital in trade. Sir John was writing in 1470–1, at the age of eighty and after sixty years' experience in the profession. Was he correct? The sceptic will point to his great age and his ten years' exile from England and the courts. On the other hand, Fortescue clearly knew his lawyers; if anybody could tell us about them he could, provided he was not recalling a mythical golden age and provided that he told the truth, not what should have been the truth.

About the time Fortescue wrote *De Laudibus Legum Anglie*, a young lawyer was beginning to achieve some prominence, Thomas Kebell of the Inner Temple. He had been born about 1439, the third son of Walter Kebell of Rearsby, a village seven miles north-east of Leicester.[2] His father was the local squire, but this was no distinction – Walter was the complete *parvenu*. A number of Kebles (the name is variously spelt) were prominent in the south of England during the fifteenth century, but Walter had no connection with any of them.[3] As Bertha Putnam suggested, his most likely link is with a Coventry family whose earliest known member, John Kebell, contributed to the royal loan of 1424 and can be followed in the town's Leet Book until 1450.[4] John never reached municipal office but was prominent in Bishop St Ward and from 1432 was summoned whenever the mayor of Coventry wished to consult citizens of middle rank.[5] This John

1. Fortescue, *De Laudibus*, 118.
2. See below, p. 33.
3. John Keble, coroner of Hampshire; Andrew Keble, controller of the pipe; Richard Keble, brother to Andrew, clerk in chancery: *Cal. Patent Rolls, 1422–36*, 396; *Cal. Close Rolls, 1435–41*, 370; *ibid., 1441–7*, 260; *ibid., 1447–54*, 61, 295; Wedgwood, *Biographies*.
4. *Coventry Leet Book*, 82, 246.
5. *ibid.*, 143. Collector of fifteenth, 1431; fourth in Bishop St Ward assessments: *ibid.*, 139, 142, 241.

would be much of an age with Walter Kebell of Rearsby, and it would be consistent with all that is known for them to be cousins, or even brothers. The connection between Walter Kebell and Coventry is only circumstantial, and for twenty years after 1450 the Leet Book is silent, but in 1471 a Henry Kebell, mercer, appears among those loaning money to the town. Although he occupied a different house and possibly followed a different trade, he was presumably the son of John Kebell, and Henry can be tentatively linked with Thomas Kebell.[6] He became mayor of Coventry in 1484, and it was in the next year, when as immediate past mayor Henry had enormous importance, that Thomas was invited to become the town's recorder.[7] On the other hand, although Henry Kebell went on to become lord mayor of London, Thomas had no further contact with him and did not mention him when he drew his will.[8]

The first mention of Walter Kebell occurs in the will of Sir Hugh Burnell, dated 2 October 1417, where he was appointed an executor, together with Joan Beauchamp, Lady Burgavenny, and a number of others.[9] Subsequent documents show that Walter and these others were there as feoffees to Lady Joan, to whom Sir Hugh had conveyed all his property.[10] That Walter is thus first found in the service of Lady Burgavenny is a further hint of some Coventry connection; her husband owned an estate a few miles away and Lady Joan played some part in Coventry affairs.[11] What Kebell's connection with Lady Burgavenny was becomes specific when, with another of her feoffees, Bartholomew Brokesby, he was admitted, on 20 May 1420, to the Gild of Holy Cross, Stratford-upon-Avon.[12] Walter is described as *seneschallus dominae Johannae, dominae de Bergavenny*, that is, steward of the honour of Burgavenny, Lady Joan's dower. He had probably held the office as early as 1418, when, again with Brokesby, he was commissioned to enquire into some estates in Shropshire and the March, and since he witnessed a Monmouthshire deed in 1434 as steward of Burgavenny, it seems safe to assume that he kept the post at least until his employer died in 1436.[13]

6. *ibid.*, 368.
7. *ibid.*, 518–21, 524–28; see below, p. 135–7.
8. *Cal. Patent Rolls, 1494–1509*, 516; *L. and P.*, i. 438(1) m.19.
9. *Register of Archbishop Chichele*, ii. 217.
10. *Cal. Close Rolls, 1419–22*, 86–90.
11. *Register of the Guild of the Holy Trinity*, ed. M. D. Harris, Dugdale Soc. 13 (1935), 4, 74, 108.
12. Shakespeare Birthplace Trust BRT1/1 – Stratford-upon-Avon Gild Register, f. 16v. Lady Burgavenny resided at Snitterfield, a nearby village.
13. *Cal. Patent Rolls, 1416–22*, 207; *Cal. Ancient Deeds*, vi. C4537.

Little is known of Walter's duties as steward, or of his life in this period. At some time he visited France, for at Easter 1440, a Leicestershire enquiry into alien residents returned that Walter had a son, Robert, who was unmarried and had been born in France.[14] Alien taxation began at the age of twelve, so that this son must have been born by 1428 at the latest, but nothing further is known. Alien subsidies for 1442 and 1453 are blank, which suggests that he had left the county or, more likely, was dead.[15] Robert may have been the son of an unrecorded first marriage, in which case Walter must have lived abroad or else have married a Frenchwoman. An alternative is that Robert was illegitimate, but it seems unusual for the father to have custody of the boy especially if begotten by a member of an invading army. More significant than these conjectures is the fact that Walter had travelled abroad. That he had done so in the retinue of William, Lord Burgavenny, Lady Joan's husband, is unlikely, but their son Richard, later earl of Worcester, went to the Normandy campaign in 1418. Perhaps the steward of his marcher lordship went with him.

It is, however, in the service of the earl's mother that Walter Kebell appears most frequently. He acted as one of Lady Burgavenny's main agents, both during her lifetime, and in settling her estate after death; he was still acting as executor as late as 1457.[16] But Walter Kebell was more than a mere land agent. Lady Joan's will, dated 10 January 1434, treats him as an esteemed confidential servant.[17] Kebell was one of six executors, chosen because her 'singler trust' was upon them 'afore other', and asked to act 'as they wolde I sholde do for hem in lyke caas'. Walter Kebell, Bartholomew Brokesby and Robert Darcy were to control her wardships and the custody of those goods which she specified should go to her grandson when he attained the age of twenty. Kebell and Brokesby were also to visit Hereford annually to distribute £10 for masses for Lady Joan's soul 'after here discrecion'. The responsibility placed on Kebell makes one provision of the will seem strange; he and one other of the executors were forbidden to act alone. Presumably this reflected on Kebell's status rather than his

14. E179/133/71 m.3.

15. *ibid.*, 133/74; 235/29, 53.

16. *Warwickshire Feet of Fines*, 2516, 2539; *Register of Archbishop Chichele*, i. 232; Leicestershire Record Office: 5D33 – Farnham Mss., *passim*; *Hastings Mss.*, i. 1, 7; *Cal. Patent Rolls, 1416–22*, 302, 305; *ibid., 1422–36*, 506; *ibid., 1436–41*, 435, 446; *ibid., 1452–61*, 199, 355; *Cal. Close Rolls, 1435–41*, 317, 322, 323, 327, 422; V.C.H., *Worcestershire*, iii. 133; CP25(1) 126/75/39.

17. William Dugdale, *Warwickshire* (1730), ii. 1031; *Register of Archbishop Chichele*, ii. 536–8.

capacity or his honesty, but the restriction seems all the more surprising in view of the large bequest which Lady Joan made to him. Kebell was to receive – in addition to the £20 assigned to each executor – one hundred marks in cash, three of Lady Joan's best horses, her best black bed of silk and 'alle the apparell of a Chambre of the best blak Tapeter that I have', a quantity of linen and bedding, and:

my rounde basyn of sylver with bolles and a ewer that longeth therto; and my litle saler and vj spones of sylver that byn in my Maner atte the Snyterfeld and my best stayned halle with a potel pot and iij pece of sylver and a grete maser covered that was Sir Adam Persales.

If, as seems likely, this was intended to equal the legacies of Brokesby and Darcy, the total value was probably in the region of £600. Despite his obscure background, Walter Kebell had gained considerably from his service with the Beauchamps.

Before the death of his patroness, indeed, Walter Kebell had been able to set up as a landowner, by the traditional method – marrying an heiress. In 1433 he appears in Leicestershire as the husband of Agnes, eldest of the three daughters and heiresses of John Folville of Rearsby, the royal coroner for the county.[18] The Folvilles had been notable – and notorious – members of Leicester society for over a century, and the match was no mean achievement for an estate steward.[19] Once again we may suspect a Beauchamp connection. Lady Burgavenny had close ties with the religious house at Kirby Bellars, near to Rearsby, and her servants, Brokesby and Darcy, who worked constantly with Walter, were Leicestershire men.

The property which Agnes Kebell inherited, although only a third of her father's estate, was by no means negligible. In her right Walter Kebell received one of the two manors in Rearsby, Chamberlain's Manor, which consisted, in the time of his son, of ten messuages, five cottages, five tofts and twenty-two virgates of land.[20] The other manor passed to William Cotton, the husband of Agnes' sister Mary, and the remaining land, made up of holdings in nearby villages, went to the

18. CP40/688 m. 373 – *Walter Kebell of Rearsby* v. *Richard Hanslade of Queniborough*, Hil. 1433. The first notice of Kebell's marriage occurs on 6 May 1437, when Walter was pardoned as executor to Lady Burgavenny and his wife Agnes, one of the daughters and co-heiresses of John Folville, late of Rearsby, but it is obvious that his style in 1433 was after his marriage: C67/38 m. 26; cf. Farnham, *Medieval Pedigrees*, 74–9.

19. E. L. G. Stones, 'The Folvilles of Ashby-Folville', in *Trans. Royal Hist. Soc.*, 5 ser., 7 (1957), 117–36.

20. *Cal. inquisitions post mortem*, i. 164.

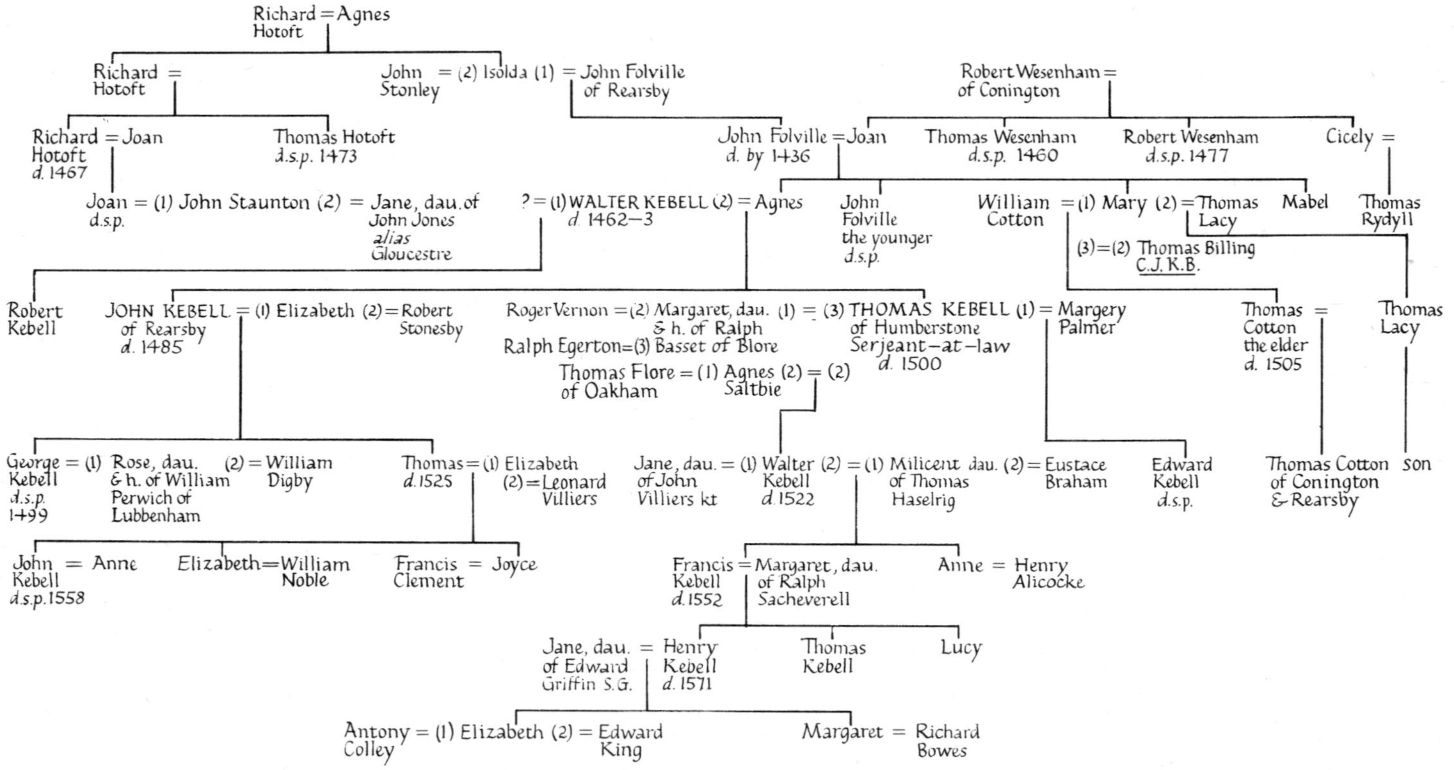

Fig. 1. The Kebells of Rearsby and Humberstone

third sister, Mabel.[21] After some years Mabel died without heirs and her property was divided between the two surviving sisters, and by the date of Walter Kebell's own death (1462–3) it had become obvious that his union with Agnes was to produce yet another windfall.[22] Joan Folville, his mother-in-law, had belonged to the Wesenham family of Conington in Huntingdonshire, and when in 1460 Thomas Wesenham died without heirs, only the life of his seventy-year-old brother stood between her daughters and the Wesenham fortune.[23]

Only slight evidence remains of Walter Kebell's new role as a landowner in Leicestershire, where, from the start, Folville prestige enabled him to adopt the style of 'esquire'. His absorbing interest would seem to have been litigation. For example, in a single term, Hilary 1447, and in a single court, the common pleas, Kebell had no fewer than seven suits in progress.[24] Nor did this passion decline with age; in the Michaelmas term of 1461 Walter was pressing actions against twelve people, was defending in another, and had at least two more writs out.[25] Sometimes he was protecting his wife's rights. When Mabel Folville died, Kebell and his brother-in-law, William Cotton, had to go to chancery to prise her share of the family estates away from John Folville's executor.[26] In 1447, likewise, the two went to law to discover documents concerning the manor owned by Richard Hotoft in Humberstone (where Serjeant Kebell was later to live); Richard's heir was a girl, his brother Thomas had no children, and the Folville sisters, although very distant relatives, had a plausible claim to the succession – clearly their husbands had to investigate.[27] Other litigation against drovers, butchers and small farmers suggests that Walter was grazing and selling stock, often, apparently, for the Leicester market.[28] Indeed, he seems here to have taken over John Folville's connections. In 1435, for example, Walter sued Hugh Catesby of Arthingworth, 'drover', and William Catesby of Sutton, a husbandman, for £36, and the following year Folville's executors sued the same Hugh for £30 owed to John.[29] In 1435 the executors went to law

21. Farnham, *Medieval Pedigrees*, 74–9.
22. For the division of Mabel's estate, see below, n. 26.
23. See below, p. 33. Cf. *Visitation of Huntingdon, 1613*, ed. H. Ellis, Camden Soc., 1 ser., 43 (1849), 24–7, 75–7.
24. CP40/744 mm. 8d, 76d, 260d, 321.
25. Plaintiff: CP40/803 mm. 205, 286d. Defendant: *ibid.*, 803 m. 190d. Writs: *Cal. Patent Rolls, 1467–77*, 4, 81.
26. C1/72/24.
27. CP40/744 m. 321.
28. *ibid.*, 743 mm. 8d, 277.
29. *ibid.*, 699 m. 50; 700 m. 398. Hugh Catesby: *Cal. Fine Rolls, 1422–30*, 294, 329.

to recover £12 from Richard Whytteley, a Leicester butcher, and in 1446, Whytteley and another Leicester butcher, William Peweman, were sued by Kebell for ten marks.[30] Nor was Kebell only supplying meat for the local market. He had interests in wool, or so his pursuit through the courts of two woolmen, a shepherd and a small London merchant would suggest.[31] He also sued such a miscellany of debtors that the suspicion is aroused that he was a money-lender. It is difficult otherwise to account for the sums he claimed from a schoolmaster, a coalman, a smith, two chapmen, and a variety of labourers and small country gentlemen.[32]

Despite his fortunate marriage and comfortable circumstances, Walter Kebell did not play the part in Leicester society that John Folville had. He was not made a justice of the peace and never held county office. Only rarely, indeed, did he act as a feoffee.[33] Walter, it seems, was far more at home with his peasant debtors, or in quarrelling with the parson of Rearsby. Tithe was presumably the issue there, for Walter's son, John, accused the parson of having walked off with one hundred marks' worth of Walter's chattels.[34] Kebell's rare appearances as a feoffee would alone dispose of one of the most persistent legends about him – that he was a lawyer, even that he became a serjeant in either 1452 or 1482. The story arose from an attempt by Sir William Dugdale to rationalise an error by William Burton; it has been established and developed by repetition and is without foundation.[35] As a former estate steward, Kebell must have had a smattering of law, but there is no evidence that he was a professional.

It must not be supposed that once Walter Kebell became established as a country gentleman he abandoned the calling which had brought him success. His patroness died in 1436 and Walter was soon

30. *ibid.*, 699 m. 578d; 743 m. 277; 744 m. 76d. Kebell was pursuing another suit against Peweman at the same time: *ibid.*, 743 m. 277; 744 m. 8d.
31. *ibid.*, 744 m. 76d; 797 m. 157; 803 mm. 205, 286d; 804 m. 272d; 805 m. 153.
32. *ibid.*, 744 m. 8d; 743 m. 277; 803 mm. 205, 286d; 805 m. 153; 715 m. 197; 713 m. 212.
33. *Cal. Close Rolls, 1447–54*, 43; Farnham, *Quorndon Records*, 145; Leicestershire Record Office: Rothley Mss. 44/28/164–6.
34. CP40/850 m. 162.
35. Burton, *Leicestershire*, 128, misnamed Thomas as Walter. Dugdale listed both Thomas and Walter, giving a year-book authority for the appointment of Walter Keble as a serjeant in 1482; the reference is to an appearance of 'Keble' in king's bench, i.e. Thomas, the future serjeant. A copying error then introduced the alternative date, 1452: e.g. W. R. Williams, *The Welsh Judges* (Brecknock, 1899).

replaced as steward of Burgavenny, but he found employment with Lord Cromwell, the treasurer of England.[36] Unlike his post with the Beauchamp estates, Kebell's work for Cromwell was certainly in the household. He left during the year beginning Michaelmas 1443, but it does not follow that even this was the end of his professional career. In 1443 Cromwell had himself retired from much of his government work and Kebell's departure may be connected with a consequent reduction of the household. Yet although Walter remained pretty active in his own affairs for a decade at least, no hint has yet appeared of any new patron after 1443–4.

Walter Kebell, father of Serjeant Thomas Kebell, was, thus, very much a *nouveau riche* in fifteenth-century Leicestershire. His ancestry was undistinguished and his fortune small; his prosperity was almost entirely owed to his service to the house of Beauchamp, which, in turn, opened the way to a lucrative marriage. Walter's career represents the first stage in the rise of one family to the ranks of the gentry. The father had succeeded in setting up as a landowner on the basis of his own good fortune and successful enterprise, coupled with his wife's money, and left sons and grandsons to consolidate and improve upon the position.

Sir John Fortescue's claim that few lawyers were not *nobilis aut de nobilium genere egressus*, was, thus, certainly not true of Thomas Kebell.[37] Fortescue's own ancestry suggests that by *nobilis* he meant 'gentry', but Thomas can hardly be said even to have had much gentry blood in his veins, certainly not on his father's side.[38] Was he an exception? Seven other serjeants were called with him in 1486 – William Danvers, John Fineux, John Fisher, John Haugh, Richard Jay, Robert Rede and Thomas Wode. Danvers was the second son of John Danvers of Banbury; John was himself undistinguished, but his elder son, Sir Thomas, a lawyer and servant of Bishop Waynflete, was knighted and became a member of parliament.[39] John Fineux is supposed to have been the son of William Fineux, esq., of Swingfield in Kent, but record evidence for this is hard to find.[40] Fisher's ancestry is, if anything, even more elusive – according to the

36. *Register of Archbishop Chichele*, ii. 536–8. A new steward is mentioned in 1446: E. Price, 'Ralph, Lord Cromwell and his household', M.A. unpublished thesis, University of London (1948), 106–7. Kebell's work for Lady Burgavenny had brought him into contact with Cromwell: *Cal. Close Rolls, 1435–41*, 317.

37. Fortescue, *De Laudibus*, 118.

38. *ibid.*, lxix.

39. Wedgwood, *Biographies*.

40. *ibid.*; *Visitations of Kent, 1530 etc.*, i. 128. Cf. below, p. 461.

Table A. *The social origins of serjeants-at-law created 1463–1521*

I	Close relation a knight or peer	6		
II	Family represented in the commission of the peace	8		
III	Father or grandfather styled 'esquire' or county M.P.	4		
			18	28%
IV	Family estates held for more than one generation	12		
			12	19%
V	Urban background	11		
VI	Legal background	4		
			15	23%
VII	Family estates not known before previous generation	6		
			6	9%
VIII	Origin insignificant or unknown	13		
			13	20%
	Total of sample		64	100%

genealogists his father was John Fisher of Fishall in the parish of Hadlow in Kent, a person of no note whatever.[41] John Haugh belonged to the numerous family of Walsham-le-Willows in Suffolk, but his place in the pedigree cannot be established.[42] Richard Jay of Basing in Hampshire was the son of a Thomas Jay, possibly customer of Sandwich, and Robert Rede was the son of a William Rede, burgess of Calais; neither were persons of any quality.[43] Most obscure of all is Thomas Wode; although he became chief justice of the common pleas, his family, even his county of origin, are a mystery.[44] An octet less *de nobilium genere egressus* would be hard to find.

It must be admitted that such a complete lack of distinction is unusual; most generally a call included one or two middling gentle-

41. *Visitations of Essex, 1552 etc.*, ii. 568.

42. *East Anglian Pedigrees*, ed. A. Campling, Harleian Soc. 91 (1939), 101 *sqq.*; *Miscellanea Genealogica et Heraldica*, 5 ser., 5 (1923–5), 208 *sqq.*; C. Coodforde, *The Norwich School of Glass Painting* (1950), plate xxiii, 101, 119–20.

43. Jay: PROB11/10 ff. 52v–54. Rede: *ibid.* 11/19 ff. 97–100.

44. At the end of his life he was associated with Berkshire, but this was probably consequent on his marriage to a Berkshire widow. The only likely tradition regarding his origin suggests Cambridge, but his early legal associations suggest London: Wedgwood, *Biographies*; *Cal. inquisitions post mortem*, ii. 374; *Visitation of Cambridge*, ed. J. W. Clay, Harleian Soc. 41 (1897), 101; *Cal. Patent Rolls, 1476–85*, 10–11, 124; *Cal. Close Rolls, 1468–76*, 1151; PROB11/13 ff. 161–2.

men. For example of the eight summoned in 1463, probably the first call Kebell witnessed, three at least belonged to established families. Others, nevertheless, were again of quite insignificant origin – John Grenefield was the grandson of a franklin.[45] The 1495 call, the last in Kebell's lifetime, is similar. The origins of all but one are known; two were of very minor importance, another was the son of a knight who was really a merchant, one was heir to a modest estate, two were related to justices of the peace and two came from important county families.[46] Thus, although the 1486 serjeants were unusually plebeian, the upper ranks of the legal profession always included a sizeable number of men of humble origins. Sixty-four men in all were called to the coif between 1463 and 1521, and thirteen, more than one in five, had only minimal claim to gentility.[47] Add the eleven townsmen and the four lawyers' sons, and fewer than three serjeants in five are left with any social consequence. Even of these, half were from the middling or lesser gentry; few, perhaps three in ten, belonged to a family which served on the commission of the peace or had equivalent status.[48] Thomas Kebell, therefore, had no reason to find his birth a disadvantage; the socially superior were clients, not colleagues.

The fact that many men of insignificant parentage should essay the law, establishes the role which the profession performed in fifteenth-century society.[49] It was an opportunity for a family to rise within or into the ranks of the gentry, for the small landowner to make the transition to the substantial squirearchy in one bound. That this was the objective of many, if not all, lawyers is confirmed by the use which they made of any success. They bought land in their home county, or in another shire in which they had the entrée (often by marriage), and settled down to play the part of the country gentleman. The family which could afford to send the heir to be trained as a lawyer was placing its money where it could yield the most rapid and considerable social dividend. It is not an accident that the habitual designation of the lawyer was 'gentleman of London'.

For a man like Walter Kebell to think of the law as a career for his

45. Guy Fairfax, Richard Pigot, John Catesby and, possibly, Richard Nele of gentry families; Thomas Yonge, son of the mayor of Bristol; William Jenney, son of a lawyer; Thomas Bryan, origin unknown; John Grenefield, grandson of William Grenefield, franklin.

46. Ives, *Trans. Royal Hist. Soc.*, 5 ser., 18. 157.

47. See table A.

48. The view that 'the majority came from families which were the backbone of county society' (E. W. Ives, 'Some aspects of the legal profession', in *Bull. Institute of Hist. Research* 31 (1958), 100) now seems optimistic.

49. See p. 374.

son was, thus, obvious to the point of cliché. That he should choose the career for the younger of his two sons by Agnes Folville – John the elder was probably born about 1436, and Thomas a year or two later, probably by 1439, certainly before 1446 – is, however, less expected.[50] Given the value of the law in establishing the fortunes of a family (and the initial outlay it required), eldest sons predominated in the profession. Genealogical tables are decidedly unreliable, but of forty serjeants called from 1463 to 1521 whose position in the family can be established more or less satisfactorily, twenty-five were eldest sons – a ratio of five in eight. The reason why Thomas, rather than John, followed the law may have been a personal one, that John was not able enough, but the probability is that Thomas had found a patron in that distant cousin, Richard Hotoft of Humberstone; Richard certainly patronised Thomas Kebell as a young man, and could well have kept him at the inns of court as a student.[51] But whatever the reason, the decision was taken; Thomas entered the law while John, the elder brother, stayed at home.

Walter Kebell died litigious to the end, and John entered upon his inheritance as a Leicestershire landowner.[52] By 1472 he was married (his son George was born about that date), but the family of his wife, Elizabeth, is unknown.[53] 1475 and 1477 saw John occupied, with his aunt Mary, in litigation to recover the entailed estates of the Hotoft family, following the demise, without heirs, of Richard Hotoft's brother, Thomas.[54] In 1477, the long-awaited Wesenham estates arrived.[55] Mary took the property at Conington in Huntingdonshire, but John's share is not certain. Presumably he disposed of what he could and purchased land in Leicestershire instead. It was probably at this time that John bought two messuages, four virgates of land and ten acres of meadow in the village of Sileby from William Bret of Rotherby.[56] It was not a straightforward purchase; Bret's feoffee

50. The dates of birth for John and Thomas are conjectured upon the marriage date of Walter *c.* 1433. Thomas was certainly over 21 in 1467: see below, p. 332.

51. See below, pp. 332–5. Richard Hotoft was one of John Folville's executors: CP40/699 m. 578d. In 1495 Brian Roucliffe left £20 p.a. to support Guy Palmes at the Middle Temple; in 1523 John Caryll left his son £10, claiming that this was enough if he lived 'honestly': *Testamenta Eboracensia* iv. 105; PROB11/21 ff. 75–6.

52. Walter was alive in Trinity term 1462, but deceased by Trinity 1463: CP40/805 m. 153; 809 m. 161.

53. John's inquisition *post mortem* gives George as thirteen years old in 1486: *Cal. inquisitions post mortem*, i. 164.

54. Farnham, *Village Notes*, ii. 370; *Medieval Pedigrees*, 38.

55. C140/64/71.

56. C1/61/73

refused to disgorge the land until Kebell began a suit in chancery. On another occasion he and his cousin, Thomas Cotton, had to go to law to protect their interest in a couple of hundred acres in Little Ashby against one of the villagers.[57]

All told, these transactions left John Kebell with a very comfortable estate, small properties in a dozen or so villages, worth, even on the unrealistic inquisition *post mortem* assessment, £85 per annum.[58] There was now a second son, named after his uncle and godfather the lawyer, and the succession seemed secure.[59] In local affairs, John Kebell seems to have been, like any sensible man in Leicestershire, a client of William Hastings, the lord chamberlain, and in January 1483 the arrival of the Kebells of Rearsby, and also, by implication, their acceptability to the court where Lord Hastings was at the height of his influence, was signalled by the appointment of John to the commission of the peace.[60] After half a century, at least some of the status of the Rearsby Folvilles had been recovered.

The triumph did not last long. On 21 August 1485, as the combatants gathered at Bosworth, twenty miles away, John Kebell of Rearsby died.[61] His heir, George, was only thirteen years old and the interest of the family was challenged almost at once.[62] But the uncle, now a prospective serjeant-at-law, took over leadership of the clan and acquired the wardship of his young nephew.[63] John's widow, Elizabeth, was associated in this, but she remarried soon afterwards, and it was, presumably, Thomas who carried the principal responsibility and who found a wife for George in the person of Rose, the daughter and reputedly the sole heiress of William Perwich of Lubbenham.[64] What wealth might have accrued from this marriage is not clear; George died without heirs at the age of twenty-seven, and the estate passed to his brother Thomas, the serjeant's godson.[65] Thomas was more fortunate and enjoyed his inheritance from 1499 until 1525, but on his death, the estate again passed to a minor, his twelve-year-old

57. CP40/882 m. 7d.
58. *Cal. inquisitions post mortem*, i. 164.
59. Twenty-eight years *et amplius* in 1506: *ibid.*, iii. 1166.
60. John appears as a witness to a Hastings' deed in 1474: Farnham, *Village Notes*, iii. 142. Commission of the peace: *Cal. Patent Rolls, 1476–85*, 563.
61. *Cal. inquisitions post mortem*, i. 164.
62. *Elizabeth Kebeel, widow* v. *Thomas Holand, gent.*, *re* injury to stock at Thrussington: CP40/896 m. 194.
63. *Cal. Patent Rolls, 1485–94*, 157.
64. Elizabeth had married Robert Stonesby by 1488: Farnham, *Village Notes*, iv. 335. Rose Kebell: Farnham, *Medieval Pedigrees*, 49, 51.
65. *Cal. inquisitions post mortem*, iii. 1166.

son, John.[66] John held Rearsby for even longer than his father – thirty-three years – but he had no male heir and when he died, the estate was broken up amongst his daughters.[67]

After the brief acceptance of John Kebell in 1483, the Kebells of Rearsby made no mark on the county. No other member of the family was selected to be justice of the peace, and, apart from George, no one married money, and the property was not extended. Indeed, the estate became heavily encumbered. Even when George died, the *post mortem* valuation had fallen to £40, less than half the figure fourteen years before. The actual amounts may not mean much, but George was certainly assigned only 17s. 3d. a year from Rearsby where his father's interest had been valued at twenty marks. The remainder was, presumably, settled on his mother, as a life interest. George's widow, too, had a claim and in 1515 she and her second husband were suing for common-law dower of one third of the estate.[68] When George's brother, Thomas, died in 1525, matters were clearly worse. Not only was John, his son, a royal ward, but the estates had also to bear an annuity of four marks settled on Thomas' sister, provision for his widow and the raising of £120 to provide marriage portions for his daughters. When, after nine years, John came of age, his mother and step-father who had been running the estate had still not cleared the legacies. First John began a chancery suit to recover his inheritance and then, in desperation, took matters into his own hands, ousted his step-father and ended up in star chamber.[69]

The transfer of the Rearsby estates three times in forty years, with provision for dependants in each case, plus the occurrence of two minorities in that time, clearly sapped the fortunes of the family before these were really established. In 1555 John Kebell was selling part of his estate and disposing of the reversion of his mother's dowry.[70] Eventually he possessed only the manor at Rearsby, and the estate which Walter Kebell had obtained in 1434 was finally broken up in 1558 on the death of his great-grandson.[71]

66. Farnham, *Medieval Pedigrees*, 79. 67. *ibid.* 68. *ibid.*
69. STAC2/27/95. 70. Farnham, *Medieval Pedigrees*, 79. 71. *ibid.*

3

TRAINING AT THE INNS OF COURT

In the fifteenth century, training for a legal career began early – many students joined an inn of court or chancery as young as fifteen.[1] Thus it may have been about 1454, and certainly not long after, that Thomas, Walter Kebell's younger son, left Leicestershire for London where he had been entered for the Inner Temple. The choice of society was not haphazard. The four inns of court each took members from all parts of the country, but they also had from time to time special connections with particular regions. The Middle Temple was then much patronised by men from Bristol and the south-west, while Lincoln's Inn had a high proportion from East Anglia and the fenland. The midlands favoured the Inner Temple, and something like half the prominent lawyers from that region studied there. This was not regional particularism, but a practical matter of sponsors.[2] An entrant had to find a 'mainpernor' to pay his bills if he defaulted and, in consequence, students tended to go where they had relatives or acquaintances. Who backed Kebell is not recorded. His background gave him links with several Inner Templars, but a likely person was John Catesby of Ashby St Leger in Leicestershire, who was prominent at the inn during the last years of Henry VI's reign.[3] Catesby must have been acquainted with the Kebells, and Thomas was later to work with his nephew.[4] A very few law students attended university before entering their inn of court, and many more spent their first year in London at an inn of chancery learning elementary law and clerical procedures.[5] It is unlikely that Kebell ever went to Oxford or Cam-

1. Putnam, *Early Treatises*, 129 n. 8.
2. This is demonstrated by the alteration in regional majorities over the years. Cf. Lincoln's Inn, Black Book 3 f. 31 [*Black Books*, i. 161].
3. John Catesby of Whiston, Northants., serjeant 1463, J.C.P. 1481, d. 1487: see below, Appendix D.
4. See below, pp. 108–9. John Catesby, however, never appears with Kebell in feoffeeships etc. Failing Catesby, Kebell may have been sponsored at the Inner Temple as in other things by his mother's relatives: see below, pp. 332–5.
5. John Kingsmill J.C.P. had been a fellow of New College: Emden, *Biographical Register of Oxford to 1500*, ii. 1074.

bridge, but he may well have belonged to an inn of chancery, probably Clifford's Inn, Clement's Inn or Lyon's Inn, houses which frequently prepared students for the Inner Temple; however, no evidence of his membership has survived.[6]

The life which Thomas Kebell and other law students led is tolerably well documented. The records of the Inner Temple go no further back than 1501 – hence the doubt about Kebell's admission – but the Black Books of Lincoln's Inn (the only continuous inn record to survive for the fifteenth century) date from 1422 and reveal a style of life which was probably much the same in all the inns. Students lived as a community, paying a termly 'pension' to cover overheads, and weekly 'commons' for food and residence; in addition there was 'coal-money' for fuel, and fines for special permissions, privileges or offences committed. Conditions were cramped – two to a chamber was the usual minimum – and in the later fifteenth century Lincoln's Inn was energetically building more accommodation. Students lived cheek by jowl with established lawyers, for the distinctive feature of the English common law was that those who practised it also supervised – and supervised minutely – those who were learning it. This tight professional community gave the common lawyers great strength and helps to explain their sheer professional competence, yet the close control of students must frequently have been irksome. It may account for some unexplained withdrawals from the society, and goes a long way to explain the outbreaks of disorder which marred inn life.[7] That behaviour by students – and established lawyers also – was no worse is accounted for by the chronology of the legal year; at no time was residence compulsory for more than twenty-eight weeks, and frequently twenty-three or so only were required. At the close of the fifteenth century the longest continuous residence was seven weeks, whenever Hilary term ran to the start of the Lent 'learning vacation', giving a period from mid-January to the fourth week in Lent; earlier there had been two possible seven weeks of residence, from mid-September to the end of the Michaelmas term and from the eve of Palm Sunday to the end of the Easter term.[8]

6. He is not mentioned *ibid.* or in A. B. Emden, *Biographical Register of the University of Cambridge to 1500* (Cambridge, 1963).
7. Analysis of the earliest run of entries to Lincoln's Inn (1428–35 inclusive) reveals a drop-out/death rate of nearly 20% in three years: Black Book 1. ff. 11v, 12, 20v, 21v, 22, 23, 23v, 28v, 29, 34, 35.
8. For changes in the inn calendar, see below, p. 41.

By no means all who entered the inns stayed for more than the minimum time required to become a fellow, even in the early fifteenth century, and by the beginning of the sixteenth the drop-out rate was, perhaps, as high as six in seven.[9] Some of these may have gone into quasi-legal employment, but most were like Antony Fitzherbert's brother, John, whose four years at the inns went to make him a successful farmer, estate manager and justice of the peace.[10] Nor was a grounding in the basics of law all that such men took away. Men valued the inns, much as the Victorians valued the universities, for the social training to be found there. The communal activities of the inns, regulated and formal like those of other societies of the time – colleges, gilds, livery companies and corporations – were concentrated on the Christmas festival, and at Lincoln's Inn this was regularly celebrated with a lord of misrule and professional players and minstrels.[11] Revels were also held at other times, and although Lincoln's Inn reduced the total in 1431, this still left one a term, plus Christmas.[12] There was too, so Fortescue said, instruction in music, dancing and knightly sports, 'a kind of academy of all the manners that nobles learn', but scant reference to this remains in the Black Books; such activity may have been *around* rather than provided *by* the inns.[13] Lincoln's Inn also had a grammar school to teach Latin and the standard curriculum of late-medieval learning.[14] A less earnest advantage offered by the inns was proximity to the city of London, and increasingly many students saw them as agreeable *pieds à terre* for tasting the delights of the metropolis. There already was to be found in embryo the polite society of the town, although hostility existed as well, akin to the town and gown friction at Oxford and

9. An accurate count of the residents at the inns is not possible as in the great majority of cases there is no evidence of dates of death or departure. In 1574 figures submitted to the government gave 125 utter barristers against 585 gentlemen in the inns of court (1 to 4.7), but the latter included *bona fide* students below the bar: SP12/95/91. 24 men were admitted normally to Lincoln's Inn from 1 Nov. 1510 to 30 Jun. 1513; 8 were called to the bar (1 to 3.0). Calls to the bar 1521–37 numbered 34; all admissions 1 Jul. 1515 to 30 Nov. 1531 totalled 224 (1 to 6.58), but vagaries of record-keeping make accuracy impossible. Black Book 3 & 4 *passim*; *Admission Book*, i. 34–46.
10. Ives, in *Profession, Vocation etc.*, 183 and n. 12.
11. *ibid.*, 185, n. 26.
12. Black Book 1 f. 20 [*Black Books*, i. 4]. In the mid-sixteenth century lesser revels were held each Saturday during term: D. S. Bland, *The Vocabulary of the Inns of Court* (privately printed, Liverpool, 1964), 20.
13. Fortescue, *De Laudibus*, 119.
14. Black Book 2(2) f. 82 [*Black Books* i. 140].

Cambridge, and some bloody encounters are on record.[15] In London, too, the pleasures of low life could be sampled. The reflections of the raffish Justice Shallow are not simply Shakespearean licence; the exclusion of vice was a perennial problem, and a gentleman might easily find his convenient back door being walled up.[16]

Educational arrangements at the inns of court are less easy to describe with confidence.[17] It has long been assumed that the pattern of learning exercises found in the early sixteenth century was in operation before the Black Books open. The evidence, however, suggests that legal education at the inns of court was a development of the fifteenth century and that Thomas Kebell's generation was the first for whom anything like the later system was available.

Inns for lawyers had existed in the London area since the early fourteenth century – the first mention of 'the apprentices in their hostels' is in the year book for 1329 – but there is no reason to believe that any training was provided.[18] That was a matter for the courts, where students had a place reserved for them ('the crib'), and judicial comment was at least partly for their benefit.[19] In *De Laudibus*, Sir John Fortescue still saw this as the main means of instruction:

> the laws of England . . . are read and taught in these courts, as if in public schools, to which students of the law flock every day in term-time.[20]

Professional education is found first at the inns of chancery. From the latter part of Edward III's reign some senior chancery clerks began to provide instruction for the juniors who resided in 'inns' under their charge. Law students began to attend also to learn useful basic skills, such as the management of writs.[21] Despite the objections of the chancellor, this infiltration continued, and by the turn of the century the chancery clerks were dropping out and the 'inns of chancery' were housing and training primarily lawyers. We know little in detail about the curriculum. By 1408 'readings' were being given in 'learning vacations' which fell between the law terms of Hilary and Easter, and Trinity and Michaelmas, but on what subject, and whether the combination of lecture and seminar found in later inns of court

15. *Chronicles of London*, ed. C. L. Kingsford (Oxford, 1905), 154–5, 169. In 1457–8 the queen's attorney was killed in a riot in Fleet Street.
16. *Black Books*, i. 158, 216, 238.
17. For the following see Ives, in *Profession, Vocation etc.*, 197–208.
18. J. P. Dawson, *The Oracles of the Law* (Ann Arbor, 1968), 36, n. 4.
19. *ibid.*, 36.
20. Fortescue, *De Laudibus*, 117.
21. T. F. Tout, *Collected Papers* (Manchester, 1934), 154–9, 162–5.

readings is unknown.[22] By mid-century there is evidence of moots, in effect mock trials, and it was no doubt at these that *la forme de pleding en Innes de Chauncerie* was learned.[23] Other exercises included 'bringing in a writ', 'reporting' and 'the declaration of the opening', and a student was clearly expected to become familiar with the *Natura Brevium*.[24] Although some of these activities are more than a little mysterious, they clearly made up a useful training in the 'principles of the comen lawe of englond'.[25]

By contrast to the inns of chancery, the early inns of court seem to have been nothing more than arrangements to live communally, made by provincial lawyers who needed to be near Westminster for the law terms; in addition to the four inns which survived, there may well have been others where occupation did not produce the continuity of custom.[26] A lawyer probably moved to an inn of court when he had learned all he could in his clerically dominated inn of chancery, but recruitment was very much a private matter. Why such societies should take up educational work and how this came to eclipse the already established teaching of the inns of chancery is obscure to a degree. One possibility is that once the latter ceased being hostels run by chancery clerks and became self-governing communities with elected principals assisted by the 'ancients' of the house, the trained lawyer would have had less incentive to leave. This would then threaten the economy of the inns of court and force them to recruit younger members by offering more advanced education than the inns of chancery, something they could do if, as seems probable, they then still had among their members a majority of important lawyers.

The few facts certainly support this hypothesis. It is clear from the Black Books that to become a fellow at Lincoln's Inn in the 1420s it was only necessary to attend three successive Christmas celebrations; initiation was what mattered, not educational exercises.[27] Moots were held, although attendance was voluntary and the exercises received little attention. Law readings were provided in the two weeks before Easter and in the three weeks around Michaelmas, but attendance was again voluntary and such texts as have survived suggest that instruc-

22. Bland, *Furnival's Inn*, 23. 23. *ibid.*, 29; *Y.B.* Mich. 37 Hen. VI, 4, f. 14.
24. Simpson, *L.Q.R.* 87. 103–5. 25. Spelman, *Reports*, ii. *128* n. 6.
26. The hypothesis that educational activity was taken up by the inns of court at a late stage in their development was first advanced by S. E. Thorne, 'The early history of the inns of court, with special reference to Gray's Inn', in *Graya* 50 (1959), 79–96.
27. Ives, in *Profession, Vocation etc.*, 202–3.

tion was brief, elementary and standard in form.[28] Nevertheless, the fact that these readings were noted down and preserved, while inns of chancery readings were not, does suggest that the inns of court had discovered something which the chancery houses could not match and which automatically gave them the edge. Inns of court may always have had seniority in the professional status of members; now they eclipsed the inns of chancery in teaching as well.

The first effort at Lincoln's Inn to provide more than basic readings came in 1436.[29] Nineteen of the fellows, including John Fortescue, agreed to attend a variety of Christmas celebrations and especially learning vacations over the next four years. The object was clearly to provide senior men to train new recruits and particularly to assist with the readings. As a result of this initiative, entrance requirements at Lincoln's Inn were tightened up in 1442; henceforward, not only Christmasses, but three Lent vacations (extended to three weeks) and three autumn vacations were to be kept in three years.[30] Whether similar attempts were made at the other inns is not known, but the general quality of the readings certainly changed about this time; they became fuller, frequently associated with named individuals, and the discussion which took place was much better recorded.[31] In 1464 Lincoln's Inn revised the procedure for electing its readers, and it was perhaps at this time that the dates of learning vacations were changed again, to the first four weeks of Lent and the four weeks following Lammas (1 August).[32] Also in the 1460s, a further attempt was made to improve attendance of seniors. The 1436 arrangements had been too ambitious and had not worked as planned, so sixteen long-established fellows agreed in Easter 1466 to cover the immediate learning vacations and a rule was made that in future, anyone called to the bench of the inn should assist at learning vacations for three years after call.[33] Even that was not final. The plan got into difficulties after

28. Black Book 1 f. 17 [*Black Books*, i. 2–3]; Thorne, *Readings and Moots*, i. lxvii–lxviii.
29. Black Book 1 ff. 31–2 [*Black Books*, i. 6–7].
30. *ibid.*, 2(1) f. 3 [*Black Books*, i. 12]. In this order the period of residence in the spring is described as from the vigil of Palm Sunday for three weeks; in 1428 the period was the last two weeks of Lent: see above, p. 37.
31. Thorne, *Readings and Moots*, i. lx, lxviii.
32. Black Book 1 f. 134; 2(2) f. 60 [*Black Books*, i. 38, 125]; *Minutes of Parliament*, i. 21; Bland, *J.S.P.T.L.* 10. 185.
33. Black Book 1 ff. 144v–147 [*Black Books*, i. 41–3].

1470, and in 1475 attendance at learning vacations was made an obligation for three years after reading.[34]

The appearance of benchers in the 1466 order points to another development which had taken place. The first recorded members of Lincoln's Inn were divided into masters and clerks, and among the latter were certainly some of the younger students. A bench existed on which men sat to play the part of judges at the moots, but there was no separate category of 'benchers'; government of the inn was, and for a century would remain, in the hands of annually elected governors.[35] The first mention of a category 'fellows of the bench' is in 1441 when they were allowed to have clerks in commons at special rates, and it seems highly likely that the rank followed from the 1436 order on vacation attendances.[36] Once certain fellows had accepted an obligation to assist during learning vacations – once, in fact, they regularly occupied the bench at moots – they became accepted as a senior grade, the benchers. And when their position had become recognised it would be natural to expect the benchers to provide the fellows to deliver new 'readings'. This call tended to come between two and five terms after call to the bench, although some men were called to the bench by being elected to read.[37] Parallel definition soon followed below the bench. In 1455 the term 'barrister' is found, and in 1466 the division into 'utter [that is, outer] barristers' and a remainder who were, or soon were to be, labelled 'inner barristers'.[38] Again the topography of the moot explains the terms. The most junior men sat behind the bar in front of the bench; from the view-point of the benchers they were 'within' it. More senior men sat at the sides of the room, that is 'outside' the bar. Formal transfer from one to the other

34. *ibid.*, 2(1) f. 30v. The 1466 agreement produced reasonable attendances at vacations until autumn 1470, though numerous defaulters; a gap in the record ensues to Easter 1475, when attendance was down to one: *ibid.*, 1 ff. 147v, 149v, 152v, 155, 156, 159; 2(1) f. 30v.

35. On the early constitutional changes within the inns see Simpson, *Camb. Law Journ.* 28; *Camb. Law Journ.* 34; Ives, in *Profession, Vocation etc.*, 204–8; J.H. Baker, 'The old constitution of Gray's Inn', in *Graya* 81 (1978), 15–19.

36. Black Book 1 f. 45 [*Black Books*, i. 11].

37. William Donington, called autumn 1466, read autumn 1467; William Briscowe, listed as bencher autumn 1467, read autumn 1468; John Haugh, listed as bencher and reader autumn 1469; Richard Whitley, listed as bencher autumn 1469, read autumn 1470; James Hobart and Kenelm Digas, called Easter 1470, read autumn 1471 and 1472, or 1471 and 1473, or 1472 and 1473; Thomas Jenney, called autumn 1475, read autumn 1476. Black Book 1 ff. 147, 149v, 152v, 156, 159; 2(1) ff. 30v, 33v [*Black Books*, i. 43, 45, 46, 48, 50, 58, 60].

38. Black Book 1 ff. 95v, 144v; 2(2) ff. 60v, 61v [*Black Books*, i. 26, 41, 125, 127].

existed by 1494, and soon this was known as 'call' to the bar.[39] The result was a *cursus honorum* into which existing offices at Lincoln's Inn such as the pensioner, and new creations such as the treasurership, were progressively fitted.

How much of this was common to the other inns we do not know, but it is evident that Thomas Kebell entered the legal profession during a genuine 'period of transition'. The inns were by no means uniform – Gray's Inn had no benchers until the seventeenth century, and the Inner Temple did not formalise the call to the bar until 1556.[40] The Inner Temple was similar to Lincoln's Inn in having governors, but these had less importance and served for several years at one time. When records begin there, real power was with the benchers, who could meet as the governing body or 'parliament' without having any governor present.[41] This may imply that benchers had been longer established than at Lincoln's Inn, which was still affirming their subordination to the governors.[42] The Inner Temple, however, also had an established rota of attendants on the Lent and autumn reader which could have begun as an alternative way of securing attendances at learning vacations and was certainly imitated in 1507 by the Middle Temple, where the status of bencher was very underdeveloped.[43] There is, however, no evidence that the Inner Temple had ever been dominated by former readers, as was the case at the Middle Temple until at least 1525 and at Gray's Inn until almost the Civil War.[44]

Given both our ignorance and the evident variety amongst the inns it is impossible to deduce the probable pattern of Thomas Kebell's education. Even though in about 1539, as part of the reforming impulse following the dissolution of the monasteries, a general report was drawn up for Henry VIII on the curriculum of the inns, it is not until the middle of the century that it is possible to generalise.[45] At Lincoln's Inn (and the two Temples appear to have been similar,

39. *ibid.* 2(2) f. 27 [*Black Books*, i. 100]. The formal term was 'admission'. The reference to the bar in the 1494 order is an insertion into an order *re* benchers in a hand other than the main text and may, therefore, be of later date.
40. Simpson, *Camb. Law Journ.* 28. 254; 34. 139–42.
41. Ives, in *Profession, Vocation etc.*, 208.
42. Black Book 2(2) f. 48 [*Black Books*, i. 117]. Lincoln's Inn benchers were, however, becoming associated with the governors (Simpson, *Camb. Law Journ.* 28. 248–9).
43. *Inner Temple Records*, i. 1, 5 etc.; *Minutes of Parliament*, i. 20–2; Simpson, *Camb. Law Journ.* 34. 142.
44. *ibid.*, 34. 138–42.
45. Bland, *J.S.P.T.L.* 10. 183–94; Fisher, *J.S.P.T.L.* 14. 111–17; R. M. Fisher, 'Thomas Cromwell, humanism and educational reform, 1530–40', in *Bull. Institute of Hist. Research*, 50 (1977), 151–63.

although figures for them cannot be presented) the pattern was then for the new entrant to spend five or six years as an inner barrister.[46] This was true in about sixty per cent of cases, and only a handful of men waited for longer than eight years. Call to the bar gave the now outer barrister a more important role in the learning exercises, but the right to plead at Westminster was a matter for the king's justices. Orders on this point were variously issued by benchers, judges and the privy council, beginning in 1518. In that year, Lincoln's Inn ruled that barristers should attend the four learning vacations after call, and in 1529 this was extended to six; these provisions may suggest that the inns then considered that new outer barristers still needed two or three years' more study.[47] In addition barristers were expected to moot regularly, although a confused order of 1543 suggests that this requirement lasted for only five years.[48] In 1547 a royal proclamation expressed similar views, requiring a pleader to have eight years' continuance at his inn before beginning to practise; given five years as an inner barrister this meant two or three years' further training after call.[49] Of course this was a counsel of perfection. If proclamations were needed to insist on eight years' training, men must have been on their feet long before that.

The one educational activity which we know much about in the fifteenth century is the reading.[50] The pattern in all the inns seems to have been for an autumn reading to be assigned to a novice and a Lent reading to follow some five or six years later; this was a more notable affair, delivered at a busier time of the year, probably in the presence of a serjeant or a judge who had belonged to the inn. The pattern could be broken by accidents – if the expected Lent reader died a novice might be substituted, while should a call of serjeants be scheduled, the serjeant elect, or the junior if there were two, was expected to read. When only one serjeant was chosen from an inn and he was fairly senior, this could mean his third reading, and this rare achievement sometimes fell to other venerable figures who stepped in to fill a gap in the normal rota.

46. The following is based upon an analysis of the Black Books.
47. Black Book 3 ff. 85, 184 [*Black Books*, i. 188, 225].
48. *Black Books*, i. 263–4.
49. *Tudor Royal Proclamations*, ed. P. L. Hughes and J. F. Larkin (1964–9), i. 408–9. This proclamation repealed one issued in 1546 which limited appearance to readers and to men licensed by the chancellor and the two chief justices on the advice of two 'benchers and ancients' from each inn: *ibid.*, i. 371–2.
50. For the following see Thorne, *Readings and Moots*, i. ix–xviii.

The earliest evidence for the chronology between entry as a student and the call to read is contemporary with Kebell's own career, but from Lincoln's Inn.[51] It shows that the average interval was getting steadily longer. Students entering in Kebell's decade, 1451–60, had to wait for fewer than ten years, while by the decade in which he died, 1491–1500, the waiting period had crept up to nearly sixteen years. In each sample, individual careers varied, but even for the most rapid, the call to read was coming later. Whereas in 1458, John Sulyard was chosen to read after only eight years, Walter Stubbes, the 1491–1500 entrant who took least time before being elected to read, had to wait for over thirteen.[52] The reason for this must be an increase in those attempting to make the law their career; more aspirants meant a longer queue. This might have little influence in Lincoln's Inn (and probably the Inner Temple), where call to the bench anticipated the call to read, but at Gray's Inn and the Middle Temple, where the readers ruled, it would have meant increasing delay in reaching the governing body. And overall it must indicate increasing professional competition. Thomas Kebell clearly took up law at a fortunate time. Allowing him to have entered the Inner Temple between the ages of fifteen and eighteen – *c.* 1454 and *c.* 1457 – he would (judging from Lincoln's Inn) have reached sufficient status to give his first reading in the mid-1460s. This would tally with what is known of other men advanced to the rank of serjeant with him in 1486. Richard Jay of Gray's Inn is supposed to have read in 1466 and John Fineux in 1469.[53] John Haugh, admitted to Lincoln's Inn in 1460, read in 1469; Robert Rede, the second serjeant from that inn, had been admitted in 1467 and read in 1481, but he was clearly a much younger man.[54] Kebell's second reading would have been given in the Lent vacation of, say, 1470 or 1472.[55] He may also have read for a third time; either

51. The following is based upon an analysis of promotions within Lincoln's Inn.

52. Sulyard: admitted 1451, 4th governor 1459, and thus probably elected reader Easter 1459 for the following autumn; Stubbes: admitted 1492, elected reader Mich. 1505 for autumn 1506: Black Book 1 ff. 80, 116; 2(2) f. 18; 3 f. 5 [*Black Books*, i. 34, 94, 138; *Admission Book*, i. 11, 26]. Sulyard seems to have had the rare distinction of reading four times: 1459, 1466, 1470 and 1478 on election as serjeant.

53. Thorne, *Readings and Moots*, i. xxxiii.

54. Black Book 1 ff. 118, 149, 156; 2(1) f. 48 [*Black Books*, i. 48, 71; *Admission Book*, i. 14, 16].

55. Thomas Fitzwilliam read at the Inner Temple in Lent 1466 (Thorne, *Readings and Moots*, i. xxxiv–xxxvii), and would in the normal course have read a second time in Lent 1471. Kebell may have been just ahead or just behind Fitzwilliam in ancienty and so have read in 1465 and 1470 or in autumn 1466 and Lent 1472; the latter is marginally more probable.

he or his colleague William Danvers gave the reading for Lent 1486 on call to the coif and Kebell was probably the junior.[56]

As we have seen, there grew up at Lincoln's Inn a *cursus honorum* which the successful lawyer pursued. He did so according to a system of precedence or 'ancienty'.[57] The Lincoln's Inn Black Books are explicit on this from the 1520s, when it seems to have regulated even the order in which men were called to the bar. Although not explicit earlier, the system was well established by the closing years of the previous century. The order in which fellows gave their first reading was the order in which they had served, a year or so before, as marshal for the Christmas festival, and this was much the order in which fellows had served as pensioner of the house a year or two earlier than that. An individual's precedence was fixed, and it was perfectly possible to predict the date of the call to read. There were, of course, some variations; personal circumstances such as ill-health might effect changes – especially if accompanied by a douceur to inn funds – while a man could lose seniority by refusing office and, perhaps, by absence from too many vacations.[58] By and large, however, promotion by seniority was the rule. The effective date seems to have been, quite literally, the date of admission to the society, not the date when the initial vacations had been completed or, in houses where this applied, the date of becoming an outer barrister; when two fellows who had entered the inn in the same year approached their first readings, they were called to serve according to the month and even the day of the month of their admission.[59] Whether or not a similar system was

56. The suggestion that Danvers was the elder rests on general probability: e.g. he was J.P. eighteen years before Kebell and became a judge almost immediately on becoming a serjeant.
57. For the following, see Ives, *L.Q.R.* 75. 351–4.
58. Edmund Jenney was excused his reading because of sickness, which accelerated the election of Robert Rede in 1481. Edward Redman followed Richard Heigham as marshal in 1480–1 and should have read in the autumn following Heigham's reading, given in 1483; Robert Morton took his place, but when Morton died between the Lent and autumn vacations of 1486 a gap was created for Lent 1490 in the rota of second readings which Redman filled: *Edward Redmayn lector pro Quadragesima hac vice* [5 Henry VII, 1490] *primo electus est eo quod antea secundum cursum suum pro diversis solicitudinibus perturbat et alijs societatis monentibus eligi non potuit et gratiam* [*sic*] *ei pro diversis consideracionibus datur quod custodiet nisi tamen in tribus annis jam proximo futuro*. The long delay in William Elys' first reading may be explained by his turbulent career at the inn. Plague could also lead to a vacation being cancelled, e.g. autumn 1479. Black Book 2(1) ff. 37v, 42, 42v, 45v, 47, 47v, 48, 81v; 2(2) ff. 3v, 10v, 59, 60 [*Black Books*, i. 63, 66, 68, 70, 71, 90, 124, 125].
59. Ives, *L.Q.R.* 75. 352.

completely operative in the Inner Temple in Kebell's student days, it is impossible to say. There is evidence that seniority operated at Lincoln's Inn from an early date. The rota for readings existed by the 1420s, and the Lent reading was already associated with election as the third, and the autumn reading with election as the fourth (and junior) governor of the house.[60] But there were exceptions to anciently throughout the fifteenth century – John Turpin, admitted in 1460, read behind three of his puisnes, while John Thornborough, admitted in 1469, read in autumn 1487 after men admitted three years later – and irregularities continued to occur even in the sixteenth.[61]

The existence in the inns even of a norm of progress by seniority may appear to discredit the claim that, in Yorkist and Tudor England, the law presented the great opportunity for ability. But progress in the inns and promotion in the profession were different matters, one deriving from the other. Paucity of evidence elsewhere has led historians to concentrate upon promotion in the inns, but this followed success in the courts. Advance to reader was certainly automatic, but automatic only for those who had established themselves at the Westminster bar. A list of common-law pleaders survives from about 1518, and includes forty-nine names, thirty-six belonging to inns where records survive.[62] All thirty-six were, or became, benchers and readers. Fortescue implied that academic success was what counted in a legal career, and the very terminology of 'calling' juniors to bar and bench suggests that the inns governed promotion. But the brutal reality was that a lawyer's practice determined his status in his inn; only the successful climbed the promotion ladder. The small coterie

60. Thorne, *Readings and Moots*, i. xii; Ives, in *Profession, Vocation etc.*, 60.

61.

John Turpin admitted	5 Jan. 1460 read	autumn 1480
Thomas Jenney	Mich. 1461	autumn 1476
Thomas Appulton	Hilary 1463	autumn 1478
Thomas Lovell	Mich. 1464	autumn 1475

(No reader for autumn 1477 is known; in autumn 1479 no reading was held.)

John Thornborough	Easter 1469	autumn 1487
Richard Heigham	Trinity 1469	autumn 1483
Robert Morton	Mich. 1471	autumn 1484
William Frost	Mich. 1471	autumn 1485
Thomas Gigges	[Mich.] 1472	autumn 1486

Thornborough was allowed to spread his initial vacations over five years. The date of Turpin's reading is established by his keeping of vacations *ad bancum* to Easter 1483. Gigges kept the Christmas vacation of 1472 but not the autumn vacation. Black Book 1 ff. 117v, 126, 129v, 134, 155v, 156v, 170v, 177v; 2(1) ff. 25v, 30v, 33, 38v, 42, 48, 53v, 56, 59v, 61v [*Black Books*, i. 58, 60, 63, 66, 77, 79, 81, 83, 85; *Admission Book*, i. 14, 15, 17, 18].

62. c82/473/36; see below, pp. 448–50.

of Westminster pleaders governed, as benchers or readers, the education of students and the behaviour of their lesser colleagues, whether court clerks, attorneys or counsel who had failed to make the grade. The failure rate was, in fact, high. Of those involved in the earliest recorded calls to the bar, at Lincoln's Inn, fifty-five per cent failed to reach the bench.[63] Some certainly did not live to achieve this, most abandoned the inn to carve out a new career in the provinces, but a minority hung on without the slightest distinction – men such as Edward Beaupre, who was called in 1523 and in 1560 was admitted to eat with the benchers as 'an ancient utter barrister'.[64] Natural selection governed a career in law.

In the absence of Inner Temple records, nothing can be said of Thomas Kebell's educational exercises. A text of one of his readings, however, does survive, and as ostensibly anonymous readings reveal identifications on the basis of internal evidence, the other two may be discovered. The known reading is on the statute of Westminster I, chapters one to four, but this was not a topic chosen by Kebell. A reader had to expound the next chapters of the statute which had been tackled by his predecessor or, if this had been completed, to begin whichever was the next of the 'old' statutes, those prior to Edward III, which formed the whole syllabus of the readings.[65] A long text of Kebell's reading belonged to the Inner Temple library but disappeared in the course of the 1939–45 war, and a shorter version still exists in the Hargrave manuscripts of the British Library.[66] There is nothing to indicate which of Kebell's readings this is. Bertha Putnam suggested that it was the third, *eo quod ad gradum servientis ad legem electus sit*.[67] The conjecture, however, now seems excluded by Professor S. E. Thorne's demonstration that the 'old' statutes were taken in a rough sequence. It is known that Thomas Marowe began *Westminster I* at the Inner Temple in 1503 and John Salter the statute of Gloucester in 1508; since Richard Hall lectured on *Gloucester* cc. 1–3 in 1481, on the presumption that the same order was followed as twenty years later, *Westminster I* could not have occupied Kebell in 1486.[68] The likeliest subject for a reading in that year is the latter part

63. See above, p. 38.
64. Ives, *L.Q.R.* 75. 353–4.
65. Thorne, *Readings and Moots*, i. xvi–xviii.
66. The Inner Temple ms. was described by Bertha Putnam: *Early Treatises*, 154–5; B.L. Hargrave Ms. 87 ff. 302–8.
67. Putnam, *Early Treatises*, 179.
68. Thorne, *Readings and Moots*, i. xvi, 136. This argument would not apply if third readers, were, exceptionally, able to choose their subject. Cf. *ibid.*, i. xvii.

of *Magna Carta*, and a reference in William Hudson's 'Treatise of the Court of Star Chamber' implies that a Kebell reading on *Magna Carta* was extant in the early seventeenth century.[69] S. E. Thorne conjectured that the Kebell manuscript represented a first reading, delivered in the 1460s, but this also involves difficulties.[70] Thomas Fitzwilliam is known to have taken the opening of the statute of Merton in Lent 1466.[71] If *Westminster I* had immediately preceded this, its first chapters would have been covered in 1461, too early for Kebell to have been involved. The latter half of the 1460s is also excluded by the evidence of a student's note which shows that *Westminster I* c. 20 was being studied at the Inner Temple in 1474.[72] This would suggest that examination of the statute would have commenced some four or five readings earlier, that is in 1472 or thereabouts, when Kebell's second reading can be presumed to have taken place.[73] Further discoveries may bring down this house of cards, but until then it seems probable that the extant reading is Kebell's second, delivered in the early seventies.[74]

A law reading of the second half of the fifteenth century was spread over three to four weeks, probably occupying two hours a day, four days a week.[75] Sessions followed a set pattern; first came exposition of a section of the statute, and then the reader's commentary, illustrated with examples and larded with doubtful points for discussion. Benchers and readers in the audience and any visiting serjeant or judge

69. See below, p. 59.
70. Thorne, *Readings and Moots*, i. xlvi.
71. *ibid*., i. 38.
72. *ibid*., i. lvii n.1.
73. See above, p. 45. There was no set number of clauses dealt with at a reading, even on the same statute; Thomas Marowe spent the whole of one reading on *Westminster I* c. 1 where Kebell covered cc. 1–4 or 5 (see below, p. 57). *Westminster II*, however, seems to have averaged four or five clauses a reading: Thorne, *Readings and Moots*, i. xvi.
74. Readings so far identified at the Inner Temple during Kebell's membership are:

Lent 1466	*Merton*, 1–4	Thomas Fitzwilliam	1st
[Lent 1472 or 1470]	*Westminster I*, 1–4	Thomas Kebell	2nd
1474	*Westminster II*, 20	[ ]	
Lent 1481	*Gloucester*, 1–3	Richard Hall	3rd
[?]	*Magna Carta*, 1–11	[?] Heruy	[?]
Lent 1483	*Magna Carta*, 11–12	Morgan Kidwelly	2nd

Thorne suggests that *c*. 1475 William Catesby read on *Magna Carta*. It seems more probable that this was his second reading, delivered in series with Morgan Kidwelly, possibly Heruy and probably Kebell in the early 1480s. Other readings which can plausibly be dated to the Inner Temple during Kebell's residence are *Prerogativa Regis* (*post* 1475), *Winchester, Articulis super Cartas, Marlborough* and *Westminster II*. Thorne, *Readings and Moots*, i. lvii, 10 n. 5, 38, 136; J. H. Baker, *English Legal Manuscripts* (1975 *sqq*), i. 11.
75. Putnam, *Early Treatises*, 171–2; Bland, *J.S.P.T.L.* 10. 185–6.

would next enter into debate with the reader while the students scribbled away at their notes, often recording the names of the contributors as a handy index of value. A reading was also a festive occasion, an opportunity for 'wining and dining the right people'. In the early sixteenth century the Inner Temple system of attendants gave the reader the support of the bencher next in line to give a second reading and the barrister due to deliver the next first reading, but he also had an escort of friends and colleagues, sometimes inconveniently large.[76] The reader's dinner was an elaborate affair, and he often entertained outsiders as well as members and former members. During his term of office he had precedence over most other seniors, and special rights to admit new members. This patronage was some recompense for the heavy expenses a reader had to meet, even though his inn often helped by providing wine.

The conduct of a law reading during Kebell's time at the Inner Temple can be followed exactly in the manuscript of Richard Hall's reading in 1481 on the statute of Gloucester. This, fortunately, preserves the names of those who contributed to the debate on the points he raised, and some eighteen of these 'reader's cases' were included in Keilwey's *Reports*.[77] The reading began early in March, although the report which survives does not indicate precisely how many lectures Hall gave or, always, where the divisions came.[78] He seems to have devoted three or four sessions to each chapter of the statute, and the text reaches 19,000 words before it breaks off in mid-sentence in the discussion of chapter three.[79] Hall took each chapter section by section with discussion after each, but whether he

76. See above, p. 43.
77. Thorne, *Readings and Moots*, i. xlvii n. 2, 136–70; Robert Keilwey, *Relationes quorundam casuum selectorum ex libris Roberti Keilwey*, ed. John Croke (1602), was reprinted, page for page, in 1688 and issued under the title *Reports d'ascuns Cases*, with added matter: new title page; allowance; epistle to the reader; list of abbreviations; original preface (a2, a2v, b1, b1v); table of contents; ff. 1–203 as 1602 edn; ff. 204–6, reports by Dalison et al.; ff. 207–15, reports by Bendlows; index. There are additional references incorporated in the text of the 1688 volume, but it would be more correct to list it as an edition of the 1602 text.
78. The reading is dated *in quadragesima Anno E.4 21*. The regnal year 21 Edward IV began on Quinquagesima 1481 and included the whole of Lent 1481; it ended on the second Saturday of Lent 1482. Hall's reading can thus be assigned to 1481 or to 1482. However, from the start of Edward IV's reign, Lincoln's Inn had always treated the Lent vacation as belonging to the new regnal year; hence Lent *Anno* 20 was 1480, Lent *Anno* 21 was 1481 and Lent *Anno* 22 was 1482. By analogy Hall's reading would belong to 1481: Black Book 2(1) ff. 45v, 48, 50v.
79. For the text of Hall's reading see Thorne, *Readings and Moots*, i. 136–70.

invited this or the audience interjected is not clear. In this way two or three sections could be dealt with in a morning. The report of the first chapter is much the fullest, occupying some two-thirds of the whole. This may have been because it was intrinsically more important, with a broad discussion of disseisin and a substantial treatment of *mortdancestor*; it may also reflect a special importance of the opening week of the reading (Lincoln's Inn regulations imply that busy men were reluctant to attend throughout a reading) or simply that notes are taken more enthusiastically when a course is beginning.[80]

The first chapter of the statute is concerned with the working of the Angevin possessory assizes. Richard Hall opened by outlining the change brought about by this in the award of damages on disseisin, and went on to distinguish various kinds of disseisin and to discuss remedies and penalties. He suggested that the possessor of estovers in a wood (minor perquisites of common, hedging and the like) would only recover damages against a grantor who destroyed the wood, not any freehold. Here he had his first challenge. Thomas Fitzwilliam, the future recorder of London, cited the rule that unless the realty (the freehold) was recovered, then the associated personalty (the damages) could not be recovered either, although the converse did not apply.[81] 'Baker', probably John Baker, agreed, pointing out the uselessness of the assize as a remedy in the stated circumstances, and further, that an assize jury had to give a verdict *per visum*, and the wood had ceased to exist! Kebell also entered the debate; if the interest no longer survived, then damages only could be recovered. He made, however, an important distinction between a wood which had been wholly destroyed and one which had simply been cut down and left to grow again. As for the remedy, if the wood had been destroyed after the writ had been taken out, then the plaintiff would recover his losses in damages only, otherwise he should bring an action on the case. The reader disagreed. Where the original grant had been by deed, an action of covenant applied, but if the estovers were appendant to another title, then an assize should be the remedy. The benchers, however, would not yield – the proper action was case. Hall took up his thread again with a consideration of the peculiar difficulties raised with multiple defendants in cases of disseisin and the various complications with single, double and triple damages. Kebell did not speak in the brief debate on a technical error in pleading which

80. Black Book 1 f. 145; 3 f. 74v [*Black Books*, i. 42, 183].
81. Thorne, *Readings and Moots*, i. 138–9.

followed this exposition – Fitzwilliam and Baker against Edward Grantham and Richard Hall.[82] The reader then examined specific difficulties in the operation of the assizes, but there was no discussion – presumably time had run out.

The second day opened with a demonstration that the statute of Gloucester made available for the first time to mesne tenants damages in assize, calculated from the start of the disseisin. Where, however, the lord had entered on escheat from the disseisor and the disseisee recovered against the lord, damages dated only from the lord's entry. Fitzwilliam immediately disagreed – damages would be assessed back to the original expulsion.[83] Baker supported the reader and Kebell argued a third position – that no damages at all were payable, the lord had done nothing improper, why should he pay for the delay of the claimant? Richard Maryot spoke next to suggest that the disseisee should recover in part from the lord, leaving the rest of the profits in recompense for rent lost by the escheat. But the reader stuck to his point: *nest reason mesque [le seignior] rendra damagez al meins del temps son entre*, and back-dated to the original intrusion if he resisted the claim. Kebell repeated his opposition; the lord could not prevent the disseisin as the claimant could have done, *et il serroit a mischif a perder lez profitz . . . quaunt nul necligens ne foly poet este deme en luy*. The lecture continued with a section on the availability of the assize to tenants. Both Fitzwilliam and Kebell challenged an example Hall had taken from the Kentish custom of gavelkind, but the reply is not recorded.[84] Hall then went on to possessory remedies in relation to heirs and widows, and so the morning concluded. The next day saw a long analysis of *mortdancestor* with even more interventions by Fitzwilliam, Baker and Kebell, during one of which the student taking notes observed that Kebell contradicted himself![85] And so the reading continued. Apart from the single interventions by Maryot and Grantham and a later one by 'Grene barester', only Fitzwilliam, Baker and Kebell argue with the reader, and it could well be that they were the benchers assigned by the inn to be present.[86] A reading could not succeed as a monologue; there must be discussion, even, perhaps, prepared discussion.

82. *ibid.*, i. 140.
83. *ibid.*, i. 142–3.
84. *ibid.*, i. 145–6.
85. *ibid.*, i. 150–8; the contradiction is p. 152.
86. Cf. the practice at Lincoln's Inn, above p. 41–2. It is strange that no judge or serjeant is mentioned in the extant ms.; Hall was reading not only in Lent but for the third time. The reader's cases which may belong to this reading show, however, interventions by Serjeant John Vavasour: Keilwey, *Reports*, ff. 106v, 107v.

It is ironic that the longer text of Kebell's own reading should have survived for four-and-a-half centuries, only to disappear at the very time historians had begun to be interested in such long-forgotten material. The only information on the manuscript was recorded in 1924 by Bertha Putnam.[87] She was studying a 1503 reading on *Westminster I* given at the Inner Temple by Thomas Marowe, the future serjeant, and was interested in Kebell's reading as a possible source for Marowe. Unfortunately she relied on the shorter British Library text, only discovering the better version late in the day – too late, indeed, to make more than a cursory report. Her description, however, is enough to establish the importance of the text in the evolution of the law reading.[88]

By the middle of the century, as we have seen, readings were no longer the unoriginal scripts they had been, where the reader had only to 'repeat the work of his predecessors, the short and elementary lectures . . . customarily given at his inn', altering, deleting or adding if he wished, but usually copying, often verbatim.[89] Instead, a reading became a seminar on an agreed text with all the brilliance in the raising of issues and the cut and thrust of debate. The weakness, however, was the strict requirement to read on an 'old' statute, which excluded from consideration a great deal of modern law. The answer was to continue with the ostensible text but to use it as a jumping-off point to discuss an area of law of the reader's own choice. In the case of Thomas Marowe the opening of the first clause he had to expound – 'the king wills and commands that the peace of Holy Church and the land be well guarded . . .' was developed into a major discourse on the justices of the peace.[90] The reading was becoming an inaugural lecture, and this was the case in other inns as well; by the 1520s it became possible to read directly on recent law.[91] Of this new approach Kebell's reading on *Westminster I* was an early example, suitable enough for a second reader whose experience warranted a claim to speak unfettered by tradition. Commenting on the text now lost, Bertha Putnam wrote:

> It is clear that Keble has produced a reading altogether different from other early readings on this statute, which ordinarily treat almost exclusively of abuses in houses of religion.[92]

87. Putnam, *Early Treatises*, 154–5. The text was in an unnumbered volume of manuscript readings which had been owned by a member of the Middle Temple, and it occupied ff. 74–96.

88. *ibid.*, 184–5 and n. 1.

89. Thorne, *Readings and Moots*, i. lxvii–lxviii.

90. Putnam, *Early Treatises*, 167.

91. Thorne, *Readings and Moots*, i. xvii.

92. Putnam, *Early Treatises*, 185 n. 1.

Kebell, instead, led the way in initiating discussion of 'the peace', and his material was an important source for Marowe.

> One is forced to believe that Marowe was thoroughly familiar with Keble's sections on surety of peace, riot, rout and assembly, escapes and gaoler by inheritance.[93]

Thomas Kebell's reading on *Westminster I* was 'a legal treatise on the peace nearly twenty years earlier than the *De Pace*'.[94]

Putnam sought to explain the connection between Kebell and Marowe by suggesting that Marowe might have been an assistant at the reading, or else a pupil. The first, however, is unlikely. Marowe was twenty-five or less in 1486, the latest possible date for a Kebell reading, with some years to go before being 'attendant on the reader'; he would clearly have been out of the question for a reading *c.* 1472.[95] On the other hand, Marowe and his friend Thomas Frowyk, the future chief justice, joined the Inner Temple in the mid-seventies, and they must have mooted and performed other learning exercises before Kebell in the years prior to his call to the coif, and have attended any final reading in 1486. There is also every reason to suppose that Marowe could have used a text of Kebell's reading. Such texts circulated, and even though the old habit of verbatim repetition had died out, the tradition that a reader should have available the work of his predecessor could well have continued.[96]

The knowledge that forty years ago the Inner Temple still possessed twenty-two folios of Kebell's lectures, with the seventeenth-century comment, 'Keble, lector, a very good reading', may discourage interest in the 368 lines of Hargrave Ms. 87 ff. 302–8.[97] How this manuscript differs from the lost version can only be conjectured. Although the pages of Hargrave 87 are more than two-and-a-half times larger than were those of the Inner Temple volume, by examining other material known to have been there also, we can calculate that

93. *ibid.*, 184; cf. 203: 'The main outline [of Marowe's account of surety of peace] closely resembles that presented by Kebell many years before.'
94. *ibid.*, 185 n. 1; Putnam dated Kebell's reading 1486.
95. For Marowe and Frowyk see *ibid.*, chapter v.
96. The only period for a reading on *Westminster I* at the Inner Temple between those of Kebell and Marowe would have been 1483–91 (see above, pp. 48–9, and Thorne, *Readings and Moots*, i. xvi), but this would have been out of order. Thus Kebell's reading was probably the immediate predecessor on the subject to that of Marowe. Marowe is known to have made at least one collection of legal material and to have been familiar with the greatest Inner Temple text, Littleton's *Tenures*: *ibid.*, i. xliii; Putnam, *Early Treatises*, 190.
97. *ibid.*, 155.

it preserved a text of Kebell's reading three or four times as long as the surviving version but only about half as long as the fullest form of Thomas Marowe's reading on *Westminster I*.[98] The explanation would seem to be that Kebell's reading was not, even in this manuscript, *in extenso*; Putnam reported:

We have the authority of the scribe of the Inner Temple volume that Keble's reading was not a perfect copy but only certain notes made by a student; f. 96. But he makes no such comment on Marowe's reading.[99]

On this basis, Hargrave 87 might be supposed to preserve perhaps a third of a reading already in note form. But what seems likely is that the extant and the lost manuscript each represented different versions of Kebell's reading. This is definitely so in the case of Thomas Marowe's *De Pace,* which is also found in both sources.[100] Hargrave 87 condenses that reading to half the length of the copy text which Miss Putnam used and which was identical with the text of the lost Inner Temple volume; all explanation and illustration had been stripped away to leave the basic legal points, sometimes in so compressed a form as to be now obscure.[101] It is tempting to suggest that this is also the explanation of the amputated version of Kebell's *Westminster I* in Hargrave 87. It too has been stripped to the bone and large sections have been omitted entirely, for example on riot, rout and assembly.[102] It cannot be a direct precis of the lost manuscript since it is of an earlier date, but it could be a condensation and selection from the notes which the Inner Temple volume copied, or others like them; less likely, it could be a rigorous selection from the reading, taken down at the time or, least likely of all, an abridgement of Kebell's original script.

Thomas Kebell opened his reading by announcing the text of his first subject:

le roy voit et commaunde que le peas del' terre et Seint Esglise soit bien gard . . .[103]

98. Putnam gives the Inner Temple ms. as 6 × 8½ inches and Hargrave 87 as 9½ × 14½ inches. The latter is loosely written with short measure on two sides. In the Inner Temple ms., which was apparently copied as a whole, ten lectures of Marowe's reading and part of the eleventh covered 29 ff.; the best text of the *De Pace* [Cambridge U.L., Ms. Hh.3.6] covers the same portion in some 32,000 words [ff. 74–102]. The length of Kebell's reading in the lost ms. was 23 ff., that is, about 24,000 words. The text in Hargrave 87 is about 6,500 words. The full text of Marowe's *De Pace* runs to 48,000 words.

99. Putnam, *Early Treatises*, 161 n. 4.

100. *ibid.*, 145–6.

101. *ibid.*, 154–7, 160–2.

102. *ibid.*, 184–5; cf. below, p. 56.

103. B.L. Hargrave 87 f. 302.

followed by the customary explanation of the relation of the statute under discussion to the common law:

cest estatute est affirmans del comen ley del' terre.

The common law, he said, provided the writ *de vi laica removenda* to remedy disturbance of the church, so that this provision of the statute was a confirmation of existing law, not the substantive authority for new. A discussion of remedies against *les extorcouns et oppressions faitz sur lez persons de Seint Esglise* followed, and this led to the first major section, *In primez est a voier as quex persones le commandment de ce estatute extende*.[104] Pointing out that the statute laid general penalties and a general obligation on all citizens, Kebell then enumerated those 'to whom the conservation of the peace more especially belongs'. In the lost version, Putnam described this as a 'long list of officials', but Hargrave 87 mentions first judges of courts of record (from the chancellor to the J.P.s) and then those not 'of record', ending with the constable.[105] This led to a discussion of the giving of surety to keep the peace which in the extant text occupies some ten per cent of the total but in the other version was even more substantial.

The next subject Kebell covered in his lectures was probably 'riot, rout and assembly', but only a sentence has survived, and there is a clean break before the next topic.[106] This was the arraignment of clerics and the pleading of benefit of clergy, and it broadened into a general consideration of clerks convict. The reporter noted an ingenious subtlety over the problem of benefit of clergy of blind persons, who could not be expected to prove clergy by reading:

If he knows how to speak Latin from having learned it and not as his native tongue, like the Italians, he shall have the advantage of his clergy . . . because the act of speaking Latin presupposes that he knows how to read and is more noble and worthy than it is merely to read.[107]

This discussion occupies a quarter of the extant text and the next subject, imprisonment, also survives at some length. Escape from custody is first discussed, covering a great variety of possible situations:

Persons hanged and after revived: [Here] the gaoler is liable to a fine as it is an escape, but if he revives in consequence of a miracle, no penalty will follow.[108]

104. *ibid.*, f. 302. 105. Putnam, *Early Treatises*, 184.
106. *ibid.*, p. 185; B.L. Hargrave 87 f. 303. A half page is blank. 107. *ibid.*, f. 304.
108. *ibid.*, f. 305. There is no catchword on f. 304v, so that material before the start of *escape* on f. 305 may have been lost.

The remainder of the Hargrave 87 text is relatively brief: notes on what Kebell said about right of wreck and market offences; while a final paragraph on elections shows that his discussion strayed into clause five of the statute.[109]

With his second reading behind him, Kebell settled to the role he was to play for the next fifteen years, that of a master of the Inner Temple bench. His duties would most probably have been those found when records begin in 1501. The benchers met four or six times a year for routine business – election of officers, the educational programme, special admissions, pardons and exemptions, and general supervision of the finances and business interests of the house.[110] By contrast with Lincoln's Inn, the records of the Inner Temple 'parliament' show few cases of indiscipline being dealt with. It was not that disorder flourished in Holborn and peace by the Thames; Inner Temple benchers apparently handled such matters, along with simple admissions, at 'the bench table', an *ad hoc* executive session held after dinner. Bench table orders were either not recorded in Kebell's day (the record only starts in 1668) or else have been lost, whereas action by Lincoln's Inn benchers out of full council was entered in the Black Books and hence has been preserved. Kebell also took his turn as governor of the inn, one of three or four benchers in office at a time, and he must certainly have held the other offices of the inn, including a spell as treasurer.[111]

Education at the Inner Temple also continued to occupy Kebell after his readings, and here we are not dependent upon conjecture, as Hall's reading has shown. Keilwey's *Reports*, which contains the reader's cases belonging to that reading, also includes moot cases up to 1486, when Kebell took the coif, and these show him busy with the regular moots and exercises after dinner which made up the continuing element in a young lawyer's training.[112] Kebell's comments are

109. *ibid.*, f. 308v. There is no catchword after the end of *imprisonment* etc. on f. 306v, nor after the end of the main discussion of *wreck* on f. 307v; ff. 308, 308v consist of 18 and 14 lines only.

110. The role of outer barristers at the Inner Temple is not clear; they may have had some duty to attend parliaments and take decisions: Simpson, *Camb. Law Journ.* 28. 254–5.

111. Kebell is, curiously, listed as a governor in Michaelmas 1486: CP40/898 m. 97d. I owe this reference to Dr J. H. Baker.

112. Thorne, *Readings and Moots*, i. xlvii n. 2, xlviii; Keilwey, *Reports*, pleas 12, 14, 15, 16, ff. 104v–105, p. 19 f. 106, p. 21 f. 106v, p. 23 f. 107v, pleas 25, 26 f. 108, pleas 39, 41–5, 47, 48, 50, 52, 54, 55, 57, 58, ff. 112–17v, pleas 67, 70–80, 83–6, 88, 90, 91, 93–100, 102–9, 111–14, 116–21, ff. 120–36. This group includes at least one non-Inner Temple item, a case in king's bench, p. 39 f. 112.

noted with respect throughout, and he appears as the most prominent contributor, far more vocal than William Danvers, his fellow serjeant in 1486. What is not known is whether Kebell took private pupils as well. Leading lawyers sometimes did, apparently as a kind of apprenticeship. John Grenefield, the future serjeant, was approached to act as 'master' to Judge Paston's son, and in Henry VIII's reign Humphrey Browne, later J.C.P., also took students.[113] If Kebell did the same it would not be surprising, for he certainly seems unusually committed to teaching, to the extent that his interest in the Inner Temple exercises did not fade even when he had left to join Serjeants' Inn. His presence is recorded at William Grevill's first reading in Lent 1492, on *Westminster II* cc. 3–5.[114] Perhaps more unexpected was his attendance at Inner Temple moots in the 1490s, and there may be surprise as well as respect in the entry *Keble semble a un mote in le Temple quant ill fuit seriant que. . . .*[115] His informal influence persisted also, for it is plausible that the post-adjournment discussion of *The Abbot of Hyde* v. *Benger*, with Kebell's explanation of an affectionately remembered catch-phrase of the late Edward Grantham, took place in the Inner Temple.[116]

Here, quite clearly, is one of the principal importances of the career of Thomas Kebell – his major role in the training of an influential generation of lawyers: two chief justices, Robert Brudenell and Thomas Frowyk; Humphrey Coningsby, whose long tenure of judicial office took him to the Reformation and the breach with Rome; Justice William Grevill, and Thomas Marowe with his significant work on J.P.s; William Rudhale, serjeant and former attorney to Catherine of Aragon, and Thomas Pigot, king's serjeant, who together reminisced about Kebell; others where the connection with Kebell is circumstantial, but strong nevertheless – John Port the future J.K.B., and John Caryll, king's serjeant and prominent reporter.[117] And, even more influential, preserved in the notes of students and in the pages of year books, Kebell's opinions reached beyond his immediate juniors to become generally current in the profession, a monument far more enduring than the one erected over his tomb. When William Hudson of Gray's Inn prepared his 'Treatise

113. *Paston Letters and Papers*, i. 41; *L. and P.*, iv. 4442(1).
114. Thorne, *Readings and Moots*, i. xxii; Putnam, *Early Treatises*, 181 n. 1.
115. *ibid.*, 172 n. 6; Thorne, *Readings and Moots*, i. xlviii; Constable, *Prerogativa Regis*, l n. 223.
116. *Y.B.* Trin. 13 Hen. VII, p. 6 f. 28; Thorne, *Readings and Moots*, i. xlvi n. 7.
117. Keilwey, *Reports*, p. 15 f. 86.

concerning the Court of Star Chamber' towards the end of James I's reign, he still thought it worth while to add to his comment on the writ of privy seal what 'Mr Keeble *in temporem Henrici Septimi* in his reading upon this law plainly declareth'.[118] 'Law schools', in Maitland's famous dictum, 'make tough law.'[119] It was in the teaching of its senior members that the common-law profession of pre-Reformation England had its strength.

118. William Hudson, 'A Treatise of the Court of Star Chamber', in *Collectanea Juridica*, ed. Francis Hargrave (1792), ii. 4. I owe this reference to Dr D. R. Mummery.

119. F. W. Maitland, *English Law and the Renaissance* (Cambridge, 1901), 25.

4

PROFESSIONAL ADVANCEMENT

Legal education in late-medieval England was a matter of private concern to the inns and the courts. Not until the religious legislation of 1563 did statute recognise the rank of outer barrister as a 'degree of learning in the common laws' and not until 1590 was it established that call to the bar was an essential qualification for practice as counsel.[1] In Kebell's day, therefore, status depended on advancement to public office within the legal system. The most numerous openings were to be found in the three great royal courts at Westminster, but there were substantial opportunities elsewhere. The highly developed legal system of the duchy of Lancaster had a court at Westminster and two provincial courts at Lancaster, while the county palatine of Chester, the quasi-independent palatinate of Durham, the duchy of Cornwall, the royal franchises in Wales and the Marches, and the households of members of the royal family also offered scope for the lawyer, as did the arrangements increasingly being made for regions of special difficulty, the north, Wales and the west.

A number of the posts offered were primarily of local significance and could be a virtual monopoly of a nearby dynasty – the Birkenhead family occupied the post of chief clerk and prothonotary at Chester for more than a century.[2] Other positions were of value for the contact they gave with royalty and the chance that favour would result in more considerable rewards. Morgan Kidwelly, who became king's attorney in 1483 on the accession of Edward V, had been the personal attorney of Richard, duke of Gloucester; Richard Eliot became a serjeant-at-law in 1503 after serving as attorney-general to Queen Elizabeth, as did William Rudhale, attorney-general to Queen Catherine, in 1521.[3] Certain of the legal posts outside the three central courts, however,

1. *5 Elizabeth I*, c. 1; Baker, *Camb. Law Journ.* 27. 214–18; 'Solicitors and the law of maintenance, 1590–1640', in *Camb. Law Journ.* 32 (1973), 60–6.
2. Ormerod, *History of Chester*, i. 82–3.
3. Kidwelly: *Cal. Patent Rolls, 1467–77*, 275; Eliot: Nicolas, *Privy Purse Expenses*, 100; Rudhale: *L. and P.*, i. p. 43.

conferred a national status, notably the chancellor, vice-chancellor and attorney-general of the duchy. The justices at Lancaster and Chester exercised considerable influence over the two palatinates, while the councils developing at York and Ludlow and the reorganisation of the Welsh judiciary in 1543 were to add more posts of importance.

Among contemporaries and later historians alike, most attention has been given, in all these courts, to the activities of judges and counsel, but since the Second World War major studies of king's bench and common pleas have emphasised that the law was also a machine worked by officials.[4] The senior clerks, in particular, not only managed the business of the court but were also experts on procedure and were recognised as such by the judges; they were also directly concerned with settling the form of pleadings in an action.[5] Since they were always based in London they were among the most constant attenders at their inns, generally inns of court, and so exercised a considerable influence in legal education; to be taken on as one of their private clerks was 'the best available advanced training'.[6]

Some clerical posts were in the royal gift. The king's bench was divided into the crown side and the civil side, and the clerk of the crown, alias the coroner and attorney, was regularly appointed by patent.[7] This meant that the post could be competed for and afterwards bought and sold like any other crown appointment. Thus on 1 March 1458 William Brome secured the reversion of the office after the tenure of the incumbent, Thomas Greswold, but when Greswold went in July, the post actually was filled by Thomas Croxton. What seems to have happened is that Croxton bought out Brome by securing for him the post of chief clerk or prothonotary, the officer in charge of the civil side of the court.[8] There was, however, a reserve on the auction, as Croxton found to his cost.[9] In 1465, a fortnight before he died, Croxton secured the reversion of his office for Thomas Vynter as a marriage portion for his daughter Etheldreda.[10] On claiming the office, however, Vynter found himself debarred by the judges

4. M. Hastings, *The Court of Common Pleas in Fifteenth Century England* (1947); M. Blatcher, *The Court of King's Bench, 1450–1550* (1978); cf. Spelman, *Reports*, ii. *361–7*, *374–82*; Baker, *Journ. Legal Hist.* 1; Meekings, 'King's bench files', 128–39.
5. Spelman, *Reports*, ii. *97–8*.
6. *ibid.*, ii. *129*.
7. Blatcher, *Court of King's Bench*, 34–9.
8. The details of the patents are in Spelman, *Reports*, ii. *361*.
9. Blatcher, *Court of King's Bench*, 37; Hastings, *Common Pleas*, 101.
10. PROB11/5 f.72v.

for lack of experience, and the post went to John West, with twenty-six years' clerical work in the court behind him. Clerks of the crown had regularly been recruited from clerks already in the court, and it may be that Croxton was trying to by-pass a convention that the reversion had to be kept within the 'club'. In the court of common pleas crown patronage applied to two offices, the custos brevium and the chirographer, and the former especially was held by men of rank, working through a deputy. From the start of the sixteenth century, however, the tendency was for the chirographer to be a trained lawyer.

On the civil side of king's bench all offices were in the gift of the chief justice.[11] In common pleas, the same was true, with the exception of the custos brevium and the chirographer and two other posts – the second prothonotary, where the custos was able to nominate, and the clerk of the outlawries, appointed by the king's attorney.[12] Thus the C.J.K.B. had fourteen and the C.J.C.P. twenty-six offices in his gift. In practice this meant that offices changed hands by purchase or from father to son, with the chief justice receiving a percentage every time or intervening to nominate, at a price. The clerk of 'hell', who was directly responsible to the chief justice for custody of the common pleas records, could even be discharged at will.[13] The most striking illustration of all this is the appointment by Chief Justice Fineux in 1498 of his son-in-law, John Roper, as chief clerk and prothonotary of the king's bench, and his agreement (to Roper's 'no lytell charge') to resettle the office in 1518 on John and his son William.[14] Money, however, was not everything. Many of the lesser clerks were clearly bred up in the court, acted as attorneys and, in the case of the filacers who handled business on a county basis, often had personal and professional ties with that area.[15] The Ropers, of course, were prominent at Lincoln's Inn, and it seems that all the prothonotaries, although beginning in humbler jobs, were expected to be a cut above other clerks. Roper went on to become attorney-general; William Mordaunt, chief prothonotary of the common pleas from 1490–1518,

11. Blatcher, *Court of King's Bench*, 40.
12. Hastings, *Common Pleas*, 107–8. However on 30 Nov. 1506 the filacership of Leicestershire passed to Babyngton on the resignation of Clerkson after payment of £20 to the crown: B.L. Lansd. Ms. 127 f. 33. Since the post of C.J. was unfilled between 7 Oct. and 26 Nov. 1506, Henry VII may have been asserting the right to nominate to posts in C.P. during vacancies.
13. Spelman, *Reports*, ii. 381–2.
14. *ibid.*, ii. 55.
15. Blatcher, *Court of King's Bench*, 44.

was the brother of Serjeant John Mordaunt; Humphrey Coningsby, third prothonotary there from 1480 to 1493, himself became a serjeant, and John Caryll, who bought the post from Coningsby, followed him to the coif.[16]

With administrative posts in royal courts it is relatively easy to identify the movements of offices between individuals. With counsel, however, the position is much less clear. Thomas Kebell's first public office came in May 1483, when he was created duchy attorney-general.[17] He had, for the previous five years, been retained by the duchy, and his seniority made him ripe for advancement, but there is something unexplained about this Lancaster appointment.[18] It was at the expense of one of the most obviously able of English administrators, Richard Empson of the Middle Temple, who had held the post since the end of 1477, and this is confirmed by events after Bosworth; Kebell was dropped and Empson reinstated, to remain in office until promoted in 1506 to chancellor of the duchy.[19] The most probable explanation of this 'Box and Cox' episode is the competition which took place in April 1483 for control of the young Edward V. Empson was associated with the queen's brother, Antony Woodville, Earl Rivers, while Kebell's patron, William, Lord Hastings, swung to support Richard, Duke of Gloucester. What more natural than the rewarding of Hastings by promoting one of his men at the expense of a protégé of the fallen Woodvilles?[20] The timing of the grant bears this out, setting it firmly in the context of the rewards given to those supporting Gloucester in the coup of April 30.[21] Kebell's survival when Hastings himself was destroyed in June can also be fitted into the political picture. William Catesby, Kebell's colleague at the Inner Temple, stood sufficiently near the monarch to inhibit any move against the recently appointed attorney of the duchy.[22]

Thomas Kebell's good fortune did not desert him in 1485. Although he had been appointed to one of the commissions of December 1483, confiscating the property of Buckingham and his suppor-

16. Roper: *L. and P.*, iii. 1389; Mordaunt: PROB11/14 f. 173; Coningsby, serjeant 1495; Caryll, serjeant 1510; for the sale see Spelman, *Reports*, ii. 377 n. 17.

17. Somerville, *Duchy of Lancaster*, i. 406. 18. *ibid.*, i. 454. 19. *ibid.*, i. 406.

20. For Empson's connection with Rivers, see S. Bentley, *Excerpta Historica* (1833), 248.

21. Kebell was appointed 28 May: *Grants of Edward V*, ed. J. G. Nichols, Camden Soc. 60 (1854), 65–6. For grants between 14 and 30 May to Norfolk, Buckingham, Lord Stanley, Gloucester's supporters (Kidwelly, Kendale and Miles Metcalfe) and to Hastings and his men (Catesby, Chauntry and Dynham), *ibid.*, passim.

22. See above p. 36; below pp. 108–11.

ters, and to the commissions of array of May and December 1484 (which should have involved him in despatching troops to Bosworth) he escaped retribution.[23] Although Empson was restored to his former post, Kebell was summoned on 11 November to take the degree of serjeant-at-law the following Trinity term. Again his standing was sufficient to warrant the call without our needing to assume compensation for the duchy post; there is little evidence, moreover, to suggest that former law officers had advantages in selection for the coif.[24] Nevertheless Kebell's call in 1485 was in marked contrast to the beheading of Catesby and the sacking of Kidwelly. He had not been too deeply involved with Richard III, and he had maintained his primary connection with the Hastings family; when the victory of Henry Tudor restored the fortunes of the second lord, Kebell yet again had patrons in high places.

The order of serjeants-at-law, to which Kebell was promoted in 1486, had been in existence for some two hundred years. Appointment to it continued until 1877, but the serjeants had their great importance during the first two, or two-and-a-half, centuries of the order. By 1600, as we have seen, a judge might be appointed without serving as a serjeant, and the law officers of the crown were the accepted leaders of the bar. But when Kebell lived, all this was in the future. The greatest honour which the law knew was the call to the coif, and this was demonstrated in the magnificence of the ceremonies which marked the occasion. No account of the 1486 creation survives, but full descriptions from other years indicate the usual pattern.[25]

The ceremony probably began on Sunday 2 July 1486 and was the high point of the entire legal year.[26] It involved the whole profession, from the chief justice of England down to the students of the inns of court and the humblest clerks in the Westminster courts. The first event was the formal leave-taking by the serjeants of their inns. At the Inner Temple, Thomas Kebell and William Danvers faced the rest of the house in the hall to receive an oration and a gift – perhaps ten marks each – and respond with a suitably grave and improving reply. Then the two of them were escorted by the fellows to Ely House, or wherever they were to be installed, and likewise the new serjeants

23. *Cal. Patent Rolls, 1476–85*, 393, 400, 489.

24. See below p. 79.

25. The following is based on the accounts for 1503 and 1521: Dugdale, *Origines*, 113–17; cf. *Minutes of Parliament*, i. 7–9. We await the study of the order of serjeants-at-law promised by Dr J. H. Baker.

26. Kebell's writ was dated 20 Nov. 1485 for 4 July 1486 (C54/346 m. 7), but the preliminary ceremonies in 1503 began two days before the date of creation.

from the other inns.[27] The next day each serjeant feasted his old society and the actual investiture began on the third morning, about ten o'clock, in the chapel. There, in the presence of all the judges, the serjeants made formal declarations on writs presented to them by the prothonotaries William Copley and Roger Brent, after which Sir William Hussey, C.J.K.B., invested each with the coif, the cap of white lawn which was the serjeant's *primus et precipuus de insigniis*, and a scarlet hood, in the manner of a university doctor.[28]

Later that day, or more probably the following morning, the newly invested serjeants processed to Westminster Hall in the splendour of their fresh liveries of blue ray, with an impressive escort, much of it newly attired at their expense. Each in turn – Danvers, Richard Jay of Gray's Inn, John Fisher of the Middle Temple, John Fineux of Gray's Inn, Kebell, the two Lincoln's Inn men, Robert Rede and John Haugh, and finally Thomas Wode of the Middle Temple – was led to the bar of the common pleas by John Vavasour and William Callow, and made a formal 'count' to which Thomas Tremayle, the third and senior of the existing serjeants replied.[29] Later the new serjeants went to St Paul's to be assigned pillars at which to practice, and everywhere there were offerings to make at shrines and gifts to be given. Fortescue gave three hundred rings at a total cost of £50, and in 1531 each serjeant gave rings to the chancellor, lord treasurer, lord privy seal and all the justices, a total of eleven, worth £8.12s., to say nothing of smaller rings to the lesser lights of the profession.[30] The climax of the call (responsible for even more of the four hundred marks which Fortescue estimated was the least that each serjeant had to lay out) was the great feast where they entertained the justices and prominent members of the profession as well as the notables of the day – in 1495 and 1503, the king himself was among the guests.[31] As a

27. In 1464, 1495, 1510, 1521, 1531 the place was Ely House, in 1503 Lambeth Palace, in 1541 St John's, in 1547 Lincoln's Inn (where the ceremonies were crammed into one day because of the change of sovereign). Hastings, *Common Pleas*, 73 n. 79; *Minutes of Parliament*, i. 8–9; *Great Chronicle of London*, ed. A. H. Thomas and I. D. Thornley (1938), 261, 326; John Stowe, *Survey of London*, ed. C. L. Kingsford (Oxford, 1908), ii. 36–7; Hall, *Chronicle*, 839; *Black Books*, i. 278–81.
28. Fortescue, *De Laudibus*, 124.
29. This is the order in which the calls of 1478 and 1486 list the serjeants chosen, and may reflect their seniority, but see below, pp. 80–1.
30. Fortescue, *De Laudibus*, 123–5; Spelman, *Reports*, i. 80. If Fortescue gave 300 rings at £50 with gold valued 40s. an ounce, the rings to lesser recipients must have contained mostly alloy or else been of gold wire.
31. Fortescue, *De Laudibus*, 122; Putnam, *Early Treatises*, 132 n. 1; *Minutes of Parliament*, i. 9.

serjeant, Kebell entered the select group which monopolised the court of common pleas where the most lucrative property litigation was heard. As a serjeant, Kebell would command the highest fees – 'there is no advocate in the wide world who makes so much out of his office as the serjeant does'.[32] To be chosen to proceed *ad gradum servientis ad legem* was both an honour in itself, and a promise of future profit.

The importance of attaining the coif is pointed by the contrast between the ceremonies on that occasion and the brief formalities when a serjeant was advanced to the judicial bench. Serjeants and judges were all members of the one order, differenced in function, but hardly in character. This, despite his dragging in confusing academic terms, was the truth behind Fortescue's description of a judge holding 'not any sort of degree in the faculty of law', but 'only an office and magistracy, terminable at the will of the king'.[33] In court the serjeants argued and the judges decided, but they were brethren of the coif, and treated each other as such; the judge was more a chairman than a referee. Indeed, in exchequer chamber, judges and serjeants met as a single order on equal terms. A common pleas case of 1489 brings out the relationship very clearly. The chief justice, Thomas Bryan, called to the coif in 1463 and C.J. since 1471, had accepted one of Kebell's arguments. John Vavasour, the opposing counsel, with barely eleven years' standing as a serjeant, said to Bryan, 'Sir, I may not be at odds with you here, but were we in exchequer chamber, I should insist that this plea is clearly inadmissible.'[34]

But the contrast between a serjeant's installation and the workaday reception of a new judge was not only because serjeants and judges shared the same dignity or degree. The essential function of the whole order, both judges and serjeants, was judicial.[35] It was when the lawyer received the coif that he achieved judicial rank, not when he was appointed to a particular court. The serjeant was a reserve justice, called on for occasional tasks, until a vacancy at Westminster brought him promotion to the first team.

Although it is nowhere stated by contemporaries, that the essential *raison d'être* of the order of the coif was judicial can be amply

32. Fortescue, *De Laudibus*, 124.

33. *ibid.*, 127–9.

34. *Y.B.* Trin. 4 Hen. VII, p. 3 f. 9. *Crofts* v. *Beauchamp* saw the unusual spectacle of the justices in exchequer chamber yielding to the serjeants and apprentices: *ibid.*, Trin. 1 Hen. VII, p. 6 ff. 28–9, p. 9 ff. 30–1.

35. Ives, *L.Q.R.* 75. 357–62.

demonstrated. Not only did the serjeants play a full judicial part in exchequer chamber, but they had an integral role in the assize system.[36] Quite commonly one-third of the assize commissions were supplied from the serjeants, and sometimes, as in the spring of 1507 and 1508, one-half. Without the serjeants, the whole pattern of regular itinerant royal justice would have broken down, and since assize judges also carried the heavy burden of the *nisi prius* system – by which cases in the central courts went to jury trial – Westminster Hall would rapidly have ground to a halt also. As juniors, the serjeants were, appropriately, assigned to the less attractive circuits; on forty-seven assizes held under Henry VII in the western circuit, only twice were both commissioners judges from the Westminster courts; in thirty cases both were serjeants-at-law. Only on the home, Norfolk and Oxford circuits was there a probability that the assize would be taken by a judge.

That serjeants belonged to the judiciary rather than the bar is also seen in the pattern of appointments. This was governed, not by merit, nor by professional pressure, but by the need for replacements for the judicial bench. Although a call of serjeants was made, on average, every eight or ten years, the actual timing was determined by the longevity, or otherwise, of the Westminster judges.[37] Kebell received his writ barely seven years after the previous call of 1478, yet before that, fourteen years had passed without a summons. The call of 1478 had brought the number of serjeants to twelve, three of whom were retained by the crown and so only available for a limited private practice. By the end of 1481 the number was down to eight, three of them in royal employment, and in 1483 and 1484 further deaths and promotions reduced the total to four, three under the king's retainer; a new call had to be made immediately Henry VII came to the throne. The call, indeed, had been overdue; before the installation there was already an unfilled vacancy in common pleas and John Fisher had to go on assize and be retained by the crown when still, technically, only a serjeant elect. A similar pattern can be seen with the next call of serjeants in 1495. In the early 1490s the order of the coif was static, with a full complement of judges, three serjeants under royal retainer and three others, including Thomas Kebell. However, the deaths of Roger Townshend J. in November 1493 and Serjeant Richard Jay in January 1494, and the promotion of John Fineux in Townshend's

36. See Table B and below, p. 74.

37. See Appendix E.

Table B. *Appointments as justices of assize etc. 1483–1513*

	HOME		WEST		NORFOLK	
1483 L	BRYAN C.J.C.P.	Sulyard	CATESBY J.C.P.	Callow	HUSSEY C.J.K.B.	NELE J.C.P.
1484 S	BRYAN	Sulyard	CATESBY	Callow	HUSSEY	NELE
L	BRYAN	Sulyard	[CATESBY]	[Callow]	HUSSEY	NELE
1485 S	BRYAN	SULYARD J.K.B.	CATESBY	Callow	HUSSEY	NELE
L	BRYAN	SULYARD	CATESBY	Callow	HUSSEY	NELE
1486 S	BRYAN	SULYARD	CATESBY	Callow	HUSSEY	NELE*[3]
L	BRYAN	SULYARD	CATESBY[4]	Callow	HUSSEY	CATESBY J.C.P.
1487 S	BRYAN	SULYARD	CALLOW J.C.P.	Wode	HUSSEY	HAUGH J.C.P.
L	BRYAN	SULYARD	CALLOW*[6]	Wode	[HUSSEY]	[HAUGH]
1488 S	BRYAN	SULYARD*[7]	Wode	Rede	HUSSEY	HAUGH
L	BRYAN	TOWNSHEND J.C.P.	Wode K.Sjt	Rede	HUSSEY	HAUGH
1489 S	BRYAN	TOWNSHEND	Wode	Rede	HUSSEY	HAUGH*[8]
L	[BRYAN]	[TOWNSHEND]	Wode	Rede	HUSSEY	Fineux
1490 S	BRYAN	TOWNSHEND	Wode	Rede	HUSSEY	Fineux K.Sjt
L	BRYAN	TOWNSHEND	Wode	Rede	HUSSEY	Fineux
1491 S	BRYAN	TOWNSHEND	Wode	Rede	HUSSEY	Fineux
L	BRYAN	TOWNSHEND	Wode	Rede	HUSSEY	Fineux
1492 S	BRYAN	TOWNSHEND	Wode	Rede	HUSSEY	Fineux
L	BRYAN	TOWNSHEND	Wode	Rede	HUSSEY	Fineux
1493 S	BRYAN	TOWNSHEND	Wode	Rede	HUSSEY	Fineux
L	BRYAN	TOWNSHEND*	Wode	Rede	HUSSEY	Fineux
1494 S	BRYAN	DANVERS J.C.P.	Wode	Rede	HUSSEY	FINEUX J.C.P.
L	BRYAN	DANVERS	Wode	Rede K.Sjt	HUSSEY	FINEUX

MIDLAND		OXFORD		NORTH	
FAIRFAX, G. J.K.B.	Vavasour K.Sjt	STARKY C.B.Ex.	Tremayle K.Sjt	NELE[1] J.C.P.	Townshend K.Sjt
FAIRFAX	Vavasour	[STARKY]	[Tremayle]	Townshend K.Sjt	*Kidwelly* A.G.
FAIRFAX	Vavasour	STARKY	Tremayle	Townshend	*Kidwelly*
[FAIRFAX]	[Vavasour]	STARKY	Tremayle	Townshend	*Kidwelly*
FAIRFAX	Vavasour	[STARKY]	[Tremayle]	Townshend	*Kidwelly*[2]
FAIRFAX	Vavasour	STARKY	Tremayle	TOWNSHEND J.C.P.	Fisher Sjt.elect
FAIRFAX	Vavasour	[STARKY]*[5]	[Tremayle]	TOWNSHEND	Fisher K.Sjt
FAIRFAX	Vavasour	*HODY* C.B.Ex.	Tremayle	TOWNSHEND	Fisher
[FAIRFAX]	[Vavasour]	[*HODY*]	[Tremayle]	TOWNSHEND	Fisher
FAIRFAX	Vavasour	*HODY*	Tremayle	TOWNSHEND	Fisher
FAIRFAX	Vavasour	*HODY*	TREMAYLE J.K.B.	DANVERS J.C.P.	Fisher
FAIRFAX	Vavasour	*HODY*	TREMAYLE	DANVERS	Fisher
FAIRFAX	Vavasour	*HODY*	TREMAYLE	DANVERS	Fisher
FAIRFAX	VAVASOUR J.C.P.	*HODY*	TREMAYLE	DANVERS	Fisher
FAIRFAX	VAVASOUR	*HODY*	TREMAYLE	DANVERS	Fisher
FAIRFAX	VAVASOUR	*HODY*	TREMAYLE	DANVERS	Fisher
FAIRFAX	VAVASOUR	*HODY*	TREMAYLE	DANVERS	Fisher
FAIRFAX	VAVASOUR	*HODY*	TREMAYLE	DANVERS	Fisher
FAIRFAX	VAVASOUR	*HODY*	TREMAYLE	DANVERS	Fisher
FAIRFAX	VAVASOUR	*HODY*	TREMAYLE	DANVERS	Fisher
FAIRFAX	VAVASOUR	*HODY*	TREMAYLE	DANVERS	Fisher
FAIRFAX	VAVASOUR	*HODY*	TREMAYLE	Fisher K.Sjt	Kebell
FAIRFAX	VAVASOUR	*HODY*	TREMAYLE	Fisher	Kebell

Table B. *continued*

	HOME		WEST		NORFOLK	
1495 S	BRYAN	DANVERS	Wode	Rede	HUSSEY	FINEUX
L	[BRYAN]	[DANVERS]	[Wode]	[Rede]	HUSSEY*	FINEUX
1496 S	[BRYAN]	[DANVERS]	WODE J.C.P.	REDE J.K.B.	FINEUX C.J.K.B.	Oxenbridg
L	BRYAN	DANVERS	WODE	REDE	[FINEUX]	[Oxenbridg
1497 S	BRYAN	DANVERS	WODE	Mordaunt K.Sjt	FINEUX	REDE
L	[BRYAN]	[DANVERS]	[WODE]	[Mordaunt]	[FINEUX]	[REDE]
1498 S	BRYAN	DANVERS	WODE	Mordaunt	FINEUX	REDE
L	[BRYAN]	[DANVERS]	WODE	Mordaunt	[FINEUX]	[REDE]
1499 S	[BRYAN]	[DANVERS]	WODE	Mordaunt	[FINEUX]	[REDE]
L	BRYAN	DANVERS	WODE	Mordaunt	[FINEUX]	[REDE]
1500 S	[BRYAN]	[DANVERS]	[WODE]	[Mordaunt]	FINEUX	REDE
L	BRYAN*	DANVERS	WODE	Mordaunt	[FINEUX]	[REDE]
1501 S	WODE C.J.C.P.	DANVERS	Mordaunt[10] K.Sjt	Frowyk	FINEUX	REDE
L	WODE	DANVERS	Frowyk	Constable*	[FINEUX]	[REDE]
1502 S	WODE	DANVERS	Frowyk K.Sjt	Butler	FINEUX	REDE
L	WODE*	DANVERS	Frowyk	Butler	FINEUX	REDE
1503 S	DANVERS J.C.P.	Kingsmill K.Sjt	FROWYK C.J.C.P.	Butler	FINEUX	REDE
L	DANVERS	KINGSMILL J.C.P.	FROWYK	Butler	FINEUX	REDE
1504 S	DANVERS*	KINGSMILL	FROWYK	Butler	[FINEUX]	[REDE]
L	FROWYK C.J.C.P.	TREMAYLE J.K.B.	Butler	Marowe	FINEUX	REDE
1505 S	FROWYK	TREMAYLE	Butler	Marowe*	FINEUX	REDE
L	FROWYK	TREMAYLE	Butler	Grevill	FINEUX	REDE
1506 S	FROWYK	TREMAYLE	Butler	Grevill	FINEUX	REDE

MIDLAND		OXFORD		NORTH	
FAIRFAX[9]	VAVASOUR	*HODY*	TREMAYLE	Fisher	Kebell
VAVASOUR J.C.P.	Fisher K.Sjt	*HODY*	TREMAYLE	Kebell	*Hobart* A.G.
VAVASOUR	Fisher	*HODY*	TREMAYLE	Kebell K.Sjt	*Hobart*
VAVASOUR	Fisher	*HODY*	TREMAYLE	Kebell	*Hobart*
VAVASOUR	Fisher	*HODY*	TREMAYLE	Kebell	*Hobart*
[VAVASOUR]	[Fisher]	[*HODY*]	[TREMAYLE]	[Kebell]	[*Hobart*]
VAVASOUR	Fisher	*HODY*	TREMAYLE	Kebell	*Hobart*
VAVASOUR	Fisher	[*HODY*]	[TREMAYLE]	Kebell	*Hobart*
VAVASOUR	Fisher	[*HODY*]	[TREMAYLE]	Kebell	*Hobart*
VAVASOUR	Fisher	*HODY*	TREMAYLE	Kebell	*Hobart*
VAVASOUR	Fisher	[*HODY*]	[TREMAYLE]	Kebell*	*Hobart*
VAVASOUR	Fisher	*HODY*	TREMAYLE	*Hobart*	Coningsby
VAVASOUR	Fisher	*HODY*	TREMAYLE	*Hobart*	Coningsby K.Sjt
VAVASOUR	Fisher	*HODY*	TREMAYLE	[*Hobart*]	[Coningsby]
VAVASOUR	FISHER J.C.P.	*HODY*	TREMAYLE	*Hobart*	Coningsby
VAVASOUR	FISHER	*HODY*	TREMAYLE	*Hobart*	Coningsby
VAVASOUR	FISHER	*HODY*	TREMAYLE	*Hobart*	Coningsby
VAVASOUR	FISHER	*HODY*	TREMAYLE	*Hobart*[11]	Coningsby
[VAVASOUR]	[FISHER]	[*HODY*]	[TREMAYLE]	Coningsby K.Sjt	Cutlerd
VAVASOUR	FISHER	*HODY*	KINGSMILL J.C.P.	Coningsby	Cutlerd
VAVASOUR	FISHER	*HODY*	KINGSMILL	Coningsby	Cutlerd
VAVASOUR	FISHER	*HODY*	KINGSMILL	Coningsby	Cutlerd*
VAVASOUR	FISHER	*HODY*	KINGSMILL	Coningsby	Brudenell K.Sjt

Table B. *continued*

	HOME		WEST		NORFOLK	
L	FROWYK*	TREMAYLE	[Butler]	[Grevill]	FINEUX	REDE
1507 S	TREMAYLE J.K.B.	Butler	Grevill	Eliot	FINEUX	REDE C.J.C.P.
L	TREMAYLE	Butler	Grevill	Eliot K.Sjt	FINEUX	REDE
1508 S	TREMAYLE	Butler	Grevill	Eliot	FINEUX	REDE
L	TREMAYLE*	BUTLER J.C.P.	[Grevill]	[Eliot]	FINEUX	REDE
1509 S[13]	BUTLER J.C.P.	More	[Grevill]	[Eliot]	[FINEUX]	[REDE]
L	BUTLER	More	Eliot K.Sjt	Pollard K.Sjt	FINEUX	REDE
1510 S	BUTLER	More	[Eliot]	[Pollard]	FINEUX	REDE
L	BUTLER	More	Eliot	Pollard	FINEUX	REDE
1511 S	BUTLER	More	[Eliot]	[Pollard]	FINEUX	REDE
L	BUTLER	More	Eliot	Pollard	FINEUX	REDE
1512 S	[BUTLER]	[More]	Eliot	Pollard	FINEUX	REDE
L	BUTLER	More	Eliot	Pollard	FINEUX	REDE
1513 S	BUTLER	More	Eliot	Pollard	FINEUX	REDE
L	BUTLER	More	ELIOT J.C.P.	Pollard	FINEUX	REDE

Notes

This table is compiled from the patent roll entries of assize commissions, writs associating the clerks of assize with the justices, and commissions of gaol delivery. * = died before next assize. [ ] = patents not enrolled; appointment presumed. Names of judges in capitals, of non-serjeants in italics.

1. The assize was probably ridden by Kidwelly, but no patent has survived; Nele moved to the Norfolk circuit.
2. Not reappointed A.G. by Henry VII.
3. Nele died 11 Jul. 1486 and so did not serve.
4. Thomas Wode was appointed nominally as clerk of assize for this occasion, so releasing Catesby for the Norfolk circuit.
5. Starky died 27 Jul. 1486.
6. Callow died 29 Jul. 1487.

MIDLAND		OXFORD		NORTH	
VAVASOUR*	FISHER	*HODY*	KINGSMILL	Coningsby	Brudenell
FISHER J.C.P.	Palmes, G.	[*HODY*]	[KINGSMILL]	Coningsby	Brudenell
FISHER	Palmes	*HODY*[12]	KINGSMILL	BRUDENELL J.K.B.	Coningsby K.Sjt
FISHER	Palmes	KINGSMILL J.C.P.	Pollard K.Sjt	BRUDENELL	Coningsby
FISHER	Palmes	KINGSMILL	Pollard	BRUDENELL	Coningsby
[FISHER]	[Palmes]	[KINGSMILL]*	[Pollard]	[BRUDENELL]	[Coningsby]
FISHER	Palmes	BRUDENELL J.K.B.	GREVILL[14] J.C.P.	CONINGSBY J.K.B.	Fairface, W.[15]
FISHER*	Palmes	BRUDENELL	GREVILL	CONINGSBY	Fairfax
CONINGSBY J.K.B.	Palmes	BRUDENELL	GREVILL	FAIRFAX, W. J.C.P.	*Erneley* A.G.
[CONINGSBY]	[Palmes]	BRUDENELL	GREVILL	FAIRFAX	*Erneley*
CONINGSBY	Palmes	BRUDENELL	GREVILL	FAIRFAX	*Erneley*
CONINGSBY	Palmes	BRUDENELL	GREVILL	FAIRFAX	*Erneley*
CONINGSBY	Palmes	BRUDENELL	GREVILL	FAIRFAX	*Erneley*
CONINGSBY	Palmes	BRUDENELL	GREVILL*[16]	FAIRFAX	*Erneley*
CONINGSBY	Palmes K.Sjt	BRUDENELL	Newport	FAIRFAX	*Erneley*

7. Sulyard died 18 Mar. 1488.
8. Haugh died 14 Mar. 1489.
9. Fairfax was not appointed for the Lammas assize, but did not die until Michaelmas 1495.
10. Mordaunt was not appointed for the assizes again but remained active until 1504.
11. Hobart was not appointed for the assizes again but remained A.G. until 1507.
12. Hody was not appointed for the assizes again but remained C.B.Ex. until 1521.
13. The Home circuit patent was renewed on 9 Oct. 1508 following Tremayle's death, but it is doubtful whether assize commissions actually operated in spring 1509.
14. Initially Pollard was continued: *L. and P.*, i. 54(8).
15. Initially Brudenell was continued: *ibid.*, i. 54(1).
16. Grevill died 9 Mar. 1513.

place, reduced the serjeants to four, with only Kebell not restricted by a royal retainer. More serjeants had to be made, and in November 1495 nine more apprentices were promoted, which freed two of the existing serjeants for the bench and Kebell for promotion to king's serjeant. What happened when turnover was less rapid is seen in the early years of Henry VIII's reign. The justices, and the serjeants called in 1510, were in general so long-lived that no further call was made until 1521. To the crown the order of the coif was a reservoir of justices, to be replenished only when the working of the judicial system of the country was imperilled.

The clearest indication of the judicial character of the call to the coif is the fact that vacancies on the bench could only be filled by serjeants; even when, in later years, lawyers were promoted directly to the rank of judge, tradition (as we have seen) dictated that they should be invested as serjeants-at-law prior to joining the bench. This monopoly of promotion is usually interpreted as a privilege, but it is more correct to see it as an obligation; every serjeant knew, when he took the coif, that he was committed to a judicial future. Immediately he would be liable for the assize commissions, and the major part which serjeants played made it almost inevitable that a serjeant should serve on them at one time or another. Soon after being chosen for the coif, Kebell wrote to a prospective client, 'I couth not be with you at thassises tyme. Parauentur I shulde be Justice of assise in som other contrey', and he was clearly not exaggerating the possibility.[38] Thirty serjeants served in Henry VII's reign, and twenty-two of them acted, while serjeants, as justices of assize. Of the remainder, Haugh and Danvers were rapidly promoted to the bench and so went on assize as full judges, two more were commissioned for the first assizes of Henry VIII, and three others died before a circuit became vacant, leaving John Yaxley with the doubtful distinction of being passed over for the task. It was also inevitable that a serjeant would later join the Westminster bench. Seventy-four serjeants in all were appointed by Henry VI, Edward IV and Henry VII. Fifty-one became judges and all the rest died before sufficient vacancies had occurred. Depending upon the death rate among the judges – and upon his own life-span – every serjeant could expect an appointment as a judge in due course. To be called to the coif was, in effect, to be nominated for judicial office.

The judicial character of the coif in pre-Reformation England

38. *Coventry Leet Book*, i. 52; cf. Richard Clerk: *Black Books*, i. 181, 184.

justified that other feature of the legal profession, the serjeants' monopoly of pleading in common pleas. This was the sugar on the pill of judicial duties, as is clearly seen in the case of William Ayscough. Raised to the bench after only two years as a serjeant, he complained to the council in 1441 that this had robbed him of his 'winnings' as a serjeant.[39] The inevitability of a judicial appointment also accounts for the reluctance of some lawyers to take the coif at all; even the exclusive common pleas bar might not be a sufficient inducement, especially as a call to the bench might put an abrupt and premature end to this privileged position.[40] Of Kebell's colleagues in 1486, John Haugh was made a judge after one term, and William Danvers after five; their 'winnings' cannot have covered the cost of their installation. It is small wonder that some men insured against the coif by securing a patent of exemption.

In all ways, therefore, the connection between the serjeants and the judiciary is plain. The work which the serjeants did in exchequer chamber and on assize, the way judicial vacancies determined the whole promotion pattern, the way in which every serjeant was destined to be a judge, all the evidence points in one direction. That Fortescue makes no mention of this is hardly surprising. Intent on portraying the legal profession as a community of academics, he could hardly admit that the serjeants he cast for the role of university dons were, in fact, busy magistrates.

How long Thomas Kebell would enjoy his 'winnings' as a serjeant depended on the extent and the immediacy of the judicial work he had to do. Here he was enormously fortunate.[41] The first assize vacancy had been allotted to John Fisher even before the actual ceremony of the coif had taken place. Thomas Wode was called in immediately afterwards for the Lammas assizes of 1486 and Robert Rede eighteen months later, while in the summer of 1489 John Fineux followed. William Danvers and John Haugh had already been promoted to the judicial bench, so that within three years of becoming serjeants, six of Kebell's seven colleagues were engaged in the judicial machine. For the next four years, however, no gaps appeared amongst the assize judges, and Kebell, with Richard Jay, remained on the side-lines. In the winter of 1493–4 the situation changed with the deaths of Townshend and Jay, so that Kebell was appointed an assize commissioner on 1 February 1494. He did not take over the plum home circuit

39. Ayscough, *Archaeologia* 16. 3–4.
40. Ives, *L.Q.R.* 75. 355–7.
41. See below, pp. 493–7.

which Townshend had ridden; Danvers took the opportunity to escape from the northern circuit, leaving the newcomer to take his place, or, rather, John Fisher to take over as senior justice and Kebell to come in as the junior. After eighteen months Fisher escaped to the midland circuit and, in the absence of any available serjeants, James Hobart of Lincoln's Inn, the king's attorney, came in to partner Kebell. Kebell and Hobart rode the circuit from then on until the serjeant died. It may be asked, why did not Kebell escape from the northern assize; he served on it for nearly seven years.[42] He might have secured Norfolk in the spring of 1496, but he had only recently taken over the north and, more important, he had been appointed justice at Lancaster.[43] Justices at Lancaster seem always to have served – as common sense dictated – on the north, the midland and the Oxford circuit, each of which took assize judges near to the county palatine. The next vacancy was for the west – again unsuitable – and this was the last in Kebell's lifetime.[44]

Thomas Kebell was thus fortunate in having seven years' freedom before judicial duties caught up with him, and his situation was even happier than this suggests. While his colleagues of the coif adorned the bench or rode the circuits, he remained free to take clients, and as the other serjeants were one by one taken into royal service, Kebell began to enjoy first a near and then an actual monopoly of business. From the spring of 1490 to early 1494, he and Jay were the only serjeants available at assize time. A parallel situation existed in term-time. From Michaelmas term 1489, only three serjeants were without royal retainer and thus free to appear against the crown, and Kebell was one of them. In January 1494 the number fell to two, and in April Kebell was left with a monopoly of employment which endured for the next six law terms. It is not surprising that the early 1490s saw some of his most substantial investment in land.[45] Such a profitable situation could not last. As the assize circuit had caught up with Kebell in 1494, so, with the decision to call new serjeants in 1495, did work for the crown during term. In July came the appointment as

42. *Cal. Patent Rolls, 1485–94*, 459. His patents as justice of gaol delivery and justice of the peace in the northern circuit counties can be traced regularly until his death. *ibid., 1485–94*, 476, 478, 479, 480, 506; *ibid., 1494–1509*, 15, 28, 31, 51, 68, 89, 147, 149, 160, 179, 194, 634, 664, 666, 667, 668.
43. See below, n. 46.
44. Kebell took the spring assize at York on 23 Mar. 1500, the last assize before his death. *Cal. Patent Rolls, 1494–1509*, 207.
45. See below, p. 338.

second justice at Lancaster, and by the end of the year he had been retained as a king's serjeant.[46] Four years later he added the other judicial prize of the north-west when he became justice at Chester.[47]

Thomas Kebell was clearly among the ablest lawyers of his generation, and it may appear curious that he did not go on to judicial office at Westminster. As has been seen, the ultimate reason for this was fortuitous; a vacancy did not occur. Kebell had been appointed in a call which raised the number of serjeants to eleven. During his fourteen remaining years, eight judicial places had to be filled and one of his contemporaries died, leaving John Fisher and Thomas Kebell as the two senior serjeants. No further vacancy occurred until four law terms after Kebell's death, when Fisher was promoted. But if Kebell was so good, why had he not been chosen earlier? Why, of the 1486 call, was Fisher immediately picked as a king's serjeant but promoted to the bench behind all the rest? Why was it John Haugh who was chosen a puisne justice of common pleas after less than six months? Indeed there is an even earlier question – why were these particular men selected to be serjeants in the first place?

The ultimate choice in promotion to the coif was undoubtedly that of the monarch himself. The practice at the end of Henry VIII's reign was for the king to be furnished with a list of suitable men, from which he 'pricked' the required number, much as sheriffs were pricked.[48] That this was the custom earlier may be inferred from the council minute of 1437: 'the names of them that shal be maade sergeantes to be send unto the King'.[49] The role of the council in the selection of serjeants – presumably agreeing a short-list – is stressed in many sources. An account of the call of 1521 declared that the 'new Ser-

46. Somerville, *Duchy of Lancaster*, i. 473; *Final Concords of the County of Lancaster*, ed. W. Farrer, Lancashire and Cheshire Record Soc., 39, 46, 50, 60 (1899–1910), i. 146–8. The patent for Kebell as king's serjeant was not enrolled, but he was probably appointed 25 Nov. 1495 with John Mordaunt to replace Wode and Rede, promoted to the bench the day before; he was paid from that date. *Cal. Patent Rolls, 1494–1509*, 43, 44; Spelman, *Reports*, ii. *386*. He was not summoned as king's serjeant to parliament in October 1495, but had been sworn of council to the king in 1494. *Cal. Close Rolls, 1485–1500*, 845; see below, p. 229.

47. Ormerod, *History of Chester*, i. 230; 'Calendar of Warrants [etc.] Chester, Henry VI to Elizabeth', in *Annual Reports of the Deputy Keeper of Public Records* 26 (1865), 52.

48. *L. and P.*, xxi(1). 1165. 'Documents signed by stamp, June 1546.' These included 'a roll containing the names of certain learned men of the four principal Inns of Court, whereof 8 names are pricked by your Majesty to be serjeants-at-law, subscribed by my Lord Chancellor'.

49. *Proceedings and Ordinances of the Privy Council*, ed. H. Nicolas (1834–7), v. 80.

jaunts, for ther konnynge, discrecione and wysdome be calide by the Kyng's Highnes and his honorabill Councelle to the gret promocyone and dignytie of the office of a Serjaunt of the lawe', while writs of summons refer to the call as being made by advice of the council.[50] Fortescue stated that serjeants were chosen by the chief justice of the common pleas, but this is not incompatible with conciliar responsibility.[51] Since the serjeants had a special association with his court, the chief justice was the obvious councillor to prepare a provisional list for discussion. Evidence suggests, however, that in the sixteenth century the chancellor took the lead, a natural consequence of the closer association of that office with the common law following the fall of Wolsey. The final list submitted to the king in 1546 was subscribed by the chancellor, and in 1547 the chancellor brought before the council the need to fill a vacancy among the king's serjeants.[52]

The comparison with the pricking of sheriffs again stresses that serjeants were chosen at the will of the crown and in its interests. This is further emphasised by the clear evidence that the individual concerned was not consulted. The reaction of John Packington of the Inner Temple to a writ of summons was to point out that he had a patent of exemption and that 'he did not intend to undertake it if his letters could discharge him'.[53] Some men secured patents in order to postpone rather than to avoid the coif, but others wanted permanent protection from the inconvenience of judicial duties.[54]

The criteria upon which names were put forward to the king is hard to establish. Common sense would suggest that judicial capacity must have been high on the list of qualifications, so also professional skill and reputation, and probably general standing with the crown and the important magnates, but evidence is mainly negative. Social standing counted for little; as we have seen, men a good deal less well-born even than Kebell made the grade. Seniority in the profession was likewise no guarantee of promotion; with calls coming at seven- to ten-year intervals, and including a wide range of ages in the six to a dozen men selected, prominent lawyers were bound to be passed over.[55] Family connections were similarly unimportant. A family

50. Quoted in Dugdale, *Origines*, 114.

51. Fortescue, *De Laudibus*, 121.

52. See p. 77; *Acts of the Privy Council, 1547–1550*, ed. J. R. Dasent, (1890), 25; cf. *L. and P.*, xii(2). 805.

53. *Inner Temple Records*, i. 98.

54. One temporary refusal was by Thomas Yonge in 1443; he accepted in 1463.

55. Ages of serjeants are hard to estimate, but a rough order among the members of

persistent in the law sometimes provides more than one serjeant, but often only after a long interval; William Jenney became a serjeant in 1463 but the next of the family to reach the coif did so only in 1531. The sons of serjeants were sometimes called, but the sample is small. Another possible reason, success in a prominent legal post, turns out to be equally inconclusive. The attorney-generals had no close connection with the coif, and, as might be expected, the record of the solicitors is no better.[56] Outside the central courts the two offices which carried most prestige were those of attorney-general of the duchy of Lancaster and recorder of London, but neither were passports to the coif.[57] If a royal lawyer was on the short-list he might have a good chance of being pricked by the king – this could explain the success of Kebell, Eliot, Rudhale or John Port – but there is no evidence that he had any prescriptive claim to be there in the first place.

On grounds of probability, patronage might be expected to operate in the law as elsewhere. Yet if selection for the coif was arbitrary, then the function of patronage was less to advance men than to protect them from an unwanted summons. In 1521, Baldwin Malet was excused 'by his own labour and industry' and 'by the special endeavours of his friends', most probably John Port the solicitor-general, who, with 'all the others of the [Inner Temple] did not believe that [he] wished to exercise that office'.[58] Influence of some kind must lie behind the escape of another fellow of the Inner Temple, John Caryll junior, from three successive writs of summons.[59] The most notable 'reluctant serjeant' of all, Edmund Dudley, exemplifies the impossibility of reducing selection to the coif to any firm rule. Called in the spring of 1503 (possibly 'pricked' by Henry VII following his service as under-sheriff of London), he was

each call is suggested by the dates in which men first served as reader of their inn. In 1521, the call included men elected to read in 1494, 1503, 1507, 1514, 1516, 1517, 1518, and 1520.

56. Of 18 attorneys between 1429 and 1559, 2 became serjeants, 2 secured patents of exemption, 3 died in office before advancement could come, and 11 were passed over for the coif or took promotion in other ways. Of the 16 solicitors who held office before 1559, 5 became attorney (none of whom reached the coif), 2 became serjeants, 4 received other posts, 2 died after a brief tenure of office, 3 were retired.

57. Of 14 attorneys to the duchy between 1471 and 1566, 3 died before any call to the coif was possible, 6 became serjeants, one secured exemption from call and 4 were passed over. Of 10 recorders of London between 1450 and 1552, 4 became serjeants, 2 were already serjeants on appointment, and 4 were passed over.

58. *Inner Temple Records*, i. 60, 63.

59. In 1540, 1552, 1555.

excused six weeks before the creation ceremony, barely leaving time to find a replacement.[60] This sudden change was perhaps because a parliament had been decided on and Dudley picked to be speaker; governments do alter decisions, and quite possibly this was all that was involved here. But was Dudley only a pawn? A few months after the parliament he entered Henry VII's service in an administrative capacity.[61] Was this a *quid pro quo* for losing the coif; had the announcement of a parliament allowed Dudley and his patrons to agitate for a transfer to a more promising avenue of promotion; were the judicial members of the council competing with the administrators for Dudley's services, or was the crown really making an arbitrary change of plan?[62]

Turning from the promotion of apprentices to the coif to the promotion of serjeants to the bench, the final voice is once more that of the king. This is made explicit in one of Thomas Cromwell's memoranda about a replacement for Justice Thomas Englefield.[63] On what grounds selection was made is again difficult to say. Circumstances varied, and a presumably important point was suitability by comparison with others available. There was also chance – being noticed at the right time; Thomas Audley, attorney of the duchy, was chosen speaker of the Commons in 1529 after nineteen years in the profession, and within three he was lord keeper.[64] It is, however, clear that forms of seniority existed among the serjeants. One, which was unchallenged in Kebell's day, was between calls; only four out of the eighty-three serjeants created between 1425 and 1510 were promoted to the bench while men called to the coif before them were still available, and one of these was a promotion to chief justice.[65] Within each call there was also an order of seniority; this determined precedence in court and was apparently fixed by the dates of admission to an inn of court.[66] There is, however, no relationship observ-

60. c82/252/1/14.

61. B.L. Lansd. Ms. 127 f. 1.

62. B. P. Wolffe, *The Crown Lands* (1970), 76–8 suggests that there was rivalry between 'administrators' and 'lawyers' in the royal council.

63. *L. and P.*, xii(2). 874.

64. *Inner Temple Records*, i. 19–20; Somerville, *Duchy of Lancaster*, i. 407; cf. S. E. Lehmberg, 'Sir Thomas Audley: a soul as black as marble?', in *Tudor Men and Institutions*, 3–31. Note also his opportune views on uses: see below, p. 257.

65. Hussey (1478), C.J.K.B. 1481, passing over Jenney and Catesby (1463); Haugh and Danvers (1486), JJ.C.P. 1486, 1488, over Tremayle and Vavasour; Brudenell (1503), J.K.B. 1507, over Butler and Coningsby (1495). In each of these cases the next vacancy/ies went to the men passed over.

66. Dugdale, *Origines*, 115, 116, 119; *Minutes of Parliament*, i. 9; cf. Bland,

able between this and promotion to the bench in the calls of 1521 and 1531, the earliest point where the order can be generally established, although the situation may have been different in the previous century. One other possible correlation can also be dismissed, length of professional experience. The first serjeants promoted from the 1521 call were the second and third eldest and then the youngest; the man with longest service was passed over three times for puisne justiceships while the most junior but one, also passed over three times, was then elevated to the post of chief justice.[67] Kebell was evidently senior to Robert Rede, but was promoted king's serjeant eighteen months later than Rede, the day after Robert had been promoted J.K.B.

One group of judicial appointments beneath the serjeants were the posts of puisne baron in exchequer. In 1461 there were four of these, designated the second, third, fourth and fifth barons, but their special functions have yet to be established; in the fifteenth century there is some evidence of promotion from one to another, but in the sixteenth, men stayed in the post to which they were first appointed.[68] When in 1471 Edward IV cut down the size of the judiciary, the puisne barons of the exchequer were reduced to two, although the post of fourth baron was restored in 1478. Their position was always an anomalous one. Barons were individually junior to serjeants, indeed sometimes presided when a serjeant elect was feted by his inn on call to the coif. Equally, however, they were members of a court before which the serjeants appeared. Nor did the move after 1579 to appoint only serjeants solve the dilemma; Edward Coke still claimed that barons were not judges on a par with king's bench and common pleas.[69] Appointment was, nevertheless, one of the lesser plums of the

J.S.P.T.L. 10. 186–7. In the call of 1547, however, the stated seniority is not that of initial admission to an inn. In the fifteenth century, the order of names of serjeants-elect on the close roll may be their order of seniority [cf. *Cal. Close Rolls, 1461–8*, 172–3 and *Y.B.* 3 Edward IV, p. 7 f. 12], but in 1486 Haugh is listed after Rede who was definitely his junior at Lincoln's Inn.

67. Fitzjames: read autumn vacation, 1504, C.B.Ex. 8 Feb. 1522; John Port: read autumn 1507, J.K.B. 10 Jul. 1525; Thomas Englefield: read autumn 1520, J.C.P. 12 Nov. 1526; Rudhale: read autumn 1494, passed over by Port, Englefield and Shelley, J.C.P. 1526; Norwich: read autumn 1518, passed over as Rudhale, C.J.C.P. 22 Nov. 1530. *Minutes of Parliament*, i. 10, 61; *Inner Temple Records*, i. 7; *Black Books*, i. 184; Thorne, *Readings and Moots*, i. xvi; Spelman, *Reports*, ii. *359*, *372–3*, *383*.

68. E.g. Roucliffe, Goldesborough, Holgrave, Lathell; cf. Spelman, *Reports*, ii. *382*.

69. *Black Books*, i. 87, 89, 90, 92, 104; *Admission Book*, i. 19; E315/486/40; *Cal. Patent Rolls, 1485–94*, 35; *ibid., 1494–1509*, 106, 339.

profession, and puisne barons could be men of standing in the law. John Allen, appointed fourth baron in 1504, had entered Lincoln's Inn in 1476, read twice (most recently in 1496) and had been re-elected as treasurer no fewer than three times; Andrew Dymmock of the Middle Temple was appointed third baron in 1497 after eleven years as solicitor-general.[70]

A number of barons had, it is true, held clerical posts in the exchequer. Nicholas Lathell, created third baron in 1488, had been clerk of the pipe; Robert Blagge, third baron from 1511, had been king's remembrancer; Edmund Denny, fourth baron in 1513, had been the lord treasurer's remembrancer.[71] Others had a background in royal fiscal administration. This was especially true of Bartholomew Westby, appointed second baron in 1501 but deeply involved in Henry VII's chamber administration.[72] It could be that these instances show that it was still possible to rise to the exchequer bench through service as a royal financial expert, but it is more reasonable to assume that just as members of the inns went into clerical posts in king's bench and common pleas, so they did into exchequer and royal fiscal administration generally, and that the able and fortunate reached the rank of baron; for example, Blagge belonged to the Inner and Westby to the Middle Temple. That this was the case is suggested by what happened later in the sixteenth century, when serjeants began to be appointed as puisne barons. The lack of expertise led to the emergence of the cursitor baron, chosen from the revenue officers of the exchequer but without judicial duties.[73] Under Henry VII and Henry VIII the barons seem to have needed no such assistance.

From the middle of Henry VIII's reign there is much more light on the whole question of judicial promotion, thanks to the survival of the state papers. The chancellor would appear then to have had the principal influence in traditional legal posts just as he had in calls to the coif. It was Lord Chancellor Audley who, on the erroneous news that Walter Luke J.K.B. was dead, proposed to the king that Humphrey Browne, king's serjeant, should be promoted and that Edward Montagu should succeed Browne; only then did he ask Thomas

70. Bryson, *Equity Side*, 16, 47–50.

71. *Cal. Patent Rolls, 1477–85*, 406; Spelman, *Reports*, i. 150; *Cal. Patent Rolls, 1494–1509*, 420.

72. *ibid., 1494–1509*, 237; *Minutes of Parliament*, i. 8; W. C. Richardson, *Early Tudor Chamber Administration* (Baton Rouge, 1952), 250, 252, 256–8.

73. Bryson, *Equity Side*, 50–1.

Cromwell to add his influence to the proposal.[74] Cromwell, however, did have some part in suggesting names for promotion. It was to the minister that Christopher Hales M.R. applied for the promotion of Montagu to the assize circuit made vacant by the death of Thomas Englefield.[75] In more recently created legal posts, Cromwell seems to have taken the lead, fittingly enough as their architect. It was Audley who wrote to him when the augmentations was involved, asking Cromwell to 'move' the king to promote Robert Southwell from solicitor to attorney and to secure the junior post for John Lucas.[76] The same deference to Cromwell, but also an example of the discussion and interchange which must have gone on, is seen in the choice for a traditional post which had been given a new status by the legislation of 1536, that of justice of Chester.[77] Immediately upon the death of Thomas Englefield, Bishop Roland Lee wrote suggesting Thomas Bromley as a suitable replacement; the next day, John Packington, one of the Welsh judges, applied to Cromwell, offering him one hundred marks.[78] Cromwell consulted Audley, who suggested Justice Fitzherbert or Serjeant Edmund Knightley. Knightley had come into wealth

> and needeth not to extort; and though he be wilful and full of fond inventions, yet it is to be thought if ever he will be an honest man, that now he hath these great possessions, and may have the estimation of a judge, he will leave all his old fond fancies and become a new man.[79]

None of these candidates were, in the end successful; the post went to William Sulyard of Lincoln's Inn, master of requests and judge in the Marshalsea, a man Cromwell had his eye on.[80]

Evidence from the 1530s and later is valuable, but it cannot automatically be projected back into the previous century. By the middle of Henry VIII's reign the settled order of the pre-Reformation profession was beginning to change. The most obvious signs are the advent of the common-law chancellor and the rise of the law officers. Just as significant is the breakdown of precedence between calls of

74. *L. and P.*, xii(2). 805. Some appointments to the bench in 1485 were 'by advice of the council': *Cal. Patent Rolls, 1485–94*, 18, 33.

75. L. and P., xii(2). 873.

76. *ibid.*, xii(2). 1160.

77. The post of justice of Chester was long established, but the palatinate had not been under the chancellor in medieval times and the reconstruction of county, Wales and the March in 1536 would have brought the Chester posts within Cromwell's purview; cf. the post of judge of North Wales, *ibid.*, xii(2). 775.

78. *ibid.*, xii(2). 770, 775.

79. *ibid.*, xii(2). 805.

80. Fisher, *J.S.P.T.L.* 14. 111–17.

serjeants. In contrast to earlier convention, after 1521 serjeants are all too frequently leap-frogged by their puisnes; when William Coningsby became a judge in 1540, he went over the heads of one serjeant of 1510, two of 1521 and four of 1531.[81] A further factor is the appearance of a more varied career prospect for the lawyer; a curriculum such as that of Richard Rich was entirely novel – attorney-general for Wales, solicitor-general, chancellor of the augmentations, speaker of the Commons, lord chancellor. In 1540, in addition to Rich at the augmentations, we find a second former law officer (Sir John Baker), as chancellor of the court of first fruits and tenths, a third, Christopher Hales, as master of the rolls, and on the woolsack, Thomas Audley, a former king's serjeant; twelve years earlier these posts for common lawyers had simply not existed. Religious conformity also enters the picture. Coupled with the political upheavals of the mid-century it played havoc with the traditional ordering of the profession and led in the end to a man like Edmund Plowden being forced into semi-retirement.

There remain the ultimate leaders of the common law, the presidents of the three great courts of king's bench, common pleas and exchequer. All told, there were only twenty-one holders of these three posts in the period between the crisis of 1471, when Edward IV replaced the chief justice of the common pleas and the chief baron, and the crisis of 1553, when Mary Tudor replaced the heads of all three courts. With such a small sample, and positions of immense prestige and prominence, it is natural to expect that personal and private factors would prevail rather than a career pattern. The personal relationship with the monarch was far more immediate than with lesser posts. Thomas Urswick, appointed chief baron by Edward IV on 22 May 1471, can have done his chances no harm by energetic leadership of the Londoners against the Bastard of Fauconberg a week before.[82] These men, moreover, were at the heart of government; they not only presided over courts which were important instruments of royal policy, but were also influential members of the royal council, by no means only present for judicial matters. There is, for example,

81. John Rowe (1510), Humphrey Browne and Thomas Fairfax (1521), Edmund Knightley, Edmund Mervin, Roger Cholmley and John Hinde (1531). The next vacancies were filled by Mervin and Browne, after which Knightley, Fairfax and Rowe died, and then Hinde and Cholmley were promoted.

82. *Cal. Patent Rolls, 1461–7*, 259; C. Ross, *Edward IV* (1974), 174–5.

contemporary witness to the value Henry VII put on William Hussey.[83]

With these senior posts, individual canvassing and patronage could operate much more simply and obviously than at lower levels. Both can be seen in the career of Edward Montagu. It is hardly surprising that a lawyer so well thought of by both chancellor and master of the rolls went to the head of king's bench at the first opportunity.[84] Six years later the death of John Baldwin gave Montagu the chance to agitate for a transfer to common pleas, and this allowed Chief Baron Lyster to move to king's bench.[85] Montagu's excuse was old age – 'I am now an old man, and love the kitchen before the hall, the warmest place best suiting with my age' – but what he really sought in the kitchen of the common pleas was the greater opportunity for profit.[86] Nor was such jockeying characteristic only of the sixteenth century. A note in the Paston correspondence suggests that William Yelverton had been counting on succeeding John Fortescue as C.J.K.B. and had been disappointed in 1461 by John Markham, and that Markham had, as a consolation, secured a knighthood for him.[87] We find what appears to be a typical patronage manoeuvre behind the promotion of Thomas Frowyk to C.J.C.P. in 1502. John Heron, the treasurer of the king's chamber, reported to Henry VII that:

> Sir John Shaa hath written to Sir Reynold Bray and offred for the chieff Justice of the comyn place as largely as he that last was gaff therefor as by his lettres apperethe – V^c marks

– clearly the lord mayor of London doing his best for a favourite son via a prominent royal counsellor well known to him (Bray had already named Shaa as one of his executors).[88] On the other hand, the entry must also mean that Henry VII was paid for promoting Frowyk, and this is by no means an isolated case. Robert Rede, Frowyk's successor, paid the same amount, five hundred marks, 'for the kinges most gracious favour to him shewed in thoffice of the chief Justice of the comon place'.[89] Dr John Yonge paid £1,000 on appointment to the post

83. See below, pp. 257, 310, 378.
84. See above, pp. 82–3. Cf. the traditional story of the discussion between Henry VII and Archbishop Morton over the appointment of Fineux as C.J.: Foss, *Judges*, v. 163; David Lloyd, *State Worthies*, ed. C. Whitworth (1766), i. 91–6.
85. 'London Chronicle', ed. C. Hopper, in *Camden Miscellany* iv, Camden Soc. 73 (1859), 18.
86. Quoted in Foss, *Judges*, v. 310.
87. *Paston Letters and Papers*, ii. 236.
88. B.L. Add. Ms. 21480 f. 185; Condon, 'Ruling elites', 127–8; Wedgwood, *Biographies*.
89. B.L. Lansd. Ms. 127 f. 33.

of master of the rolls, while minor officials such as clerks of the peace paid between twenty and forty marks.[90] It should, nevertheless, not be assumed that Henry was selling to the highest bidder. These payments by Shaa and others must be put in the context of the king's distinctive fiscal methods, in at least the latter years of his reign: a approach to government which even allowed him to charge John Erneley £100 for the highly sensitive post of attorney-general.[91] We should see this less as simony than a system of 'annates', a premium to the grantor from anyone appointed to an office of profit. The £100 down and £233.6s.8d. by instalments which Rede paid would not have excluded from consideration any puisne or serjeant-at-law fit to be chief justice.[92]

The evidence on the calling of serjeants must lay stress on the intention of the crown to secure the expert services it required, whereas at the level of chief justice, appointments were much closer to those of any other lucrative crown office. It is, nevertheless, possible to see shared characteristics among the men who stood at the summit of the common-law hierarchy, and some contrasts, for king's bench, common pleas and exchequer were all different.[93] Without the requirement to appoint a serjeant, exchequer had the widest range of recruits; of the nine men concerned in the years 1471 to 1553, only one was a former judge, only two were serjeants of any seniority, while Fitzjames had worn the coif for six months; none had served as king's serjeant.[94] By contrast, five had been attorney-general and four recorder of London, and it appears that the post went normally to the attorney of the day, unless recently appointed or in poor health, when the position went to the recorder of the City. In 1483, for example, Chief Baron Nottingham retired; Huddersfield, the attorney-general, had also left, perhaps in political disfavour, and the post went to Humphrey Starky the recorder. In 1486 Starky died, and was suc-

90. *ibid.*, ff. 32, 33, 33v, 44, 45v.

91. *ibid.*, f. 45v. Cf. the bidding in 1504 for the post of speaker of the Commons: Condon, 'Ruling elites', 128. William Esyngton paid 250 marks down on appointment for life as A.G. to the duchy in 1506 [B.L. Lansd. Ms. 127 f. 16], but the grant was held to have been voided in 1509 by the death of Henry VII: Constable, *Prerogativa Regis*, *l* n. 216.

92. These payments to Henry VII indicate a different order of morality from the early Stuart tariff of £5,000 to £17,000 for a judicial post (even allowing for inflation).

93. For this discussion of chief justices and chief barons, see Table C. For appointments before 1510 see Appendix E; after 1510 see Spelman, *Reports*, ii. *351–96*; see also London, *Cal. Letters Books* K and L; *Recorders of London*.

94. For Cholmley as K.S. see below, p. 134.

ceeded by Hody A.G., until 1522. The attorney then in office had only six months' seniority, and his predecessor Fitzjames, now serjeant, was appointed instead.[95] The next vacancy again saw a new attorney in post and the exchequer went to the ex-recorder, Richard Brook, J.C.P.; the recorder in office, disappointed of the place of chief baron, was within the year promoted to common pleas.[96] After Brook the succession went 'attorney', 'recorder', 'attorney'. In the whole period 1471 to 1553, no chief baron was appointed who had not served in one or other of these offices. The exchequer was especially concerned with the fiscal rights of the king, and it is clear that the state expected the chief baron to have political experience, either as a law officer of the crown or as the law officer of the most populous unit of local government.[97]

The other court with a political dimension was the king's bench. Here all appointees had to be serjeants at least, and two of the three men in office between 1469 and 1526, Billing and Fineux, had judicial experience also. After joining the coif all three had given the crown special service as king's serjeants and Hussey had served earlier as attorney-general. A change took place, however, on the death of John Fineux. His successor was Chief Baron Fitzjames, and the transfer initiated a novel pattern in king's bench promotion, for two of the next three chief justices also came from the exchequer, and at the time of appointment they were not even serjeants. What was in later years to be achieved by promotion of the attorney-general immediately to the post of chief justice of England *per saltum* (as in the case of a man like Edward Coke) could be achieved under Henry VIII by promotion through the exchequer. By the time the king died, the coif was no longer the established way of promotion in king's bench. In common pleas, however, tradition was still fairly secure, although Attorney-General John Erneley, the first ever promotion *per saltum*, was appointed to this court. Royal service was a *sine qua non* here as in the other courts, but with the exception of Erneley it was in the post of king's serjeant. The common pleas was also different in that many more of its chief justices had had prior judicial experience, either in the court or in king's bench. There were no transfers from the exchequer, and Montagu, the only C.J.K.B. to descend to the lower court, had been a serjeant of some experience before his first judicial

95. The attorney passed over was John Roper.
96. The attorney passed over was Richard Lyster, the recorder William Shelley.
97. This breaks down in the confusion about religious conformity after 1553.

Table C. *Career patterns of chief justices and chief barons, 1471–1553*

	I	II	III	IV	V	VI	VII
KING'S BENCH							
Billing	1469–81	J.K.B.	K4½	11	√		√
Hussey	1481–95	S.		3	√	√	
Fineux	1495–1526	J.C.P.	C2	7½	√		
Fitzjames	1526–39	C.B.Ex.	[see section B]				
Montagu	1539–45	K.S.		7	√		
Lyster	1545–52	C.B.Ex.	[see section B]				
Cholmley	1552–3	C.B.Ex.	[see section B]				
EXCHEQUER							
Urswick	1471–9	Rec.Lond.					√
Nottingham	1479–83	'royal counsellor'				√	
Starky	1483–6	S.		5			√
Hody	1486–1522	A.G.				√	
Fitzjames	1522–6	S.		½		√	
Brook	1526–9	J.C.P.	C6	9½			√
Lyster	1529–45	A.G.				√	
Cholmley	1545–52	Rec.Lond.		14			√
Bradshaw	1552–3	A.G.				√	
COMMON PLEAS							
Bryan	1471–1500	S.		7½	√		C.S.
Wode	1500–2	J.C.P.	C5	9½	√		
Frowyk	1502–6	K.S.		7	√		C.S.
Rede	1506–19	J.K.B.	K11	9½	√		
Erneley	1519–21	A.G.				√	
Brudenell	1521–31	J.C.P.	K14	3½	√		
Norwich	1531–5	J.C.P.	C½	9½	√		
Baldwin	1535–45	K.S.		3½	√		
Montagu	1545–53	C.J.K.B.	[see section A]				

Column II Position at time of appointment
Column III Judicial experience (K = K.B., C = C.P.) in years
Column IV Length of time as a serjeant before promotion to bench
Column V Patent as king's serjeant
Column VI Patent as attorney-general
Column VII Appointment as recorder of London (C.S. = common serjeant only)
(All years are rounded to the nearest half-year)

appointment. It is almost as though the courts were becoming professionally distinct, with the king's bench and exchequer requiring political experience and the common pleas weight of legal learning.

There is little profit in discussing average lengths of service in a profession where promotion was a matter of dead men's shoes. Puisne justices chosen from the 1463 call averaged just over thirteen years as serjeants – those called with Kebell in 1486 averaged a month over seven; chance mortality determined the difference. But with chief justices (and even more chief barons) where royal choice was much more open, it is significant that the crown chose men of widely differing experience. John Fitzjames (appointed C.B.Ex. after six months as a serjeant) and John Erneley were obviously exceptional, following service as law officers. But Humphrey Starky became C.B.Ex. after five years and John Baldwin C.J.C.P. after three-and-a-half. As for Thomas Frowyk, not only had he worn the coif for fewer than seven years, but he was also barely forty when appointed to head the common pleas; he had given his first reading at the Inner Temple only ten years before.[98] But Frowyk's successor, Robert Rede, had been as much a prodigy as Frowyk, and he spent more than twenty years as serjeant and puisne judge, only becoming chief justice at the third opportunity.[99] On Rede's death in 1519, and after a brief interlude for Chief Justice Erneley, Robert Brudenell was appointed; he had seventeen-and-a-half years behind him as serjeant and puisne judge, and it was nearly twenty-nine years since he had read for the first time at the Inner Temple, the year before Frowyk![100] There is no pattern here.

For the biographer of even a recent historical figure it is often hard to decide why his subject's career flourished – or failed to flourish – and this despite ample material. With individuals from five centuries ago, and little information beyond positions held and appointments made, it is impossible. The infinity of personal interactions – chance, influence, hard work, aptitude – must always be beyond our knowledge. Nevertheless, the pattern and chances of a career in law are clear, and so too the one dominant influence, the needs of the crown. How and when serjeants were called, who was chosen, who omitted, assize duties, promotion to the bench, advancement to the rank of chief justice, it was what the state required that mattered. Promotion in the legal profession in the fifteenth and early sixteenth centuries reflected the *raison d'être* of the law itself; in the ultimate it served the king.

98. Putnam, *Early Treatises*, 127; Thorne, *Readings and Moots*, i. xvi.
99. See above p. 45.
100. Thorne, *Readings and Moots*, i. xvi.

PART II

LEGAL PRACTICE

5

THE FOUNDATIONS OF A LEGAL PRACTICE

The landmarks of a successful legal career are chronicled in professional and public records; less easy to uncover are the stages in building the law practice on which this success is founded. The professional papers of the pre-Reformation lawyer are a rare find; clients record the results of litigation, not the names of their advisers, and the courts are interested in cases, not the advocate who conducts them. It is thus no surprise that the first notice of Thomas Kebell in a professional role does not occur until he was over thirty, when in November 1470 he stood surety for a royal grant enrolled on the fine roll.[1] Nevertheless, in this entry he is described as 'gentleman of London', a sufficient indication that he was already an established lawyer. What had occupied Kebell in the years before is a matter for surmise. Some men, such as his junior at the Inner Temple, Humphrey Coningsby, secured employment as a clerical officer in the royal courts; others such as John More, William Rudhale or Walter Rowdon practised as attorneys – there was as yet no apartheid between the branches of the profession.[2] Another possibility is that Kebell 'devilled' for some more established lawyer.[3] After 1470 he begins to appear more and more frequently in the records of legal business until, in 1474, he was prominent enough to be appointed J.P. for Leicestershire.[4]

I

In the absence of news reporting, the ambitious lawyer could not hope to attract public notice by his conduct in some *cause célèbre*. Instead,

1. *Cal. Fine Rolls, 1461–71*, 276.
2. Hastings, *Common Pleas*, 266–7, which explains Coningsby's comments in *Broke* v. *Latimer*, *Y.B.* Mich. 12 Hen. VII, p. 5 f. 8 (he had also been an attorney in common pleas in the 1470s, *ex inf.* J. H. Baker); Blatcher, 'Working of king's bench', lv, lxvi.
3. e.g., Henry Saunders, bencher of Lincoln's Inn from 1505–6 had at one time been clerk to William Donington of the same inn, who left him all his law books: *Black Books*, i. 139; PROB11/7 f. 126v; see above p. 61; below p. 453, Brook, R.
4. See below, p. 227.

he had to rely upon recommendation within the profession and upon the good offices of his relations, friends and neighbours. That Kebell became known as a promising young man must be assumed, but his good fortune was to attract the attention of the lord chamberlain, William Hastings, the boon companion of Edward IV and the principal nobleman in the midlands. The lord chamberlain's chief power lay in Leicestershire, and the famous castle which he built in the 1460s at Kirby Muxloe was less than ten miles from Kebell's home. Bartholomew Brokesby, the friend and companion of Kebell's father, had a son who married William Hastings' sister, and Kebell's cousin and friend, Richard Hotoft, was also well known to Hastings.[5] Local and family connections were reinforced by professional ones. Kebell clearly knew John Catesby, the serjeant-at-law, and John Catesby was a member of Lord Hastings' council.[6] John's nephew, William, who entered the service of the peer – obviously on his uncle's introduction – a year or so after Kebell, was with Thomas at the Inner Temple and was apparently his friend.[7] Certainly, both William's father, Sir William Catesby, and later William himself, made use of Kebell's professional services, and after William's execution in 1485 Kebell was largely concerned in the disposal of those estates which had escaped confiscation.[8] With all these advantages of locale and mutual acquaintance, Thomas Kebell could approach the lord chamberlain with some confidence.

No papers have survived from the litigation which Thomas Kebell promoted for his patron, but a good deal of the non-controversial legal work can be reconstructed from the lists of the feoffees who handled the Hastings property. His first appearance for Lord Hastings was in November 1472 as co-plaintiff in a fine concerning the estates of Eleanor, Lady Hungerford and Moleyns.[9] The action was designed to secure the inheritance of Eleanor's grand-daughter, Mary, who had been betrothed to Lord Hastings' young son and heir, Edward, and the feoffees included two bishops, and the dean of the chapel royal, two knights of the king's body, three simple knights and an esquire besides. But such important personages could not be expected to concern themselves with technicalities: they were there to provide prestige and publicity. For the real work, a small body of close

5. *Hastings Mss.*, i. 2, 300.
6. C1/90/34–5.
7. Roskell, *Bull. John Rylands Lib.* 42. 153; Thorne, *Readings and Moots*, i. lvii.
8. See below, pp. 108–11.
9. *Warwickshire Feet of Fines*, 2700; cf. *Hastings Mss.*, i. 233, 238, 267, 303–4.

friends, employees and lawyers was usually included – sometimes, indeed, the notables were left out altogether.

It was as a 'working feoffee' that Kebell appears most frequently for the Hastings family. Thus the trust to which Lord Hastings conveyed his estates in 1475 during the Picquigny campaign included both archbishops, the chancellor, the keeper of the rolls, the master of the horse, the two chief justices and a puisne judge, a serjeant-at-law, the chancellor of the duchy of Lancaster and the king's attorney, and, as expert members, William Moton and William Grymmesby, esquires, William Chauntry, dean of Newark College, and the lawyers, William Eland, John Eltonhead, Robert Staunton and Thomas Kebell.[10] Moton, Grymmesby, Kebell and Chauntry, plus another cleric, Robert Mome, canon of Lincoln Cathedral, were the 'working feoffees' most used by Lord Hastings during the last eight years of his life, with Kebell clearly providing legal expertise. On 16 September 1476, for example, Chauntry, Grymmesby and Kebell were associated with Lord Hastings in the receipt of some property in Braunstone, Leicestershire.[11] In January of the next year, Chauntry, Grymmesby, Moton and Kebell were granted property near Market Harborough on Hastings' behalf, while in the July, Chauntry, Grymmesby and Kebell again appeared with Hastings, this time as grantees of the reversion of the hundred of Framland in Leicestershire.[12] 1478 saw considerable activity of the same sort. At Ascensiontide, Chauntry, Grymmesby, Moton, Mome and Kebell were plaintiffs in a fine for the advowson of Lubbenham.[13] A month later, on 25 June, the same group registered title to part of the manor of Lubbersthorpe (a further portion of this was added in the next year) and in December took seisin on behalf of Hastings of property in the town of Leicester.[14]

Before the end of 1478, Kebell was once more involved, as he had been in 1472, with the affairs of Lady Mary Hungerford. On 16 November, he, together with William Chauntry, William Grymmesby, John Mounpesson and Robert Baynard, was associated with Lord Hastings in receiving a grant of the wardship of the eleven-year-old heiress.[15] Although the daughter of an attainted Lancastrian family,

10. *Cal. Patent Rolls, 1467–77*, 517. In 1478 Grymmesby is listed as clerk to Lord Hastings: E405/66 m.3.
11. Leicestershire Record Office, DG5/19–20.
12. *Hastings Mss.*, i. 144, 87.
13. CP25(1) 126/79/36.
14. *ibid.*, 126/79/40, 46; *Hastings Mss.*, i. 303–4. For later transactions for Hastings see *Cal. Ancient Deeds*, iv. 8407; *Hastings Mss.*, i. 3, 99, 138; CP40/880 m.1.
15. *Cal. Patent Rolls, 1476–85*, 129.

the barons of Hungerford and Moleyns, Mary was heiress to the Botreaux barony through her great-grandmother, Margaret, Baroness Botreaux, and a notable matrimonial prize. Hastings had, indeed, been granted the wardship long before, as the 1472 fine specifically indicates.[16] The repetition in 1478 was needed because of the death in that year of Baroness Botreaux, Mary's last close relative, and indicated that Hastings had now taken personal charge of the heiress.[17] For Kebell to be involved was unconsciously prophetic, for Mary Hungerford was later to become his patroness – his 'most singular good lady' – and the guardian of his son and heir.[18]

Kebell remained in the service of the Hastings family despite the sudden execution of his employer in June 1483. In May 1484 he acted with other feoffees of the late peer to provide for the widowed Lady Katherine Hastings according to her husband's will.[19] The following autumn, he was entrusted with one of the last payments ever made towards the building of Kirby Muxloe.[20] Easter 1486 saw Kebell busy with three of the most prominent lawyers of the day – Sir Guy Fairfax, J.K.B., Sir Richard Nele, J.C.P. and Sir Thomas Fitzwilliam, recorder of London – assuring the title of Lady Katherine and her son, the second baron, to manors in Leicestershire and other counties.[21] At the same time, Kebell was engaged with other feoffees in conveying estates in Sussex and Nottinghamshire to Lord Hastings, while in July 1488 he was once more active about the dower lands of Lady Katherine.[22] With the reversal of the Hungerford and Moleyns attainders after Bosworth, additional property came to Lord and Lady Hastings – and further work to Kebell.[23] Purchase of land continued as well; in February 1493, for example, land in Buckinghamshire was released to Lord and Lady Hastings and Thomas Kebell.[24] But by now Kebell had given twenty years' service to the family; thus it was, perhaps, a satisfaction to him when a Hastings

16. *Hastings Mss.*, i. 303–4.
17. G.E.C., *Peerage*, vi. 622.
18. See below, pp. 411–12.
19. *Hastings Mss.*, i. 297; no doubt it was Kebell whom Hastings relied on to ensure that his feoffees should never be less than four in number: PROB11/7 f. 76v.
20. A. H. Thompson, 'Building accounts of Kirby Muxloe, 1480–4', in *Trans. Leics. Arch. Soc.* 11 (1913–20), 214.
21. *Cal. Close Rolls, 1485–1500*, 63.
22. *Cal. Patent Rolls, 1485–94*, 210; *Hastings Mss.*, i. 297.
23. *Cal. Charters and Rolls in the Bodleian Library*, ed. H.O. Coxe and W.H. Turner (Oxford, 1878), 23; *Cal. Close Rolls, 1485–1500*, 731.
24. *ibid.*, 671.

enfeoffment of 15 February 1500 included not his own name, but the name of his son.[25]

The actual positions which Kebell occupied from time to time in the Hastings entourage are not easily determined. Among the numerous letters of retainer issued by William, the first baron, there is none for Kebell, although there is one for the apprentice Lawrence Lowe, 'to be of his councelle learned'.[26] This, however, means little; John and William Catesby were certainly members of the baron's council and no letters survive for either.[27] Indeed, in all probability Hastings retained lawyers in addition to Lowe, Kebell and the two Catesbys – his son Edward had more than a dozen in his pay.[28] But while Kebell was obviously *de concilio domini*, the regularity with which (in marked contrast to these other known councillors) he served in the land transactions of the peer does suggest that he was more than a retained adviser: that he was the legal and business agent of Lord William.[29] The most usual title for such an officer was 'attorney' or 'attorney-general', and although no lists of the fees paid by Hastings have survived to put the matter beyond doubt, it is highly probable that this was the post Kebell held; certainly Thomas Jakes who was the attorney for Edward Hastings, the second baron, did the same sort of work as Kebell had done for Edward's father.[30] Of the serjeant's own place in the household of the second baron there is no doubt, for lists have survived for 1489–90 and 1499–1500.[31] In each he appears as the third of the principal officers, following the steward and the receiver-general; although his post is not described, quite clearly he was the director of legal and business affairs. This change to a more senior post is reflected in the work done. While attorney-general, Kebell had generally acted in concert with some or all of the 'working feoffees'; under Edward, Lord Hastings, he seems to have served as

25. *Hastings Mss.*, i. 5; Kebell's last appearance for Lord Hastings is recorded in 1496: *Warwickshire Feet of Fines*, 2751; 'The Farnham bequest', in *Trans. Leics. Arch. Soc.* 17 (1933), 46.

26. Dunham, 'Indentured retainers', 123.

27. John Catesby: C1/90; William Catesby: Roskell, *Bull. John Rylands Lib.* 42. 160–1. For baronial councils, see below, pp. 139–40.

28. Huntington Library, HA16250, William Dugdale, 'History of the Hastings Family (1677)', 31–2; Hastings used William Hussey C.J.K.B. and Richard Pigot K.S. as his executors.

29. The reference to him as of Hastings' council in 1480 is not conclusive.

30. Nichols, *Leicestershire*, iii. 574. Nichols records Kebell's fee as £20, the same as those of Bray the steward and Sacheverell the receiver-general. B.L. Harl. Ms. 433 f. 57, however, gives £5, the same figure that Dugdale recorded for 1500.

31. Huntington Library HA16250, 31–2.

an individual.[32] It is rather as if the routine work which he had done was now left to Jakes, with Kebell intervening as was necessary.[33]

With the Hastings family the historian has to rely largely upon deeds and land settlements; other families, however, can supplement the picture. Thomas, Lord Darcy, employed, as his principal legal agent, Richard Lyster of the Middle Temple (later chief baron of the exchequer and chief justice of king's bench), though apparently with the title of receiver.[34] Lyster was responsible for collecting and dispersing money, for borrowing against the security of plate and for redeeming the pledges, for collecting debts and pursuing lawsuits, for miscellaneous business such as the preparation of the king's new year gift, for the sending of news and for advice of all sorts.[35] His employment with Darcy began, at the latest, in 1507 and lasted, despite Lyster's appointment as solicitor-general in July 1521, to at least the end of the financial year Michaelmas to Michaelmas 1522–3; even after that Darcy used his services from time to time.[36] The record for 1521 is typical. Lyster paid the rent for Darcy's house in Stepney, paid for wine purchased at Calais, supplied the peer's two sons at court with their allowances and some delicacies and paid the final portion of his daughter's dowry to Sir Robert Constable, under strict instructions to get a full receipt, 'for he is something trowbillus and dengerous'.[37] Routine receipts and payments continued, and April's instructions included the delivering of a fine primer, sending a consignment of wine, spices and onions to Hull, the collection of rent arrears, the conduct of various lawsuits, and a request to search for a likely wardship to buy.[38] In June the peer sent to Lyster a poor relative

32. Moton died 1482, Grymmesby 1482–3, Chauntry 1485, Mome 1502: *Cal. Fine Rolls, 1471–85*, 664, 667; A.H. Thompson, *Newark College* (Leicester, 1937), 117–19, 232, 237.
33. e.g. *Hastings Mss.*, i. 194, 269; *Cal. Close Rolls, 1500–9*, 436, 480. Jakes: pardoned 1509 as gentleman of London, of the Inner Temple, of Finchley, Middx, and Wellsborough, Leics., *nuper clericus inferni* (i.e. keeper of the treasury of the common pleas), also his wife Elizabeth, widow and executrix of Thomas Frowyk C.J.C.P.; she was daughter and heiress of William Carnevyle: *L. and P.*, i. 438 (1) m.7; *Cal. inquisitions post mortem*, iii. 463; Hastings, *Common Pleas*, 256–60; PROB11/18 f. 12v; Spelman, *Reports*, ii. *379*, *381*.
34. *L. and P.*, Add. i. 389.
35. *ibid.*, i. 1482, 1502; ii. 1261; iii. 1090, 2273, 2656, 2733, 2982, 3374; Add. i. 211, 233(21), 240, 280, 1233(12), and below.
36. *ibid.*, iv. 2527, 4732; Add. i. 1233(21). Lyster would have met Darcy following his appointment as clerk of the peace for the West Riding in 1507: B.L. Lansd. Ms. 127 f. 33v.
37. *L. and P.*, iii. 1172, 1236, 1250; Add. i. 327 (11–13, 15, 16).
38. *ibid.*, iii. 1260.

who was facing a chancery *subpoena* and in July Lyster reported on the business he had in hand; he also warned Darcy that Wolsey was expecting the commissioners on their way to Scotland to be entertained, and sent word that the cardinal himself was going to Calais to arbitrate between Francis I and Charles V.[39] Later in the same month Darcy was instructing him to discover a sure and good carrier for the plate which had been redeemed from pawn.[40]

Lyster's two last letters of 1521 sum up the enormous variety of business a lawyer was expected to take on. Subjects dealt with on 12 October were the progress of the hospital Darcy hoped to found, the despatch of plate, the current financial position and the poor prospects for the immediate future, his inability to get any wine for his employer, the latest news from the cardinal at Calais and the court at Windsor, technical advice on a land transaction with the earl of Westmorland, and advice of a different sort on the need to find Darcy's heir a wife, with notes of possible brides still on the market.[41] In his letter of 2 November, Lyster had to meet some criticisms by Darcy of the accounts he had submitted, criticisms which seem to have reflected on Sir Arthur, the heir, as well.[42] The slow arrival of rents was again a problem, but the plate could be despatched securely. The plague was rampant in London so that common pleas and king's bench had been adjourned, and several courtiers and royal officers had died. There was more news of the Calais negotiations, since More and Fitzwilliam had come over to report to Henry VIII, and information about a treaty to protect English shipping in the channel.

Lyster's service to Lord Darcy can be paralleled by the career of Antony Dymmock a generation earlier. Like Lyster, Dymmock became a law officer of the crown and later a baron of the exchequer, and he too had earlier been an agent for a prominent magnate, in his case Antony Woodville, Earl Rivers.[43] Dymmock was Rivers' 'attorney', but he clearly did the same work that Kebell did for Hastings and Lyster was to do for Darcy. He supervised feoffeeships, pursued law cases, gave advice, collected news and acted as the earl's agent at court. Just as Kebell handled some money for Hastings, so the fuller record shows that Dymmock, like Lyster, acted as 'banker' to the peer's entourage. Kebell, Lyster and Dymmock stand out only because the record of their activities has survived or can be recon-

39. *ibid.*, iii. 1407; Add. i. 317.
40. *ibid.*, iii. 1436.
41. *ibid.*, iii. 1669.
42. *ibid.*, iii – Appendix 31.
43. Ives, in *Bull. Institute of Hist. Research* 41. 216–29.

structed. There is little room to doubt that if the sources were extant and there was labour to tackle them, a majority of the magnates in pre-Reformation England would be found employing a lawyer in this way.[44] Of the importance of such employment to the lawyer there can be no doubt either. We cannot know whether the heights of the profession could be scaled without enjoying such a position at some stage. It is certain, however, that to do so conferred very great advantages.

II

The patronage of the first and second Lord Hastings laid the foundation of Thomas Kebell's success. It seems also to have introduced his services to others, for Kebell found considerable business among Hastings' retainers. The full detail of this cannot be recovered – the documentation of the retinue comes to an end in 1483, and many of Kebell's engagements date only from the reign of Henry VII – but the connection is obvious.[45] In Michaelmas 1479, for example, a group of known Hastings supporters, including William Catesby and Thomas Kebell, was concerned with the marriage settlement of Elizabeth, the daughter of a recently indentured retainer, Richard Boughton.[46] Three years later, on 4 September 1482, Kebell and Thomas Entwysell, esquire, indentured to Lord Hastings in 1474, were among the feoffees of another retainer, John Griffin.[47] How much of this can be accounted for by instructions from Hastings cannot be determined. However, in 1481 William Moton, one of the peer's retinue and also a 'working feoffee', chose to appoint Thomas Kebell as executor of his will.[48]

In the June of 1483, the execution of William, Lord Hastings, broke up the retinue which he had built up over the preceding twenty years. Some of his men attached themselves to the duke of Buckingham, but after his disgrace and execution later in the year their fortunes become obscure; that they returned to the Hastings allegiance when the accession of Henry Tudor had restored the family's influence, although likely, is not at all certain. Nevertheless the connections between Thomas Kebell and the members of the former

44. Cf. Rawcliffe, *The Staffords*, 144–63.
45. For the Hastings' retinue, see Dunham, 'Indentured retainers'.
46. *Cal. inquisitions post mortem*, ii. 123; cf. *Cal. Close Rolls, 1476–85*, 665.
47. *Cal. inquisitions post mortem*, i.37.
48. c67/53 m.13.

retinue persisted. Indeed, as late as Michaelmas 1494, the largest property transaction in which Kebell was ever concerned seems to have come to him through the Hastings connection. This was a fine and recovery in king's bench by one of the earliest of William Hastings' retainers, Sir Simon Montfort of Hampton in Arden and Coleshill, as agent for his neighbours, the Bromes of Baddesley Clinton, with Thomas Kebell to assist him.[49] In the following Christmas vacation, however, circumstances changed drastically. Sir Simon, suddenly exposed as one of the conspirators with Sir William Stanley against Henry VII, was executed, and in the parliament of January 1495 he was attainted and his property confiscated.[50] The confusion seems to have put a stop to the Baddesley Clinton case for more than a year. Perhaps, even, Kebell was engaged during that time in guarding against any mistaken confiscation of Baddesley Clinton. Not until April 1496 did he regrant the estate to the Bromes.[51]

This episode was unique in Kebell's legal career. His other activities for former Hastings retainers were a good deal more mundane. In 1488 he served as the legal expert in a group of feoffees, among them two Hastings retainers, which sued a fine on behalf of a third, John Turvyll, esquire.[52] In the next year Kebell was associated with another former Hastings man, Sir John Babington, as one of the beneficiaries of a chantry founded jointly by Sir John and by Ralph Savage at North Wingfield, Derbyshire; in 1495 additional beneficiaries were named including Lord Hastings' former esquire, now Sir Ralph Longford.[53] Before this, in 1493, Kebell and Babington had been associated with Sir Henry Willoughby in the settlement of the Warwickshire lands of John Cokeyn on a relative Thomas, and both the Cokeyns, as well as Willoughby, Babington and Kebell, had belonged to the Hastings entourage.[54] Willoughby had already employed Kebell in his own behalf on at least one occasion. This was in 1490 when the serjeant was enfeoffed with him and with others of the estate in Derby and Nottinghamshire which John Zouche, es-

49. Shakespeare Birthplace Trust, DR3/277, 278, 282; cf. *Warwickshire Feet of Fines*, 2744.
50. Polydore Vergil, *Anglica Historia*, ed. D. Hay, Camden Soc., 3 ser., 74 (1950), 72; *Rot. Parl.*, vi. 503–7.
51. Shakespeare Birthplace Trust, DR3/282.
52. CP25(1) 126/80/3. The other retainers were Ralph Shirley, kt, and Thomas Entwysell, esq.
53. *Records of the Borough of Nottingham*, i. 429; *Cal. Patent Rolls, 1485–94*, 264.
54. *Cal. inquisitions post mortem*, ii. 942; iii. 284.

quire, had purchased from another Hastings man, Henry, Lord Grey of Codnor. The occasion of the enfeoffment was, apparently, the marriage of John's son and heir to one of Willoughby's daughters. But some mistake was clearly made in the legal arrangements, whether by Kebell or another we do not know. Grey had died in 1495 before the transfer to Zouche was complete, but matters proceeded normally until a few months after Kebell's death when the crown discovered that Grey had provided in his will that the same property should be sold to the king for the use of his younger son, Henry, Duke of York. The council promptly stepped in, forced the surviving feoffees to surrender the estate and confiscated Zouche's enfeoffment. Willoughby protested the priority of the Zouche sale but had to buy back the estate for a premium of £400 above the price paid by the king.[55] No such repercussions followed the other appearances of Kebell for Henry Willoughby. In 1495 he was a feoffee for land in Warwick and Staffordshire, and in March 1496, Kebell and his servant William Bret, together with Sir John Babington, witnessed a further land transaction, involving Sir Henry and Sir Gervase Clifton; Clifton was also a former Hastings man.[56]

It could be argued that this work did not come to Kebell through the influence of the Hastings retinue but simply from midland gentry to a prominent midland lawyer. But such criticism is over-sceptical. Sometimes association via the Hastings family is direct. William, the first baron, was a feoffee for John Norwich, esquire, of Brampton Dingley in Northamptonshire.[57] His co-feoffees included his brother, Sir Ralph, Thomas Kebell, and a Northamptonshire gentleman occasionally found in the Hastings circle, William Lane of Orlingbury.[58] Norwich is not among the known Hastings retainers, but when he later became insane, Edward, the second baron, obtained the custody of his person and lands, which indicates that some client relationship existed.[59] In other cases the Hastings influence worked at one remove. Thus Kebell was appearing in 1494 for the Hubaude family of Astwood in Worcestershire, and it is surely significant that the unfortunate Sir Simon Montfort knew the head of the family, Edward Hubaude, well.[60]

55. *Cal. Ancient Deeds*, v. 10747; *Cal. Patent Rolls, 1494–1509*, 583–4; *Cal. Close Rolls*, *1500–9*, 160, 782.
56. *ibid.*, *1485–1500*, 823; *Cal. Ancient Deeds*, iii. c3270.
57. *Cal. inquisitions post mortem*, ii. 882, 929.
58. *ibid.*, ii. 621; *Hastings Mss.*, i. 99.
59. *Cal. Patent Rolls*, *1494–1509*, 272.
60. V.C.H., *Worcestershire* (1901–24), iii. 115; *Cal. Close Rolls, 1485–1500*, 127.

For at least one family of Hastings supporters – the Shirleys of Staunton Harold – Thomas Kebell became a permanent legal adviser. His first recorded professional contact with them was in 1480 as an agent for Hastings, but he soon went on to work for the family. Kebell almost certainly became one of John Shirley's trustees, and it was no accident that, on the latter's death in 1486, Kebell, assisted by William Basset, a former Hastings retainer, and two others, obtained the commission to draw up the inquisition *post mortem*.[61] In the same year Kebell presided over a group of family friends who mediated between the widow, Eleanor, and the son and heir, Ralph, in a dispute about Eleanor's jointure and dower and the portions due to Ralph's sisters.[62] Having settled the matter, Kebell and the others took the necessary legal steps to embody their decision in due form.[63] A decade later, although now a king's serjeant, Kebell was still busy in Shirley family affairs as a trustee of the marriage settlement of Ralph Shirley, now a knight, and Anne Vernon, the daughter of another former Hastings retainer, Sir Henry Vernon of Haddon.[64]

III

In the later years of Kebell's association with the Shirley family, an additional bond was forged when Ralph Shirley became a member of the Inner Temple.[65] The date is not known, and Kebell was in any case considerably his senior, but the society of the inns did encourage real friendship which transcended barriers of age or rank. Already connected as lawyer and client, sharing a loyalty to the same locality, Kebell and Shirley were now members of the same club. It seems unlikely that Sir Ralph was ever in practice – his career was that of a country gentleman and a courtier – yet he certainly maintained his connection with the Inner Temple long after the serjeant's death. But if Shirley was not a professional lawyer, Kebell had plenty of clients who were. Lawyers were well placed to compete for land, grants and privileges, and were obvious partners for business deals, to say nothing of suspicions that they indulged in money-lending.[66] Hence,

61. CP25(1) 126/79/49; *Cal. Patent Rolls, 1485–94*, 132–3.
62. Leicestershire Record Office: DE170/60, 61; 26D53/83; 53/315.
63. CP25(1) 126/80/3.
64. Leicestershire Record Office: 26D53/2552.
65. Mentioned in 1507: *Inner Temple Records*, i. 8, but a fellow by 1491 (mentioned in a plea roll, *ex inf.* J.H. Baker).
66. See below, pp. 119–20.

in their own behalf, they were amongst the busiest of the nation's conveyancers and litigants.

Early in his career Kebell acted with Richard Choke, probably the son of Sir Richard, J.C.P., in receiving a conveyance in the family home town, Bridgwater.[67] A few years later, in 1480, he was a feoffee for Richard Danvers senior, brother to another common pleas judge, Sir Robert, and himself almost certainly a lawyer.[68] In 1489 Thomas Kebell was bound in one hundred marks to a King's Lynn merchant, Thomas Thoresby, together with another serjeant-at-law, John Fisher.[69] The occasion was the purchase by Fisher of Thoresby's manor of Clopton in Cambridgeshire, and Kebell provided the security for Fisher's repayment of the purchase price.[70] Although there is no reason to believe that Kebell was particularly intimate with Choke, Danvers or Fisher, instances of this sort could be accounted for by friendship. There is, however, ample evidence that the legal profession was honeycombed with agreements and deals of various kinds. Kebell, for example, together with John Mordaunt of the Middle Temple and Richard Heigham of Lincoln's Inn (both of whom later became serjeants-at-law), John Jenour, filacer of the common pleas and fellow of the Middle Temple, and William Gascoigne of the Middle Temple, recovered land from the feoffees of Thomas Huntington of Trumpington. The transaction was connected with the marriage of one of Huntington's two daughters and heiresses with Mordaunt's brother William, another officer of the common pleas and member of the Middle Temple.[71] A few days before his death, Kebell was named in the settlement of an estate

67. *Bridgwater Borough Archives*, v, 1468–85, 912.
68. B.L. Add. Ch. 38757, 38758; Wedgwood, *Biographies*.
69. *Cal. Close Rolls, 1485–1500*, 443.
70. *ibid.*, 442.
71. *Cal. inquisitions post mortem*, ii. 448. John Jenour – clerk of assize and filacer, later prothonotary of the common pleas, son and heir of William Jenour of Stonham Aspall, Suffolk: *Cal. Patent Rolls, 1485–94*, 476 *sqq.*; Hastings, *Common Pleas*, 189, 257; *Inner Temple Records*, i. 462; *Visitation of Essex, 1612*, 221; *Minutes of Parliament, passim*; PROB11/29 f. 81. William Gascoigne – of Cardington, Beds., sheriff of Bedfordshire and Buckinghamshire 1506–7, excused his obligations at the Middle Temple on account of his engagements to an unnamed employer: *L. and P.*, i. 438 (1 m.26); *Cal. Fine Rolls, 1485–1509*, 871; *Minutes of Parliament*, i. 1, 3. William Mordaunt – clerk of assize and prothonotary of the common pleas, son of William Mordaunt of Turvey, of Hempstead in Essex in right of his wife, treasurer of the Middle Temple 1506, executor, with William Gascoigne, of the will of his brother John, serjeant-at-law: *Cal. Patent Rolls, 1485–94*, 350 *sqq.*; Hastings, *Common Pleas*, 256; PROB11/19 f. 57; *Minutes of Parliament*, i. *passim*; *Cal. Patent Rolls, 1494–1509*, 430. Cf. Spelman, *Reports*, ii. *103*, *130*, *219*, *375*, *377*.

upon Henry, grandson and heir of Edmund Thwaits of Lund by Watton, and his prospective bride, a daughter of another Yorkshireman, Robert Constable of North Cliffe.[72] Constable was a Lincoln's Inn lawyer who had become a serjeant-at-law in 1495, and Edmund Thwaits was legal adviser to the earl of Northumberland.[73]

Among these transactions which Kebell undertook for lawyers, by far the largest number are in favour of members of his own inn, the Inner Temple.[74] Soon after he was made a serjeant, Kebell became a feoffee for one of the senior men of the society, Richard Maryot of Sherington in Buckinghamshire.[75] Equally he was a feoffee for a young member, Gregory Adgore of Brantham in Suffolk, who became a serjeant three years after Kebell's death.[76] Each house, indeed, seems to have acted as a business, as well as a social and educational community, with the members employing one another, providing guarantees or running in partnership.[77] In the Easter term of 1482, for example, Thomas Tropenell, esquire, of Great Chalfield in Wiltshire (*c.* 1405–88), 'a perillous covetous man' and an incurable litigant, came to London to see his lawyers.[78] He went first to Lincoln's Inn to consult three of the fellows there, the attorney John Nethersole, and two apprentices, William Donington and Robert Rede.[79] Their opinion was then passed to one of the judges, William Jenney, significantly a former member of the society.[80] Then, so it seems, Tropenell's Lincoln's Inn advisers took him to meet a

72. *Cal. inquisitions post mortem*, ii. 573.
73. Edmund Thwaits: *Testamenta Eboracensia*, iii. 308–10.
74. Edmund Thwaits may be the 'Thwaytes' who attended Inner Temple moots: *ex inf.* J.H. Baker.
75. *Cal. inquisitions post mortem*, i. 724. For Maryot, see Thorne, *Readings*, xliv-xlv; his daughter married Humphrey Catesby, son of Justice John Catesby, formerly of the Inner Temple: *Cal. inquisitions post mortem*, i. 723–4.
76. *ibid.*, iii. 357.
77. E101/414/6 f. 2v shows Robert Constable and Percival Lampton of Lincoln's Inn co-operating in the purchase of a ward. Lampton – attorney-general of the palatinate of Durham: *Admission Book*, i. 24; *Black Books*, i. 97, 106, 113; 'Cursitors' rolls of the palatinate of Durham', in *Annual Reports of the Deputy Keeper of Public Records* 35 (1874), 20.
78. *Tropenell Cartulary*, i. x-xiii.
79. *ibid.*, i. 265. Nethersole acted for Tropenell earlier: *ibid.*, ii. 303–5, 308, 312–13. Nethersole – see above, p. 22. William Donington – admitted Lincoln's Inn 1458; reader Lent 1473 and Lent 1485; J.P. Surrey from 1474; died 1485: *Admission Book*, i. 14; *Black Books*, i. 45 *et passim*; *Cal. Patent Rolls, 1467–77*, 631; PROB11/7 f. 126.
80. *Tropenell Cartulary*, i. 265.

team of experts at the Cardinal's Hat, a tavern near to the Old Bailey frequented by lawyers who specialised in real property law.[81]

This influence of an inn of court upon the professional life of its members can be clearly seen in the career of Thomas Kebell. In 1488, he was associated in a common pleas recovery with Robert Sheffield of the Inner Temple, a future recorder of London, and John Eliot of Clement's Inn, an inn of chancery associated with the Inner Temple.[82] Some years later, in 1496, Kebell was involved in a most revealing transaction on behalf of an Inner Temple colleague, when he became a feoffee of the manor of Haslingfield, near Cambridge, owned by Sir William Tyndale.[83] The purpose of the settlement was to secure repayment to one of the feoffees, Serjeant Humphrey Coningsby, of the substantial sums which he had lent to Sir William. Seven feoffees represented Tyndale's interests, four more were judges (presumably selected as neutrals), while Coningsby was supported by four feoffees, at least three of whom – Kebell, Frowyk and Brudenell – were connected, as Coningsby himself was, with the Inner Temple.

Some Inner Temple connection is probable in the 1489 appearance of Kebell to receive, on the behalf of a Reynold Sonde, the release of property in Berkshire from Peter Peckham, esquire.[84] This was the outcome of a lengthy lawsuit between Peckham and Sonde over the will of Robert Strongbone, gentleman, a battle which involved Peckham in a charge of *praemunire* and a session in the Marshalsea

81. *ibid.*, ii. 348; for other consulations at the Cardinal's Hat, see *Paston Letters and Papers*, ii. 594–5. The lawyers consulted were Thomas Tremayle, William Huddersfield and Richard Jay. Huddersfield – of Shillingford, Devon; Lincoln's Inn, admitted 1455, reader 1465, 1469, 1476; attorney-general; exempt from becoming a serjeant, 1486; died 1498: *Cal. Patent Rolls, 1476–85*, 37, 349; *ibid., 1485–94*, 86; *Admission Book*, i. 13; *Black Books*, i. 39, 48, 60; Wedgwood, *Biographies*; PROB11/11 f. 298; *Cal. inquisitions post mortem*, i. 264.
82. Farnham, *Quorndon Records*, 170. It is possible that the Sheffield in question was the recorder's father. There were two Robert Sheffields, father and son, both of Butterwick, Lincolnshire, both J.P. and M.P., both of the Inner Temple; the elder died in 1502, the younger, born *c.* 1462, recorder of London, kt, speaker of the commons, died in 1518: Wedgwood, *Biographies*; Thorne, *Readings and Moots*, i. xvi; *Inner Temple Records*, i. 13 *et passim*; *Cal. inquisitions post mortem*, ii. 566; *L. and P.*, i. 438 (1 m.8, 3 m.18). John Eliot, fellow and possibly principal of Clement's Inn, was related to Richard Eliot, serjeant and J.C.P.: Williams, *Early Holborn*, ii. 1506, 1510–13A; *L. and P.*, i. 1836(14).
83. *Cal. inquisitions post mortem*, ii. 11; cf. *Cal. Patent Rolls, 1494–1509*, 140.
84. *Cal. Close Rolls, 1485–1500*, 461.

prison, not, however, his first taste of gaol.[85] Peckham was a chancery clerk, Strongbone almost certainly a lawyer, while Sonde was chief clerk of the king's bench.[86] Which inn Sonde belonged to is not known, but the feoffees appointed on his behalf suggest a strong link with the Inner Temple – Kebell, William Danvers, J.C.P., Thomas Danvers, and Humphrey Coningsby; the other feoffees were John Cheney, a Berkshire knight and one of Henry VII's council, and John Easyngwold, who was an attorney.[87] Further evidence of the influence of the inns is Kebell's participation, in 1499, in a recovery to redistribute the interests in the properties of Sir William Littleton in Stafford and Worcestershire.[88] Sir William was the son of the most famous Inner Templar of the fifteenth century, Sir Thomas Littleton, justice of the common pleas and author of *The Newe Tenures*, the first textbook of the common law. Associated with Kebell in the recovery were Sir William's brother, Richard, for whom the *Tenures* was written, and three Inner Templars, Sir Ralph Shirley, Thomas Marowe and Robert Brudenell.

With at least two fellows of the Inner Temple, Thomas Frowyk and William Catesby, Kebell approached the position of a regular legal

85. *Y.B.* Mich. 2 Ric. III, p. 8 ff. 3–4; p. 45 ff. 17–18; p. 51 f. 22; London, *Cal. Letter Books*, L, 89–90.

86. Peckham – London citizen and mercer, clerk of chancery (so described in a pardon roll, *ex inf.* J. H. Baker); Holborn resident; 'gentleman of London', 1463, receiving gift of goods (see below, p. 119); died 1501: *Cal. Close Rolls, 1461–8*, 195, 377; *Cal. Fine Rolls, 1471–85*, 144; Williams, *Early Holborn*, 613 *et passim*; *Cal. inquisitions post mortem*, ii. 482. Strongbone – third cousin to Peckham; 'gentleman'; receives gifts of goods; feoffee with lawyers: C1/75/68; *Cal. Patent Rolls, 1461–7*, 254, 538; *ibid., 1467–77*, 435; *Cal. Close Rolls, 1461–8*, 75; *ibid., 1468–76*, 944; London, *Plea and Memoranda Rolls, 1458–82*, 158. Sonde – prothonotary of the king's bench; of Throwley, Kent; son of William Sonde, prothonotary, and his wife Elizabeth; J.P. 1481–91; possibly M.P. 1483, 1484; died 1491: *Y.B.* Mich. 2 Ric. III, p. 51 f. 22; Spelman, *Reports*, ii. *363*; *Cal. Patent Rolls, 1476–85*, 563; *Cal. Close Rolls, 1485–1500*, 231; Wedgwood, *Biographies*; *Cal. inquisitions post mortem*, i. 735, 738, 739; C1/108/67.

87. Thomas Danvers – of Waterstock, Oxon.; M.P., J.P.; servant of Bishop Waynflete; no specific statement of his membership of the Inner Temple has yet been discovered, but it is inconceivable that he would have belonged elsewhere: Wedgwood, *Biographies*; *Paston Letters and Papers*, i. 430, 586; ii. 378–9, 424, 583; MacNamara, *Danvers Family*, 155–70. Cheney – of Falstone-Cheyne, Wilts.; Lord Cheyne: Wedgwood, *Biographies*. Easyngwold – of Newark: Baker, *Journ. Legal Hist.* 1, 193.

88. *Cal. inquisitions post mortem*, iii. 517, 530; cf. *ibid.*, ii. 326, 909; iii. 559. Littleton – of Pillatonhall, Staffs.; J.P., M.P.; married Alice, daughter and heiress of William Wynnesbury; reader for Lent 1493; several times governor of the Inner Temple: *ibid.*, ii. 537, 622; *Cal. Fine Rolls, 1485–1509*, 734; Thorne, *Readings and Moots*, i. xvi; *Inner Temple Records*, i. *passim*. Shirley – see above, pp. 101, 103.

adviser. In 1494 Kebell had joined with Frowyk and Nicholas Tichborne of the Inner Temple, to obtain the custody of the land of John Grey, the minor heir of Edward, Viscount Lisle.[89] By 1500 they were again co-operating in the acquisition of a grant of wardship, this time of the heir of one of Kebell's relatives, Robert Moton.[90] It is not thus surprising that in 1496 the serjeant should have executed a fine, with other Frowyk trustees, for property in East London, or that Frowyk's inquisition *post mortem* should reveal Kebell (with four other lawyers) as a feoffee of Ypres Inn in Knightrider Street and also a feoffee for substantial Frowyk property in and around Harrow on the Hill in Middlesex. In the latter case Kebell headed a group of nine, eight of whom were lawyers, six trained at the Inner Temple.[91]

With William Catesby, Kebell's professional association lasted much longer, and his work was correspondingly more extensive. Kebell's earliest appearance for his colleague was in January 1477, when, with their common patron, Lord Hastings, Catesby's father, three of Catesby's other relatives and a neighbour, Kebell began to acquire land on William's behalf in the Northamptonshire village of Watford.[92] The next year, Catesby, with his father, Sir William, an uncle, John Catesby of Althorp, Thomas Kebell and Everard Digby, a notable midland gentleman, secured associated property in Great Creaton, and later in the same year Kebell assisted Catesby in activities on behalf of the latter's dependent, Maud Knightley.[93]

With Kebell and Catesby working side by side for the lord chamberlain, it might be expected that they would bring each other employment. Definite evidence of this is difficult to discover, but one

89. *Cal. Patent Rolls, 1494–1509*, 3. Tichborne – 'gentleman of London'; M.P., J.P.; read Inner Temple 1509, 1516; treasurer 1517–19: *Cal. Close Rolls, 1500–9*, 11(xxxi); Wedgwood, *Biographies*; *Inner Temple Records*, i. 14, 36, 41, 43 etc. Although, on Wedgwood's reckoning, the member of the Inner Temple would not be the M.P. but probably his son, it is likely that only a single person is involved.

90. B.L. Add. Ms. 21480 f. 61. This entry in John Heron's accounts only identifies the payment as 'for the warde of Mutton'. No inquisition *post mortem* survives, but a writ of *diem clausit extremum* was issued 4 Jul. 1498 for 'Robert Moton of Leicestershire': *Cal. Fine Rolls, 1485–1509*, 593; see below, p. 118.

91. *Calendar to the Feet of Fines, London and Middlesex*, ed. W. J. Hardy and W. Page (1893), ii. 8; *Cal. inquisitions post mortem*, ii. 195, 243.

92. *Cal. Ancient Deeds*, iv. 7033, 6644, 10268, 8350. William Lord Hastings, William Catesby, kt (father), John Catesby, serjeant (uncle, query cousin), John Catesby of Althorp (uncle), Thomas Wyndesore (cousin by marriage) and Edmund Newnham, gent., of Stuchbury, Northants. Wyndesore – Wedgwood, *Biographies*. Newnham – *Cal. Close Rolls, 1476–85*, 905; *Cal. inquisitions post mortem*, iii. 458. For the Catesbys see below, pp. 234–5, 383–4.

93. *Cal. Ancient Deeds*, v. 10792, 9827, 9074; *Cal. inquisitions post mortem*, iii. 994.

transaction does suggests the sort of thing which may have happened. William Catesby was, in addition to his work for Lord Hastings, also in the regular employ of the duke of Buckingham, and in 1480 he, together with three known associates in the Buckingham service, took a feoffment of the manor of Tilbrook in Huntingdon.[94] Also a feoffee was Thomas Kebell, and it seems highly probable that he had been brought in through William Catesby. Kebell's private work for Catesby continued also. In 1480 he acted as a feoffee in the acquisition of land in Long Buckby, and in April 1483 he became a feoffee for property in Hollowell, another village near to Catesby's home at Ashby St Legers.[95] This same month of April had, of course, enormous significance in English politics with the death of Edward IV and the coup of Gloucester, Buckingham and Hastings, and no small consequence for their followers. For Kebell it brought professional promotion, but for Catesby it began two years of convulsive activity, passing from treachery to affluence and power but ultimately to disaster.[96] Kebell's activity for Catesby lessens in these years, and he avoided political gambles, but his one recorded service does reflect the fortunes of Richard III's feline assistant. This was in February 1484 when, illegally, as he well knew, Catesby purchased the Leicestershire manor of Kirby Bellars (using as one of his agents another Inner Templar, Thomas Danvers). The property was vested in Catesby and his two associates in royal service, Viscount Lovell and Sir Richard Ratcliffe, his uncle, Judge Catesby, Thomas Kebell, Roger Wake and William Ashby; Kebell's servant William Bret was one of the attorneys who received seisin on behalf of the trust.[97] Eighteen months later, perhaps to the very day, William Catesby was beheaded at Leicester. Ratcliffe was already dead, two days earlier at Bosworth Field, and Lovell and Wake were proscribed fugitives.[98]

After the disaster of 1485 the laws of attainder and forfeiture put an end to Kebell's position as a Catesby trustee. Two associated prob-

94. Roskell, *Bull. John Rylands Lib.* 42. 156; *Cal. Ancient Deeds*, iv. 8480. John Geffrey – feoffee of Henry, duke of Buckingham: *Cal. Patent Rolls, 1476–85*, p. 257. Thomas Garth – executor of Anne, duchess of Buckingham: Wedgwood, *Biographies*. Richard Harper – receiver of Henry, duke of Buckingham: *ibid.*

95. *Cal. Close Rolls, 1476–85*, 671, 672; *Cal. Ancient Deeds*, iv. 8415.

96. See above, pp. 63–4, below, pp. 231, 234–5.

97. *Cal. Close Rolls, 1476–85*, 1209.

98. Accepting Polydore Vergil's date for the execution. Catesby's will, however, is dated in the Prerogative Register as 25 August: Roskell, *Bull. John Rylands Lib.* 42. 170–1. Lovell and Wake were attainted in Henry VII's first parliament.

lems, however, remained – the title to Kirby Bellars and the inheritance of the manor of Althorp in Northamptonshire – and both involved Kebell in chancery suits. The Kirby Bellars case began soon after Bosworth with a petition from William Kyrkeby, the prior of the Augustinian house at Kirby Bellars.[99] William Catesby, he alleged, had wrongfully purchased the manor which belonged to the priory, but had ordered, in his last will, that the property should be restored; however, despite this, his trustees had refused to deliver the estate. It is, at first sight, surprising that Prior William should expect the feoffees of an attainted traitor to have any rights at all; anyone claiming wrongful eviction would normally have expected to make their case to the crown. That this did not happen may be explained by the alleged confession that Kirby Bellars had been wrongfully acquired, or more probably by the conjecture that William's wife, Margaret, held a life interest in Kirby as elsewhere.[100] Another complication (which explains the feoffees' refusal to heed Prior William) rapidly emerged with a counter-claim by the Charterhouse of Axeholme.[101] Kebell and the other surviving feoffees, Sir John Catesby, William Ashby and Roger Wake (pardoned but not yet restored to his lands) were stakeholders with the sure knowledge that should both contenders fail to establish a claim, the crown would oust the feoffees at the first opportunity![102] The chancellor retained consideration of the major issue but remitted part of the dispute to arbitration. Chief Justice Hussey and Guy Fairfax, secondary justice in the court of king's bench, were selected for the task, and they reported on 4 February 1486 in favour of the Charterhouse.[103] The chancellor, deciding the principal question similarly, instructed the feoffees to enfeoff accordingly, and by 16 June he had ratified the decision of the arbitrators.[104] On that date, the priory of Kirby Bellars reported that the feoffees had already complied, but the actual demise by Kebell and his associates is dated 16 October 1486.[105]

The dispute about Althorp seems a good deal more complex, and it certainly took longer to settle. The beginning can be traced to an

99. C1/77/86.
100. PROB11/7 f. 114v, but the will makes no specific mention of Kirby Bellars, only of the general restoration of wrongs. Cf. *Cal. inquisitions post mortem*, i. 1109, 1113, 1131.
101. This is apparent from the final settlement: *Cal. Close Rolls, 1485–1500*, 152.
102. Wake was restored to his estates between June 1488 and March 1496: *Cal. Patent Rolls, 1485–94*, 228; *Cal. inquisitions post mortem*, ii. 847.
103. *Cal. Close Rolls, 1485–1500*, 152. 104. *ibid.*, 152. 105. *ibid.* 149.

enfeoffment of the manor made by John Catesby of Althorp, esquire, in about 1480, to John Catesby the judge, Thomas Kebell, Thomas Wyndesore and William Catesby the younger.[106] When the feoffor himself died on 4 November 1486, only Justice Catesby and Thomas Kebell still survived, and the judge died very soon after.[107] Thus Kebell was left as sole feoffee to face a dispute about the intentions of the late squire of Althorp. Hardly was Justice Catesby dead before John Catesby, the brother of William, Richard III's councillor, and nephew to John Catesby of Althorp, entered a bill in chancery against Kebell.[108] He alleged that Althorp had been bequeathed by its last owner to him, but that the serjeant refused to surrender the estate. Kebell was subpoenaed on 4 February 1487, and replied that he had no knowledge of the will, a response obviously intended to delay proceedings, pending the arrival of the rival claimant. He duly appeared in the summer of 1487 in the person of yet another John Catesby, a minor, son of the William Catesby who was executed after Bosworth, and thus the nephew of the first claimant. This new contender alleged that John of Althorp had invited his mother to Althorp for the birth of her child, had become the godfather and had sworn to make the boy his heir, but that Kebell refused to perform the oath. There was yet a third party, the bishop of Ely, who claimed that part of the property was his on account of an agreement with John of Althorp, and sued Kebell accordingly. The *subpoena* following the second bill was dated 22 November 1487, and enabled Kebell to request that the parties should inter-plead. The first claimant produced witnesses who stated that the original enfeoffment had been to his use, but the younger John could only offer circumstantial evidence. The court therefore decided for the first petitioner and ordered Kebell to hand over the estate to him; the defeated John Catesby was to be for ever excluded from any title to the property. Kebell obeyed with alacrity. Judgement was given on 18 June 1488, and on 4 July the serjeant executed the transfer; with this, Kebell's connection with the Catesby family came to an end.[109]

106. Depositions of Everard Derby [*recte* Digby] and others in chancery. The whole of the case, including the depositions and the final judgement, is summarised from the exemplification on the patent roll in *Cal. Patent Rolls, 1485–94*, 232–4; the chancery documents are C1/87/53–60. Cf. Althorp Park, Spencer Mss. 863–81.

107. *Cal. inquisitions post mortem*, iii. 1003. Wyndesore died 29 September 1485, a month after Catesby's execution: *ibid.*, i. 12. There may have been other feoffees; if so, they must have been dead by 1486 as none are named.

108. The Catesbys are difficult to disentangle; this John may be William's half-brother.

109. *Cal. Close Rolls, 1485–1500*, 301.

It was not, however, the end of the vicissitudes of the manor of Althorp. The successful plaintiff remained in possession until the death, in 1505, of George Catesby, son and heir of William and so elder brother of that John who by the 1488 decision had been 'forever' barred from any claim.[110] The inquisition following George Catesby's death took place in January 1506 and returned that the reversion of Althorp had been sold by John Catesby of Althorp to George's father, William, for £200, and that Kebell and the others had been seised to the use of John during his lifetime and then to the use of William and his heirs. When John died, therefore, Althorp should have passed to the crown. Equally, when George Catesby obtained a reversal of the attainder and restoration of his father's land in 1495, Althorp should have been returned to him. But, the jury declared, a certain John Catesby of Althorp, that is, the successful plaintiff of 1488, had taken over the lands, 'by what right or title' they did not know. George's heir was a royal ward and the crown, relying on the verdict of the jury, occupied Althorp – despite the fact that the 'right and title' was none other than the judgement of the court of chancery.[111] The Catesbys never farmed the manor again; by 1508 it had been sold to the Spencer family and became the principal seat of their increasing importance.[112]

The point of interest for Thomas Kebell is the truth, or otherwise, of the jury's story. If the 1506 verdict was correct, then the 1487 suits had been fabricated to evade the laws of forfeiture, and Kebell must have been involved, if only tacitly. John Catesby left only a nuncupative will, a notorious source of testamentary dispute.[113] This certainly supports the case argued for the successful plaintiff and makes no mention of any sale to William Catesby, but as the witnesses to the will were also the witnesses produced by the plaintiff in court, it is not surprising that the versions tally.

That something odd was afoot seems clear. John Catesby of Althorp died in London on 4 November 1486, and his will was admitted to probate on 11 November, before other possible claimants in Northamptonshire can have had time to digest the news.[114] Add the fact that the witnesses to the will were largely his servants, that when giving evidence in chancery not all of them reported the making of the will

110. *Cal. inquisitions post mortem*, iii. 1003.
111. *Cal. Fine Rolls, 1485–1509*, 850.
112. Finch, *Northamptonshire Families*, 39.
113. PROB11/7 ff. 208, 208v; B.L. Add. Ms. 16172.
114. It is also odd that the nuncupative will was allegedly made three weeks before the testator died. Witnesses for the losing claimant denied there was a will at all.

which they had previously witnessed, and that one of the two who did listed as present only two of the signatories and two others who were not signatories, and the matter becomes suspicious. Neither claimant would want a sale of Althorp to William Catesby to leak out – immediate confiscation of the property by the crown would advance nobody – but witnesses for each side do almost let the cat out of the bag. Thomas Aynesworth of Cliffe told of William Catesby building a costly windmill at Althorp, more the action of a future owner than, as another witness implied, of a parent seeking a legacy for his child. Robert Catesby, a London parson and cousin of the testator, hinted that the marquess of Dorset had counted upon receiving the manor as forfeit until he was assured that it was not due to descend to the attainted William's heir. Most suggestive of all, Richard Dryland let slip that Althorp had been granted to William Catesby and his heirs.[115] If the 1506 report that William had bought Althorp is correct, as these straws in the wind suggest, then it is easy to explain why his son's witnesses told such unconvincing stories. A true title by inheritance was barred by attainder, and a distinctly second-best had to be fabricated out of vague promises and circumstances. The impossibility of the elder son telling the truth may, indeed, explain why the successful John Catesby could bring his case at all.

Government evidence is divided. John Catesby, the successful party in 1488, was certainly in trouble over his claim to the property following the 1506 jury report.[116] On the other hand, George Catesby, a loser by the 1488 judgement, had married Richard Empson's daughter in 1496, and it is hardly likely that his father-in-law would have ignored a chance to recover Althorp.[117] Edmund Dudley certainly believed that the chancery judgement was sound; he wrote in 1509 that 'one Catesby of Northamptonshire was in a manor vndone vpon a light surmyse'.[118] Instrinsically, too, the risks may appear to make a major deception less probable, although no-one in 1487 could have

115. William Catesby was 'of Althorp': *Cal. Ancient Deeds*, iv. 10792. His son John quitclaimed Althorp to William's brother as late as 1502: Spencer Ms. 889.

116. B.L. Lansd. Ms., 127 f. 32 records his payment on 6 Nov. 1506 of 400 marks (100 down and the rest by obligations) 'for the kingis gracious favour for the confession of his travers for the mannour of Althorp and for treasure trove, and for his pardon'.

117. *Cal. inquisitions post mortem*, iii. 101. It might, however, have been difficult to raise a claim in 1496, so soon after the first judgement, and with the necessity of admitting to an attempt to evade crown rights. In 1506 it was in the crown's interest to accept the claim to Althorp.

118. C. J. Harrison, 'The petition of Edmund Dudley', in *E.H.R.* 87 (1972), 88.

anticipated the meticulous royal scrutiny which characterised the later years of Henry VII's reign. Nevertheless, ambiguity does remain, and with it the possibility that Kebell was at least acquiescing in a fraud for the benefit of the family of former clients.[119]

119. There may be some relationship with *Burnly* v. *Halewel*: *Y.B.* Mich. 9 Hen. VII, p. 5 ff. 8–10.

6

THE LAWYER AND HIS CLIENTS

The primacy of local allegiance was one of the enduring features of English life before the Industrial Revolution. Provincial feeling served to rally the population in days before the nation meant a great deal outside the governing circles, and it also was associated with the simple matter of bread and butter. Until the Reformation, openings for service in a monastic administration were as important to the sons of neighbouring gentry as was the promise of what Milton called 'convenient stowage' in the nearest nunnery to their 'withered' daughters. Amongst lawyers, just as local connections often determined the inn a man entered, so local connections played a significant part in bringing the work that he needed.

The most famous family of lawyers to exploit local connection were the Pastons. Judge Paston founded his success on his Norfolk clients while John Paston made a killing from the estates of his deceased employer and distant relative, John Fastolf of Caister. Nor was this only a one-way traffic. A lawyer with local knowledge and connections was a powerful and dangerous man, an ally well worth the gaining. The legal clans of Heydon, Jenney and Yelverton were substantially responsible for the prolonged tribulations of the Paston family, and not until they had been mollified by bribery or marriage alliances was Paston wealth secure. Something of the threat a lawyer might pose comes out in a king's bench case in which Kebell appeared, dated 1493.[1] Humphrey Coningsby of the Inner Temple brought a writ of trespass alleging that a tenant of his had been driven out by threats to life and limb. What had actually happened was that Coningsby had put in the tenant as part of a claim to the property, only to see him depart hastily when the rival claimant threatened to take the tenant to court! Where circumstances permitted, violence might be a way to deal with an inconvenient lawyer. In Devon, in 1455, the recorder of Exeter, Nicholas Radford, was dragged from his house and murdered

1. *Y.B.* Mich. 9 Hen. VII, p. 4 ff. 7–8.

by a gang of sixty under the command of the heir to the earl of Devonshire on account of his service to the earl's arch-enemy, Lord Bonville.[2] Snobbery, too, reinforced self-preservation; Margaret Paston observed:

> it is thought the more lerned men that ye haue of yowr owyn contre of yowr councell the more wurchepful it is to you.[3]

I

Thomas Kebell's service with Lord Hastings was another example of this, but the influence of locality can be seen at work in many other instances in his career. Apart from the transactions already considered (predominantly from Leicestershire and the neighbouring shires), the interests of nearly forty more of Kebell's non-litigious clients can be pinned down to a particular locality.[4] Of these, a third fell in Kebell's home county and a further fifth from close at hand. Of the remainder, one in four came from the semi-circle of counties between Humberstone and London. There were also a handful of engagements for northern clients, but these clearly arose from the serjeant's connections with York and Lancaster. Apart from these, the rest of England was represented by only three or four examples. Too much cannot be made of figures which may be determined simply by accident of survival – a lawyer's practice was certainly not limited to one area. Indeed, a predominance in the profession of men from the midlands and the south-east meant that in many areas to consult a prominent lawyer was to approach an outsider. Sometimes, even, the crown sent counsel to accompany the assize judges, presumably in the absence of sufficient local men.[5] Nevertheless, the foundations of a lawyer's practice were laid among his family, his friends and his acquaintances. Very frequently, indeed, local men established a monopoly of even the better-known legal positions in an area; the recorder of Norwich was usually a Norfolkman, the abbot of Peterborough had a predominance of lawyers in his service from the shires around the soke, while London gave preference to local men

2. Radford, *Trans. Devon Assoc.* 35. 251–78.
3. *Paston Letters and Papers*, i. 275.
4. This is not to say that the clients necessarily came from the area where the land in question lay.
5. Lincoln's Inn, Hale Ms. xii (77).

like Frowyk, Marowe and More, despite the wide range of alternative talent available, close at hand.[6]

The majority of these midland legal matters which involved Thomas Kebell were in no way remarkable.[7] Yet minor items sometimes reveal considerable ramifications. In 1483 and 1485, Kebell was a defendant in two chancery suits brought by a John Chester to recover a small property in Loughborough which Kebell and two others, William Dunthorn and Richard Knyveton, held as feoffees.[8] Neither case went far, but investigation of this flurry of litigation reveals the activity of a group of London money-lenders. William Chester, father of John, was a City merchant, a stapler, with ostensible interests in bell-founding as well as wool and skins. He was also an usurer, so too was his relation, John Chester senior, and so, possibly, a third of the family, Richard Chester, both London citizens interested in wool.[9] With the established credit trading of the wool business, such a clan were well placed to lend for gain. In this instance, William Chester had advanced money to a John Farnham, and the Loughborough property had been conveyed as security via Richard Chester and two lawyers, John Stok and John Haugh, to Dunthorn, Knyveton and Kebell.[10] They were to hold the land while Farnham repaid Chester £7 a year for ten years, after which control would be returned to Farnham. He defaulted, and John Chester, William's son, backed by John Chester senior, brought an action in 1483 to enforce the forfeit, and a second in 1485 to compel the feoffees to obey his instructions. Kebell's role is difficult to disentangle. Someone among the feoffees must have proved awkward. It was not

6. For the abbot of Peterborough, see *Peterborough Monastery*, 17.
7. e.g. 'Mss. of Leicester Corporation', in H.M.C. *Eighth Report* (1907–9), i (2), 415b; *Cal. Close Rolls, 1476–85*, 1176; *Cal. inquisitions post mortem*, iii. 1002; Bateson, *Leicester*, ii. 433.
8. C1/58/128; C1/79/78.
9. William Chester – merchant of the Staple, citizen and woolman of London; skinner and bell-founder; pardoned 1472; receives gift of goods 1475 (see below, p. 119): *Cal. Patent Rolls, 1467–77*, 347; London, *Plea and Memoranda Rolls, 1458–82*, 172. John Chester – citizen and woolman of London; merchant of Calais; pardoned for offences against the usury statute, *3 Henry VII* c. 6: *Cal. Patent Rolls, 1485–94*, 471. Richard Chester – of Stowe St Edward, Glos.; chapman, woolman, citizen and skinner of London; pardoned 1472; sheriff of London, 1484; executor of William Chester; no direct evidence of money-lending, but clearly involved in the Farnham business: *Cal. Patent Rolls, 1467–77*, 347; *ibid.*, *1476–85*, 499; London, *Plea and Memoranda Rolls, 1458–82*, 123 *et passim*.
10. John Stok – described here and elsewhere as 'gent' and so probably a lawyer, although there were London merchants of the same name.

Dunthorn, town clerk of London and probably a fellow of Gray's Inn; later an executor of William Chester, he clearly represented the creditors.[11] Of the connections of the Derbyshire lawyer, Knyveton, little is known. Kebell, however, like Farnham, was a Leicestershire man, and his father Walter had worked with Farnham's father, so it seems likely that it was he who represented the debtor's interests.[12] Certainly the Farnhams survived this brush with London finance.[13]

Sometimes in his provincial practice Thomas Kebell worked with men of distinction, but more often, his associates were connected in some way with the parties concerned.[14] In other instances, Kebell represented men who were obviously his own friends, neighbours or employees – William Ashby of Lowesby, Sir Thomas Pulteney of Misterton or William Bret of Rotherby.[15] It is characteristic that the serjeant, with one of his agents, William Smith of Withcote, and with Sir Thomas Pulteney, should be a feoffee for William Ashby; that Ashby and Smith should be among the serjeant's own feoffees; that Kebell, in turn, should act for Pulteney; and that Ashby's son should be executor for both Pulteney and Smith.[16] Kebell also acted for relatives. He took over the management of his deceased brother's estate and obtained a grant of the wardship and marriage of the heir, his nephew George.[17] He was likewise executor of the will of 'his cousin', Robert Moton of Peckleton, in addition to being co-grantee with Frowyk of the wardship of the heir.[18] It is difficult, however, to distinguish such work from more usual professional activities. In the late 1470s, for example, Kebell became a feoffee for Thomas Billing, chief justice of the king's bench, who about the same time married his

11. William Dunthorn – town clerk 1461; associated with several Gray's Inn men, Richard Welby, John Watno, Thomas Urswick and William Laken, executor of William Chester; died 1490: London, *Cal. Letter Books*, L, 11; *Cal. Patent Rolls, 1476–85*, 208; *Cal. Close Rolls, 1468–76*, 1579; *ibid., 1485–1500*, 72; London, *Plea and Memoranda Rolls, 1458–82, passim*; *Cal. Fine Rolls, 1485–1509*, 279; PROB11/8 f. 276.

12. Dunthorn and Kebell did have one link via Thomas Lovet; Kebell was his feoffee in Hunts., and Dunthorn in Northants.: *Cal. inquisitions post mortem*, i. 749, 753. The connection is complicated. Kebell's uncle by marriage, Thomas Billing C.J.K.B., formerly of Gray's Inn, had a granddaughter Joan who married John Haugh, Dunthorn's associate (see above, p. 117) and, secondly, Thomas Lovet (see below, p. 465): Farnham, *Quorndon Records*, 145.

13. *ibid., passim*.

14. *ibid.*, 170.

15. Ashby – CP25(1) 126/79/38. Pulteney – Farnham, *Village Notes*, iii. 228. Bret – see below, p. 347.

16. *Cal. inquisitions post mortem*, ii. 334, 497; iii. 204, 269; *L. and P.*, i. 438 (3 m.6).

17. *Cal. inquisitions post mortem*, i. 164; *Cal. Patent Rolls, 1485–94*, 157.

18. See above, p. 108.

aunt Mary, but whether his employment by Billing was the result of this match we do not know.[19] In any case, it may be false to try to draw a distinction between work for professional clients and work for relations. Kebell's services were in demand by his family, but we need not assume that he offered them for nothing; Moton, for example, left the serjeant a legacy of five marks.[20]

The record of Thomas Kebell's non-litigious work beyond the circle of family, friends and locality can briefly be told. He had few exceptional clients or cases to disturb the even tenor of his practice; with a considerable clientele in Leicestershire to provide the backbone of his conveyancing and advisory work, he extended similar activities elsewhere. He was, with other royal lawyers, made a feoffee of the king in 1496.[21] For twenty years until his death, he was feoffee for the marquess of Dorset, successively step-son to Edward IV and brother-in-law to Henry VII.[22] Kebell was briefly engaged in the notorious process by which William, Marquess Berkeley, disposed of the family estates to spite his brother and heir, but the connection did not persist.[23] In the last years of his life he acted for the Willoughby family. Kebell was a trustee for the marriage settlement of the heir in 1495, and four years later was one of a group of feoffees called in as part of a settlement of the feud between Robert Willoughby, Lord Broke, and Richard Nevill, Lord Latimer.[24] These notable figures apart, most of the serjeant's casual clients were gentry of the lesser sort, scarcely one a merchant or townsman.

The only substantial connection between Kebell and a merchant was his loan of £38 to Roger Wyggeston, stapler of Calais and citizen of Leicester.[25] The circumstances, however, are not known, and the fact that the lawyer rarely appears as the recipient of a gift of goods (a concealed form of mortgage) suggests that Kebell was not habitually a lender of money. Some lawyers, by contrast, made this a main

19. Leicestershire Record Office: 26D 53/653; cf. *Cal. inquisitions post mortem*, i. 749.
20. PROB11/11 f. 200
21. *Rot. Parl.*, vi. 510b.
22. *Cal. Close Rolls, 1476–85*, 719; *Cal. inquisitions post mortem*, iii. 929.
23. *ibid.*, i. 800. See John Smith, *Lives of the Berkeleys*, ed. J. Maclean (1883), ii. 126–49.
24. *Cal. Patent Rolls, 1494–1509*, 198; *Cal. Close Rolls, 1485–1500*, 791, 1201; *ibid., 1500–9*, 181; see below, p. 121.
25. CP40/962 m. 267. The bond was dated 27 Aug. 1500, two months after Kebell's death, but as it was executed between Wyggeston and Kebell's executors it presumably referred to a debt contracted in the serjeant's lifetime. The executors also sued five Derbyshire yeomen for miscellaneous amounts totalling £31 6s. 8d. but these were probably farming debts: CP40/961 m. 465.

business.[26] William Callow's testament tells of one pledge (a silver salt) 'lying in my deske vppon my countre', for all the world as though he kept a pawnshop.[27] In all he listed eleven outstanding or partly repaid loans made against obligations or on the security of plate, ten of which added up to £155.13s.4d.; the profit he could make on pledges is clear from his restoring a royal (10s.) to one customer whose spoons and coral beads had brought him more than the £1 advanced. Callow's experience was not unique. Nicholas Stratham gave instructions that:

> Loue the grocer at the Stokkes in London haue xxxs. in recompence of his plegges that he did forfitt to me, or els that he haue the same plegges of plate of the same price that he leide theym to me, at his eleccion, for I did wyn more thenne xls. of the Arras that he did forfitt to me.[28]

With money advanced against security of land – Gregory Adgore made four separate loans to one client totalling £111.13s.4d. – there was always the chance of a more enduring profit.[29] William Callow appears to have acquired forfeited property in Canterbury worth five hundred marks, including Shafford's Court where he lived; William Catesby lent seven hundred marks to the courtier Richard Haute and ended up with the manor of Welton in Northamptonshire.[30] William Vampage, already £80 in debt and needing to raise money to follow Clarence to Picquigny, mortgaged his Worcestershire property to Thomas Brugge and eventually, having raised further sums from the future serjeant, parted with the land for a total of £240; Brugge's son restored the property under the terms of his father's will 'that by ne for hym his soule shall bere any parell afore God'.[31]

Thomas Kebell was connected with one mortgage, but as a trustee, not a principal. In 1491, together with John Carnwallis, esquire, Robert Ellyngton, John Brown and Reynold Pegge (the latter two at least being lawyers), Kebell was granted the manor of Manuden, then in Hertfordshire, by Thomas Bassingbourne of Hatfield. This transaction was part of a sixteen-year mortgage of the property to Robert Hawkins of London, a hatter or haberdasher who is better described as a money-lender. The mortgage was redeemed in December 1493

26. e.g. Richard Jay: C1/81/2; *Cal. Close Rolls, 1476–85*, 27, 92, 710; London, *Plea and Memoranda Rolls, 1458–82*, 178.
27. PROB11/8 ff. 57, 57v.
28. PROB11/6 f. 53.
29. PROB11/14 f. 159v; cf. Coningsby, above, p. 106.
30. PROB11/8 f. 58; *Cal. Ancient Deeds*, iii. A5360.
31. *ibid.*, i. C1765; iii. C3279; vi. C4539; *Cal. Close Rolls, 1476–85*, 51, 139.

by Bassingbourne's brother-in-law, Sir William Say, but the improvement in the owner's fortunes did not last. By 1505 Bassingbourne had sold Manuden to John Gardiner, presumably John Gardiner of the Inner Temple.[32]

By contrast with the detail which it is possible to assemble about Kebell's non-contentious practice, his litigious work remains indistinct. Thanks to the problems of the sources, only some fifty disputes can be isolated where at least the client Kebell appeared for is known. Certain litigants, not surprisingly, fit into the pattern of his non-litigious clients. He appeared for Edward, Lord Hastings, and his wife Mary (Kebell's 'good lady'), in a *quare impedit* to secure her right to part of the Hungerford inheritance.[33] The former retinue of William, Lord Hastings, is represented by Sir Thomas Grene, for whom Kebell appeared on three occasions, and by Sir Henry Vernon (whose manor of Aylestone Kebell also took over when William Moton, the former steward, died).[34] He played a prominent part in the pleading of *Broke* v. *Latimer* and acted for several colleagues from the legal profession, including Sir Roger Townshend and fellows of the Inner Temple such as Robert Sheffield.[35]

Close analysis, however, is precluded by the nature of the evidence. The only reason parties are named is the personal interest or curiosity of the lawyer who reported the case, which explains why the names of lawyers crop up so frequently. Identifying Kebell's clients does reveal that he had a wider practice in the courts than in non-contentious work; people employed him from as far apart as York, the west

32. *ibid.*, *1485–1500*, 742; *ibid.*, *1500–9*, 472, 530; *Cal. Ancient Deeds*, iii. D800. John Brown – apprentice-at-law; retained by duchy; offered recordership of Coventry; died *c.* 1497; probably of Berkhamsted, Herts.; possibly an officer of the common pleas: *Cal. Close Rolls, 1485–1500*, 333; *Cal. inquisitions post mortem*, ii. 627; Somerville, *Duchy of Lancaster*, i. 454; *Coventry Leet Book*, 528; *Cal. Fine Rolls, 1485–1509*, 562; *Cal. Patent Rolls, 1461–7*, 69; Hastings, *Common Pleas*, 124, 126, 261–3, 265–6. Reynold Pegge – of Rothersthorpe, Northants.; attorney and officer of king's bench; clerk of assize; died 1510: *L. and P.*, i. 438 (2 m. 7); Farnham, *Quorndon Records*, 171; Blatcher, 'Working of king's bench', lx; *Cal. Patent Rolls, 1485–94*, 161; PROB11/16 f. 263v. Ellyngton – probably an associate of Hawkins: *Cal. inquisitions post mortem*, iii. 63. Hawkins – London, *Cal. Letter Books*, L, 211; *Cal. Close Rolls, 1485–1500*, 159 and *passim*; *ibid.*, *1500–9*, 385, 425. Gardiner: *ibid.*, *1500–9*, 63.

33. *Y.B.* Hil. 13 Hen. VII, p. 24 f. 18.

34. *ibid.*, Pas. 4 Hen. VII, p. 7 f. 8; Hil. 13 Hen. VII, p. 14 f. 16; Mich. 14 Hen. VII, p. 19 f. 7; Pas. 11 Hen. VII, p. 1 f. 17; the information about Aylestone I owe to the kindness of my former student Dr S. M. Wright.

35. *ibid.*, Mich. 12 Hen. VII, p. 5 f. 8; Trin. 11 Hen. VII, p. 4 f. 25; Hil. 6 Hen VII, p. 3 f. 14; Pas. 11 Hen. VII, p. 4 f. 19.

country, East Anglia and the south coast.[36] But this is hardly surprising; Kebell would have been an unlikely choice as a working feoffee in an area he did not know and which did not know him, but litigation at Westminster was different. Counting the courts where he appeared produces equally little. Two-thirds of his cases in the year books were in common pleas, as might be expected both of a serjeant and of the known balance of civil work between the courts at that period; just over a quarter were king's bench matters. There are similarly small gains in any study of the issues and the law in Kebell's cases. Without evidence of the original grievance it is impossible to explain why a particular form of action was chosen. Moreover, year-book reports are normally concerned with a particular point of interest which was often not so much raised by the case as contained in the argument of one of the lawyers taking part. It is impossible to decide whether certain types of case held particular difficulties, and the year books certainly do not indicate in any way the content of legal practice. They are no more likely to chronicle the normal pattern of activity in Westminster Hall than case-notes on the complications of pregnancy are to reflect the normal course of childbirth. Neither do the sources allow us to trace the development of individual skill and experience from year to year, or the growth of a lawyer's practice, nor do they make it easy to enquire into specialisation or partnership, to probe into conventions of the bar, into a system of seniors and juniors or relationships between clients, attorneys and counsel.

It is, therefore, of more than passing interest that a contemporary account has survived for one suit in which Kebell was for a time engaged, *Pilkington* v. *Ainsworth*. The narrative, which in itself deserves to be better known, tells of the struggles which the Pilkingtons of Rivington in Lancashire had with the Ainsworths over an estate in the Derbyshire village of Mellor – struggles which lasted from before 1463 until at least 1511.[37] The narrator, Robert Pilkington, gives very much a plaintiff's view – his claim is always just and his enemies always motivated by evil – but as a description of late fifteenth-century litigation, his account is probably unique.

Thomas Kebell, as will be seen, had been on the fringes of the

36. e.g. *Dean of York* v. *Rex*: *Y.B.* Hil. 3 Hen. VII, p. 10 f. 3; *Cary* v. *Gilbert re* the manor of Clovelly: *ibid.*, Mich. 10 Hen. VII, p. 1 f. 1; *Rex* v. *the Sheriff of Suffolk*: *ibid.*, Hil. 3 Hen. VII, p. 1 f. 1; *Thomas Combs* v. *Simon Erlington*: *ibid.*, Pas. 13 Hen. VII, p. 1 f. 18, cf. Wedgwood, *Biographies*.

37. North Yorkshire Record Office, ZDV XI, printed in 'Wombwell Mss.', in H.M.C., *Various Collections* (1901–14), ii. 28–56. References below are to the printed text.

Pilkington case for some years as a potential arbitrator when, in July 1498, Robert Pilkington had to face the surprise hearing of a writ of assize at Derby.[38] He had very little chance even if he had received proper warning. Behind the Ainsworths was the Savage family, notably Thomas Savage, bishop of London and 'lord presedent of the kynges noubull counsayle courte'; and at an earlier hearing of the assize in February 1498 Bishop Savage had sent 'tender letters' to all the jurors and during the case James Savage, his brother, had 'stode at the barre and maintenyd Aynesworth matter in all his pouere both prevely and openly'.[39] On that occasion Pilkington had been able to produce 'dyvers wrytynges from his gud lorde of Derby' and this had led to an attempt to get a settlement out of court. But in July a corrupt jury and Savage influence carried the day. The assize judges disliked the result, especially John Vavasour, Kebell's colleague as justice at Lancaster; damages were reduced by three-quarters and judgement respited until the Michaelmas term in London. Pilkington was also given copies of the court record, and the judges held a private discussion with him and his counsel at Derby Abbey in an attempt to have the jury attainted. Pilkington preferred the less hazardous writ of error, and he came to London in good time for the Michaelmas term to discuss his case once more with Vavasour. For the July assize Pilkington had secured Robert Brudenell of the Inner Temple, at short notice, but Vavasour clearly suggested he should now consult Thomas Kebell. He took the advice and:

> shewyd his mater and copese of his forther prosses at Derby unto Mayster Kebull, that tyme one of the chefe sergandes to the kyng and the secunddare juge at Lancaster and mone othere placys, and there and then reteynyd hym of counsayle with the said Robert and gave hym xld. and delyverd hym all copes to stede the mater agaynys the myghalmas terme.[40]

Brudenell was kept on as well, and Kebell's 'prinotare clerke', William Reynold, was engaged as attorney, making a powerful team.[41] They lost no time. The writ of error was taken out on Tuesday 16 October for return in king's bench the following Monday; on the next Saturday William Reynold removed all process from common pleas to

38. See below, pp. 128–9.
39. For the Savage family see Ives, in *On the Laws and Customs of England*, 303–11; 'Wombwell Mss.', 40–1.
40. For the following see 'Wombwell Mss.' 51–5.
41. Reynold – 'of London'; associated with John Muscote of the common pleas; witness to Kebell's will: *Cal. Close Rolls, 1468–76*, 562; *ibid., 1500–9*, 715; see below, p. 341.

king's bench and before term was over a *scire facias* was issued for John Ainsworth's appearance on the first day of the ensuing term. Pilkington returned home, leaving a bastard son, John, to act for him, and he was probably well satisfied with his progress.

Ainsworth appeared as ordered and proceeded to engage his own team of lawyers, three serjeants 'cheve of counsayle with the Byschope of London' – Thomas Frowyk, John Kingsmill and Robert Constable – and as his attorney (a shrewd move) one of the senior officers of the court, John Fisher 'prinotore next Mayster Roper at the kynges bench'.[42] Clearly they decided to procrastinate, for it was not until Kebell had appeared once, and a second and third time with Brudenell, that Fisher answered. As Pilkington said, Ainsworth's counsel:

> mad so mych craft in delays that thay wold none onswar make unto the last day of hyllore terme and that was no more but made dymynscions agaynys the furst day of ester terme then next.

On the first day of Easter, 1499, Kebell 'was at the barre' but delays continued almost to the end of the term. Eventually:

> Mr. Kebull and Mr. Brytnell had moche to doo with Aynesworth counsell, notwithstandying my lord chefe juge had said whether thay wolde or not they schuld rejoyne, and so they dyd generall, by thies wordes *Nullum est erratum*.

In the second week of the Trinity term Kebell and Brudenell again appeared in court but then they apparently decided to change tactics. With Reynold in attendance they spent the afternoon of 10 June in planning 'how they schuld mynystir the matter', and the next morning they were at the bar at half past eight suing a new writ against Ainsworth, alleging that he was wasting the estate. The case occupied the judges for the next two-and-a-half hours, but it was then adjourned for two days in succession, and when renewed, it was discovered that Vavasour's clerk had brought in an incorrect record. Brudenell went to St Bride's in Fleet Street himself to secure a correct copy, but the case had lost priority with the justices and Ainsworth's lawyers were able to frustrate many of Kebell's appearances. Eventually, on 25 June, the Pilkington side did secure an appointment with

42. The identity of Fisher is not clear. Dr J. H. Baker suspects that he may have held the post that is later described as that of the 'secondary'; the earliest named secondary is John Lucas, early in Henry VIII's reign: Spelman, *Reports*, ii. 364–5. A *William* Fisher was filacer and a very active attorney in king's bench *c.* 1490: Blatcher, 'Working of king's bench', xxxvi; *Court of King's Bench*, 142 n. 19.

the chief justice to scrutinise the records, but it was then discovered that Vavasour's clerk had forgotten to supply a crucial document and Pilkington himself had to make two copies, one for Fineux, the chief justice, and one for Rede, his colleague. The outcome was that they were ordered to 'bryng in presedence from the comyn place of othere maters in like case adjugyt'.

Damage to the manuscript makes it hard to be sure what happened next, but it seems that the search for precedents was a failure and there was talk of dropping the case in the Michaelmas term. But something must have convinced Kebell that there was life in the suit, because it was not abandoned, and, indeed, the opposition began to show signs of concern. The Hilary term opened with an approach from the bishop of London to Kebell, first by 'a credabull and a well lernyd gentylmon' and then in person, announcing that he had bought out Ainsworth and so owned Mellor himself, but that he was prepared to compensate Pilkington's claim. The latter certainly saw this as a trick and complains that:

> when the said Robertes counsayle hade grauntyd to heng stylle his accyon, then the byschope schewyd Mr. Kebell that yf the said Robert wolde not aggre to sell his ryght and tytyll of Mellur, the said byschope and Aynesworth wolde sewe grete accyons of dettes and for costages of damagis agaynys the said Robert.

Kebell's response to these threats, however, looks like the effort of counsel to secure at least half a loaf for his client, for at their meeting at the Lancaster spring sessions:

> Mr. Kebull desyryd the said Robert to wryte such onswar as he schuld make to the said byschope at the Ester terme then next sewyng, that he myght be syght of the said wrytyng be fresch in his remembrance agaynes the terme aforesaid.

The reply Robert sent by Kebell was a plea to the bishop to relent, and the inducement that for a secure title to Mellor he would hand over the marriage of his son and heir, worth £40 and more. Kebell, however, fell ill and gave no answer to Bishop Savage that Easter term; Pilkington transferred his suit to Vavasour, but the royal court went abroad that summer, the bishop included, and a serious outbreak of plague occurred in London so that no further action was possible for the rest of 1500 or Hilary 1501. By that time, Bishop Savage had been raised to the see of York 'and thus he come to, to ryse in dyngnete and ay the gratter and the more in the kynges favor'; Kebell was dead and for a decade the Pilkingtons gave up.

As the only account we have of Kebell's conduct of a case, this tale is hardly flattering. In fairness it must be remembered that the Pilkington–Ainsworth feud had been in progress for a quarter of a century before Kebell was called in and was to be revived in 1511, eleven years after his death. It is important also to note the influence of the values, attitudes and methods of contemporary society; it was not the law which was at issue so much as spheres of magnate influence. As for the business of litigation itself, the account confirms the influence of the inns of court connections, with Vavasour, Kebell and Brudenell all associated with the Inner Temple, and certainly implies that the latter two were acting as senior and junior in a team which relied for clerical work on Kebell's own clerk, Reynold; perhaps it is not improper to see a 'firm' here, at least in embryo. Yet the principal impression is of the personal involvement of lawyers in the affairs of their clients. In part this was the result of professional immaturity, with no hint of a divided profession or of deliberate attempts to make the law impersonal. In part, too, it was inevitable, given that lawyers themselves were active in the propertied community of the time. Assuming Pilkington to have been in the right, Kebell's actions were certainly an attempt to use the law against, and to protect the law from abuse by, the over-mighty, but they may also have been influenced by the fact that as justice at Chester and at Lancaster Kebell had his personal relation with both Bishop Savage and the earl of Derby who, in any case, had their own relationship as nephew and uncle. And if involvement with clients was the rule and not an exception, then we have an important clue to the pressures which could and did bring change to the weight of accumulated case-law.

II

Thomas More wrote of his professional work in the opening of *Utopia*:

> I do daily bestow my time about law matters: some to plead, some to hear, some as an arbitrator with my award to determine, some as an umpire or a judge with my sentence to decide.[43]

The emphasis which More put upon action as an arbitrator or as an umpire corresponds to the importance which such activities had in the fifteenth and sixteenth centuries. The high cost and the unreliability

43. More, *Utopia*, 22.

of litigation would, in itself, explain the popularity of arbitration and the frequent provision in wills, contracts and so forth, that any disputes should be settled by agreement.[44] But settlement by negotiation was also deliberately encouraged by authority. In 1500, for example, a boundary dispute broke out between the city and the abbot of St Mary's, York.[45] The citizens wished to negotiate from the start, but it was only after two royal officials and the cathedral officers had added their voices that the abbey agreed. In an example from the previous reign, a dispute between the lawyer John Burgoyne and two Cambridge monasteries was settled by the direct intervention of the royal council.[46]

The crown was not alone in these efforts: magnates would often try to patch up a quarrel in an area specially under their influence. In another of the city of York's disputes, this time with the dean and cathedral chapter in 1487, the earl of Northumberland intervened to force a settlement, and set up one of his own lawyers, Edward Redman, to lead the discussions.[47] Kebell's patron, Lord Hastings, acted similarly. In the early 1480s a dispute between Joan Chesylden, a widow, and her step-son John Chesylden over an annuity due from the manor of Allexton in Leicestershire was settled by Hastings' intervention and the award:

> demised & made by Master Kebill, sergeaunt of the lawe, and other the said Lord Hastinges counsell.[48]

This was not Kebell's only experience of arbitration. In 1480 an agreement between two cousins, Sir Humphrey Talbot and Sir Robert Willoughby over the property of a common ancestor specified that:

> if anything concerning the premises be omitted or otherwise written than was the intent of the parties, it shall be reformed by John Broune or Thomas Kebell.[49]

In 1481 he was engaged for an arbitration between the city of Coventry and the priory; Serjeant John Vavasour was to lead for the city

44. e.g. after *Broke* v. *Latimer*: *Cal. Close Rolls, 1485–1500*, 1201.
45. *York Civic Records*, ii. 146 *sqq.*
46. *Cal. Close Rolls, 1476–85*, 737.
47. *York Civic Records*, i. 178. Redman – Wedgwood, *Biographies*; *Testamenta Eboracensia*, v. 23. Cf. Rawcliffe, 'Baronial councils', 92–3.
48. REQ3/4. The date is established by other documents in the case. Hastings is referred to as deceased and hence must be William; cf. the arbitration of John Catesby between two Hastings men in 1467–8: C1/90/34–5.
49. *Cal. Close Rolls, 1476–85*, 720.

with Kebell to support him, and they were opposed by the Catesbys, John the serjeant and his nephew William.[50] A meeting at Coventry was arranged for Passion Week, but before this the prior died and the arbitration had to be abandoned. Indeed, one great disadvantage of settlement by negotiation was its uncertainty. Not only was determined good will required from both sides but good fortune as well. For one party to die was particularly bad luck, but hazards were legion – lawyers might not turn up, necessary evidence might be missing, no decision might be announced in the time allocated, and when a decision was reached, one or other party might refuse to honour it. In an attempt to avoid this last danger it was normal to provide a penalty clause. Thus in the same year, 1481, a crown-sponsored arbitration was reinforced with bonds of £100 each from the contestants, Richard St George and William Wentworth, who were disputing the title of some Cambridgeshire manors.[51] Thomas Kebell led for Wentworth with John Baker as his junior, while John Turpin and Robert Morton represented St George.[52] But the prospects were not good. The four men had to complete their work in two weeks and if they could not agree, the archbishop of York and Sir Thomas Grey were to decide within the following week. Such speed was desirable but hardly realistic and whether anything ever came of the arbitration is doubtful.

The frustrations and difficulties of arbitration are strikingly illustrated in Robert Pilkington's narrative. In all, the dispute with its various side issues went to arbitration at least four times, all to no effect. Before he became Pilkington's counsel, Kebell had been concerned on two occasions. The earlier was arranged in 1495 by friends of the contestants, and both parties agreed:

> to abyde the dome of lerned counsayle . . . in the furst, the chefe juge of england, who so eyvere he was or ells Mayster Kebull, Mayster Woddes, Mayster Rede, Mayster Cunesbe, sergeandes of the Coyfe, Mayster Hawardyne, justys of Chester.[53]

Such a panel might be thought to be somewhat ambitious, but the negotiation collapsed for a different reason – Ainsworth 'forsoke this

50. *Coventry Leet Book*, 474.
51. *Cal. Close Rolls, 1476–85*, 781.
52. Baker – Inner Temple: Thorne, *Readings and Moots*, i. xlvii; see above, p. 51–2. Turpin and Morton – Lincoln's Inn: *Black Books*, i. *passim*.
53. 'Wombwell Mss.', 36–7. There is some difficulty in dating this agreement. It was apparently made between 12 Nov., when Coningsby became a serjeant, and 24 Nov., when Wode and Rede were promoted to the bench. Pilkington, however, implies that the arbitration had broken down before All Hallows, 1 Nov.

poyntment'. The other attempt, three years later, was more realistic.[54] It followed the confrontation at the Derby assize in February 1498 between the influence of the Savages and the influence of the earl of Derby.[55] Each side was persuaded by the judges to be bound in £100 to accept the award of the earl of Shrewsbury and 'Mayster Thomas Kebull, that tyme on of the kynges sergendes and the ton of the jugges at Lancaster', the bonds to expire at Corpus Christi (14 June). The critical question was then the arranging of a meeting. First Robert obtained letters of introduction from the Stanleys to the earl of Shrewsbury. The earl 'toke grete credencez to' Robert and 'made hym gud chere for his lordes sakes' and then sent him to the Lent sessions of the duchy court at Lancaster to find when Kebell could visit the earl; Kebell arranged to meet Shrewsbury at Wingfield, halfway between Chesterfield and Derby, on the Thursday before Trinity Sunday – that is 7 June 1498 – a bare week before the bonds expired. Pilkington came as arranged, only to find that Kebell had not arrived. Seeking to save something from the 'treyte', the earl advised Pilkington to go himself to Kebell, and whatever the latter decided, since he was 'learned in the law', the earl would accept. With time running out, Pilkington hurried the forty miles to Humberstone only to discover that Kebell:

> was not comyn home from London, and so that labur was wast and the obligacions expiret and voyde at the Corpuskyrste day then next sewying.

It would, however, be wrong to make too much of the difficulties and disappointments of arbitration as against litigation – its popularity is sufficient witness to its attractions. However great the frustrations of negotiation, a lawsuit could be even more chancy. Again the Pilkington saga has pointed the moral. Once the 'treaty' had failed, Pilkington, with Kebell's best efforts, strove to establish his claim at heavy expense, but Savage influence frustrated all attempts at legal redress. 'To folow the meanys of the law' could be a sad fate.[56]

The arbitrations in which Kebell was involved once again illustrate the dominance of local interests in much legal practice. In addition to his work for the city of Coventry, he acted in an arbitration involving the city of Nottingham and in a minor dispute in Leicester.[57] In about 1498 the corporation recorded:

54. *ibid.*, 40–1. 55. See above, p. 123. 56. 'Wombwell Mss.', 35.
57. Nottingham – *Cal. Ancient Deeds*, vi. 6834. The presence of Sir Gervase Clifton and Lawrence Lowe among the other arbitrators suggests that the influence of Lord

be it had in mynde yat Thomas Wygston of Belgrave promised afore Mr. William Wygston senior, Mayor, that Richard Eyre should have a ground of his behind the house of Robert Sapcote so that he would give as much for it as he gave before.

No agreement was reached and Thomas Wygston agreed to stand the award of the mayor and Serjeant Kebell. Since Eyre was remembered in Kebell's will, it could even be that the lawyer was representing the interests of one of his own servants.[58] Arbitration also came Kebell's way in consequence of his official position. In March 1499 a dispute in Lancashire went to arbitration and the award was to 'stond the dome' of the earl of Derby, John Vavasour and Thomas Kebell, the justices at Lancaster, or any one of them.[59] Similarly, as justice of assize, Thomas Kebell was called in to advise Serjeant Robert Constable and the apprentice William Fairfax in yet another of the attempts to settle the quarrel between the city of York and St Mary's Abbey.[60] Justices of assize were regularly expected to pacify such local disputes, and after Kebell's death his colleague James Hobart and his successor Humphrey Coningsby continued the efforts to resolve the York troubles.[61] As in the rest of his practice, personal factors played an important part in bringing him work as an arbitrator. Thus in 1499 an award was announced between Robert Strange and Charles Rypon over the manor of Clewer in Berkshire in which the terms of a sale had been determined by Sir Robert Drury and Thomas Kebell, presumably representing Strange, and two other serjeants, Butler and Constable, apparently representing Rypon.[62] The connection between Strange, Kebell and Drury was through the duchy of Lancaster: Strange was duchy receiver in East Anglia and Cambridgeshire, Drury, a Lincoln's Inn barrister, was deputy chief steward of the south parts of the duchy, while Kebell, of course, was second justice at Lancaster.[63]

Hastings was involved: Dunham, 'Indentured retainers', 123, 130. Leicester – Bateson, *Leicester*, ii. 442.

58. See below, p. 347.
59. *Palatine Chantries*, ed. F. R. Raines, Chetham Soc., 1 ser. 59, 60 (1862), i. 157.
60. *York Civic Records*, ii. 158.
61. *ibid.*, ii. 165, 170. For other examples of justices of assize acting similarly, see *L. and P.*, v. 988; xii(2), 20.
62. *Cal. Close Rolls, 1485–1500*, 1094.
63. Somerville, *Duchy of Lancaster*, i. 596, 431, 473.

III

Service in a seigneurial household coupled with a wide range of legal services for a numerous clientele – litigation, land transfer, advice, feoffeeship or arbitration – was a healthy recipe for a lawyer's success. It is also obvious that such a career had gone far beyond the traditional link between lawyer and client – touting for employment at the parvis or porch of St Paul's Cathedral in London. Throughout Kebell's lifetime St Paul's was still in use as a meeting place between lawyer and client but it is unlikely that many lawyers actually searched for employment there.

Among the wealthiest employers it was usual to retain legal advice on a long-term basis by the grant of an annual fee and, very often, a livery or cash in lieu, 'fees and robes', to use Chaucer's phrase. In 1422–3, John Mowbray, the earl marshal, had two serjeants and four apprentices on annual retainer, together with an attorney in the common pleas and another in the county of York.[64] A century later, Henry VIII's close friend, Sir William Compton, retained six men *de consilio*, one already a serjeant and three who were to reach the coif later; another was an exchequer official, and retainers were also paid to two attorneys and a solicitor.[65] Corporations followed suit. Bridgwater, for example, retained one regular learned counsellor in the first part of the fifteenth century, until in 1468 a new charter provided for a recorder; the much larger city of Norwich had correspondingly more advisers – a recorder, a serjeant-at-law and an apprentice.[66] York, which appears to have had a recorder and four other counsel by 1454, even tried to stem the tide in 1490 by discharging all lawyers of fee.[67] Ecclesiastics were equally active. In Henry VII's reign the bishop of Worcester feed a serjeant, three apprentices and an attorney in common pleas and exchequer.[68] Peterborough Abbey in 1504–5 had at least seven lawyers on its pay-roll, and an attorney as well.[69] The *Valor Ecclesiasticus* would have revealed the full extent of legal retaining by the church but for the king's determination to disallow all such

64. B.L. Add. Ch. 17209.
65. Compton Muniments, Castle Ashby, 995.
66. Alexander Hody: *Bridgwater Borough Archives*, iii, iv, *passim*, v. xii; Norfolk and Norwich Record Office, Chamberlains' Accounts, 13–14 Edward IV, f. 54.
67. *York Memorandum Book*, ii. 199; *York Civic Records*, ii. 54.
68. Worcestershire Record Office, 009:BA2636/192 no. 92627/$\frac{7}{12}$. I owe this reference to the kindness of Dr C. C. Dyer.
69. *Peterborough Monastery*, xlviii–xlix.

expenses, yet something is suggested by those claims which were submitted nevertheless. In parts of the diocese of Lincoln an almost concerted effort was made – notably by the Oxford colleges – to have legal expenses recognised which 'byn annuall and perpetuall and of no lesse necessite then the fees and chargis of auditors, receyvors, and baylyffs and other annuall charges' which the crown did allow.[70] Generally a lump sum was stated for fees and legal costs – £60 at Magdalen, £10 at New College, £6.13s.4d. at All Souls, £40 at Corpus Christi, £5 at Lincoln – but Oseney Abbey, which claimed £20 in expenses also, claimed for one serjeant, two attorneys in the exchequer and one each in king's bench and common pleas.[71]

Retainers of this sort were for a term, or more usually for life, and were often executed by deed. As we have seen, the relationship between the lawyers and the bastard feudal world was close, and it is highly likely that the commonest of these deeds, the indenture of retainer, developed from that system. The indenture between William, Lord Hastings, and Lawrence Lowe, the future recorder of Nottingham, in 1474, is drawn for life, as the statutes on retaining specified. It is in the same form as other indentures for non-lawyers – 'to ride and go [with Lord Hastings] and him assist and aid against all persons, his said ligeance only except . . . accompanied with such persons as is according to his degree'; the requirement 'to be of his councelle learned' appears only as an extra, and there is no mention of any retaining fee.[72] In form Lowe was a retainer like the rest.[73] Legislation suggests a similar conclusion. The earliest statute regulating livery ignored the peculiar position of the lawyer, even though remuneration in 'fees and robes' was so characteristic of the profession.[74]

But although these non-feudal associations can still be seen in Kebell's day, lawyers were more generally retained *pro consilio impendendo* in return for an annual fee.[75] Many of these engagements were still by deed, often with the fee secured upon the revenue from a

70. *Valor Ecclesiasticus*, ii. 223.
71. *ibid.*, ii. 224, 238, 241, 249, 264, 288. Cf. *Oseney Abbey*, 101. 251, 281, where the house retained one serjeant-at-law, two apprentices and two Westminster attorneys in 1509–10, but one apprentice and two Westminster attorneys only in 1520–21.
72. Dunham, 'Indentured retainers', 119, 123.
73. Cf. the form of John Pullen's retainer, see below, p. 139.
74. *13 Ric. II, St. III*, c. 1. The first exception was made in 1399 by *1 Hen. IV*, c. 7.
75. For other connections with clientage, see above, pp. 115–16. Radford, *Trans. Devon Assoc.* 35. 257.

particular piece of property. Sir Thomas Grene, Kebell's client, made two grants by charter in June 1502 for 20s. each in favour of Edmund Hasilwode and John Muscote, both of the Middle Temple, and enfeoffed some of his lands for the purpose.[76] A distraint clause was frequently included for further protection. Thus, in 1429, John Bellars, esquire, settled a life annuity of 13s. 4d. on Thomas Palmer of Rockingham, great-uncle of Kebell's future wife, *pro bono consilio suo impenso et impendendo*, charged half-yearly on property at Holt, with power to distrain for non-payment.[77]

Patrol retainers for a year or longer were also common. The 1448–9 accounts of the duke of Buckingham have against payments of £2 to Serjeant Robert Danby and ten marks to Thomas Berston, the authorisation '*per dominum concessum ut patet per compotum receptoris*'.[78] The accounts of Elizabeth Woodville, Edward IV's queen, show retaining both by patent and by parol. Her attorney-general, John Dyve, and her attorneys in king's bench and common pleas were retained by patent; her learned counsel – two serjeants and two apprentices – were paid '*per litteram dicte domine regine de warranto*'.[79] Where a town was the employer, the equivalent was a resolution of the governing body, as at York, which resolved in 1484 that Edmund Thwaits should be 'of counsell with thys cite and have soch fee as his father had afor hym, that is to say xxs. yerly'.[80] Another variant was the will and testament. Walter Grene, an exchequer clerk and father-in-law to Justice John Catesby and Baron John Holgrave, left John Blofield £20 'for his good counsel to my executors'; Sir Edmund Gorges appointed the Middle Templar 'Thomas Jubbes, lerneman, supervisor and overseer [of his will] having for his labour 40s.'.[81] Although no term was expressed, the contract presumably lasted until the testator's estate was settled. Others were more specific. John Ellerker left £20 in 1438 to be held for five years in the

76. *Cal. inquisitions post mortem*, iii. 259; *L. and P.*, i. 438 (1 m. 26, 2 m. 12), 1803 (1 m. 6); *Minutes of Parliament*, i. 3, 4, 8, 11 *sqq*.
77. Leicestershire Record Office, DE221/4/6/42.
78. J. H. Markland. 'The rent roll of Humphrey, duke of Buckingham, 1447–8', in *Archaeological Journal* 8 (1851), 280–1.
79. Myers, *Bull. John Rylands Lib.* 50. 456–7, 461–2.
80. *York Civic Records*, i. 90. Cf. London, *Cal. Letter Books*, L, 82.
81. Williams, *Early Holborn*, 1210–11; *Somerset Medieval Wills, 1501–1530*, ed. F. W. Weaver, Somerset Record Soc. 19 (1903), 151. Cf. the bequest of £3 6s. 8d. to John Brook to supervise a will: *Trans. Bristol and Gloucestershire Arch. Soc.* 50 (1928), 202. Lady Burgavenny left over £1400 [sic] to defend the property of her grandsons: *Register of Archbishop Chichele*, ii. 536.

Charterhouse at Hull as a fighting fund to protect the family estates, to be released at the discretion of the prior and his executors (who included Serjeant John Portington); the prothonotary William Copley stipulated that the attorney Thomas Rayner should be paid 6s. 8d. a year to complete an action of *formedon*, with a further 13s. 4d. a year for other litigation, apparently for life.[82]

The retainer for counsel could also be used where a lawyer retired or was promoted to royal service. Towns particularly saw advantage in this. When Thomas Billing retired as recorder of London in 1454 on appointment to the coif, he was given a gift and retained of counsel at 20s. a year.[83] His successor Urswick was granted two tuns of wine and a tun a year thereafter.[84] When in 1545 another recorder, Roger Cholmley, resigned, he was granted twenty angel nobles in gold yearly, or their equivalent.[85] Provincial cities did the same. In 1449 William Donington retired as recorder of Coventry and was granted £10 a year for life with a retainer as counsel *ex officio*.[86] In some circumstances an annuity was the equivalent of a golden handshake. In 1442, Robert Danvers took over as recorder of London, and his predecessor, 'old and infirm', was granted 20 marks a year.[87]

The most important retainer enjoyed by Thomas Kebell came, of course, from the Hastings family. Added to that, Kebell was probably retained by Sir James Harrington of Preston in association with William Cutlerd of Lincoln's Inn – a connection which may have resulted from Kebell's service at Lancaster.[88] His most exalted client was Sir Charles Somerset, illegitimate son of Henry Beaufort, duke of

82. *Testamenta Eboracensia*, ii. 69; iv. 49; cf. v. 47. Rayner, clerk of assize: Blatcher, 'Working of king's bench', lxv; Baker, *Journ. Legal Hist.* 1. 199; *Cal. Patent Rolls, 1485–94*, 105, 163, 215, etc.
83. *Recorders of London*, Jor. 3 f.141.
84. *ibid.*, Jor. 7 f.243; Jor. 8 f.7.
85. On appointment as C.B.Ex.: Spelman, *Reports*, ii. *384, 390, 395*. Foss, *Judges*, v. 294–5 and *D.N.B.* describe Cholmley as king's serjeant, and he is so named in an undated Middlesex commission for 1544–5: *L. and P.*, xx(1). 623 p. 325. However, when noting his resignation, the City of London specifically described him as 'knight, serjeant-at-law and recorder', *pace Recorders of London* citing the same reference, Rep. 11 f.244 (now f.231). Wriothesley confirms that he was promoted to C.B.Ex. from recorder: Charles Wriothesley, *Chronicle*, ed. W. D. Harrison, Camden Soc., n.s. 11, 20 (1875, 1877), i. 162. The patent as king's serjeant cited in Dugdale, *Origines*, as 36 Hen. VIII p. 18 has not been traced.
86. *Coventry Leet Book*, 235–6.
87. *Recorders of London*, Jor. 3 f. 141; cf. *York Civic Records*, iii. 151, 153; *York Memorandum Book*, ii. 266–7.
88. *Abstracts of inquisitions post mortem*, ed. W. Langton, Chetham Soc., 1 ser., 95, 99 (1875–6), ii. 167–9.

Somerset, later to be lord chamberlain and earl of Worcester.[89] Somerset engaged Kebell in November 1489 at 26s. 8d. a year, secured on the manor of Dufton in Northamptonshire, which was leased to the abbey of St James outside the town. But Sir Charles did not give Kebell power to distrain, and when after 'divers years' the abbot stopped payment, the serjeant was forced to appeal to chancery for his money. Kebell also found the church a considerable source of employment. His one recorded post was that of chief steward to the prioress of Langley at an annual fee of 13s. 4d., a position he held by 1485 at the latest.[90] His will, however, refers to 'places of religion in the cuntre as I have had fees of', and although these are not specified, provisions for requiems and the like suggest the abbey of Leicester, very much an expected patron, only a mile or two from Kebell's house, and the College of Newark, also in Leicester, again no surprise considering his ties with its master, William Chauntry.[91] It is also likely that he had some connection with Launde Priory, for which he was acquiring land in 1491, and with Stoneleigh Abbey in Warwickshire, where he worked for the abbot in 1480, perhaps as his attorney-at-law.[92] Another possible link was with Christ Church, Canterbury, for which Kebell worked in 1499, but no mention of this house was made in the will.[93] A probable employer who is named in it, is the convent at Clerkenwell, but the bequest to the Whitefriars of London probably reflects not business but long years of worshipping there.

Thomas Kebell's retainers also included engagements by two of the most important urban corporations in his part of the midlands, Coventry and Leicester. Most is known of his connection with the former. His earliest appearance in the town's Leet Book was for the 1481 arbitration with the priory of St Mary, and by 1485 he was under permanent retainer.[94] As he could then write of favour and kindness shown 'to me of long time passed', he had clearly enjoyed more employment than this, probably back into the 1470s. The climax of his professional connection with Coventry came in December 1485, when he was approached with the offer of the next vacancy of the

89. C1/210/66.
90. SC6 988/11.
91. See above, p. 95; below p. 429.
92. *Cal. Patent Rolls, 1485–94*, 343; *Cal. Ancient Deeds*, i. B140.
93. *Christ Church Letters*, 65–6.
94. *Coventry Leet Book*, 527.

recordership of the city.[95] Henry Butler, the rather assertive recorder in office, had fallen ill and 'was not expected to live', and the mayor and his brethren had decided to make immediate arrangements for a successor.[96] Thomas Kebell was not the only lawyer canvassed for the post. He was given the first opportunity, but John Smith, the town's messenger, also carried a letter asking John Brown, another Inner Temple bencher, to accept the post if Kebell declined it. There seem, indeed, to have been two factions among the corporation on this issue. In his reply to the town, Brown wrote that he understood (clearly from John Smith) that 'ther will be labour made of Maister Tho. Kebell', but that he knew nobody except the mayor, Robert Onely, and John Symondes who had been mayor in 1477. This suggests that Brown was the candidate of Onely, Symondes and their supporters, but that a majority wanted Kebell. No doubt this was, in part, because of their experience of his work for the city, but there is also the suspicion about the role played by Henry Kebell, who enjoyed in 1485 the very considerable influence Coventry allowed to its immediate ex-mayor. As a victim of Henry Butler's insolence, Henry Kebell had a personal interest in the promotion of a successor, and as a relative had a family interest in Thomas Kebell.[97] As in so many other aspects of this lawyer's career, personal and local connections went together.

With the office of recorder so much in its infancy, there were wide variations between town and town in the arrangements for the position.[98] An especial problem, at least in Coventry, was the relationship between the needs of the recorder's own practice and the interests of the town. Not only did the council insist that the recorder should be resident in the city, but, when debating the invitation to Kebell and Brown, even agreed to require the recorder, henceforth, not to appear against any private Coventry citizen. Such restrictions inevitably interfered with a lawyer's private practice, and this was the burden of Kebell's reply to the city.[99] Residence in Coventry, he explained, was out of the question, and since he had recently been

95. Except where otherwise indicated, this discussion of the Coventry recordership is based upon the account in the Leet Book, where the correspondence is recorded in full: *ibid.*, 524–8.

96. *ibid.*, 520–1.

97. See above, p. 24.

98. See below, p. 289.

99. Kebell's reply indicates that he had, on a previous occasion, been asked to reside in the city. As no vacancy in the recordership had occurred since 1455, this request must have been made in connection with another appointment or an unrecorded proposal to replace Butler before 1485.

chosen to become a serjeant-at-law, it was clear that his presence in the town would be restricted to what was professionally necessary; in particular, he could not commit himself to be present for the assizes and the sessions. Suitable alternative arrangements, however, could certainly be made; other towns, Kebell pointed out, found it possible to have a serjeant as recorder – York, London, Bristol – so why not Coventry? As for the limitation on appearing against individual citizens, this Kebell declared was 'to streyte, not resonable, ne in eny Citie vsed'; it was clearly unrealistic for a lawyer to insist in arrangements with all his other clients, that they could not rely on him in suits with any individual Coventry citizen. Kebell's refusal was firm – the conditions were too high a price to pay. The city stood by its requirements; any relaxation 'the said Mair and his said brethourn thowt that hit myght not be for the wele & profet of this Cite, & specially to suffer his absens at the tyme of the assise or the sessions of the peace'. In contrast to Thomas Kebell, John Brown had no reservations and so the office was promised to him on Butler's death.

In the event, the demise of Henry Butler proved to be less imminent than the citizens of Coventry thought, and he survived until late in 1489.[100] Even then Brown did not obtain the recordership over which there had been such debate. The king asserted his interest and the next occupant of the office was not Brown, but Richard Empson.[101] Whether Empson accepted any of the restrictions offered to Kebell may be doubted, but well into the next century Coventry was still attempting to have its recorder in residence; in 1524, however, when the recorder, Ralph Swillington, became attorney-general, the town allowed him the liberty it had earlier denied to Serjeant Kebell to be non-resident and to be absent from assizes and sessions as the king's business required.[102] The principal reason for Kebell's failure to get the recordership was the self-esteem of the Coventry burgesses, but the tone of Kebell's letter suggests that he was himself lukewarm about the offer. The status he had achieved in his profession allowed him to pick and choose as it suited him.

With the substantial corporation of Leicester only a few miles from Kebell's home at Humberstone, it was natural for him to have a considerable professional connection with that city. Kebell acted for individual Leicester citizens, arbitrated in a town dispute, maintained a residence in the city, and in 1482–3 was admitted a freeman.[103] By

100. *Coventry Leet Book*, 537. 101. *ibid.*, 537, 547. 102. *ibid.*, 642, 688.
103. See above, pp. 119, 129–30; Kebell's house was in Humberstone Gate St, but he

1494 he enjoyed the office of recorder which he had refused at Coventry.[104] Leicester had been granted a recorder by the charter of 1464, and Kebell is the first known holder of the post. The Leicester recordership was much less developed than the post at Coventry – the principal task, on the surviving evidence, was holding the sessions of gaol delivery alongside the mayor – and the position was much more suited to Kebell's opinions on municipal office.[105] The town also may have had more than his legal qualification in mind. The Thomas Jakes who succeeded Kebell as recorder of Leicester was the same Thomas Jakes who followed the serjeant in the household of Lord Hastings.[106]

What did Kebell and lawyers like him do in return for these long-term retainers? In the case of some, it is clear that the payment reflected their importance and nothing more. Six months after rising to favour with Richard III, William Catesby was feed at five marks a year by Lord Stanley 'for his good will and counsel, past and to come'; in 1498, John Grevill granted £5 a year to Richard Empson 'for his good counsel past and to come' while in 1505 the receiver of Peterborough Abbey wrote against the fee paid to Edmund Dudley the significant phrase '*de secreto consilio domini regis*'.[107] Such payments no more indicate services performed than do the many fees received by Thomas Cromwell in his hey-day – most strikingly the £10 paid him by his rival, the duke of Norfolk.[108] Yet in law the liabilities of the genuine retainer for counsel were hardly greater. *Pro consilio* meant nothing more than advice if asked, certainly no obligation to conduct litigation or other business, and in *Oliver* v. *Emsonne*, decided early in Henry VIII's reign, it was held that an annuity to Richard Empson 'for counsel' remained in force even though he was a prisoner in the Tower.[109] But in practice clients expected a good deal for their money. Even the mere duty to give advice could be onerous. At Nottingham

had property elsewhere at different times. *Cal. inquisitions post mortem*, ii. 497; Bateson, *Leicester*, ii. 333, 351; *Freemen of Leicester, 1196–1770*, ed. H. Hartopp (1927), 54.

104. KB9/401/22.

105. Kebell was probably in office from December 1486, since he was then placed second to the mayor in the commission of gaol delivery, the precedence enjoyed from 1500 by Thomas Jakes as recorder; cf. Empson at Coventry: Bateson, *Leicester*, ii. 280, 452; *Cal. Patent Rolls, 1485–94*, 164, 212, 398; *ibid., 1494–1509*, 194, 230, 286, 288, 580.

106. See above, pp. 97–8.

107. *Cal. Ancient Deeds*, iv. 10182, 8418; *Peterborough Monastery*, xlviii.

108. H.M.C., *Mss. of the Marquess of Bath* (1904–8), ii. 7.

109. Baker, *Camb. Law Journ.* 27. 209.

in 1484–5, the recorder was being consulted, on average, once a month (sometimes for several days on end), and this in addition to other work for the city.[110] Some clients went to the lengths of spelling out the duties expected, as the abbot of Fountains did in 1484 when retaining John Pullen for life at 60s. 8d. a year (i.e. twopence a day).

Johannes Pulleyn, pro concessione premissa, in causis et negociis predicti Abbatis et successorum suorum, ad sumptus et expensas eorumden, quociens et quando oportune requisitus fuerit et commode potuerit, laborabit et equitabit et eorundem negocia fideliter sollicitabit et procurabit, et suum fidelem consilium in omnibus premissis semper impendet, ac sic semper pro fidele vassallo et serviente familiari dictorum Abbatis et suorum successorum per eosdem reputabitur et acceptabitur.[111]

More riskily, conditions could be imposed by word of mouth. William Langford of Stanton Harcourt apparently contemplated litigation to break his retainer of John Butler of Lincoln's Inn (serjeant in 1495),

to whom i recauntyd a annutye of xx marks soo that he schold do certayne thynges for me & myne, the wych he never dede nether performyd hys promisse in no thynge.[112]

For many lawyers, *pro consilio* meant not only being available for consultation, but also serving on a client's council, that executive board which assisted in the running of a major estate. As with the royal council, contemporary usage was innocent of any such distinction as a matter of degree, not kind, and it is anachronistic to try to divide counsellors from councillors. But for those concerned, a retainer *pro consilio* would involve attendance at periodic meetings, such as the attendance of the two Norfolk lawyers, John Heydon and Henry Spelman, at the meeting of Lord Grey's council in 1467–8, and a multitude of other duties.[113] In the six months before his arrest in April 1521, the duke of Buckingham paid Thomas Jubbes of Bristol and Thomas Matston of Wotton under Edge, two 'learnedmen' of his council, for, respectively, thirty-nine and forty days' attendance at Thornbury, to give 'advise and counseill in the said duke's causes'.[114] Given the duke's substantial employment of lawyers, it is not surprising to find the impersonality of the year books breaking down at the time of his execution:

110. *Records of the Borough of Nottingham*, ii. 229–41.
111. *Fountains Abbey*, i. 231–2. 112. *Bridgwater Borough Archives*, iv. 142, 861.
113. *Grey of Ruthin Valor*, 139; see below, p. 287.
114. E36/220 [*L. and P.*, iii. 1285(4)]. For a major discussion of the role of lawyers in a magnate's council, see Rawcliffe, *The Staffords*, 144–63, and 'Baronial councils', *passim*.

Dieu a sa ame graunte mercy car il fuit tresnoble Prince & prudent & mirror de tout courtoisie.[115]

Another activity which may have been remunerated by the permanent retainer was the sort of service Kebell did Lord Hastings as a 'working feoffee'. Clearly such work was not done gratis, and its enduring nature would make an annuity more appropriate than an initial, once-for-all payment.[116] Litigation too was expected of the retained lawyer, whatever the letter of the law said. The Mowbray account for 1422–3 includes among the costs of a plea to oust a royal nominee from a post properly in the earl marshal's gift, 6s. 8d. paid to:

divers servants, apprentices-at-law, retained with the lord in that case, because the serjeants-at-law who were of fee with the lord were king's serjeants-at-law, and for that reason could not plead in the aforementioned case.[117]

IV

Retaining for shorter periods – for a particular suit or particular duration – did not require the variety of service expected in the long-term contract, but the variety of forms is very similar. The best known retainer by indenture is that between Sir Robert Plumpton and John Yaxley in 1501, retaining the serjeant to appear at the Lammas assizes at York, Nottingham and Derby.[118] Traditionally, however, the majority of retainers are thought of as being by payment of a cash fee in advance.[119] The serjeant-at-law had an obligation to be of counsel on demand, and quite reasonably expected the security of payment at the time of hiring, but the custom was general. George Empson, apparently Sir Robert Plumpton's attorney, gives a precise description of such a retainer in a letter of 1500:

I received your letter by Mr. Sygskyke clerk and 2 ryals closed therin, and acording to your commandement I have retained in the Exchequer, by the

115. *Y.B.* Pas. 13 Hen. VIII, p. 1 f. 11.
116. R. H. Helmholz, 'The early enforcement of uses', in *Columbia Law Rev.* 79 (1979), 1509 shows that feoffees might be paid on appointment.
117. B.L. Add. Ch. 17209. This translation of *diversis servientibus apprenticiis ad legem* seems preferable to 'various serjeants apprentices-at-law' (J. L. Kirby, 'An account of Robert Southwell, receiver-general of John Mowbray, earl marshal, 1422–3', in *Bull. Institute of Hist. Research* 27 (1954), 198). Alternatively, the word *et* may be missing.
118. *Plumpton Correspondence*, 152–3.
119. Baker, *Camb. Law Journ.* 27. 210–13; cf. Kebell in *Y.B.* Pas. 5 Hen. VII, p. 1 f. 20.

advice of Mr Blakewall, Mr Denny, [and] in the Chauncry, Porter, and given unto them their fees.[120]

On the other hand it is certainly not true that all clients paid in advance. Richard Clavelleshay wrote from Somerset to John Brokhampton of Strand Inn, enclosing four bonds for a total of £36 13s. 4d.

Sir, I pray yow take actions accordyng to this obligacions aboverehersed, for the iiij obligacions ben due, savyng vij^{li} xiiij^{s} that y have receyvid . . . Also y pray yow sue this othir wrytte in Maister Brounyng ys name, and y wyll paye yowr feys for bothe.[121]

Lawyers were even prepared to do favours.[122] Sir William Plumpton's London agent wrote to him in 1469 in confusion over what, if anything, would be charged:

Mr. Midleton had great labour therewith; I profferd him no rewards because ye may reward him yourselfe as it please you. Maister Fairfax had x^{s} for that matter, all on. Mr. Suttill labored effectually; I tould him he shold be rewarded of the mony in his hands and [he] said lightly he would have none; so I wot whether he will take or no – he hath nott all paid yett. I pray you, against the next terme, send me word how I shall be demened in rewards giveing, for and it go to matter in law, it will cost mony largely.[123]

Particular factors might explain this instance – Thomas Middleton of Gray's Inn and Henry Sotehill, the attorney–general, were both related to Plumpton.[124] But at the Gloucester assizes of July 1453, Sir John Fastolf provided a breakfast for two lawyers '*quia non aliud regardia*' and in the 1470s Reginald Goldstone, writing to the prior of Christ Church, Canterbury, asked 'I pray yow send me word whedyr I shall pay Townysende and Vyncent Vinche [sic] theyr fees, and howe moche'.[125] Professional regulation was in its infancy and it was a

120. *Plumpton Correspondence*, 145. 121. *Bridgwater Borough Archives*, iv. 858.

122. In addition to their charitable obligations to the poor, or on other grounds; cf. 'Guy Fairfax said openly att the barre that he knew so, verily, they were not guilty – that he wold labor their deliverance for almes, not takeing a penny': *Plumpton Correspondence*, 35. 123. *ibid.*, 23.

124. *ibid.*, lxxi–lxxii, lxxxi–lxxxii; Thorne, *Readings and Moots*, i. xix; *Cal. Patent Rolls, 1461–7*, 6.

125. B.L. Add. Ms. 28206 f. 124; *Christ Church Letters*, 31. Roger Townshend was the future J.C.P.; Vincent Finch was chirographer of the common pleas. Hastings, *Common Pleas*, 281; Wedgwood, *Biographies*.

126. Cf. the report of the duke of Buckingham's Welsh estates *c.* 1500: 'The Courte Clerk [of Newport] ys spoken with and thurghly appoynted with for his attendaunce to kepe the shires and courtes betwene this and Michelmas, but from thensfurth he graunteth not to geve ferther attendaunce yn that rome enlesse then

matter for individual calculation when and indeed whether to claim a fee from a known and valued, or potentially valuable employer.[126] The corollary is equally true; for anyone outside the circle of known clients or a lawyer's own social group, counsel might be hard to find, as Robert Pilkington had discovered when called unexpectedly to the Derby assizes of July 1498:

> the said Robert come to Derby and hade no space to gete no frendes nore counsayle owte of his cuntre but his ij servandes, and when he come to Derby hade non acuayntancez with no lerned mon, but with gret labur and gret cost gete on lernyd mon calde Mayster Robert Byrtenell that neyver afore herde tell of his matter.[127]

Later, however, Pilkington was more fortunate, for he records that Brudenell and Kebell sometimes waived their fees.[128]

The most striking evidence that lawyers in pre-Reformation England saw employment in commercial rather than professional terms was their willingness to work on credit. An annual fee was normally paid in arrears and not always promptly. Christopher Jenney, the future judge, was retained by the Le Strange family in the 1520s; his fee, due at Michaelmas, was sometimes as late as 31 December, and once he was paid nothing at all for twenty months.[129] Attorneys and general legal agents were particularly obliging. The accounts of Fastolf's executors show that the fee of John Jenney, their attorney in the London Guildhall, was at one time seven years in arrears.[130] These managers had also to carry the day-to-day expenses of their clients, much as a solicitor does today. In consequence, where payment in advance was insisted on by a pleader, it was more often than not the manager who put up the money, and likewise with court fees and clerical charges. Sometimes there is a specific reference to litigation being financed by the lawyer, as in the Le Strange account which notes a payment in March 1523, 'to Mr. Knyghtley for his fee & for that money that he leyde oute for suyng Symon Holden'.[131] More frequently credit is implicit, as in the Le Strange account where

he may be thenne ascirtayned what fee he shall perseve for the same.' Staffordshire Record Office, D641/1/5/3.

127. 'Wombwell Mss.', 39.

128. *ibid.*, 53–4.

129. 'Le Strange', *Archaeologia* 25. 475, 494.

130. Magdalen College, Fastolf Ms. 42. *Plumpton Correspondence*, 115 shows one attorney refusing to finance a client further.

131. 'Le Strange', *Archaeologia* 25. 467. Cf. the action brought by Hugh Jones, attorney of common pleas, to recover money 'leyd owt' for a client: C1/529/39.

Knightley presented a bill for 'costs of sute for iij termes'.[132] In major litigation a client might pay by instalments. The bill which Thomas Playter of Lincoln's Inn presented to the Fastolf executors, covering the year 1459–60, indicates that he met the £6 9s. 9½d. spent in the Michaelmas term out of his own pocket, and it was not until Hilary that any sums from the executors reached him.[133] That term meant additional payments, including the arrears of several attorneys, but eventually sufficient was paid to Playter to put the executors a few shillings in credit. Easter term saw Playter once more dipping into his own resources as instalments fell behind, and the gap widened still further during Trinity. The end-of-year tally gave a deficit against the client of £6 10s. 10d. on the four terms, plus Playter's fee of five marks and a livery gown, a cash equivalent of nearly £10.

V

The most obscure area of legal employment remains to be considered: the miscellaneous duties for which lawyers were required. Payments for drawing documents show that such work was normally the province of the lower ranks or even the fringe members of the profession. In 1530, William Brereton, a prominent Cheshire gentleman at the royal court, had agreements with his bailiffs put into legal form by the clerk to John Skewys, Wolsey's former adviser.[134] The Carpenters' Company of London employed a scrivener from 1480 to 1483 to write the rules of the craft, to read and see acquittances, to provide a copy in English of a testament and to write the annual accounts, and the scrivener's servant was paid for overseeing bonds.[135] But if the matter was significant, then major figures would be involved. Following the death of Thomas Stonor in 1474, the family consulted John Twyneo, the recorder of Bristol, over the inquisition *post mortem*; in Henry VIII's reign the Le Stranges of Hunstanton employed William Yelverton of Gray's Inn to draw up an agreement, and the Manners family called upon a serjeant-at-law to advise on the earl of Rutland's funeral in 1543.[136] For this non-litigious work lawyers must often have

132. 'Le Strange', *Archaeologia* 25. 468. On an earlier occasion Christopher Jenney advanced money to buy land: *ibid.*, 455. Cf. the loan by Thomas Stotevile of Lincoln's Inn to the priory of Ely to secure the union of a living with the priory: PROB11/5 f. 167v.

133. Fastolf Ms. 71.

134. SC6 Henry VIII/404 f. 24.

135. *Carpenters' Company*, ii. 58–9, 60–1, 64–5.

136. *Stonor Letters and Papers*, i. 145; 'Supplementary Stonor letters and papers', 11; 'Le Strange', *Archaeologia* 25. 541; *Rutland Papers*, iv. 343.

agreed terms in advance or simply submitted a bill, but there are signs that such services were originally remunerated by a gratuity or reward, not an agreed fee. The payment for the York charter of 1442 includes the costs incurred but describe the remuneration of the lawyers involved as for 'advice, favour and work in the said matter'.[137] Yet this point cannot be made too confidently as the terms 'fee' and 'reward' were becoming synonymous.[138]

An area of legal work where information is particularly scarce is the land market. That lawyers were in demand is clear from contract after contract specifying that a sale must be executed 'by advice of learned council'. Details, however, are hard to find. The Le Strange accounts refer to several land purchases, but the legal costs do not appear; perhaps Christopher Jenney's annual retainer covered such work.[139] The limited case-law adds little. Kebell was engaged in a thrice-reported case arising from the failure of an agreement to make an estate to the plaintiff 'in fee, by enfeoffment or by fine or otherwise as his counsel learned in the law advised'.[140] The plaintiff's story was that his counsel was John Wekes or Wilcks, possibly the Wiltshire escheator, who had advised procedure by deed, and that the plaintiff had informed the defendant.[141] The latter seems to have claimed that no advice was given, even though asked for.

In the years before the dissolution of the monasteries, the purchase of land was probably a less important source of legal employment than family settlements were, but evidence is no more plentiful there. The accounts of Fastolf's executors record the charges for a new enfeoffment of Sir John's manors of Dedham and Runham, made in 1457–8.[142] The cost was £10 9s. 0d., over half going on the royal licence necessary, with 20s. being paid for counsel; unfortunately no details are given. But even this limited evidence must suggest that legal business which amounted overall to a very considerable total is eluding investigation.

Slightly more can be said of the terms for the engagement of

137. *York Memorandum Book*, iii. 130.

138. Baker, *Camb. Law Journ.* 27. 207.

139. Cf. *Fountains Abbey*, iii. 36, 77.

140. *Y.B.* Trin. 6 Hen. VII, p. 3 f. 4; Hil. 11 Hen. VII, p. 15 f. 17; Trin. 11 Hen. VII, p. 1 f. 23.

141. *Cal. Patent Rolls, 1485–94*, 471; cf. the John Wykes employed by the Pastons. *William* Wylkes was prothonotary of the common pleas 1487–98: Spelman, *Reports*, ii. 377. Another John Wykes was an attorney and possibly of Gray's Inn: Baker, *Journ. Legal Hist.* 1. 203.

142. Fastolf Ms. 42.

lawyers for arbitration. Where this was arranged by mutual consent of the parties there seems to have been no necessity to secure prior agreement from those named as arbitrators; this, at least, is the inference from the 1495 Pilkington arbitration.[143] The 1498 arbitration, involving Kebell, suggests that judges would sometimes propose arbitrators with equal ignorance of their willingness or availability.[144] There was greater involvement, perhaps, when arbitrators were imposed upon disputants at the behest of the king or one of the magnates. The representatives whom the earl of Northumberland sent to settle the quarrel between the city of York and the dean and chapter arrived within days and took the opportunity to settle a dispute among the aldermen at the same time.[145] On the other hand, Mayor Shillingford of Exeter found in the 1440s that the eminent, even when willing, were not necessarily reliable as arbitrators – time after time distractions and political considerations delayed settlement of a quarrel between the city and the cathedral.[146] One related device which he tried as 'the reule of the lordis' dragged on was a direct settlement out of court, 'a day of entrety, ij of their counseyll y called to and ij of oures'.[147] Each side attempted to engage a powerful team:

> They nempted Coplestone yn certeyn, Hengston or Wode for their part. Y, Mayer, nempted Radeforde in certeyn, Hody, Beef or Douryssh as y myghte gete, and so departed. The whiche dey at Seynt Peter's we mette with bothe counseill, but they fayled of Hengston and broghte Copleston and More. We faylled Radeford and broghte Beef and Douryshe.

But this assembly of legal talent was not a success; the dean called off any agreement because William Hyndestone was absent. There is no evidence of the way either party attempted to ensure the attendance of counsel. When Kebell represented Coventry his appointment was entered in the town books, but given the personal involvement of the mayor in this Exeter loveday, parol retainers seem probable. However, certain of the counsel named by Shillingford may have been in receipt of a regular retainer by fee and livery although the one who certainly was, Nicholas Radford the recorder, was the very one who would not, or could not, turn up.

The historian's hardest task is not to establish the facts about the past but to understand the past in its own terms. It is one thing to survey

143. See above, p. 128. 144. See above, p. 129. 145. See above, p. 127.
146. *Letters of Shillingford*, 69–72. 147. *Ibid.*, 45–6.

Thomas Kebell's law practice but quite another to attempt to reach a general conclusion on the shape of law practice in pre-Reformation England. If anything, the evidence suggests that there was no such thing as a characteristic or consistent pattern to professional work. The enormous range of a lawyer's activities, his integration with his own particular community and the Westminster dimension which took him outside that community, the absence of professional regulation and the consequent market economy in legal skills, all this produced an atmosphere of opportunity and *laissez-faire* in marked contrast to contemporary assumptions about place, hierarchy and regulation. Indeed, this in itself suggests what must have drawn men to the profession, over and above the material opportunities which it offered – the variety and challenge of the law. It may be hopelessly anachronistic to write of 'job-satisfaction', but it is difficult to imagine that Kebell's career was not a satisfying one. Travel, contact with men and affairs, a place in events, sometimes great events, responsibility, initiative, argument and intellectual combat – this was what the law was about, as well as making money. The law was not simply a way to get rich, it was a profession with glamour.

7

THE LAWYER AND THE YEAR BOOKS

The picture of Thomas Kebell's law practice drawn in the previous chapters has frequently stressed his connections with his community – social and topographical. He has appeared the servant of Leicestershire folk in general, and the Hastings and their retinue in particular, as much as or more than a 'gentleman of London'. Given the evidence, this is inevitable, but it distorts the picture. Local connections were the backbone of practice, but it was successful practice at Westminster which helped to bring local clients; Leicestershire people went to Kebell not simply because they knew him or some friend knew him, but because he was successful in the central royal courts. And what was true of practice will also be found to be true of the rewards of practice; Leicestershire connections enabled Thomas Kebell to set up as a squire, but his Westminster practice gave him the means to do so. Centre and locality each informed the other.

Anyone wanting to study the role of the lawyer in the central courts faces serious problems. Court records are uniformly silent upon judges and counsel and, except in equity, compress the actual suit into a few lines of a formulary. Some letters survive, occasionally a few bills of legal costs; cause papers and the miscellanea of litigation rarely. The only material preserved by the lawyers and the only material of any quantity at all is provided by the year books.

In their most familiar form, the edition of 1678–80, the year books are eleven large folio volumes covering every reign from Edward II to Henry VIII, with the exception of Richard II; each is divided by regnal years and subdivided into the law terms – hence the title used in Kebell's inventory, 'a book of years and terms'.[1] But despite this impressive appearance, year books present enormous problems.[2]

1. See below, p. 445.
2. For the following, and reference to previous discussion of the problems of the year books, see Ives, *L.Q.R.* 89. 64–86 (alternatively 'The origins of the later year books', in *Legal History Studies 1972*, ed. Dafydd Jenkins (Cardiff, 1975), 136–51). Cf. Simpson, *L.Q.R.* 87. 94–118; Abbot, *Law Reporting*, 9–36; Spelman, *Reports*, ii. *164–78*.

They are in law-French, abbreviated, corrupt and sometimes unintelligible. For the later fifteenth and the early sixteenth century, authoritative manuscripts have virtually disappeared, and the printed text took fifty years of publishing before it reached its present form. To confuse matters still further, manuscripts do exist outside the canon, and printed material too of a variety of kinds, and the relationship with the received text is anything but clear. Dating is often totally inaccurate; Kebell died in June 1500 but he figures in twenty-nine cases for the year 1500–1 and in two cases of 1505.[3] Some years and terms are missing, and within each term by no means all cases are noted, perhaps one or two, perhaps several dozen. Thus Kebell's last thirteen terms as an apprentice are covered by fourteen cases from the single term of Edward V's reign, eleven cases labelled Michaelmas 1 Richard III, fifty-three described as Michaelmas 2 Richard III and sixty-four cases from 1 Henry VII. The great majority of year-book cases come from only one court, the common pleas, there is no standard form or length of entry, and it is rare to be told the names of the litigants. Indeed, although it is convenient to describe the later year books as 'law reports', the term is misleading. Their interest is not in cases so much as in pleading, and the reporter noted as much of a suit as served this interest; the decision of the court is all too rarely given.

Even more disquiet is roused by the question 'how were year books produced?' There is almost no external evidence, but textual criticism suggest that they originated in the private notes which lawyers took of cases for their own information. These might be copied up in year-book form or according to some other arrangement or none, and both the original notes and the copies might circulate among the profession. Borrowers would organise, omit or conflate at will, and add, abbreviate and annotate. A further complication was the arrival of the printed year book. Publishers obtained what copy they could and licked this into commercial shape, improving and expanding their text in successive editions. Whether or not there was organised year-book production in the fourteenth century, by Kebell's day it had disappeared. It is impossible to talk of 'the' year book for *anno* this or that or to assume that year books reflect the calendar of the courts. They reflect only the interests of the succession of individual lawyers who contributed to that text which finally was put into print.

3. The figure of 30 in Ives, *L.Q.R.* 89. 75 is an arithmetical error; the cases in *Y.B.* 21 Hen.VII are Mich., p. 55 f. 39 and p. 67 f. 41.

I

This review of the sources indicates clearly that many questions about the pre-Reformation lawyer in court cannot be answered satisfactorily. With Kebell there are even problems in accounting for his appearances in the year books. Not only is Thomas Kebell the most noticed counsel in all the year books of Henry VII, but in the whole history of these reports, few lawyers, if any, have received such attention. He speaks in four, six and even ten times as many cases as other serjeants, and his opinions are more often noted than those of the chief justice of the common pleas himself. His obvious importance and skill are suggested in the deference regularly accorded him, yet this degree of attention must raise a question. Of 566 entries for his period as a serjeant where the names of lawyers are given, Kebell appears in 314. Why should he receive such overwhelming notice?

The answer seems to lie in this vexed puzzle of year-book bibliography. Analysis shows that there are significant differences within the text in the attention paid to the serjeant. The reports for the relevant years reached the printing press at five different dates; years 3 to 8 Henry VII were published in 1505 along with part of year 1 and year 2 which reached essentially their present form after additions in 1530; 9 and 12 Henry VII appeared in 1509 and 14 and 15 Henry VII in 1529. A°10, 11, 13 and 16 did not appear until 1555. This piecemeal publication clearly indicates that the reports for the reign did not circulate as a single corpus and, indeed, those published in 1555 need to be divided into A°10, 13 and 16, which Fitzherbert knew and used for his *Graunde Abridgement*, and A°11, which he did not.[4] In most of the books for Henry VII's reign, Kebell's name occurs in between twenty and fifty per cent of cases where lawyers are recorded – not excessive proportions for a prominent advocate. Material outside the year-book canon is similar. In Harleian Ms. 1624, a miscellaneous collection of early Tudor cases, Kebell is the pleader most in evidence, but he appears in fewer than half of the cases where lawyers are named; in the reports associated with Robert Keilwey, Kebell again leads: he is named in ten cases out of nineteen, but John Mordaunt occurs seven and Thomas Frowyk six times.[5] In the year books for 10, 13 and 16 Henry VII, however, the situation is entirely

4. Abbott, *Law Reporting*, 18.
5. For B.L. Harl. Ms. 1624, see Simpson, *L.Q.R.* 73. 103; Ives, *L.Q.R.* 89. 77–8, 80.

different. Kebell appears in seventy-five per cent of cases; in total he takes part in 125 discussions, and two-fifths of all his notice in the year books are concentrated in these three years. The best that Chief Justice Bryan can make is 67 appearances, and the other serjeants are nowhere. One explanation of Thomas Kebell's unnatural prominence therefore, is that the year-book canon includes a collection of reports peculiarly concerned with him.

An attractive hypothesis is that this collection was Kebell's own. But although certain entries do appear to be *obiter dicta* of Kebell, and others show awareness of his motives, it is unlikely that the text as it is today stemmed from him. In the report for Trinity 10 Henry VII an interchange between Kebell and Bryan ends with a retort by the chief justice and the reporter's comment, *ad quod non responsum*; in 13 Henry VII the reporter inserts a comment into one of Kebell's speeches and an *ideo quaere bene de hoc* into another; 16 Henry VII had Kebell asserting a congruency and Bryan expressing doubt, 'Kebell said that those cases were clear, therefore query'.[6] An alternative suggestion is that these reports originated at the Inner Temple. Support for this comes from one entry in 13 Henry VII where the common pleas case of *The Abbot of Hyde* v. *Benger* is followed by a discussion out of court, probably at, and certainly between members of the Inner Temple, in which Kebell explained the line he had taken; a discussion which recalled affectionately the favourite maxim of a former fellow, Edward Grantham.[7] Two facts, however, argue against this. First, the year books for 10, 13 and 16 Henry VII do not concentrate on other fellows and former members of the Inner Temple; the interest is personal to Kebell. Secondly, there is good evidence of Inner Temple material in other sources where Kebell's pronouncements receive more restrained attention.[8] Kebell's clerk or one of his pupils may, of course, have been responsible. A personal connection is implied in a postscript to a case entered under 10 Henry VII:

Kebell veniendo de Westminster dit, si le barre ne soit bon, & le title ne soit bon, donques le recover sur seisin & disseisin trove &c, car cest bien trove. Et icy est mieux pour le plaintiff que recovera in Assise que ne sera amende: car donques est mal barre & mal title & il recovera sur le residue trove. Quod nota.[9]

6. *Y.B.* Trin. 10 Hen.VII, p. 13 f. 27; Mich. 13 Hen.VII, p. 3 f. 7; Pas. 13 Hen.VII, p. 8 f. 22; Pas. 16 Hen.VII, p. 4 f. 6.
7. *ibid.*, Trin. 13 Hen.VII, p. 6 f. 28.
8. Simpson, *L.Q.R.* 73. 95–103; Thorne, *Readings and Moots*, i. xlvii; Spelman, *Reports*, ii. *166*, *169*, *171*.
9. *Y.B.* Pas. 10 Hen.VII, p. 27 f. 23. Cf. Hil. 6 Hen.VII, p. 8 f. 15: '*Nota per*

The Grantham reference might suggest the same. But against this is the brief entry under 10 Henry VII of a statement by Kebell which ends *quaere quia non interfui* and for 16 Henry VII the note '*et Kebell dit que cest fuit adjuge, sed non dixit ubi*'.[10]

Kebell himself, admirers at the Inner Temple, personal colleagues and friends, none can be credited with the year books for 10, 13 and 16 Henry VII as they now stand. Of course the composite nature of the books is as true for these years as for any others, and it would be quite possible for any or all of these contributors to have responsibility for items in the existing texts. It would, however, require detailed bibliographical analysis to disentangle the constituents of each year book, if, indeed, this could ever be done. Until then it is possible only to note that the excessive response to Thomas Kebell in the reports is a bibliographical peculiarity of certain sources.

II

Stripped of the excessive prominence of the year books for A°10, 13 and 16 Henry VII, Kebell remains, but more credibly, the leading member of the bar; from his debut as a serjeant he rapidly became the most talked-of counsel in the land. One factor was undoubtedly professional success; we must believe, with Burton, that Kebell was 'one of the greatest practice in those days'.[11] Another was the particular advantage he enjoyed between 1489 and 1496, when anyone seeking a serjeant was bound to consider him.[12] But Kebell's contributions are also partially explained by the method of discussion in the late-medieval courts. The initial speeches in a report seem normally to be by the counsel engaged in the case; sometimes this is stated, sometimes it can be inferred. Yet not all debate is confined to them. Kebell's first reported remarks in common pleas were in a case of dower in 1486.[13] This was opened by Jay and Vavasour, but they were followed by Wode, Fineux, Kebell, Rede and Fisher, before the judges gave their opinions. On occasion the whole order of the coif

Townshend *veniendo de* Westminster *quod* . . .'; Mich. 20 Hen. VII, p. 18 f. 9: '*Et veniendo de* Westminster *jeo ouy Monseignier* Fineux *dire* . . .'.

10. *ibid.*, Hil. 10 Hen.VII, p. 14 f. 16; Mich. 16 Hen.VII, p. 2 f. 1. Cf. Hil. 13 Hen.VII, p. 15 f. 16: 'Kebell *mouva l'court a aver un brief a l'evesque de luy assoiler ove un peine in mesme le brief. Mes ascuns semble q'il aura primes un brief sans peine*.'

11. See above, p. 3.

12. See above, pp. 75–6.

13. *Y.B.* Pas. 1 Hen.VII, p. 3 ff. 17–19.

might speak; *Broke* v. *Latimer*, in common pleas in 12 Henry VII, saw Kebell and Yaxley representing the parties, and their submissions were followed by comments from all the other serjeants and the four judges.[14]

The status of these subsequent speakers is not easy to determine. Sometimes they were counsel engaged by the parties (for example, king's serjeants in crown suits). This is clear in a report from 5 Henry VII where Kebell was opposed by *touts les serjeants retenus encontre luy*, and is implied in a common pleas case of 12 Henry VII where Mordaunt, speaking first, and to the same effect as Kebell's opening, used this illustration:

the manor of Northsoure is the manor of Soure, and North is only an addition. For example, if there were a manor of D which is Mordaunt's manor and another manor of D which is Kebell's manor, in that case one is called Mordaunt's manor and the other Kebell's manor; in that case a fine of the manor of D levied by Master Kebell is good without calling it Kebell's manor – for the manor of D is the name and the rest is only a usage to know one from the other.[15]

Co-operation was not only between serjeants; John Butler and Thomas Kebell appeared together for Sir Roger Townshend in the late 1480s when Butler had almost ten years ahead of him before he reached the coif.[16] In some cases serjeants were engaged in support of apprentices already retained, as in a king's bench case of 9 Henry VII where William Grevill appeared with Humphrey Sedgewick against Humphrey Coningsby and William Rudhale but where Serjeant Rede was also engaged with Coningsby and it was Kebell's intervention which secured a last-minute respite by asserting precedents in Grevill's favour.[17] Most strikingly, when Thomas Marowe was counsel in a chancery case in 8 Henry VII, he left the entire conduct of the plea to a serjeant.[18]

Many of Kebell's year-book appearances fall into these two categories, acting as leader or as one of a team. In other reports, however, his contribution seems to be spontaneous. A suit over an annuity was being conducted between Wode, Fineux and Vavasour, and Kebell intervened to point out that *nos livres* were ambiguous; in another example where Thomas Oxenbridge was pleading, Kebell suggested

14. *ibid.*, Mich. 12 Hen. VII, p. 7 ff. 11–13.
15. *ibid.*, Trin. 5 Hen. VII, p. 3 f. 36; Mich. 12 Hen. VII, p. 4 ff. 6–7.
16. *ibid.*, Trin. 11 Hen. VII, p. 4 f. 25.
17. *ibid.*, Mich. 9 Hen. VII, p. 3 ff. 6–7.
18. *ibid.*, Mich. 8 Hen. VII, p. 4 ff. 7–8. Cf. Brudenell and Kebell, above, p. 123.

a tactic he could employ.[19] Kebell was not alone in what can only be sheer professional enthusiasm – on occasions it could lead a whole court far from the matter in hand. Thus in 1491 the king's bench had little difficulty in rejecting the claim of a defendant who had been dispossessed of his lands but, on re-entering after harvest, had seized wheat which the disseisor had sown and reaped.[20] Justice Fairfax, however, went on to reminisce about a nice distinction which had been sustained in 1471–2 when he was practising as a serjeant, between the product of man's energy – such as corn grown from seed – and the product of nature – such as hay, logs, apples or nuts. Thomas Tremayle and other serjeants standing by agreed that this was good law, although when Fairfax was asked whether the goods could be recovered after removal from the disputed property and he answered no, the reporter records his own and perhaps his neighbours' doubts. Thomas Kebell then posed an even more elaborate conceit; given that the disseisor sowed the land and that then the disseisee entered, only to be expelled again by the disseisor who reaped the crop, if the disseisee then re-entered a second time he could not take the harvest for himself! The reporter challenged this, perhaps reflecting the debate in court, and after this the rights of feoffee of a disseisor were discussed. The whole debate is hypothetical but it gets a high commendation in the year book, *quaere bene de ceste matter quia bona*.

Not all interventions, however, were inspired by casual professional curiosity. It is clear that the serjeants were expected to argue as *amici curiae*. A case of trespass reported under Trinity 13 Henry VII reads, '*apres que les serjants avoient peruse le barre (quibus argumentis non interfui)*, Vavasour . . .', and so continues with the judges' opinions.[21] In a *quare impedit* dated Easter 1490, Kebell so destroyed the argument of the opposing counsel, Richard Jay, that '*tout le court tient cler &c nul question . . . purque de cest mater les serjants &c juges furent discharges de argument*'.[22] The formal nature of this consultation comes out in a suit of 14 Henry VII to enforce an annuity.[23] Kebell opened for the plaintiff, Constable replied and Kebell demurred; on a second day, when the reporter was absent, *fuit argue per les serjeants* and on a third day by the justices, with Wode,

19. *ibid.*, Hil. 9 Hen. VII, p. 10 f. 17; Pas. 10 Hen. VII, p. 30 f. 24. Cf. Mich. 9 Hen. VII, p. 6 f. 10.
20. *ibid.*, Hil. 5 Hen. VII, p. 9 ff. 16–17.
21. *ibid.*, Trin. 13 Hen. VII, p. 5 f. 26. The new serjeants also appeared together: *ibid.*, Pas. 1 Hen. VII, p. 2 ff. 14–17.
22. *ibid.*, Pas. 5 Hen. VII, p. 1 f. 20.
23. *ibid.*, Trin. 14 Hen. VII, p. 8 f. 31.

the puisne, rehearsing *tout le matier*, presumably both the case and the arguments of the coif. The results of these discussions are possibly to be found in year-book entries such as *fuit tenus per les serjeants & touts les justices*' or 'Bryan, chief justice, *auxy dit expressement & agre per le grander part des justices & serjeants*.[24] Bryan put this collective responsibility in a striking way when he demolished a contention of Thomas Wode in a discussion about *capias*:

> and that for a single argument, the counterpart of what, in manner, is agreed by all my fellows as well on the bench as at the bar.[25]

An even more important though less regular involvement of the serjeants in the construction of the law was their work in exchequer chamber, that 'assembly of all the judges of England for matters of law'.[26] Points for discussion could arise from litigation and be forwarded by the court concerned, or be raised by the judges in principle or be put by the crown or its officers. During Kebell's years as a serjeant, exchequer chamber meetings took place at least two or three times a year, though most frequently in the earlier years, in the wake of the political upheaval of 1485. In many reports individual contributions are not recorded, but Kebell spoke in twelve of the fifteen cases where names are known. The most completely reported, *Sir William Stonor's Case*, includes perhaps twenty speeches by three apprentices, the king's attorney, five serjeants (Kebell included) and six of the seven judges.[27] Where the serjeants were united in exchequer chamber, their influence could be decisive. In *Crofts* v. *Beauchamp* 'the justices were not of one mind . . . and so the justices yielded to the serjeants and apprentices'.[28] Exchequer chamber decisions passed rapidly into circulation. *Higford's Case* was argued in Hilary 1487 and in Michaelmas 1488 in *Lord Dacre's Case* Kebell stated the ruling 'as it was adjudged in the case of Hickford lately'.[29] It is possible also that the concurrence of the serjeants is implied where decisions are annotated *per bon advis*. 'To be advised' is already used to describe adjournment for further consideration by the bench, and justices

24. *ibid.*, Pas. 9 Hen.VII, p. 11 f. 24; Trin. 14 Hen.VII, p. 2 f. 28. Cf. Keilwey, *Reports*, f. 24v: 'quod *fuit dedictum per touts les serjeants & per* Vavasour *adonques solement en le* benche'.
25. *ibid.*, Pas. 14 Hen.VII, p. 2 f. 21.
26. Hemmant, *Exchequer Chamber*, i. xiii.
27. *Y.B.* Trin. 12 Hen.VII, p. 1 ff. 19–22; Mich. 13 Hen.VII, p. 3 ff. 4–9, p. 12 ff. 11–12. See below, pp. 248–57.
28. *ibid.*, Trin. 1 Hen.VII, p. 6 f. 29.
29. *ibid.*, Hil. 2 Hen.VII, p. 14 f. 12; Trin. 2 Hen.VII, p. 3 ff. 17–19. See below, p. 240.

would certainly discuss a case privately before and during a hearing.[30] But *bon* may imply something more. When Kebell claimed that the common pleas could issue *certiorari* against justices of the peace:

the court said to him that they would be advised until the next day. And then the next day the justices of the common pleas sent Vavasour to the king's bench, who came back and said that those of the king's bench were divided in opinion and said that the case was one on which it was good to be advised (*fuit bon d'estre avise*). And for this doubt the matter was adjourned to the next term.[31]

III

The obvious importance of exchequer chamber rulings and decisions taken after deliberate discussion immediately raises the general question, what was authority for the pre-Reformation legal profession? There is no simple answer since year-book debates are so very varied. As against the items warranted *per bon advis* are others where doubt is implied, and not only because the reporter has added 'query'. The absence of justices is carefully noted, and the bench certainly thought that security lay in numbers. In 1491 Tremayle was alone in king's bench and gave his views with the proviso 'I wish to be advised until Fairfax comes'.[32] Special attention is given to the whereabouts of the two chief justices, and without them what a bench said was clearly tentative.[33] In *The Corporation of Waterford* v. *Thomas Thwaytes* in exchequer chamber:

Hussey, chief justice, said that statutes made in England bound those in Ireland, which was not seriously challenged (*moult dedit*) by the other justices, notwithstanding that some of them were of the contrary opinion the previous term in his absence.[34]

Most year-book cases, moreover, do not go beyond discussion. Sometimes the report tells of procedural arguments (often hypothetical), which the court held 'clear' or 'denied utterly'.[35] There are occasions

30. *ibid.*, Mich. 10 Hen.VII, p. 14 f. 7, p. 18 f. 8.
31. *ibid.*, Pas. 13 Hen.VII, p. 7 ff. 21–2.
32. *ibid.*, Trin. 10 Hen.VII, p. 10 f. 27; Mich. 10 Hen.VII, p. 15 f. 8; cf. Hil. 6 Hen.VII, p. 6 f. 14: 'Kebell *estants absent*'; Pas. 6 Hen.VII, p. 1 f. 1; cf. Trin. Edw. V, p. 2 f. 2: 'Starky *ne poiet tarier &c pur ceo* Bryan *ne arguoit plus.*'
33. *ibid.*, Hil. 6 Hen.VII, p. 9 f. 15, p. 6 f. 14: 'Danvers *fuit de mesme l'opinion absente* Bryan.'
34. *ibid.*, Mich. 1 H.VII, p. 2 f. 3.
35. *ibid.*, Pas. 5 Hen.VII, p. 1 f. 20; Trin. 6 Hen.VII, p. 5 f. 5; Mich. 9 Hen.VII, p. 3 f. 7; Pas. 9 Hen.VII, p. 2 f. 23, p. 11 f. 24; Hil. 10 Hen.VII, p. 1 f. 12.

when justices or counsel will claim this or that as 'clear law', 'common knowledge', 'common erudition' or the 'common course', but are these more than *obiter dicta*?[36] At other times agreement is claimed *in maniere* which appears to mean 'in effect', or the reporter records a majority opinion – '*l'opinion des touts les justices* (except Bryan & Jenney) *fuit*' – or a reserved position – '*mes* Bryan & Wode *disoient expressement que* . . .'.[37] But it is a rare example which ends, as a *capias* case of 14 Henry VII, in collective discussion followed by a ruling by one of the bench:[38]

Vavasour . . . Wode to the contrary . . . Bryan to the contrary . . . with which Danvers agreed. Therefore it was awarded by Vavasour *ex assensu sociorum suorum* that . . .

Far more typical is the common pleas case, probably from 1489–94, where Vavasour J. said:

We have all in effect (*in maniere*) agreed some time ago (*devant celle temps*) that . . .

Bryan replied:

This has been held (*tenu*) as you say within the last two years before us ourselves, but it was not a judgement (*ne fuit pas adjuge*) and perhaps never will be . . .[39]

This fluid attitude becomes even more apparent when bench and bar turn to the year books. Appeal to *nos livres* is routine: '*Est un question in nos livres si* . . .'; '*il ad este tenu in nos livres* . . .'; '*ceo ad este souvent fois adjuge en nos livres* . . .'; '*il vouldroit montrer livres de cest ple* . . .'.[40] But what is being referred to, and how?[41] In almost half the reports in which Kebell cites precedents he did provide some approximate reference, generally the regnal year, but sometimes the circumstances or the names of the parties. For example, in a *praecipe quod reddat* of 1489 to 1493 he said:

36. *ibid.*, Mich. 11 Hen.VII, p. 19 f. 5; Pas. 14 Hen.VII, p. 2 f. 20; see below, pp. 160–1.
37. *ibid.*, Pas. 14 Hen. VII, p. 2 f. 21; Mich. 1 Ric. III, p. 9 f. 4; Hil. 14 Hen. VII, p. 6 f. 17. Even a judgement could be by a majority and so vulnerable: Hil. 6 Hen.VII, p. 6 f. 15: 'Bryan *dit que il ne vouloit donner judgement . . . mes si un de ses compagnons vouloient donner il vouloit agreer entant que chescuns este incontre luy mesme*.'
38. *ibid.*, Pas. 14 Hen.VII p. 2 f. 21; cf. Pas. 10 Hen.VII, p. 24 f. 23.
39. *ibid.*, Trin. 11 Hen.VII, p. 2 f. 24.
40. *ibid.*, Mich. 9 Hen.VII, p. 3 f. 7; Hil. 9 Hen.VII, p. 10 f. 17; Pas. 9 Hen.VII, p. 3 f. 23; Mich. 14 Hen.VII, p. 15 f. 7.
41. Cf. Hemmant, *Exchequer Chamber*, i. lxxix-lxxxiii, ii. xviii-xxiii; Lewis, *L.Q.R.* 46. 207–24, 341–60; 47. 411–27; Spelman, *Reports*, ii. *159–63*.

that this case . . . was adjudged good, now of late in the case of Wilmer in the time of the present king. And he showed a copy of the record (*le copie del' record*). And the court said that this case was adjudged *per bon advis*, and therefore they thought this case good law.[42]

It may be, also, that Kebell provided citations more frequently than this, for a reporter in one case noted Kebell as saying '*il ad est adjuge*' and then added '*sed non dixit ubi*'.[43] Certainly in Trinity 5 Henry VII plea 5 folio 41, a case printed by Pynson within fifteen years of being heard, Kebell is credited with saying:

et iij H[enry] VI Littilton tient que ceo va en barre. Et en xxj E[dward] IIII aiuge est que . . .

and Bryan, agreeing, with '*et issint est aiuge* vij E[dward] IIII'.[44] It is, however, impossible even with a text that early in print to be sure how much of the reference was added by editors, and much citation remains quite imprecise.[45] Kebell, appearing for the prior of Newark by Guildford, claimed: 'in our books a rent was granted to a man and his heirs on condition . . .', hardly an adequate direction.[46]

This lack of any reliable citation was compounded by the absence of any single text, and the fact that texts were not necessarily congruent or expected to be so.[47] These points are obvious in *Sudberth* v. *Agard* (1486–93).[48] The court had ruled unanimously that Kebell's client, the plaintiff, had to produce a particular deed:

Kebell: 'Sir, the contrary has been often adjudged', and he alleged divers books and divers years [to the effect] that [the defendant] is responsible for showing the deed. And the court held entirely against him. And he prayed the justices to hear what he would say.

Another account of the case adds to what was clearly a lively exchange:

42. *Y.B.* Trin. 13 Hen. VII, p. 1 f. 25. Wilmer's Case was probably heard in exchequer chamber (see above, pp. 154–5) and may be the case cited also at Hil. 5 Hen. VII, p. 4 f. 14. Kebell's statement may imply that a copy of the roll was produced or, equally, a copy of the report; in Henry VI's reign, texts of the reports were produced: Lewis, *L.Q.R.* 46. 342.
43. *ibid.*, 344–5; *Y.B.* Mich. 16 Hen. VII, p. 2 f. 1. Hemmant, *Exchequer Chamber*, ii. xxi-xxii, draws attention to the contrast in citation between the Long Quinto of 5 Edward IV and the texts of other year books.
44. *Y.B.* Trin. 5 Hen. VII, p. 5 f. 41; ed. Pynson (S.T.C. 9928.5, Harvard Law Library, 1505), sig. k6. Later eds. give the first reference as 35 Henry VI.
45. Lewis, *L.Q.R.* 46. 343; Hemmant, *Exchequer Chamber*, ii. xix-xxi.
46. *Y.B.* Hil. 10 Hen. VII, p. 4 f. 13.
47. Ives, *L.Q.R.* 89. 67–8.
48. *Y.B.* Pas. 10 Hen. VII, p. 20 f. 22.

Kebell: The distinction in our law is where . . . And so it is in the case of four husbands and their wives, A°11 Henry IV.
Bryan: We will look in our books ready for tomorrow.
Kebell said that he had seen many books and all the books state . . . he is not bound to produce the deed at the voucher.
Bryan: And I have seen many books contrary to that, and answer me this . . .[49]

Furthermore, even when the court was presented with irrefutable evidence of previous decisions, it was not bound to take notice. Kebell was arguing, not appealing to authority, when he said, again in *Sudberth* v. *Agard*, that:

he believed that the justices would not wish to alter the opinions of all the books which have been adjudged.[50]

In a *quare impedit* of 5 Henry VII Kebell cited *The Bishop of Lincoln's Case* of 33 Henry VI.[51] The chief justice replied that:

if the case in 33 Henry VI were to be judged now, the law would be [as the chief justice had already stated], for he would never be of the opinion that [was in] the book of 33 Henry VI.

Year-book citation was, nevertheless, taken seriously.[52] In at least fifty-four cases, Kebell himself referred to earlier decisions, sometimes several references on one occasion, and this takes no account of cases where the citation came from other counsel. Lawyers were also prompt to rebut precedents made against them. In *Rede* v. *Capell* in chancery, Coningsby for the defendant opened the second day by saying that the plaintiff had adequate remedy at common law 'and this had been adjuged in 20 Edward III – see the book'.[53] Kebell replied, 'as to the book, it is not adjudged as has been said'. In a formedon case in 8 Henry VII, Vavasour said from the bench, '*voiez cy un president Anno 6 Edward IV vel circa* . . .', and Kebell retorted, '*c'est auter case, car come Fineux ad dit, ce prove que* . . .'.[54]

Lawyers thus had no doctrine of binding precedent, but the fixed habit of quoting authority. To resolve this paradox we need to notice another characteristic, their reliance on personal recollection.[55] A case from 1488–9 has Kebell saying:

49. *ibid.*, Mich. 11 Hen.VII, p. 12 f. 4.
50. *ibid.*, Pas. 10 Hen.VII, p. 20 f. 22; Hemmant, *Exchequer Chamber*, ii. xxi.
51. *Y.B.* Pas. 5 Hen.VII, p. 1 ff. 20–2; ed. Pynson (1505) sig. h1^v.
52. Lewis, *L.Q.R.* 47. 422–3.
53. *Y.B.* Pas. 7 Hen.VII, p. 2 f. 12.
54. *ibid.*, Mich. 8 Hen.VII, p. 3 f. 7.
55. For the following see Ives, *L.Q.R.* 89. 69–71.

And, Sir, as to the case which was put the other day, where the [royal] pardon was granted to all men for [all] felonies and robberies except to men who were with Queen Margaret; Sir, if someone pleaded such a pardon against the king I agree entirely that he must submit that he was not with Queen Margaret. And the case was judged, as I heard, that in such a case . . .[56]

On one occasion this exchange took place between the judges:

Vavasour: I was forced by the court when I was a serjeant to say *Mon franktenement, absque hoc que* . . .
Bryan: I grant well [that it was] as you say. For there he did not say . . .[57]

The most extreme example is the reference by the elderly Guy Fairfax J.K.B. to a point he remembered from the time of Richard Newton who had died forty years before.[58] But what is significant about these reminiscences is that they are accorded the same status as precedent from the reports and claims that this or that has been adjudged or is good law. In discussing when a writ of error abated for the death of one of the recipients, Kebell sought analogies:

this has been adjudged many times in our books where *Audita Querela* is sued and one of the plaintiffs dies, the writ does not abate because it is directed to discharge [the plaintiff of his obligation] and not to recover anything; but if it was error in *praecipe quod reddat*, as the case was before you recently, then death does abate the writ, because the plaintiffs will have judgement to restore them the land . . .[59]

In a discussion dated 9 Henry VII, Constable 'alleged a judgement in the time of Richard III . . . and he said in Mich. 38 Henry VI it was adjudged also. See the book.'[60] In the *Prior of Newark's Case* Kebell's argument includes all the following: 'it is clear law', 'it is adjudged in 30 E[dward] III', 'also this case is adjudged 2 H[enry] IV' and 'I have seen this case adjudged.'[61] A king's bench case from 1485–95 ends:

Hussey: In my own time I have seen a party taken by a *capias pro fine* in a redisseisin, and he was also in execution by the party.
Kebell: Certes! I was counsel in the same case.
Constable: Certes, the contrary was held *Anno* 6 or 7 Edward IV.
Hussey: See your books against the morrow, and then you will have your award.[62]

56. *Y.B.* Pas. 4 Hen.VII, p. 9 f. 8.
57. *ibid.*, Trin. 10 Hen.VII, p. 5 f. 26.
58. *ibid.*, Mich. 4 Hen.VII, p. 1 f. 16; cf. Mich. 3 Hen.VII, p. 30 f. 15; Trin. 10 Hen.VII, p. 27 f. 29; Pas. 15 Hen.VII, p. 2 f. 8.
59. *ibid.*, Hil. 3 Hen.VII, p. 2 f. 1.
60. *ibid.*, Mich. 9 Hen.VII, p. 1 f. 5.
61. *ibid.*, Trin. 16 Hen.VII, p. 2 ff. 9–10; cf. Trin. 11 Hen.VII, p. 2 f. 24: 'Bryan: "*Ceo ad este tenu in noz livres . . . et issint fuit adjuge in temps* Edward *le 4 quand jeo fus serjant a le barre*".'
62. *ibid.*, Hil. 11 Hen.VII, p. 11 f. 15.

The debate moves from personal recollection to report without distinction. A few years after Kebell's death, Justice Tremayle made the equation specific: 'in all my life, nor in all the books that I have seen, have I seen that . . .'.[63]

If reports of past cases were regarded as the equal, but no more, of what professional training and experience suggested, a number of facts are explained about the year books, why the early printers concentrated on texts from the generation prior to that currently in practice, and why the number of manuscripts in circulation was low, measured either by survivals or by the size of known collections.[64] More important, it explains the attitude of lawyers and the courts to the law. Reports were valuable as a guide to what the profession had felt in similar or analogous circumstances in the past; they provided continuity of experience. On the other hand, the past imposed no necessary constraint on the present; training and personal experience were guides equally as valuable. Together they built up a *formation générale*, the 'common learning' of the profession. The usual term for this was *erudition*, but *maxim* was also used. Appeal to this common learning was final. A formedon case, allegedly from 1497, reports:

Kebell a le contrary. 'Et me semble que on poit conditioner ove un feffee in fee simple que il ne alienera.'
Bryan fist a luy interruption & dit que ils ne vouloient luy ouir a arguer a cest conceit. 'Pur ceo que il est merement incontre nostre comon erudition, & est or in maniere un principal; purque per cest mesne nous duissomus transposer touts nostres anciens precedents. Purque ne parlez plus de cest point.'[65]

In a case of assize from the late 1490s it was Kebell's turn to allege:

A le premier point, pur ce que le party ne purrait avoir nulle tielle execution come le roy ad, scilicet de son corps, le contrary de ceo ad este souvent fois adjuge & est en manniere comon cours si bien en Assize come en redisseisin trove ove force.[66]

In another case Kebell was the victim. He attacked a plea which alleged that a sheriff had awarded a *withernam* (a stage in the machinery of distraint), and not, as was pedantically correct, the suitors of the county court:

And the court said to him that it was not a new case, for the common usage is

63. *ibid.*, Hil. 21 Hen.VII, p. 30 f. 19.
64. T.F.T. Plucknett, *Early Legal Literature* (Cambridge, 1958), 112; Abbott, *Law Reporting*, 11, 17, 256; Ives, *L.Q.R.* 85. 108.
65. *Y.B.* Pas. 13 Hen.VII, p. 9 f. 23.
66. *ibid.*, Pas. 14 Hen.VII, p. 2 f. 20.

to allege that the sheriff himself made the award, and not the suitors; and this had been allowed as a sound form of pleading many times before this.[67]

By its nature, this common mind was more a consensus of approach than a catalogue of specific rulings. Christopher St German did list two or three dozen 'maxims' in *Doctor and Student*, but there was never a formal list.[68] Fortescue remarked that maxims were acquired 'through the senses and the memory'; they were learned at the inns, in court and in the year books, which, as he said on another occasion, reported the business of the courts *ad futurorum eruditionem*.[69] Kebell could, therefore, appeal to this common learning in a very imprecise fashion: 'if the law is as I have always taken it . . .'; 'I have often seen that . . .'; 'and further it was said in this case by Kebell that . . . he took it as a principle that . . .'.[70] But loose though it was, this common agreement was there and woe betide counsel who alleged *un erudition* without justification. Kebell replied to Robert Constable:

There is neither ground nor erudition for what you say, for in many cases the party will be recompensed where the defendant is taken by *capias pro fine*, even though no *capias* lay in the original. But this has been an erudition: that the party shall only have *capias ad satisfaciendum* where *capias* lies in the original. But this erudition you speak of, I have never heard it before.[71]

To minds familiar with *stare decisis*, such a general understanding and no more seems an invitation to uncertainty, but it was, in fact, a recipe for vitality. Authority lay in the collective mind of the profession, past and present.

IV

There are, not surprisingly, similarities between this approach and the handling by Kebell and his fellows of statute law. The regular consideration of statute at the inns of court provided a basis of knowledge, and manuscripts of past readings were certainly available, possibly even an official collection; many lawyers also kept notes of enacted law or had a volume of statutes; and printed sets were increasingly available.[72] Kebell made a minimum of fifty-six citations

67. *ibid.*, Mich. 16 Hen.VII, p. 6. f. 2.
68. St German, *Doctor and Student*, 57–71; Ives, in *Profession, Vocation etc.*, 191.
69. Fortescue, *De Laudibus*, 21, 114.
70. *Y.B.* Pas. 1 Hen.VII, p. 2 f. 15; Mich. 10 Hen.VII, p. 6 f. 4; Keilwey, *Reports*, f. 19.
71. *ibid.*, Hil. 11 Hen.VII, p. 11 f. 15.
72. E13/170 vi^r; see above, pp. 48–54.

to statute, but allowing for multiple citations and the continuation of cases from report to report, some forty separate discussions can be isolated, mentioning twenty-seven statutes in all. Legislation from the period 1322 to 1430 appears rarely in the list, and for 1430 to 1483 only two private acts caused discussion, although there are eight citations of more recent legislation.[73] The bulk of reference, however, is to the old statutes, those prior to Edward III, which formed the inns of court curriculum, with the two statutes of Westminster, 1275 and 1285, in pride of place. Citation is too much at the mercy of chance factors in the year books to warrant much analysis, but Kebell's calendar does hint at the frequent citation of a few crucial clauses, rather than a wider use of statutes; of eleven references to the fifty clauses of *Westminster II*, one is general, two clauses are cited once, two twice and one four times.[74] The actual method of reference is imprecise and chapter numbers are rarely found, but a particular section could be indicated by its opening, as it was at a law reading. In *The Countess of Richmond* v. *the Dean of Windsor*, Kebell referred to part of clause five of *Westminster II* as 'Westminster the second which commences *cum pax fuerit reformata*'.[75] Quotation tends to be approximate also, but verbatim reference was possible if required. In *Everard Digby's Case*, Kebell said:

> The statute *Westminster II* c. 3 lays down that the woman shall have *cui in vita* for land recovered by default against her husband. And, expressly it is said, '*habeat suum recuperare per breve de ingressu*'.[76]

Yet on this citation of statute caution is needed more, perhaps, than in all year-book problems. Much of the reference has been added later, and even where references seem integral, extensions, tampering

73. *1 Ric.III* c. 1 (uses): *Y.B.* Mich. 8 Hen.VII, p. 4 f. 7, Hil. 14 Hen.VII, p. 4 f. 15; *1 Hen.VII* c. 1 (uses): *Y.B.* Hil. 14 Hen.VII, p. 7 f. 17; *3 Hen.VII* c. 2 (uses): *Y.B.* Trin. 4 Hen.VII p. 1 f. 9; *4 Hen.VII* c. 17: *Y.B.* Trin. 12 Hen.VII, p. 1 f. 20, Mich. 13 Hen.VII, p. 3 f. 6 (reports of Stonor's case); unidentified act of restitution: *Y.B.* Trin. 4 Hen.VII, p. 6 ff. 10–12, Pas. 10 Hen.VII, p. 24 ff. 22–3 (reports of the same case).
74. *Y.B.* Hil. 3 Hen.VII, p. 1 f. 1; Hil. 4 Hen.VII, p. 4 f. 2; Trin. 5 Hen.VII, p. 3 f. 36; Pas. 7 Hen.VII, p. 2 f. 11; Mich. 10 Hen.VII, p. 1 f. 1, p. 12 f. 6; Trin. 10 Hen.VII, p. 24 f. 29; Mich. 12 Hen.VII, p. 3 f. 4; Hil. 14 Hen.VII, p. 7 f. 17 (*bis*); Pas. 16 Hen.VII, p. 11 f. 8.
75. *ibid.*, Pas. 16 Hen.VII, p. 11 f. 8. The statute reads: '*et cum aliquando inter plures clamantes alicuius ecclesie pax fuerit reformata*.' Cf. the custom in readings: see above, pp. 55–6, and Thorne, *Readings and Moots*, *passim*.
76. *Y.B.* Hil. 14 Hen.VII, p. 7 f. 18. The reference in c. 3 is: '*quod mulier . . . habeat recuperare per breve de ingressu*'. Cf. the citation in the same case of several statutes by other counsel.

or plain error may have crept in.[77] In a case dated 10 Henry VII, Bryan asked Kebell to quote the words of the statute of Gloucester.[78] The serjeant replied:

It is permitted to no man to make waste, sale or destruction in houses, woods or gardens

a reasonable approximation to:

Farmers, for the duration of their farm, shall not waste, sell or remove houses, woods or men, or anything.

But the quotation is not from the statute of Gloucester; what Bryan wanted and what Kebell gave him was the statute of Marlborough.[79]

The use of statute in the courts has been studied by historians and lawyers in search of the principles of statutory construction.[80] In brief, Kebell's generation was familiar with the distinctions Coke described – between statutes affirmative and negative, general and particular, those making new law and those affirming existing law – and with the interpretation appropriate to each.[81] The general trend was towards equitable construction according to the intentions of the legislators, but it was still possible to argue for narrow verbal interpretation, and the days of the equitable extension of statutes were not yet over. Thus a pleader could take the line which suited his current client. In *John Colt's Case*, Kebell argued for rigorous construction, to which Fisher replied, 'the statute will be taken according to generous construction. And divers matters will be taken within a statute which are not named by it.'[82] In *Sir William Stonor's Case* Kebell occupied the modern position; the statute concerned was *De Prerogativa Regis*.

Donque, quand cest Statut est fait, que est doubteous, il sera construe solonque l'entent de l'fesors de meme le Statut.[83]

In *Everard Digby's Case* Kebell took the third possibility – equitable extension. The point of the exact quotation from *Westminster II* was

77. See above, p. 157. The court, however, could call for sight of the text: *ibid.*, Hil. 9 Hen.VII, p. 17 f. 21.
78. *ibid.*, Mich. 10 Hen.VII, p. 8 f. 5.
79. Statute of Marlborough, *52 Henry III* c. 23. The error 'Gloucester' is found in the earliest known version of the year book for 10 Henry VII, by Pynson (1555) at f. 5v.
80. Thomas Egerton, *A discourse upon the exposition and understanding of statutes*, ed. S.E. Thorne (San Marino, U.S.A., 1942); Chrimes, *Constitutional Ideas*, 192–299.
81. *ibid.*, 249–64.
82. *Y.B.* Pas. 5 Hen.VII, p. 12 f. 31.
83. *ibid.*, Trin. 12 Hen.VII, p. 1 f. 20; see below, p. 253.

to show that despite the precise words, the heir 'by the equity of the statute will have a formedon', and by analogy a similar conclusion would result in *1 Henry VII* c. 1:

Although the statute speaks of vouching the pernors of profits, this will be understood as if the act was such that . . .[84]

Everard Digby's Case was not the only example of argument from statute by construction or analogy. In A°9 Henry VII Kebell is found arguing from *5 Richard II* st. 1 c. 7 and *8 Henry VI* c. 9 to rules applicable in a case of trespass; the court denied his argument 'utterly'.[85] Sometimes the substance of the statute and of the suit were far apart. In *The Shepherd's Case*, concerned with the loss of sheep by carelessness, Kebell argued that nonfeasance was no ground for action, on the analogy that before the 1349 statute of Labourers a master had no redress where a servant who had been retained refused to serve.[86] The same statute was used on another occasion by Kebell to argue a distinction in a case of livery.[87] In a number of examples, counsel adduced the common law which existed before a statute. In *Cary* v. *Gilbert* Robert Rede sought to establish that a particular recovery had been fraudulent and pointed to the situation in *praecipe quod reddat* as it existed before the passing of *Westminster II*. Kebell replied *'le Comon Ley devant le Statut de* Westminster *le 2 ne fuit come ad este pris'*.[88] Awareness of the common law behind the particular enactments of parliaments had long been a characteristic of the legal profession.[89] It comes out clearly in a case Kebell took in the years 1489 to 1493.[90] A mill had fallen into disrepair and he was contrasting damages for waste at common law and damages under the statute of Gloucester c. 5:

the recovery will be entirely in damages at common law which are enlarged by statute to recover the thing wasted and treble damages in place of the single damages at common law; but the same nature of the action which was at common law lasts to this day, notwithstanding the penalty is enlarged by statute.

The astute pleader could go from statute into common law and from common law to statute as it seemed best.

84. See above, p. 162; cf. *Y.B.* Mich. 8 Hen.VII, p. 4 f. 8: *'per l'equite de le Statut de* Richard *le 3'*.

85. *ibid.*, Mich. 9 Hen.VII, p. 3 f. 7.

86. *ibid.*, Hil. 2 Hen.VII, p. 9 f. 11.

87. *ibid.*, Mich. 6 Hen.VII, p. 13 f. 13.

88. *ibid.*, Mich. 10 Hen.VII, p. 1 f. 1.

89. Chrimes, *Constitutional Ideas*, 255.

90. *Y.B.* Pas. 13 Hen.VII, p. 3 f. 21.

V

Given the contemporary approach to authority, argument in court in Kebell's day was more to the particular case than to the weight of authorities, and the consequence was a perceptible fluidity in the law. Counsel recognised this. In the same case in which Kebell rapped Constable's knuckles over *capias*, this exchange took place:

Hussey: Certes Anno 2 Henry IV a man prayed a *capias ad satisfaciendum* for damages recovered in a writ of dower, and he was not allowed it because *capias* was not in the original; but I have never heard such erudition about the *capias pro fine*. And before *Anno* 36 Henry VI, in debt or trespass after the year, if the party was taken by *capias pro fine* it was current in all books that he would answer the party as well as the crown. But there is a new opinion taken, as you say, that after the year, because the party cannot have execution without a reply, that he should be put to his *scire facias*. But although such an opinion has been taken on this point it has not yet been adjudged, although the contrary has many times been adjudged.
Kebell: It seems to me that older opinion was better, because . . .[91]

In *The Abbot of Hyde* v. *Benger* Kebell had some difficulty because he was not sufficiently up-to-date. He treated the court to an historical disquisition on disclaimers in avowry, pointing out what was *le consideration des anciens sages de l'Ley*, and quoting cases from as far back as the reign of Edward I.[92] Jay replied:

Your case of disclaimer in an assize of rent is an ancient example; but show us such a case adjudged in recent years (*in novel termes*).[93]

Kebell admitted that this was impossible, but nevertheless stuck to his point:

I have put to you a judgement from the time when such matter was more commonly in use.

Vavasour's memory then came to the rescue:

When I was a serjeant . . . the person who disclaimed brought *assize*; and I was counsel in this assize, and for this [very] difficulty the assize was adjourned. And the matter was well argued and in the end, *per bon advis* . . .

The justices accepted Vavasour's reminiscence thankfully.

91. *ibid.*, Hil. 11 Hen.VII, p. 11 f. 15.
92. *ibid.*, Trin. 13 Hen.VII, p. 6 ff. 27–8.
93. Jay may have meant 'in recent year books': Ives, *L.Q.R.* 89. 72. Cf. Kebell, 'come est adjuge souvent fois en ancient ans': *Y.B.* Hil. 14 Hen. VII, p. 5 f. 16.

The late-medieval year books are the great forgotten sources for social history, a neglect which they invite by being alternately incomprehensible and frustrating, or both together. But attention brings its rewards. There are the the books themselves, the notes and jottings of many men assembled by processes of editing and redaction we are only beginning to understand. Then there is the search for law in the collective mind and memory of the profession, in statute and in the year books themselves. But over and beyond is the contact with judges and counsel in the cut and thrust of the court room. For no other occupational group in England do we have recorded so much direct speech; what lives in year books is not the law, but the lawyers.

8

THOMAS KEBELL AS AN ADVOCATE

The heart of the English legal system in Thomas Kebell's day, and for centuries afterwards, was the great hall of the palace of Westminster. Provincial courts there were in plenty, but just as the lawyers who worked them were part of a profession centred on the inns of court, so litigation in them was increasingly subject to the central royal courts.[1] Rebuilt less than a century before Kebell read for the bar, Westminster Hall housed the chancery, the king's bench and the common pleas. The exchequer met in a room off the north entrance, near which was the Exchequer Chamber, and buildings around were to house the family of courts that grew up by the middle of the sixteenth century; already the Star Chamber was in use for judicial and conciliar discussions and hearings. In the hall proper, common pleas had the draughtiest position, against the western wall towards the northern end; king's bench filled the south-eastern and chancery the south-western half of the dais at the upper end of the hall.

Each court was arranged in a similar fashion. King's bench, for example, occupied the three southern bays of the hall, and from the western wall to the centre where stood the king's marble chair, which the chancellor, and possibly the chief justice, used on formal occasions. The judges sat on a raised bench some twenty-seven feet long against the southern wall, with the royal arms painted above them and a canopy overhead; over the canopy stood Richard II's statues of the kings of England, watching the court below. The court was separated from the body of the hall by a barrier along the front of the dais; depicted in the mid-1450s as a rail, it was in fact made of oaken planks and in the late sixteenth century was a solid wooden partition. Below the justices, the court was divided from side to side by the bar, again a solid partition, but, like all the fittings of Westminster Hall, removable for state occasions. On the side nearest the bench was a twenty-foot 'exchequer' table, covered with a green cloth, round

1. Henderson, *English Administrative Law*, 83–93.

which the court clerks sat and on which the court criers perhaps stood to see out into the hall. On the other side stood litigants and counsel. The court was closed on the east by the wall of the hall, against which there was seating, possibly for a jury when necessary or for persons attending the court or mere spectators.[2] The west of the court was closed by bars and doors, but by the end of the sixteenth century a small stand had been added, level with the justices; who sat there is not clear – possibly others required to attend, or more of the spectators who also crowded the gangway and hung over the rail at the edge of the dais. By then, too, a double-tiered box had been added for them in the fourth bay of the hall, but it is not known whether this provision existed in the fifteenth century. Chancery was similar in lay-out and presumably also common pleas, although the latter was closed off by barriers on both sides. The surroundings of the exchequer are not known, but the bench, table and bar were as in the other courts; the one exception was that the exchequer boasted a 'cage' for prisoners awaiting trial where the king's bench merely kept them in leg irons, shackled together at the back of the court.[3]

What makes possible such a description is the survival of four remarkable miniatures, probably of the 1450s, showing each of the Westminster courts, and a drawing of the upper part of the hall at the turn of the seventeenth century, as well as architectural and archive evidence.[4] Together they give an overwhelming impression of the congestion of the courts. King's bench measured some thirty feet wide by fifty-six feet deep, and in this space were crowded nearly two dozen judges and court officials plus counsel and, perhaps, half-a-dozen litigants or defendants, possibly a jury and a press of spectators.[5] In common pleas the suspicion is of a worse crush when the serjeants were there in force. This intimacy is reflected in the informality of the court and the immediacy of the interchange between counsel, and between the bar and the justices, who were certainly not loath to intervene. In a case of error in king's bench Kebell

2. In the fourteenth century, common pleas had a special 'crib' for students: J.P. Dawson, *The Oracles of the Law* (Ann Arbor, 1968), 9, 36.
3. The cage may be an artist's embellishment.
4. Inner Temple Ms. Add. 188, reproduced in *Archaeologia* 39 (1863), 357–72; B.L., *Catalogue of British Drawings*, pl. 6; *History of the King's Works*, ed. R.A. Brown etc. (1963–), i. 543–5.
5. Westminster Hall is 67½ feet wide, but a gangway separated king's bench and chancery. For an attempt to reconstruct the king's bench seating plan in 1532 when staff had risen to 26: see Spelman, *Reports*, ii. *354–7*.

was disputing with his fellow serjeants, Richard Jay and Thomas Wode, whether the two original defendants should have pleaded separately or jointly.[6] Justice Fairfax interjected on Kebell's behalf:

You say well, for I pose that someone brings a writ of trespass against two individuals for fouling his grass by trampling it; one replies that it was the highway to the church and he came with a corpse to the church, and the other pleads the same. This [plea] is sufficient, for there is only a single trespass against the demandant and yet with respect to those who have done the default it is multiple and each of them has justified [their doing of] all that the demandant has alleged, viz. that they fouled his grass by trampling on it.
Hussey C. J.: Certes, it is only a single trespass. And I pose that . . .
Jay: Yet it is still error, for they pleaded individually, but the damages were collective. . .
Kebell: What you say is true if the issue had been taken on their separate torts as if they had pleaded *not guilty*, but here . . .

and the debate continued between counsel.

How discussion in court was handled can only be inferred, given the meagre evidence.[7] Clearly only a minority of cases could be discussed in detail; much business must have been put through in a routine fashion. In the fifteenth century this was expedited by paper pleadings, which were in frequent use by the reign of Edward IV. A list of fees, probably from 1457, distinguished the 'comyn declaracion, comen plea in barre, comen replicacion and comen reioynder in pleas personall', entered by a defendant or his attorney, from pleas 'pleded by a Serjaunt', and the Edward IV year books confirm that submitting a 'paper' directly to the clerks was a recognised way of entering a plea.[8] Little is so far known of the reason for this development, whether it was simply to save the pockets of litigants or whether it reflects increasing formalities in oral pleading or the increasing bureaucracy of the courts, but it was to have considerable importance for the legal profession. By 1600 pleadings were normally exchanged in the form of 'books', and the erstwhile pleader was now turning his attention to arguing the law before the bench or presenting evidence to the jury. 'The lawyer who appeared in court was now an advocate.'[9]

But it would be wrong to place too much emphasis in the fifteenth century on this change; the profession was paying more attention to

6. *Y.B.* Mich. 11 Hen.VII, p. 27 f. 7.
7. For an important technical discussion of pleading, see Spelman, *Reports*, ii. *142–59*.
8. Hastings, *Common Pleas*, 185–90, 251.
9. Milsom, *Historical Foundations*, 39.

substantive law, but most time was still spent in the technicalities and problems of pleading. Although a plea had been made, it was still subject to attack or amendment in open court. One example was a case of debt on obligation from the period 1486–93. This was the frequently reported case arising from an agreement to transfer an estate before a given date as the purchaser's counsel directed.[10] What the entry under 11 Henry VII suggests is that the plaintiff had requested the defendant to make over the estate without bringing in a lawyer, and Kebell for the defendant pressed Richard Jay to assert in his plea that the request had been in the form required by the indenture. The court supported him and Bryan ruled, '*Amendez votre ple.*' Not only could pleas be changed, but pleading in open court still had plenty of vitality. One report of *Pind* v. *Eriche* shows Kebell insistent on securing a particular form of traverse from the defendant's counsel, Robert Rede. In the end the chief justice said to Rede, '*Prenez son papiers de luy et avisez vous bien envers le prochein jour s'il luy travers ou nemy.*'[11] The situation in Kebell's lifetime seems thus to have been that paper pleading and pleading *ore tenus* existed side by side. A straightforward plea could be entered in writing in the knowledge that if difficulty arose it could still be taken onto the floor of the court. On the other hand it was possible, and for problem issues perhaps desirable, for counsel to present the plea in the first place in court.[12] In the one case the drafting was, apparently, done by the court clerks, in the other by counsel, but neither was binding until the term was out.[13]

When the court was to debate any question the starting point was an argument by the counsel involved. On occasions, however, a discussion was deliberately set up by counsel posing a hypothetical question. In Easter term 9 Henry VII:

> Kebell came to the bar in the common bench and asked this question: 'If a single woman of full age is disseised, married, the disseisor dies and then her husband, can the woman then enter [on her property]?' And it was said by all the justices that [she could not], for when the woman was disseised she was of full age and could have entered before she married . . . But it would have been different if the disseisin was effected during the marriage . . . But all the justices said in the first case . . ., and also all the justices and serjeants agreed

10. See above, p. 144.
11. *Y.B.* Pas. 11 Hen.VII, p. 10 ff. 21–2, p. 12 f. 22; Trin. 11 Hen.VII, p. 11 f. 27. The quotation is from Pas. 11 p. 10; cf. *ibid.*, Trin. 10 Hen.VII, p. 5 f. 26.
12. *ibid.*, Trin. 10 Hen.VII, p. 5 f. 26.
13. See above, p. 61.

this for good law. And they also said . . . which was agreed by the serjeants also.[14]

In these discussions the serjeants spoke in order of seniority, by turns *pro et contra*; they knew the openings of the two parties, and any adjourned session would start with a recapitulation of the previous arguments. Whether the serjeants were prepared in any way beyond this is not clear. Certainly in exchequer chamber, prior warning was not always given. Early in Henry VII's reign the crown challenged a grant by Edward IV of a shrievalty for life.[15] Preliminary opinions were ventured:

but because this was the first occurrence, the justices, serjeants and king's attorney agreed that they would study the matter well and they would hear [what could be said], and what they had [already] said was tentative (*pour nient*) as they wished to be free to say what they wanted to and thought, notwithstanding what they had said on this occasion.

The physical congestion of the Westminster courts and the involvement of the senior members of the bar in thrashing out the law together had a direct effect upon the working of the late-medieval courts. The common impression is that what happened there was a gigantic gamble. Nobody can deny that there were pitfalls and technicalities in plenty, but the close and easy relations of judges and counsel were in some instances a real protection to the litigant. Bench and bar could if they wished work together to secure fair representation for both parties. This is well demonstrated by the readiness with which Thomas Kebell sought – and was given – the benefit of the court's advice. In one of the earliest of his reported cases, from the time when he was still an apprentice, Kebell:

asked advice of the justices [of the king's bench]. 'If the plaintiff [in an appeal of murder] had had the original writ with proclamation [in the county court], according to the statute, and if now she wishes to have an *exigent* [to outlaw the accused], must she have another writ with proclamation or not?' And he thought not, since the statute has been complied with on this point in the original [writ]. *Jenney Justice*: 'Is your *reattachment* general or special?' *Kebell*: 'The words are *quod sit in eodem statu quo fuit tunc*, but how process was awarded is not recited in the reattachment.' *Fairfax*: 'Then this is in form only a general *reattachment* and so process *de novel* will be awarded.' *Jenney*: 'You must understand that if an *appeal* or *reattachment* should be sued, then the plaintiff is unable to vary from his plea and so at each stage (*chescun nature*) of the action. But if it should be general, then the law is

14. *Y.B.* Pas. 9 Hen.VII, p. 10 f. 24.

15. *ibid.*, Mich. 2 Hen.VII, p. 20 f. 7.

contrary; and so if your *reattachment* should be special it is then not necessary to have the writ proclaimed, and if general, then it is necessary. So *avises vous bien*.'[16]

This readiness was still found when Kebell was a serjeant. In Trinity term 1496 when he was faced with a difficulty in pleading he disclosed the facts and said:

I would have your guidance as to how I should plead this matter. *Bryan*: 'It seems that you will have special matter entered [*viz.*] . . .' *Vavasour* thought that this would only appear in evidence and not be entered. Note, *Vavasour* is against all such special entries. *Bryan* said that it is right that he should show special matter or else . . . *Kebell*: 'So it seems to me.' And then he pleaded the special matter *scilicet* . . .[17]

Predictably the co-operation of bench and bar was not always as fruitful. Sometimes, with the best will in the world, the court was unable to help. The suit arising from the agreement to convey property as the plaintiff's counsel directed is a clear example.[18] The year-book report for Trinity 1496 begins:

Kebell came to the bar and put to the justices that he was at issue for a poor man, and prayed their discretion because he would not willingly commit a *jeofail*.

The defendant had claimed that 'counsel had not given advice', but Kebell argued that this was too general. Bryan C.J. agreed, but not the puisne justices, Townshend and Vavasour. Bryan would not move and said to Kebell, 'thus you see our opinions'. Kebell then reported his plea that J. Wilks had been the plaintiff's only counsel, that he had given advice and that the plaintiff had informed the defendant, and also the defence plea that Wilks gave no advice.

Vavasour: Have you alleged that the advice was given to the plaintiff by his counsel, or by the counsel to the party due to make over the estate?
Kebell: We have alleged neither, but we have said that counsel had given advice that the defendant should make a particular [conveyance] of the estate.
Townshend: You should have said that the plaintiff's counsel had given advice to the defendant to make such an estate.
Bryan: No, certes! He has said better . . .; it is sufficient to say that the plaintiff's counsel had given their advice and the defendant must take notice . . . at his peril.
Kebell: We would make this to be most sure, for if the law should be that the

16. *ibid.*, Trin. Edw.V, p. 4 f. 3.
17. *ibid.*, Trin. 10 Hen.VII, p. 25 f. 29.
18. *ibid.*, Trin. 11 Hen.VII, p. 1 ff. 23–4; cf. above, pp. 144, 170.

defendant must take notice, this [Townshend's formula] would make the plea good.

Vavasour then reverted to the *consilium non dedit advisamentum* issue, only to have the last of the common pleas judges, William Danvers, deny his case flatly. Bryan has the last word, '*soit de cest comme estre peut*' and the report ends, *et puis Kebell alla in Banc le Roy per auter matiers.*[19]

From time to time, however, the bench could be blunt, when checking a particular flight of fancy or a counsel who seemed intent on a dangerous course. Thus in 1492 in a complex case of formedon, Kebell (for the tenant) wanted to demur on the counterplea, so risking adjournment to the next term with the consequence that his client would be prevented from pleading further.[20] Justice Vavasour and Chief Justice Bryan both reiterated Kebell's peril:

Vavasour said to *Kebell*, 'Be well advised, for if [your demurrer] is adjourned it is peremptory [binding]. Each voucher is in place of the tenant entering a bar, and if he vouches and puts his case and that case is insufficient and it is adjourned to another term, then that is binding for the tenant.

If he demurs on the counterplea this is peremptory if it is adjourned, but in the same term it is not peremptory . . . Therefore, be well advised if you would demur.

And see here a precedent *Anno* 6 Edward IV or thereabouts, where a man was vouched as heir to a woman, as the case is before us, that the demandant said . . .

Kebell: This is a different case . . .
Bryan: Guard yourself well, for it is peremptory . . .

On occasion the court would insist. A report dated Hilary 11 Henry VII has Bryan forcing Rede to plead in a particular way, despite insistent support from both Thomas Wode and Thomas Kebell.[21] In the *Case of the Chapel of Ronceval*, Rede, this time opposing Kebell, was threatened by the chief justice in most explicit terms:

to expedite your case, grant [that your opponent] can have aid or otherwise make the papers [as you are arguing now] and I know that judgement will go against you.[22]

Kebell himself was frequently criticised. For every instance when 'to avoid all doubts' he changed his plea, there were many others

19. For the decline of tentative pleading and judicial counselling, see Spelman, *Reports*, ii. *152–6*.
20. *Y.B.* Mich. 8 Hen.VII, p. 3 f. 7.
21. *ibid.*, Hil.11 Hen.VII, p. 10 ff. 14–15.
22. *ibid.*, Pas. 10 Hen.VII, p. 5 ff. 18–19.

where the court ruled against him – as he sometimes pointed out.[23] The following exchange took place in a *cui in vita* in 1494–5 (the action by a widow to recover lands alienated by her husband), where Kebell (for the widow) was opposing the tenant's request to be shown the land in question because this had already been allowed on an earlier but defective writ.[24]

Vavasour thought that he should have the view. For the Statute is: 'Where the writ is abated . . .' [*Westminster II*, c. 48]
Bryan to the contrary: For the party had the view twice recently; therefore the view is a matter well in our discretions. So he moved *Fineux* and *Danvers* privately and, without further argument said, 'Answer without the view'.
Vavasour said that all this matter would be entered [on the record] if the tenant wanted, and on that he could have a writ of error, if the law would assist him. Otherwise he and his colleagues would give him a statement [of the ruling] under seal.
Kebell: The matter is not to be entered in this case. For I was overruled in a similar case this term, to take a bill [of particulars] at my own risk but no mention was made of any record of the denial of view.
The next day *Wode* moved the court that the whole matter should be entered [of record]. And this was granted him.

Sometimes a note of exasperation creeps into what the judges say. 'No, by God' says Hussey to Kebell.[25] Bryan becomes particularly brusque when Kebell ignores the delicate position of attainted land early in Henry VII's reign.[26] A Yorkist beneficiary had brought a writ of trespass against the previous owner who had entered on his lands in anticipation of parliamentary restoration:

Bryan said that all the justices were of one opinion and also the justices of the king's bench for they had talked together on this matter. And therefore he said to Vavasour (Townshend [the senior] being absent), 'Give judgement.' And judgement was given that the plaintiff should take nothing by his writ.
Kebell: By this it seems that the party restored could bring an action for trespass covering the whole intervening period [of the forfeiture], which is nonsense.
Bryan: And so he could have an action and, as I have heard, so he would have.

A few of the many instances where the court overruled counsel followed mistakes by the pleader. One of his 'posthumous cases' shows Kebell persuading the bench that a writ was adequate, alleging that the wording in the register of writs took a particular form; when the register was produced and found to be different 'the judges

23. *ibid.*, Mich. 10 Hen.VII, p. 4 f. 4.
24. *ibid.*, Mich. 10 Hen.VII, p. 18 f. 8.
25. *ibid.*, Hil. 7 Hen.VII, p. 2 f. 9.
26. *ibid.*, Pas. 10 Hen.VII, p. 24 ff. 22–3.

changed their opinions'.[27] In general, however, an advocate's task is to argue the contentious, and it is inevitable that he will lose as well as win. Indeed, it is evidence of Kebell's professional standing that his name should occur so frequently, attached to this challenging submission or that. Very few of these were overtly concerned with substantive law, almost all with procedure, but as an artist in procedural subtlety Kebell well deserved the respect he received.

One notable instance is the five times reported *Case of the Chapel of Wanborough*.[28] In 1483 the advowson of the free chapel of Wanborough, near Swindon, had been transferred to Magdalen College, Oxford. Subsequently a rent of fourteen marks a year, due from the Wiltshire rectory of Edington, was withheld, and when arrears reached £28, the college distrained. The tenant of the rectory recovered his animals by a writ of replevin and Magdalen 'avowed', that is, justified the distraint and asked the common pleas to reimpose it. The tenant had an impossible case on the facts; witnesses could testify to years of uninterrupted payment to the free chapel.[29] Legal nit-picking promised little either; the transfer had been carefully done – there exist no fewer than fourteen of the deeds produced in the process. Nevertheless Kebell demurred, arguing that Magdalen had no claim because the transfer of the advowson was invalid.

The serjeants listed at least eight separate defects in the college's title, so that the chief justice said 'Take the exceptions one after another.' Most is known about those that failed at the first discussion. The contention that rent was only due from the date of the hand-over, not the date of the union, collapsed when both dates were found to coincide. Kebell's claim that royal licence had been given to a union of the chapel and the *college* whereas the suit had been brought by the *president and scholars* was less easy to dismiss, but the weight of opinion was hostile. In particular it was objected that the academic body *was* the college:

> if the scholars and the president were destroyed, the whole college is destroyed; but if the walls and buildings are destroyed, the college endures.[30]

Many of Kebell's arguments exploited the frontier between canon and common law, always fruitful in litigation about church property. He

27. *ibid.*, Trin. 16 Hen.VII, p. 1 f. 9.
28. *ibid.*, Hil. 6 Hen.VII, p. 2 ff. 13–14; Pas. 10 Hen.VII, p. 7 ff. 19–20, p. 12 f. 20; Mich. 11 Hen.VII, p. 30 ff. 8–9; Trin. 11 Hen.VII, p. 10 ff. 26–7.
29. Magdalen College, Wanborough Deeds *passim*.
30. *Y.B.* Pas. 10 Hen.VII, p. 7 f. 20; cf. *ibid.*, Trin. 11 Hen.VII, p. 10 f. 27.

suggested that to plead that the union had been 'with the concurrence of those who are required by the law' was far too general, and he was supported by Justice Townshend. Vavasour J., however, replied that the manner of the union was a question for canonists, and it is hard to see how a lay court could have tried a claim that the due forms of the church had not been observed.

In these initial stages Kebell got furthest with a second foray into the borderland between spiritual and temporal. Since the Magdalen plea had stated that the union was 'with the assent' of the bishop and other interested parties, it must follow that a third party had effected the union, and who that was must be stated too. This would have forced the college to start from scratch with a writ correctly stating that the bishop had united the foundations, and the argument was accepted, on first hearing, by a majority of the bench, including the chief justice. At a later discussion, Roger Townshend maintained the objection to union 'by assent':

> This is a good cause [to void the union] as it seems to me, and I have talked with those of the spiritual law and they say that the words of the union are 'we unite and make one', which proves that the plaintiff must allege who made the union and not say it was done by his assent.[31]

This time, however, the other justices changed their opinions, swayed by William Danvers, who pointed out that royal authorisation of a parliamentary bill was in the form 'I assent', while Vavasour followed this up by saying:

> If an act of parliament should be in the form that 'by the assent of the king, the lords spiritual and temporal and the commons it is ordained and enacted . . .', that is a valid act of parliament, yet it would not be an act if the king and the lords and the commons had not made it. But because it says it was ordained by their assent it is understood that they have made the act.[32]

Townshend gave way when it was pointed out that the phrase 'by assent' was only a late insertion, and Bryan clinched the discussion:

> It was said by Bryan that it had seemed to him earlier that the union was not good [in law], seeing that it did not state who had made the union, but he said that a doctor of spiritual law had changed his mind.[33]

On all these objections, therefore, Kebell lost the argument in common pleas, but he was nevertheless able to force the bench to take

31. *ibid.*, Trin. 11 Hen.VII, p. 10 f. 27.
32. *ibid.*, Pas. 10 Hen.VII, p. 7 f. 20; Trin. 11 Hen.VII, p. 10 f. 27.
33. *ibid.*, Pas. 10 Hen.VII, p. 7 f. 19.

the case to exchequer chamber. This was presumably because of the weight of his other objections about which no common pleas discussion is known. Two dealt again with the conjunction of canon and common law. The deeds had spoken of the agreement of the warden of the chapel, but a union could only take place if the benefice was vacant. In common pleas Bryan had accepted this:

'As to the union, seeing that there was a warden at the time the union was made, I do not know what the law of the church is on that point, but we will discuss with the doctors of [canon] law. But according to our law' he held the union void.[34]

The second argument was that free chapels could be of two kinds, those with cure of the souls, where the bishop had an interest, and those without, where he did not:

so [the matter] can be spiritual and it can be temporal and it will be taken by the court that it is temporal unless the contrary is shown.[35]

There was also a point which Kebell described as 'the force of the matter', that the royal approval of the union had taken the form of a pardon and release for unlicensed alienation in mortmain (inadequately drawn, Kebell said). A union, however, had to be licensed not only because of mortmain but because it terminated a corporation, and a retrospective pardon could not do this; if the bailiffs of an unincorporated town purchased land and were pardoned for the acquisition, this did not make them a corporation. Here, at least, was the stirring of an issue of substance.

Unfortunately no text of the exchequer chamber discussion is known, and the outcome is also in doubt. An observer noted that the judges in exchequer chamber agreed 'in effect' that the avowry was bad, presumably because the union was void.[36] Yet he also noted – and this is clear elsewhere in the year books – that the common pleas announced that the avowry was good; and his confusion is seen in his comment 'therefore query this matter'. A possible resolution is supplied by a comment which Bryan made twice, that even if the union were void, the college, as the occupier of the chapel, was still entitled to distrain. Thus, even if exchequer chamber had agreed with Kebell that the union was invalid, as it apparently did, this might not have stopped the college. The serjeant had, however, imposed considerable delay, thrown up numerous complex issues and forced the

34. *ibid.*, Hil. 6 Hen.VII, p. 2 f. 14.
35. *ibid.*, Hil. 6 Hen.VII, p. 2 f. 14.
36. *ibid.*, Pas. 10 Hen.VII, p. 12 f. 20.

case before the highest judicial consideration then known, and he had yet one more trick up his sleeve. When the college was on the point of getting judgement in its favour, Kebell asked whether it was represented in court. It was not, and despite all that had gone before, Magdalen was nonsuited. Kebell's client had won, and we hear next of the college suing in chancery.

Ingenuity in the service of injustice condemned the profession in the eyes of moralists, but clients no doubt thought otherwise. Willingness to exploit the law to the limit, and beyond, comes out time and again in the year books. When defending Henry Vernon in an advowson case, and under great pressure from Chief Justice Bryan, Kebell openly admitted what he was about: 'All I have to do is to disable [the plaintiff's] candidate either on a question of fact or a question of law.'[37] Nor was it simply a matter of genuine loopholes in the opposition case. Raising objections could be a psychological tactic. Kebell tried this with Robert Rede in another advowson case where he first tried to oblige Rede's client to produce a deed which he did not have, then argued a technical defect because a date had been omitted from his plea and then another defect because a name had been omitted; Rede, however, was not stampeded – he carried the court on the first point and coolly amended his plea instead of arguing on the other two.[38] At the least, such tactics gained time. When pleading the record of a lower court, Kebell once found himself told that no such record existed.[39] This clearly took him by surprise, but he responded with a request that a writ of *certiorari* should be sent to 'the justices of the peace before whom the record had been made' – a novel request since *certiorari* was, at that time, sued through chancery, not issued directly by either bench.[40] The court warned of the risks:

> Take good care that you do not lose your costs over this; why will you pray this at your peril?
> *Kebell*: Yes, truly, for you have the authority to write to all inferior justices.

The result was that common pleas stood the case back a day and then consulted the king's bench, which suggested a reference to exchequer chamber. The matter was thereupon adjourned to the next term and in the meanwhile Kebell's client was able to obtain a *certiorari* from chancery to the justice of assize, the real court concerned, and to have the record produced in due form.

37. *ibid.*, Pas. 11 Hen.VII, p. 1 f. 18.
38. *ibid.*, Pas. 9 Hen.VII, p. 3 f. 23.
39. *ibid.*, Pas. 13 Hen.VII p. 7 ff. 21–2.
40. Henderson, *English Administrative Law*, 91.

The psychological battle was particularly evident in demurrers, pleas on the law, not on the facts. There the key was gaining the support of even one or two justices, which immediately put pressure on the opposition. We find, for instance, Robert Rede not daring to demur because of the opinion of a court impressed by Kebell's arguments.[41] Much, of course, depended on a lawyer's assessment of his own case. In an action for waste, following the lease of a watermill, the judges were divided on Kebell's submission, and so:

> he did not dare to demur but [did so] with respect to a single load of clay, and said that he would put so much at risk to press the question in law. And for the rest, he pleaded further.[42]

Apparent confidence, however, could itself be a weapon. In the case where the court warned Kebell so firmly that his demurrer for the defence would be binding, he knew that Bryan and Townshend thought as he did, stuck to his point, and said to the demandant:

> If you think your counterplea is sound, I am ready to [enter my] rejoinder . . . But the demandant did not dare to jeopardise the issue because if the counterplea was bad in law, the issue would then be nothing but a *jeofail*.[43]

In a case fought out on the facts, rather than the law, the key was the traverse. Skill in selecting the issue on which to go to jury trial was essential for the pleader; he had to avoid being forced to assert what was uncertain or deny what was verifiable; and to evade issues where the opposition was bound to win. Pleading was akin to the game 'Poison Spot' where children try to force one another to step on a forbidden area. The point is well seen in a case Kebell conducted for his friend Robert Sheffield, part of a much larger and longer dispute about common rights on his land.[44] Among the claimants was a certain 'Alice', possessor of a neighbouring manor, but Sheffield discovered that one of her servants was putting his own beasts in to common and brought a separate action against him. Since the issue was the ownership of the cattle, it was important for the servant to maintain that he was acting for his employer, whose right to pasture was not being questioned in this particular suit. Serjeant John Fisher, his counsel, therefore entered the reply that his client had put in Alice's beasts.

41. *Y.B.* Pas. 13 Hen.VII, p. 8 f. 22.
42. *ibid.*, Pas. 13 Hen.VII, p. 3 f. 21.
43. *ibid.*, Trin. 13 Hen.VII, p. 1 f. 25; see above, p. 173.
44. *ibid.*, Hil. 6 Hen.VII, p. 3 f. 14; Mich. 11 Hen.VII, p. 31 f. 9; cf. *ibid.*, Pas. 11 Hen.VII p. 4 ff. 19–20.

Kebell avoided this by affirming 'you put in your own beasts' and if this had been traversed the jury would have had to decide simply whether the servant had or had not done so, the very question Sheffield wanted. Fisher therefore tried to impugn the plea:

This is not a proper plea. How if these are beasts owned by the defendant but leased to Alice to dung the land? They can then properly be put in to graze.[45]

Kebell pointed out that it was for Fisher to allege such special title but the other serjeant replied with a more dangerous argument.

You must take a traverse here; our side has said that we put in the beasts belonging to Alice and you have said that the beasts are ours. Therefore you must traverse, that is, say *without that the beasts belonged to Alice*.

The trap is obvious; to go to a jury denying that animals in the pasture belonged to Alice would invite defeat since, as everybody knew, some of them did. The defence, however, is equally clear, and Kebell had barely begun his reply when Bryan interjected:

he need not traverse, for the defendant perhaps put in Alice's beasts and also his own.

Kebell, nevertheless, was not to be stopped, and spelled out the matter, concluding:

When I say that he put in his beasts where he has said that he put in Alice's beasts, the putting in of her beasts will not be understood as denied by implication.

Bryan then said to Fisher,

if there is going to be any traverse it must be taken on your part, saying that you put in the beasts of the said Alice, *without that you put in your own*.

It would not be surprising, given the complexities of pleading, if parties often settled out of court. The year books are rarely concerned to note the outcome of any case, but occasional notes indicate that settlements certainly did take place. One such was *The Abbot of Hyde* v. *Benger*, a complicated action in which the abbot tried to recover rent and services from Benger and the defendant denied that he held land from the abbot.[46] Kebell appeared for Benger, and it was this case which saw his lecturing common pleas on feudal law in the reigns of Edward I and Edward II until Jay asked for up-to-date examples.[47] At

45. This and subsequent quotations are from *Y.B.* Mich. 11 Hen.VII, p. 31 f. 9.
46. *ibid.*, Trin. 13 Hen.VII, p. 6 ff. 27–8; Mich. 15 Hen.VII, p. 8 f. 16; Mich. 16 Hen.VII, p. 2 ff. 1–2.
47. See above, p. 165.

one point Kebell appears to have won wide support for his argument, and the discussion turned to the matter of damages, but the bench was deeply divided. Then, at a late stage, Bryan found a new problem, so although each party entered its position on the record, neither could be confident; thereupon they came to an agreement out of court.

In any study of the reports of court-room debates in the lifetime of Thomas Kebell, what comes out most strongly is the dominant influence of the chief justice of the common pleas, Thomas Bryan. It is he who, present or absent, dominates discussion, not simply by his obvious learning nor by his responsibility to speak last and sum up, but by his personality.[48] Indeed, in the interchanges between Bryan and Kebell we see the quality of the early Tudor legal profession at its best and at first hand. In *Sudberth* v. *Agard*, a case turning on voucher to warranty, Bryan said after the debate on year-book precedent:

Answer me this, if [the defendant] . . . is . . .?
Kebell: Perfectly reasonably, just as if . . .
Bryan [to *Rede*]: By this reasoning he will delay [your client] for a long time, so do what you want.
Rede: To this plea I plead etc.
Bryan [to *Kebell*]: Have a care, for this will be binding for the tenant [your client] but for the demandant it is no more than having a voucher.
Vavasour: If it were at another term, it has been held that it would then be binding.
Kebell: Even if it is another term, there is no reason why it should be binding.
And then Kebell of his own volition showed that . . .[49]

Another exchange took place in the action brought by Richard Broker to recover goods wrongfully taken from him.[50] The shorter of the two reports pays attention only to one point, raised for the defence by Kebell: if X takes goods from Y (Broker), can Y subsequently transfer ownership to X? Bryan thought that the removal of the goods by X destroyed Broker's possession and so his ability to make any gift. Kebell, however, thought the gift good in law, and, even if it were not, Broker's gift must at least have the effect of a release to X:

Bryan asked *Kebell*: If the owner in law is outlawed, are his goods forfeit?
Kebell: Yes Sir, as I understand it.
Bryan: If the real tenant is disseised and the disseisor is outlawed for felony, who will have the land? I consider that the disseisor retains responsibility for the land for all time.

48. The actual judgement was pronounced by the senior puisne judge.
49. *Y.B.* Mich. 11 Hen.VII, p. 12 f. 4; see above, pp. 157–8.
50. *ibid.*, Trin. 10 Hen.VII, p. 13 f. 27; cf. Mich. 6 Hen.VII, p. 4 ff. 7–9.

Kebell: Under your correction, the lord could enter and take the land.
Bryan: If a man is disseised of his rent and afterwards grants that rent away, that grant is void.

And to this, the report concludes 'there was no reply'.

Bryan was certainly master in his own court. Thomas Wode began an adjourned case by demurring for the plaintiff on Kebell's earlier pleas; Kebell replied with another argument and asked for judgement in his favour.[51] The chief justice enquired what pleas Kebell had made.

Wode: 'He has pleaded another bad plea just as the others are.' And he rehearsed to [Bryan] the pleas and would have argued that the latest plea was worthless. *Bryan* would not hear him but said that it was perfectly good. But he said to *Kebell* that he would not hold with him in his plea that [the defendant] had the freehold rights unless he said . . .[52]

Equally, Bryan would stand no nonsense. In the *Case of the Chapel of St Mary of Ronceval* Kebell argued (as he had over the chapel of Wanborough) the difference between being incorporate as 'the Master, Wardens, Brothers and Sisters of Ronceval' and pleading, by virtue of royal letters patent, as 'the Master and Wardens' only.[53] Thomas Wode disagreed, and Kebell replied:

I say that if the king had not granted the chapel that it should be impleaded by the name of 'the Master and Wardens' that it would be impleaded by the name of 'the Master, Wardens, Brothers and Sisters', according to the first words of the incorporation.
Bryan: What you say is true, but yet that does not prove that when the king granted the chapel that it should be impleaded by another name that it should necessarily plead according to that title, and I know very well that there are twenty religious houses in England in the same situation, and Windsor is one. So make your reply [to the plea].[54]

Bryan was adept at sticking to the point. In a case of replevin Kebell appeared for the prior of St John, against a tenant who claimed he owed a rent of 6d. for two acres instead of 12d. for one.[55] Arguing that the plea was double, the serjeant claimed that the tenant had to plead either the difference in area or the difference in rent.

Bryan said that, without any question, the plea was not double because the tenant must plead what his tenure really is.

51. *ibid.*, Trin. 10 Hen.VII, p. 1 ff. 24–5, p. 5 f. 26, p. 22 ff. 28–9.
52. *ibid.*, Trin. 10 Hen.VII, p. 22 ff. 28–9.
53. *ibid.*, Pas. 10 Hen.VII, p. 5 ff. 18–19, p. 11 f. 20; Trin. 11 Hen.VII, p. 12 ff. 27–8.
54. *ibid.*, Trin. 11 Hen.VII, p. 12 f. 28.
55. *ibid.*, Trin. 13 Hen.VII, p. 2 ff. 25–6.

John Fisher, for the tenant, remarked that although the extra rent was the point of the action 'we do not agree that we hold the acre the plaintiff refers to'.

Kebell: Then you can plead this other matter relating to your tenure by way of protestation [that is without prejudice to the main plea].
Bryan: That he will not do but, rather, what the tenure is in reality.
Others said that the protestation would not help in this case.
Kebell: I posit that if we had said . . . so I think that he must traverse the rent of the acre we are referring to.
Bryan: That he will not, but he must show the truth about his tenure [and plead] *without that he held from you in manner and form* [*as you have avowed*].

When Kebell produced yet another objection, Bryan cut the discussion short:

Yet the traverse seems sound [in law] if we leave out any response on the differences in services [claimed], for this is not the nub of the matter.

Kebell then took issue in the words suggested by Bryan and dropped the attempt to get the services specified in the plea.

In a debt on obligation case we find Bryan resisting not only Thomas Kebell but Wode and Rede as well – two future chief justices.[56] Required to make an estate worth £10 a year before a certain date, the defendant had, he claimed, transferred one manor in Somerset and another in Wiltshire, worth £10 together. Rede was about to reply when Bryan stopped him:

Take care what you are doing. For I ask, if the party traverses and says that the two manors are not worth £10 a year, where will such an issue be tried?
Wode: By both counties.
Bryan: No Sir, or so it seems to me.
Rede: If one person claims someone to be a ward by virtue of a manor in one county and a second person claims by virtue of a manor in another county, the issue of priority will be tried by both counties.
Bryan: I grant that, certainly, because it cannot otherwise be tried which is held by the older title. But in this case one county cannot try the value of a manor in another county, nor vice-versa. So it seems to me that he must show in his plea what each manor is worth annually, and if he wants to traverse the value of each manor it will be triable in the county where the manor lies.
Kebell: I pose that should one plead assets of a certain value in different counties this will be tried in both.
Bryan: Again I say, think very carefully what you reply to this.

Rede's answer was to say by protestation that together the two manors

56. *ibid.*, Hil. 11 Hen.VII, p. 10 ff. 14–15.

were not worth £10 a year, and that no estate was transferred in one manor before the date due, but to plead only to the lateness of the other, thus avoiding a double plea. Bryan, however, was not satisfied:

> This is no plea for you do not deny that he made an estate in the first manor [only reserve your position on this by protestation], and that manor, for anything that has been said, could by itself be worth £10 and so the liability is discharged. For although the defendant has said that these two manors are worth £10, this would be a true statement if they were worth £100. Therefore, either the defendant in his bar [to your action] or you in your replication must allege the full value of each manor or otherwise the pleading will be defective.

Townshend supported him and Rede gave in. Thomas Bryan had, as so often, carried the day.

Sir John Fortescue began the final chapter of *De Laudibus Legum Anglie* by putting into the mouth of the young prince of Wales an eulogy of the common law.[57]

> I am fully assured, chancellor, from your exposition in this dialogue that these laws are not only good but the best. And if some of them need improvement, the rules of parliament teach us that it can quickly be done there. Hence that realm is always really or potentially governed by the most excellent laws.

But the way justice is administered, and by whom, is as much part of the test of any system as the 'real or potential' laws. And in later medieval and early sixteenth-century England it is the part which, thanks to the year books, we know most about. The story is not as black as contemporaries and scholars working under their influence have supposed. The year books show us lawyers as able as any before or since, on the bench and at the bar. They reveal an intimacy of atmosphere where little could get by by default or sleight of hand, and where court and counsel could combine in the interest of litigants. The court, and especially the chief justice of common pleas (and presumably of king's bench as well) had a much greater control over litigation than is often supposed, and insisted on having the final say. But it is equally clear that Fortescue's encomium is wildly at variance with the facts. Pleaders could exploit technicalities to an alarming degree and the court had all too often to wring its hands in despair. The first is, perhaps, justifiable (one man's delay is another man's justice), and it must be remembered that many of the problems of pre-Reformation English law resulted from the attitudes of contem-

57. Fortescue, *De Laudibus*, 135.

porary society to the legal machine and the role of law. The courts, too, deserve sympathy, because what was defeating them was the weight and technicality of the law itself. It was precisely the failure of Fortescue's corrective parliamentary mechanism to work which condemned men of the calibre of Bryan and Kebell to grapple with outmoded procedures, new issues which had to be fitted into old forms, and the slow strangulation of finer and finer distinctions as brilliant minds were confined to traditional approaches. The comment which is at once saddest and the most revealing of the career of advocates such as Thomas Kebell is the remark made to him by Thomas Bryan, 'Make of this what you can.'[58]

58. See above, p. 173.

PART III

THE LAWYERS AND THE LAW

9

THE LEGAL SYSTEM

The English common law, which was served so assiduously by Thomas Kebell and his fellows, seemed both venerable and secure. Although its tradition dated only to the custom of the royal court of Angevin days, triumph over alternative laws had been complete. Even the law of the church, which had provided such resistance in the days of Henry II, now operated under the licence of the common law.[1] In parliament, the judges and serjeants took precedence over all commoners in the royal procession to the House of Lords, and sat in a tight group on and around the woolsack in the centre of the chamber.[2] On circuit the majesty of the law was recognised by the ceremonious welcome, housing and entertainment of the justices, while at the opening of the assize the commissioners were met by the notables of the shire and were expected to provide a grave discourse suitable to the occasion.[3]

I

Appearance and reality are, nevertheless, not the same, and the founding father of English legal history, F.W. Maitland, argued that behind this apparent security, the English common law was in a parlous position.[4] Across the channel, Europe was experiencing one of its periodic resurgences of Roman law. Communities everywhere, and especially the princes, were turning under the pressures of new political and economic stresses to the chief legacy of the Roman empire, the *lex civilis*; in country after country, 'the reception of Roman law' was undermining and even sweeping away the ancient laws and customs of the continent. Did England alone escape? The devastation of the flood, yes, but not, so Maitland claimed, the

1. See below, pp. 272–5.
2. S.E. Lehmberg, *The Reformation Parliament* (Cambridge, 1970), 76–8.
3. A description of assize ceremonies under Elizabeth I is given in J.S. Cockburn, *A History of English Assizes, 1558–1714* (Cambridge, 1972), 65–9.
4. F.W. Maitland, *English Law and the Renaissance* (Cambridge, 1901).

danger; unique in Europe, the English common law had resisted inundation by the civil law, but the pressure had been intense and the dykes had only just held.

Compelling though Maitland's analysis was – supremely as presented in the Rede lecture at Cambridge in 1900 – the evidence he used has been steadily eroded by his pupils and successors. He relied heavily on Thomas Starkey's advocacy of a 'reception', but Starkey's argument attracted little attention at the time.[5] Maitland cited a complaint by so-called 'students of the common law' against the encroachments of chancery in 1547, but this turns out to have been part of a sordid political attack on the chancellor.[6] The significance which he attached to the ending of the published year books has been undermined on bibliographical grounds.[7] As T.F.T. Plucknett suggested in 1932, in the sixteenth century demand for the older year books grew, and it is now known that reporting of cases was on the increase.[8] Some years before Plucknett wrote, Sir William Holdsworth published a careful critique of Maitland's evidence, showing that the law administered by the newer courts such as star chamber was not some dire foreign import, but the common law applied as and where possible.[9] Subsequent studies have only reinforced these objections, while in Europe scholars have shown that the 'reception' was a phenomenon not found outside Germany, and only partial even there.[10] On the continent, indeed, the story seems to have been more of a revival of national laws against the restrictions of the medieval romanist tradition, and the reform of the civil law which did go on remained confined to the studies and lecture rooms of the universities.

5. G.R. Elton argues that Starkey's unpublished treatise recognised that a reception of Roman law in England was unrealistic but did encourage (abortive) proposals to codify the common law: 'Reform by statute: Thomas Starkey's *Dialogue* and Thomas Cromwell's policy', in *Studies*, ii. 246–50.
6. A.J. Slavin, 'The fall of Lord Chancellor Wriothesley', in *Albion* 7 (1975), 265 *sqq*.
7. T.F.T. Plucknett, 'The place of the legal profession in the history of English law', in *L.Q.R.* 48 (1932), 328–40.
8. *ibid.*, 331–2; Abbott, *Law Reporting*, 108–9.
9. Holdsworth, *H.E.L.* iv. 217–93. The *coup de grâce* to Maitland's theory has been given by S.E. Thorne, 'English law and the Renaissance', in *La Storia del diritto nel quadro delle scienzi storiche* (Florence, 1966), 437–45, but N. Pronay, in *British Government and Administration*, 90–2, 102–3, has drawn attention to the appointment of civil lawyers to the staff of the chancery in the reign of Edward IV.
10. W. Kunkel, 'The reception of Roman law in Germany: an interpretation', and G. Dahm, 'On the reception of Roman and Italian law in Germany', in *Pre-Reformation Germany*, ed. G. Strauss (1972), 263–315 and the works cited in Spelman, *Reports*, ii. 27 n. 2.

The handful of sixteenth-century commentators who argued the desirability of transferring Roman law to England were as realistic about England and about Roman law as such experts usually are.

Following the destruction of Maitland's hypothesis, it has become fashionable to dismiss danger to the English common law in the sixteenth century as a canard. The matter, however, cannot be disposed of so easily. Developments in continental legal systems, in whatever direction, were not fortuitous. They were not self-generating but a response to defects in the existing legal arrangements. And among the inadequate, antiquated legal systems of Christendom, the common law was no exception; England, too, was growing in economic and social complexity; in England, just as much as on the continent, more efficient and sophisticated government was on the way.

Popular dissatisfaction with the English common law was widespread. In 1450 the Kentish rebels roundly declared:

> the law serveth of right and nought else in these days but for to do wrong, which for no thing almost is sped but false matters by colour of the law, for meed, dread or favour.[11]

A popular broadside, probably of Henry VIII's reign, *Questions worthy to be consulted on for the weale publyque*, asked:

> Whether euell order long abused myght be redressed by good lawes well obserued?
>
> Whether the lawes of the kynges of Englande made before the conquest be the common lawes of this Realme, and myght be reuiued agayne?
>
> Whether the proces at the common lawe is grounded on anye lawe positive?
>
> Whether the said proces is daylye abused as wel in courts as at the Shriffs his handes, by manifest collusion or not?
>
> Whether manyfest calumnye to sue false plees be suffred at the common lawe?[12]

Not only were the common folk, when we can hear them, disparaging; powerful critics can be found among the common lawyers themselves. Thomas More wrote of the contradiction between the unending stream of new laws and a country which was never 'well and sufficiently

11. H.M.C., 'Mss. of Magdalen College' in 8th *Report*. 1 (1881), 267A.
12. *Questions worthy to be consulted on for the weale publyque* (n.d.).

furnysshed with lawes . . . which thing the infinite controuersies in the lawe, dayle rysinge, neuer to be ended, playnly declare to be trewe'.[13] Sir Thomas Eliot, the humanist, was an enthusiast for the clarification of the law, and this in a book:

> wherin I wyll rendre myne offyce or duetie to that honorable studie wherby my father was aduanced to a iuge and also I my selfe haue attayned no lytle commoditie.[14]

There was clearly ground for such opinions. Sir John Fortescue selected four features of English law to demonstrate the innate superiority of the common law over its European counterparts. One was feudal wardship. Sir John waxed lyrical on the humanitarian concern this showed for the orphaned heir, while the English landed classes did everything in their power to avoid so happy a possibility.[15] Another of Sir John's superior features was the English jury, a mode of proof so much less corrupt than witnesses, the proof at civil law.[16]

> Feeble indeed in power and of less diligence may he be deemed, who cannot find, out of all the men he knows, two who are so lacking in conscience and truth that for fear, love, or advantage, they will contradict every truth.[17]

But 'fear, love or advantage' is an unconscious echo of the men of Kent, 'for meed, dread or favour', and it was the common law they were describing. As soon as it was known that Sir Robert Plumpton was to appear at the Lammas assize in York in 1499, his lawyer advised 'special labour', 'privily', to the potential jurors to secure their voices or their absence from the trial, and the advice was the merest commonplace.[18] But the most outrageous of all Fortescue's comments is his assertion at the end of *De Laudibus* that delay in common law litigation was only what was necessary and reasonable.[19] Modern

13. Thomas More, *Utopia*, 67.
14. Eliot, *The Gouernour*, i. 144–5. Thomas Eliot was the son of Richard Eliot J.C.P.; he was, early in his career, the clerk of assize to the western circuit and later clerk to star chamber: Lehmberg, *Sir Thomas Elyot*, 22, 27–31. For the views of another humanist critic, Richard Morison, see Thorne, in *La Storia del diritto*, 440–2.
15. Fortescue, *De Laudibus*, chapters xliv, xlv: see below, pp. 247–8, 275–6.
16. *ibid.*, chapters xx-xxxii.
17. *ibid.*, 45. The two remaining contrasts between English and French law were differing attitudes to the legitimisation of bastards and to social status by descent (*ibid.*, chapters xxxix-xliii). Fortescue's argument amounts to nothing more than prejudice.
18. *Plumpton Correspondence*, 132–4. Plumpton's counsel was John Pullen of Lincoln's Inn: see, pp. 139, 266.
19. Fortescue, *De Laudibus*, chapter liii.

scholarship has revealed an adjournment to consult counsel which was ultimately extended over eight and a half years, and another over six and a half, and this was after the tedious procedure of mesne process had been gone through to get the case before the court at all.[20] *Vox Populi, Vox Dei*, a popular ballad from the late 1540s, commented:

For pawre men thay doe crye
And saye it is a-wrye;
They saye thay cannott be herde,
But styll frome Daye to daye Differed;
When they haue any swtte,
They may gowe blowe ther flwtt;
Thus gothe the comon brewtt.[21]

The only hope of progress was to do what Sir John Fastolf did, to pay for 'expediting' the suit.[22] England was ripe for law reform.

If the pressures upon an antiquated law were similar in England and in Europe, it might, at first sight, seem that bringing Roman law across the Channel would have gained more support than it did. The reason why advocating a reception would not have been relevant in England is the particular form which the inadequacy of the medieval law took. The common law was not inadequate in doctrine. The best known instance where the reception was encouraged on the continent was by German princes seeking to escape the limitations of existing law upon the power of the state; for them Roman maxims such as *quod principi placuit legis habet vigorem* were highly attractive. But such notions were not needed in England. The common law was the king's law, administered by judges holding office at his pleasure; it was tender towards his rights, responsive to his wishes and always ready to grant his procedural privilege. The common-law equivalent to the maxim about the will of the prince declares, just as effectively, *ea interpretacio sequenda sit que pro rege fecit*.[23] English law needed no injection of Roman-law concepts.

20. Hastings, *Common Pleas*, 215; Blatcher, *Court of King's Bench*, 49–62 gives examples of appearance to answer a criminal charge after forty years and a response to outlawry in a civil case after twenty-one. For the dilatoriness of sheriffs see *ibid.*, 71–81, and 'Distress infinite and the contumacious sheriff', in *Bull. Institute of Hist. Research* 13 (1936), 146–50.
21. *Ballads from Manuscript*, ed. F.J. Furnivall, Ballad Soc. 1868–72, i. 136.
22. See below, p. 310.
23. Stephen Gardiner, *Letters*, ed. J.A. Muller (Cambridge, 1933), 390.

Where the common law needed reform was in procedure. It was excessively complex, it was dilatory and above all it was vulnerable. Delays, impediments and downright injustices could be bought for cash or secured by influence; 'angels work wonders in Westminster Hall'.[24] The two vital links in the judicial chain were the sheriff and the jury, and it was expecting too much in the fifteenth century for the one to be incorruptible and efficient at all times and the other to be composed of men of iron. Of even more importance was the lack of resilience within the system; the arteries of the common law were hardened. To leaf through the voluminous records of the common-law courts is to enter an unreal world where men are summoned and do not come, outlawed and do not care; where a progressively less and less significant group of problems is handled, and the sorrows and wrongs of real people are far away. Quite clearly the common law needed to be reformed or else given new vehicles in which to work.[25]

The source of such new machinery could only be the king. The tradition that the sovereign was the fount of justice with an almost sacramental obligation to right the wrongs of his people was still a vital one. Just as the common-law courts had emerged in the late twelfth and the thirteenth century to discharge this obligation in a regular manner, so two hundred years later the process was repeated to produce a new generation of courts – the chancery and the so-called prerogative courts, star chamber, requests and the like. 'Prerogative court' is, in fact, a dangerous term; it suggests some arbitrary executive interference with normal justice, whereas the truth is that these prerogative courts administered common law as far as possible, and that the 'common-law' courts of the sixteenth century had been the 'prerogative courts' of Angevin days. The origin of each generation of courts was the same, the royal household; constitutionally each represented in an institutionalised form the delegation of royal responsibility for justice to the king's counsellors.

The chancery, the first of the second family of courts, had its origins towards the end of the fourteenth century. Suitors who could not secure justice through the existing courts presented a 'bill' or petition to the crown asking for redress, and it became the custom for the king to commit to his chief executive adviser, the chancellor, as many bills for settlement as possible, mainly the civil ones. By the

24. Brant, *Ship of Fools*, f. xv.
25. For a judicious criticism of common-law procedure, see Hastings, *Common Pleas*, 211–44.

middle of the fifteenth century this 'bill procedure' had become a well-developed process; a petition (in the vernacular) is followed by an answer from the defendant, a rejoinder and then a replication, until all the story of each side is revealed, and this is followed by the taking of depositions by witnesses, all of which allows the chancellor to give judgement on the evidence or, very frequently, send the case to arbitration or to umpires. Direct responsibility for petitions involving criminal or political matters was normally retained by the royal council, which employed a similar 'English bill' procedure and became institutionalised in the sixteenth century as the court of star chamber. Other prerogative courts also appeared on similar lines but with more particular terms of reference, notably the conciliar tribunals in the north and the marches of Wales. All this was at the time procedurally superior to the common law. Defendants were brought to answer immediately by *subpoena*. Disputes were decided by the evidence. New wrongs and new remedies could be recognised, jury trial, with its potentialities for corruption, was by-passed, and the council could deal effectively with bribery, maintenance and embracery and all the various devices of judicial manipulation. The problems which led arm-chair theorists to advocate the reception of Roman law were in fact dealt with in England by a fresh initiative of the crown to provide new procedural opportunities for common-law principles.

II

From the first, these new courts were complementary to the older courts of common law in that they did what the ancient courts could not do. An important factor in the growth of chancery was service to the mercantile community, most strikingly a method of raising capital against interest 'which skated over the laws of usury'.[26] They were complementary also in that, in theory, matters normally 'determinable at common law' came into their purview only where some technicality or personal status hindered the existing courts. They did not set out to interfere with what these courts could do. Yet, despite this, the chancery and the prerogative courts were a very real alternative to the king's bench, the common pleas, the assize system and the jury. The advantages which they offered led litigants so to present their cases, that they would fall within the reference of one of the newer courts, and not in the traditional bench or *coram rege*.

26. Pronay, in *British Government and Administration*, 94–6.

The legal fiction has always been an important method by which common-law machinery has been adjusted. By 1500 the exchequer had already toyed with *quominus*, which was later to gain it a general jurisdiction; king's bench was developing the *latitat* procedure which eventually enabled it to oust the common pleas as the principal tribunal for civil actions.[27] Fictions could as readily extend the jurisdiction of the newer courts. One such which seems to have been developing in the chancery was the action for the detention of deeds. An entirely proper part of the chancellor's work was to assist litigants who could not sue at common law because the relevant documents were in the possession of their adversaries or third parties. Chancery, however, did more than secure the disclosure of the documents, it determined the title to them, and this inevitably led on to the title to the land concerned. Where the claim to the documents had been purely exploratory or, worse, vexatious, action of this sort was well justified; any chancery decision on title was, moreover, always provisional, and only the common-law courts could give a final judgement. Nevertheless, the regular trial of land titles in chancery in the early sixteenth century went far beyond these discretionary limits.[28]

The extent of chancery involvement in title to land is well illustrated in *Daubeney* v. *the Abbot of Ford and Tibbes*.[29] This was one of the last cases handled by Thomas More, and judgement was given by his successor, Thomas Audley, in July 1532. Henry, Lord Daubeney, claimed that he was seised of property by title of descent, but that not only were the charters concerning the estate in the hands of the abbot of Ford and a John Tibbes, but that Tibbes, backed by the abbot, was claiming title, and Daubeney was unable to enjoy peaceful receipt of the profits. The abbot replied that he was guardian for John Tibbes, the minor heir of Robert Tibbes who had died seised of the estate in his own right. Daubeney repudiated this; his own grandfather had once been disseised by the Moleyns family and had recovered by novel

27. For *latitat* procedure, see below, pp. 210–11; for *quominus* see Spelman, *Reports*, ii. *63–4*.
28. Ives, *Trans. Royal Hist. Soc.*, 5 ser., 18. 167–70. It is, however, important to note that some chancery suits were additional to a suit at common law, either to be vexatious or on the principle of trying everything possible: i.e. the provision of extra courts could encourage litigation. One weakness in chancery procedure was the uncertain effectiveness of the injunction: Jones, *Chancery*, 466–7. For the general question of the pressures on the common-law system and the role of the lawyers see also Ives, *Trans. Royal Hist. Soc.*, 5 ser., 18. 164–73.
29. C1/626/33–7. This, and other late examples, have been cited because decrees for earlier cases do not usually survive.

disseisin, but since the descent of the property to Daubeney, the Moleyns had again made a disseisin and had sold the land to Robert Tibbes. The abbot responded that long before the recovery – if any – indeed, in the time of Richard II, the Moleyns were seised and the property descended from father to son until it was sold to Tibbes. Not to be outdone, Daubeney then entered a descent from heir to heir in the male line back to Edward III. The significant point about the reaction of chancery is that it did not dismiss this pleading to common law, where it palpably belonged. Instead the decree recorded that Daubeney had failed to establish his claim; the abbot and his protégé were dismissed and the plaintiff ordered to pay costs.

Chancery was not alone in handling issues previously sacred to the common-law courts. C.G. Bayne demonstrated that more than half of the known cases heard in star chamber under Henry VII were land suits, and the discovery of additional material for the reign has only confirmed the conclusion.[30] Again they were brought in by a fiction, not of detention of deeds but of riot. Dr J. A. Guy's study of star chamber during the ascendancy of Cardinal Wolsey tells the same story; disputed title was by far the largest category of suit dealt with.[31] The later restriction of star chamber to criminal matters proper (a change still requiring elucidation) was a reduction of the original jurisdiction. Lord Chancellor Hatton said, *c.* 1590, that 'noe matter of tytle is now dealt with in that Court, albeit since the errection of the Court that was very common'.[32] Although there were again limits to the finality of titles established, star chamber would enforce them. In many cases, too, litigants were not looking for a judicial decision but for a negotiated settlement registered by the court and enforceable by it, thus avoiding the weaknesses of private arbitration.[33] With star chamber active in the field of land litigation no less than chancery, there was a real possibility that two sorts of title to land might have emerged; one, solemn and neglected, enforced by traditional remedies, the other – accepted in usual circumstances – granted outside the courts of common law.

Without doubt, the greatest threat to the common-law system before the Reformation was the 'use'.[34] This device effectively took the management of land settlements out of the traditional courts by vesting seisin at common law in a group of nominees, feoffees, but

30. Bayne, *Council of Henry VII*, cxxxvi, cxxxix, clv; Guy, *Cardinal's Court*, 15–17.
31. *ibid.*, 51–9.
32. Bayne, *Council of Henry VII*, clv.
33. Guy, *Cardinal's Court*, 56–7.
34. See below, pp. 247–8, 275–6.

leaving the beneficiary in control of the property, his interest protected by chancery. In this way all the common-law rigidity on the devise of land was evaded, and so too in effect the feudal obligations which followed from seisin in knight service. The position of the beneficiary presented the common law with a conundrum of a person who enjoyed the land but had no title to it; Littleton speculated that he was a tenant-at-will.[35] In the end, the use was accepted as an interest which could exist, and some forms fell under the jurisdiction of the common-law courts, especially after legislation in 1484; but the commonest and most important variety, a use established on a will, remained with chancery. The popularity of the device grew apace; if statistics derived from the sample of cases from Essex and Kent can be taken as typical, by 1460 ninety per cent of petitions to the chancery concerned uses.[36] The sort of multiple and conditional settlement which uses could achieve comes out in case after case. For example, in 1530 and 1534 chancery decrees settled two cases arising from the death of Hugh Lightfoot of Writtle in Essex.[37] Predictably, a family quarrel brought the settlements to court, but in the end the court disentangled an entail in the male line, an enfeoffment to Hugh, another to his second wife with remainder to their daughter, an enfeoffment to female heirs of his deceased eldest grandson, and a collusive enfeoffment to that grandson, backed by a fraudulently secured chancery degree aimed at evicting the widow. Through such arrangements, what really mattered in family and property law began to be handled in chancery. This was no victory for 'equity' over 'common law'; it was a matter of an 'up-to-date' procedure. When in 1464 the judges refused to recognise an equitable estate in the court of common pleas, rejecting the plea of Serjeant John Catesby that 'the law of chancery is the common law of the land', they were tacitly recognising that new remedies could only with difficulty be accommodated in the ancient courts.[38]

A key factor in determining the pace of this provision of equity and prerogative court procedures was the attitude of individual chancellors and their willingness to listen to matters which might be dismissed to common law. With star chamber, for example, it is clear that the arrival of Thomas Wolsey inaugurated a period when litigants

35. Holdsworth, *H.E.L.*, iv. 430; Milsom, *Historical Foundations*, 184; McFarlane, *Nobility*, 68–70.
36. Jacob, *Fifteenth Century*, 457, quoting the work of Miss M. Avery.
37. C1/498/9–12; 510/46–53.
38. *Y.B.* Pas. 4 Edw.IV, p. 9 f. 8.

were positively encouraged to turn for help to the royal prerogative. It is impossible to be exact, but it does seem that the number of cases begun before Wolsey in fifteen years totalled nearly 1,700 as against 300 for the whole reign of Henry VII.[39] As Sir Thomas Smith remarked, the court 'tooke great augmentation and authoritie' when Wolsey was chancellor.[40] With chancery, expansion had begun long before.[41] Under Edward IV, chancery petitions ran at about 360 a year; when Morton and Warham were chancellors the figure was 500, and for Wolsey 540. The real upward surge, however, came with his successors. If Wolsey's encouragement of business made the court of star chamber, it was More and Audley who made the fortunes of chancery. In two and a half years More received an average of 900 bills a year, while Audley had 1,200. In eighty years, that is, from 1460 to 1540, chancery business had increased threefold.

III

The counterpart to vitality in chancery and star chamber was decline in the common-law courts. There is considerable difficulty in any attempt to estimate the amount of business in any court, still more the range of its activity. The common law hardly looks in difficulties in the late fifteenth century when the common pleas might have seven hundred pleadings or imparlances in one term as against chancery's 360 petitions in one year.[42] And yet, as early as 1415, parliament was complaining in vain at the extension of chancery jurisdiction by the use of *subpoenas*; mere numbers may not tell the whole truth.[43] It is also hard to get behind pleas at common law to the reality of the issue. The common pleas enjoyed some seventy or eighty per cent of common-law business and the overwhelming bulk was pleas of debt; in Michaelmas 1481, five out of every seven suitors whose case was advanced enough to enter warrant of attorney alleged debt.[44] *Prima facie*, therefore, the court's concern with land was much less than with money, but land suits could be shaped in debt, and without adequate modern study of the case load it is hard to be sure what the proportion was. The accumulation of business by a court can also be a

39. Guy, *Cardinal's Court*, 51.
40. Quoted *ibid.*, 139.
41. For the following see Ives, *Trans. Royal Hist. Soc.*, 5 ser., 18. 116–17; cf. Guy, *Thought* 52. 282.
42. Hastings, *Common Pleas*, 190; Ives, *Trans. Royal Hist. Soc.*, 5 ser., 18. 166.
43. *Rot. Parl.*, iv. 84.
44. Hastings, *Common Pleas*, 16, 27; Ives, *Trans. Royal Hist. Soc.*, 5 ser., 18. 166.

reflection of its efficiency or otherwise; the effectiveness of the bench, the appropriateness of the remedies, the speed of the court, streamlined or clumsy procedure, all need to be considered. A complicating factor is that, as we have seen, a majority of common-law cases never reached trial.[45] Plenty, no doubt, were lost in the jungle of mesne process, but, for many litigants, starting a suit was enough to bring the other party to terms out of court.

One guide through this complex problem does, however, promise some element of objectivity. This is the docket roll of the king's bench, in which the chief clerk kept an index of all the procedural steps he took each term in cases at issue in his court.[46] The chief clerk was absorbing mesne business from other officers of the court by the *latitat* procedure, but this can be excluded; so, too, can the increasing number of private matters entered on the rolls to be of record and labelled *Anglia*. Finally a check can be made on the chief clerk's diligence by detailed comparison of the docket roll with the *coram rege* roll, the master record of the court. Handled in this way, this source offers reliable figures not of cases or litigants but of the number of stages by which suits at issue in the king's bench were advanced each year; it measures the bureaucratic 'through-put' of the chief clerk.

The first point the docket rolls make obvious is the considerable short-term fluctuation in the work of the court. In the first extant roll, the busiest year, 1448/9, has half as many entries again as the lightest, 1450/51. Individual terms varied even more; Michaelmas 1448 has 248 entries, Michaelmas 1450 only 120, Trinity 1448, 192, Trinity 1450 a mere 60. The archive is complete enough, however, to allow the calculation of a running mean which can absorb the impact of freak years and casualties such as the loss of a term's entries, adjournment in mid-term, or the occasional closure of the court for plague.[47] Taken in this way the docket rolls suggest that between 1444/5 and 1450/1 the mean load on the chief clerk was of the order of 560 procedural steps a year. The second roll covers the years 1 to 10 Henry VII, where, after the first two thin years of political disturbance, the

45. Hastings, *Common Pleas*, 183.
46. For the following see the references in Ives, *Trans. Royal Hist. Soc.*, 5 ser., 18. 165–7, and Table D.
47. Blatcher, *Court of King's Bench*, 23, 168, 169; IND1325 ff. 10v, 15v, 16; 1333 ff. 2, 2v (adjournments for Pas. 1489, Mich. 1490 and 1528). It is important to include freak returns in any calculation since casual interruptions were a normal part of the life of the court.

load is about 460. The roll for Michaelmas 1495 to Michaelmas 1497 has been lost, but the mean for the rest of Henry VII's reign was 520–30, with extremes of 421 and 586. Omitting the first two terms of the next reign, and also Michaelmas 1512, which precedes another break in the record, the mean for 1510–12 is nearer 550, with actual entries in 1511/12 reaching 704, the highest total on the docket rolls to that date. But between 1522/23 and 1529/30 a fall begins, with the mean declining to 357 between extremes of 535 and 222. In the next decade, the mean is even lower, ending at 321 with limits of 396 and 258. For the rest of Henry VIII's reign the trend stays almost always below 350, but a recovery set in later in the 1540s, with the mean breaking 400 in 1550, and from 1550/1 until the death of Mary, rapid advance brought the mean to about 780, and in one year, 1555/6, actual docket roll entries reached the new record of 902. The trough of this evident depression seems to have lasted from 1526/7 to 1549/50, with the eye of the storm in the years 1536/7 to 1539/40; in the trough business was always below 400 items a year, and in the eye this sank to a nadir of 320. The plea rolls of the court confirm the records of the chief clerk's dockets, with their numerous blank membranes, extraneous entries and exaggerated spacing.[48] All the evidence suggests that the king's bench had fallen on hard times.

Counting docket roll entries is open to the objection that any change in the way business is recorded will necessarily falsify figures so obtained. This is not a serious problem. The count shows both decline and recovery, so that if change in the customs of the court explains the fall in entries, we have to account for the subsequent rise either by yet another, and compensating, change in procedure, or by an even more massive injection of new business. Furthermore, work by Dr Marjorie Blatcher on an entirely different set of records, those of the clerk of the hanaper, has confirmed the trend indicated by the docket rolls.[49] Every judicial writ had to be sealed at a fee (almost always seven pence), and since a court writ was required at every stage of common-law process except the first, the amount raised is an indicator of business which is exempt from changes in record keeping. Unfortunately the series of hanaper profits is very defective. As with

48. Blatcher, in *Elizabethan Government and Society*, 200–1.
49. Blatcher, *Court of King's Bench*, 15–21. The contrast between the detailed variation of the graph, *ibid.*, 21 and Table D reflects the difference between calculating decennial averages on the basis of surviving figures (complete years only) and indexing the actual figures or plotting them directly; cf. the graph in Ives, *Trans. Royal Hist. Soc.*, 5 ser., 18. 167.

Table D. *Docket roll entries in king's bench, 1444/5–1557/8, compared with the profits of sealing judicial writs*

	King's Bench Docket Rolls		Fees for Sealing Judicial Writs		
	I Total	II Mean	III King's Bench Index	IV Common Pleas Index	V Total Index
23 Hen.VI 1444/5	267/2				
24 Hen.VI 1445/6	508				
25 Hen.VI 1446/7	529				
26 Hen.VI 1447/8	637				
27 Hen.VI 1448/9	685	579*	100	100	100
28 Hen.VI 1449/50	472	566			
29 Hen.VI 1450/1	458	556			
1451–1485[1]					
1 Hen.VII 1485/6	286		52	41	43
2 Hen.VII 1486/7	213		42	34	35
3 Hen.VII 1487/8	469				
4 Hen.VII 1488/9	393				42
5 Hen.VII 1489/90	580	388			
6 Hen.VII 1490/1	426	416	65	46	49
7 Hen.VII 1491/2	416	457	66	47	49
8 Hen.VII 1492/3	518	467	75	46	50
9 Hen.VII 1493/4	466	481	74	47	51
10 Hen.VII 1494/5	432	452	69	43	46
1495–1497[2]					
13 Hen.VII 1497/8	291/3				

Table D *continued*

	I	II	III	IV	V
14 Hen.VII 1498/9	442		64	56	57
15 Hen.VII 1499/1500	441		62	45	48
16 Hen.VII 1500/1	421		54	54	54
17 Hen.VII 1501/2	528	444*	62	57	58
18 Hen.VII 1502/3	521	471	60	54	55
19 Hen.VII 1503/4	582	499	64	60	61
20 Hen.VII 1504/5	553	521	60	76	74
21 Hen.VII 1505/6	512	539	62	78	76
22 Hen.VII 1506/7	586	551			
23 Hen.VII 1507/8	498	546			
24 Hen.VII 1508/9	335/2	516 (bracketed with 1 Hen.VIII)			
1 Hen.VIII 1509	98/2				
1/2 Hen.VIII 1509/10	550	516			93
2/3 Hen.VIII 1510/11	669	547			
3/4 Hen.VIII 1511/12	704	571			
4/5 Hen.VIII 1512/13	189/1	622*			
5/6 Hen.VIII 1513/14			80	81	81
6/7 Hen.VIII 1514/15					
7/8 Hen.VIII 1515/16			95	65	69
8/9 Hen.VIII 1516/17					
9/10 Hen.VIII 1517/18			53	31	34
10/11 Hen.VIII 1518/19	270/2		75	47	51
11/12 Hen.VIII 1519/20	659		74	40	45

Table D *continued*

	I	II	III	IV	V
12/13 Hen.VIII 1520/1	574				
13/14 Hen.VIII 1521/2	456		65	29	34
14/15 Hen.VIII 1522/3	535	553*	55	29	33
15/16 Hen.VIII 1523/4	413	527			
16/17 Hen.VIII 1524/5	431	482	44	20	23
17/18 Hen.VIII 1525/6	222	411			
18/19 Hen.VIII 1526/7	365	393	62	21	27
19/20 Hen.VIII 1527/8	353	357			
20/21 Hen.VIII 1528/9	457	366	68	56	57
21/22 Hen.VIII 1529/30	394	358			
22/23 Hen.VIII 1530/1	331	380			
23/24 Hen.VIII 1531/2	378	383			
24/25 Hen.VIII 1532/3	372	386	36	77	71
25/26 Hen.VIII 1533/4	396	374	44	75	71
26/27 Hen.VIII 1534/5	373	370	39	74	69
27/28 Hen.VIII 1535/6	346	373	37	68	63
28/29 Hen.VIII 1536/7	258	349			
29/30 Hen.VIII 1537/8	308	336	38	55	53
30/31 Hen.VIII 1538/9	322	321	36	51	49
31/32 Hen.VIII 1539/40	373	321	36	51	49
32/33 Hen.VIII 1540/1	194/3	304*	38	53	51
33/34 Hen.VIII 1541/2	389	330*			
34/35 Hen.VIII 1542/3	382	345*			
35/36 Hen.VIII 1543/4	292	339*	129	52	63

Table D *continued*

	I	II	III	IV	V
36/37 Hen. VIII 1544/5	386	342*			
37/38 Hen. VIII 1545/6	236/3	352*			
38 Hen. VIII 1546	147	338* (38 Hen. VIII and 1 Edw. VI together)			
1 Edw. VI 1547	166				
1/2 Edw. VI 1547/8	465	354*			72
2/3 Edw. VI 1548/9	470	390*	211	50	72
3/4 Edw. VI 1549/50	413	395*	211	43	66
4/5 Edw. VI 1550/1	621	456			
5/6 Edw. VI 1551/2	660	526	308		100
6/7 Edw. VI 1552/3	523/3	572*	400	75	120
1 Mary 1553/4	669	612*	355		
1 & 2 Philip & Mary 1554/5	800	689*			
2 & 3 Philip & Mary 1555/6	902	746*			
3 & 4 Philip & Mary 1556/7	824	778*	355		
4 & 5 Philip & Mary 1557/8	685	776	277	108	131

Column I — Totals of entries on the king's bench docket rolls, exclusive of *latitats* and those marked *Anglia*. Where figures are not available for four terms in a year the number extant is indicated as /2 etc.

Column II — Figures from Column I expressed as a five-year running mean. Points affected by averaging up defective returns are asterisked.

Columns III–V — Totals of net hanaper profits from the sealing of judicial writs, expressed as an index (base = 1448/9).
All figures are to the nearest whole number.
All figures are calculated Michaelmas to Trinity.

Notes: 1. Hanaper receipts survive for 11 years in this period. Index figures are as follows (K.B.: C.P.: Total): 1457/8–135:88:94; 1461/2–83:70:72;

1465/6–103:96:97; 1468/9–88:84:85; 1470/1–19:18:18; 1474/5–59:65:64; 1475/6–54:70:67; 1476/7–58:78:76; 1478/9–30:42:41; 1479/80–54:72:69; 1480/1–37:57:54.
2. No hanaper receipts are available for these years.

Sources: 1444/5–1450/1: IND 1324; 1485/6–1494/5: IND 1325, 1326; 1497/8–1512/3: IND 1327, 1328, 1329, 1330; 1518/9–1557/8: IND 1331–1338; Blatcher, *Court of King's Bench*, pp. 138, 167–71. See also the graph in Ives, *Trans. Royal Hist. Soc.*, 5 ser., 18. 167.

the docket rolls, totals vary from year to year quite significantly, and with only fifty-five complete sets of figures available for the 114 years from 1444/5 to 1557/8 and a maximum continuous series of eight years (1498/9 to 1505/6), long-term trends cannot be reduced to statistics. What is significant, however, is that the figures Dr Blatcher assembled for the profits of sealing king's bench writs suggest the same story as the docket rolls. If indexed to a base of 100 in 1448/9 the first year when docket rolls and hanaper receipts coincide, king's bench totals for sealing writs in the reign of Henry VII work out in the 60s, are somewhat higher early in the next reign but settle back in the 1520s before declining between 1532/3 and 1540/1 to a figure in the 30s. What is more, since income from the seals was generated by the whole court, it is clear that the overall work of king's bench declined, not simply the work of the chief clerk recorded on the docket roll.[50]

The hanaper profits also add a new dimension to the story because they include figures for the common pleas, whose docket material is entirely inadequate. In consequence it is possible to compare the fortunes of the two courts. Some error may be built in by indexing again on the base 1448/9, since we do not know how typical the balance between the two courts was in that year. But even admitting the possibility of some distortion, the figures show that the fortunes of

50. But note the exception after 1542: see below, p. 213 n. 80. It will be noted that while hanaper profits and docket roll entries agree on the *fact* of decline and recovery, they differ on the degree, with the former tending to accentuate both processes. Thus, in 1539/40 the index for profits is 36, but an equivalent for the entries would be 54; in 1557/8 the figures are 276 and 118. The counts, however, reflect different aspects of the court's work. During the decline, since the chief clerk was using the cheaper *latitat* to poach from the filacers, the overall profits of the court can be expected to have declined faster than his own. During the recovery, the more rapid rise in the figures for total profits may suggest that in the 1540s business is beginning to be omitted from the docket rolls, along with *latitat* entries themselves (which occur only occasionally after Mich. 1545).

common pleas were in decline in the early Tudor period and were clearly worse than those of the king's bench, although on a different time-pattern. For much of Henry VII's reign the index was already down to between 40 and 50, improving between 1503/4 and 1515/16, but then dropping disastrously over the next ten years to the low 20s, while its sister court still had the worst to come. In the 1530s, when the storm really broke about king's bench, common pleas was starting a modest recovery, but this was overtaken when king's bench began to pull out of the trough in the late 1540s. The hanaper receipts establish that common-law decline was not confined to king's bench.

IV

If in the later fifteenth and early sixteenth centuries the traditional courts were in danger of being relegated to a position second in importance to new courts such as chancery and star chamber, why was the danger averted – for averted it was? In the eighty years or so on either side of 1600, old and new courts lived side by side in reasonable co-operation and harmony.[51] In part the explanation lies in the clearer definitions which, as we have seen, took chancery and star chamber out of land law. In part, too, these courts suffered from their own success. More litigation meant more paper-work, while allegations of a free interpretation of equity by chancellors like Wolsey led to attempts to systematise and regulate judicial discretion. Courts which had come to prosperity by offering better justice, or justice where there was none, became notorious for procrastination.[52] Another factor was that these courts had in the injunction and decree a flexible weapon to secure equity but one which was less effective in securing finality.[53] There was also the hallowed position of common-law process. Its methods were engrained in English life, and civil administration depended on them as much as the courts did.[54] To have dropped below a base of common-law activity would have undermined the foundations of state and community, notably the jury.

51. Jones, *Chancery*, chapter xiii.
52. *ibid.*, chapter vii; T.G. Barnes, 'Due process and slow process in the late Elizabethan and early Stuart star chamber', in *American Journal of Legal History* 6 (1961), 221–49, 315–46.
53. See above, pp. 196–7. Injunctions and decrees were not 'of record' and so could not prevent reopening of the same issue. This reflects the conciliar origin of the prerogative courts with the tradition of political settlement by arbitration and influence. This is an objection made by Edward Hall, *Chronicle*, 585.
54. See above, pp. 9–10.

Each of these factors played a part in preserving tradition, but an important ally was the profession of common lawyers.[55] In the first place, the new courts were from the start serviced by, and depended on, the existing common-law profession. As Dr J. A. Guy has written of Wolsey:

the minister was only able to implement his policies in the first place because he had secured the co-operation of the leading professionals . . . As councillors, justices of king's bench, common pleas and assizes, commissioners of inquiry, *oyer et terminer* and gaol delivery, their support was essential to the success of Wolsey's aims and government, and they gave energetic assistance irrespective of personal antagonisms.[56]

In consequence, one common bar accepted and served all the courts, 'prerogative' and 'common-law' alike. The claim by defendants in chancery that they ought to be being sued at common law was mere form, but it did enshrine an attitude antagonistic to the decline of the older courts. With the Reformation, the colonising of chancery by the common lawyers was demonstrated at the highest level. Thomas More became in 1529 the first common lawyer for 150 years to be chancellor, and in 1534 Thomas Cromwell became master of the rolls.[57] Courts practising modern judicial procedures were under the control of a legal profession which saw their function as complementary to, not destructive of the work of the two benches. A critical stage in achieving this *modus vivendi* was the statute of uses.[58] Secured in 1536 by a combination of judicial subservience and self-interest, in effect it transferred to common-law courts much of the litigation on uses which had belonged to the chancery. At one blow they had recovered the dominant role in land suits. Four years later the common-law courts added, again at the expense of the chancery, the devise of land by will, their first substantial stake in testamentary jurisdiction.[59]

The lawyers, therefore, controlled the newer tribunals and saw them as part of a single judicial machine. Equally important, the older courts began a programme of self-reform.[60] The development of

55. For the following, see also Ives, *Trans. Royal Hist. Soc.*, 5 ser., 18. 170–3.
56. Guy, *Thought* 52. 287–9.
57. For Cromwell as M.R., see below, p. 257. Thorp C.J.C.P. and then Knyvet C.J.K.B. held the great seal from 1371 to 1377.
58. *27 Henry VIII* c. 10; see below, pp. 257–9.
59. *32 Henry VIII* c. 1.
60. On the question of law reform, see now the seminal study of J.H. Baker; Spelman, *Reports*, ii. *passim*, especially *51–64*.

'actions on the case' enabled the common law to grope towards the consideration of modern problems such as slander, contract and liability. This seems to have been true particularly of king's bench, although it must be said that most is known about that court. Between 1500 and 1550 it entertained, largely in the variety of 'case' known as *assumpsit*, a significant number of new issues.[61] Many were of a commercial kind, such as marine insurance, bills of exchange, freight, contracts and partnership.[62] This is not to suggest that such actions were common, but it is to say that less and less could the king's bench be accused of irrelevance and the inability to meet the needs of the day. And as the century progressed, reform proceeded. It even became possible to wonder whether the whole second generation of royal courts had not become superfluous.[63]

How the process of change operated in Thomas Kebell's day will be touched on in a later chapter, but it is worth at this point probing more deeply a reform in common law which took place against a background of the rise of the newer courts.[64] How far was this a deliberate competition with equity and prerogative and between the common-law courts themselves, and how far a response to other factors? The late C. A. F. Meekings, after a lifetime's experience of king's bench records, put the problem thus:

> Perhaps, most of all, one would like to know if it was the development of the equity side of the Chancery that stimulated the King's Bench to develop the classic bill procedure under Chief Justice Fortescue, Markham, Billyng and Huse; or rather, whether the development of the equity (and later prerogative-court) bill and the classic King's Bench bill are not part of an early-Renaissance development of new ways of litigation.[65]

Contemporaries who were aware of what was going on saw the changes in king's bench in particular as a dishonest attempt to attract business, and some recent studies have suggested that courts in pre-Reformation England were in competition.[66] Conscious willingness by king's bench to expand reached a peak, it is argued, when the court was dominated for nearly half a century by a *mafia* from Kent

61. *ibid.*, ii. *60–1*.
62. *ibid.*, ii. *286*.
63. Henderson, *English Administrative Law*, 70 n. 41.
64. See below, pp. 276–81.
65. Meekings, 'King's bench files', 106.
66. Most recently Blatcher, *Court of King's Bench*, 6–9, 103–6, 164–5. For the Fineux connection see *ibid.*, 145–6, 149–50; Spelman, *Reports*, ii. *54–7*.

whose 'godfather' was John Fineux, chief justice from 1495 to 1525, and whose principal members were his relatives by marriage, the Roper family, which passed the office of chief clerk from father to son for 118 years. Guilt by association is clear, and it was obviously in the interest of Fineux and John Roper not to turn away business in time of dearth. Still more was this true in 1539 when Edward Montagu, another of the clan, became C.J.K.B., with his brother-in-law William Roper, son of John and grandson of John Fineux, as chief clerk. Suspicion is strengthened by the far-reaching reform in procedure which king's bench developed alongside its new remedies, based on the issue of a writ of *latitat* arising on a fictitious 'bill of Middlesex'. This allowed the court to offer quicker and cheaper remedies over the whole range of common-law jurisdiction, including title.

The device of bill and *latitat* certainly did involve successive chief clerks (indeed, it allowed them to poach fees from the lesser clerks, the filacers).[67] It must also have had the approval of the bench. The first step towards turning a genuine procedure for Middlesex grievances into this most fruitful of legal fictions was a ruling in 1452 that defendants who had surrendered and been released on bail were still in the custody of the court. Thus an individual could be brought to answer an alleged trespass in Middlesex by a bill and a writ of *latitat*, which cost less and cut out several stages of process on original writ; the trespass could then be quietly abandoned and the real action begun against a prisoner 'in custody', which again had financial advantages. The court also felt an effect because bills could raise matters not otherwise handled in Westminster Hall; they forced the judges, as Dr Blatcher so acutely phrased it, 'to think the legally unthinkable more often'.[68] The device 'involved minimal effort and outlay' and by the start of the sixteenth century was so popular that John Roper had to reorganise the filing system of the chief clerk's office.[69] The next land-mark was also a clerical one and came in 1542, early in Montagu's period as chief justice; clients using *latitat* were no longer required to pay for sealing the artificial bill and writs to the sheriff of Middlesex and for having these enrolled, so saving cost and delay. King's bench could now offer the litigant:

67. For the following, see Blatcher, *Court of King's Bench*, 111–35.
68. *ibid.*, 160.
69. *ibid.*, 120, 125; there were other bureaucratic developments also: Meekings, 'King's bench files', 100–12.

an escape from the inconvenience involved in suing by original, a highly expeditious first process, and a defence against jurisdictional quibbles.[70]

Judges faced with and willing to consider new remedies; a bench and clerks ready to contrive and connive at new procedures. It is tempting to see common law courts here calculatingly bringing in reform to counter economic decline.

Not all the evidence, however, reads this way. In 1452 the judges did not rush to seize extra business; the issue had been argued twice before and in the end they may have been forced to approve a procedure which had grown up unofficially.[71] This, as Dr Blatcher would point out, necessarily implicates the court clerks, yet the initiative must have lain in part with litigants and their counsel.[72] Reform, too, was piecemeal and did not yield the courts immediate dividends. The fictitious bill of Middlesex was in substantial use after the middle of the fifteenth century but did not, as we have seen, prevent king's bench business from declining.[73] The changes of 1542 may-have been more productive, but they can fairly be seen as a logical clumination of previous advances. Manoeuvre here is hard to envisage; king's bench had been quietly developing a new procedure, but this implies only that the court tolerated a development which litigants found useful and which diverted fees to the chief clerk at a time when the total load on the court was falling. John Fineux could have gained only accidentally from co-operation with the Ropers; unsupported tradition, indeed, suggests that he disapproved of bill procedure.[74]

Willingness to consider new remedies can have brought Fineux no great material return either. It did, however, agree closely with his known personality and ideas. Today we should class him as an 'interventionist' judge. His attack on sanctuaries, albeit at Henry VIII's investigation, radically revised Hussey's judgement in *Humphrey Stafford's Case*, and Thomas More noted that Fineux had the firm opinion that 'who so taketh from a justice the order of hys dyscrecyon

70. Spelman, *Reports*, ii. 54.
71. Blatcher, *Court of King's Bench*, 119–20; see below, p. 277. Dr Blatcher, however, points to the important activities of court clerks as legal advisers: *ibid.*, 141 n.16.
72. *ibid.*, 144–6.
73. Blatcher, *Court of King's Bench*, 128; see above, pp. 201, 206.
74. The profits of sealing writs in king's bench are known for sixteen of Fineux's thirty years as C.J. In only four did profits rise more than 11s.od. (1.28%) above those of the first year; in nine they were more than £1 lower: *ibid.*, 169–70. For Fineux's opinion of bill procedure: *ibid.*, 150.

taketh surely from hym more thanne halfe hys office'.[75] For a judge of this temper, close relations and family ties with court officers and other important lawyers were less a sinister network than a source of support. As for Montagu, it appears that he too was willing to innovate:

sessions at the Guildhall before Mountague C.J. . . . in the 1540s already had the strong mercantile bias which typified the seventeenth-century King's Bench.[76]

Too personal an association of Fineux and Montagu with deliberate expansionism by king's bench may be more than the facts warrant. We must allow for genuine professional initiative in reform, both procedural and substantive.

It is clear, also, that reform in king's bench did not engender serious contention with common pleas. Though apparently distinct, the courts operated much more as separate functions of a unified bench. Not only was this institutionalised in the meetings of exchequer chamber, but during the sittings of king's bench and common pleas the justices regularly communicated about difficult cases.[77] Existing statistical evidence certainly does not suggest that reform in king's bench was at the expense of the sister court.[78] Figure 2a shows that although the volume of litigation expanded and contracted in the short as well as the long term, there is nothing to indicate that either court squeezed the other. When common pleas was in trouble in the 1520s, king's bench only succeeded in maintaining the level of profits it had enjoyed over several decades; in the 1530s the recovery of common pleas was significantly in excess of any king's bench losses. Nor are conclusions different if the data are reassembled to show the share each court took of available litigation (Figure 2b). In the 1530s

75. Ives, in *On the Laws and Customs of England*, 298–301; Spelman, *Reports*, ii. *41*, *343–5*.
76. *ibid.*, ii. *286*.
77. *Y.B.* Trin. 9 Hen.VII, p. 2 f. 1; Hil. 9 Hen.VII, p. 1 f. 14; Mich. 14 Hen.VII, p. 6 f. 2. The same was true of chancery: *ibid.*, Hil. 4 Hen.VII, p. 3 f. 2; Pas. 8 Hen.VII, p. 3 f. 11.
78. The difficulties which, as Dr Blatcher stressed (*Court of King's Bench*, 133–7), remain in accounting for the rapid popularity of *latitat* and for the slowness of the process to attract business to king's bench (and for the coincidence of both phenomena) are significantly reduced if less emphasis is placed on competition with common pleas. Cf. S.F.C. Milsom: 'The diversion of jurisdiction was not deliberately aimed at by anybody. The king's bench of course welcomed the end and connived at the means; but the force behind it was the plaintiff's desire for other qualities of the new procedure': *Historical Foundations*, 56.

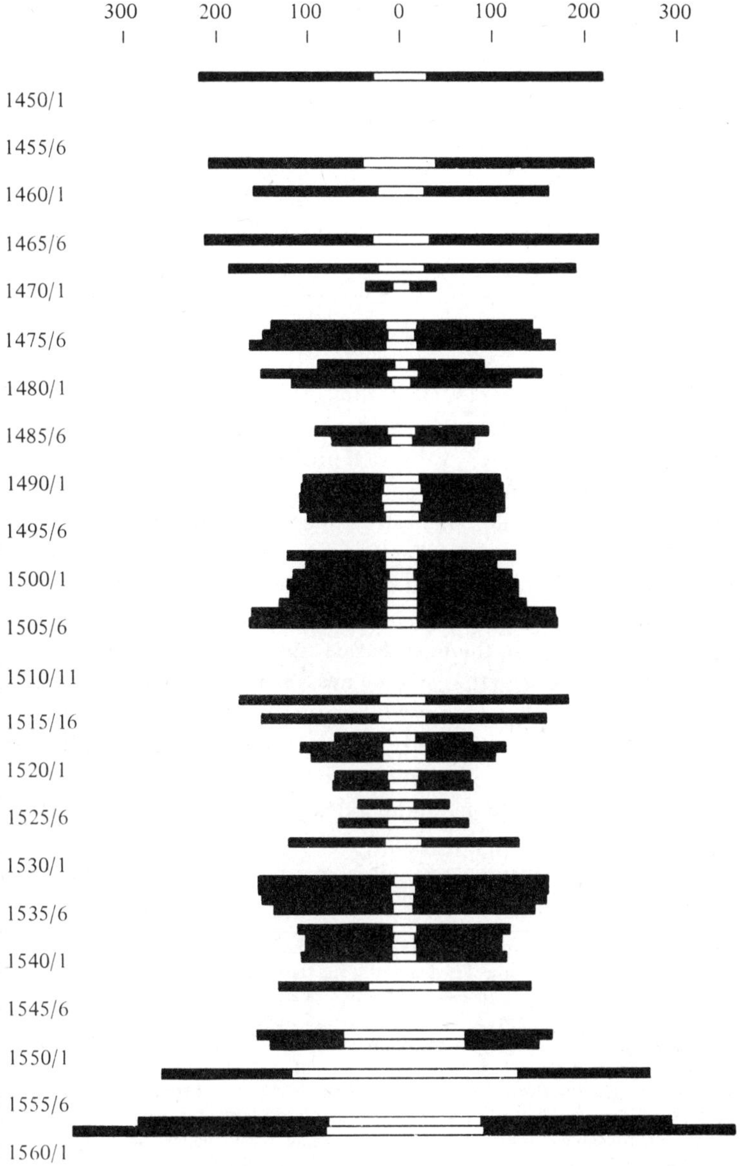

Fig. 2a. Graph showing the relative movements of hanaper profits for the sealing of judicial writs (common pleas shown in solid). (Source: Blatcher, *Court of King's Bench*, 168–71)

the common pleas was taking over ninety per cent of business – hardly evidence of retreat.

The one hint of poaching comes with the revival of king's bench in the late 1540s. Whereas in three periods – 1474–7, 1532–6 and 1548–50 – the average annual profit from sealing judicial writs was the same, some £307 or £308, the common pleas' share in the earlier periods, £273 and £282 respectively, dropped in the third to £178, and this despite the reduction in king's bench charges for sealing process by bill.[79] The result was that the latter was taking a significantly larger share of total business, rising in 1552/3 to forty-six per cent. But this may be an aberration; Edward Montagu was quite convinced in 1545 as to which court was the more profitable. In any case, in the last of the series of hanaper receipts for the sealing of judicial writs (for 1557–9), common pleas is once more well ahead, and although king's bench does have nearly a quarter of the total profits, it has clearly made that gain by attracting new litigants.[80]

It is similarly difficult to read straight competition into the story of buoyant prerogative and weakening common-law courts. It might, for example, seem plausible that the problems of common pleas in the 1520s reflected the competition of Wolsey's chancery, and the weakness of king's bench in the next decade, the rivalry of star chamber. However, we have seen that Wolsey made his principal thrust in star chamber and that chancery was taking more cases under More and Audley than under the cardinal. Even a suggestion that Wolsey was discouraging resort to common pleas by a lavish use of injunctions falls before the evidence that injunctions were not used by him in any novel way.[81] Similarly, the recovery of common pleas in the 1530s antedated the defeat inflicted upon chancery in 1536 by the passage of the statute of uses. It is also important to see these common-law

79. Blatcher, *Court of King's Bench*, 168–71; see above, p. 210. The contrast of the 1548–53 figures with those of earlier years, and the dominance of the common pleas in litigation before 1542, is clear in Figures 2a and 2b.

80. Calculations after 1542 are affected by the loss of crown profits following changes in sealing practices in king's bench: see above, p. 210. Thus it could be argued that later receipts of the court must reflect, pound for pound, a larger amount of business, that the drop in common pleas profits by 11% between 1537–41 and 1548–50 is the result, and that king's bench business *post* 1542 is much underestimated in the tables. But since common pleas profits (on unchanged charges) were in 1557–9 240% above the 1537–41 average, this must argue that that court's work too had expanded in actual terms. Throughout these calculations the costs of sealing have been assumed to be in constant proportion to the net profits and so have been ignored. Cf. *ibid.*, 138 n. 3.

81. Guy, *Thought* 52. 280.

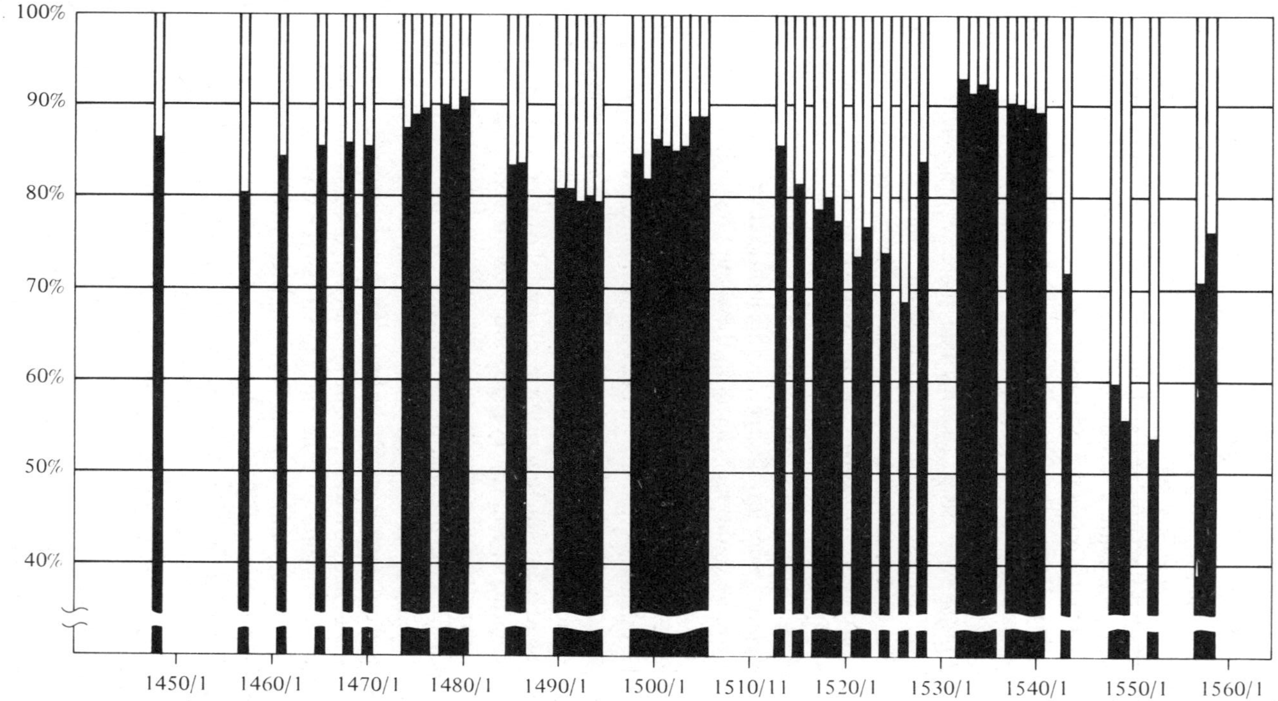

Fig. 2b. Graph of the relative movements of hanaper profits for the sealing of judicial writs (common pleas shown in solid), expressed in terms of a constant level of litigation. (Source: as Fig. 2a)

fluctuations of Henry VIII's reign in the context of a long-term decline which went back to at least the third quarter of the previous century; by 1474/5 to 1476/7, total profits from common-law sealing had already dropped to sixty-nine per cent of the 1448/9 level. It is impossible that the rising but still modest total of chancery petitions plus those to the council was the only cause. We need a new model; simple 'confrontation' is not adequate.

Fifteenth-century Englishmen were unquestionably litigious; even sixty-nine per cent of the 1448/9 level of business represented in excess of 12,000 judicial writs each year, over and above those which defrayed office costs. But it seems that there was, nevertheless, a reduced willingness to waste time in litigation which got nowhere, or even, perhaps, an increased resort to the alternative remedies offered by good lordship – still plenty of litigants, that is, but increasing numbers staying away. And if so, prerogative remedies did not so much divert business from the common law as pick up business which the older courts were losing. Seen in this light, reform was a belated response by the traditional courts to the same pressures which had called for the expansion of prerogative jurisdiction. Our model of relations between the pre-Reformation courts should be industry, not the stock exchange. What threatened common pleas and king's bench was not a take-over bid but the loss of customers; it was public demand which compelled the king to expand the operations of equity and prerogative jurisdiction; reform allowed the older courts to 'update' their product and to 'diversify' into new areas of litigation.

Relations between courts were not, of course, uniformly tranquil. There is some evidence that by the last third of Henry VIII's reign common pleas had become critical of some king's bench innovations, but this was quite fraternal, on the lines of 'what is tolerated elsewhere is not going to happen here!'.[82] The jurisdiction of the council too was challenged from time to time; in 1506 a lawyer was barred from appearing before it and threatened with imprisonment for advising a client not to answer in a suit about land.[83] Complaints are found especially during the reaction after Henry VII's death.[84] How far these were against the judicial activity of the council is not clear, but in some cases the objection was to calling defendants before individual counsellors. What is evident, however, is that the council continued to attract clients and to exercise its jurisdiction without hindrance,

82. Spelman, *Reports*, ii. 297–8.
83. Bayne, *Council of Henry VII*, 46.
84. Spelman, *Reports*, ii. 71–4.

and that the common lawyers continued to support it and to plead before it. Where title was at issue in star chamber the custom from Henry VII's reign was to refer the substance to a panel of common-law judges, and for their report to form the basis of the council's final decree.[85] In the fifteen years of Wolsey's supremacy almost seventy lawyers are known to have practised in star chamber (a substantial proportion of the common-law bar), and the four who did so most frequently included one future judge, one serjeant and one serjeant elect.[86]

Chancery came in for criticism as well. To a backwoodsman like the author of the *Replication of a Serjaunte at the Lawe* (written to refute Christopher St German) the discretion of the chancellor, especially a non-lawyer like Wolsey, threatened the very survival of the common law, while at a less apocalyptic level the relationship of the equity of chancery and the equity of common law was bound to arouse professional discussion.[87] Counsel and judges had long been aware that litigants were having to go to chancery, and they were not above pointing out the alternatives available in common law and also the disadvantages of equity – for example Humphrey Coningsby's remarks in 1505 on the lack of finality in chancery judgements.[88] This was the thrust of one of the most famous of common-law pronouncements, that an action of *assumpsit* could be brought for failure to convey land to a purchaser; enunciated by Fineux at Gray's Inn in 1499, it concluded with the comment 'and I will not need to sue out a *subpoena*'.[89] In king's bench nearly twenty years earlier, Guy Fairfax had argued the potential of *action on the case* in more general terms:

> The *subpoena* will not be used as often as it now is if we rely on *actions on the case* and maintain the jurisdiction of this court and of other courts.[90]

In the case of *Thomas and Alice Russell*, Hussey C.J.K.B. objected to a chancery injunction to the point of promising to get the plaintiff or his attorney out of the Fleet prison should the chancellor's wrath put them there.[91]

But once again this friction with chancery was no more than we might expect of overlapping competence and alternative remedies.

85. Guy, *Cardinal's Court*, 96–7.
86. Guy, *Thought* 52. 278.
87. Spelman, *Reports*, ii. 37–43.
88. *Y.B.* Mich. 21 Hen.VII, p. 40 ff. 34–5.
89. *ibid.*, Mich. 21 Hen.VII, p. 66 f. 41. For the dating 1499, see Spelman, *Reports*, ii. 267.
90. *Y.B.* Pas. 21 Edw.IV, p. 6 f. 23.
91. *ibid.*, Mich. 22 Edw.IV, p. 21 f. 37; cf. Blatcher, *Court of King's Bench*, 5–6.

Fairfax was making only a passing comment in the course of a debate on procedure. *Thomas and Alice Russell* for all its strong language, was settled by discussion; we should presume an instance of tactlessness or an error somewhere, as in 1536 when Fitzjames, C.J.K.B., challenged Lord Chancellor Audley.[92] Few litigants argued the jurisdictional limits of chancery and, as with star chamber, common lawyers were deeply involved in the operation of the court.[93] The commission set up in 1529 to exercise the jurisdiction of the chancery during Wolsey's absence at Blackfriars included half a dozen of the most prominent counsel of the day and three judges.[94] Common lawyers consistently recognised the need for chancery. *Rede* v. *Capel* arose from a fraudulent recovery engineered by one London alderman, William Capel, to free land from an unexpected tenant (another alderman, Bartholomew Rede) whose 'term of years' had some time yet to run.[95] Thomas Kebell said:

It is inconvenient that the termor [Rede] should upset the recovery of the freehold . . . to save his term while the demandant [Capel] cannot have any remedy . . . And so, perhaps, because of this inconvenience, the termor will not overturn it at common law, but yet in conscience he shall have right done. For here [in chancery] the inconvenience is not material, for the logic (*cause*) of the [common law] judgement is not being reversed, but an alternative way found in conscience.

The two chief justices, Hussey and Bryan,

thought expressly that it was good conscience to restore [Rede] to possession if there was no remedy for him by common law. For this recovery was by covin, and recovery by covin is abhorred in our law, and nothing more so.

Even when Fineux as a serjeant was disputing with the chancellor, Archbishop Morton, about the scope of chancery, he argued the impossibility, not the impropriety, of an equitable remedy for every grievance. The case followed the unilateral payment of a debt by a co-executor so that the will could not be performed.[96]

Fineux: The matter cannot be remedied. Each executor has full power in himself and can do all that his colleagues can do, so that the release he made is good [in law].

92. Spelman, *Reports*, ii. *83*. 93. *ibid.*, ii. *75*.
94. Guy, *Thought* 52. 278–9. Dr Franz Metzger has kindly furnished me with an analysis of chancery litigation which shows that nearly forty known common lawyers appeared twenty times or more in chancery in the period 1515–29; more than twice that number appeared less frequently.
95. *Y.B.* Pas. 7 Hen.VII, p. 2 ff. 10–13; cf. below, p. 269.
96. *ibid.*, Hil. 4 Hen.VII, p. 8 ff. 4–5.

Chancellor: 'No one shall leave the court of chancery without remedy.' It is contrary to reason that a single executor should have all the property [of the deceased] and make a release independently.
Fineux: Sir, then if 'no one shall leave without remedy', therefore 'no one needs to be confessed'! But Sir, the law of the land is for many things and many things are to be sued here which are not able to be remedied at the common law, and others are in conscience between a man and his confessor, and so in this matter.

Over all, common lawyers, judges and counsel alike, were content, as their predecessors had been, to see chancery as part of the system, not its enemy.[97]

The relationship between common law, chancery and law reform was revealingly demonstrated in the famous meeting which took place between Thomas More and the judges. Historians who have accepted the 'confrontation' model have usually seen the appointment of More as an olive branch to the common lawyers, ending the excessive interference which had marked Wolsey's chancellorship.[98] In particular it can be argued that More was personally and professionally hostile to arbitrary discretion.[99] Nevertheless, as we have seen, Wolsey's excesses have been much exaggerated, and whatever lawyers thought of Wolsey as a person, they had co-operated with his chancery, while the court was to grow even faster under his successor. It is clear, too, that More spent half his time on land law, just as Wolsey had done.[100] It should not be surprising, therefore, to find that the riposte of the anonymous serjeant to *Doctor and Student* can be dated to More's chancellorship, not Wolsey's, or to recognise that it was

97. See above, p. 208. S.F.C. Milsom makes the important point that 'judge and chancellor both saw themselves as concerned to secure the application of the same absolute justice, rather than to do justice seen as a product of human thought about which men might differ . . . But even when this [change in attitude] had happened, and when the visibly substantive rules of the common law were being overridden at the discretion of the chancellor, the dialogue between the two sides often shows true perplexity rather than true conflict between the two sides committed to their causes': *Historical Foundations*, 83.
98. Spelman, *Reports*, ii. *81*.
99. Cf. Dr J.A. Guy's favourable interpretation of Wolsey in *Thought* 52. 280–1, with a more traditional and critical assessment by Dr J.H. Baker, Spelman, *Reports*, ii. *77–80*. Friction between Wolsey and certain common lawyers existed at a personal level; see the interview between William Shelley and the cardinal: Cavendish, *Wolsey*, 117. Nevertheless the fact that senior common lawyers signed the complaints against Wolsey (Spelman, *Reports*, ii. *79*) need not suggest that these were more than the general commination extrapolated from individual grievances, expected on such occasions: *L. and P.*, iv. 6075 (20, 21, 26, 31). A detailed study of the factional element in Wolsey's fall is much needed.
100. Guy, *Thought* 52. 282–3.

unrealistic and reactionary.[101] Of course More handled the common-law courts with greater tact than the cardinal of York, but he was criticised for his use of injunctions, as earlier chancellors had been.

The meeting with the judges was the outcome.[102] After dinner, More took his guests through a detailed consideration of all the injunctions he had issued and 'they were all enforced to confess that they, in like case, could have done no other wise themselves'. But the chancellor did not leave the matter there. He suggested that the common-law courts could take on the burden of much of his equitable activity; he was offering, in effect, to stop or even reverse the rise of chancery. They refused. As More explained to his son-in-law William Roper, reform might radically have changed the role of the judges, making judicial decision more vulnerable to criticism by litigants, and still more, one presumes, by the crown. But someone had to 'mitigate and reform the rigour of the law'; as Morton had reminded Fineux, complainants could not be left 'without remedy'. The old archbishop had been More's first patron, and he would have approved the response of his erstwhile page:

> Forasmuch as your selves, my lords, drive me to that necessity for awarding out injunctions to relieve the people's injury, you cannot hereafter any more justly blame me.

So instead of Thomas More accelerating the reform of common-law procedures by the judicious admixture of discretion, he had to strengthen chancery. Indeed, his very presence on the woolsack as a common lawyer 'gave doctrinal validation' to the alternative system.[103] He took significant steps to improve chancery machinery and so too the effective enforcement of final decrees, there and in star chamber.[104] Common-law reform was a slow and stumbling business, and until it made more progress, equity had to step in to meet the needs of many litigants. As this episode reveals so sharply, what the common-law courts had to overcome was not other competition but a self-imposed handicap.

The English legal profession in the eighty years before the Reformation was involved at a turning-point in English legal history. It

101. *ibid.*, 285; D.E.C. Yale, 'St German's *Little Treatise Concerning Writs of Subpoena*', in *Irish Jurist*, n.s. 10 (1975), 324.
102. Roper, *Lyfe of Moore*, 44–5.
103. Guy, *Thought* 52. 285.
104. *ibid.*, 287–8. Since the above was written, Dr Guy has expanded his analysis in *The Public Career of Sir Thomas More* (Brighton, 1980).

was the position of the common lawyers, their attitudes and their activity, positive and negative, which ensured the survival of the common-law process; which delimited the judicial role of the royal prerogative; which made possible the modernisation of the law in substance and procedure and established the dichotomy between equity and law. They guaranteed that, in the end, tradition would assimilate the new and not give way to it, that reform came from within the time-honoured procedures, not in spite of them. Whether this was, in the long run, to the advantage of the country is a matter of value judgement, although we are less certain than past generations of the innate superiority of Anglo-Saxon legal procedures over systems which have answered the same questions in different ways. But the responsibility for the survival of the English common-law courts, for good and ill, belongs, in great measure, to the common lawyers.

10

THE CROWN AND THE PROFESSION

Without 'the roote of Justice', 'the tree of comonwelth cannot contynew', so wrote Edmund Dudley of Gray's Inn as he whiled away his long imprisonment in the Tower. 'And this roote of justice must nedes come of our souereigne lord hym self, for the whole auctorite thereof is gyven to hym by God.'[1] The occasion was unusual but the sentiments commonplace. Forty years earlier, John Fortescue had quoted with approval the text, *regis namque officium pugnare est bella populi sui, et eos rectissime iudicare*, and a generation later, John Ponet would write that 'thende' of a king's authority 'is determined and certain, to maintene iustice, to defende the innocent, to punishe the euil'.[2] In the words of the oath offered to the monarch at his coronation,

> You shall make to be done after your strength and power, equal and rightful justice in all your dooms and judgements and discretion, with mercy and truth.[3]

I

The relationship between the king and law and justice, which was a commonplace at a metaphysical level, can also be looked at in historical and constitutional terms. English common law was, initially, the custom of the king's court, and the king's proprietorial interest continued long after this custom had come to be accepted as the common law of the realm. He was privileged at law, and the courts were always tender to his interests. In most cases the crown was not open to process except of grace, and the general principle was, *le melior sera pris pur luy*.[4] This regulated even royal bounty; as Kebell

1. Dudley, *Tree of Commonwealth*, 34.
2. Fortescue, *De Laudibus*, 2; John Ponet, *A Shorte Treatise of Politike Pouuer* (1556), sig. c.
3. *Select Documents in English Constitutional History 1307–1485*, ed. S. B. Chrimes and A. L. Brown (1961), 354.
4. *Y.B.* Hil. 5 Hen. VII, p. 10 f. 17.

said, '*le graunt le roy prendra effecte forsque strictement*', or in the fuller statement by John Fineux in the same case of 1487, '*le construccion des patents le roy par implication ne sera pris car construction des patents le roy par implication sera pris mieux pour le roy*'.[5] The justification was spelled out by Kebell in common pleas *circa* 1493:

> The grant of the king will be taken in the way most beneficial to the king and most strictly against the grantee, because the king is the conservator of the law, which is the common weal, and because he is the governor of [the law] it will be more favourable than [to] another person.[6]

Even in the minutiae of pleading, royal privilege was accepted. This comes out in a trespass case of the same period in which Kebell claimed *aid du roy* (the association of the crown in the defence of his client's title).[7] Richard Jay, the opposing counsel, objected that *aid* did not lie in trespass, and even if it did, it could only be asked for when issue had been joined. Kebell's reply was to call in royal privilege. *Aid de common person* was, he argued, available only after issue, but not so *aid du roy*; the king had to be brought in from the start, he was at the beck and call of no-one. Although Chief Justice Bryan rejected the suggestion that the king could not be brought in later, he did so on the same ground:

> I postulate that I plead not guilty in an action for trespass [and so go to trial without further pleading], and I put in evidence that the king leased the land to me; in that case we [the judges] ought not to proceed without consultation with the crown.

Prohibitions *rege in consilio ulterius non praecedente* were, indeed, a regular feature of litigation.[8] The crown could also pursue both a demurrer and a transverse in the same case: that is, dispute the law and at the same time deny the facts. As Kebell remarked to the attorney-general when defending the sheriff of Coventry, '*vous poies demurre* & *apres prendre issue* & *faire si comme vous plait*, & *cette ne poimes nous*'.[9] In his own courts the king certainly was *de le melior part*.[10]

The prerogatives of the crown did not exist only in this sense of

5. *ibid.*, Hil. 2 Hen. VII, p. 16 f. 13.
6. *ibid.*, Trin. 8 Hen. VII, p. 1 f. 1.
7. *ibid.*, Mich. 11 Hen. VII, p. 29 ff. 7–8.
8. e.g. *ibid.*, Mich. 2 Ric. III, p. 35 f. 13.
9. *ibid.*, Trin. 10 Hen. VII, p. 17 f. 28.
10. Among other crown advantages in litigation were the amending of pleas and the pursuit of double pleas: *ibid.*, Edw. V, p. 12 f. 7; Pas. 14 Hen. VII, p. 4 f. 26; Trin. 16 Hen. VII, p. 5 f. 12.

technical advantage. The king also had special claims on his subjects, in particular his feudal dues, and these raised issues of the most complex kind. For example, probably in Hilary 1489, a case of dower was argued in common pleas (with William Hussey C.J.K.B. in attendance), in which a father and son had died in quick succession, leaving a grandson who had been taken into royal custody as a minor.[11] The crown granted the estates away for the duration of the minority and the son's widow sued the grantee for dower, only to be told that as her husband had failed to sue livery, his negligence extinguished her rights. At least half-a-dozen serjeants, including Kebell, argued the case, while *divers bons estudients* made their views clear. The matter was between party and party, but as it turned on the capacity of common pleas to grant dower as well as chancery, and also on the interpretation of the 'statute' *De Prerogativa Regis* and the right of primer seisin, the interest of the crown was obvious. Divided on the law, the king's serjeants united to secure an adjournment for consultation with the crown.

The dominant position of the crown, taught by political theory and accepted in daily practice by the courts, was reinforced by what we have seen was the implication of a career in law – that a lawyer would inevitably be drawn into royal service. Because they served the law and the law was the king's law, all lawyers were in a sense king's men; politics, law and government were one.[12] That Henry VII signed his own accounts is well known, but his 'chief financial officer' was Thomas Lovell of Lincoln's Inn, treasurer of the king's household for thirty years and the man 'probably pre-eminent in the general political sense' among the advisers of the first Tudor.[13] From 1469 to 1558 the chancellor of the exchequer was almost always a common lawyer, and so too the chancellor of the duchy; after 1484 the speaker of the commons invariably was.[14]

The court of augmentations stands as a good example of what this involvement in government could amount to. As created in 1536, it had four principal officers, each of whom was a lawyer, as was also the clerk of the court.[15] The reorganised court of 1547 had eight senior posts shared between eleven men, and nine of them had legal experience.[16] In the middle and lower ranks of the augmentations (or

11. *ibid.*, Pas. 1 Hen. VII, p. 3 ff. 17–19; Hil. 4 Hen. VII, p. 1 f. 1.
12. See above, pp. 9–10.
13. Chrimes, *Henry VII*, 111.
14. See Ives, *Trans. Royal Hist. Soc.*, 5 ser., 18. 153–4 for these and other examples.
15. W. C. Richardson, *Court of Augmentations* (Oxford, 1962), 492–3.
16. *ibid.*, 155.

for that matter any Tudor organisation) it becomes more and more difficult to identify the background of the men involved. Furthermore, inn records are such that the education of perhaps three-quarters of the common lawyers cannot be traced for the period when the augmentations staff were beginning their careers. Yet despite this, half of all the administrators in the court's London establishment can be shown to be lawyers.[17] Provincial posts are even harder to check, but one district receiver in eight belonged to either Lincoln's Inn or the Inner Temple.[18] By 1536 Kebell and his fellows had long been dead, but the role of lawyers in the augmentations was only a repetition of the position in his day. The earliest of Henry VII's enquiries into his land rights was carried out by John Venables, esquire, and the Bartholomew Westby of the Middle Temple who went on to become a principal figure in the system of general surveyors, a system which was to a considerable degree staffed by the legal profession.[19] Again, when in August 1504 Henry VII set up a committee to clear away arrears in the payments owed by the crown, four of the seven members were common lawyers.[20] As we have seen, in the great provincial departments, notably the duchy of Lancaster, the role of the lawyers was equally prominent and equally important.[21]

It is thanks to duchy material that it is possible to show what administrative work for the crown really entailed for Thomas Kebell. Fifteen folios have survived of duchy council minutes for 1484 and 1485 when he was attorney-general; eight meetings are recorded in fair copy with Kebell appearing at all but the last, 27 June 1485.[22] The series is incomplete, but the pace of work is suggested by the evidence for the Hilary term of 1484 when the council met (always at Westminster) on the 13, 16, 20, 23 and 25 February, effectively twice a week.

For the first meeting two items are minuted – the claim of the abbot of Kirkstall to the duchy manor of Barnoldswick, and the complaint of the feodary of Tickhill that he had been ousted from office. In the

17. This was true of both the first and the second courts (*ibid.* 155, 492–4). Ushers, messengers, craftsmen etc. have been discounted.
18. This was true of both the first and the second courts (*ibid.* 49–50, 281–2).
19. *Cal. Patent Rolls, 1485–94*, 71; W. C. Richardson, *Early Tudor Chamber Administration, 1485–1547* (Baton Rouge, 1952), 66. Cf. the suggestion of B. P. Wolffe, above, p. 80, although the principal victim of reaction against the policies of Henry VII was the council learned (see below, pp. 230–1).
20. *Cal. Patent Rolls, 1494–1509*, 380.
21. See above, pp. 60–1.
22. DL5/2 ff. 1–15. This duchy material was drawn to my attention by Dr J. A. Guy.

latter case, John Kendale, the king's secretary, brought confirmation of the dismissal, but on Barnoldswick the council arranged to search the duchy records; the various repositories were allocated to individual counsellors, and Kebell with Richard Empson was assigned the collection at St Bartholomew's in London. Three days later the main item was a complaint by the tenants of Castle Donington in Leicestershire against an encloser. The council appointed a commission with instructions to enquire and report next term; given the county, Kebell was the obvious head for this. A similar course was taken with a second item at the meeting, a complaint from the tenants of Sutton in Lincolnshire about interference with their fishing rights by the bishop of Ely, although the lawyer heading the commission was this time William Hussey of Sleaford, C.J.K.B. On Friday, 20 February the council heard of the problems of Pevensey arising from an inundation of the sea in the autumn of 1482, and appointed yet another commission. The following Monday a complaint from Thetford was heard (alleging the wrongful sale of property), and a *subpoena* issued. On the last of these Hilary term meetings the council made a payment of £4 18s. 0d. to the duchy bailiff of Hartington in recompense for his losses following an assault the previous January when 'the said bailiff was commaunded to warne the court there to bee holden'; no action against the assailant is recorded. Thomas Lyster of Wakefield also appeared that day for the prior of Monk Bretton in his claim for the forest of Holcombe in Lancashire. Later meetings continue certain of these items. The Barnoldswick search, due by Trinity term 1484, was deferred on 22 November following to Easter 1485 and although some searches, including Kebell's, had been completed by then, the full report was not available until the end of June. The Pevensey matter also came up again, with a complaint in May 1485 against the original petitioners.

The continuity of this sort of work even after Kebell had become a serjeant is illustrated from his involvement in the duchy enquiries into the abbey of Burton-on-Trent. In 1488 he was appointed with the steward of the honour of Tutbury to investigate complaints by duchy tenants and officers against the abbot, and at the end of his life he was directing the prosecution of the abbey before the duchy council on the complaint of the tenants of Burton under Needwood and Rolleston.[23] The issue was once again enclosure, and Kebell took personally, or at

23. *Materials for the Reign of Henry VII*, ii. 361; DL3/6 T3 ff. 31–46.

least signed, the evidence of the ancients of each village in turn. He then seems to have drawn up a formal statement of the allegations, and perhaps he organised the collection of relevant charters for the court. Nor was Kebell concerned only with duchy administration. He served also on the council of Prince Arthur, and a minute of the late 1490s tells of similar activity for the properties of the duchy of Cornwall: orders to collect relief in the south-west from Sir Humphrey Fulford; the hearing of a complaint of the tenants of Newport in Essex, respited to next term 'for certen doutes what the lawe will therin'; investigating complaints against the lieutenant of the honour of Wallingford; approval of the seizure of a ward's lands, but further action to await directions; a decision to prosecute those who had embezzled the goods of the vicar of Bodmin, due to the prince on his suicide, and poachers in the Gloucestershire lordship of Bruern; a summons to the parson of Rising to answer complaints by the prince's bailiff there.[24] And Kebell is, it must again be stressed, by no means unique. Six signatures are attached to this minute, and every one is of a lawyer – two serjeants in addition to Kebell (John Mordaunt and Humphrey Coningsby), William Grevill, who was to be called to the coif in 1503, Sir Robert Sheffield, recorder of London, and John Chaloner of Gray's Inn.[25]

This involvement of lawyers in government was not only in formal employment. One of the significant characteristics of Tudor England was the simplicity of the royal administrative machine and the consequent reliance upon the voluntary service of the wealthy and prominent.[26] For many Englishmen, indeed, the king's authority was experienced only through his commissions, and here the crown made one of its greatest calls upon the expertise of the profession. A lawyer could expect to be placed upon the commission of the peace of his county once his status in the profession had become recognised, not when his position in the county justified the appointment. When Thomas Kebell became a Leicestershire J.P. in 1474, he anticipated his elder brother by some eight years.[27] And although frequently absent at Westminster, Kebell was no sinecurist. In January 1487, for example, he was second to Lord Hastings when the Leicestershire J.P.s indicted two local gentlemen for a major riot.[28] Kebell was also

24. E163/11/27.
25. Chaloner: Putnam, *Early Treatises*, 33 n. 2; Sheffield: see above, pp. 179–80.
26. J. P. Dawson, *History of Lay Judges* (Oxford, 1960), 293–9.
27. *Cal. Patent Rolls, 1467–77*, 619; *ibid., 1476–85*, 563.
28. KB9/372/20.

custos rotulorum.[29] Lawyers were just as heavily in demand for the numerous *ad hoc* commissions which were issued, and not only those, like oyer and terminer or gaol delivery, which were judicial in character. In, for example, the regnal year 21 Henry VII (22 August 1505 to 21 August 1506), sixty-seven commissions were entered on the dorse of the patent roll in addition to the routine commissions of the peace and for the assizes.[30] Thirty-nine were judicial commissions of one sort and another but twenty-eight were administrative, involving thirty groups of commissioners. Known lawyers were appointed to nineteen of these, and possibly a twentieth. Very often it is clear that it was the lawyers who were expected to do much of the work. The commission of 20 April 1506 to investigate royal rights and crown officers in Yorkshire and the north-east consisted of the archbishop of York, Lord Darcy, Sir John Hussey, Sir Marmaduke Constable and three lawyers, Brian Palmes, Thomas Grice and Thomas Meryng.[31] Archbishop Savage was president of the council, Darcy warden of the East March, and Hussey master of the wards, so that the actual work inevitably fell on the lawyers, perhaps with Constable, a knight of the body, in the chair.[32]

What this might mean for the individual lawyer can be particularly illustrated from the career of Thomas Kebell, since by comparison with some of his colleagues he was let off fairly lightly by the crown. He served on the Leicestershire commission to raise an alien subsidy in April 1483, and again in the summer.[33] In the following December he served with William Catesby, Henry Butler, recorder of Coventry, and three local gentlemen to root out the duke of Buckingham's supporters in Warwick and Leicester.[34] Twice in 1484 he was placed on the Leicestershire commission of array, and in May 1485, with Viscount Lovell, Sir Thomas Stanley and seven others, all lawyers, Kebell was commissioned to suppress coinage offences in the central and west midlands.[35] In 1486 he was placed on a casual gaol delivery at Guildford, and in December of that year made the first of his regular appearances at the delivery of Leicester gaol which lasted until 1496.[36] In 1495, Sir William Stanley's treason sent the serjeant into the

29. KB9/376/1.
30. *Cal. Patent Rolls, 1494–1509*, 439–91.
31. *ibid., 1494–1509*, 489.
32. Cf. the commissions into 12 counties in 1509 following the death of Viscount Beaumont; 18 of the 36 men involved are known lawyers: *L. and P.*, i. 132(26).
33. *Cal. Patent Rolls, 1476–85*, 354, 396.
34. *ibid., 1476–85*, 393.
35. *ibid., 1476–85*, 400, 489, 544.
36. *ibid., 1485–94*, 162, 163, 164, 213, 398, 475; *ibid., 1494–1509*, 86.

midlands on a commission of oyer and terminer.[37] Two years later he was again on a royal investigation, this time into the escape of prisoners from Nottingham gaol, and by then, of course, he was regularly engaged, spring and autumn, in the northern assize circuit and judicial duties at Lancaster and Chester.[38]

All in all it would be hard to discount the involvement of the common lawyers in the government of pre-Reformation England. The climax was their activity in the king's council. At this stage the council was a large body which never met as a whole, but whose members formed an advisory and executive pool employed entirely as the king wished for the business in hand. One third of the commoners on Edward IV's council were common lawyers; under Henry VII the proportion rose to nearly two in five, while between 1509 and 1527 almost a third of all counsellors were common lawyers.[39] Kebell was admitted to the council on 18 June 1494, and the next year he was appointed to the post of *serviens ad legem domini regis*.[40] A king's serjeant had two functions beyond those of the ordinary counsellor. He was, in the infancy of the attorney-generalship, inferior only to the chief justices as a legal adviser to the crown. Secondly, he led for the crown as required, although the law officers, court officials and others might handle cases also. Thus in Michaelmas 1499, Thomas Kebell was both present with the judges and the other king's serjeants at the council meeting which decided the fate of Perkin Warbeck and the hapless earl of Warwick, and also active in king's bench to enforce the penalty due to the crown against a plaintiff who had sued on the same issue both there and in the city of London.[41] Just over half the serjeants were retained by the crown at some point in their careers.[42] There were two or three king's serjeants at a time in the first half of the fifteenth century, three was the usual number under Edward IV and Henry VII, and three or four under Henry VIII. The increase may be explained by the need for increased legal assistance, and as a corollary

37. *ibid., 1494–1509*, 31.
38. *ibid., 1494–1509*, 92.
39. Ives, *Trans. Royal Hist. Soc.*, 5 ser., 18. 154 n. 2. Lawyers made up one-third of the most regular councillors under Henry VIII: Guy, *Cardinal's Court*, 28–9; the proportion of lawyers at each council meeting also averaged one in three, although on occasion it could be nearly 50%: W. H. Dunham, 'Members of Henry VIII's whole council, 1509–1527', *E.H.R.* 59 (1944), 205–7, revised; *L. and P.*, iv. 1082. Cf. Condon, 'Ruling elites', 130.
40. El.2652 f. 3v; see above, p. 77.
41. Bayne, *Council of Henry VII*, 32; *Y.B.* Mich. 14 Hen. VII, p. 15 f. 7.
42. *Acts of the Privy Council, 1547–50*, ed. J. R. Dasent (1890), 25 suggests that promotion to king's serjeant was by seniority.

to the reduction of the number of judges from the wasteful ten or so before 1470 to a later norm of seven or eight.[43] One occasional duty which was expected of judges as well as king's serjeants was attendance upon the Lords in parliament time. Normally all were summoned, along with the king's attorney, although names are occasionally missing and an ordinary serjeant was sometimes also required to attend.[44] Only the 1497 parliament coincided with Kebell's service as king's serjeant, and he duly attended, although in common with many lawyers he had sat previously as an M.P.[45] No particulars have survived, but he was very probably concerned with legislation transferring certain crown lands to feoffees, himself among them.[46]

Some lawyers on the king's council were of principal importance. The chief justices were amongst the most regular attenders, and a royal order of 1494 provided that William Hussey C.J.K.B. should be with the king on his summer progress.[47] Even when the smaller 'privy' council appeared it took time before the exclusion of the chief justices was final. Lawyers without judicial office who were major counsellors include William Catesby, Thomas Lovell, Richard Empson, Edmund Dudley, Thomas More, Thomas Audley and Thomas Cromwell, a notable tally. Perhaps the most obvious evidence of the common lawyers in the pre-Reformation council is the 'council or counsel learned in the law'. Sometimes this term merely indicates the king's legal advisers, who might be instructed to prepare a technical brief or to arbitrate in a dispute. In this sense it is a synonym for 'counsellors with professional training', even perhaps 'counsellors in professional posts' – the king's serjeants, the law officers and other lawyers retained of council – including from time to time the judges.[48]

43. See above, p. 16. For the early fifteenth century see *Select Cases in the Court of King's Bench*, vii, ed. G. O. Sayles, Selden Soc. 88 (1971), lxii–lxiii.
44. J. C. Wedgwood and A. D. Holt, *History of Parliament: Register 1439–1509* (1938), lix, lx and *passim*.
45. *Cal. Close Rolls, 1485–1509*, 969. He had sat for the duchy of Cornwall seat at Lostwithiel in 1478 and possibly subsequently, but not in 1491, the only year for which lists are at all complete: Wedgwood, *Biographies*; cf. Ives, *Bull. Institute of Hist. Research* 41. 222–3. In view of the work of the History of Parliament Trust, no examination of the profession in parliament has been attempted here.
46. *Rot. Parl.*, vi. 510b.
47. Bayne, *Council of Henry VII*, xxxii.
48. Royal requirements took precedence over judicial business: '*En l'eschiquer chambre devant touts les Justices at serjeaunts (Hussey et Bryan esteants absents ove le Roy a son concel a Windsor)*'; '[*les justices*] *surrexerunt et allerent al' chancelier et seigneurs de star-chambre*'; '*Et le roy mit pour les Justices et luy* [Townshend] *interrupt de sa raison*': *Y.B.* Hil. 6 Hen. VII, p. 9 f. 15; Mich. 2 Hen. VII, p. 9 f. 13; Trin. 4 Hen. VII, p. 8 f. 12.

However, the term, as we have seen, also describes certain meetings of counsellors where the particular business of crown prosecutions and debt-collecting was undertaken.[49] Information is scanty, but the names of eleven attenders are known for the last nine years of Henry VII's reign, and eight of these were common lawyers. The profession was the nearest the crown came to having a body of trained administrators on which it could rely.

II

The pre-eminence of the crown as an employer raises the whole problem of the legal profession and politics. We have observed how Thomas Kebell's own career was affected by the crises of 1483 and 1485, and the same could be said of Richard Empson, Thomas Lovell, William Catesby or Morgan Kidwelly. Empson and Lovell suffered in the first crisis and recovered in the second; Kidwelly had a brief prominence as Richard III's attorney-general and had to work his way back to a measure of favour after 1485; Catesby backed the winning side in 1483 but was summarily executed in 1485.[50] Political involvement was something which no aspiring lawyer could avoid – to refuse to serve the crown was to eschew the area of opportunity, to hamstring a whole career. Much ink has been used in attempting to explain Thomas More's entry into royal service when he expressed dislike for the work. No doubt an importance attaches to his convictions about the obligations of the humanist to his prince, but more significance belongs to the sheer career logic of the legal profession. Any man who took up the law could be certain that success would bring him into royal service, indeed this was the great attraction; even Erasmus, writing of More's reluctance, had to admit 'there is no better way to eminence [in England]; for the nobility are mostly recruited from the law'.[51] Assertions of dislike for politics and the court should,

49. James Hobart A.G., Thomas Lucas S.G., Serjeants John Mordaunt, Humphrey Coningsby and Robert Brudenell, Richard Empson, Middle Temple, and Edmund Dudley and Richard Hesketh, Gray's Inn. See above, p. 9.
50. For Kebell, see above, pp. 63–4. Empson continued to work for the duchy after his discharge as A.G. in 1483: DL5/2 ff. 1–15; Somerville, *Duchy of Lancaster*, i. 392. Lovell was attainted in 1484: Wedgwood, *Biographies*. Kidwelly A.G. was not reappointed in 1485 but eventually was sworn a counsellor to Henry VII: J. R. Lander, 'Council, administration and councillors, 1461–85', in *Bull. Institute of Hist. Research* 32 (1959), 179–80.
51. Quoted in Chambers, *More*, 85.

perhaps, be treated much as the longings of the business tycoon for the simple rural life.

If the king was dominant in the law, and lawyers were inexorably drawn into his service, the consequence for the profession and for litigants was profound. This was before the days of secure judicial tenure, lawyers as members of political parties and an autonomous Bar Council; the individual lawyer of Kebell's day was on his own. The king's judges did, it is true, find some protection in the technicalities of the law. Warned by the fate of Tresilian C.J. in 1388, the judges avoided any decision on Richard of York's claim to the throne in 1460, first by treating this as a dispute between parties in which judges could not properly take part, and then by taking the constitutional point that judges deriving their authority from a king could give no opinion on that king's title.[52] In 1485, likewise, they avoided by a neat fiction all adjudication of Henry VII's erstwhile status as an attainted rebel.[53] But technical evasion did not always serve. A judge held office 'at the king's pleasure' and this meant what it said. For bringing in a verdict of misprision of treason where Edward IV had determined on treason, Chief Justice Markham lost his post.[54] Lawyers in the royal administration were just as vulnerable. The crown needed managerial skills and offered tempting rewards, but security there was none.

Some conventions did exist. It was not expected that a lawyer need go down with his principal. Thomas Cromwell's determination to 'make or mar' on the fall of Wolsey was the characteristic response of the managerial expert to the loss of a patron.[55] Past activities were not necessarily held against a lawyer either. Kebell himself was a witness to this, with his involvement with William Catesby and his profiting by the misfortunes of Richard Empson in 1483. But, conventions allowed, there was only one way to survive, complete deference to royal wishes. It did not always guarantee safety. In 1553, Cholmley C.J. and Montagu C.J. had to abandon their legal objections to Edward VI's 'device' for the succession at the king's express personal command; Mary Tudor deprived each of his place, notwithstanding.[56] But a changeover of monarchs was always a touchy busi-

52. M. McKisack, *The Fourteenth Century* (Oxford, 1959), 457–8; Jacob, *Fifteenth Century*, 521; *Rot. Parl.*, v. 375–9.
53. *Y.B.* Mich. 1 Hen. VII, p. 5 f. 4, presenting the decision as the long-held view of the bench.
54. Hastings, *Common Pleas*, 88–9, 94.
55. Cavendish, *Wolsey*, 105.
56. Montagu's own account stresses the pressure from Edward, not from Northumberland alone: H.M.C., *Mss. of Lord Montagu of Beaulieu* (1900), 4–6.

ness, and in 1553 more touchy than ever before. In all normal circumstances, profit and survival lay in ensuring that the law gave the king what he wanted; once again, as the tag put it, 'whatever interpretation is in the king's interest, that is the one to follow'.[57]

The judges gave the lead. Markham, Cholmley and Montagu were very much exceptions in falling foul of the crown. When Edward IV wrested the throne from Henry VI, only Fortescue was replaced, and he was in flight after the battle of Towton; 1483 made no difference to the judges, and at the accession of Henry VII John Catesby, the uncle of Richard III's beheaded counsellor, was reappointed along with the rest of the bench.[58] Only the action of Edward IV in 1471 is an exception. On his restoration in October 1470 Henry VI had reappointed all the judges, retaining the most junior, Richard Nele, in king's bench. But the following March Edward renewed the patents of only four of the judges who had been in office when he fled the country, moved the senior puisne, Nedeham, to king's bench and the less experienced Nele to common pleas. Danby C.J.C.P. and four puisnes were retired altogether. Why this unique step was taken is not known, but on balance it seems that only in Danby's case was royal displeasure the cause. Apart from Thomas Yonge it was the longest serving puisne judges who were omitted, and since they were not replaced, the probability is that advantage was taken of the need to renew patents to reduce both the age and the size of the bench.[59] The likelihood that this is the correct explanation is increased by the concurrent reduction of exchequer barons from five to three.

1471 apart, historians have often taken judicial continuity as evidence of independence or a reflection of the shortage of alternative talent, but more realistically it demonstrates subservience.[60] Judges were royal officers; their accepted duty was to support the king. This

57. See above, p. 193.
58. Prisot C.J.C.P. was not reappointed in 1460, but was clearly ill or already dead: Hastings, *Common Pleas*, 130 n. 13. The statement, found in Foss, that in 1485 Catesby's reappointment was delayed is incorrect. Six Yorkist judges were reappointed on 20 Sept. 1485, the seventh, Richard Nele, on 13 Oct.: see Appendix E.
59. Appendix E. At least three of the former justices continued to be used or favoured by the crown. However, Walter Moyle's quitclaim to the king of all actions, dated 11 Dec. 1471, is curious unless it refers to his arrears of salary, which constantly appear in exchequer records of the 1460s; *Cal. Close Rolls, 1468–76*, 829. The retirement of Thomas Yonge and Ralph Wolseley B.Ex., each a former Yorkist partisan and each later reappointed, also argues that economy, not retribution, was the motive.
60. Foss, *Judges*, v. 1; Hastings, *Common Pleas*, 92–4; Chrimes, *Henry VII*, 158–9.

did not imply that they had to countenance injustice; as well as the more material interests of the crown they had to guard its reputation as the fount of justice. But open subversion of royal policy was out of the question. Indeed, Markham may have been less a martyr for justice than an obstructive person, inclined more to tell the king what could not be done than to find ways to do it.[61] Where the bench led, the bar followed. Edward Hall records that counsel were loath to plead against Henry VII's fiscal devices.[62] It is this, too, which explains the apparent sycophancy of Thomas Audley or Richard Rich, although they were in sixteenth-century terms hardly more sycophantic than the modern civil servant.

The way in which the facts of professional life served to augment the dominance of the crown is emphasised by the careers of men like Catesby, Empson, Dudley and Cromwell which ended in disaster. Why, for example, was William Catesby beheaded in 1485? He expected no such fate, as his will clearly shows.[63] Why was Empson executed in 1510 but Lovell not even in danger? Why did Audley and Rich die full of years and honour, while More and Cromwell fell to the headsman's axe? Something must be allowed to casual political and personal circumstance. This played a large part in the fall of More, and the misfortunes of Fortescue, Lovell and Catesby were ultimately a consequence of the turbulence of the 1450s and the 1480s; Empson and Dudley, like Cholmley and Montagu, were overtaken by a change of monarch. But bad luck is not the whole explanation. Vulnerability was another factor. A lawyer could easily become identified with a particular policy and incur the hatred of those who suffered from it; with no protection but royal favour, he could easily be cast aside or even used as a scapegoat. The attack of the Pilgrimage of Grace on Thomas Cromwell, no less than execution of Empson and Dudley in 1510, makes this clear. Yet lawyers who came to grief were not only victims of chance or of the loss of royal favour. They were, quite precisely, men who had abandoned the safety of self-effacing obedience and had entered the world of politics.

Sir John Fortescue, Thomas Lovell and William Catesby, for example, had engaged personally in the struggles of Lancaster and York, the first at the Parliament of Devils, Lovell in Dorset's rebellion in 1483 and Catesby, most noticeably, in the fall of Lord Hastings, and they had even been present on the field of battle. It is small

61. Cf. Hussey's comment on Markham in *Y.B.* Mich. 1 Hen. VII, p. 5 f. 4.
62. Hall, *Chronicle*, p. 503.
63. PROB11/7 f. 114v.

wonder that Catesby, Fortescue and Lovell should have been treated like the political and military leaders whose role they had adopted; Catesby, taken at Bosworth, was 'headed', Fortescue, with better luck, was spared after Tewkesbury and was able to make his peace with Edward IV; Lovell escaped from the fiasco of Buckingham's revolt to return on the victorious side in 1485.[64] Thomas More and Thomas Cromwell, likewise, had long left the ranks of the lawyers when they went to the scaffold.[65]

The same seems also to be the explanation of the Empson and Dudley arrests in 1509. No doubt their death sixteen months later was a sacrifice to buy popularity for a new king, but this explanation does not meet the facts of their arrest, regularly though historians repeat it.[66] Henry VIII succeeded on 22 April 1509; on 23rd Henry VII's general pardon was reissued and by the 30th, at the latest, Empson and Dudley were excluded by name – some sources even suggest that they were arrested on the 23rd.[67] It is impossible that, in Edward Hall's words, they lost royal favour 'to shifte the noyse of the straight execucion of penall statutes in the late kynges daies . . . for to satisfie and appeace the people'. At the time, most of the nation was unaware that Henry VII was dead. Furthermore, even if the public had had time to complain, how could it have distinguished between the supposed illegalities of the two fallen ministers, and similar actions by Sir Thomas Lovell, John Erneley the attorney-general, and others like them – until, that is, arrests pointed the finger. Hall's alternative explanation must be nearer the mark: 'whiche attachement was thought to bee procured by malice of theim, that with their authoritie, in the late kyngis daies wer offended'.[68] Empson and Dudley, in other words, fell because they were politically exposed at the accession of the new king. Theirs was not the fate of the lawyer-administrator but the fate of the unsuccessful politician. The new king's influential grandmother was quite possibly Dudley's enemy, and it may be significant that Sir Henry Marney, who replaced Empson as chancel-

64. Cf. the execution of [John] Archer of the Inner Temple, counsel to the duke of Exeter, after the fall of the Tower to the Yorkists in 1460; Nicholas Hervy, recorder of Bristol, was a casualty at Tewkesbury: 'John Benet's Chronicle', ed. G. L. Harriss, in *Camden Miscellany* 24, Camden Soc., 4 ser., 9 (1972), 227, 233; William of Worcester, 'Annales', in *Letters and Papers Illustrative of the Wars of the English in France*, ed. Joseph Stevenson (Rolls Ser. 1864), ii. 773.

65. G. R. Elton, 'Sir Thomas More and the opposition to Henry VIII', and 'Thomas Cromwell's decline and fall', in *Studies*, i. 155–72, 189–230.

66. Chrimes, *Henry VII*, 316–17.

67. *L. and P.*, i. 2, 11(10); Hall, *Chronicle*, 505.

68. *ibid.*, 505.

lor of the duchy, was one of her executors.[69] Lovell's security may be also explained – far from having antagonised Margaret of Richmond, he too was an executor.[70] The countess, it is true, died at the end of June but by then Empson and Dudley had been cast as scapegoats.

III

The evidence from the legal profession, therefore – whether from that minority which lost favour or from the conformist majority – suggests once again that in the law the king was supreme. The consequence was the ability of the crown to use the courts to enforce its will. The obvious example is law and order, and Kebell's career offers a number of illustrations. In 1490 he was concerned in an indictment for illegal liveries which had failed to allege that the clothing had been worn.[71] Kebell attempted to have the case thrown out: 'if a man takes livery but does not wear it, this is no damage at all'. Thomas Wode, for the crown, drove at the reality:

> The statute was made for the damage which ensues, viz. when one gives liveries, he will have a great company at his command, and for this men will not dare to execute the law on any of them. If a man takes a livery and does not use the livery, yet he is named his man, and is in mischief of the statute.

Although the 1468 statute was less explicit, perhaps, than the 1504 act would be, Kebell was in a weak position and the court probably ruled against him.[72]

More important than the famous evils of bastard feudalism was the good behaviour of sheriffs and other royal officers. A complicated case, listed under Michaelmas 1487 and Easter 1490, demonstrates the point.[73] After some executors had been successfully sued in debt, the sheriff of Surrey was ordered to levy the required sum from the testator's goods. He passed the order to the bailiff of Kingston and then returned the bailiff's reply that there were no goods, a return flatly against the verdict. The truth seems to have been that the jury was mistaken, and Kebell argued that the return was legitimate, but the court saw a challenge to the finality of verdicts and demanded a new one. That too was attacked as inadequate: Thomas Wode, for the

69. Brodie, *Trans. Royal Hist. Soc.*, 4 ser., 15. 160; Somerville, *Duchy of Lancaster*, i. 393.
70. Wedgwood, *Biographies*.
71. *Y.B.* Mich. 6 Hen. VII, p. 13 ff. 12–13.
72. *8 Edw. IV* c. 2; *19 Hen. VII* c. 14.
73. *Y.B.* Mich. 3 Hen. VII, p. 1 f. 11; Pas. 5 Hen. VII, p. 9 ff. 27–8.

crown, claimed that the sheriff was trying to evade his responsibilities. Kebell replied that the sheriff was bound to tell the truth, and if the chattels were not there they were not there, but the court was hostile – there were adequate ways of making a return, the sheriff (and, some argued, the bailiff) was being obstructive, and he was fined and forced to make a proper return.

In the Michaelmas term of 1482 Kebell took part in a case which helped to sign the death warrant of the sheriff's tourn as an efficient instrument of criminal justice.[74] Already, in 1461, parliament had enacted that all indictments and presentments at the tourn should be transferred by the sheriff to the justices of the peace, but the 1482 case limited the sheriff's right even to take presentments.[75] The issue was presentment in the case of rape, and the king's bench, led by the chief justice, quashed the return. The powers of the tourn were at common law, so that rape, as a felony by statute, was beyond its reference. Kebell, still an apprentice, argued that the sheriff had a right at common law to enquire into matters concerning the king, and Serjeant Callow that the duty to enquire into felony (except homicide), must extend to felony by statute, but they failed. One reason, perhaps, was the justices' equation of the tourn and the leet, making the tourn the sheriff's private franchise. This was certainly argued in 1491 when Kebell appeared for a person indicted four days outside the period prescribed for the tourn by *31 Edward III* c.15.[76] Kebell claimed the indictment was void, but Wode, probably again for the crown, argued that while the sheriff lost his profit if the tourn was late, the king's interest survived. Kebell's reply was that the tourn was indeed the king's, but was granted to the sheriff, so that void under the statute meant entirely void. A more important reason for hostility to the tourn was stated by Justice William Jenney in the 1482 case, when he said that any increase in the power of the sheriff would be detrimental to the commissions of the peace and of oyer and terminer. It is commonplace to note the encouragement of the justices by the crown; the courts seem to share this. In 1498, for example, servants of Sir Thomas Grene J.P. were sued for having assisted him in quelling a local riot.[77] The plaintiffs argued through Serjeant Kingsmill that the defence had to produce written orders from Grene, but Thomas

74. *ibid.*, Mich. 22 Edw. IV, p. 2 ff. 22–3; cf. Trin. 6 Hen. VII, p. 4 ff. 4–5, Pas. 11 Hen. VII, p. 11 f. 22.

75. *1 Edw. IV* c. 2.

76. *Y.B.* Pas. 6 Hen. VII, p. 4 ff. 2–3.

77. *ibid.*, Mich. 14 Hen. VII, p. 19 ff. 7–10.

Marowe, who was to read in 1503 on the J.P.s, countered that this was unnecessary where the justice was present in person. Serjeant Frowyk disagreed, but Kebell reiterated the need for justices to have freedom to act. The significance of the powerful judgement which vindicated Grene's men needs no emphasis.

IV

A glance at even this one area of law shows the law and the lawyers committed to serving the king, but even in the sensitive field of public order the crown was, strangely, not always successful. This was sometimes due, of course, to non-legal factors. Among Kebell's earliest known cases was one arising from a feud in East Anglia.[78] A servant of William Jenney, serjeant-at-law, had been murdered, and because the initial verdict was unsound in law Jenney had the coroner dig up the body and return a correct indictment, naming among the accessories William Wingfield. This extreme step aroused *gravis clamor*, although exchequer chamber backed up the coroner. A second element in the case, however, was that the defendants were 'gentlemen and esquires of the king's household'. William Brandon, Wingfield's nephew and himself an esquire of the household, attempted in open court to overawe William Hussey with tales of the accused's service to the king. The chief justice ordered him out, 'or verily you will be where he is'. The next stage was for Wingfield to exploit technicalities, claiming that the indictment described one defendant incorrectly; Kebell argued for him, but opposition was strong. So, clearly, were politics, and the court adjourned, declaring the problem 'subtle'. The crown, similarly, was unable to secure the correction of Sir Thomas Grene of Norton Davey in Northamptonshire. Sir Thomas, the justice whose men were to be protected in 1498, was a person of power and some independence who was to die in the Tower, suspected of collaboration with the earl of Suffolk.[79] Early in Henry VII's reign he had entered into a bond to keep the peace which the crown claimed was forfeit. Kebell again appeared for Grene but it was not eloquence but the jury's respect for Sir Thomas which carried the day.[80]

78. *ibid.*, Mich. 21 Edw. IV, p. 56 ff. 71–2; Mich. 2 Ric. III, p. 5 f. 2. Cf. *Cal. Patent Rolls, 1476–85*, 242.
79. Polydore Vergil, *Anglica Historia*, ed. D. Hay, Camden Soc., 3 ser., 74 (1950), 138–40.
80. *Y.B.* Pas. 4 Hen. VII, p. 7 f. 8.

Yet even when such factors were absent the crown did not always win. In Hilary 1488 the king's bench tested an indictment against Thomas Gire, bailiff to Edmund Bedingfield, sheriff of Suffolk.[81] John Lenthorp, the Suffolk escheator, had seized animals belonging to an outlaw, despite a royal order of *non molestando*. Gire, with two others, went on the sheriff's orders to recover the property, and their first visit yielded a hundred sheep. No doubt fearing trouble on the second visit, Gire took with him three hundred men from adjacent villages, *modo guerrino arraiati*. The case ostensibly turned on the freedom of the bailiff to raise such a posse, but it is clear from the strenuous efforts of the royal lawyers to inculpate Gire that royal authority was being abused for private ends. Richard Jay and Thomas Kebell argued that Gire's action was entirely in order. The king's serjeants replied that a sheriff could have only 'reasonable support', to which the counter was that he might take as many men as he felt he needed. The crown next claimed a limitation of a sheriff's power under *Westminster II* c. 39, but Jay and Kebell retorted that a sheriff also had power at common law. The king's attorney then intervened, but without success. The court had to quash the indictment. In 1490 Kebell again defended a sheriff, this time against the allegation that he had allowed a prisoner to escape.[82] The prisoner was being taken to execution after the Coventry gaol delivery when the procession was attacked by a Roger Draycott and others, and the felon released. The city sheriff mounted a pursuit, never lost sight of the felon, and eventually captured and hanged him. The attorney-general, nevertheless, brought an action against the sheriff. Kebell argued that to call this an escape was to stretch words and that, in any case, there had been no escape, only a forcible rescue. Although Kebell eventually found the easier way of pleading a technical flaw in the indictment, this was not before the court was inclining to his view.[83]

The paradox that the crown, which had such privilege in law and such veneration from lawyers, had to fight hard for what it wanted is not confined to matters of law and order. One obvious problem was the complex and even contradictory nature of its interests. Soon after taking the coif, Kebell was engaged in two suits arising from royal

81. *ibid.*, Hil. 3 Hen. VII, p. 1 f. 1; Trin. 3 Hen. VII, p. 4 f. 10.
82. *ibid.*, Mich. 6 Hen. VII, p. 9 ff. 11–12; Trin. 10 Hen. VII, p. 3 ff. 25–6, p. 17 f. 28.
83. Kebell was engaged for another sheriff (*ibid.*, Hil. 3 Hen. VII, p. 11 f. 3) but the report is insufficient to determine whether the crown was concerned in the accusations against him.

feudal rights, *Higford's Case* and *Dacre's Case*. John Higford of Emscote, near Warwick, died in December 1485, and his inquisition *post mortem* returned a grandson and two daughters as joint heirs, all under age, and, hence, wards of the crown.[84] Thereupon his brother, William, petitioned chancery for a new inquisition, claiming that many of the estates were entailed. Kebell opposed this, arguing that William should have made his title to the first enquiry and that to grant, in effect, a second *diem clausit extremum* was to risk an infinity of heirs, with the consequent jeopardy to royal rights. The suit went to exchequer chamber, probably in Hilary 1488, where the precedents were found to be poor, two examples in 1436–7 and one the previous Michaelmas term in the concurrent Dacre plea, still *sub judice*. Eventually, helped by the warnings of the chancery clerks of impending chaos, Kebell's opinion prevailed.

Within the year *Dacre's Case* came to trial.[85] Joan and Philippa, daughters and heirs of Lord Dacre, had married two brothers, Richard and Robert Fiennes; as Joan was the elder, Richard had taken the peerage, but the estates were settled between the couples. Richard and Philippa died, and, in March 1486, Joan also, and the inquisition for Suffolk returned that the Dacre lands in the county were occupied by Robert Fiennes, her brother-in-law. This was in November 1486, but within the year a new inquisition was granted on the ground that Joan had actually died seised of the Suffolk property and that Robert's title was feigned to deprive her grandson (a royal ward) of his rights. The king's financial interest therefore was precisely contrary to the Higford judgement, and the whole question of commissions subsequent to a *diem clausit extremum* was thrown into the melting pot once more.

John Brown opened for Robert Fiennes, claiming that the Higford decision had settled the matter, but Thomas Wode, newly appointed king's serjeant, objected that without a second commission the king would lose his right. Kebell would have none of this; a straight rejection of an inquisition was allowable neither to the king nor the heir – elucidation, yes, but not setting aside the original. Higford's ruling must stand. The king's serjeants were on shaky ground, but first John Fisher and then the senior, John Vavasour, did his best.

84. *ibid.*, Hil. 2 Hen. VII, p. 14 f. 12, and (with variations) Trin. 2 Hen. VII, p. 3 f. 17; *Cal. inquisitions post mortem*, i. 136. The sources do not agree on all the facts.
85. *Y.B.* Mich. 4 Hen. VII, p. 1 ff. 15–17; *Cal. inquisitions post mortem*, i. 189, 190, 261, 336, 662; *Cal. Patent Rolls, 1485–94*, 165–6.

Vavasour: I pose that should the *diem clausit extremum* say, when returned, that she died seised of no land, or if it should be found that someone was the heir to a tenant in chief where [in fact] he died without heirs, what remedy is there for the king unless he has a new commission?
Fairfax [J.K.B.]: The king can enter, and otherwise he has no remedy.
Vavasour: This seems marvellous!
Kebell: You and your fellows will say anything to earn your fee from the king.

Fairfax, with Tremayle J. in support, now proceeded to lecture the king's serjeants on the five sorts of inquisition after the death of a royal tenant. But Vavasour was not cowed.

'There is a further writ in the exchequer which is called *dum fuit infra aetatem*, of which you have not spoken.' *Brown* & *Kebell* & *others* wondered what writ this was. But *Brown* said to *Robert Fiennes*, 'Enter on the land in good hope of the court's opinion.' And then, at another occasion, *Hussey Chief Justice* was of the same opinion, *sc*. that the commission was wrongly awarded . . . And so it was held clearly by all the justices.

With the Higford and the Dacre cases so near in time and in matter it would have been difficult for the crown to win both. Yet the Dacre case reveals another element in the paradox that the crown which was the master of the law still had to fight for what it wanted; this is the sarcastic and critical attitude towards the king's lawyers. It appears in more than this example. In a case dated as Easter 1496, but probably from the period Michaelmas 1488 to Trinity 1489, Kebell appeared for the claimant in a plea of formedon to recover an inheritance.[86] Serjeant Robert Rede objected that the existing tenant held only for life by 'curtesy of England', but that the reversion belonged to three girls, one of them a royal ward, and so he prayed the crown in aid. Kebell objected – the royal right arose from an entirely separate estate, and when Rede raised the spectre of prerogative wardship, Kebell pointed out that no inquisition had ever suggested that the royal ward was concerned in the disputed lands; the support of the crown could not be dragged in by surmising that the state had a claim, a point which John Vavasour, for the king, had to concede. 'Our case is clear', said Kebell,

It appears that [this estate] descended to him from another ancestor, and so the king is entitled to no wardship of these lands. For the statute is *de quibus*

86. *Y.B.* Pas. 11 Hen. VII, p. 2 ff. 18–19. The debate can be dated after 30 June. 1488 and before 14 Aug. 1489 by the joint appearance of Wode and Vavasour for the king, unless Vavasour is speaking as a judge, in which event the date lies between 14 Aug. 1489 and the death of Townshend, 9 Sept. 1493. For prerogative wardship see pp. 247–8.

ipse tenens obiit seisitus, and this cannot be if the lands descended through another.

The judges agreed, but the king's serjeants would not easily yield the chance to add to the lands already in royal custody. Thomas Wode produced a conveyance which gave the deceased tenant-in-chief a reversionary interest, and Bryan C.J. agreed that royal wardship would then apply. But Kebell would not be shifted.

But suppose it is as [Wode] says, yet this must be found in the inquisition, or otherwise there is no ground to pray the king in aid.
Rede: We ask that we may have a day [a respite] to see if any other office is found for this.
Kebell: You know very well that there is no other office, but you are doing this to delay us.
Wode: You need not be as hasty as you are; for if there is no other office so that the king cannot have this, yet if the land is recovered against the heir, the marriage which is in the king ['s hands] is impaired, and this is a sufficient cause to grant aid.
Kebell: We will not burden ourselves much for that!

In exchequer chamber in 1493, the chief justices publicly criticised the king's serjeants.[87] The defendant in a novel disseisin had produced a succession of investigations by the escheator to the ultimate effect that all the land in question had been forfeit to the crown following the attainder of William Catesby. He then proceeded to pray the crown in aid. Brudenell and Kebell made a concerted assault on this, arguing that the successive inquisitions cancelled each other out, that the assize had been awarded before this additional material was introduced, and that to allow this would be to allow an infinity of delay. John Butler, James Hobart A.G. and the three king's serjeants presented a solid phalanx of opposition, but the judges finally tired of their ingenuity. Bryan C.J.C.P. said,

You will never let this come to *procedendo* [the writ which sent the case back for trial], for you will feign each day another case.

Sir William Hussey's rebuke to John Fisher still has a sting after six hundred years: 'Sir, you argue much not to the purpose.' Indeed, Hussey:

pour ce que il fuit passe le temps pur touts les Juges or devant moves, & pour ce cause ne voulait souffrer ascun juge a arguer.

The machinations of royal lawyers are not confined to those cases

87. *ibid.*, Mich. 9 Hen. VII, p. 5 ff. 8–10.

where colleagues or the bench were compelled to protest. In 1490, the crown had secured an exchequer judgement against certain merchants of the Steelyard for evading customs.[88] They sued a writ of error as provided by the statute of 1357, but on two successive occasions the writ lapsed on the failure of the judges to appear. Before a third writ could be implemented, the crown sued to have execution of the original judgement. This suit was considered in exchequer chamber, where Thomas Kebell, probably with Serjeant Robert Rede, appeared for the merchants against the attorney-general, James Hobart. Hobart argued for the strict letter of the law – the default was not caused by the successful plaintiff (the crown), and so execution had of right to be granted. Kebell replied that it was not the defendants' job to produce judges on time. There was also common sense in holding back execution; 'otherwise they are without remedy'.

> For if the money should be paid to the king and in his coffers, you [the court] do not have the power to give judgement for restitution as you can with the case of a common person.

The year before, Kebell had had another experience of royal deviousness when he fought unsuccessfully for Sir Thomas Grene to prevent the crown invalidating a trial going in his client's favour by tactics so blatant as to draw year-book comments.[89] A similar case, dated Michaelmas 1494, saw royal lawyers abandon their plea as they saw the court about to pass against the crown.[90] It was in order to forestall this sort of thing that the crown, like any other litigant, tried to manipulate sheriffs and juries. The Paston evidence is notorious; involved in a suit against Lord Moleyns, the family was told by the sheriff that Henry VI had ordered him 'to shewe favour to the Lord Molyns and hese men'.[91] Edward IV paid for the 'labouring' of at least one jury in the west country.[92] In Reformation treason trials the crown had to select juries carefully, and even in the aftermath of the Pilgrimage of Grace or Wyatt's rebellion any slackness might lead to the acquittal of manifest traitors.[93] Criminal procedure was sacro-

88. *ibid.*, Hil. 6 Hen. VII, p. 9 f. 15.
89. *ibid.*, Pas. 4 Hen. VII, p. 7 f. 8. The king's solicitor first prayed '*respect pur l'avauntage le Roy*' on the illness of the attorney, and was granted four days' respite; the king's serjeants then challenged the jury.
90. *ibid.*, Mich. 10 Hen. VII, p. 33 f. 11.
91. *Paston Letters and Papers*, ii. 73.
92. C. L. Scofield, *Edward IV* (1923), ii. 373, quoted Hastings, *Common Pleas*, 95.
93. G. R. Elton, *Policy and Police* (Cambridge, 1972), 314–21; D. M. Loades, *Two Tudor Conspiracies* (Cambridge, 1965), 97–8.

sanct, and only in the rare circumstances of martial law could it be dispensed with.[94] Civil procedure, likewise, bound king as well as subject, and even the king's prerogative outside the common law did not allow him to touch life, limb or real property.[95]

V

On the one hand, therefore, the English common law and the English legal profession were wholly subservient to the crown; on the other, the crown had to act within the recognised limits of due legal process, so much so that royal lawyers used all the tricks they knew and royal ministers all the devices of maintenance and embracery. To modern eyes this is a contradiction, but it would not have seemed so to men familiar with the ideas and assumptions given form and order in the works of Chief Justice Fortescue. His insistence that the English constitution combined both regal dominion and political dominion leads directly to an identification of justice with due process; as he wrote in *De Laudibus*:

> St Thomas [Aquinas] . . . desired that a kingdom be constituted such that the king may not be free to govern his people tyrannically, which only comes to pass when the regal power is restrained by political law.[96]

The king was no less supreme, but royal power operated through fixed and accepted machinery.[97] Edmund Dudley said much the same in his advice to Henry VIII:

> Let it not be seen that the prince himself for any cause of his own, enforce or oppress any of his subjects by imprisonment or sinister vexation, by privy seal or letters missives, or otherwise by any of his particular counsellors, but to draw them or entreat them by due order of his laws. For though the matter be never so true that they be called for, though their pain or punishment should be sorer by the due order of the law, yet will they murmur and grudge because they are called by the way of extraordinary justice. Wherefore the most honourable and sure way for the prince to have his right of his subjects, or to punish them for their offences, shall be by the due order and course of his laws.[98]

There was not the antithesis between 'Tudor Despotism' and the rule of law and king-in-parliament which has sometimes been supposed;

94. On this see Elton, *Policy and Police*, chapter 7 *passim*.
95. The prerogative powers of the crown were limited to arrest, interrogation (and torture), fine and imprisonment.
96. Fortescue, *De Laudibus*, 27.
97. *ibid.*, 27.
98. Dudley, *Tree of Commonwealth*, 36–7.

rather, the royal will operated through due legal process and the 'High Court of Parliament'. Thus the prejudice of the law towards the crown and the need for crown lawyers to fight for royal rights were both aspects of the one fact that the king governed by the law. Equally, royal justices who rejected royal policies or applications which infringed the law were, in the ultimate, not acting as guardians of liberty or justice so much as protecting the authority of the crown. The Tudor courts rendered the power of the crown legitimate.

Henry VII's reign opened with a classic instance of the common lawyers serving the interest of the crown: the case of Sir Humphrey Stafford, in which Kebell may have had a voice. Attainted in November 1485, Stafford had evaded arrest by taking sanctuary at Colchester, only to sally out at Easter 1486 in abortive revolt. He took refuge again, this time in the abbot of Abingdon's sanctuary at Culham, but he was forcibly removed and taken to the justices of oyer and terminer at Worcester on 22 May.[99] The abbot also appeared to protest his privilege, and the whole matter was referred to the council in London. It was clearly impossible for the state to tolerate a repetition of events, and Henry VII was personally anxious for the judges to rule against the abbot's charter. On 13 June, orders were given 'for Judges to deliver upon the priveladg shewed by the Abbot of Abbendon and to aunsweare in goodly hast', and an exchequer chamber debate was held on the 15th.[100] Unfortunately for the king, eagerness had outstripped due process (neither chief justices nor chief baron had been at the council which called for the judicial opinions), and the puisne justices at the exchequer chamber meeting had to protest against being asked for an opinion on a case already begun. This was not judicial independence; judges could legitimately be consulted on policy or hypothetical cases, or they could have an actual case referred to them in exchequer chamber, but it was not due process to start a case and then to seek an opinion.[101] Later that day, Chief Justice Hussey arrived in London and on the 16th he went to the king and persuaded him to let

99. For the following, see *Y.B.* Pas. 1 Hen. VII, p. 15 f. 22; Trin. 1 Hen. VII, p. 1 f. 25; Hemmant, *Exchequer Chamber*, ii. 115–24; Bayne, *Council of Henry VII*, 8, 13; C. H. Williams, 'The rebellion of Humphrey Stafford', *E.H.R.* 43 (1928), 181–9.

100. The names of the speakers in the exchequer chamber debates on Stafford's case are not recorded; although Kebell and the other new serjeants were not formally invested until 4 July, it is unlikely that they were not among those consulted.

101. This interpretation was at least 35 years old and had been advanced in 1460 *re* the duke of York's claim to the throne: Myers, *English Historical Documents, 1327–1485*, 416.

the judges handle the matter in king's bench where 'they would do what of right they should do'. The king, however, urged haste and was displeased when Hussey immediately gave Stafford a week to prepare the case. In fact it was not until 29 June that the actual trial was held and the issue duly remitted to a meeting of the judges the next day. There, at last, they did everything Henry had hoped; not only did they strike down the Culham sanctuary and return Stafford to the Tower to die, but their judgement invalidated all but the most exceptional of sanctuaries as refuges for traitors.[102] The king's will had been done, handsomely, but 'by the due order and course' of the law.

102. I. D. Thornley, 'The destruction of sanctuary', in *Tudor Studies*, ed. R. W. Seton Watson (1924), 198–200. Formal condemnation of Stafford was pronounced on 5 July. In the very comparable *Savage's Case* the judges restricted sanctuary still further: Keilwey, *Reports*, ff. 188–92; Ives, in *On the Laws and Customs of England*, 297–303; cf. Spelman, *Reports*, ii. 341–6.

11

THE INTEREST OF THE STATE

Convention has established the years around 1500 as a watershed in English history, when either the strong government of medieval times was recovered, or a qualitative change achieved to a new sort of rule. Whatever the interpretation and whatever dates should be assigned to the process, the fact is clear, and at the heart of it was a determination by the crown to interpret its rights at law in the most liberal fashion and then to enforce them with rigour. Just as social and economic change was beginning to put pressure on accepted legal notions, so the search for strong rule required a reconstruction of the law. Able to rely on the profession and the courts to execute its will within the limits of due process, the crown also turned to the lawyers to reinterpret the law.[1]

The condemnation of Humphrey Stafford involved the striking down of a privilege allowed, perhaps, for six centuries, but the prime example of legal manipulation is the attack by the crown on the greatest of the recent advances in property law, the use.[2] The reason for the hostility of a reinvigorated government is well known. Enfeoffment to uses which gave wide powers to settle estates also had the effect of defeating feudal obligations, notably the right of the lord to wardship of the heir's body, marriage and lands when a minor succeeded to land held in knight service.[3] The crown was the chief loser – never a tenant, always a lord – and even more so because of its rights of 'prerogative wardship'. These provided, as we have seen, that if a

1. See above, Chapter 10.
2. See above, pp. 245–6. For the following see Constable, *Prerogativa Regis*; Bean, *Decline of Feudalism*; Spelman, *Reports*, ii. *192–203*. For limited action in the exchequer to enforce crown interests see the work of Dr D.L.J. Guth quoted in Chrimes, *Henry VII*, 191–2 and his article, 'Notes on the early Tudor exchequer of pleas', in *Tudor Men and Institutions*, 101–22.
3. In law, wardship of the body and wardship of the lands were distinct. Tenants-in-chief needed royal licence to alienate, and the crown could insist that a token minimum of land in knight service was retained, so preserving the obligations under feudal law; mesne lords, however, could not prevent total alienation by tenants. But see the qualification made in Spelman, *Reports*, ii. *192–3*.

military tenant-in-chief died seised, leaving an heir under age, the crown would have wardship of all the land he had held, both of the crown and of lesser lords by knight service, socage and any other tenures. But the seisin of lands enfeoffed to use lay with the feoffees, so that even where the crown's rights over land held in chief survived, prerogative wardship would bring it nothing. These losses the crown could not tolerate, and early in Henry VII's reign the courts began an exercise in reinterpreting the law which was to last into the reign of his son and produce repercussions to 1660 and beyond.[4] The accompanying executive reforms are well known, but the heart of the process was a rigorous probing of existing law, law based on the thirteenth-century quasi-statute, *De Prerogativa Regis*. S. E. Thorne comments on the opening years of the campaign, 1485 to 1495:

> The few straightforward situations in which the prerogative had always been applicable, precisely envisaged by the clauses of *Prerogativa Regis* and long familiar to escheators, had quickly been surrounded and all but overshadowed by a great variety of variant situations that had not hitherto fallen within its scope. Stringent literal application and extension by analogy, powerful instruments in the hands of the crown's lawyers, had broadened its reach. Interpretations in the light of reason, which abstracted *Prerogativa Regis* from its historical milieu and gave its words their current meanings and connotations, had transformed its obsolete clauses into essentially new provisions. Fragmentary statements and *dicta* in the earlier Year Books had been used with ingenuity to give colour to what were in fact not old rules but new departures.[5]

How, in Thorne's phrase, 'new departures' were made to reverse the decline in feudal profits can be seen by watching Thomas Kebell and his fellow lawyers in a number of cases, most notably in *Dormer* v. *Rex & Fortescue*, known to contemporaries as *Stonor's Case*.[6]

In origin the case was simple. Sir William Stonor – a knight of the body, first to Edward IV and then Henry VII, who had built up large estates on success with wool and wives – had purchased in 1481–2 the manor of Bury, near Gosport, held in socage of the crown, and the manor of Nursling Beaufo, near Southampton, held of St Swithin's,

4. See below, pp. 257–9, 262.

5. Constable, *Prerogativa Regis*, vii.

6. *Y.B.* Trin. 12 Hen.VII, p. 1 ff. 19–22; Mich. 13 Hen.VII, p. 3 ff. 4–9, p. 12 ff. 11–12; Keilwey, *Reports*, Mich. 13 Hen.VII, p. 5 ff. 32–33v; Pas. 21 Hen.VII, p. 15 f. 86; Hemmant, *Exchequer Chamber*, ii. 175–82. The report *ibid.*, ii. 161–75, transcribed from B.L. Hargrave 105, is the printed report of Mich. 13 Hen.VII, p. 3. The case began in Trinity term 1495 and ended at Easter 1496: *ibid.*, ii. 179, 182. The reports, however, are all dated 1497: see below, p. 251 n. 16. Not all the details in the reports agree with each other or with the king's bench record.

Winchester.[7] As Stonor well knew, title was also claimed by the vendor's relatives, Thomas Hargrave and his sons-in-law Thomas Dormer and John Wells.[8] Possession was disturbed immediately on purchase and again in 1491, and after Stonor's death in May 1494, the inquisition *post mortem* returned that the manors had been occupied by Dormer, although at the time of death, feoffees were seised to Stonor's use.[9] Sir William's claim descended to his twelve-year-old son, John, and the crown claimed wardship on the grounds of other property held in chief. Stonor, however, had sold his son's marriage to Sir John Fortescue of Ponsbourne, and the boy had married, in 1491, Fortescue's daughter Mary. To protect his investment, Sir John promptly purchased the wardship and marriage of his son-in-law.[10] Dormer thereupon appeared in chancery in July 1495 to traverse the inquisition and assert his own claim. The crown called Fortescue to answer the next Michaelmas *pro nobis aut pro se ipso*, and he and Dormer then pleaded to issue, whether Dormer had been disseised prior to Stonor's purchase.

There is nothing in this to suggest a leading case in feudal law. The crown stood neither to gain nor to lose. It had Sir John's money and, in any case, its right to wardship over the rest of the Stonor land was not in doubt; Sir William had died seised of two Somerset manors held in chief by knight service.[11] And yet the case could be manipulated to the king's interest. Already the seizure of the Hampshire manors had been cause for comment, for they had been seized by the escheator in virtue not of lands held in chief outside the county, but of the advowson of the church of Penton Mewsey (near Andover), held in chief by knight service, and for this reason alone. The escheator's

7. Stonor – *Stonor Letters and Papers*; Wedgwood, *Biographies*; *Cal. inquisitions post mortem*, i. *passim*. The date of the purchase is established by *Cal. Close Rolls, 1476–85*, 841, 899; *Stonor Letters and Papers*, ii. 153–4.
8. Kingsford, *E.H.R.* 35. 421–32.
9. *Stonor Letters and Papers*, ii. 139; Kingsford, *E.H.R.* 35. 425–6; *Cal. inquisitions post mortem*, i. 961.
10. *ibid.*, i. 977, 1175; Constable, *Prerogativa Regis*, 5, 127; *Cal. Patent Rolls, 1494–1509*, 21. Stonor's daughter at the same time married Fortescue's younger son, Adrian. *Stonor Letters and Papers*, i. xxxv, represents this as healing a breach between the Fortescues and Stonors, but Fortescue was one of Stonor's executors: *Cal. Close Rolls, 1500–9*, 129. A marriage where the parties had passed the age of consent (14 years for boys, 12 for girls) extinguished the right of the crown to wardship of the body of the heir. But if the heir was *infra annos nubiles* the marriage was voidable and the lord could offer an alternative marriage: Constable, *Prerogativa Regis*, xxxi, xxxiv-xxxv.
11. *Cal. inquisitions post mortem*, i. 1129.

law was good, but stringent enough to raise professional eyebrows. When Robert Constable read on *Prerogativa Regis* at Lincoln's Inn eighteen months later he commented:

solement per reson d'avouson en grose, tenuz de roy en chief, claime le roy le garde de Sir W. Stoner; & solement pur cel cause Sir John Fortescu fuit coarte a redemer l'eir dell roy, quell il avoit achate del pier l'eir & il marie einz annos nubiles.[12]

A second factor was that in 1490 parliament had passed the first national legislation on uses as these affected royal feudal rights.[13] Couched in confirmation of the statute of Marlborough, it had blocked a loophole in the 1267 act by providing that where a *cestui que use* (beneficiary) died leaving a minor heir and without making a will of his lands, his overlord could sue by writ to have the land and wardship of the heir, notwithstanding the use.[14] Stonor had left no will, and Bury and Nursling were enfeoffed to uses; Dormer's traverse was, thus, the opportunity to test – and exploit – the implications of the statute for prerogative wardship. Other points could be teased out, too; for example, the inquisition had returned that Nursling was held of the Prior of St Swithin's, Winchester, 'by service unknown' – what did that imply?

When, therefore, Fortesque and Dormer had pleaded to issue, James Hobart, the king's attorney, intervened to raise the whole question of the royal title in Bury and Nursling. The next stage, the jury trial, was arranged not in Hampshire, as would have been usual, but at Westminster in the Easter term of 1496. Although Dormer appeared in person, Fortescue, by this stage, had sunk into the background, and Hobart was presenting the case. Faced with the determination of his sovereign, Dormer abandoned his traverse. Further, in a way that is not entirely clear, Hobart secured exchequer chamber discussion of the king's rights. There was certainly no formal advisement on the

12. Constable, *Prerogativa Regis*, 5.
13. *4 Henry VII*, c.17, 'An Act agaynst fraudulent feoffmentes tendinge to defraude the Kinge of his wardes'. A previous act of 1481 referred only to the duchy of Lancaster: *Rot. Parl.* vi. 207–8.
14. For comments on the inadequacy of this act see Holdsworth, *H.E.L.* iv. 448–9; Chrimes, *Henry VII*, 182–3; Milsom, *Historical Foundations*, 187–8; Bean, *Decline of Feudalism*, 248; Simpson, *Land Law*, 173. But these may underestimate the technical and conceptual difficulty of reform, which could also (*pace* Holdsworth) account for the first steps being undertaken within the compass of *Marlborough*. Cf. Bean, *Decline of Feudalism*, 193; see below, pp. 253–6. Dr J.H. Baker does not see the act as 'a foretaste of royal policy': Spelman, *Reports*, ii. *194*.

Dormer plea, for there was no need, and this explains the absence of any exchequer chamber ruling in *Stonor's Case*.[15] The record ends:

> Thereupon, one and all of the aforesaid premises having been understood and considered by the court here, the serjeants-at-law of the lord the king and the king's attorney being present, having been summoned for this purpose, it is awarded that the aforesaid Thomas Dormer take nothing by his aforesaid traverse and plea.

What seems probable is that having seized on this case to test important points in feudal law, the crown overawed Dormer before whisking the lawyers into exchequer chamber for a hypothetical discussion of royal rights.[16] Dormer clearly did not feel that his case had been tried and found wanting. In 1502 he was again contesting the title to Nursling.[17]

Transmuted into an opportunity to test royal feudal rights, *Stonor's Case* first addressed itself to the effect of *4 Henry VII* c. 17 on prerogative wardship.[18] Counsel opposed to the crown benefitting under the act were Thomas Marowe and Humphrey Sedgewick, apprentices, and two of the recently appointed serjeants, John Butler and Thomas Frowyk.[19] They argued first for strict construction. When this statute provided that the lord should have custody, it intended the immediate lord of the fee; even where the crown was able to claim prerogative wardship, lands in use would under this act be enjoyed by the mesne lord. Where the statute specified wardship of lands in knight service it meant those lands only, not any claim

15. Cf. Bean, *Decline of Feudalism*, 253; Constable, *Prerogativa Regis*, 20 n.48.
16. It is probable that all the reports of the case refer to the same discussion(s), not to different stages. *Y.B.* Trin. 12 Hen.VII, p. 1 and Mich. 13, p. 3 each note a discussion by Frowyk which refers to a case in 9 Henry IV; Mich. 13, p. 3 and p. 12 have the same material attributed to Butler and Sedgewick respectively. Fineux's remarks in Mich. 13, p. 3 cross-refer to those of Kebell in Trin. 12, p. 1 and are probably the same as in Keilwey, *Reports*, f. 33v and probably the ruling noted by Rudhale and Pigot: *ibid.*, f. 86. The adjournment after Mich. 13, p. 3 may be an editorial insertion to rationalise this report with p. 12 which probably precedes it. There is no reason to believe that Trin. 12, p. 1 represents an argument prior to adjournment to exchequer chamber: Bean, *Decline of Feudalism*, 252.
17. Kingsford, *E.H.R.* 35. 425.
18. Each speaker dealt with the four points of the case in turn, but all saw the construction of the statute as *le premier point*. The following integrates all four reports.
19. Humphrey Sedgewick – of Lincoln, but connections with Yorks. N.R.; Lincoln's Inn, admitted 1482, reader autumn 1497; J.P. Yorks. N.R. and Ripon; died December 1500/May 1501: *Cal. Patent Rolls, 1485–94*, 507; *ibid., 1494–1509*, 667, 669; *Cal. Close Rolls, 1485–1500*, 323, 1227; *ibid., 1500–9*, 548; *Admission Book*, i. 22; *Black Books*, i. 109, 122.

through them to prerogative wardship over socage lands in use. Similarly with basic rule of *Prerogativa Regis* c. 1; royal rights only arose when a tenant died seised, and the words of the new law, 'as if their tenants had died seised', would not do. Frowyk even claimed that the statute was irrelevant to the Stonor case because it referred to feoffments to the use of the tenant, whereas Stonor had enfeoffed 'to himself and another'.[20] In the second place the argument was that royal prerogatives existed at common law. Thus, where a statute made law what before did not exist at common law, royal prerogative could not exist. As John Butler said:

This is a new wardship given to lords which did not exist at common law, and, because of this, the king shall not have his prerogative.[21]

In Sedgewick's view, the royal prerogative applied wherever an ordinary person was entitled to wardship at common law; any extension of royal rights came by specific provisions in an act.[22] Thomas Marowe in particular developed this approach:

To my mind the king can have no prerogative unless in something which has always been given to him by prerogative, for a prerogative cannot [just] start today; thus prescription is an essential element in a prerogative. Thus it appears in this case that if the royal prerogative is upheld, this will be [a right] starting from today, which to my mind cannot be.[23]

If Sedgewick and Marowe were to triumph, there was an end to royal efforts to amplify the prerogative.

The crown's case was argued by an unnamed lawyer, possibly an apprentice, by John Kingsmill, another of the new serjeants, and by James Hobart A.G. and the king's serjeants, John Mordaunt and Thomas Kebell.[24] One obvious argument was put immediately by Hobart, that the king did not only enjoy prerogative rights but also rights as a lord himself, and hence was in benefit by the statute.[25] It would not, however, bear much weight as the distinction between

20. Hemmant, *Exchequer Chamber*, ii. 164. Mordaunt dismissed this as not material since title descended in conscience only to the heir: *ibid.*, ii. 166.
21. *ibid.*, ii. 167. Sedgewick also argued that the act established a custody by statute, not wardship at common law: *Y.B.* Mich. 13 Hen.VII, p. 12 f. 12.
22. *ibid.*, Mich. 13 Hen.VII, p. 12 f. 12.
23. *ibid.*, Trin. 12 Hen.VII, p. 1 f. 19.
24. *ibid.*, Mich. 13 Hen.VII, p. 12 f. 11 identifies this counsel as Danvers, but neither the place of the speaker nor his opinions indicate that he was William Danvers J.; cf. *ibid.*, Mich. 13 Hen.VII, p. 3 f. 8. The first edition of this year book was, however, not until 1555.
25. *ibid.*, Trin. 12 Hen.VII, p. 1 f. 19.

royal rights by prerogative and as *dominus* was well established.[26] A stronger point opened by Hobart and Kingsmill and developed by both Mordaunt and Kebell was on the construction of statute. A statute, they argued, 'will be construed according to the intent of the those who made the statute, not always after the words of the statute'; parliament intended feudal lords to benefit, and obviously intended the king not to be in a worse case than other lords.[27] Lack of specific mention of the crown was immaterial; only specific reference in a statute removes the king's rights, but he benefits positively from all legislation, for this is implied in his assent to bills. Viewed in this way, royal benefit by *4 Henry VII* c. 17 was clear. Kebell said:

> The statute *A°4 Henry VII* c. 17 [says] 'Chief Lords', and the king clearly is a lord, for all lands are held of him, mediately or immediately. Thus, the intent in making the statute was because the lords were being ousted by this sort of feoffment, for which reason the statute was made as a remedy so that such a feoffment would not have the effect of ousting lords from their wardships. Hence, if such feoffments will not have the effect of ousting the lords it follows that it is not now reasonable but that the king should be within the provisions of the statute.[28]

The statute had to be construed as removing an obstacle to the operation of the common law, putting lords, and the king, where they would have been before the enfeoffment.[29]

What is perhaps most indicative of royal policy is the implication that enfeoffment as a device to hand on the succession to property was *ipso facto* fraudulent. It was more than helpful that *4 Henry VII* c. 17 had been drafted as a re-enactment of the statute of Marlborough, which had established the notion that uses could be collusive.[30] Since *Prerogativa Regis*, said Mordaunt:

> a deceit was devised by the common law to keep the tenant's heir out of the wardship of the King or of other lords, to wit, a feoffment to the use of the tenant and his heirs, the which was against reason, and notwithstanding this feoffment the right of the land in conscience descended to the feoffor's heir,

26. Constable, *Prerogativa Regis*, xv–xvii.
27. *Y.B.* Trin. 12 Hen.VII, p. 1 f. 20. This was probably the occasion when Kebell declared 'for clear law' that the crown was not bound by a general prohibition in a statute: Keilwey, *Reports*, Hil. 13 Hen.VII, p. 3 f. 35.
28. *Y.B.* Trin. 12 Hen.VII, p. 1 f. 20.
29. So 'Danvers', *ibid.*, Mich. 13 Hen.VII, p. 12 f. 11.
30. See below, pp. 255–6. Holdsworth, *H.E.L.*, iv. 448 suggests that this was a propaganda device. Cf. Bean, *Decline of Feudalism*, 193. For the culmination of the argument on collusion, see *ibid.*, 280.

and he could compel the feoffees to suffer him to take the profits or to make estate to him of the land as heir to his father, and yet he shall not be in ward.[31]

Care was also taken to argue into the statute socage land in use, held of mesne lords. Kebell pointed out that the statute provided for wardship as if the tenant had died seised, and since prerogative wardship would have applied to land in socage if he had died seised, socage land in use had been caught by the statute.[32] In fact the text did not mention socage, but the crown asserted the equity of the statute; unless the king were allowed prerogative wardship of enfeoffed socage land held of mesne lords, he alone would be excluded from the restoration of common-law rights provided by the act. The prerogative was to be interpreted 'largely'; Kebell even argued that the statute gave rights of wardship even when the crown had licensed the alienation to feoffees.[33]

Apart from the scope of the 1490 statute, three other questions were debated in *Stonor's Case* – whether if he claimed by the statute the king had to proceed by writ, what meaning should be read into the return that the land held of St Swithin's was 'by service unknown', and whether the form of the inquisition was adequate, given the wording of the statute.[34] The positions are predictable. Opponents of the crown argued that if the royal claim were allowed, it would still have to be sued – there was no right of seizure. If the king came in by the statute he was bound by the procedure of the statute; he had no right of entry on a feoffee at common law. Secondly, 'by services unknown' must mean socage tenure; if Stonor held from the prior of St Swithin's it must at least be by fealty, and tenure by fealty was socage. The doctrine that tenants would normally hold by the tenure of their overlord argued likewise; the assumption was that the prior held in frank tenement, and therefore that his tenants did also, which meant socage tenure.

The royal lawyers replied that a tenant-in-chief 'by services unknown' was always assumed to hold by knight service, and analogy would extend this to mesne tenants. By this rule, too, the prior's tenure would not be frank tenement but military service, and the assumption about sub-tenants would then make Stonor hold by knight service, which, in any case, was the most usual tenure. Only Kebell declined to speculate:

31. Hemmant, *Exchequer Chamber*, ii. 165.
32. *ibid.*, ii. 168–9.
33. *ibid.*, ii. 168.
34. Keilwey, *Reports*, Mich. 13 Hen.VII, p. 5 f. 32.

whether it be held in socage or by knight service, the king shall have the wardship, therefore I shall not argue about that.[35]

On the matter of process, the king had a right to enter where common people could not; an inquisition was a matter of record and the king could enter on a record; his common-law right to enter on tenants-in-chief after office found was undoubted, so why not on the tenants of others? In any case, claimed Kebell, not only the king benefited; feoffees ousted by the crown would be better placed than those sued by mesne lords.[36] What counsel said on the sufficiency of the inquisition attracted less notice from reporters, and the discussion has not survived on the large point that the statute only operated on intestacy, and the inquisition had not mentioned whether or not a will existed. It was, however, argued that 'tenure by services unknown' was void; it was repugnant to state a tenure but claim ignorance of the services which established the tenure, and hence tenancy-in-chief by knight service should be understood.[37]

The reception of the crown's arguments by the judges was not unanimous. Wode and Rede accepted royal benefit under the statute in respect of all lands held by the tenant, and also the royal right of entry. Rede said:

the statute shall be construed as though it were said, to wit, 'he who would have the wardship of the land if he had died seised, shall now by the statute have the wardship of the heir'.[38]

Vavasour, on the other hand, argued for the exclusion of the king as not covered by the word 'lords', for the exclusion of socage land, and for process by *scire facias*. Danvers stressed the need to interpret the new statute in relation to the statute of Marlborough. The rationale for wardship under *4 Henry VII* c. 17 was fraudulent enfeoffment; where the king had licensed alienation he was not defrauded, and so he had no claim under the statute (and for unlicensed alienation he had protection already), and if he had no wardship of lands in chief it was hard to allow wardship of land held of other lords.[39] For Chief Justice Bryan the inquisition was crucial. The crown had established its entitlement provided the office was sound, but omitting any mention of a will defeated the right of the feoffees to traverse, and 'by

35. Hemmant, *Exchequer Chamber*, ii. 169.
36. *ibid.*
37. So 'Danvers', *Y.B.* Mich. 13 Hen.VII, p. 12 ff. 11–12.
38. Hemmant, *Exchequer Chamber*, ii. 172.
39. For *Marlborough* and fraud, see Constable, *Prerogativa Regis*, 19–20 *et passim*.

services unknown' was void for uncertainty. On this latter point, Fineux C.J.K.B. agreed, but he persuaded Bryan to accept that as the advowson had been returned in chief by knight service, the uncertainty should be taken to the king's advantage.[40]

Fineux did not, however, accept that omitting the will was fatal to the crown. The inquisition could be traversed in chancery, and as the office stood, it should be construed as returning a simple use without a will, in line with royal privilege under the statute of Marlborough. Indeed, like Danvers (but to the opposite effect) Fineux saw *Marlborough* with its concept of fraudulent uses as the context for *4 Henry VII* c. 17. The 1267 statute provided that: 'if the king's tenant in chief for one acre holds from another [lord] a second acre which he puts in feoffment collusively and this is returned by the inquisition, then the king shall have his prerogative, and for the same reason in this case here', and the reporter added 'which was not denied'.[41] The Tudor act alone could not have given the king rights, but the claims allowed under the act were grounded in existing feudal lordship: 'the impediment which put the king from his prerogative was the enfeoffment, which is taken away by this statute'.[42] It was the governing position of *Marlborough*, too which led Fineux to his one limitation on the crown's claims. *Marlborough* specifically excluded socage lands when defining collusive enfeoffment, and therefore enfeoffments of socage lands could not be upset by the 1490 legislation. The chief justice's general argument seems to have carried the exchequer chamber, and certainly did so on this matter of socage lands. The report in Keilwey of a case in 1506 notes that:

> the king will have wardship of the acre held from him [in chief by knight service and enfeoffed to uses] and also of the other acre held by knight service of the common person but not of the acre held [of a common person] in socage. And thus was the statute of 4 Henry VII construed by the advice of all the justices of England when Kebell was king's serjeant, as Rudhall and Pigot said who had heard them arguing.[43]

40. This seems implied by a comparison of Hemmant, *Exchequer Chamber*, ii. 173 and Keilwey, *Reports*, Mich. 13 Hen.VII, p. 5 f. 33.
41. *ibid.*, Mich. 13 Hen.VII, p. 5 f. 33v.
42. *ibid.*, Mich. 13 Hen.VII, p. 5 f. 33v.
43. *ibid.*, Pas. 21 Hen.VII, p. 15 f. 86. William Rudhale: Wedgwood, *Biographies*. Keilwey's report here probably derived from Serjeant John Caryll, formerly of the Inner Temple: Simpson, *L.Q.R.* 73. 89–105. The memory is in error, unless it is intended that the acre in socage was also enfeoffed. The king's right to prerogative wardship of socage lands of which the tenant died seised was clear in Kebell's day.

The limitation, however, did not frustrate the crown for long. In an addendum to the same case it it noted that:

today, *sc*. Michaelmas term 6 Henry VIII [1514] the common experience is that the king, by his prerogative, will have wardship as well of lands of which the ancestor died seised [and enfeoffed] in use, as [of those] in possession, as well land held in socage as by knight service.

Detailed observation of Kebell and his colleagues in *Stonor's Case* can be paralleled in other litigation involving Henry VII's feudal rights.[44] It is, however, to the generation after Kebell's death that we must look for the climax of the story and the most blatant example of lawyers construing the law in the interests of the crown. In 1529 Henry VIII determined to secure by statute the comprehensive restoration of feudal rights towards which crown policy had been working for forty years.[45] The house of commons was intransigent. After five sessions of frustration, the king moved in 1533 to engineer a test case in chancery arising from the will of Lord Dacre of the South. The chancellor, Thomas Audley, could be relied on to support the crown, even though the interest of his court lay in maintaining the use.[46] The master of the rolls, Dr John Taylor, might have proved more difficult, but either by invitation or good fortune he resigned in the autumn of 1534 and Thomas Cromwell took his place.[47] It is highly likely that this was principally in order to play a part in the Dacre case, for three months after the resulting statute received the royal assent, Cromwell resigned.[48]

Immediately on his appointment to the rolls, Cromwell was busy in discussions with the judges; the case opened in Easter 1535, and in Trinity:

in exchequer chamber by appointment of the chancellor and the secretary, all the justices and the chief baron [of the exchequer] were assembled to put their

44. See above, pp. 240–2.
45. For the following see Ives, *E.H.R.* 82. 673–97. For a comprehensive examination of the legal issues in Dacre's case, see Bean, *Decline of Feudalism*, 277–84 and Spelman, *Reports*, ii. *200–3*.
46. Audley's appointment as lord keeper (later chancellor), 20 May 1532, at the height of the parliamentary campaign to recover royal rights, may well have been influenced by his known (and probably calculated) hostility to uses: Ives, *E.H.R.* 82. 682–3; Spelman, *Reports*, ii. *198–9*.
47. Taylor was possibly a sick man; he died soon after resigning: *D.N.B.* Cromwell was appointed 8 Oct. 1534: G. R. Elton, *Tudor Revolution in Government* (Cambridge, 1953), 99.
48. His successor took office 10 Jul. 1536: *ibid.*, 127 n.2.

opinions on this case privately (but Justice Englefield was not there because he was on royal business in Wales).[49]

The crown offered two contentions, that uses were unknown at common law, and that the *cestui que use* could not devise an estate by his will. The first was a forlorn hope and possibly a bargaining tactic, for since the statute of Richard III the common law had become thoroughly accustomed to the use.[50] The second issue, however, the right to devise, was explosive; if decided in the negative it would throw into doubt many, possibly most, landed titles. Audley and Cromwell pressed the idea, along with John Baldwin C.J.C.P., Richard Lyster C.B.Ex., and Walter Luke J.K.B., and they had behind them a decade of legal thought critical of the use: 'no land is devisable by will except by a custom, for it is contrary to the nature of land to pass in such a manner'.[51] The other chief justice, John Fitzjames, with his colleague John Spelman, and William Shelley and Antony Fitzherbert of the common pleas, rejected this:

such a will is a declaration of the trust and a showing to the feoffee of his intent how the feoffment shall be, and the feoffee is obliged in conscience to perform this. And the devisee has no remedy by the law to compel him to perform this. And he gives nothing in the land by his will, but only his use, and the estate of the feoffee is not impaired in any way by this.

What happened next is told only by John Spelman, and highly evocative it is:

Port, another justice of the king's bench, was of the same opinion, but he spoke so low that the said chancellor and secretary understood him to be of the contrary opinion. And because of this they thought that the greater number of the justices were of the opinion with them. And for this reason, all the justices were commanded to appear before the king. And he commanded them to assemble to agree on their opinion. And those who were of the opinion that the will was void should have of the king hearty thanks. And then the justices reassembled before the said chancellor and secretary and debated this question; and Fitzjames, Fitzherbert and Spelman, seeing the opinion of the said chancellor, secretary and the other justices who were men of great sense and the number of them was greater, they conformed themselves to their opinion; but Shelley was not there because he was ill, and Englefield was in Wales.

49. Quotations are translated from the account by Spelman in B. L. Hargrave Ms. 388 ff. 96–7. Attention was first drawn to the passage in A. W. B. Simpson, 'The equitable doctrine of consideration and the law of uses', *University of Toronto Law Journal* 16 (1965), 8–9. The text and a translation of the complete passage can be found in Spelman, *Reports*, i. 228–30.

50. *ibid.*, ii. *195–8*.

51. *ibid.*, ii. *198–200*.

Faced with a decision which threw countless settlements into doubt, the Commons capitulated and accepted the statute of uses, with all the consequences for land law which followed.

The part lawyers played in 'the revival of feudalism' is the most explicit example of the profession moulding the law to suit the monarch. Less obvious, but of equal importance, were the frequent calls which the crown made for legal elucidation or judicial advice. These were, in Professor Chrimes' phrase, 'the key to some of Henry VII's actions at the time of his accession and in ensuing years', but they were no Tudor invention.[52] In 1465 it was the exchequer chamber which handled the delicate issue of complaints against the earl of Warwick for exceeding his jurisdiction as constable of Dover Castle; it was likewise exchequer chamber which ruled in 1467 against the power of the pope to exempt clergy from royal taxation of the church.[53] Similarly, when Edward IV's government was faced with a challenge to the control of bullion it enjoyed under moribund fourteenth-century statutes, it was exchequer chamber which vindicated royal authority.[54]

The most remarkable of all Yorkist consultations with the legal profession occurred in June 1485. Richard III summoned the judges *in interiora camera stellata* to advise him in person on three judicial issues, apparently with the royal council in attendance.[55] The first problem was what to do when a chancery judgement was deliberately defied and a counter-attack commenced in common law; to the king's apparent desire to see the vexatious suit immediately penalised, the judges replied that this was impossible until the action was proved false, but they recommended instead that the chancellor should imprison the offender for contempt. The second matter concerned abuse of process by a justice of the peace, and the judges concluded, after long debate, that this was a serious offence punishable by fine and dismissal, a decision which anticipated the concerns of the 1489 statute.[56] The third item was clearly the most serious. A fraudulent alteration of common pleas records (involving no less a person than the custos brevium with three other lawyers and the beneficiary of the trick as well), the episode raised a host of legal problems. The judges quickly construed the offence as felony under the statute of amend-

52. Chrimes, *Henry VII*, 160.
53. *Y.B.* Pas. 5 Edw. IV, Long Quinto, f. 127; Hemmant, *Exchequer Chamber*, ii. 11.
54. *Y.B.* Pas. 4 Edw. IV, p. 4 f. 4, p. 19 f. 12.
55. Hemmant, *Exchequer Chamber*, ii. 86–94.
56. *4 Henry VII*, c. 12.

ments, *8 Henry VI*, c. 12, but found that statute unenforceable in the particular circumstances; the offenders had to be allowed instead to plead guilty to misprision of felony only. Richard III was so angry that he sat in person in king's bench and, apparently, wished himself to assess the fine; the judges persuaded him otherwise but probably only after promising exemplary sentences.[57]

The accession of Henry VII saw this level of consultation increased to deal with a number of unusual problems, ranging from an attainted king with a prospective wife who had been declared illegitimate, to a speaker elect of the Commons who was dead in law.[58] It was the lawyers who declared that the king, *ex officio*, was incapable of being under attaint; who devised a procedure to allow attainted M.P.s to take their seats; who oversaw the difficult restoration of Henry's supporters to their lands.[59] In all there were probably more than twenty meetings of the leading lawyers in the first year of the new king's reign, mostly in exchequer chamber but elsewhere as well (including a working dinner with Chief Justice Hussey), although not all were for discussion of policy matters.[60] The tempo slackened as the dynasty became more established, but reliance on the law was never far away. It was, for example, the judges to whom the king looked in or about 1505 to resolve the politically sensitive disagreement between the duke of Buckingham and his younger brother over the latter's marriage to a widow under the king's feudal guardianship.[61] In the next reign, too, lawyers played an important part in the reaction against Henry VII's fiscal policies, while it was to be a lawyer who

57. The report (Hemmant, *Exchequer Chamber*, ii. 90) ends with the ambiguous *Et hoc est voluntas Regis, videlicet per justiciarios suos et legem suam unam est dicere etc.* which may indicate (as Hemmant translates) that Richard III accepted the opinion of the judges that assessing a fine was a matter for the court concerned. But translated – 'And the king's will was this, viz. to speak the same by both his justices and his law' – it may imply that the king expected the courts to impose the sort of penalties he expected.
58. The principal issues are listed in Chrimes, *Henry VII*, 160–1.
59. *Y.B.* Mich. 1 Hen. VII, p. 5 f. 4; see above, p. 174.
60. *ibid.*, Mich. 1 Hen. VII, p. 2 ff. 2–3, p. 3 f. 3, p. 4 ff. 3–4, p. 5 f. 4, p. 6 f. 4, p. 7 f. 5; Hil. 1 Hen. VII, p. 1 f. 5, p. 2 f. 6, p. 5 f. 8, p. 6 f. 9, p. 10 f. 10, p. 11 f. 10, p. 12 f. 10, p. 13 f. 10, p. 25 ff. 12–13, p. 26 f. 13; Pas. 1 Hen. VII, p. 5 f. 19, p. 6 f. 20, p. 12 f. 22, p. 15 f. 22; Trin. 1 Hen. VII, p. 1 f. 25, p. 5 f. 27, p. 6 f. 28, p. 9 f. 30. Some cases appear more than once.
61. *ibid.*, Mich. 20 Hen. VII, p. 20 f. 10; *Cal. Close Rolls, 1500–9*, 414, 435, 471, 479; cf. Rawcliffe, *The Staffords*, 161–2. The close roll suggests a marriage date in 1505, but the *Y.B.* report, dated Mich. 1504, refers to the marriage being arranged by Reynold Bray who died 5 Aug. 1503.

tried to frustrate and a lawyer who made possible Henry VIII's break with his first wife Catherine.[62]

The importance of the guidance which these meetings gave the crown can be summed up in the origination of that most famous of Tudor statutes, the so-called Star Chamber Act of 1487.[63] Henry VII had proposed to open his reign, as had Edward IV, with a formal oath taken in parliament and administered by commission to gentry throughout the country, binding them to good behaviour.[64] The commissioners, in fact, may already have begun work before parliament met on 9 November.[65] When, therefore, the crown came to submit the business for the forthcoming session to a meeting of the judges at Blackfriars, the views which were expressed on the oath must have been unwelcome.[66] The judges also looked back to the reign of Edward IV. At some time, probably during a session of the 1472–5 parliament, the peers and 'others' had drawn up, at royal command, a programme of law enforcement, and orders had been sent to all J.P.s to put into effect an agreed list of statutes. This the judges were certainly prepared to endorse in 1485, with the addition of the statute of sheriffs of 23 Henry VI. But the chief lesson which they drew from the episode was the futility of proceeding by oaths and promises. Although the peers had then sworn to abide by the list of statutes, as far as retaining was concerned, they had, William Hussey recalled, broken their oaths within the hour. The value of a fresh round of promises was illusory. The law, Sir William declared,

> will never be properly enforced until all the peers, both spiritual and temporal are in agreement, for the love and dread that they have of God or the King, or both, to execute it effectively. Then, when the King for his part and the peers for theirs are determined to do this and do it, everyone else will obey readily, and if they will not they will be punished, and then everyone will take warning from them.

Everything depended upon executing the law, and this depended upon compelling magnates to behave.

This plain hint that the problem required a political rather than a

62. See above, p. 80; G. R. Elton, 'Sir Thomas More and the opposition to Henry VIII', and 'King or minister? The man behind the Henrician Reformation', in *Studies*, i. 155–72.
63. *3 Hen. VII*, c. 1.
64. Bayne, *Council of Henry VII*, 1; Dunham, 'Indentured retainers', 91; Williams, *English Historical Documents, 1485–1558*, 332–4; Chrimes, *Henry VII*, 64–5.
65. Dunham, 'Indentured retainers', 91.
66. *Y.B.* Mich. 1 Hen. VII, p. 3 f. 3.

judicial solution came to fruition two years later with the *pro camera stellata* act. This was drafted to meet the very point of the judges' objection to the 1485 oath, and the method adopted, a special group of counsellors, was the only one which could put the dread of the king, if not of God, into the minds of over-mighty subjects; even the language of the statute, that 'the lawes of the lond in execucon . . . take litell effecte', seem to echo Hussey. Another connection of the act with the Blackfriars debate of 1485 is the terms of reference laid down, which seem to reflect the statutes approved by the justices on that occasion. The most famous of Henry VII's measures to restore order to England was at least in line with advice given to the crown by the judges.

Francis Bacon remarked that Henry VII governed his law by his lawyers, but the comment reflects more the fifteenth- and sixteenth-century norm than the preference of a single monarch.[67] The support of the profession and the courts offered a principal means to secure the powers and policies of the crown, to make the country, again in Bacon's phrase, 'to dance more often and better to the tune of the prerogative'.[68] The consequences need not be laboured; they are the stuff of history over the next two hundred years. When the early Stuarts turned to the judges to construe the law, they were following a long-standing precedent; when the Long Parliament abolished star chamber, feudal dues and the fiscal rights of the domestic prerogative, it was smashing a machine constructed for the state by Yorkist and early Tudor lawyers; whenever a landowner sought to provide for his family, or whenever his conveyancer took up a quill, it was to grapple with a law hammered out by the same lawyers – Hussey and Fineux, Mordaunt and Kebell and a hundred and more like them.

67. Francis Bacon, *Historie of the raigne of King Henry the seventh*, ed. J. R. Lumby (1882), 131.
68. Quoted in Constable, *Prerogativa Regis*, ix.

12

A CHANGING COMMUNITY

To litigants and to general observers, lawyers apply known principles to the particular; the problem is simply to ascertain what the law is and then to make sure it is implemented. But 'what is the law?' can only to a limited degree be kept separate from a second question, 'what ought the law to be?', and when an issue is raised which is in some respects novel, the courts will be forced to, in a sense, 'make' law. In England today this possibility is limited, but in the centuries before parliament became a massive legislating institution, the scope for judge-made law was much more considerable. As social and economic development brought to light questions which necessitated new answers, these answers were given more by the courts than the legislature. Thomas Kebell's generation stood at the start of this. The pace of change was quickening, and frequent though parliaments were (and wide though their competence was recognised to be), legislative change in the law was occasional and spasmodic. If the law was to adapt, the lawyers had to adapt it.

Yet although this proposition is true, it is no simple task to trace non-statutory change in law, or even to be sure that the lawyers understood wholly what was at stake. As Professor Milsom has argued, the notion of the substantive element in law was late to develop.[1] Obviously it could have little meaning while trial consisted in the proper presentation to God of the contradictory oaths of rival claimants, through either the ordeal or battle. Nor would it necessarily be raised in the sort of litigation which dominated the later middle ages. This was directed at putting a dispute to a jury, not at arguing what the law was; 'the essence of a law-suit was still the formulation of a question to be put to some deciding mechanism'.[2] Of course asking 'how can a defendant introduce into his plea this point or that?' could invite the query 'ought he to be allowed to introduce it?' and hence,

1. S. F. C. Milsom, 'Law and fact in legal development', *University of Toronto Law Journal* 17 (1967), 1–19.
2. Milsom, *Historical Foundations*, 37.

'what ought the law to be?', but raising substantive matters in this indirect way was hardly encouraging. The nature of litigation determines the concept of law which is possible, and medieval concentration on procedure inhibited the development of substantive doctrine. Another inhibiting factor was the dominance of 'the general issue'; wherever possible the litigant had to make a general denial of his opponent's claim (which survives today as the sweeping 'not guilty' plea in criminal trials). Special pleas with the consequent discussion of general points of the law were only gradually admitted. When Thomas Kebell, defending Sir Henry Vernon in a *quare impedit*, couched certain facts as a matter of law in an attempt to avoid taking a traverse, John Vavasour J. said to him, 'we would do better to give this in evidence to the jury'.[3]

These conceptual obstacles to the appreciation of substantive law were, to some degree, offset for Kebell's generation by changes in pleading and the appearance of the paper plea.[4] At the very time when the country was entering a period of accelerated change, the courts and the profession were beginning to be both freer to consider substantive law and more concerned with advocacy. The full development of this lay beyond the lifetime of Thomas Kebell, and much of his work continued to centre on the admissibility of pleas. Nevertheless, substantive law was beginning to emerge.

Change in substantive law by court action is gradual and erratic; it is a process of sedimentation, the laying down of one judicial decision upon another. It is also a retiring process – there are no publicised revolutions. In Kebell's day, and for long after, change was less in terms of principle than in the adaptation of existing remedies to new situations. The best example in the pre-reformation period is in the area of contract. Traditional remedies to enforce agreements, actions of covenant and debt, were 'stunted by technical rules'.[5] Lawyers, therefore, turned to other actions to see what could be substituted. Eventually, by the mid-fifteenth century the possibilities of *assumpsit* were being exploited – an action on the case which brought in contract by alleging that the defendant had 'undertaken' to do this or that. A whole range of issues was opened by this notion (and it took another

3. *Y.B.* Pas. 11 Hen. VII, p. 1 f. 18.
4. See above, pp. 169–70; cf. *Y.B.* Trin. 16 Hen. VIII, p. 13 f. 15: 'Kebell *monstra al' court le ple in barre & demurrera sur le ple in arrest de jugement, entant que ce est matter in ley.*'
5. C. H. S. Fifoot, *History and Sources of the Common Law: Tort and Contract* (1949), 330.

century and a half before the action was fully developed, as signalled by *Slade's Case* in 1602), and Kebell was at the bar in the critical early years. The problem at that stage was the application of *assumpsit* to nonfeasance (failure to perform a contract), as well as the accepted misfeasance (improper performance). The principal case, and one in which Kebell argued, was *The Shepherd's Case* of Hilary 1487.[6] The defendant had been in charge of one hundred sheep and had, it was claimed, negligently allowed them to drown; was he liable under *assumpsit*? Robert Rede thought not; covenant was the appropriate action (although since this depended on a sealed deed it was unlikely to be of any use). Wode disagreed, but Kebell took a conservative line – misfeasance, yes; nonfeasance, no. Roger Townshend, from the bench, was much less restrictive, trying to bring the case within misfeasance by arguing a positive obligation to care for the animals; but he reiterated the rejection of *assumpsit* where there was only the failure to execute a promise. Two other brief reports of *assumpsits* have survived for the same year, with the bench each time repeating Townshend's cautious extension of misfeasance, but in the year before Kebell's death, nonfeasance received powerful endorsement.[7] Fineux C.J. declared:

> if one makes a covenant . . . and he does nothing about it, I shall have *Action sur mon cas* on this nonfeasance as much as if he had been guilty of a misfeasance; for I am damaged by this.[8]

The ground was now established for a more sophisticated law of contract enforceable at common law, with all that this implied for the community.

Thanks to a succession of scholars, it is possible to detail the development of particular actions such as *assumpsit*. But in a less specific way it is also possible to explore the relation between the lawyers and the law by considering the sort of issues which were being brought before the courts. This is essentially the approach of the social historian of law and not the historian of legal development. It explores the inter-relation of society, legislation and litigation, and not the emergence of doctrines or the rationale of legal ideas. It is, however, close to the way the law appears to the layman who cares little for theory and much for practicality, for the one question, 'what

6. *Y.B.* Hil. 2 Hen. VII, p. 9 f. 11.
7. *ibid.*, Hil. 2 Hen. VII, p. 15 f. 12; Mich. 3 Hen. VII, p. 20 f. 14.
8. *ibid.*, Mich. 21 Hen. VII, p. 66 f. 41; for the date see Spelman, *Reports*, ii. 267.

can the law do about this wrong that I have suffered?' or its positive variant, 'how can the law assist or hamper me in what I wish to do?'

Scrutiny of the many cases argued by Thomas Kebell shows clearly the wide range of problems which contemporaries looked to the law to solve. A number of these arose on penal bonds with conditional defeasance, the device most commonly used in his day to enforce written contracts. It combined an acknowledgement of debt with a condition specified in an accompanying indenture; compliance with the condition made the debt void.[9] In 1489, for example, a common pleas action was heard for the supply of bread to 'the vicars of Sarum'; the lessee of one of their rectories paid part of his rent in bread and did so by arrangement with a baker who was forced to sue for his money.[10] The discussion in the report is concerned with pleading, not with the substance of the contract, but this is very usual. Indeed, the absence of argument on substance was one of the attractions of the device. As Kebell remarked in a case reported under 1491, 'what binds the plaintiff is not the indenture, for the indenture is not used here by way of covenant, but as a reference as to the condition'.[11] That case was one of debt on obligation to secure a marriage contract, and this was one of the commonest uses of the system. Another example was *Vavasour* v. *Pullen*, in which Kebell represented John Pullen of Lincoln's Inn who was being sued following the marriage of his relative, Richard Banks, with the daughter of William Vavasour.[12] Like many cases involving members of the profession, it rated considerable interest.[13] Pullen had bound himself to see that Banks and his father would make certain feoffments to secure the wife's interest, but Richard apparently made a single more major settlement of property upon himself and his bride. His father-in-law objected – or saw the chance to get more – and sued Pullen. The question was, had Banks satisfied the conditions? Kebell argued that one settlement was comprised within the other, but Rede, for Vavasour, claimed that Pullen as a third party was not protected by Banks' initiative. Wode and Fineux agreed with Kebell, and although Justice Vavasour predictably supported his relative, Danvers and Bryan C.J. favoured Pullen.

9. Thorne, *New York Law Rev*. 26. 19–21; A. W. B. Simpson, 'The penal bond with conditional defeasance', in *L.Q.R.* 82 (1966), 392–422.
10. *Y.B.* Trin. 4 Hen. VII, p. 8 ff. 12–13. Cf. Mich. 5 Hen. VII, p. 18 f. 8.
11. *ibid.*, Mich. 6 Hen. VII, p. 11 f. 12; Hil. 6 Hen. VII, p. 1 f. 13.
12. *ibid.*, Hil. 9 Hen. VII, p. 11 ff. 17–18, p. 16 f. 20. John Pullen: see above, pp. 139, 192.
13. Many of the names of parties preserved in year-book reports are those of lawyers.

One of the more unusual of these cases proved a stage in the growing interest of the common law in the world of commerce. Probably from 1489–93, the case originated in an attempt to guarantee a sea captain's payment for a trading voyage.[14] The agreement was that if the *Trinity* was sailed via Lynn to pick up a cargo in Norway and delivered the freight safely in London, then the bond would become payable; in the event some cargo was lost at sea and the skipper sued for his money. The issues were complex. First there was the question of using conditional defeasance in this way; the debt was already good in law, and although it could clearly be voided, how could a condition bring it more into force than it was already? Then there was the possibility of a bond which was sound in itself but a condition which might be defective. Was the bond still valid, or were both void? Kebell argued the latter; he was supported by Wode, and the court agreed. But the principal issue was the doctrine of venue which had inhibited the maritime jurisdiction of the common law for generations. Common-law trial was by a jury of the locality, and no English jury had knowledge of Norway. Kebell argued that the condition depended upon departure from a given point in England and return, and this could be tried perfectly well. Fineux developed this into a distinction between cases 'fulfilled *ultra mare*' and those partially fulfilled '*citra mare*', but Bryan claimed that this latter sort were only admissible by special provision of parliament. Vavasour and Townshend JJ. argued that the English component in the condition could be tried – and later claimed a precedent – but Bryan was firm. Parliament had laid down that certain actions abroad were prohibited, and these could be tried in England, but not private contracts. In the case of the *Trinity* only part of the condition could be tried, and since the condition was a unity it was void. If the condition was to 'convey to Norway', the defendant must reply that 'he did not convey to Norway', which was quite un-triable at common law; 'and this disposes of the case put by my brother Vavasour'.

And it was adjudged in my time where a man had a royal licence to carry all the merchandize he had in Bruges to London without paying customs, and when he landed the goods at Billingsgate they were seised as uncustomed. In exchequer he pleaded his licence and because it could not be tried, Illingworth, then chief baron, gave judgement for the king. And if I retain a man to

14. *Y.B.* Hil. 11 Hen. VII, p. 13 f. 16; Pas. 10 Hen. VII, p. 21 f. 22. But John Fisher, counsel for plaintiff, had lent money on a ship called *The Trinity* in 1475; see below, p. 462.

go with me to Brittany, if he returned here without my permission, that can be tried here. But if he served me there or not cannot be tried. So in this case, if he delivered the goods at any port in England can be tried, but whether he conveyed them satisfactorily by sea or not and whether they were drowned in the sea or not, cannot be tried here.

No ruling is recorded, and Holdsworth went too far in suggesting a majority decision in favour of the *ultra mare/citra mare* distinction, but clearly the weight of the argument was against Bryan.[15] In king's bench in the same period, Kebell had argued in similar vein to Fineux, and Hussey C.J. (though not the reporter) had made no objection.[16] Finally, in 1505–8, Fineux was able as C.J.K.B. to repeat his distinction as a dictum, unopposed.[17]

If Thomas Bryan recalled the keenness of the crown over customs in the 1460s, it was no less eagle-eyed twenty years later when an information was laid in the exchequer against the prominent London financier Sir William Capel.[18] The charge was that he had sold cloth and general merchandise to aliens on credit, contrary to an act of 1430. The matter was difficult and went to exchequer chamber. Hussey C.J. said to Kebell, who was representing Capel: 'I and my companions have been discussing this matter amongst us beforehand, so show us your objections.' The cloth in the consignment, Kebell claimed, was exempt from the 1430 statute because an act of 1431 had allowed cloth sales on credit so long as no royal proclamation to the contrary had been made. The remainder of the merchandise he sought to excuse by pointing to the dilemma the statute posed. Delivery of goods was unavoidable at common law following a valid sale, and since the law compelled Capel to hand over possession, he was no longer liable to the crown. In a comment on this Bryan claimed that even without mention of amount and date of payment a sale was good, although the court agreed only '*in maniere*'. John Mordaunt, however, had complete support when he said that with date and amount stated, a sale must transfer possession.

The report of *Rex* v. *Capel* is brief, and there was probably no judgement in the case, given Capel's purchase of a royal pardon.[19] It does, however, suggest the problems which the increasing use of credit posed for the law, as does another occasion when Kebell

15. Holdsworth, *H.E.L.*, v. 119.
16. *Y.B.* Hil. 7 Hen. VII, p. 1 f. 9.
17. *ibid.*, Mich. 21 Hen. VII, p. 32 f. 34.
18. *ibid.*, Mich. 10 Hen. VII, p. 14 f. 7. The case may be dated between Hobart's appointment as attorney and Hussey's death, i.e. 1486–95.
19. *Cal. Patent Rolls, 1494–1509*, 43, dated 7 Nov. 1495.

appeared for the financier.[20] Capel was occupying, by statute staple, the Essex lands of a debtor until the sum due had been recovered. He was disseised and brought a writ of trespass. Robert Rede alleged for the defendant that Capel had bought some of the London property of the debtor which had also been under occupation, and so the execution was discharged. But the claim of Rede's client was a weak one, and Kebell in blistering form carried the court with him; 'Rede, therefore, did not dare to demur on account of the opinion of the court.' Another action concerned with finance was brought by Kebell on behalf of Lord Dudley against Sir Richard Pole, represented by John Vavasour.[21] Dudley was seeking the return of a gold chain which, it would appear, he had given to Pole as security for a loan of one hundred marks. The report is concerned only with Kebell's attack on the defence plea to retain the chain, but underneath, the real issue was forfeiture in cases of debt.

Among the commercial cases in which Kebell took part were some more connected with trade and finance. One of these survives only in his opinion that a partner selling on behalf of a joint concern was liable to account to the other party; the report ends, *quaere quia non interfui*.[22] Three other reports seem to be of a single case concerning goods for sale at Grocers' Hall in London, brought by Richard Broker against John Wimbish or his bailee.[23] The reports, however, are concerned with technicalities of bars and property in bailment. A case of a different sort was the writ of trespass brought by the prior of Southwark.[24] A stream ran through his property in Southwark which tenants used to dye cloth, for baking and brewing, and for cattle. Now the defendant had, he claimed, made a lime-pit for tanning skins so close that it had polluted the water and forced the tennants to leave. Kebell appeared for the defendant but the report does not give the outcome of this struggle between old and new commercial interests.

It would be wrong to give the impression that Kebell was continuously involved with cases which reflected the quickening of overseas trade, business and urban finance. Economic pressures on the countryside are represented by a number of actions arising from the popularity of pasture farming – the nature of foldage and the peculiar-

20. *Y.B.* Pas. 13 Hen. VII, p. 8 f. 22.

21. *ibid.*, Mich. 5 Hen. VII, p. 1 f.1

22. *ibid.*, Hil. 10 Hen. VII, p. 14 f. 16.

23. *ibid.*, Mich. 6 Hen. VII, p. 4 ff. 7–9; Trin. 10 Hen. VII, p. 13 f. 27; Mich. 16 Hen. VII, p. 7 ff. 2–3.

24. *ibid.*, Trin. 13 Hen. VII, p. 4 f. 26.

ity of the Norfolk fold-course, the grazing rights of the citizens of York, the rights of common for tenants-at-will, the extinction of common and the destruction of hedges following enclosure of common.[25] One case which drew the reporters, either for its interest or the fact that Robert Sheffield of the Inner Temple was plaintiff, suggests the economic pressures on the highland zone.[26] Sheffield, represented by Kebell, claimed that his close had been broken into, 3,000 of his fish caught and the pasture ruined by horses and pigs. The defence was that the area was a large moor over which the next manor had right of common. The jury passed with Sheffield, but there was much debate on technical issues when Kebell prayed judgement; although he secured this, a writ of error was brought on the action in 1502.

Another sign of change in the countryside is seen in the cases Kebell took arising from the creation of parks. In litigation in which he represented the duchess of Norfolk against the earl of Suffolk, the extent of a licence to hunt was tested.[27] In 1494 or thereabouts, Thomas Kebell was the successful counsel in an action against the bailiff of a park to enforce a reckoning for the deer there, a case which helped to open the remedy of an action of account to owners of parks, and revised the law on game.[28] Serjeant John Fisher, for the bailiff, made two substantive points – firstly a park is only a boundary from which no profit can arise, and so no account is possible; secondly, deer are wild animals in which nobody has any property:

> if someone kills deer in my park or coneys in my warren, the only action I shall have against him is for entry into the close.

Kebell replied that a park is more than its paling, as the wording of licences to empark and the law on poachers each demonstrated. The court accepted his definition.

Kebell then proceeded to defend the novelty of an action of account for a park. It was not, he said, a valid objection to say that an action of account had not been brought before. A rehearsal of the statute of Westminster II would show that the action had then lain for many

25. *ibid.*, Pas. 1 Hen. VII, p. 17 f. 24; Trin. 4 Hen. VII, p. 11 f. 13; Mich. 11 Hen. VII p. 27 ff. 6–7; Trin. 16 Hen. VII, p. 4 f. 11.
26. *ibid.*, Hil. 6 Hen. VII, p. 3 f. 14; Mich. 11 Hen. VII, p. 31 f. 9; Pas. 11 Hen. VII, p. 4 ff. 19–20. For Sheffield, see above, p. 106.
27. *ibid.*, Trin. 12 Hen. VII, p. 5 f. 25; Hil. 13 Hen. VII, p. 1 ff. 12–13, p. 2 f. 13.
28. *ibid.*, Mich. 10 Hen. VII, p. 12 ff. 6–7.

cases no longer in use; once the writ had passed the chancery it would not abate, provided it could be maintained by argument.

In my opinion, in every case where a person has anything in his care, if he does not hold it to his own use, then he will render an account for it.

To the argument that there was no property in wild beasts, Kebell had to admit that this was the view of no less an authority than Bracton.

However, by common law, before the statute of Westminster [I], if a stranger killed a deer in my park, the jurors ought to award damages for the value of the deer, as for the breaking in. So, today, I shall recover damages if a stranger kills a deer in my close, because when the deer is in my close nobody has any right to meddle with it, for I am nearer in possession of the beast than anyone else.

Even though there was no right of property, provided there was an interest, then there was action of account. The two other serjeants present, Rede and Wode, gave Kebell unanimous support. The puisne judges were more cautious. The junior, John Fineux, agreed that a park-keeper was accountable for grass, wood and the like, but for deer only if trapped and sold on instructions, while John Vavasour produced a powerful statement of the strict Bractonian view. Bryan C.J., on the other hand, accepted the whole of Kebell's argument; if the defendant was bailiff, he was as such liable to account for the deer. Of the further discussion there is no record, but the final decision was for Kebell. An owner could call his bailiff to account for the profits of his park, including deer, herons, hares and rabbits, although not, so Bryan added as an afterthought, pheasants and partridges.

In reading the later year books, the twentieth-century eye is drawn to cases which hint at the social and economic future of the country. But it is just as significant to notice lawyers at work on cases concerning the church, cases which in Kebell's massive list occur again and again. Frequent actions of *quare impedit* – the writ brought to recover a patron's right to appoint to a living – tell of the identification of the church with the world of property.[29] Some produced very substantial professional interest, notably *Rex* v. *the Bishop of Coventry and Lichfield*, from the late 1490s, which covers more than eight folios spread over two reports, and in which John Mordaunt enumerated no fewer than six points of difficulty.[30] This was, perhaps, exceptional as it arose from the king's interest as guardian of the patron, a minor in

29. Some 15 of the reports involving Kebell arose on *quare impedit*.
30. *Y.B.* Pas. 14 Hen. VII, p. 4 ff. 21–7; Pas. 15 Hen. VII, p. 2 ff. 6–8.

wardship, with Mordaunt and Kebell arguing for the crown. But a single report of an anonymous *quare impedit* could nevertheless run to three folios. The most interesting from Kebell's point of view was that brought by Edward, Lord Hastings, and his wife Mary against Sir Walter Hungerford, the local bishop, the incumbent and others unnamed.[31] This clearly arose from a dispute between Lady Mary and her uncle Sir Walter over the division of the family property to which he was heir male and she heir by blood, following his restoration after a Yorkist attainder. Kebell, for the Hastings, claimed seisin by a title conveyed from an earlier enfeoffment, and the defendants that the enfeoffment was to Sir Walter and his male heirs. The report is brief and without conclusion, but shows that Kebell first attacked the line-up of patron, bishop and parson as a conglomeration of separate rights which had to be pleaded separately, and then went on to pick holes in the technical correctness of Hungerford's case.

Property litigation arising from ecclesiastical titles was, however, not confined to lay patrons. Ecclesiastical foundations were frequent parties in court. This was not only because of the size of church endowments but because they raised the whole question of the corporation in law. How should a corporation sue and be sued; was a corporation liable for debts contracted by its head or its former head; how were the charters, letters patent and acts of parliament endowing corporations to be construed?[32] Religious corporations were also more dependent than many laymen on agents, leases and agreements, and so embroiled in litigation that this produced.[33]

Perhaps of more interest than the church as a great estate, and certainly more significant for future history, were actions which raised the conflict of laws with the state. Testamentary business was a fruitful source of friction between the two. One case of special interest to the profession was *Sonde* v. *Peckham*, arising, as we have seen, from a dispute between Reynold Sonde of the king's bench and a London citizen and chancery clerk over the will of Robert Strongbone.[34] After years of litigation, the case arrived in 1489 at the

31. *ibid.*, Hil. 13 Hen. VII, p. 24 f. 18.
32. e.g. v. abbot of Westminster, *ibid.*, Mich. 6 Hen. VII, p. 2 f. 7; v. prior of Dunstable, *ibid.*, Mich. 13 Hen. VII, p. 2 f. 2; v. abbot of Battle, *ibid.*, Mich. 9 Hen. VII, p. 6 f. 10.
33. e.g. *ibid.*, Hil. 7 Hen. VII, p. 2 ff. 9–10, probably v. Magdalen College, Oxford; cf. below, p. 345.
34. *ibid.*, Mich. 2 Ric. III, p. 8 ff. 3–4, p. 45 ff. 17–18, p. 51 f. 22; Trin. 4 Hen. VII, p. 12 ff. 13–14. For Sonde, Strongbone and Peckham, see above, pp. 106–7.

king's bench. The issue was now the forty marks for usury paid to Strongbone which Peckham had returned '*in discharge de conscience le dit R.S.*' when acting under an earlier church authority now set aside in favour of Sonde. Several of the leading apprentices of the day took part: John Brown for Peckham, supported by Thomas Oxenbridge, and Humphrey Coningsby for Sonde, supported by William Grevill; Kebell and Wode, the serjeants consulted, were inclined against Peckham, especially on the quixotic repayment of usury. The majority of the bench was also against Peckham, but the problem of jurisdiction was clearly felt. Hussey refused to meddle with 'the authority of the bishop of Rome' and concluded, 'we will be advised on this matter for it is the first motion [of this sort]'.

Some years later, in the problem case of *Purrie* v. *Magdalen College, Oxford*, Kebell was even more involved in canon law.[35] The suit, better known as '*The Case of the Chapel of Wanborough*' turned, as we have seen, on the validity of the annexation of the chapel to Magdalen, with Kebell attacking on a number of grounds, some referring to the technicalities of annexation. Townshend J. agreed with the criticism, saying that he had checked with the canon lawyers, and Bryan concurred, but on another point the chief justice expressed doubt: 'I do not know what the law of Holy Church is on this point, but we will consult with the doctors of the law.' In a later hearing, however, he withdrew his agreement with Kebell and Townshend, saying 'that a doctor of canon law had changed his mind', though the reporter did not know the reason. The Wanborough case was an example of canon law being drawn into a common-law property suit, but in 1497 a direct issue was joined between the church and the lay courts over defamation.[36] The executor of a defendant condemned in the church courts for slander was sued for the sum awarded the plaintiff, and replied by suing a prohibition, which removed the case to the secular courts for adjudication on jurisdiction. The discussion became a debate on the right of church courts to exact a penalty for defamation. Kebell, as the senior serjeant, spoke last, in favour of withdrawing the prohibition:

> Seeing that the spiritual law admits such a libel was made, we have nothing here to dispute whether this is the law of Holy Church or not, or if they [the

35. *ibid.*, Hil. 6 Hen. VII, p. 2 ff. 13–14; Pas. 10 Hen. VII, p. 7 ff. 19–20, p. 12 f. 20; Mich. 11 Hen. VII, p. 30 ff. 8–9; Trin. 11 Hen. VII, p. 10 ff. 26–7; cf. above, pp. 175–8.
36. *ibid.*, Trin. 12 Hen. VII, p. 2 ff. 22–4.

church courts] are right or not, for nothing belongs to us or otherwise follows in all matters which belong etc. or are in their authority to discuss.

The court agreed unanimously.

Occasionally in Kebell's litigious work for or against the church there were rumblings of the distrust which was to swell to the storm of the Reformation. A common pleas case of 1495 had distinct foreshadowings of the Hunne affair twenty years later.[37] A Londoner who had broken out of the bishop's gaol brought a suit for false imprisonment against the arresting officers. The defence took its stand on the provision of the 1401 statute *de haeretico comburendo* that a person defamed for heresy or holding opinions contrary to the canons of the church should be arrested and held until, within three months, he had purged himself or abjured. Church law, the officers continued, required every parishioner to pay tithes to his local parish, but the plaintiff had declared that he ought not to pay tithes to St Dunstan's in the West where he lived. His boast led to his being defamed to the bishop, who ordered his arrest. For counsel, the plaintiff had, significantly, another Londoner, Serjeant Frowyk, and he brought out all the lay hostility to clerical authority. The defence, he claimed, had omitted to identify the accuser so that the plaintiff could challenge the defamation, a reference to lay dislike of the secret accusation of the church law. Nor had the church produced the necessary written authority for the arrest. In substance, too, the defence was bad. The 1401 statute was aimed at matters *enconter le Faith*, not *enconter lour constitutions* – another standing grievance of the laity that the church used spiritual sanctions to enforce its administrative will. The church authorities, he said, using an example calculated to appeal to the court, 'have a canon that no priest should be impleaded at common law, for no cause; if a man holds opinions contrary to such a canon, he is not within the scope of this statute!' The allegation, in itself, was also insufficient; many reasons might make a man claim not to pay tithes – a papal exemption, payment to another qualified person, or quite simply he might already have paid. Frowyk also seems to have gone behind the officers to the bishop: he had not brought about purgation or abjuration within the time limit, so he was in breach of the statute on which his men were relying.

Serjeant John Mordaunt, for the defence, attacked the technical objections: defamation could be by '*common voix ou fame*', not

37. *ibid.*, Hil. 10 Hen. VII, p. 17 ff. 17–18.

necessarily by an individual, and arrest without warrant was valid. Kebell then intervened, first with comments on the right of arrest at common law, and then on the case as a whole – whether by arrangement with Mordaunt or as *amicus curiae* is not clear. The defence, he held, was good. The bishop was not liable for the failure to clear a plaintiff whose own escape had precluded this. Even if the bishop were liable, the officers were not, for subsequent negligence did not make the original arrest illegal – a point of importance for lay authorities which Chief Justice Bryan confirmed. As for the matter, the statute lay against all opinions contrary to the canons. Before the Lateran Council, Kebell explained, tithes could be paid to any priest, hence the canon that an individual should pay tithe only in his immediate parish. Thus the plaintiff's opinion clearly brought him within *2 Henry IV* c. 15. It was the opinion that tithes should not be paid which was crucial; Frowyk's speculations might excuse a man who said he would not pay, but that was not the same as saying he had no obligation to pay. The year-book argument ends at this point, but Frowyk's remark about suing priests seems to have rankled with the reporter, for he put in as an afterthought Bryan's remark:

> that a wise doctor of the law said to him once, 'priests and clerks can be impleaded at common law perfectly well by the usage of that law', for he said, 'that the king is *persona mixta*, for he is a person united *cum sacerdotibus*', in which case he can maintain his jurisdiction by prescription.

Within a generation, an argument used to justify a long-standing convention was to take on a very different complexion.

To Thomas Kebell, these glimpses of the relationship between society and the law would have seemed wildly perverse in leaving until last the land law, but the most obvious example here we have already noticed, the development of the use.[38] Instead of estates descending without complication from heir to heir, the use made possible flexible family settlements which permitted the management of land in the sophisticated manner demanded by the age. At a late stage statutes were provided to meet specific difficulties with the device, but statute did not lie at the heart of the development.[39] This was the work of generations of the profession, quietly drawing conveyances to achieve

38. See above, pp. 197–8, 247–8.

39. *1 Ric. III* c. 1 was crucial in admitting the idea that the *cestui que use* could have power in law over the estate. Statutes regulating uses were passed in five of the seven parliaments of Henry VII: *1 Hen. VII* c. 1; *3 Hen. VII* cc. 5, 16; *4 Hen. VII* c. 17; *11 Hen. VII* c. 20; *19 Hen. VII* c. 15.

what their clients wanted. In Kebell's case, he was counsel when the rights of feoffees to employ counsel, the power of executors to manage land enfeoffed to third parties, the legality of re-enfeoffment of the *cestui que use* and the position of charges under statute merchant on enfeoffed estates were all debated.[40] He also tried to challenge settled doctrine by arguing that a feoffee could be bound by the original grant not to alienate, but the court would not listen to an argument which would have made trustees so obviously the servants of the grantor.[41] Kebell was also involved in the equally significant testing of the rights of the growing body of men who held land on lease.[42] A case dated 1489 saw him maintain the traditional position that the lessee was vulnerable to eviction if the estate came into the hands of the lord by wardship or some other title; Townshend J. queried this, however, and later his became the accepted view.[43] In another leasehold case (dateable to the years 1489–93), Kebell was concerned with the availability of an action of ejectment to permit a lessee to recover his lease rather than damages for eviction, something that became settled in 1499.[44]

Assumpsit and debt on obligation, finance and commerce, agriculture and parks, corporations and canon law, the use and the commercialising of land title: these examples amount to a substantial demonstration of the involvement of the courts and the lawyers in the problems of a changing society. Examples confined to cases taken by one counsel, albeit the most frequently reported, can, of course, give only an impression; they are no substitute for a comprehensive analysis of common-law litigation. They may, indeed, be positively misleading if an assumption is made that Thomas Kebell should join the ranks of the 'makers of English law'! But even an impressionistic survey of this sort establishes the simple but telling proposition that the professional activity of lawyers in pre-Reformation England helped to determine the evolution of society.

However, what a demonstration of the significance of law for the process of social change does not do, is to explain precisely how the needs of society were mediated to the courts. Did lawyers respond to

40. *Y.B.* Pas. 8 Hen. VII, p. 3 f. 11; Hil. 14 Hen. VII, p. 4 f. 14; Pas. 10 Hen. VII, p. 13 ff. 20–1; Mich. 8 Hen. VII, p. 4 ff. 7–8; Pas. 11 Hen. VII, p. 10 f. 21; Trin. 11 Hen. VII, p. 11 f. 27.
41. *ibid.*, Mich. 10 Hen. VII, p. 28 f. 11; Pas. 13 Hen. VII, p. 9 ff. 22–4.
42. Spelman, *Reports*, ii. *180–4*.
43. *Y.B.* Trin. 5 Hen. VII, p. 3 ff. 35–8; Spelman, *Reports*, ii. *182*.
44. *Y.B.* Pas. 13 Hen. VII, p. 3 f. 20; Spelman, *Reports*, ii. *181*.

pressure from clients, and from different sorts of clients, and if so, how? Did the social and professional background of the lawyers themselves play a part, perhaps a schizoid one? How far did the law change society, and how far did it respond to changes in society? These questions may always defy comprehensive answer, but they cannot be ignored.

The weight of recent opinion would stress the influence of the client. The lawyer can only survive if he satisfies the need put before him. The position is well illustrated by a letter of *c.* 1500 which shows a complainant being directed to ask Richard Higham (possibly the serjeant) how to arrest an adversary 'by *latitat* or otherwise' – and no doubt if Higham had not been able to help, another lawyer would have been.[45] It was this readiness of the suitor to demand a remedy if needs be 'otherwise' which was the dynamic of change. It must, for example, lie behind Dr J. H. Baker's demonstration that while before the second quarter of the sixteenth century there were relatively few *assumpsit* cases which went to trial, many were commenced and went no further than the original writ, no doubt being in the main settled by the defendant after this warning of serious intent.[46] That these *assumpsits* might not have been admitted if they had come to court mattered little; parties wanted a settlement, not a test case to benefit historians. Evidently, therefore, a novel form of action might not be seriously tested until it had gained some currency and an expectation had grown up that it did rightfully lie. Here, perhaps, we have a clue to the way in which legal change worked. Given a genuine need such as nonfeasance, continued use of an original would raise a presumption that the process was valid. Even if the court reacted unfavourably when the action was eventually tried, only an exceptionally emphatic and well-publicised decision could have put an end to the use of similar original writs, still less to a suitably modified version. A second test case would be thrown up in due course. It might again produce a rejection but it might, perhaps, secure a modified or even a divergent judgement; at the least it would indicate points to be covered before the writ was tried again. And so the process would go on.

It is possible, therefore, to see how demand by the public could set up pressure for legal change. What of the profession? It not only had a

45. SP1/231 f. 164 [*L. and P.*, Add. i. 90].
46. Spelman, *Reports*, ii. 256. Some actions which remained at the original stage were possibly ignored, but the number implies success.

financial incentive to assist clients; more important, it had the means. First of all, in the inns of court, and especially in the readings as developed in Kebell's day, there was a forum for and an incentive to creative legal thinking.[47] We have seen the respect given to Kebell's dicta at the Inner Temple, and there is plenty of similar evidence; Gray's Inn material, for example, is common in the year books, such as the note under 15 Henry VII of a pronouncement which Chief Justice Fineux made at Thomas Thatcher's reading there.[48] In litigation too, as we have again seen with Thomas Kebell, there was always the possibility of utilising old remedies in new situations.[49] Little-used actions could also be revived; thus Kebell was counsel for the plaintiff in *Beauchamp* v. *Crofts*, one of a handful of *scandalum magnatum* cases which presaged a revival of interest in this remedy for defamation during Henry VIII's reign.[50] Ideas could also be tested effectively through newer procedures. Actions on the case had as yet no set form, and permitted counsel to experiment with new issues which could be framed in trespass.[51] The king's bench bill worked in the same direction.[52] Continuity of experiment was encouraged by gossip and rivalry within the profession, but of equal or greater importance was the method of reporting of which the year books are the surviving evidence. The careful noting there of variant opinions and argument served to build up a repository of alternative interpretation, encouraging lawyers to recommend hitherto unsuccessful forms of action which had, nevertheless, been supported by one of the giants of the past or, perhaps, by a current judge at an earlier stage of his career. When a reporter added '*me semble parva est differentia . . . Quaere*' to a note of Kebell's failure to persuade the court that his client's bailment plea fell within cases they did allow, he was almost inviting further litigation.[53]

Outside the courts, conveyancing and drafting generally were even more open to experiment. In the matter of entails, for example, every new technique for preventing the permanent disposition of property was met by counter efforts. Thus an action reported under both 10

47. *ibid.*, ii. *133–5*.
48. See above, p. 150; *Y.B.* Trin. 15 Hen. VII, p. 21 f. 11; Ives, *L.Q.R.* 89. 82–3.
49. See above, pp. 165, 402.
50. *Y.B.* Mich. 13 Hen. VII, p. 1 ff. 1–2; Keilwey, *Reports*, ff. 26–29v. For *scandalum magnatum* see Spelman, *Reports*, ii. *244–5*.
51. *ibid.*, ii. *86–9*; for the mechanics of drawing pleas see *ibid.*, ii. *96–100*.
52. See above, p. 210; Spelman, *Reports*, ii. *88*.
53. *Y.B.* Hil. 5 Hen. VII, p. 11 f. 18.

and 13 Henry VII has Kebell successfully justifying one of the early clauses designed to prevent alienation by the tenant in tail.[54] It was in this same action that he wanted to argue that a feoffee to uses could be bound not to alienate, and this reminds us that another important factor in assisting change was the fluid nature of court-room debate and the possibility of tentative pleas which by their very nature were bound to probe both law and procedure.[55] When in the action for waste against the lessee of a mill Kebell did not dare proceed with a plea that agreement with the tenant precluded the lessor from bringing an action, he did, as we have seen, say that he would put one load of clay 'at risk to chase the law'.[56]

Thus clients and counsel together had reason and means to bring new problems to the courts. Why did the courts respond? The difficulties in assuming a primarily commercial motive have already been considered.[57] The assumption that judges crudely represented class interest, whether conscious or unconscious, need not detain us long either. It would be wrong to assume that even in the manorial court the steward of the lord could always ignore or control the jurors; as for major litigation, this took place within a unified propertied community where it is anachronistic to contrast 'feudal' and 'bourgeois' or 'land' and 'commerce'. It is true that, from time to time, there is evidence that judges were aware of social implications. In a well-known comment, Bryan C.J. rejected the notion that the copyholder had no remedy against eviction by the lord:

> This was never my opinion, and as I believe, it never will be, for if it were, all copyhold in England would be defeated. Therefore, I hold that always, provided the tenant pays his customary services, should the lord dispossess him, he will have an action of trespass against [the lord].[58]

His remained a minority opinion, and sixty years later the royal council had to intervene to forestall a ruling that eviction could not be challenged.[59] But all this time chancery and the conciliar courts did protect the copyholder, and by the second half of the century Bryan's support of unfree tenures was beginning to be accepted at common law.

54. *ibid.*, Mich. 10 Hen. VII, p. 28 f. 11; Pas. 13 Hen. VII, p. 9 f. 22. Simpson, *Land Law*, 196–7.
55. See above, pp. 165 and 171–2.
56. *Y.B.* Pas. 13 Hen. VII, p. 3 f. 21.
57. See above, pp. 209–11.
58. *Y.B.* Hil. 21 Edw. IV, p. 27 f. 80.
59. Spelman, *Reports*, ii. *184–7*; cf. E. Kerridge, *Agrarian Problems in the Sixteenth Century and After* (1969), pp. 74–5.

The influences which *did* affect the judicial bench were sometimes jurisdictional. It was, for instance, evident in Henry VIII's reign that Westminster had to take on cases which were not being brought, perhaps could no longer be brought, in county, borough and church courts.[60] This was not the straightforward story of jurisdictions under forty shillings being eliminated by inflation, or ecclesiastical authority undermined by Reformation changes; but the shift of business is clear, and so too the need to respond.[61] The statute of uses similarly presented new issues to king's bench and common pleas.[62] But receptivity was as important as challenge, and here we must try to penetrate the mind of the judges. In the last resort, it was their attitudes and assumptions, the way they saw the law and their place in it, which must account for the readiness to entertain change.[63]

In creating this readiness, chancery played a continuing role which it is easy to overlook. Here, cheek by jowl with the common-law courts, was an institution which existed to receive and consider relief for all wrongs, old and new, real and imagined.[64] In consequence, lawyers became familiar with the notion that wrongs should, if possible, be righted somewhere. It was widely recognised that the common law alone could not attain this, but the approach of the judges and successive chancellors was to ask, 'how can justice be achieved within the legal system as a whole?' This could lead them to agree that a complainant must and would be relieved, before deciding amongst themselves 'how' and 'by whom'.[65] When More faced the judges with the issue of equity and common law he was only articulating a contrast which was obvious every day in Westminster Hall.[66] This is not to raise again the spectre of competition but to suggest that there was an almost gravitational attraction between chancery and common law. This was the ethos which lay behind Kebell's remark that a writ, once issued, ought not to abate 'if it can be maintained by argument'.[67] The philosophy of the chancery challenged the metaphysics of the common law, and as long as emphasis in all courts lay on justice this favoured the raising of new problems.

It would be too much to say, of course, that the climate of legal thought *c.* 1500 actually favoured the acceptance of new doctrines;

60. Spelman, *Reports*, ii. *258*.
61. *ibid.*, ii. *53*; Blatcher, *Court of King's Bench*, 155–6.
62. See above, p. 208.
63. See above, pp. 395–403.
64. See above, pp. 218–19.
65. See above, p. 218.
66. See above, pp. 219–20.
67. *Y.B.* Mich. 10 Hen. VII, p. 12 f. 6.

the status quo must always have been worth an initial advantage in the discussion of new remedies. Common learning, too, could be a barrier, as Kebell found.[68] But what mattered was the possibility of new questions. Provided a problem could be technically presented, a court would examine it according to 'the reason of the law'. And once that problem had been raised, change was often only a matter of time.

The only instance where this model of legal change under pressure can be completely tested is that of the crown and its feudal revenues, already considered.[69] The sequence which brought movement there certainly agrees with the model. A powerful and persistent client demanded redress, and with some reason. This produced a professional debate which extended over years, not days, and led to a gradual piecemeal reconstruction of the law. The case, admittedly, was special, with a unique, continuing, influential client with the longest of purses. Equally, our clear picture of the process may be a compound of the distinctive issues involved and hindsight – reading steady policy into what at times was probably not more than an instinctive seizing of immediate advantage. Nevertheless, the episode is instructive. Wider legal change probably followed a similar pattern, as needs and pressures led litigants to face the courts again and again with the obligation to do justice in this novel circumstance or that. The process of social transformation through the law was, as S. E. Thorne has described it, not a matter 'of sharp reversals of earlier rules' but:

> a shift in emphasis, a choice of alternatives, a heightened importance given to a case formerly ignored, the sudden blossoming of a doctrine barely hinted at earlier, the broader construction of statutory words.[70]

And tantalising though such nuances are, they 'mark the transformation well enough'.

68. See above, pp. 160–1. 69. See above, pp. 247–59.
70. Thorne, *New York Law Rev.* 26. 15.

PART IV

THE PROFESSION AND SOCIETY

13

THE REWARDS OF THE PROFESSION: FEES AND PAYMENTS

Chaucer's 'Man of Law' begins his 'tale' with a diatribe against the 'hateful harm' of poverty, an opening entirely in character with a serjeant-at-law who:

> For his science and for his heigh renoun
> Of fees and robes hadde he many oon.
> So great a purchasour was no-wher noon.
> Al was fee simple to him in effect,
> His purchasing mighte nat been infect.[1]

The audience would have caught the allusion at once; wealth was the goal of the lawyer, the measure of success. It would have enjoyed, also, the serjeant's praise of wealthy merchants:

> O riche marchaunts, ful of wele ben ye,
> O noble, o prudent folk, as in this cas!
> Your bagges been nat filled with *ambes as* [a pair of aces],
> But with *sis cink* [a six-five], that renneth for your chaunce;
> At Cristemasse merie may ye daunce . . .[2]

This identification of the law and wealth is universally made, and generally in terms less urbane than Chaucer's. The besetting sin, almost the trade-mark of the lawyers, is avarice. Refusing to share knowledge except for money appears a simple lack of charity, and the esoteric language and exclusiveness of the profession seem a conspiracy to fleece the layman.[3] In medieval England this was a stock theme of the moralist, increasingly heard as lawyers became better organised and more influential. When Thomas Kebell joined the profession, the anonymous *London Lickpenny* was in circulation:

1. Geoffrey Chaucer, *Complete Works*, ed. W.W. Skeat (Oxford, n.d.), 423.
2. *ibid*., 477.
3. Ives, *Univ. Birmingham Hist. Journ*. 7. 130–42.

In Westminster I found one
Went in a longe gowne of ray;
I crowched, I kneled before them anon,
'For Mary's love', of helpe I gan them pray.
As he had be [en] wrothe, he voyded away;
'Bakward', his hand he gan me byd.
'I wot not what thou menest', gan he say,
'Lay downe sylvar or here thow may not spede.'[4]

At the end of his life Kebell may have watched the interlude *Mundus et Infans* where the character 'Folye' also appears as a serjeant-at-law:

For I am a seruant of the lawe,
Couetous is myne owne felowe.
We twayne plete for the kynge,
And poore men that come from vplande,
We wyll take theyr mater in hande;
Be it ryght or be it wronge,
Theyr thryfte with us shall wende.[5]

I

But complaint is one thing, evidence another, and evidence is hard to find. Lawyers did submit itemised bills, as is shown by frequent reference in accounts, but clients rarely thought it worth keeping these original vouchers once the final audit had been taken. And however satisfactory to the auditor, there is little value to the student in entries such as the 1444–5 account of Durham Priory:

Diversis jurisperitis apud London per manus Johannis Gatisheued in causa de Queryngdonmour; vicecomiti pro regardo suo pro seisina liberata Priori Dunelm in dicta mora; clerico vicecomitis pro uno replegiari vocat 'tociens quociens'; Johanni Blenkarn pro execucione ejusdem; et duobus hominibus vicecomitis pro imparcacione animalium Willelmi Elmedon chivaleri super dictam moram, ac aliis – summa xxvij^{li} xi^{s} j^{d} [6]

Fortunately, a number of complete statements were from time to time copied into accounts, especially where going to law was an unfamiliar experience; sometimes, as in the accounts of Sir Edward Don of Sanderton in Buckinghamshire for November 1532, the original voucher may be attached, and in court records itemised statements

4. E.P. Hammond, 'London Lickpenny', in *Anglia* 20 (Halle a. S., 1898), 413. This extract is from the lesser-known but earlier version of eight-line stanzas.
5. *Select Collection of Old Plays*, ed. Robert Dodsley, xii (1827), 325. The first known edition was printed in 1522, but the text is clearly earlier.
6. *Account Rolls of Durham*, i. 144–5.

can be found supporting claims for costs or damages.[7] In a few instances a major original bill has survived, as in the account submitted by Thomas Playter to the Fastolf executors or, even more unusual, the survey of legal costs incurred by Fastolf in the decade 1448–58, although in its later portions this degenerates into block payments to individuals *per billam suam*.[8]

For the permanent retainer, the principal source is different – the accounts of the client's receiver-general. Again some entries can be unhelpful – the Durham account for 1536–7 lumps retainers to one canon and three common lawyers in a single total of £5 – but normally individual fees are given, sometimes with descriptions of the work done.[9] Bailiffs' accounts can also yield details of permanent retainers where these were secured upon particular properties – the 1467–8 valor of the Greys of Ruthin is one such instance – although there is no means of telling how many lawyers in addition had unsecured retainers.[10] There are other difficulties as well. A problem with accounts is separating retainers for legal work from retainers for estate work where the recipient happens to have been a lawyer, especially as certain men would couple both functions under the one appointment. What significance is to be placed on the 40s. fee paid by the earl of Surrey in 1501–2 to John Mordaunt '*legis perito, capitallo senescallo de* Wyllingston', or the retaining of John Butler by Maxstoke Priory in 1494–5 as 'in counsel and steward of the convent'?[11] Descriptions also can be misleading. When the earl of Surrey retained James Hobart in 1501–2 by letters patent as his chief steward in Suffolk, he was retaining the king's attorney for his legal expertise and influence, not as an estate manager.[12] Usage, too, was idiosyncratic; 'attorney', 'attorney-general', 'serjeant-at-law', 'steward', 'receiver', all can designate a principal legal agent.[13] In the early 1520s the earl of Oxford was paying fees by letters patent to Sir Robert Drury as 'chief steward' and to Humphrey Wingfield as 'of counsel and his attorney at law' and by 1529–30 the earl's executors had also engaged Thomas Audley as their 'attorney' at Westminster.[14] The titles obscure a trio of the best legal brains in the country; each was a ruler of his inn; Drury had been

7. Warwickshire Record Office: CR895/106.
8. Magdalen College, Fastolf Mss. 71, 42.
9. *Account Rolls of Durham*, ii. 703.
10. *Grey of Ruthin Valor*, 68–9, 137, 139.
11. Philipps Mss. sold at Sotheby's, 26 Jun. 1967, no.691; SC6 Henry VII, 1701.
12. Philipps Mss. sold at Sotheby's, 26 Jun. 1967, no.691.
13. Sometimes 'secretary' is also used: *Plumpton Correspondence*, 89.
14. Philipps Mss. sold at Sotheby's, 26 Jun. 1967, no.695.

speaker of the house of commons, Audley was so currently, and Wingfield was to succeed him; each was or was to be a royal counsellor, while Audley was to receive the great seal in 1532. One final difficulty is that the weight of evidence favours the important and the corporate employer. It is probable that such clients set the standard for fees at Westminster, but it is likely that legal services at less sophisticated levels were paid on a lower scale, an area of the subject which remains almost totally obscure.

II

With these caveats in mind it is possible to examine lawyers' receipts, starting with the permanent retainer. No overall statistic is possible, but fee lists have been collected for the century from 1422 to 1534 from twenty-five employers of two or more lawyers on permanent retainer, excluding known estate officers; the list is made up of three queens, eight peers, three leading commoners and one bishop, and ten religious corporations. In all one hundred and fifty-six separate contracts are covered.[15] Payments range from 6s. 8d. to £13 6s. 8d., but the overall concentration is clear; the great majority of fees (seventy per cent of the sample) fall between £1 and £2, with the 26s. 8d. paid to Kebell by Sir Charles Somerset as almost the precise median.[16] Furthermore, many of the fees above £2 can be explained as payments to a single principal legal agent and adviser, in the same way as the £5 a year which Lord Hastings paid Thomas Kebell.[17] Scarcity of accounts for smaller employers prevents the drawing up of a parallel table, but what evidence there is suggests fees of the same order with, as might be guessed, an emphasis on the lower end of the range. In 1453–4, the priory of St Thomas at Stafford was paying 40s., and in the statutes for Tattersall College (founded under the will of Lord Cromwell, *ob.* 1456), one or two counsel were to be retained with the fee of £1 apiece.[18] In the 1490s, Maxstoke Priory paid 13s. 4d. and Tattersall 6s. 8d., as did Great Dunmow Priory in the years before the Dissolution.[19] From early in the fifteenth century the London Goldsmiths' Company retained a counsel at 40s. a year, until

15. Table E: retainers continued over a number of years are only given once.
16. See above, pp. 134–5.
17. B.L. Harl. 433 f. 57.
18. H.M.C., *Tenth Report* (1885), iv. 358; *ibid.*, *De L'Isle and Dudley* (1925–42), i. 183.
19. sc6 Henry VII, 1701; H.M.C., *Various Collections* (1901–14), i. 195; B.L. Add. Ms. 20,021.

in 1443 the post was upgraded to that of common clerk at 53s. 4d.[20] Among non-corporate employers, Sir Thomas Lovell retained Robert Wroth in 1522–3 at 20s. *per annum* and the Le Strange family early in Henry VIII's reign engaged Christopher Jenney at 20s. a year, later increased to 53s. 4d., as well as an attorney whose fee was apparently 3s. 4d. a term.[21] Such a low fee was not always appreciated. As a correspondent reported to Sir Robert Plumpton in 1490, Robert Blackwall, his attorney in the exchequer

> hath sent to you a pattent to seale, as appeareth by the same, shewing to him your pleasure of vj^{s}viij^{d} by yere; and that he toke to no regard. The world is so covettus, I wott not what to say, nor I wyll: *parum sapienti sufficyt*![22]

Plumpton understood and is later found paying Blackwall 10s. a year.[23]

The position of lawyers retained by urban corporations was broadly similar. Bridgwater paid Alexander Hody 13s. 4d. in Henry VI's reign; in 1484, Cambridge was paying 20s.[24] Even the greater towns followed the common rates. London paid 20s. to Thomas Marowe and Edmund Dudley as it had to Serjeant Billing forty years earlier.[25] Many towns also had an equivalent to the 'attorney-general' of the individual or monastic client. Increasingly fashion was designating him 'the recorder', but usage was not yet uniform – not surprisingly, given the various sources from which recorderships developed. In the earlier fifteenth century the work which would later be done for Southampton by a recorder appears to have been done by the town clerk at a fee of £5, while at Cambridge the recorder, who had developed as a keeper of the archives, was still, in 1494, being paid 6s. 8d. a year.[26] Sometimes, even though a town follows fashion and obtains a recorder by royal charter or simply adopts the name, the amount paid suggests no special duties; Plymouth was paying only 26s. 8d. in 1487 and Leicester the same in 1511.[27] But the trend

20. T.F. Reddaway, *Early History of the Goldsmiths' Company* (1975), 101–2.
21. *Rutland Papers*, iv. 260; 'Le Strange', *Archaeologia* 25. 467–8, 479.
22. *Plumpton Correspondence*, 93.
23. Blackwall was a cleric and a master in chancery as well as an attorney in exchequer: *ibid.*, 99, 115, 145, 147.
24. *Bridgwater Borough Archives*, iv. *passim*; Cooper, *Cambridge*, i. 231.
25. Putnam, *Early Treatises*, 133 n.5; see above, p. 134.
26. *Stewards' Books of Southampton*, ed. H.W. Gidden, Southampton Record Soc. 39 (1939), iii; Cooper, *Cambridge*, i. 244.
27. *Plymouth Municipal Records*, ed. R.N. Worth (1893), 91; Bateson, *Leicester*, iii. 8.

Table E. *Fees paid to lawyers on regular retainer, 1422–1534*

			£13-6-8	£10	£6-13-4	£5	£4	£3-6-8	£3	£2-13-4	£2	£1-6-8	£1	13-4	10-0	6-8	
1	Mowbray	1422–3									2	1	4	1			8
2	Stafford (Countess)	1431–2						1			1						2
3	Stafford	1441–2									7						7
4	St Mary's, Warwick	1448–9										1		1			2
5	The Queen	1452–3		1		1					3	5					10
6	Fountains Abbey	1456–7											1	7			8
7	The Queen	1466–7				2					4	2					8
8	Grey	1467–8						1			5						6
9	St Augustine's, Canterbury	1468–9									1	1	2	2			6
10	Stafford	1475–6						1			1	2		3			7
11	Arundel	1482–3						1			3						4
12	St Andrew's, Northampton	Hen. VII									1		2				3
13	Wells Cathedral	1487–1508										1	3				4
14	St Augustine's, Bristol	1491–2											4	2	1		7
15	Bishop of Worcester	1497–8									1	2	2				5
16	Hastings	1501–2				1	1	1			3	3	3			1	13
17	Grene	1502											2				2
18	The Queen	1503		1							2	4	1				8
19	Peterborough Abbey	1504–5							2		3		1			1	7
20	Oseney Abbey	1509–10									1		2	2		1	6
21	St Augustine's, Bristol	1511–12											5	3			8
22	Compton	1527–8	1		1						6	4					12
23	De Vere executors	1529–30						1		1	1						3
24	Durham Cathedral	1531–2									1		3				4
25	Norfolk	1533–4								1	2	2		1			6
			1	2	1	4	1	6	2	2	48	28	35	22	1	3	156

Sources

1. B.L. Add. Ch. 17209.
2. Staffordshire Record Office, D641/1/2/13.
3. *ibid.*, D641/1/2/17.
4. *Ministers' Accounts of St Mary's Warwick*, ed. D. Styles, Dugdale Soc. 26 (1969), 23–4.
5. Myers, *Bull. John Rylands Lib.* 40. 414–16. The £5 was shared between two holders of the post of attorney in the exchequer.
6. *Fountains Abbey*, iii. 31–2.
7. Myers, *Bull. John Rylands Lib.* 50. 456–9, 461–2.
8. *Grey of Ruthin Valor*, 68, 69, 75, 137, 139.
9. 'St Austin's Abbey, Canterbury: Treasurers' Accounts', ed. C. Cotton, in *Archaeologia Cantiana* 51 (1939), 84.
10. Staffordshire Record Office, D641/1/2/26.
11. Dorset Record Office, D16/M67. I owe this reference to the kindness of Dr R. W. Dunning.
12. B.L. Harl. Roll K8.
13. H.M.C., *Mss. of the Dean and Chapter of Wells* (1907–14), ii. 105, 180, 207.
14. *Two Compotus Rolls of St Augustine's Abbey, Bristol*, ed. G. Beachcroft and A. Sabin, Bristol Record Soc. 9 (1938), 258.
15. Worcestershire Record Office, 009;1 BA 2636/192 92627$\frac{7}{12}$.
16. Huntington Library, HA16250, 31–2.
17. *Cal. Ancient Deeds*, iv. 10063, 10185.
18. N.H. Nicolas, *Privy Purse Expenses of Elizabeth of York* (1830), 100–1.
19. *Peterborough Monastery*, xlviii–xlix.
20. *Cartulary of Oseney Abbey*, vi. 251.
21. *St Augustine's*, *Bristol*, 269.
22. Castle Ashby, Compton Muniments 995.
23. Philipps Mss., sold at Sotheby's, 26 Jun. 1967, no.695. The fees of 66s.8d. (Wingfield) and 53s.4d. (Drury) were in addition to annuities under the earl's will of 53s.4d. and £6.13s.4d. respectively.
24. *Durham Household Book*, ed. J. Raine, Surtees Soc. 18 (1844), 93.
25. SC6 Hen.VIII/6305. I owe this reference to the kindness of Mr Christopher Whittick.

towards a recorder with a higher salary was strong, and such a post was normal in larger towns. Norwich, as early as 1464, paid £5, Nottingham (in 1500) 53s. 4d., Exeter (1514) £4, Bristol (1519) £10, Coventry (1522) and York (1534) £13 6s. 8d. each; Shrewsbury, which in 1511 was paying a recorder a mere 26s. 8d., was twenty years later paying £4, or £5 if resident and willing to be restricted in the freedom to take clients.[28]

The comparison of fees cannot, however, be extended into a comparison between employers or a discussion of changes over the century before serious inflation set in; lists are of varying completeness and represent only lawyers identified.[29] One pattern which can be seen is that many serjeants were among the more highly paid counsellors – 40s. a year was common – and that attorneys tended to be somewhat lower paid than the median, but this says the obvious. More interesting is the spread of retainers through the profession and the quality of the men concerned. For the reign of Henry VII, where eight employers provide sufficient evidence to begin to talk of some sort of sample, the forty-nine retainers were paid to thirty-nine individuals, including five future judges, three future serjeants, five close royal counsellors, the attorney-general, a future solicitor-general and three of the principal clerks of the Westminster courts. The sample is restricted, but it is enough to suggest that retainers were not the monopoly of a clique. This is not to say that lawyers did not accumulate fees – indeed, these could amount to a tidy income. Richard Empson enjoyed regular fees from seven known clients, was recorder at Coventry and Northampton and was chief steward of the abbey of Peterborough, and these engagements alone brought in nearly £40 a year.[30] What his total receipts were is unknown: Judge Paston, according to a critic, had nine fees in East Anglia, totalling £17 10s.,

28. Norfolk and Norwich Record Office, Chamberlains' Accounts 1470–90, f. 54; *Records of the Borough of Nottingham*, iii. 69; H.M.C, *City of Exeter* (1916), 56; *The Great White Book of Bristol*, ed. E. Ralph, Bristol Record Soc. 32 (1979), 77, 79; *Coventry Leet Book*, 681; *York Memorandum Book*, ii. 267; H. Owen & J.B. Blakeway, *History of Shrewsbury* (1825), i. 537.

29. 'Robert Northwyche', *Grey of Ruthin Valor*, 139.

30. The Queen, 26s.8d: Nicolas, *Privy Purse Expenses*, 101; John Grevill, £5: *Cal. Ancient Deeds* iv. A8418; Hastings £4: Huntington Library, HA16250, 31–2; Walter Mauntell, 13s.4d.: *Cal. inquisitions post mortem*, i. 372; John Bernard, 26s.8d.: *ibid*, iii. 568; Durham Abbey, 40s.: *Account Rolls of Durham*, ii. 306; St Andrew's, Northampton, £2: B.L. Harl. Roll K8; *Coventry Leet Book*, 537, 547; *Records of the Borough of Northampton*, ed. C.A. Markham and J.C. Cox (1898), i. 312; *Peterborough Monastery*, xlviii. In addition he was High Steward of the University of Cambridge: Cooper, *Cambridge*, i. 277.

and this omits £2 he received from the earl of Norfolk; Kebell had a minimum of £8 6s. 8d., from four clients alone.[31]

III

Turning from long-term contracts to more limited engagements, the miscellaneous non-litigious work done by the profession needs only a passing mention. Every instance was different. There was no such thing as a standard indenture, a standard search, a standard negotiation; there could be no standard fee. In 1491 a 'new dede for the termys of the hall' cost the Carpenters' Company 3s. 4d.; the next year the parish of St Mary at Hill, near Billingsgate, paid a Lombard St scrivener a similar amount but for two deeds, a copy of the bead-roll 'and for other things'.[32] The accounts of Bridgwater for 1453–4 show the town clerk, John Pole, receiving 4½d. for writing a deed and the next year 2s. for writing out the title to a tenement.[33] Much also depended on the quality required. In 1520 the duke of Buckingham spent 6s. 8d. having a recognisance written by a clerk in chancery; in 1510–11, St Mary at Hill had spent 1s. 5½d. on indentures between the parish and a bell-founder, and that included wine.[34] A handful of examples demonstrates the variety.

Fountains Abbey, 1457–8: Nicholas Gyrlyngton [going] to the bishop of Exeter about the tenths of Aldburgh – 6s. 8d.[35]

Nottingham, 1464: [To] John Fitzherbert to prolong the tyme of enrollyn of the charter for allowance of the grenewax – 10s. 0d.[36]

Canterbury, 1480–1: To John Clerk and Humphrey Starke, arbitrators, in part remuneration, so that they should give effectual work and diligence towards concluding the matter. Each of them – 6s. 8d.[37]

Canterbury, 1480–1: To deliver to Whatno in part payment or as his reward for engrossing the arbitration and judgement of the said arbitrators – 6s. 8d.[38]

Coventry, 1482–3: [The recorder, making] a papir of the awarde which sheld haue be gyffen betwixt the Cite & Briscowe – 40s. 0d.[39]

Duke of Buckingham, 1498–9: Mr William Butler, expenses for being within

31. *Paston Letters and Papers*, ii. 508–9; B.L. Add. Ch. 17209; see below, p. 323.
32. *Carpenters' Company*, ii. 88; *London City Church*, 273.
33. *Bridgwater Borough Archives*, iv. 69, 71, 83, 84.
34. *L. and P.*, iii. 1286 (p. 504); *London City Church*, 273.
35. *Fountains Abbey*, iii. 67 (Latin).
36. *Records of the Borough of Nottingham*, i. 376.
37. 'Records of Canterbury', 134 (Latin).
38. *ibid.*, 135 (Latin).
39. *Coventry Leet Book*, 515.

the lordships by order of the duke for the true examination and noting of what lands and tenements are held in chief – 57s. 5d.[40]

Drapers' Company, 1508–9: Payd to Robert Olneys counceill for makyng of the indenture – 26s. 8d.[41]

Canterbury, 1513–14: To Mr Hales . . . for his counsell & to remember to speke in the parliament that Mr Mayer myght haue gaole delyverye by the charter without commyssion – 13s. 4d.[42]

Duke of Buckingham, 1521: To one John Collis of Bristowe, lernedman, for his advise and counsaille in drawing and writing the copie of a pair of indentures of defesauntes bitwene the said duc and . . . John Serjeaunt – 3s. 4d.[43]

Le Strange, 1526: To my lorde of Brynckenell [Robert Brudenell C.J.] for ye knowledge of the releasse of Ms Woodhous & Mrs Banyard at Thetford at ye cises for Rustens in Snetisham – 6s. 8d.[44]

Great Dunmow Priory, 1534: To a man of law for sekyng of evydens – 3s. 4d.[45]

St Mary at Hill, 1536–7: To a lernyd man for serchyng in ye kynges escheker for the chauntries longynge to the chirche – 1s. 4d.[46]

Earl of Rutland, 1542: To Serjante Molenax for makynge of my lord's wyll when my lorde went into the northe – 40s. 0d.[47]

Earl of Rutland, 1543: To Mr Sergjant Mullinex for commyng to Belvoyer to gyve his advice that the funeralles might procede – 22s. 6d.[48]

St Mary at Hill, 1547–8: To Mr Clerke, counsellour, for the view of the churche evidences consernyng the chauntry landes – 20s. 0d.[49]

St Mary at Hill, 1548–9: To Clarke, the man of law, for the makynge of a draught of wrightinge betwene Mr Parsone and ye masters of ye parische for the new howse in the chirche yarde – 1s. 8d.[50]

By the nature of things the crown was one client with particularly varied requirements. How these were remunerated is not always clear. Judges, barons of the exchequer and law officers often enjoyed annuities in addition to regular fees, but even so would receive lump sums from time to time.[51] In 1474–5 the judges received £50 'for divers matters and great labours' as well as £50 for attendance at parliament; the king's serjeants and attorney shared £40 for their work in parliament.[52] Sometimes crown service was an incident of office.

40. Staffordshire Record Office, D641/1/2/27 (Latin).
41. A.H. Johnson, *History of the Worshipful Company of Drapers* (1914–22), i. 481–2.
42. 'Records of Canterbury', 150.
43. E36/220 f. 9.
44. 'Le Strange', *Archaeologia* 25. 479.
45. B.L. Add. Ms. 20021, f. 13.
46. *London City Church*, 373.
47. *Rutland Papers*, i. 337.
48. *ibid.*, i. 343.
49. *London City Church*, 387.
50. *ibid.*, 389.
51. e.g. William Hussey, 40 marks p.a. as C.J.K.B.: *Cal. Patent Rolls, 1485–94*, 13.
52. E405/58 mm.2, 5v.

This was the case for the clerk of the crown in king's bench although even then Henry Harman (in office 1480 to 1502) had a life annuity of £10.[53] On occasion, payments were channelled via the law officers. In 1452–3 Margaret of Anjou paid her attorney-general nearly £30, which covered, among other things, *solucionibus diuersis hominibus legis-peritis pro auisamento et consilio suo habendis*; in November 1466, Richard Fowler, the king's attorney, was reimbursed 'for the costes and expenses of our counsaill lerned' which he had paid out of his own pocket.[54] Payments by direct warrant were also made: to John Markham C.J.K.B. in 1465, 40 marks in costs and reward for twenty-four days at an oyer and terminer at Gloucester plus twenty-eight days attending the council at Stafford; £3 6s. 8d. in 1498 and £14 6s. 8d. in 1499 to Coningsby and Frowyk for writing 'certayn bokes' for the king; £100 to John Port J.K.B. in 1527 'for special considerations'.[55] Some amounts were quite small. Thomas Tremayle received 40s. in 1475 as a reward *pro scripcione diuersum materium concernante les Esterlinges*, Hussey for a related matter 20s. and Jenney '*pro diversis laboribus*' 6s. 8d.[56] In the account for Easter 1480, John Wydeslade, the common pleas filacer for Devon, received 6s. 8d. for his work in securing a favourable verdict in the crown's action against an Exeter merchant.[57]

IV

Comparison of costs again becomes a possibility with the fees for individual lawsuits. Here there is, for once, clear guidance in the year books. In 1452, Serjeant Walter Moyle declared that, where no other arrangements had been made, 3s. 4d. was the 'common right' of the serjeant and 1s. 8d. of the attorney, and the court apparently concurred.[58] But how frequently was a fee paid? Did 'refreshers' differ from initial retainers? How far was 'common right' a minimum rather than the standard? Was there variation according to the work done?

As an initial retainer normally paid in hand, Moyle's 'common

53. E403/2558 m. 1.
54. Myers, *Bull. John Rylands Lib.* 40. 421; E404/73/47.
55. E404/73/6,96/64; Putnam, *Early Treatises*, 134. For the employment of legal counsel by one of the newer courts, see W.C. Richardson, *History of the Court of Augmentations* (Baton Rouge, 1961), 387–91.
56. E405/60 m. 7.
57. E405/69 m. 5v.
58. *Y.B.* Mich. 31 Hen.VI, p. 1 f. 9; cf. Baker, *Camb. Law Journ.* 27. 213; Hastings, *Common Pleas*, 76.

right' *was* quite common; in Michaelmas 1491, the parish of St Mary at Hill made initial payments to a serjeant and two apprentices at 40d. each.[59] However, other sums are frequently found. A generation later, St Mary at Hill had to pay a serjeant and a Lincoln's Inn apprentice 13s. 4d. 'for coming to the Guyld Hall'.[60] In 1459, Lord Cromwell's executors paid a total of 13s. 4d. to Richard Illingworth and Thomas Bryan; in 1501–2, Canterbury engaged John Roper for 6s. 8d.; in 1445–6, Exeter had retained William Boeff of Lincoln's Inn for 20s.[61] At the opposite extreme, the nunnery of St Radegund in Cambridge paid a retainer of 1s. 8d. in 1450–1

in regardo dato Johanni Gryton pro bono consilio suo domine impenso et in posterum impendendo in diversis materiis, et specialiter in quodam replegio prosecuto.[62]

A similar variety can be seen with attorneys. The parish of St Ewen, Bristol, engaged Richard Kayton in 1457–8 for 20d., and Sir Robert Pointz paid the same to his attorney in 1489–90; indeed, within Westminster Hall that amount was routine.[63] But in 1444–5, the duke of Buckingham retained an attorney in a case of wardship at 6s. 8d.[64] The differences are explained by the commercial element in law; a lawyer charged according to what he felt he was worth, what the market would stand, what the task would entail and how far it would exclude other clients. In 1499 Sir Robert Plumpton was warned that the services of a leading counsel from outside Yorkshire 'wilbe costly to you', and when he engaged a serjeant two years later he contracted to pay £5 down and £21 13s. 4d. later.[65] But for this he was to receive, without additional costs, the personal attendance at three northern assize towns of one of the half-dozen leading advocates in the kingdom, who would effectively be excluded from taking other major clients for several weeks on end. For Robert Pilkington to secure Robert Brudenell at the last minute for the Derby assizes required 'gret labur and gret cost', but a subsequent engagement of Thomas

59. *London City Church*, 178.
60. *ibid.*, 326.
61. H.M.C., *Various Collections*, i. 211; 'Records of Canterbury', 148; *Letters of Shillingford*, 145.
62. A. Gray, 'The priory of St Radegund, Cambridge', in *Cambridge Antiquarian Soc. Octavo Publications*, 30 (1898), 173.
63. 'Churchwardens' accounts of St Ewen's, Bristol', ed. J. Maclean in *Trans. Bristol and Gloucestershire Arch. Soc.* 15. 168; Dorset Record Office, D16/M74; STAC2/8/229–32 [*Star Chamber*, ii. 196–205].
64. Staffordshire Record Office, D641/1/2/271.
65. *Plumpton Correspondence*, 134–5, 152–3.

Kebell for Westminster, well in advance of term, cost only the 40d. of common right.[66]

The market element in fees is well illustrated in the accounts of the city of Canterbury for 1501.[67] Difficulties about the city's fishmarket made it imperative to petition the king during the summer vacation when he was at Wanstead, in south-west Essex. Arriving, the Canterbury representatives engaged 'Maister Raynold' to be of counsel (probably Henry Reynold, a clerk of the signet); he received 3s. 4d. and a reward of 1s. 8d., plus, apparently, 1s. 8d. more for drawing up their petition.[68] But greater expertise was urgently needed, and the city chamberlain and four colleagues

> rode from Stratforde to London to oure counsell, and ther was none of theym bycause it was a vacacion tyme &c. And ther abydyng in London the seid [J.W. and L.F.] for to seke and reteign counsell, and the same mornyng [the rest] . . . rode to Fyncheley to seke Maister Frowyk. And he was then riden to Walsyngham. And then [they] . . . came to London homeward ayen.[69]

The two in London had had better fortune.

> Item, the same mornyng mett with Maister Recorder of London comyng to the Tempill; besought hym to be good maister to the Cetie, and reteignyd him – 6s. 8d.

Nevertheless this did not clinch matters. The recorder's servant was treated to a good breakfast at the King's Head in Fleet Street, and the chamberlain, no doubt duly informed of the lawyer's schedule, went to Guildhall to wait. Unsuccessful there, the delegation pursued the recorder to Lord Daubeney's house and once more waited, this time

> till the seid Master Recorder had souped. And when he came out, [they] . . . besought hym to spede theym, for the tyme of the forfett passyd not iij daies, whiche answerid that he was sore occupied and myght not entende it so shortely. Wher[upon] we toke hym 6s. 8d., and then he hadde us wayte on hym on the morowe in the Tempill.

The recorder of London was a busy man; the Canterbury citizens were in a hurry and they were outsiders. But this looks suspiciously like standing out for 13s. 4d.; the recorder would be as well aware as anyone how thin London was of counsel.

Having secured his lawyer, a client had to introduce him to the

66. 'Wombwell Mss.', 39, 51.
67. Canterbury Cathedral Library, F8, ff. 336–7.
68. *Cal. Patent Rolls, 1494–1509*, 312.
69. The city had tried to engage Frowyk earlier: Canterbury Cathedral Library, F8, f. 333v.

case.[70] This might mean producing documents, and it was common for litigants to prepare statements for counsel or even to have them professionally prepared in advance, for just such a contingency.[71] The Pilkington narrative has the contemporary heading 'The tytylls of Pylkynton to Anesworthe's landes' and is clearly one such.[72] A most elaborate example is the 'cartulary' produced in Edward IV's reign for Thomas Tropenell of Great Chalfield in Wiltshire.[73] Having trodden on a good many people in assembling his estates, Tropenell was determined to leave his heirs prepared for the inevitable challenge. The book includes rambling statements of the title to various properties, gathered from family history, heraldry, reminiscence and various charters and deeds by an obvious amateur, probably Tropenell himself. It also includes formal summaries of title and prepared briefs which counsel drew up on the basis of some of those statements. The contingent nature of the professional brief on the Great Chalfield estate is made quite explicit at the end:

Memorandum, that apon the saide sight of evydences, recoverers and other thyngis concernyng the saide maner of Chaldefeld as have ben shewed unto the saide councell, hit is thought and avised by the same counsell at this tyme that the maters of the saide aunswers and barrys shall be sufficient instruccions to mynstre plees by as the case schall requyre for the suerte of the title of the saide Thomas Tropenell, his heires and assignes to the saide maner of Est Chaldefeld and other premyysses, remyttyng alwey to such personys as hereafter schall be of councell in the same title to mynystre such of the saide maters as to them schall seme moste expedyente with the avaunttage of all such evydences concernyng the same maner as to them herafter schall be schewed.

(One almost suspects the common form of a professional disclaimer here.)

Also memorandum, that all this present writyng of Chaldefeld byfore reherced is a behofull and expedient instruccion for the maner of delyng and behavyng and in ple pledyng for Thomas Tropenell and his heirs, if he or eny of theyme be empleded thereof or of eny parcell therof in tyme comyng. And also beholde and over se well all writyngis and dedes foluyng, and takith and occupieth that is most behofull and expedyente.[74]

How much a client could explain at the time of retaining is doubtful. Pilkington handed over his documents to Kebell when he paid the

70. The common expression for this was 'to ripe[n]': *L. and P.*, Add. i. 93.
71. *Plumpton Correspondence*, 151–2.
72. The title is omitted from the H.M.C. edition.
73. *Tropenell Cartulary*.
74. *ibid.*, i. 271.

initial 40d., but Canterbury paid its two fees before even getting an appointment to discuss the case. And this raises the question of further costs before and during pleading. The evidence is, for once, consistent: a standard charge in London of 3s. 4d. a consultation. Business about the Canterbury fishmarket in the spring of 1501 required meetings with counsel at Serjeants' Inn on Friday 14 May and Thursday 20 May and at St Paul's on Sunday 23rd.; two serjeants, Thomas Frowyk and John Kingsmill, and an apprentice, John Hutton of Gray's Inn, attended, and each received 3s. 4d. a time.[75] 3s. 4d. seems to have been paid per meeting, whatever the duration. Thus, although Canterbury had paid Hutton 3s. 4d. at Serjeants Inn on 14 May 1501, he received a second fee for a meeting that afternoon in St Paul's.[76] This may explain why clients so frequently fed their lawyer; breaking for meals would have meant a second fee. Charging per consultation could, equally, be a disadvantage. When Jubbes and Matston visited Thornbury to advise the duke of Buckingham they could spend up to a fortnight, but were paid at the rate of 3s. 4d. a day; true, they were no doubt accommodated free and on one occasion Jubbes received an additional 20s., but it would clearly have been possible to earn more at Westminster, provided the clients were there.[77]

Exceptions to the 40d. consultation fee are not, however, unknown. In Michaelmas 1448, Sir John Fastolf paid one fee of 3s. 4d., but two others of 6s. 8d. and one of 5s.; the following term he paid thirteen at the usual rate and two at 6s. 8d.[78] Some higher payments may be explained by a desire to keep the services of a particular individual. Thus Fastolf's executors paid 3s. 4d. in 1460 to Richard Pigot for advice about a traverse, but 6s. 8d. to William Comberford; Pigot would become a serjeant in due course, but Comberford was the second prothonotary in the common pleas.[79] There was, nevertheless, no regular bonus for seniority. At a consultation about the Fastolf traverse, John Jenney and John Grenefield received 3s. 4d. and

75. Canterbury Cathedral Library F8, ff. 334v, 335. Cf. *Paston Letters and Papers*, ii. 594–5.
76. Canterbury Cathedral Library, F8, f. 334v.
77. E36/220; 3s. 4d. a day was the standard remuneration of lawyers serving Queen Margaret and Queen Elizabeth: Myers, *Bull. John Rylands Lib.* 40. 414; 50. 457–8. By 1536, royal lawyers were claiming 6s. 8d. a day. H.M.C., *Eighth Report* (1881–1909), ii. 20.
78. Magdalen College, Fastolf Ms. 42.
79. Magdalen College, Fastolf Ms. 71 m. 6.

Serjeant Littleton the same as Comberford, 6s. 8d, but when, in 1523, the city of Oxford paid two fees at 6s. 8d. and eight at 40d., Serjeant John Spelman received the higher and Serjeant John Port the lower amount.[80] Oxford also paid a joint fee of 1s. 8d. to a serjeant and two apprentices, which has some parallel in the St. Mary at Hill accounts where two apprentices split 3s. 4d., and was probably in lieu of entertainment.[81] Fees other than 40d. could also be appropriate for additional work, over and above 'advice'. When the Carpenters' Company was petitioning parliament, William Grevill, the future serjeant, was paid 6s. 8d.[82] Canterbury paid 6s. 8d. to the recorder of London, which covered 'contriving and correcting' a star chamber bill, and 6s. 8d. to Frowyk to make a new one.[83] But a higher rate was by no means the rule. John Hutton had earlier charged Canterbury only 3s. 4d. when correcting 'the copy', and when the Fastolf executors had a copy of a record made, William Jenney 'oversaw' it for, again, 3s. 4d.[84]

The situation outside Westminster and London was more fluid. The duke of Buckingham paid Jubbes and Matston their 3s. 4d., but found it necessary to pay Serjeant Richard Brook 6s. 8d. a day to attend at Thornbury.[85] Travelling was clearly a factor here; Jubbes had to come twelve miles and Matston five, where Brook came either from London (where he was recorder) or from his home in Ipswich.[86] The position in the north can be seen in the accounts of Fountains Abbey for the years 1455–8, which include at least thirty-three payments to lawyers for work done in litigation, over and above annual fees and miscellaneous business.[87] Thirteen are at the London rate and thirteen at 6s. 8d.; two are at 20d. and five at 10s. or above. The accounts, however, are not always explicit as to work done or the distinction between consultation and appearance in court. Thus half of the fourteen payments to Nicholas Girlington, the lawyer most employed, were probably connected with court procedure or appearances.[88] Nevertheless, taking only the gifts and payments for

80. *ibid.*, m. 7; *Records of Oxford*, 52. The fee of one half mark to Spelman could have been an initial retainer.
81. *London City Church*, 178.
82. *Carpenters' Company*, ii. 116.
83. Canterbury Cathedral Library, F8, ff. 337, 338.
84. *ibid.*, f. 334v; Magdalen College, Fastolf Ms. 71 m. 8.
85. E36/220.
86. For work done for Buckingham at London and Greenwich, Brook, while an apprentice, had been paid 3s. 4d. a day: SP1/22/81.
87. *Fountains Abbey*, iii. 17–19, 50–2, 59–60, 66–7, 144, 151, 154.
88. *ibid.*, iii. 17–19, 60, 66, 151.

counsel, a higher fee than in London seems clear, and this is confirmed by the payment to Guy Roucliffe, recorder of York, of 6s. 8d. specifically *pro consilio suo cum Abbate*.[89] These higher fees are not explained by scarcity of competition, for the Vale of York was the one part of northern England which produced lawyers in the same profusion as the south. Nor, *prima facie*, was travelling the reason; most of the abbot's lawyers came from Yorkshire. But the long journey from Westminster to Yorkshire might well have led to larger fees being charged by men like Girlington with practices in the central courts, especially as these appear to have included costs; in London, Fastolf normally paid Girlington 3s. 4d.[90] On at least one occasion northern rates operated for northern business done in London. In the summer of 1442 the common clerk of York visited Westminster to secure confirmation of the city charters. Peter Arderne, the future chief baron, was understandably paid 13s. 4d. 'for his advice, favour and work', work which included personal attendance on the chancellor, and actually collecting the charter. But two other lawyers were less involved, one being paid 3s. 4d. and one 6s. 8d., and the higher fee went to Nicholas Girlington.[91]

The situation at Exeter was not dissimilar. In 1447–8, the city paid, it appears, six fees for consultations, three at 3s. 4d. and three at 6s. 8d.[92] Local rates were again paid in London; one payment to the Crediton lawyer, Thomas Dourish, annotated 'in London', was at 6s. 8d. In the same year Dourish also received a bonus of 26s. 8d. *de rewardo in Gylhalda civitatis ex consensu Majoris et sociorum suorum*. Even at the less remote Nottingham the trend to payments above 3s. 4d. is visible. In 1464, Serjeant Richard Nele was paid 20s. to visit the city, and shared a second reward of 33s. 4d. with Robert Staunton – probably £1 to Nele and a mark to Staunton – and 13s. 4d. for himself alone later.[93] Recorders also were likely to be paid lump sums. In 1445–6, Nicholas Radford, recorder of Exeter, received two sums of 13s. 4d. '*ultra pensionem suam*' for counsel in the city's suit against the cathedral, and a further 6s. 8d. *pro consilio*.[94] Two years later he received 20s. reward and 26s. 8d. *pro consilio suo habendo circa negotium civitatis ad sessionem pacis Epiphanie Domini*.[95] At Cambridge, although the recorder, John Wode, was only retained at

89. *ibid.*, iii. 52.
90. Magdalen College, Fastolf Ms. 42.
91. *York Memorandum Book*, ii. 130–1.
92. *Letters of Shillingford*, 148–52.
93. *Records of the Borough of Nottingham*, ii. 374–5, 377.
94. *Letters of Shillingford*, 145.
95. *ibid.*, 148, 152.

6s. 8d., he received as much again on a single occasion in 1501 for 'labour and counsel' in a demarcation dispute between Cambridge and the priory of Barnwell.[96]

V

Payments to the profession once litigation was under way fall under three heads: costs incurred on behalf of the client for court fees, documents and searches; any fee due to the lawyer himself for this, or for conducting formal stages in process; payment for argument or representation before the bench. The first is not strictly relevant to professional remuneration, and court costs were, in theory, on a tariff fixed by the court. Nevertheless, it is not always possible to make precise distinctions between categories, and especially between what a lawyer had to pay clerks and officials and what he charged for his own time and effort. An example of consolidated payments are those made by St Ewen's, Bristol, in a chancery suit of 1463–4 to Roger Kemys 'to sue the *dedimus potestatem* – vij^{s}ij^{d}', 'the day that this *dedimus potestatem* was executed – vj^{s}viij^{d}', and 'for the prorogyng and getyng of a newe *dedimus potestatem* – ij^{s}ij^{d}'.[97] In 1527, Worcester Priory paid John Port 11s. 'for the releassyng of our servants of the lattitat', in 1522, the Le Strange family spent 22s. 2d. 'for puttyng inne of the Niseprise at Thetford' while in 1499, Cambridge had paid 26s. 8d. to their recorder

> for the business of the town and keeping and supporting the rights of the same, and to defend the matters between the University and town of Cambridge in the pending plea.[98]

Some bills, however, are explicit. Where the business was routine it seems clear than no special fee was paid beyond the attorney's retainer, chargeable each term. This covered most mesne process. The costs of the first stages of *William Chapell* v. *Cade*, a common pleas action from 1531–2, are preserved with related star chamber papers.[99] In four successive terms a total of £4 4s. 10d. was spent, but counsel was required only twice, at an aggregate fee of 23s. 4d., to draw the replication and the joinder of issue, and never for appearance in court;

96. Cooper, *Cambridge*, i. 251, 255.
97. *Trans. Bristol and Gloucestershire Arch. Soc.* 15. 173.
98. *Journal of Prior More*, 264; 'Le Strange', *Archaeologia* 25. 467; Cooper, *Cambridge*, i. 251.
99. STAC2/8/229 [*Star Chamber*, ii. 196–8].

the attorney's 3s. 4d. a term covered the rest of the year's business. Where an apprentice or serjeant was employed in process, 3s. 4d. was usually paid. Having given Serjeant Spelman 6s. 8d. 'for his counsell in makyng of my master['s] answer in the Duchy Chamber', the Le Stranges then paid him 3s. 4d. 'for his counsell in puttyng in of the answer'.[100] Lower fees can be found. The city of Oxford in 1523 paid 12d. and 20d. respectively to the clerks of two of its counsel for 'the making of the answer' in chancery and in the exchequer.[101] But 3s. 4d. certainly became a standard fee for counting at the bar in fines and recoveries, and when in 1471 the Pastons employed William Hussey to imparl in king's bench, his fee was once again 40d., as was John Hutton's in 1501 when the city of Canterbury's representatives 'were admytted to attornys by his labour and diligence'.[102] In *Pilkington* v. *Ainsworth*, Kebell and Brudenell did much of the routine process, at 3s. 4d. for each appearance.[103]

Inevitably the line between procedural motions and argument and pleading was a fine one. The payment by the Fastolf executors in Hilary 1460 of 3s. 4d. to William Jenney 'to calle vppon the bylle a yens Seyntloo in the eschequer' might fall into either category, but certainly not the entry in the Easter term:

> to [William] Lacon at iiij tymes to go in to the exchequer to meve the court that the comission was not laufull to sese ony landes &c – 13s. 4d.[104]

Procedural motions could become ground for argument, and vice versa. Thomas Kebell appeared for Robert Pilkington on more than one occasion when the opposing side failed to turn up, leaving him little to do for his 3s. 4d. except complain to the bench.[105] It is not surprising, therefore, that 40d. should also be the standard fee for pleading *in curia*. William Laken's efforts in 1460 in the exchequer were supported by Grenefield (twice) and Catesby, each at 40d., while in the same account Grenefield, William Jenney and John Jenney were each paid 3s. 4d. for appearing in an action of trespass.[106] In the third week of May 1501, Canterbury paid counsel in Westminster Hall on Monday, Tuesday, Friday and Saturday, twelve payments all told and each at 3s. 4d.[107] In *Roger Chapell* v. *Cade* in common

100. 'Le Strange', *Archaeologia* 25. 467–8.
101. *Records of Oxford*, 52.
102. Baker, *Camb. Law Journ*. 27. 211 n. 38; *Paston Letters and Papers*, ii. 594; Canterbury Cathedral Library, F8, f. 339.
103. 'Wombwell Mss.', 53.
104. Magdalen College, Fastolf Ms. 71, mm. 3, 6.
105. 'Wombwell Mss.', 53.
106. Magdalen College, Fastolf Ms. 71, m. 6.
107. Canterbury Cathedral Library, F8, ff. 334v, 335.

pleas, five counsel were consulted in Michaelmas 1531 and four in Easter 1532 in equity, and in every case the fee was 40d.[108] This is not to say that higher fees are unknown. On 28 February 1453, Sir John Fastolf paid Choke 3s. 4d. 'for the plea re Bradwell' but the following term 6s. 8d., with the annotation 'King's Serjeant'.[109]

Most high fees, however, seem once again to have been paid in the provinces. The duke of Buckingham in 1508 paid a serjeant £6 13s. 4d., the recorder of Bristol £4, and a less prominent lawyer 40s. for attendance at the sessions at Brecon; twelve years later he paid Thomas Matston 10s. for two days' attendance at Cirencester.[110] In 1456, Girlington received 6s. 8d. for his work in a suit against John Constable on behalf of the abbey of Fountains at the Lammas assizes at York.[111] Double that amount was paid by the Stonor family to John Twyneo of Bristol in 1474 for, it appears, his attendance at Thomas Stonor's inquisition *post mortem*.[112] In 1447–8, the city of Exeter paid the recorder 13s. 4d., William Boeff 20s. and Thomas Dourish 6s. 8d. for their services at the 'love-day' between the corporation and the earl of Devon.[113] At a less exalted level, an assize taken by the churchwardens of St Ewen's, Bristol, in 1465 cost 6s. 8d. for the appearance of Roger Kemys, their 'man of lawe', and 6s. 8d. to Serjeant Richard Pigot their 'counsel'.[114]

As with consultations, a fee was payable whenever a lawyer appeared for a client. At 40d. a time, refreshers could mount up. The St Mary at Hill litigation was ended by arbitration after three years. John Mordaunt and Thomas Marowe had each made £1 1s. 8d. and, in all, £3 1s. 8d. was shared between five lawyers.[115] By comparison, the suit brought by Canterbury was much more intensive and much more profitable. In the single week 17 to 23 May 1501, the city paid Frowyk, Kingsmill and Hutton fees amounting to £1 each.[116] Regular work and emergencies, each paid appropriately. In 1457–8 Nicholas Girlington was paid eight times by the abbot of Fountains, a total of £2 3s. 4d., plus his retaining fee of 13s. 4d.[117] In March 1463 Sir John

108. STAC2/8/231 [*Star Chamber* ii. 201–3].
109. Magdalen College, Fastolf Ms. 42.
110. SP1/22/77; E36/220.
111. *Fountains Abbey*, iii. 154.
112. *Stonor Letters and Papers*, i. 145; ii. 11.
113. *Letters of Shillingford*, 152.
114. *Trans. Bristol and Gloucestershire Arch. Soc.* 15. 178.
115. *London City Church*, 178, 190, 203.
116. Canterbury Cathedral Library, F8, ff. 334v, 335.
117. *Fountains Abbey*, iii. 60, 66–7, 74.

Howard engaged Thomas Yonge for two days' 'labore att the Whyte Frerys' and paid him £1.[118]

One form of remuneration which it is easy to overlook is the entertainment which the lawyer received from the client. Food and drink were a sizeable addition to receipts in cash. In Michaelmas 1471 the Pastons spent £2 on fees for counsel and 2s. 4d. on wine and pears, a 'service charge' of nearly six per cent.[119] But that was modest. In 1481 the city of Canterbury spent 37s. 5½d. in a fortnight on entertaining counsel, court officers and others with influence, and on gifts.[120] Under the guidance of that old fox John Shillingford, the city of Exeter in 1447–8 invested 51s. 10½d. on food and drink for counsel, 25s. for an elaborate fish dinner for the judges of assize and 5s. for wine, 10s. 5d. on wine for the barons of the exchequer, 20s. on fish for the lord chancellor and 6s. 4d. on gifts to counsel.[121] And milking the expense account may not be only a twentieth-century phenomenon. The affairs of Fastolf's executors for one term at Westminster in 1460 required four free dinners, one free breakfast, wine and meat at a tavern once, drinking at taverns on eight occasions and three presents of wine or wine and pippins.[122]

Another payment in kind was the robe or livery which, Chaucer noted, was regularly part of a lawyer's retainer. The temptation is to dismiss this as a minor perquisite, but it was well worth having. In 1464 Sir John Howard provided James Hobart a 'longe blakke gown of puke' costing 42s.[123] In the case of the recorder of Bristol, the ten yards of scarlet cloth and the fur worth 60s. which he received each year represented, at £9 13s. 4d., almost a doubling of his £10 fee.[124] Liveries also meant that a man could dress well, and they had about them an element of status. Sir John Fastolf provided attorneys with a garment worth 8s. but counsel with one worth 10s.[125] The Fountains Abbey grant to John Pullen specified a robe *de sectis generosorum monasterii* while the dean and chapter of Canterbury gave their counsel a robe suitable for an esquire.[126] That accounts enter livery in money terms does not yet mean that the gift was automatically com-

118. *Household Books of John (Howard)*, 151.
119. *Paston Letters and Papers*, ii. 594–5.
120. 'Records of Canterbury', 134.
121. *Letters of Shillingford*, 148–52.
122. Magdalen College, Fastolf Ms. 71, mm. 6, 7.
123. *Household Books of John (Howard)*, 257.
124. *The Great White Book of Bristol*, 73.
125. Magdalen College, Fastolf Ms. 42.
126. *Fountains Abbey*, i. 231–2; 'Records of Canterbury', 134–5.

muted to cash. Fastolf certainly gave gowns or cloth, and as late as 1534 the grant to Pullen of the perquisites of the recorder of York specifically included clothing.[127] At Nottingham, however, a fee of 40s. to the recorder in 1462, plus a gown worth 13s. 4d., was by the end of the century being consolidated into a fee of four marks.[128] Another kind of gift was the pair of gloves. This was a common present at a serjeant's farewell to his inn, when the gloves were 'lined' with money, but gloves were also given by clients, apparently unlined.[129] In the Pilkington case, his attorney William Reynold had 22d. for his fee and for gloves, suggesting that the latter were worth two pence.[130] The Fastolf executors, however, gave Thomas Littleton a pair of gloves of 'mayll' worth 28d.[131] There were also payments in kind more substantial than either robes or gloves. John Sulyard appears to have been paid by the transfer to him of a wardship.[132] William Nottingham, A.G. and then C.B.Ex., had the life tenancy of a house in Gloucester owned by the earl of Shrewsbury; Richard Brook, also chief baron, occupied his London home by gift of the earl of Northumberland, rent free.[133]

The fee of the expert is the way he announces himself to the public, but it is only a part of the story of his rewards. Much will depend upon the chances of earning that fee, and something to the opportunities for remuneration 'on the side'. Reward, moreover, is comparative. It has to be measured against alternative careers, the lawyer against the gentleman, against the merchant, against the cleric. But even before considering all this, fees and fee levels alone do suggest interim conclusions about the common lawyers of Kebell's day. One is the comparatively low level of fees and the frequency of payment – even with prominent counsel, little and often was the rule. Another is the commercial emphasis which pervaded pre-Reformation practice; *laissez-faire* and *laissez-aller* were the mottoes, collectively and individually. But the dominant impression is, yet again, of the ubiquity of the lawyer. Our interest in the Canterbury chamberlains' account for

127. *York Memorandum Book*, ii. 267.
128. *Records of the Borough of Nottingham*, iii. 279, 417.
129. *Minutes of Parliament*, i. 8.
130. 'Wombwell Mss.', 53.
131. Magdalen College, Fastolf Ms. 71 m. 2.
132. *Cal. Ancient Deeds*, vi. c6184.
133. Wedgwood, *Biographies*; PROB11/19 ff. 97–100. William Hussey was granted a seven-year term in a Huntingdonshire property in return for maintaining its owner 'atte courte for his lernyng in the lawe': *Cal. Ancient Deeds*, vi. 6972.

1500–1 has turned on the fishmarket litigation, but in an appendix, tucked between payments for wine at a tavern and for visiting minstrels, is 3s. 4d. to the clerk of the peace for Kent for his benevolence, and elsewhere 8d. for seeing to the sealing of city warrants.[134] And similar traces hide in account after account of the time.

134. Canterbury Cathedral Library, F8, ff. 348v, 349.

14

THE REWARDS OF THE PROFESSION: INCOME AND MORALITY

When the reformers of the mid-sixteenth century drafted prayers for all conditions of men, they did not overlook the lawyer. How could they? His temptations were obvious:

> we most heartily pray Thee . . . so to rule through the governance of Thy Holy Spirit the hearts of the Lawyers, that they . . . may without partiality both faithfully give counsel and also indifferently pronounce of all such causes as be brought unto them and by no means suffer themselves to be corrupted with bribes and gifts which blind the eyes of the wise and subvert true judgment.[1]

Of course, many people felt that lawyers were past praying for anyway. The popular agreement that they were interested in fees, not justice, implied something more damning, while moralists said openly that the profession was corrupt. Alexander Barclay, anglicising the *Narrenschiff*, wrote in 1509:

> For howe beit that the lawes ought be fre,
> Yet sergeaunt, at turney, promoter, Juge or scribe
> Wyll nat fele thy mater without a preuy brybe[2]

and Hugh Latimer had at least two centuries of moral indignation behind him when he savaged the profession in his sermons.

> Loo, heare is the mother and the daughter and the daughter's daughter. Auarice is the mother, she brynges forthe brybe takynge, and brybe takynge, peruertyng of iudgement.
>
> Ther lackes a fourth thing to make vp the messe, wyche . . . if I were iudg, shoulde be *Hangum tuum*, a Tyburne typpet to take wyth hym! And it were the iudge of the kinges bench, my Lorde Chyefe Iudge of Englande, yea, and it were my Lord Chaunceloure hym selfe, to Tiburne wyth hym![3]

But how true was this?

1. Becon, *Prayers*, 25.
2. Brant, *Ship of Fools*, f. xv.
3. Hugh Latimer, *Sermons*, ed. G. E. Corrie, Parker Soc. 22 (1844), i. 179–80.

I

Bribery certainly did occur. Sir John Fastolf spent £6 13s. 4d. on a cloth of gold robe, of crimson velvet, for no less a person than John Fortescue, C.J.K.B.[4] The chief justice might write later that no English judge 'was ever corrupted with gifts or bribes', but Fastolf's gift was specifically to encourage him to be 'more favourable' in his judgement towards a prisoner in the Marshalsea.[5] But such bluntness is rare. Almost always the historian finds himself having to decide when conventional marks of respect, gifts to secure attention and gifts to improve the standing of a litigant in a judge's eyes pass over into corruption. In three years, the parish of St Mary at Hill gave the two chief justices £1 13s. 4d. in cash, meals worth £1 8s. 10d. and wine, poultry and rabbits to the value of £1 12s. 1d.[6] This was no attempt to buy a favourable decision, since many of the payments were made jointly with the other party. The purpose was to secure attention, and litigants would do anything to get their cases noticed. Mayor Shillingford was furious when a present of fish for the lord chancellor failed to arrive from Exeter:

[It] came not yet, me to right grete anger and discomfort by my trauthe, and the cause that hit was boght for myche like to be lost; for hit hadde be a gode mene and order after spekyng and communication . . . the buk horn to have be presented, and Y to have come there after, &c. and so to have sped moche the better: but now hit is like to faille to hyndryng. And so Y have helpe ynogh abakward and but litell forthward as hit at alle tyme proveth and appereth . . . Cristes curse have they bothe, and seye ye amen.[7]

Lawyers and suitors also shared the feeling that if a lawyer was being kind enough to consider a matter it was only courtesy to show gratitude. Mayor Shillingford reported another occasion when everything did go right.

Y hadde a dey to appere before the lordis for oure mater, . . . and for as moche as my lord Chaunceller bade the Justyse to dyner ayenst that same day for oure mater, seyyng that he sholde have a dys of salt fisshe; Y hiryng this, Y didde as me thoght aughte to be done, and by avys of the Justise and of oure counseill, and sende thider that day ij stately pikerellis and ij stately tenchis, for the whiche my lord Chaunceller cowde right grete thankys and made right moche therof hardely; for hit came yn gode seson, for my lordis the Duke of

4. Magdalen College, Fastolf Ms. 42; K. B. Mcfarlane, 'William Worcester', in *Studies Presented to Sir Hilary Jenkinson*, ed. J. C. Davies (1957), 214.

5. Fortescue, *De Laudibus*, 128.

6. *London City Church*, 178, 190, 203.

7. *Letters of Shillingford*, 23.

Bokyngham, the Markis of Southfolke, and other Bysshoppis divers dyned with my lord Chaunceller that dey.[8]

An uglier face to such practices is seen in Fastolf litigation. Sir John's executors had to give 20d. to a court clerk 'by cause he wold not ells entre' a release.[9] Fastolf himself paid for the 'friendship' of useful people – the clerk of the petty-bag or the clerk to a justice such as Sir William Yelverton.[10] There is, admittedly, no sign of Canterbury's double retainers; no doubt Sir John was too lucrative an employer to play that trick on. Indeed, apart from Fastolf's direct bribe to Fortescue, there is only one other suspicion of crude manipulation – the cryptic payment in a suit for wardship 'to a certain man in reward for labouring to secure the person' of that ward.[11] On the other hand there were several occasions when Sir John paid out money to 'expedite' his pleas, once to a clerk in the exchequer but most often to the king's attorney.[12] Litigants regularly solicited ministers and men in the king's confidence for their support.[13] Magdalen College was advised in 1494 to 'get Lord Husse safe . . . for his wisdom may do most for the College next the King'.[14] Clients saw no reason why what was normal elsewhere in society should be omitted because the law was involved, nor did patrons feel any inhibitions, not least the king.[15] There is evidence, too, of the employment of a large number of lawyers for a single plea, a combination of cornering the market and overawing the opposition; the Titchwell costs show twenty-five payments to counsel over two years, and to nine different individuals.[16] The value of this ploy was well known. John Fineux advised the prior of Canterbury to 'spend mony among men of lawe of [the Chancellor's] cownsell and other, and your matyers wyll be spede'.[17] In the Plumpton correspondence, one letter records the reaction of an attorney whose client was in difficulties:

The judges . . . say they understand by credible informations that these men be not guiltie, and [the accusation] is but onely your maintenance; and so one

8. *ibid.*, 8–9. Shillingford also paid the justices of assize: *ibid.*, 150. The corporation of Canterbury regularly gave gifts to lawyers from Kent, and on at least one occasion John Fineux reciprocated: 'Records of Canterbury', 148–50.
9. Magdalen College, Fastolf Ms. 71 m. 3.
10. *ibid.*, Ms. 42.
11. *ibid.*, Ms. 42.
12. *ibid.*, Ms. 42.
13. *L. and P.*, iv. 1949; ix. 656. One payment by Canterbury was to Baron Hales and Christopher Hales S.G. for favour over 40 marks forfeited by the city in an action against a local cleric: 'Records of Canterbury', 152.
14. MacNamara, *Danvers Family*, 162–3.
15. *Paston Letters and Papers*, ii. 541–2.
16. Magdalen College, Fastolf Ms. 42.
17. H.M.C., *Various Collections*, i. 232.

of them said to me out of the court. And Guy Fairfax said openly att the barre, that he knew so, verily they were not guilty, – that he wold labor their deliverance for almes, not takeing a penny; and I seing this, took Mr Pygott and Mr Collow.[18]

A refinement was to retain key court officials as well. Ainsworth engaged as his attorney against Pilkington the second prothonotary of the king's bench, John Fisher, and it may be the same man whom Canterbury feed a few years later; Canterbury, indeed, seems to have paid Fisher fees for six terms in one year, a deliberate case of overpayment.[19] Pilkington's son learned the lesson. When he re-opened the case, he paid Fisher 20d. 'for feyre of doyng me hurtt for he was agaynst my father afore'.[20]

Yet evidence of this sort is not common. Only a tiny fraction of payments raise suspicion, even in the Fastolf manuscripts, and this is significant. Fastolf was a chronic, almost a professional litigant, and his executors and agents were deeply versed in litigation. If those who knew all the tricks of the trade did not go in for wholesale corruption, the ordinary litigant was even less likely to do so. Robert Pilkington never offered any inducement to a lawyer, which cynics might suggest explains his lack of success. But Mayor Shillingford would spend where it paid him, and he was more concerned to stand well with the legal establishment than to manipulate the law. The Plumptons likewise show little faith in corrupting the profession and neither, despite their inside knowledge, did the Pastons. There is massive evidence in contemporary correspondence of attempts to pervert, or at least influence justice, but the principal reliance was on the well-established methods of good lordship, interest, recommendation and favour.

Lawyers were no more immune from such influences than any other group. Indeed, because they had professional links as well as links with society around, they were doubly open to temptation. A most extreme example of conspiracy to pervert the law occurred at the York assizes of 1502. The context was the attempt by Richard Empson to strip Sir Robert Plumpton of his lands in the interest of Empson's daughter.[21] To ensure that Plumpton lost, John Vavasour, the senior assize judge for the midlands, was specially appointed clerk

18. *Plumpton Correspondence*, 35.
19. Canterbury Cathedral Library, F8 ff. 335v, 339, 340v.
20. 'Wombwell Mss.', 56.
21. *Plumpton Correspondence*, cvi–cix; Ives, *Univ. Birmingham Hist. Journ.* 7. 150–1.

of assize for the northern circuit, as it were *in commendam*, temporarily ousting one of the two regular clerks, Thomas Strey, an attorney of Clement's Inn known to be favourable to Sir Robert.[22] Vavasour's colleagues on the midland circuit probably knew what was going on; the two northern judges certainly did, and so too did their second assize clerk, who was also vice-chancellor of the duchy of Lancaster, while collusion at Westminster must have been necessary to secure the four sets of letters patent which the scheme required.[23] But this is to say little more than that lawyers were part of the society of their day, and an important part. There was a moral case for believing that Plumpton possessed his estates as a result of his father's blatant dishonesty, just as the resentment of the Ainsworths and the Savages at the arrival of the distant cousin is perfectly understandable: the feelings of Mrs Bennet are always with us.[24] What Empson did differs from what Archbishop Savage did in *Pilkington* v. *Ainsworth* only in his ability to bring in so many colleagues, and how much that was due to his status with the king and how much to the legal old-boy network is impossible to say. The more normal focus of the bribery which did go on was the sheriff and the jury, where everyone from the king downwards felt that 'labouring' was worth the expense.[25] The weight of the accounting evidence is against the frequent corruption of lawyers. Cynics may again argue that influence offered surer returns; gross tampering with the profession would have led to an auction with the wealthier once more coming out on top and the winners being the lawyers! But whatever the motive, it does appear that although the law, as always, ran on money, it did not run on 'hot' money.

II

If this was the case, why the outcry? In part this can be explained by individual misconduct, or alleged misconduct, which helped to create suspicion of the profession as a whole. Juliana Herberd complained to the council that in treating her as he had, William Paston had been false to his oath as a serjeant:

22. *Plumpton Correspondence*, 181; *Inner Temple Records*, i. 461.
23. John Fisher, Humphrey Coningsby, James Hobart, Robert Henrison. For Henrison see Somerville, *Duchy of Lancaster*, i. 479.
24. Sir William Plumpton had sold the marriage of his apparent heirs, his grand-daughters, while at the same time concealing the (doubtful) legitimacy of his son Robert; Empson's daughter married the son of one of the grand-daughters.
25. For the bribery of sheriffs and juries see Bennett, *The Pastons*, 167–71; McFarlane, *Nobility*, 117–18.

for the whiche othe the juges delyuered hym . . . a coyfe of treuth with the appurtenauntez of clothyng for a signe to be knowen for a rightful man before an othir, the whiche coife with the appurtenauncez he hath forfet and is worthy to forswere the court.

Not only should Paston be formally degraded, but also 'othir meyntenours of the same science . . . extorcioners that thus oppressed, mischeven and ouerladen the people'.[26] Fraud, indeed, was frequent enough for a recognised punishment to exist for attorneys and the like. John Redhewe, a London grocer, found himself and his wife in grave trouble after defaming William Husey of London, gentleman, as:

a pooler, a promooter of falte [sic] causis, and [saying] that he was worthy to wer papires aboute Westminster Hall, and that he was a bastarde.[27]

In some cases fraud was undertaken in the interests of clients. Richard III's anger at the doctoring of court records has already been noted; the anger was unusual, but was the offence? The passing of an act in 1429 argues not.[28] In the Coventry courts too (admittedly not 'of record'), it had been necessary to rule in 1421 that court officers were no longer to amend the records saying 'hit is falsely entred and falsly done', but whether the penalty of 6s. 8d. and suspension for the rest of the mayoral year would have been a deterrent is questionable.[29] Corrupt lawyers could be very useful. When one client found his king's bench action stopped by chancery, his son engaged a fresh attorney, and when he was stopped, a third – and they evaded the anger of chancery by not replying when called by the usher.[30] Even the great succumbed to temptation. In 1540, Humphrey Browne K.S. found himself in the Tower accused, in part, of advising prisoners of the way to defeat royal claims to the goods of convicted felons.[31] In November 1557 it was the queen's attorney who was in the Tower facing the forfeiture of his £1,000 bond for good behaviour.[32] His offence had been that 'he had sundry ways attempted to cloake and colour' a murder and a burglary, even to the extent of setting out to discredit the justices of assize investigating the crimes. Browne had

26. *Paston Letters and Papers*, ii. 511.
27. C1/439/30. The case was heard by Wolsey; the relationship of William Husey to the former C.J. is not known.
28. *8 Hen. VI* c. 12. See above, p. 259.
29. *Coventry Leet Book*, 34–5.
30. C1/216/86.
31. For a full transcript of the record, and references to this affair, see Spelman, *Reports*, i. 183–4; ii. 351–2. The allegation about counselling prisoners appears only in Spelman's note.
32. B.L. Lansd. Ms. 639 f. 52.

also been accused of advising a client how to evade the statute of uses, and royal feudal rights certainly were a most fruitful field for chicanery; his confederates were the speaker of the Commons, Nicholas Hare, the attorney of the duchy, William Coningsby, and a reader of Gray's Inn, William Grey. The fact that family lawyers seem to have provided the escheator with a draft of the inquisition *post mortem* made it easy to enter a deceitful enfeoffment, and it was not impossible to legitimate this by securing pardon from an unwitting crown.[33] The profit is less obvious when false inquisitions were returned providing grounds for a royal claim to wardship.[34] Here, if the accusation against the bishop of Winchester and the 'crafty counsell' of Thomas More 'lernyd in lawe' is to be believed, the object was to set up a wardship which the instigator could then purchase from the crown.[35]

A more sinister danger was that a lawyer might deceive his client, something against which there was almost no defence. When a Norfolk widow could not settle her 'debate' with her husband's executors,

> ther come vnto here oon John Newman of Norwich, lerned in the temporal lawe, and took vpon him and promysed her that he shuld, if she wold take him xxs., so purvey for them in your [the archbishop of Canterbury's] spiritual court and take vp counsell for hir that she shuld recouer ayenst them and haue hir money ageyn. And after that, he come ageyn to hir and told that he hadde tidyngges from London that he must send vp iiij marks and ellys hir matier shuld be lost, and if he hadde it, hir matier wer saaff and she suld haue hir iugement and a gret recouery and hir money besiden ageyn, euery peny. Where in trouthe he toke neuer ony such accion nor counsell, but all this was a feyned thyng . . . and thus untruly he deceyued hir and put the money in his owen purse.[36]

A more sophisticated technique was to profit from knowledge of a client's affairs. Sir Sampson Meverell, a Stafford J.P., accused John Tunsted of accepting a retainer and then undermining him, and something similar was alleged against William Jenney.[37] Jenney, according to an unnamed correspondent of John Paston, had stepped in 'wyth-outyn ony knoulach of myn fadyre or of me' to purchase the Suffolk manor of Oulton, which the writer had already bought and substantially paid for:

33. *Paston Letters and Papers*, ii. 554–61; *Plumpton Correspondence*, cxvii; cf. the involvement of Richard Jay: *Cal. inquisitions post mortem*, i. 339; *Cal. Patent Rolls, 1494–1509*, 302.
34. *Cal. inquisitions post mortem*, iii. 407.
35. C1/384/6–9. Thomas More of the Middle Temple.
36. C1/124/21.
37. C1/72/112

the whech is to vs gret sorwe that wee scholdyn ben so vntruly don to; and it doth vs most evyl wheere as wee put all ouyre trost, he sonest hath deseyued vs – and that is Wylliam Jenney, for he promysyd bothyn my fadyre and me that he wold haue don hys part ther-in that wee scholdyn haue had a-state accordyng to our comenantys [*sic*], and to that entent he toke of me xxs. for j reward.[38]

Whether Paston's mediation recovered the property or the money already paid is not recorded. Before long he was himself to be accused by William Yelverton J.K.B. of forging the will of his employer, Sir John Fastolf, and thereby diverting to himself large estates in Norfolk and Suffolk. Not that Yelverton's motives were pure; as a co-executor and feoffee with Paston, he resented being cut out by Paston's death-bed 'bargain' with the old knight. Thomas Playter's report is highly revealing:

Ser, I Playter speke wyth Maister Yeluerton . . . I vnderstand he woll not be straunge to falle jn wyth you a-geyn, and also that he woll not hurte you jn your bargeyn if ye coude be frendely dysposed to hym ward as ye have ben; for wyth-oute a frendelyhood of your parte hym semeth he schuld not gretely help you jn your bargeyn, so I fele hym. He leueth sum-qwhat a-loffe, and not vtterly malycyous a-yens you.[39]

Other judges were involved also. Fortescue had been recruited to Paston's side and so had John Markham, also of the king's bench.

Yeluerton wold be glad to fall in to yow be soposyng, for Master Markam hathe sayd playnneley j-now to hym.

Nor was Jenney to be left out. Although only a feoffee, not an executor, he is soon found as Yelverton's main ally, asserting a claim to distribute Fastolf's goods as well as his lands.[40]

Lawyers were also not above hunting directly for themselves or their families. In 1504, for example, the son of a London grocer petitioned the crown to enquire into his selling of property while under age 'for right esy and smale somes of money by unlefull entisement and sinistre meanes'. The purchasers were led by that 'oracle of the law', Chief Justice Frowyk, and included a king's bench filacer, Edward Cheseman, and John Toly, a not-too-scrupulous auditor from the Middle Temple with the same ominous surname as Thomas Toly, the sheriff's clerk of the Richard III forgery.[41] We do not have

38. *Paston Letters and Papers*, ii. 268. Cf. a similar accusation against Edmund Hasilwode of the Middle Temple: C1/571/15.

39. *Paston Letters and Papers*, i. 161–3.

40. *ibid.*, ii. 259, 293.

41. *Cal. Close Rolls, 1500–9*, 328. The description of Frowyk is from Thomas Fuller,

Frowyk's reply, but he did die possessed of property bought from the complainant. As might be expected, many accusations tell of a lawyer using his inside knowledge to exploit legal process. William Paston prayed to be delivered from his adversaries, including William Aslak and Juliana Herberd, but according to them, Paston did what he could to expedite this by imprisoning them, in Juliana's case on six occasions, often in irons and for three years 'in the pitte withynne the castell of Norwiche'.[42] The Pastons, in turn, found process used against them, as when William Jenney kept the clerk of the peace away from a gaol delivery to frustrate the release of the Pastons' bailiff, Richard Calle.[43] Norfolk lawyers, however, were not exceptional – we merely know more about them. In the course of his long struggle to secure the lordship of Clopton in Cambridgeshire, Serjeant John Fisher was accused not only of violence but of indicting the 'ancients' of the village at quarter sessions (and suing them at common law) in revenge for their inconvenient memories about local custom.[44] Some years later a plaintiff in chancery on a matter of title reported that an earlier petition had been frustrated when the defendant Thomas Clement and a John Clement had fraudulently effected a recovery to William Rastell 'their secret unlaufull berer and mayntener' – clearly More's nephew looking after More's protégé (and his own future father-in-law).[45]

Corruption, therefore, can be found, or more generally, accusations of corruption – and that distinction is important. To the lawyer matters might appear somewhat different. As Thomas More was being led to execution he was, so the stories go, abused by one disappointed litigant and accosted by another whose business was still unfinished.[46] To the first he replied that justice had been done – and we must allow that not every disgruntled client is a wronged innocent. To the other More admitted that the business was outstanding, but he had neither time nor influence left. Again this gives a clue to the

Worthies of England (1662). Cheseman: Baker, *Journ. Legal Hist.* 1, 191; J.P. Middx, cofferer of the household: *Cal. Patent Rolls, 1494–1509*, 650; *Cal. Close Rolls, 1500–9*, 840. John Toly: *Minutes of Parliament*, i. 13; *Cal. Patent Rolls, 1494–1509*, 598; *L. and P.*, i. 485 (58), 1149, 1418. Thomas Toly: London, *Cal. Letter Books*, L, 236; see above, pp. 259–60.

42. *Paston Letters and Papers*, i. 7; ii. 505–7, 509–15.

43. *ibid.*, ii. 370.

44. C1/223/25, cf. 124/45, 125/78, 238/39, 40.

45. C1/946/40. Lawyers in judicial posts were especially open to accusation. Thomas Burgoyne, London: C1/40/30–2; John Fleming, Southampton: C1/106/57; Walter Rowdon, Gloucester: C1/210/67.

46. Hall, *Chronicle*, 817; Chambers, *More*, 348.

complaints against the profession; busy men do get behind and clients with a low priority can get squeezed out. Kebell did fail to keep his appointment with Pilkington, but there was nothing venal in this, and when Nicholas Statham did nothing to justify a fee for service in parliament, he arranged for it to be repaid, especially since, as an impartial M.P., he had had qualms about accepting it in the first place.[47] The will of Chief Justice Hussey made special provision for sins of omission:

I will haue iij preestis at Cambrigge to syng for this entente that where as I haue offended any manne or woman in woorde or dede and haue not doon due satisfaccion, or where as any manne hath ben putt to coost or hurte by lacheousnes and slownes of my laboures, that the suffrages of the masses may be goostly satisfaction to those persons whome I haue offendid, and wold make bodely satisfaction if I knew what persons they were and how and in what thyng I haue hurte theym.[48]

Lawyers customarily put a less sophisticated clause of restitution in their wills. Robert Morton of Lincoln's Inn was typical:

Tenderly I pray and specially require myn executours that if eny wrongis by me haue be doone to eny manner persones and dew profe therof made afore my seid executours, that they make due restitucion to the parties grevid for such wrongys by me so doon, to the vtterest that it may be knowen.[49]

Nevertheless, as William Ayloffe (also of Lincoln's Inn) made clear, such a clause was there as an insurance, not in expectation that claimants would come flocking.[50] Specific restitution is sometimes ordered, but this mostly refers to lands and goods acquired by mortgage, where the borrower is given yet another chance to repay, or to doubtful titles, which are to be arbitrated; Statham did admit to a fine wrongly levied in a court he had kept, but he had learned of his mistake only after the event and nothing suggests that he had deliberately delayed repayment.[51] Faced with the terrors of late-medieval

47. PROB 11/6 f. 53.
48. PROB 11/10 f. 256Av. A similar clause occurs in the will of William Copley: see below, p. 414.
49. PROB 11/8 f. 146v. Kebell was even less concerned: see below, p. 426.
50. PROB 11/19 f. 1.
51. Robert Sheffield: PROB 11/19 f. 116v; see above, p. 106; Richard Brook: PROB 11/23 f. 23; Gregory Adgore: PROB 11/14 f. 159v; William Callow: PROB 11/8 ff. 57–8; William Catesby: PROB 11/7 f. 114v; Statham: PROB 11/6 f. 53. Statham held the court 'for Walwyn' (Richard Walwyn of Lincoln's Inn: *Black Books*, i. 30–69), and it is significant that he had not paid over the money wrongly collected; he was told of his mistake by 'Genney of London' (John Jenney of the Guildhall: see below, p. 467).

death, most lawyers appear to have been untroubled by professional misdeeds.

In the battle for public esteem, indeed, the lawyer could not win. For Frowyk to buy land from an improvident young man was to invite criticism, even if (as is perfectly possible) his motive had been to assist the vendor. Since all lawyers were crafty, everything they did was suspicious, *ipso facto*. In practice, corruption can be matched by probity, even in the same man. Justice Vavasour, who certainly aided Empson, appeared to Pilkington as a staunch opponent of maintenance, willing to risk the hostility of the president of the king's council.[52] And more than once we find generosity. It became a proverb that 'a suit in *forma pauperis* hath no scent', but we have seen Kebell taking them and Fairfax stepping in to save poor men from Sir William Plumpton.[53] In 1477, Richard Fryston, master in chancery, joined with Justice Yonge and his brother John, alderman of London, to defeat a scheme very similar to the one which Frowyk, on an unfavourable construction, was involved in.[54] Admittedly one of the instigators was himself a chancery clerk and the apprentice set up for plucking was a relative of the Yonges – scepticism might argue that Frowyk found a young man with fewer friends. Certainly, too, the relative absence of litigation against lawyers could be explained by their limited accountability and by the difficulty of getting lawyers to plead against their colleagues.[55] But on the evidence, the case against the profession is at worst not proven. Some lawyers were honest, others were dishonest, some might be both, just like mankind generally. The safer verdict is that they shared the values and standards of the society around: no better, no worse.

III

One important factor in blackening the reputation of the lawyers was the way legal costs operated. There was no such thing as cheap litigation. Even a simple stage in mesne process could be quite costly.

52. See above, p. 123. The professional cohesion which could, as in the manoeuvres against Plumpton, lead to conspiracy, could also lead to helpful unofficial contact between parties: *Plumpton Correspondence*, 121.
53. See above, pp. 141 n.122, 172. The proverb is mentioned in E. Hake, *Newes out of Poules Churchyarde* (1575), sig. B7v.
54. *Cal. Close Rolls, 1476–85*, 126.
55. For the narrow construction of legal obligations, see Baker, *Camb. Law Journ.* 27. 209–12; for the difficulty of obtaining counsel, see *Paston Letters and Papers*, ii. 520–1.

Table F. *Analysis of legal costs (Fastolf Mss.)*

	Fastolf Account A 'Bradwell, Beyton and Tychewell' Mich. 1458		*Fastolf Account B* 'Bradwell' Mich. 1449–55		*Fastolf Account C* 'Tychewell' 1448–50		*Thomas Playter's Expenses* 1459–60	
TRAVEL AND SUBSISTENCE		24%		11%		12%		33%
CLERICAL EXPENSES								
(a) charges	60%		57%		25%		7%	
(b) gratuities and treating	3%		2%		2%		1%	
(c) expediting business	–		1%		–		–	
		63%		60%		27%		8%
TRIAL COSTS AND JURY EXPENSES		–		11%		–		12%
PROFESSIONAL COSTS								
(a) fees and rewards to counsel	11%		8%		53%		24%	
(b) fees to attorneys	–		4%		–		1%	
(c) gifts and treating	2%		1%		4%		3%	
(d) expediting business	–		5%		4%		–	
		13%		18%		61%		28%
EXPENSES NOT ITEMISED		–		–		–		19%
TOTAL	£10 1s.2d	100%	£58 4s.4d	100%	£7 16s.7½d	100%	£35 0s.10d	100%

In one term the Arundel family paid 6s. 10d. for five writs, and a *supersedeas* cost £1 17s. 1d.[56] To return to *Roger Chapell* v. *Cade*, costs over four terms at common law averaged 29s. 9½d., and £2 2s. 5d. a term for seven terms in chancery and star chamber; the related suit by William Chapell averaged 22s. 2½d. and £2 1s. 2d. respectively.[57] Pilkington spent between forty and seventy shillings a term on his writ of error, and the total came to £12 9s. 4d. or more.[58] He claimed that over twenty years his litigation over Mellor had cost £78 8s. 0d. – and this despite the fact that Kebell had often refused a fee.[59] In ten years, Sir John Fastolf's costs were estimated at a monstrous £1,085.[60]

Where did the money go? Here the Fastolf papers are of prime importance. They include four accounts for legal work which are sufficiently detailed to establish what was spent and where.[61] Reducing miscellaneous payments to some order involves artificial and sometimes arbitrary categories, but that allowed, the conclusion is clear. The weight of costs in a law suit was in general expenses, not in fees. Clerical costs – for clerical and procedural work in court and outside – were often the heaviest item, while the burden of travelling and subsistence was also considerable. In two of the four Fastolf accounts these together amount to eighty-seven per cent and seventy-one per cent of the total bill. By contrast, fees and rewards to all grades of lawyer never exceeded thirty per cent in three of the four lists. In the fourth, fees took a surprising sixty-one per cent, but the bill is short and included an unusually high proportion of meetings with counsel. The total disbursed in the four accounts is high (£111 2s. 11½d.); but professional charges amount to only £26 10s. 0½d., a mere twenty-four per cent, and even with gratuities and inducements offered for clerical work, the figure only reaches twenty-six per cent. Another Fastolf suit is still more striking. At a *nisi prius* hearing at Gloucester in 1453 when the judge and the lawyers involved received only 11s. 1d. in cash and kind, the total bill was £7 6s. 2d.[62]

56. Dorset Record Office, D16/M74.
57. STAC2/8/229–32 [*Star Chamber*, ii. 196–205].
58. 'Wombwell Mss.', 51–6.
59. *ibid.*, 44, 53. Sir Robert Plumpton was advised that £40 would be needed to undertake his defence against Empson: *Plumpton Correspondence*, 152.
60. Magdalen College, Fastolf Ms. 42.
61. Table F, A, B, C: *ibid.*, Ms. 42; Playter's Expenses: *ibid.*, Ms. 71.
62. B.L. Add. Ms. 28206/124. Cf. costs in vexatious chancery suit of 48s. 2d., including only 8s. 8d. (18%) for attorney and counsel: C1/150/44.

Certain clients did understand that a payment to their lawyer was not necessarily a payment for their lawyer; Pilkington lists his charges as 'costs' and 'expenses', although without ever defining the terms. But it would hardly be surprising if others who watched their money flow into the hands of a lawyer drew the crude and wrong conclusion; and it was this confusion which gave what substance there was to allegations of avarice. We may, for example, suspect that it was the 50s. 6d. claimed in costs which caused John Parker to deny that William Rede of Exeter had ever been retained by him:

to ride to London as a solicitor and to labor for hym before the kynges justicez at Westminster and also in the kynges chaunceri, in and for suche maters as . . . [he] then sued Richard Heydon and George Jeffron, and to reteygne lernyd councell and attorneys.[63]

Lawyers were blamed, when it was the system itself which was costly And again they had no hope of defending themselves. Their wealth was proof of guilt. A pamphlet published in 1552 asked:

Think you the laweiers could bee such purchassers if their pleas were short and al their iudgements, iustice and conscience?[64]

Another had inquired a few years earlier:

Whether a M pounds gotten yerelye by one man at lawe was truelie deserued at all mennes handes?[65]

The answer seemed inescapable.

IV

Precisely what the income of Thomas Kebell or of any other pre-Reformation lawyer was it is impossible to say. To know this it would be necessary to know the case load and the appointments book of the individual concerned, and such evidence does not survive. The nearest to it is a document relating to the practice in 1482 of Andrew Dymmock, at that time 'attorney-general' to Earl Rivers. In Trinity he seems to have been handling at least ten cases, and if Dymmock earned the same fee for each as Thomas Playter, his receipts for the term would have been £8 6s. 8d., giving an annual figure from litiga-

63. C1/558/40.
64. Gilbert Walker, *A manifest detection of the moste vyle and detestable vise of Diceplay* (n.d.), sig. Bviii, modernised in *The Elizabethan Underworld*, ed. A. V. Judges (1930), 38.
65. *Questions worthy to be consulted on for the weale publyque* (n.d.).

tion alone of £33 6s. 8d.[66] This is very probably an underestimate. An *ex hypothesi* check is the consultation rate of 3s. 4d. per day or per session. If a lawyer was able to offset those days when he was not working against days when he received more than a single fee, his receipts would have been £60 a year, with any annual retainers, robes or payments in kind on top. Such a level for earnings is not outrageous, given our partial information about Dymmock or the claim by John Rastell that he earned forty marks a year from practising the law part-time.[67] Those with particularly lucrative positions clearly earned considerably more. Thomas Jubbes had his fee as recorder of Bristol, worth £19 13s. 4d., plus the employment the post brought with it. A retainer from the duke of Buckingham brought £2 a year and considerable business on a daily basis; from October 1520 to April 1521 the duke paid him £7 10s. od. in fees and rewards for thirty-nine days' work, only half of it during the law terms, which left him very free to take on other clients.[68] In addition he had his earnings from non-litigious work, such as the 40s. he received in 1511 for supervising the will of Sir Edmund Gorges. [69] It seems not unreasonable that, for a man like Jubbes, we should think in terms of an income nearer £100 than £60. And a few outstanding men below the coif made even more, enough to refuse the honour. William Roper estimated at £400 Thomas More's income *circa* 1517 when he was the rising star of the profession and in the highly profitable post of under-sheriff of London.[70]

Another measure of income is the money paid to prominent lawyers in lieu of practice. The crown engaged counsel to attend a Devonshire oyer and terminer in 1456; Serjeant Thomas Littleton received £13 6s. 8d. and two apprentices half that amount each.[71] A serjeant

66. E315/486/61.
67. *Original Letters*, ed. H. Ellis, 3 ser. (1846), ii. 308–12.
68. Rawcliffe, *The Staffords*, 241; E36/220. The attorney-general to Margaret of Anjou was paid £21 6s. 8d. in 1452–3 for 128 days at 3s. 4d. Elizabeth Woodville's attorney-general was credited with 35 days at 3s. 4d., mostly out of term: Myers, *Bull. John Rylands Lib.* 40. 414; 50. 457–8.
69. *Somerset Medieval Wills, 1501–1530*, Somerset Rec. Soc. 19 (1903), 151.
70. Roper, *Lyfe of Moore*, 8–9.
71. Lincoln's Inn, Hale Ms. xii (77). It is possible that this commission, to deal with the Courtenay–Bonville disorder, was being paid danger-money; Nicholas Radford was murdered later in the year. However, Littleton was paid £13 6s. 8d. in 1474–5 to cover 'his great expenses' in an eyre in Monmouth, so the amount may be a usual one: E405/58 m. 5v. Administrative commissions were also paid. John Markham and Nicholas Ashton were paid £20 in 1450 to cover costs and expenses of an enquiry at Canterbury: E404/73/1; Thomas Bryan received £5 for the Bucks. and

serving as justice of assize received £10 a circuit, and a king's serjeant an annual retainer of £20, plus 26s. 11d. for livery.[72] These sums brought Kebell's known receipts to £49 13s. 7d., and this without several retainers of unknown amount and allowing nothing for income from practice.[73] A further comparison is the income of a puisne justice, which, according to William Ayscough, was initially lower than that of a serjeant.[74] The judge received fees and robes worth £108 13s. 5¼d., plus a share of court fees; evidence assembled by Dr Margaret Hastings suggests that this would bring an ordinary judge something like £50 a year minimum.[75] Over and above, he could develop or even continue private practice; Pilkington paid John Vavasour 13s. 4d. in gold to use his influence with Bishop Savage.[76] Assize commissions paid the standard £20 a year and an oyer and terminer could bring a puisne judge £20 also.[77] All in all it seems probable that a newly appointed judge might expect about £250 a year.

How much more, accepting William Ayscough's word, could a serjeant expect to earn? He was claiming compensation for 'loss of his winnings' as a serjeant, consequent on his promotion to the bench only two years after his call to the coif. He sought grants equivalent, at five per cent, to a capital sum of £500; the existing judges had averaged ten years before promotion, and if Ayscough had been counting on a similar period, he was estimating his loss at £62 10s. 0d. a year. Add this to the estimate of what a puisne judge did receive and a figure of £300+ is arrived at for the serjeant. Ten years as a serjeant was, however, a long stint; the average among Ayscough's contemporaries as serjeants was to be nearer five. For him to justify £500 for the three years which, according to this comparison, he had lost, his income would have had to be over £450 a year, something better than that claimed for More eighty years later. On the other hand, both figures are almost certainly exaggerated, Ayscough to gild his petition and Roper to exalt the standing of More; and Roper, in addition, was writing nearly forty years after the event,

Oxon. commission in connection with the 1474 benevolence, but whether for reward or expenses is not clear: E405/58 m.5v.

72. E101/203(7) [*L. and P.*, i. 2787].

73. King's serjeant – £21 6s. 11d.; justice of assize – £20; Lord Hastings – £5; Sir Charles Somerset – £1 6s. 8d.; city of Leicester – £1 6s. 8d.; priory of Langley – 13s. 4d.

74. Hastings, *Common Pleas*, 75; Ayscough, *Archaeologia* 16, 3–4.

75. Hastings, *Common Pleas*, 82–4.

76. 'Wombwell Mss.', 55.

77. Lincoln's Inn, Hale Ms. xii (77): C.J.K.B. – £40, C.B.Ex. – £26 13s. 4d., J.K.B. – £20.

Table G. *Analysis of the subsidy assessment of the legal profession (in goods), 1523*

	No	£40	£50–99	£100–149	£150–199	£200–249	£250–299	£300+	Highest	Total	Median
Inner Temple	18	6	6	1		3	1	1	£300	£ 1925	£107
Middle Temple	22	7	10	3	1		1		£250	£ 1594	£ 72
Lincoln's Inn	25	10	10	3		1		1	£666	£ 2162	£ 86
Gray's Inn	12	3	6	1	1			1	£333	£ 1167	£ 97
Total: Inns of Court	77	26	32	8	2	4	2	3	£666	£ 6848	£ 89
Inns of Chancery	30	13	11	3	1	2			£200	£ 2048	£ 68
King's Bench Clerks	7*	1	5	1					£100	£ 410	£ 59
Common Pleas Clerks	15	5	5	1		3		1	£400	£ 1645	£110
Total: Court Clerks	22*	6	10	2		3		1	£400	£ 2055	£ 93
King's Bench Justices	3					1		2	£666	£ 1266	£422
Common Pleas Justices	4					1		3	£433	£ 1339	£335
Barons of the Exchequer	3†					2		1	£400	£ 800	£267
Serjeants	5§			2		2	1		£250	£ 883	£177
Attorney-General	1							1	£500	£ 500	£500
Total: Justices etc.	16†§			2		6	1	7	£666	£ 4788	£299
Grand Total	145	45	53	15	3	15	3	11	£666	£15739	£109

* plus one clerk assessed in lands at £82
† plus one baron assessed in lands at £200
§ plus five serjeants assessed in lands or lands and fees, two at £160, one each at £140, £106 and £100

when legal fees were beginning to be quite different under the impact of inflation. Taxation records are subject to an opposite distortion. In November 1523, in anticipation of the first instalment of the recently granted parliamentary subsidy – payable on income from lands and fees or the capital value of goods, whichever was more favourable to the crown – 152 Westminster lawyers were assessed at a uniform five per cent.[78] Four serjeants were assessed on capital of between £100 and £250, indicating that they were worth less in terms of income; the two assessed on 'lands and fees' were put at £160; and the three rated on land only averaged £115. Four years later More was assessed at a mere £340 a year in lands and fees although by then he was obviously earning more than the alleged £400 of 1517.[79] It has, however, been argued that the 1523 assessment was the most careful before the Civil War; certainly in the case of the peers an attempt was made to return figures which bore some relation to reality.[80] If that is true of the lawyers, and we allow an underassessment of only fifty per cent, not the several hundred per cent of later days, we again reach the £200/£300 bracket. The whole matter is highly conjectural, but it seems possible that the income of a serjeant was about the more conservative of the figures derived from Ayscough's claim, ± £300.[81]

V

If estimates of a lawyer's income in Kebell's day can be at best only a partially informed guess, this is even more true of any comparison with wealth elsewhere in the community. The most that can be offered is a contribution to the problem. This has two parts, income and capital. On income, the clearest comparison is with the church, where fewer than one quarter of parochial benefices had in excess of £15 a year.[82] This takes no account of pluralism or of any private fortune which a cleric might have, but it is enough to explain the occasional desertion from a prospective career in the church to the

78. Table G. *Inner Temple Records*, i. 455–66. This table omits the clerks of the exchequer, some of whom were not lawyers, and the crier of the king's bench. The chancery is not included in the assessment. The lower limit for assessment was £40.
79. Elton, *Studies*, i. 138–9.
80. Miller, *Bull. Institute of Hist. Research* 28. 23–31.
81. A lawyer also received presents. Kingsmill – 40s. from Magdalen College when made serjeant: Emden, *Biographical Register of Oxford to 1500*, ii. 1074; William Rudhale – 26s. 8d. from Worcester Priory 'toward his charges when he was made seriaunt of the coyff': *Journal of Prior More*, 135.
82. P. Heath, *The English Parish Clergy on the Eve of the Reformation* (1969), 173.

law; John Kingsmill who deserted Oxford for the Middle Temple, earned the epithet 'costly', became J.C.P. and a friend of Edmund Dudley.[83] To judge by the *Valor Ecclesiasticus*, a lawyer might well earn more than the total revenue of many of the abbeys which employed him.[84] The comparison with the higher clergy is, of course, quite different. A successful pluralist archdeacon who had given good service to the crown might be in receipt of £1,000 a year.[85] The majority of episcopal incomes were even higher. The wealthiest see was Winchester, valued in 1536 at £3,885, and even allowing for the poor Welsh dioceses, the average episcopal income was £1,300.[86] Higher clerics certainly had greater overheads than lawyers, but it is extremely unlikely that even the most prominent lawyers achieved anything like this level. A cryptic document, probably concerning loans to the king in the 1523 financial crisis, gives sums of £200 to £1,000 for the bishops but £100 for the recorder of London and the king's solicitor, the same for Serjeant John Port, 100 marks each for two attorneys and £200 for the clerk of the crown in the king's bench.[87] In the light of the comparison, the hostility of common lawyers towards churchmen in Henry VIII's reign takes added point.

A comparison with higher clerics explains the envy of the church by the lawyers; comparison with landed incomes shows why men went into law. Even if the 1523–5 taxation cannot be relied on for absolute figures, it can show the relative position. It has been demonstrated that in Sussex the median assessment for an esquire was £50 in lands and fees; the one Westminster lawyer below the coif who was assessed on lands and fees was John Lucas, who came from nearby Kent, and he was rated at £82.[88] The median for five serjeants in lands and fees was £133 which, in Sussex, would have placed them well up with the knights.[89] Most lawyers, however, were assessed in 1523 in goods, not lands.[90] The mean for judges was £375, which was well above the average for all landed men, except peers. Fineux C.J.K.B. was assessed at £666, Brudenell C.J.C.P. at £433, Fitzjames C.B.Ex. at

83. Emden, *Biographical Register of Oxford to 1500*, ii. 1074; *Plumpton Correspondence*, 135.
84. The average revenue of houses suppressed in 1536 was £97. 80% of monasteries enjoyed less than £300 a year.
85. e.g. Thomas Magnus: A. G. Dickens, *The English Reformation* (1964), 44.
86. Hoskins, *Age of Plunder*, p. 127.
87. *L. and P.*, iii. 2483(2).
88. J. Cornwall, 'The early Tudor gentry', in *Econ. Hist. Rev.*, 2 ser., 17 (1965), 462; for Lucas, see *L. and P.*, iv. 214, 6125; *Inner Temple Records*, i. 462.
89. *ibid.*, i. 465–6.
90. See Table G.

£400, and the attorney-general at £500. It is probable, indeed, that these leading lawyers commanded means comparable to those of the lesser nobles. Lord Willoughby was assessed at 1,000 marks in land because that figure was 'better than the value of his moveable goodes'; Fineux, assessed at 1,000 marks in goods, clearly had the higher standard of living.[91] Lower in the scale the picture is equally impressive. Of 129 barristers, attorneys and court clerks rated in 1523 at £40 or more in goods, the median was £85; for Sussex gentry assessed on goods it was £40 and for esquires £110.[92] What little we know of actual, rather than assessment incomes corroborates this story. The small sample of feodary surveys probably gets as near as possible to statistics of real wealth. The median for esquires and gentlemen in the reign of Henry VIII was £64, for knights, £204.[93] Dymmock's hypothetical income of £60+ would thus have put an apprentice firmly in the ranks of the prosperous gentry; a puisne judge at £250, and still more a serjeant, was the equal of many a knight. Even a modest attorney could earn £5 a year, which was the accepted standard for a yeoman or estate bailiff – twopence a day, plus perquisites.[94] It is small wonder that the gentry put their sons to the law.

Comparison with merchant incomes is much less simple. Where a merchant had bought land, a figure can be suggested. Thus Sir Geoffrey Boleyn, former lord mayor of London, died in 1463 with rents valued at £115, an income well within a serjeant's reach.[95] In the 1436 tax assessment, the aldermen of London averaged £54 a year from land, where Alexander Anne, the newly appointed recorder, had £44.[96] But this takes no account of income from trade, which occupied half the capital of the wealthiest merchants and a much higher proportion with the lesser men who could not afford to withdraw amounts from stock to invest in land.[97] Hence any assessment of mercantile wealth must be made in terms of capital, not income. Merchant capital could easily surpass the wealthiest members of the legal profession, as Fortescue implied in *De Laudibus*.[98] Sir Geoffrey Boleyn was possibly worth £2,000 in money and plate, over and

91. Miller, *Bull. Institute Hist. Research* 28. 25.
92. Cornwall, *Econ. Hist. Rev.*, 2 ser., 17. 465.
93. *ibid.*, 463.
94. John Fortescue, *The Governance of England*, ed. C. Plummer (1885), 13; *Letters and Accounts of William Brereton*, ed. E. W. Ives, Lancashire and Cheshire Rec. Soc. 116 (1977), 73–4.
95. Thrupp, *Merchant Class*, 128.
96. *ibid.*, 378–86.
97. *ibid.*, 127.
98. Fortescue, *De Laudibus*, 128–31.

above his lands; Thomas Kebell was worth £796.[99] Not that Boleyn was typical. In the 1523 subsidy anticipation the total wealth of those lawyers who were assessed was £15,739 and the individual average £109; with the judges and serjeants omitted the figures are £10,951 and the average £85.[100] There were plenty of merchants worth less than that. In 1534, John Johnson began trading at Calais with £55, and in the fifteenth century a young merchant's portion was generally between £20 and £200.[101] In 1474, one third of the livery of the Mercers' Company was said to be worth only between £66 and £100.[102] Even at the end of life many merchants were relatively modestly endowed; a quarter left less than £100 and the median was £300.[103] But the key point is that there was an elite fifteen to twenty per cent of London merchants like Boleyn worth £1,000 and more, and this the lawyers could not match.[104] In the provinces the position varied from town to town. In Nottingham in 1523, only fourteen men were assessed at more than £20 in goods and the highest at only £100.[105] The recorder could well have been wealthier than most, perhaps all, the aldermen; certainly the visiting justices of assize would have been. However, in Coventry, Leicester and other towns in 1523, a few individuals were much more substantial, and the same was true of the occasional great clothier; the widow and daughters of Thomas Springe of Lavenham were assessed at £1,333 6s. 8d. in goods and his son at £200 in land.[106] Such men, along with the London elite, really were, in Fortescue's phrase, 'richer than all the justices of the realm'.

The conclusion to be drawn must be that the law offered the best chances for an acceptable level of success, but that the glittering prizes lay elsewhere. By the simple test of maximum profit, the bishops and the London aldermen outstripped the judges, perhaps by more than one hundred per cent. But neither church nor commerce offered as much to the majority as the law did. Nor was potential gross income all that mattered. When it came to disposable wealth, a lawyer could

99. Thrupp, *Merchant Class*, 128; see below, p. 447.
100. See Table G.
101. B. Winchester, *Tudor Family Portrait* (1955), 22; Thrupp, *Merchant Class*, 103.
102. *ibid.*, 108.
103. *ibid.*, 109.
104. *ibid.*, 110; Hoskins, *Age of Plunder*, 38. In 1522 45 individuals, perhaps 0.5% of London taxpayers.
105. *Records of the Borough of Nottingham*. iii. 162–81.
106. W. G. Hoskins, 'English provincial towns in the early sixteenth century', *Trans. Royal Hist. Soc.*, 5 ser., 6 (1956), 6–7; *Age of Plunder*, 39–40.

easily outclass a cleric or merchant with larger nominal receipts. A minimum of overheads (no liability for staff or the upkeep of properties so costly to the cleric), and no requirement to plough profits back into trade, probably gave the lawyer the edge in free capital; certainly merchants' sons become lawyers far more commonly than the reverse. Money was not the whole story either. Celibacy was enough to dissuade a family from sending its eldest son into the church, and there was no guarantee that a younger son in orders would be more interested in advancing his nephews than in the religious and educational interests which so many of the leading clergy developed. As for trade, this was hardly a possibility for an elder son of a landed family, requiring as it did continued residence in London, at least in the early years, and, for anyone seeking to join the aldermanic oligarchy, assiduous attention to city affairs. The law, on the other hand, never separated a man from his roots; if marriage or the purchase of land took him away, this was a migration accepted among the gentry; the legal year was planned in the expectation that the lawyer would be required on his estate in the spring and at harvest; what is more, he relied professionally on clients from his own home community. In other words, in addition to significant opportunities to make money, a career in law was congruent with the interests of a landed family in a way which the potentially more lucrative opportunities of the church and the city were not.

15

THE REWARDS OF THE PROFESSION: THE ESTATES OF THOMAS KEBELL

In fifteenth-century England, success and security were measured in one commodity – land. Coin, plate and jewels were wealth, but land was the gilt-edged investment, safe, enduring and the clearest blazon of gentility. Supply, however fell far below the demand. Much was in the dead hands of the crown, the church and the corporations, and a good deal more was subject to entail. As for demand, established landowners were always anxious to add to estates where possible, but even more vigorous competitors were younger sons of the gentry and wealthy men of humble origin. The first, deprived by primogeniture of any adequate inheritance, needed land to survive, while the second sought it as the accolade of respectability. For some, marriage with an heiress brought the land they sought – typical of these landed gentry by courtesy of their wives was Walter Kebell the elder; others turned to trade or, as Walter's youngest son Thomas did, to the law for the money to purchase an estate. Many indeed were lucky in both marriage and business but not Thomas Kebell; with one vital exception all his property was purchased with the profits of his profession.

I

By the end of his life, Serjeant Kebell owned property in some twenty villages in Leicestershire and in Leicester itself. He had also begun to look for investments elsewhere, and after his death the crown made enquiries for property he might have held in Derby, Nottingham, Rutland, Northampton, Warwick and Stafford, as well as the automatic investigation in Leicestershire.[1] Only the record of this last remains, and it seems unlikely that Kebell had, at the time of his death, acquired much of a footing outside his native shire.[2] There, however, his property was considerable and spread over a wide area.

1. *Cal. Fine Rolls, 1485–1509*, 650, 692, 720. The Leicestershire return is calendared in *Cal. inquisitions post mortem*, ii. 497.
2. See below, pp. 339–42.

+ Land occupied by Thomas Kebell
⊙ Land occupied by the Kebells of Rearsby
0 15 km
0 10 miles
NOTTINGHAMSHIRE
DERBYSHIRE
Plungar
Harby
Stathern
Hose
Eastwell
Scalford
Burton on the Wolds
Saxelby
Loughborough
Shepshed
Melton Mowbray
Barrow on Soar
Sileby
Rotherby
Kirby Bellars
Ashby de la Zouche
Ratcliffe on Wreake
Thrussington
Rearsby
Cossington
Syston
Queniborough
Barsby
RUTLAND
Thurmaston
Barkby
Cold Overton
Birstall
Thorpe
Belgrave
Hamilton
Congerstone
Humberstone
Scraptoft
Leicester
Evington
Billesdon
Market Bosworth
Kirby Muxloe
Little Stretton
Knighton
Norton
Great Stretton
Illston
Potters Marston
LEICESTERSHIRE
Hinckley
Stoney Stanton
Little Ashby
Lubbenham
Market Harborough
Lutterworth
WARWICKSHIRE
NORTHAMPTONSHIRE

Fig. 3. Map of the Kebell family properties

A good portion of Thomas Kebell's property had formerly belonged to the Hotoft family, although he did not obtain this all at once or in the same way. The Hotofts were related to the Kebells via Thomas' mother, but although he referred to them as his cousins the common ancestor was his great-great-grandfather.[3] The Hotofts had been prominent in the upper ranks of Leicester society during much of the fourteenth and fifteenth centuries, but by the time that Edward IV won the throne the family was nearing extinction.[4] The last survivors were two brothers, Richard, the elder, who held the family estates, and Thomas his heir.[5] Richard had had a daughter, Joan, and in 1455 the family estates had been settled on her and her husband, John Staunton, but Joan had died without children.[6] Thus, when Richard died in 1467, the inheritance, including Humberstone, passed to Thomas, and on his death in 1473 was broken up according to various ancient family settlements, one of which even brought John Kebell some property; none, of course, reached his younger brother.[7]

Although not benefitting under any entail, Thomas Kebell received his first Hotoft property as a gift, a bequest from Richard Hotoft, although he had to fight a lawsuit before his title was established. After the death of his daughter, Richard Hotoft had decided to use the unsettled portion of his estate in and around Great Stretton to provide for a priest to pray for his soul. He died, however, before his will could be drawn up, and a dispute over the words uttered on his death-bed brought the parties to court.

There were two claimants, Thomas Hotoft and Thomas Kebell, and each sued Richard Hewitt and William Greenham, the feoffees of the former owner. Kebell began his suit in the autumn and winter of 1467–8, soon after Richard Hotoft's death, with a bill of complain to Robert Stillington, bishop of Bath and Wells, the lord chancellor.[8] Kebell alleged that, in Richard Hewitt's presence, Richard Hotoft had 'willed and required' his feoffees to transfer to Kebell and his heirs for ever, property in Great Stretton, Queniborough, Barkby, Illston, Evington, Scraptoft and Belgrave amounting to eight messuages, fourteen tofts and a close, thirty-five carucates, six acres

3. Farnham, *Medieval Pedigrees*, 38.
4. Wedgwood, *Biographies*.
5. Farnham, *Medieval Pedigrees*, 38.
6. Leicestershire Record Office, 5D33, Ms. Pedigrees – 'Humberstone', quoting two fines of Mich. 34 Henry VI (1455).
7. Hotoft pursued a common pleas action up to and including Easter term 1467: CP40/821 m. 206d; Thomas died 5 Apr. 1473; see above, p. 33.
8. C1/42/89–92. Stillington was appointed chancellor 20 Jun. 1467; the latest document in the file is dated 13 May 1468.

of land, £11 15s. 2½d. in rent and half the advowson of a chantry at Stretton, in all a sizeable estate.[9] This gift, Kebell asserted, was to enable him and his heirs to provide a priest to say mass daily for the soul of Richard Hotoft at an altar of the Trinity and Our Lady in Humberstone Church. Hewitt and Greenham, however, had refused to enfeoff Kebell at the instigation of Thomas Hotoft, the deceased's brother, who had, in addition, refused to surrender important deeds concerning the estate. Summoned to answer, Hewitt, Greenham and Hotoft put forward a different version of the testator's intentions. What Richard had declared was that Kebell should establish a chantry and that the lands which Hewitt and Greenham held should be used to endow it. Provided the court required from Kebell security to do this, they would surrender the land. Kebell retorted that this was never Hotoft's intention. He had asked Kebell to settle the land under strict penalties should any lessee refuse to pay the priest, but he had never asked Thomas to amortise the land. Thus, according to the defendants, Hotoft had intended to endow a chantry, but according to the plaintiff, to make him a gift on the understanding that he employed a priest to say the necessary services. The 'bayle and profett' which Kebell would receive over the cost of the priest, was, so he asserted, the crux of the dispute.

While Kebell was engaged against Hewitt, Greenham and Thomas Hotoft, Hotoft began a chancery suit against the other two. Styling himself Thomas Hotoft, brother and heir to Richard Hotoft esquire, he asserted that Richard, on his death-bed, had bequeathed his land to him.[10] But the spectacle of the brother attempting to rescue the family from a rapacious lawyer stands little scrutiny. With no heir to succeed, Thomas Hotoft was trying to turn his estates into cash. He had a buyer ready in the person of Joan Hotoft's former husband. Having lost the reversion of Richard's lands on her death, John Staunton was in the market for whatever Thomas Hotoft could salvage from the confusion of Richard's legacies, and John's brother, Thomas Staunton, and another relative, Robert Staunton, came forward to assist Thomas Hotoft in his suit.[11] Whether the feoffees Hewitt and Greenham were originally involved is not clear. Their initial concern may simply have been to hand over responsibility to

9. As elsewhere in this chapter, acreages etc. must be taken as notional.
10. C1/40/290.
11. C1/58/322; *Cal. Close Rolls, 1468–76*, 931. The Stauntons were pledges for the complainant.

the court by refusing both Kebell and Hotoft, but there is no doubt where their later sympathies lay, or, perhaps, with Hotoft threatening further litigation, their self-interest. Hotoft's bill was not proceeded with. Instead, on 3 May 1468, Hewitt and Greenham interrupted chancery to report a radical change in their dispute with Kebell.[12] The case was not down for hearing until the following November, but, as they declared, after the court had set this date, it came 'to there notice and knolege' (how, they did not say) that the original deed by which they held the land specified that they should follow Richard's wishes only if declared in a written will, but that otherwise they should enfeoff his right heir, that is, of course, brother Thomas. Thus, what Richard had or had not said on his death-bed was quite immaterial; Thomas Hotoft had an indisputable title.

The opportune appearance of a long-forgotten indenture invites scepticism, but forgery seems unlikely. Hewitt, Greenham and Thomas Hotoft had all based their arguments on Richard's verbal will, a curious proceeding if all or any were contemplating a faked deed specifying a written will. More probably, an obsolete document – perhaps an uncancelled previous enfeoffment – had been discovered among the deeds Thomas Hotoft was holding, or by the feoffees, and pressed into service. Whether it was as conclusive as claimed is, however, dubious, for it was used, not to refute Kebell, but to excuse a *coup de main* by Thomas Hotoft. Tired of their repeated refusals to perform this indenture, he had, Hewitt and Greenham reported, taken the law into his own hand, ousted them from possession and installed Thomas Staunton. None of this was their fault: indeed they are at pains to show that their own conduct has been exemplary. They could not 'in law nor conscyens' make an estate according to Kebell's version of Richard Hotoft's nuncupative will (they have quietly dropped their own rival version) but neither have they surrendered the estate to Hotoft, for fear of the court's displeasure. Yet the inference is clear; Hotoft was quite justified in his action. And as if to forestall the suspicion that this was all a device to put Hotoft in possession and extricate themselves from trouble, they declare 'for trowthe that at the tyme of the makyng of theyre seyd answer nor longe tyme aftyr, they vndyrstod nott truely nor remembryd eny syche feffement made to thym by wryttyng apon condition as in the seyd deyd hys specifyed'.

Even at this distance of time their story rings false. From Kebell's

12. C1/42/89.

original bill to their informing chancery of the long forgotten indenture was, at the very most, two law terms. In this short time Hewitt, Greenham and Hotoft had reached an issue with Kebell over Richard Hotoft's last wishes and been awarded a date for trial; Thomas Hotoft had entered a counter plea; a 'long time after' this the indenture had been found and then Thomas Hotoft had had to request his inheritance 'divers times'! What seems much more probable is that it was proving difficult to maintain their version of Richard Hotoft's will. A revised brief with, if possible, Thomas Hotoft in actual possession offered better chance of success. At this point our evidence comes to an end and we do not know what the court said about this new plea. Clearly the manoeuvre did not work, for Kebell certainly established his claim to a great part of the estate, and without any requirement to found a chantry. The echo of victory is still heard forty years later when the serjeant recorded with satisfaction in his own will – fully declared in writing – that:

> my good cousin Richard Hotoft gavẽ to me and to mine heirs his lands and tenements in Much Stretton and Little Stretton and divers other places to the intent that I should for ever keep his Obit yearly and also find a priest yearly and perpetually to say divine service daily for his soul . . . And that I should bind the said land as straightly and surely as I could or might, not Amortising it.

II

Acquiring the valuable Stretton estate at the age of thirty was a stroke of fortune which entirely changed the status of Thomas Kebell; no longer the aspiring son of a parvenu, he had acres of his own. Thereafter the tale of his land purchases is the tale of his growing success in the law. By the middle of the 1470s Kebell was in high favour with his patron, established in practice, appointed to the Leicestershire commission of the peace, and his arrival had been announced by the call to read for the second time at the Inner Temple. Thus it is no surprise that the year 1476 or 1477 saw Kebell acquiring as his country seat the house and manor of Humberstone, a village two miles to the east of Leicester and only five miles south of Rearsby where he had been born.[13] In making his first purchase of land so near to his old home, Kebell was not simply influenced by having land in Leicestershire already; he was following the pattern of the great majority of his

13. Humberstone has now been engulfed by the expansion of Leicester.

fellow lawyers, who turned in their search for landed estates to their home territory. In part this was only natural – it was from their own acquaintances that they would hear most easily of land coming on the market – but it also reflected the intense provincialism of English life; lawyers chose their inns on the basis of local affiliations, looked to their neighbours for work, and sought to return as established landowners to the society to which they belonged.

Humberstone, like Kebell's property in Stretton, had originally been part of the Hotoft estate; indeed, his cousin and benefactor, Richard, had made the manor his home. But for this purchase the lawyer had to enter the open market. The manor had passed on Richard's death to his brother Thomas and thence, by sale, to John Staunton – the fate intended for Stretton. It was only on Staunton's death without heirs that Kebell was able to buy. The price was four hundred marks, £266 13s. 4d.[14] Such a figure is some indication of the capital which Kebell had accumulated, and it was the possession of ready money of this order which gave lawyers such an edge when land was for sale. The merchant's money was locked up in enterprise, the landowner might need to pay by instalments; when a lawyer might, like one of Kebell's colleagues, have £800 in the safe keeping of one monastery, raising a substantial sum in cash presented no difficulty.[15] The purchase of Humberstone also shows that Thomas Kebell had an eye for a good investment.[16] The net annual yield from the property was put at forty marks, so that Kebell was obtaining a ten per cent return, double the common rate. The price Kebell paid was, indeed, even lower than the 450 marks which Staunton had paid only a few years before, and that price was modest enough. Kebell's obvious bargain is probably explained by a lawsuit begun by Jane, John Staunton's second wife, after her husband's death. According to Jane, John had used part of her jointure to purchase Humberstone, promising to settle it on the two of them and their heirs. On John's death, however, his brother Thomas Staunton had stepped in and disposed of the land to Kebell. The lawyer has often been accused of speculating in dubious titles – 'al was fee simple to him in effect' – and it may be that Kebell saved fifty marks by accepting the risk that Jane would win the suit for her jointure.

14. C1/58/322.
15. John Vavasour J.C.P.: PROB11/15 f. 128; *Testamenta Eboracensia*, iv. 91. William Donington of Lincoln's Inn (d. 1485) had £100 in royals and £200 in gold: PROB11/7 f. 126.
16. C1/58/322.

Where Kebell lived before Humberstone is uncertain; afterwards he was described as 'late of Ashby de la Zouche', so he probably spent his time, when not in London, in the household of Lord Hastings.[17] But once squire of Humberstone he took up residence there in the large manor house.[18] Already his two properties formed a sizeable estate, and Kebell soon set about adding to it. Between 1481 and 1485, Kebell was again able to purchase land from the Staunton family (from Thomas Staunton's nephew): the manor and advowson of Congerstone, a village twenty miles to the west of Humberstone, beyond Market Bosworth.[19] About the same time the lawyer acquired another outlying property, five messuages and seven virgates at Overton in the east of the county.[20] The third largest purchase in the early 1480s was nearer Humberstone. It comprised the manor of Thrussington and six messuages, a cottage, two tofts, sixteen virgates and four bovates of land and meadow and a rent of 27s. 6d., plus an additional messuage and toft in Ratcliffe on Wreke.[21] It also made Thomas his brother's overlord, for John Kebell had a sizeable holding in Thrussington.[22]

The purchase of Congerstone, Overton and Thrussington in the space of a very few years is clearly a reflection of increasing prosperity. In 1478 Kebell was retained by the duchy of Lancaster and by 1481 his opinions begin to be noticed by the year books, although he was still only an apprentice. During the next few years, however, there comes a lull in Kebell's investment. This could possibly reflect loss of income following the eclipse of the Hastings fortunes. On the other hand, in the year of Lord William's murder, Kebell had become attorney-general for the duchy of Lancaster, and the lull may reflect only a sluggish market or the need to absorb recent purchases and build up capital. Whatever the reason, with promotion to serjeant, Kebell was soon buying again. In December 1489 he bought a messuage, two tofts and a croft and twelve bovates of land at Hose in the

17. c67/52 m. 27.
18. He probably also had a house on the Stretton estate.
19. *Cal. inquisitions post mortem*, ii. 497. The nephew, Edmund Churche, entered the Staunton lands in 1481: *Cal. Fine Rolls 1471–85*, 713. Kebell certainly held the estate before August 1485, because William Catesby and John Kebell were among the feoffees.
20. *Cal. inquisitions post mortem*, ii. 497. The purchase took place before August 1485, as John Kebell was a feoffee.
21. *ibid.*, ii. 497. The purchase took place before the autumn of 1484 when Thomas Powtrell, one of the feoffees, died: *Cal. Fine Rolls, 1471–65*, 830.
22. *Cal. inquisitions post mortem*, i. 164.

north of the county.[23] Only a few months later, in April 1490, he was again in the market, this time for a holding in Shepshed, a village near Loughborough.[24] In 1492, if no earlier, Kebell occupied, so the subsidy of that year records, property in the town of Leicester, in the Swine Market.[25] In August of the same year, the serjeant agreed with Henry, Lord Grey of Codnor, and his wife for the purchase of the manor of Stanton by Sapcote in the south of the county, near to Hinckley.[26] Lord Grey had no direct legitimate heirs and he was disposing of much of his land for cash – other purchasers were to include Sir Reynold Bray, the king's councillor, and later Henry VII himself – and with the manor were 180 acres of land and a half interest in 400 more.[27] That Thomas Kebell too was given a chance to buy some of Grey's land may have been yet another dividend from the Hastings connection: Henry Grey had been one of the most prominent of Lord William's retinue.[28]

1489 had ushered in the period, lasting to the end of 1495, during which, as we have seen, Kebell enjoyed particular advantages among the leading lawyers of the day, freedom from assize duties and from the restrictions of royal retainer. The consequences of this half-decade of near monopoly are to be seen in 1495 and 1496 when Kebell's land purchases reached their peak. The first transactions took place in 1495 when Thomas Kebell recovered from the Willoughby family of Wollaton their holding in Hamilton and Barkby Thorpe, villages only a mile or two from Humberstone – 400 acres of land, forty of meadow and 500 of pasture, plus a rent of £8, the whole valued at £28 6s. per annum.[29] In the Trinity term of 1496, the serjeant was party to two more contracts. One secured the manor of Eastwell and six messuages, ten tofts and 527 acres of arable, meadow, pasture and wood in Eastwell and the nearby villages of Scalford and Kirby Bellars.[30] The second purchase brought the lawyer eight houses and 110 acres in Leicester and the adjoining village of Belgrave.[31] In the four years of life that remained to him, the serjeant bought no more land, but the successes of 1495 and 1496 were a fitting climax to a

23. *Cal. Close Rolls. 1485–1500*, 450.
24. Leicestershire Record Offices, 5D33, Ms. Pedigrees – 'Shepshed', quoting Hastings Mss.
25. Bateson, *Leicester*, ii. 333.
26. *Hastings Mss.*, i. 54–5; CP25(1) 126/80/11.
27. *Cal. Close Rolls, 1485–1500*, 842; see above, p. 102.
28. Dunham, 'Indentured retainers', 133.
29. *Cal. inquisitions post mostem*, ii. 497.
30. CP25(1) 126/80/22.
31. *ibid.*, 80/23.

lifetime during which good fortune, useful connections, and an eye for the market, but above all success in the law, had turned the younger son of an estate steward into a man of property.

III

The record of Thomas Kebell's investment in land is contained in the dispassionate chronicle of deeds and conveyances, but on the reasons for any transaction the documents are silent. Circumstantial evidence, however, can be made to yield at least something. It seems clear, in the first place, that Kebell was very ready to speculate. This has already been seen in his purchase of Humberstone at a low price but with the risk of litigation, and is noticeable on a number of other occasions. In 1489 Kebell obtained a licence to purchase from William Elton and his wife an estate in Stathern, Harby and Plungar in the north of Leicestershire together with an associated holding in Derbyshire.[32] Nothing further was done about this at the time, but in March 1494 Kebell and Elton were able to make a contract.[33] Elton and his wife Alice agreed that should they die without heirs, the property (originally the fortune of Alice's deceased sister) should be sold to Kebell for twenty marks. The estate ran into several hundred acres plus a moiety of some hundreds more, and £13 6s. 8d. scarcely seems a market price. But quite clearly Kebell was interested in a long-term profit. He laid out 24s. 8d. for the licence from the crown, plus the inevitable gratuities, and had, presumably, also had to pay William Elton for the option. Thomas himself did not see the return for this outlay; it was left to Walter to benefit from his father's foresight.[34]

The terms under which Kebell had bought Stanton from Lord Grey were more than a little speculative. The valuation which Grey agreed with Sir Reynold Bray was calculated on eighteen and a half years' purchase, that is, eighteen and a half times the annual return, and Bray paid in two instalments, a token in advance and the rest after the transfer of title.[35] The manor of Stanton, Kebell's purchase, had an annual value of £3. Assuming, therefore, that Grey sold his other lands at eighteen and a half years' purchase, the manor should have cost Kebell £55, or at the more usual rate of twenty years' purchase, £60. The serjeant, however, paid only £25 in cash, and agreed to pay

32. Farnham, *Village Notes*, ii. 358. 33. *Hastings Mss.*, i. 11.
34. C142/39/99. 35. *Cal. Close Rolls, 1485–1500*, 842.

the balance in the form of an annuity of £3 for the lives of Henry Grey and his wife.[36] Thus if either survived for more than a decade, Stanton would become a very expensive purchase. And the gamble paid off. Grey died in 1495 after less than three years, and although his wife survived him, she was dead before 1500.[37]

Thomas Kebell was always prepared to wait. He more than once persuaded a childless owner to realise the value of property by selling it to him while retaining a life tenancy. By allowing the vendor to keep possession Kebell was able to secure a property long before it would have come on the open market. The method was not, of course, peculiar or original, but it required a long purse and the ability to wait for the investment to pay. One example appears in Kebell's will, where he recorded that certain lands and tenements in Billesdon were occupied for life by Nicholas Temple and his wife but on their decease were to pass to him and his heirs.[38] Like the land in and around Stathern, the Billesdon property duly came to Walter. A similar arrangement was proposed in abortive negotiations which took place towards the end of Kebell's life. His objective was an estate in Milton and Marholm in the Soke of Peterborough, belonging to Robert Wittilbury, esquire – the very property which the London alderman, Sir William Fitzwilliam, was to purchase in 1502 and was later to be the head of the Fitzwilliam barony. If the serjeant's attempt to establish himself outside his home county had not broken down at a very late stage, history might speak of Kebell, not Fitzwilliam, of Milton.

The negotiations for Milton throw some further light on Kebell's business methods. The story came out in a chancery suit brought by his son against Robert Wittilbury.[39] Walter alleged, quite simply, that Wittilbury had sold to his father the manors of Milton and Marholm for 1,400 marks – nearly £950 – subject to the life interest of himself and his wife. Thomas had paid £300, but since his death Wittilbury had refused to complete, despite offers of the rest of the money. The defendant's story was more complex. He had, indeed, agreed to sell the reversion of the manors to Thomas Kebell, although for the sum of 1,100, not 1,400 marks – a discrepancy of £200 – but satisfactory terms for payment could not be arranged, and 'so no bargeyn conclu-

36. *Hastings Mss.*, i. 54.

37. G.E.C., *Peerage*, vi. 131. The death of Katharine, Lady Grey, can be presumed from the absence from Kebell's will and inquisition *post mortem* of any reference to an outstanding rent charge.

38. See Appendix A, p. 430.

39. C1/328/73–6.

did'. The negotiations had, however, clearly gone a long way. Indeed, Kebell's counsel had presented a draft agreement to Wittilbury's own lawyers to have clauses inserted guaranteeing his title for life and the payment of the full sum. John Mordaunt, king's serjeant, and Robert Constable, serjeant, had added the necessary changes for Wittilbury and had also attached to the draft a paper, in Mordaunt's handwriting, setting out more fully 'there mynde and councell'. But this paper had been 'embezzled' and without it Wittilbury would not proceed.

Walter Kebell, however, still possessed this original draft of the contract and Robert's own signature was on it, a most damaging document; some plausible explanation was vital. According to Wittilbury, the draft had not been signed by him during Kebell's lifetime. After the latter's death William Reynold, one of his servants, had come to Milton from Lady Mary Hastings, Kebell's executrix, bringing the original draft but not Mordaunt's opinion, 'wherwith . . . Robert was discontentid'. However he was at the time – so he claimed – 'sore seke . . . and in Jebardie of his life', and Reynold put pressure on him to sign. If Robert were to refuse, Reynold said, 'he durst not go ageyn to his seid lady'. The threat had the desired effect; 'for the seid ladys pleasur and her desire' Robert agreed to sign. Wittilbury was perfectly aware, despite any illness, of the stupidity of this, and he attempted to cover himself by saying to those present:

> I pray you all that here be present to bere record whate so ever shalbe seid heraft I wyll neuer agre that that seid papir wherto I wyll sett my hand is not nor shall not be accepted as my dede, mynde nor entent oneless he bryng forth the seid papir of reformacon wrytten with the hand of the seid Sir John Mordaunt.

Not unnaturally Walter denied this story; Robert had signed during Thomas Kebell's lifetime, there never had been a paper of Mordaunt's opinion, and Reynold had come asking for completion and offering payment. The depositions of the witnesses have, unfortunately, disappeared, but with all relevant information collected, the case went for trial in November 1503. It was heard by William Warham, bishop of London, the keeper of the great seal, and Walter Kebell, as a minor, was represented by his cousin, George Villiers of Ashby. The decree was pronounced on 16 November. Walter Kebell was to give up all claim to Milton and Marholm and Robert Wittilbury was to return to Walter one hundred marks which Thomas Kebell had paid him for implementing certain agreements which had not, in fact, been carried out.

At this distance the facts of the case and the reasons for the decision are hard to disentangle. It is not, however, difficult to discover why Wittilbury was intent upon breaking off negotiations after Kebell's death. He was busy selling to Alderman Fitzwilliam at the very time that Walter Kebell was suing him.[40] The obstacles to an agreement during the lifetime of the serjeant are less obvious. Certainly price could have been one of them. Fitzwilliam paid 1,200 marks, whereas Kebell had agreed, so Wittilbury said, to pay only 1,100, but there is no evidence that Fitzwilliam had made his bid during the serjeant's lifetime. The defendant's statements seem to suggest that payment was the root of the trouble. Had Kebell's heavy outlay in 1495 and 1496 depleted his capital? If his widow is to be believed, the serjeant should have had the money to complete the deal, but as some was locked up in loans and in debts due to him, he may have found it difficult to raise the sum at once.[41]

More significant for Kebell's business methods is the discrepancy between the £300 he was supposed to have paid and the £66 Wittilbury was ordered to repay. Does the £300 represent a premium to induce Wittilbury to sell and the £66 the portion of this which could be closely enough connected with the sale, for chancery to order repayment? Certainly both parties were in rough agreement that about 1,000 marks were outstanding; Wittilbury, asking 1,100, admitted finally to receiving one hundred marks, and the Kebells, offering 1,400, claimed to have paid 450. Of course, Wittilbury always denied having received the full £300, but as he was equally insistent on the apparent irrelevancy that his bargain with Kebell provided for his retaining any part payment plus the property should any part of the price not be paid, he clearly had something to hang on to. Was this more than the hundred marks he was eventually compelled to return? If so, then Kebell was clearly prepared to go a long way to get what he wanted. But the final impressions produced from the suit over Milton are not simply of Thomas Kebell's persistence but equally of his obstinacy and his taste for gambling. Holding out for the terms of settlement which he wished suggests the one, and the willingness to write off at least 100 marks and to make no provision for the Wittilbury negotiations in his will suggests the other.

In common with so many in that land-hungry age, Thomas Kebell

40. Finch, *Northamptonshire Families*, 101; *Cal. Close Rolls, 1500–9*, 263, 505, 584, 804.
41. C1/329/51.

had a voracious appetite for property. But it would be wrong to suggest that he bought without discrimination. Again the evidence is circumstantial, but it is clear enough. The second half of the fifteenth century had seen a change in the pattern of small and moderate lay estates in England.[42] In the preceding century the emphasis had been on fixed and customary rents and dues. By the later fifteenth century the profits were to be made, instead, from direct exploitation of the land, notably by sheep farming, and an estate organised to yield rents was not necessarily suited to this new development. Owners now wanted compact properties, to facilitate management and to make improvement possible, and improvement in Kebell's Leicestershire meant enclosure for sheep farming. Considerations of this sort seem to lie behind Kebell's choice of investment. He certainly concentrated on large properties or ones which complemented those he already had. Apart from a town house in Humberstone Gate Street in Leicester, he bought only one small, isolated holding, a messuage and eight acres at Barrow on Soar, near to Loughborough.[43] Most of his purchases were of some size or else were near to land he owned. He bought, for example, one virgate in Thrussington to add to the sixteen he had already, and his will records that he had purchased 'divers lands and tenements' in Stretton to augment the Hotoft legacy.[44] The large estate in Hamilton and Barkby Thorpe, bought in 1495, was adjacent to Humberstone, as was the purchase in Belgrave in 1496.[45]

The clearest indication of deliberate calculation in Kebell's purchases is to be found in his property dealing in north-west Leicestershire. There, acquisition of an estate in Hose and the start, in the same year, of negotiations with William Elton for land in the three neighbouring villages of Harby, Stathern and Plungar are obviously related. In 1496 Kebell increased his interests in the area by purchasing the nearby manor at Eastwell, plus associated holdings in Scalford and Kirby Bellars to the south.[46] Although he did not live to see the Elton property absorbed into his own, Kebell had assembled in the Vale of Belvoir a block of estates which augured well for future prosperity. The policy he pursued there – acquiring a nucleus, in this case at Hose, and gradually adding other property – may explain the

42. Finch, *Northamptonshire Families*, 165–7; cf. *ibid.*, 66–72.
43. *Cal. inquisitions post mortem*, ii. 497.
44. See Appendix A, p. 430.
45. There is some suggestion that Kebell was buying other land in Barkby and Barkby Thorpe in Mich. 1494: Farnham, *Village Notes*, i. 122–3.
46. See above, p. 338.

four large purchases which Kebell made in distant parts of the county where no considerations of estate consolidation can have applied – Shepshed, Congerstone, Stoney Stanton and Overton. Each of these was of a good size, worth possessing despite the distance from Humberstone, and each was capable, like Hose, of being the kernel of a group of properties sometime in the future. Some similar consideration must also have been behind Kebell's attempt to purchase Milton and Marholm.

Thomas Kebell also had an interest in certain other land, although details cannot easily be recovered. His will refers to a farm at Stretton on a relatively long lease; his inventory shows that he occupied grazing for five hundred head of sheep in Lubbenham, a village near Market Harborough.[47] He kept smaller flocks at Barsby, six miles north-east of Humberstone, and at Birstall, north of Leicester and across the river Soar from his Belgrave land. Another flock was grazed at Rearsby, presumably on pasture rented from his nephew George or his cousin Thomas Cotton. In 1485 Kebell also took an eighty-year lease of the manor of Potters Marston, near Stoney Stanton, from the chapter at Coventry.[48] Some of these rented properties fit naturally into the pattern of Kebell's other estates; the Stretton farm obviously did, Birstall was part of Belgrave, Rearsby was adjacent to Thrussington, and Potters Marston went with Stoney Stanton. In 1481, Thomas Kebell was holding some land in Queniborough, as did also his brother John, and their cousin Thomas Cotton; how long this continued is not known, but the village of Queniborough was, yet again, close to Kebell property, this time at Rearsby.[49] A similar calculation can be seen in the acquisition by the two brothers of Cossington Mill in 1479; Cossington lies in the heart of the 'Kebell' country.[50] Occasionally, however, there were exceptions. Barsby was too distant to be an adjunct to Humberstone, while, most curious of all, the farm at Lubbenham lay in an area of Leicestershire where the serjeant had no interests at all.

47. See Appendix A, p. 427 and B, p. 440.
48. E303/16 no. 146; the rent was 20 marks p.a. I owe this reference to the kindness of Dr C.C. Dyer. Kebell owned land in Stoney Stanton, but his inventory sites his flock in this area at Potters Marston. In the ensuing discussion it is assumed that Potters Marston and Stanton were one unit.
49. Farnham, *Village Notes*, iii. 332; when he died, John owned land in Queniborough: *Cal. inquisitions post mortem*, i. 164.
50. Leicestershire Record Office: 44'28/202, 203; cf. *ibid.*, 28/200.

IV

At his death in 1500, Thomas Kebell's property was considerable, gathered by steady investment of the profits of his law practice and chosen with an eye to the latest thinking in estate administration. This up-to-date approach can also be detected in the running of the estate. A good deal was leased, particularly the more distant portions – Congerstone, Shepshed, the fragment in Barrow on Soar, and the holdings in the north-west, presumably until William Elton's land could be taken over.[51] There were, however, some distant properties which were not rented out, where the advantages of direct exploitation must have outweighed the inconveniences of distance. Thus Kebell farmed Stoney Stanton, Barsby, Lubbenham and Cold Overton, although all were some way from Humberstone. The bulk of the estate, however, fell into three compact divisions, and these were farmed directly. The lands bequeathed by Richard Hotoft, together with nearby purchases which Kebell had made himself, formed one unit, farmed from Great Stretton. The second, and, since the acquisition of Hamilton and Barkby Thorpe, the largest block clustered around Humberstone and included the manor there, eight messuages, five tofts, eight virgates and 1,050 acres of land, plus a mill, all in close proximity. Here there were main farms at Humberstone and at Hamilton. Thrussington was the centre of the third group, which included Kebell's interests in Queniborough and Syston, and also the leasehold property at Rearsby where, however, there was a separate farm.

Of the staff which Thomas Kebell employed we have little evidence. At Humberstone he certainly lodged some agricultural workers under his own roof, but of the more responsible officers there is no direct information.[52] Kebell's will provided for a dozen employees but this number included his clerk and some domestics.[53] It is not, of course, to be expected that a lay estate of this size would have required the large staff engaged by monastic houses or great magnates; as Kebell himself remarked, the owner could do much of the work himself.[54] If the owner was a lawyer, then this was doubly likely. But although Thomas Kebell no doubt did on occasions act as his own steward, court-keeper, auditor, receiver or bailiff, his long

51. Judging by the occurrence of farm animals and implements in the inventory.
52. See Appendix B, p. 439.
53. See Appendix A, p. 427.
54. *Y.B.* Pas. 8 Hen. VII, p. 3 f. 11.

absences probably forced him to employ full-time supervisors, as the better-known Paston family did.[55] How many we cannot be sure. Walter Kebell certainly employed a separate bailiff at Hamilton, but there can be no assurance that this was so elsewhere, or that the father had a bailiff at Hamilton.[56] However, among the servants named in the serjeant's will, some probable estate officers can be picked out.

Thomas Turner was obviously Thomas Kebell's accountant, his auditor or receiver-general. The will records:

> Also, where Thomas Turner oweth me by obligation certain money, and also upon arrearages of another account £15 or more (which in the whole amounteth to more than 50 marks), I bequeath and release to him all the said debts except £20.

Surprisingly, in view of the bequest, Turner may not have been long in post. Kebell's previous receiver was a Derbyshire yeoman named Lawrence Liversegge, and at the time of the serjeant's death his account was still outstanding.[57] Of Turner, however, nothing is definitely known, although it seems probable that he was of a similar status to Liversegge. This is not the case with another legatee, William Smith. A Leicestershire landowner, though in a small way, he was lord of the manor of Withcote and had further holdings in Foxton and Glen Magna.[58] He was thus Kebell's neighbour, for Great Glen was the next village to Stretton Magna while Withcote is only three miles from Cold Overton. Smith also practised as an attorney, and may have been a member of Lincoln's Inn.[59] He served the second Lord Hastings and his wife as their personal attorney and probably also the abbey of Owston and the priory of Launde, and he acted as a feoffee for a number of Leicestershire men, particularly for Kebell.[60] He was a feoffee for the lawyer's property in Barrow on Soar, Shepshed, Stanton, Eastwell and the adjacent villages, and in Belgrave and Leicester.[61] But William Smith was clearly more than a trustee. Only Smith, of the score or so of Kebell's feoffees, benefitted under his will. William's name appears at the head of the lawyer's servants with the

55. *Paston Letters and Papers, passim*. Richard Calle, their agent, married into the family, though against stiff opposition. Cf. Margaret Paston's advice to her husband, 'in feyth it is tyme to crone yowr old officere': *ibid*., i. 275.
56. Leicestershire Record Office: DE73 – Register Book 1, f. 185.
57. CP40/961m. 465; 962 m. 464.
58. *Cal. inquisitions post mortem*, iii. 1165.
59. *Black Books*, i. 101; E315/51, William Smith *jurisperitus* in a plea *re* Kirby Bellars.
60. Huntington Library, HA16250, 31–2; *Cal. Patents Rolls, 1494–1509*, 156–7, 318, 518; *Cal. inquisitions post mortem*, i. 1222; ii. 334; iii. 386.
61. *ibid*., ii. 497.

largest money bequest, five marks, plus the gift of a horse. It is accompanied by a request 'to be loving to my soul and to my son' which must indicate that Smith was in a position to influence the religious provisions of the will and the running of the estate during Walter's minority. All this suggests that Smith was the most senior member of the serjeant's entourage, probably his steward.

Less is known of the next-named beneficiary, Richard Eyre. Eyre was a burgess of Leicester who was later to be associated with the foundation of Wyggeston Hospital.[62] He received forty shillings under Kebell's will, the same as the lawyer's clerk, William Reynold, whose name comes next, but no suggestion can be made about his role in the estate or household. He certainly was Kebell's servant, for the lawyer described him as such when coming to his aid in a local feud.[63] Following Reynold are two more names, Robert Bret and Robert Gaddisby. Their lesser bequest of two marks might suggest a post of bailiff but this is mere supposition. Gaddisby was, like Richard Eyre, a burgess of Leicester (though a less prominent one) and a participant in the foundation of Wyggeston Hospital.[64] Robert Bret belonged to that class of business agents or *hommes d'affaires* whose ubiquity in Yorkist and Tudor England is only matched by their obscurity.[65] He was, however, the second of his family to serve Thomas Kebell. A brother, or possibly a cousin, William Bret of Rotherby, died in 1496 having appointed 'my Maister Thomas Kebell' as the supervisor of his will.[66] Bret's wife was the sole executrix, and he looked for help to Kebell 'in whom my singular trust is above all others alive'. William Bret, like Smith, was both a small Leicestershire landowner and a lawyer/man of business; at one time he was undersheriff.[67] It was upon Bret, Smith, Turner and others like them that Thomas Kebell had to depend. They in turn could take encouragement from his success. Walter Kebell had once been no better than they were.

But the consolidation and organisation of an estate was only one

62. Thompson, *Wyggeston Hospital*, 689, 712; Bateson, *Leicester*, ii. 351, 372 *et passim*.
63. KB27/908/19 (I owe this reference to the kindness of Mr C. Whittick).
64. Bateson, *Leicester*, ii. 353, 370, 467; Thompson, *Wyggeston Hospital*, 689, 712.
65. Probably connected with John Bret of Rotherby: *Cal. Close Rolls, 1461–8*, 190. Robert Bret acted as a feoffee for William: *Cal. inquisitions post mortem*, i. 1222.
66. PROB11/10 ff. 254v, 255.
67. Of Rotherby: *Cal. inquisitions post mortem*, i. 1222; possibly eldest son of John Bret of Rotherby and nephew of William Bret, citizen and draper of London (d. 1494): PROB/10 ff. 152, 152v; under-sheriff of Leicestershire: CP40/878 m. 532.

half of the late fifteenth-century recipe for prosperity; the other was improvement, and in Kebell's Leicestershire this meant enclosure. The county was at the heart of open-field England and with little land still to be colonised and with much soil suitable either for arable or pasture, competition produced the near classic struggle between shepherd and ploughman. Modern study has more and more revealed the complexities of the problem: the regional peculiarities, the differing advantages which enclosure offered, the various pressures involved and the diverse social groups who stood to gain. But in pre-Reformation Leicestershire, enclosure was more often than not the work of the local squire, carried through in his own interest and with the intention of turning arable into grazing land.[68] It is often suggested that this commercial exploitation was more attractive to new purchasers, perhaps with a fresh attitude to profitability and free of ties with the villagers concerned; and lawyers have been accorded a prominent place among such hard businessmen. Such a thesis is incapable of statistical support, even less of proof. But while it may not be profitable to speculate on the economic mores of the legal profession, it is clear that certain lawyers did favour enclosure, Thomas Kebell among them.

The best-known support for enclosure came from the minor lawyer John Fitzherbert, whose *boke of husbandry* (1523) represented the most advanced agricultural thinking of the day.[69] Some lawyers enclosed on a large scale. Thomas Pigot of Whaddon, the Inner Temple lawyer (created serjeant in 1510 and king's serjeant in 1513) against whom Cardinal Wolsey made his famous threat to teach 'the new law of the star chamber', enclosed nearly twelve hundred acres in his home county of Buckingham.[70] Another offender was Robert Brudenell. Like Kebell and Pigot, both a serjeant (called in 1503) and a former member of the Inner Temple, Brudenell was returned by the enclosure commission of 1517 as having enclosed 250 acres in Leicestershire.[71] Of those barristers called to the coif on the same occasion as Kebell, one at least was an encloser, and apparently a brutal one. This was John Fisher of the Middle Temple. He enclosed the manor of Clopton in Cambridgeshire and converted the land to

68. Hoskins, *Essays*, 173.

69. See above, p. 2.

70. *L. and P.*, ii. App. 38; I.S. Leadam, *Domesday of Inclosures, 1517–18* (1897), i. 162–5, 212, 278, 472. Another Inner Templar interested in enclosure was William Danvers J.C.P.: MacNamara, *Danvers Family*, 177.

71. Leadam, *Domesday*, i. 230.

pasture. Friction with the villagers grew serious, and the whole dispute ended in the court of chancery.[72]

No such drama accompanied Kebell's known enclosure, and the loss of the 1517 reports for a great part of Leicestershire has left us with little detail. Quite clearly, however, he was responsible to a considerable extent for the depopulation of Great Stretton. Great Stretton is now a 'deserted village', one of the many in the county, and is marked only by its isolated parish church. The site is now pasture, whose unevenness is attributed locally not to the foundations of houses but to the military engineering of the ubiquitous Oliver Cromwell. Thomas Kebell's will refers to the 'enclosures and approvements' which he had made on his lands in Great and Little Stretton, and to the sheep pastured there. Part at least of these enclosures can be identified with the 178 acres which retained the name 'Keble's Close' until the end of the eighteenth century.[73] The serjeant's will may, indeed, imply more changes than this, but even the enclosure of 178 acres was a substantial blow to the village. The population was probably already low, but Kebell's action made complete clearance only a matter of time. Thomas Kebell's interest is also seen in his attempt to purchase enclosed grazing land. It was their enclosed value which caused him to bid for the future Fitzwilliam sheep walks at Milton and Marholm; Potters Marston, where he acquired some grazing, was already an extinct village.[74] Most striking of all was the purchase in 1495 of Hamilton. The village had been enclosed by the Willoughby family at least twenty years earlier and provided 500 acres of pasture alone.[75]

V

With this interest in enclosure, it is no surprise that Kebell was a very considerable sheep farmer, owning at the time of his death over 3,500 head.[76] This was no mean total, even in that age of large flocks. It could not compare with Judge Townshend's 9,335 or with the hordes of Spencer sheep later in the century, but it could rival the flocks of many a substantial monastery.[77] The details are recorded in Kebell's inventory but, with only this one count, the management of the flock

72. See above, pp. 104, 316.
73. V.C.H., *Leicestershire*, v. 109.
74. Hoskins, *Essays*, 74.
75. *ibid.*, 74–5.
76. The following discussion of Kebell's flock management is based on his inventory: Appendix B, pp. 440–2.
77. Finch, *Northamptonshire Families*, 171; R.H. Hilton, *The Economic Development*

is less than easy to reconstruct – and the suspicion that some figures have been 'rounded off' does not help.

Thomas Kebell kept breeding flocks at six properties, Lubbenham, Birstall, Rearsby, Hamilton, Humberstone and Stretton, about 1,060 ewes in all. The overall total of lambs was 720, a satisfactory though not remarkable ratio. However, there was considerable variation in the number of lambs between flocks. At Birstall and Lubbenham an equal number of ewes and lambs were declared, which suggests either guesswork, or that some of the previous year's crop, yet to be shorne, have been included. On the other hand, at Rearsby, 260 ewes were recorded with only 160 lambs while Humberstone was even worse, 280 against 160. If these last figures are reliable and can be taken as averages, Kebell's sheep produced a poorish 60 lambs per hundred ewes.[78]

The compactness of Kebell's estates allowed considerable movement of sheep. The ewes and lambs of Rearsby clearly formed part of the same flock as the 429 hogs of Thrussington. The absence of all lambs at Stretton and the excess at Hamilton suggests an interchange there, as does also the absence of wethers at Hamilton and Humberstone and the large number at Stretton. Indeed, there are other signs of flock specialisation. Nowhere were ewes, wethers and hogs all kept; Lubbenham and Stretton carried the first two, Hamilton, and Rearsby and Thrussington each had ewes and hogs, Potters Marston nothing but wethers and Barsby and Cold Overton only hogs. On occasion Kebell moved his sheep over some distance. Potters Marston, Barsby and Cold Overton, which supported no breeding sheep, were the outlying properties and must have been supplied from elsewhere or by purchase. Curiously enough, no rams are recorded. It would be tempting to suggest that the other branch of Kebell's family, or his cousin, Thomas Cotton, owner of the second Rearsby manor, provided them. Certainly, they must have been imported.[79]

It seems clear that Thomas Kebell was farming, in the traditional

of some Leicestershire Estates in the Fourteenth and Fifteenth centuries (1947), 67–8; R. Trow-Smith, *History of British Livestock Husbandry to 1700* (1957), 206; A. Savine, *The English Monasteries on the Eve of the Reformation* (Oxford, 1909), 178; K.J. Allison, 'Flock management in the sixteenth and seventeenth centuries', in *Economic Hist. Rev.*, 2 ser., 11 (1958), 99–101.

78. Cf. J.F.H. Thomas, *Sheep* (1945), 58–60, 75, 89; Finch, *Northamptonshire Families*, 42; Allison, 'Flock management', 102; *Sheep Breeding and Management* (H.M.S.O., 1956), 40.

79. Cf. the suggestion that the abbey of Leicester leased rams: Hilton, *Leicestershire Estates*, 68.

fashion, for wool and not for meat.[80] He kept a high proportion (sixty per cent) of wethers which produced higher-quality fleeces than the ewes and hogs. The sheep at Potters Marston are described as 429 wethers 'young and old' which suggests a mixed-age flock where wastage was made good by an intake of hogs. On this particular farm the intake in 1500 would seem to have been 50, for although shearing had taken place, only 379 fleeces are recorded, suggesting that the remainder had been shorne elsewhere. If fifty was the average annual intake in a flock of 429, then (allowing for some loss by accident and sickness) Kebell must have kept his sheep for at least eight years, an old practice soon to be abandoned by the more advanced farmers. There is, however, a suggestion that Kebell did accept some progressive ideas; his property included a rick of peas at Humberstone, additional feed for his sheep.

Valentine Mason, who drew up Kebell's inventory, viewed the estate in the middle of shearing time – indeed, he probably arrived when Thrussington had been finished and the shearers were due to begin at Rearsby. This again gives evidence of the centralising tendency on Kebell's estate, for the wool from Thrussington, Hamilton, Barsby and Humberstone had all been brought to the manor house for storage, 1,086 fleeces in all, worth £18 2s. Of the more distant properties whose flocks had been shorne, Potters Marston stored its own wool and Cold Overton seems to have sold it already.

Thomas Kebell's interest in sheep and enclosure is clear, but he was not the enemy of tillage that the sheep master was thought to be. Either he owned land which he could not enclose or he was content with a mixed arable and pasture economy. He had two ploughs and no fewer than twenty-nine draught animals. All but one couple of oxen were kept at Hamilton, where the enclosure of the village can hardly have left a demand for such a number of working beasts. This is clearly another way in which the estate was organised as a single unit. The draught animals for the properties around must have been grazed together on the enclosed pasture of Hamilton, which would clearly be more convenient, and furnish better nourishment, than dispersal on the various village commons. There is no reason to suspect that Kebell used his teams to plough his enclosed land for up-and-down

80. For the following see Trow-Smith, *Livestock Husbandry*; Thomas, *Sheep*; Finch, *Northamptonshire Families*; Allison, 'Flock management'; J. Thirsk, 'Farming techniques', in *Agrarian History of England and Wales, iv: 1500–1640*, ed. J. Thirsk (Cambridge, 1967), 187–91.

husbandry, and no surprise in the crops that he grew in the open fields – wheat, barley and peas. But even among his cattle Thomas Kebell's interest in grazing can be seen. It is sometimes said that these were kept, at this time, principally to breed the plough oxen. Certainly this was not so with Kebell; if he ran his sheep primarily for wool, he kept his cattle for meat. In all he had 158 beside the draught animals. The fifty-eight bullocks at Lubbenham and the forty steers at Thrussington were clearly stores, and so too the majority of the fifty-three steers and heifers at Potters Marston. The only cows were kept near to Humberstone, eighteen at Hamilton and nineteen at the manor itself, although the latter figures included some heifers to provide replacements among the breeding herd, and steers to be fattened for slaughter. Households like Humberstone consumed significant quantities of produce from the associated estate, and a good number of these beef animals must have ended on Kebell's table. The cows presumably supplied the house with cheese, butter and milk, although surprisingly, Kebell's goods included no cheese- or butter-making equipment; poultry was unimportant, represented only by three swans, three cranes and a pair of geese. The obvious market for surplus store cattle was at Leicester, where a thriving leather industry reinforced an urban commodity market. Lubbenham and Potters Marston, however, lay in the south of the county, which was just beginning its rise to prominence as a supplier of the London market, and Kebell may even have inherited some of his father's droving connections.[81]

When Burton, the Leicestershire antiquary, had assembled the story of Kebell's estates and noted that all trace of the lawyer's achievement had disappeared, he was moved to comment upon the transitory nature of human success:

> of all this great estate which he left to descend, there is not one part of it belonging to any that is either of the name or blood, but all sold, dispersed, gone – *sic dii voluere*.[82]

But to the historian the metaphysical deduction is less interesting than the historical; there is irony in Kebell's acquisition of property, but there is also significance. His steady purchases give a measure of the rewards of the law, circumstantial reconstruction suggests an awareness of the economic potentialities of his day – consolidation, management and enclosure – while his inventory suggests something of the

81. See above, pp. 28–9.

82. Burton, *Leicestershire*, 128.

farming activity which he directed. All over England, wherever a lawyer chose to settle, Kebell had his counterparts, some greater in fortune, many less, but all ploughing into the land the profits of the law, to reap a rich harvest of gentility. Perhaps Thomas Kebell had exceptional drive – certainly he had, in the Hotoft bequest, considerable luck; but if even a proportion of the legal profession had the courage to speculate, the awareness of planning, the enthusiasm for enclosure, the determination to farm for the market and the social success which he can be shown to have had, then the picture of the lawyers as an extrovert economic group is at least partially true. As William Harrison, writing midway between the death of Kebell and the researches of Burton, declared:

> as after the coming of the Normans the nobility had the start, and after them the clergy; so now, all the wealth of the land doth flow unto our common lawyers.[83]

83. William Harrison, *Description of England*, in Raphael Holinshed, *Chronicles &c.*, ed. H. Ellis (1807–8), i. 304.

16

THE REWARDS OF THE PROFESSION: HUMBERSTONE MANOR

On Monday, 6 July 1500, ten days after Kebell's death, the official party came to Humberstone to schedule his goods for probate.[1] Whether or not they were actually led by Valentine Mason, general appraiser for the Canterbury archdiocese (and Kebell had been wealthy enough to attract such attention), the resulting inventory was drawn up with care. The inspection followed the lay-out of the building, room by room, and this is fortunate, for otherwise nothing would be known about the house which Kebell occupied. Not only does it no longer exist, but even the site is forgotten. The two manors of Humberstone village each had their great house, Hotoft's where Kebell lived, and Haselrigge's where the family of that name still lived, but more than this cannot be said. One of the sites is now occupied by a hospital, during the building of which medieval foundations were discovered, but there is nothing to indicate which house this was, and memory of a second site has vanished.[2] But thanks to the inventory, drawn up on that first Monday of July in the year 1500, at least a good guess can be made of what the Kebell home was like.

The house which the appraisers came to visit was a two-storey building, with a central hall and one protruding wing, a type very common at the time.[3] It was probably an old building – there is no evidence of recent work on the main structure of the house – and it was

1. Wiltshire Record Office 88:5, 17a. See below, Appendix B.
2. V.C.H., *Leicestershire*, iv. 439. G. E. Kendall, *Humberstone, a brief history of the Church and its manors* (Leicester, 1916), identifies the existing manor with the Haselrig house, and places Hotoft's Manor next to the church. The suggestion of P. Rahtz, 'Humberstone Earthwork, Leicester', in *Trans. Leic. Arch. Soc.* 35 (1959), 1–32, that the house discovered during the excavation of the earthwork, Leicestershire Ancient Monument 66, might be Hotoft's Manor, is ruled out on account of size. This covered an area 37 feet square, where Kebell's house was clearly much larger (see below).
3. The analysis which follows is conjectural, based on a close interpretation of the inventory in the light of recent work on late medieval buildings. Cf. Margaret Wood, *The English Medieval House* (1965).

perhaps much as his 'kind cousin' Richard Hotoft had known it forty years before. It was large, with no fewer than ten chambers for the family and servants, a community, therefore, of some size and significance. The inspection began with the hall, traditionally the main room and entrance of a house; presumably the party had come in through a great door at the lower end, protected by the screens passage. The inventory immediately proceeds to the room above the buttery, which shows that Kebell's house followed the usual plan where the buttery lay immediately adjacent to the screens passage, between the hall and the kitchen. Presumably the stair was reached from the passage, and the party, having surveyed the hall, was able to ascend immediately to the upper floor. Having completed their scrutiny of the chamber over the buttery, it moved to the smaller chamber next door, and thence to another bedroom which must have been above the kitchen; adjacent to this room was a privy, presumably built out beyond the kitchen wall. The next room inspected was that over the chapel which, in all probability, lay at right angles to the main block. This led to another room, also, apparently, above the chapel, and this room had access, by a stair or a ladder, to the garret above. This was itself divided into two rooms; in the outer one the clerks slept.

Having completed the upper storeys at the lower or buttery end of the hall, the officials next passed to the parlour, which would have opened from the upper end. The fact that they did not continue with a complete circuit of the upper floors must dispose of any suspicion that Hotoft's Manor was a courtyard building, and must also indicate that the hall was open to the roof, with no passage over it. From the parlour, the party ascended again to the first floor, to what was the principal room of the house, and from that to the maidens' chamber, presumably in the garret above. Sleeping female domestics beyond the chamber of the master and mistress of the house was a characteristic measure of Tudor domestic discipline.[4] With the maidens' chamber, the survey of the parlour end of the house was complete, clear evidence that there was no second wing to balance the chapel.

Valentine Mason's men went next to the ground floor rooms at the lower end of the hall – buttery, pantry and kitchen, and thence to the outbuildings. These comprised a stable – over which the yeomen had their accomodation – a new stable with a room over it, a bakehouse

4. Cf. W. Hoskins, 'The Elizabethan merchants of Exeter', in *Elizabethan Government and Society*, ed. S. T. Bindoff et al. (1961), 182.

with a chamber above for the ploughman, a barn and a garner, all, presumably, making with the kitchen a courtyard. Having completed the outbuildings, and carefully noted their contents – newly clipped wool, a stack of fodder, wheat in the barn, malt for brewing, lead for roofs, millstones, ploughs and carts – all the life of an active farm and busy household, the appraisers probably went into the parlour where they noted the farm animals and crops in the field, the serjeant's plate and apparel. They then broke off to survey the chapel (a hint that this was entered from outside the house and was probably an addition to the original plan) and perhaps to inventory the lawyer's books there.

The inventory of Humberstone, drawn up so soon after the owner had been interred from this same chapel, gives a vivid picture of the life he had enjoyed. Houses of similar standing in the area would have been generally the same – Kebell's tastes were pretty conventional – but Humberstone is not of interest only because it tells of a way of living common to the landed squires of the day. Beyond that, it shows what success in the legal profession brought.

When Kebell died, the rise in living standards which brought increasing comfort and even luxury to wealthy houses by the end of the century was in its infancy.[5] Thus it is not surprising that the furnishing in some rooms was sparse or 'sore worn'. The hall, for example, had only a cupboard, a long form and some curtains which had seen better days, and there is no mention of the great table which was the traditional centre of the household. A table must have been there; presumably it was so much a fixture that it was treated as such. But though we can assume that the servants ate in the hall, Kebell and his family followed the practice which was becoming fashionable of eating in the parlour in privacy and some comfort. The parlour was a large room, possibly twenty-seven feet by eighteen, and some twelve feet high, with the walls covered by cloth hangings of board-alexander, a luxury which had ousted, in the fifteenth century, the painted walls of earlier times, but which was, in turn, being displaced by panelling.[6] The parlour contained a table, flanked by two forms, with a chair at the head and foot, a cupboard with a green cloth, and,

5. Much of the following discussion has been informed by a study of F. W. Steer, *Farm and Cottage Inventories of Mid-Essex* (1950). For a comparative study of a fifteenth-century home, see Bennett, *The Pastons*, 87–101.
6. These, and later estimates, are merely guesses, based on the lengths of the tapestries given in the inventory.

as was usual in days before the separate bedroom, a featherbed with hangings. The ample bed-clothes – two pairs of blankets, a bolster and a pair of good quality flaxen sheets, all covered with a tapestry counterpane – suggest that someone of standing slept there, perhaps the steward, or Philip Morgan the priest. Above the parlour, and reached, presumably, by a wall staircase, was Kebell's own room. At the time that the inventory was taken, this room was in apparent confusion following the obsequies of the former owner, but when occupied it would have had a certain magnificence.[7] Expensive tapestry covered the walls, the best in the house, the principal bed was hung in red damask and sarcenet, while the second bed had a sperver of ray silk and green tartron curtains. The room had two carpets – Kebell was following the new fashion here – a cupboard, and five chests, which probably served as seats, as well as storage.[8] By contrast, the female servants in the attic above were poorly supplied, with a mattress, a bolster and a feather pillow, a pair of blankets and two old coverlets.

In addition to the parlour and Kebell's own room, two other chambers were more than mere bedrooms, the rooms over the chapel. The first, possibly fifteen feet by twelve, was hung in board-alexander and contained a table, apparently of the four-legged type, a chair, and four joint stools, with a ship chest and a worn carpet, which could suggest the room in which Kebell worked (directly above was the room occupied by the clerks). This chamber also contained the usual beds, one with a sperver to match the wall hangings, and a smaller bed without draperies. The second of the rooms over the chapel had, likewise, a table – on trestles this time – a form, two stools and a cupboard, and it could have been used by Kebell's clerks. The hanging was an inferior one, but one of the beds had a sperver and the other a reasonably good feather bed, although the sheets on the better bed were of a quality 'for yeomen and labourers', and those on the other even poorer. The attic rooms, the clerks' chamber and the inner garret chamber, were, once again, sleeping places only, although the occupants rated considerably better furnishings than the female domestics in the other attic. The clerks had a painted cloth to cover the wall, and even a chair, while the bed in the inner garret did have hangings, albeit old ones, and sheets of better than labourers' quality.

7. The following reconstruction takes into account both the furniture *in situ* on 6 Jul. 1500, and the contents of the chests.
8. Steer, *Inventories*, 18–19. Carpets were still, normally, furniture coverings.

The first-floor rooms over the buttery and kitchen were also only for sleeping. The chamber over the buttery was moderately furnished, but the little room adjoining had a single draped bed, and the chamber next to the privy two beds without hangings of any sort. Servants who slept over the outhouses had even sparser conditions. The yeomen had a pile of bedding and five mattresses, to sleep on the floor, and although anyone sleeping on the mattress in the bakehouse would not, with the two blankets and the two coverlets provided, have suffered with cold, the same cannot be certain of the ploughman with his mattress, bolster, one blanket and a single coverlet.

But if the furnishings of Humberstone were impressive only in the rooms used by Kebell himself, the same cannot be said of the linen and kitchenware which the lawyer possessed. The inventory reflects, in fact, the characteristic medieval contrast of a relative paucity of furniture coupled with a plenty, a magnificence even, of utensils and cloth of all purposes. The linen store included over two dozen pairs of sheets, most of them of the best quality, and a number of spare napkins, towels, table and cupboard cloths, and blankets. Table linen in use was kept in the buttery and pantry – board cloths, tablecloths, cupboard cloths, both plain and diaper, towels and napkins, and the score of candlesticks that lit the house after dark. The kitchen, likewise, was amply equipped. For table use there were three sets, or garnishes, of pewter, three dozen platters, twenty-seven basins and twenty-eight saucers, besides five 'great chargers'. Cooking utensils included six large brass pots and four smaller 'posnettys', six pans – the larger sort holding five gallons – and besides these, two chafing dishes and a water chafer ('somewhat broken'), a frying pan and a great kettle. The kitchen had the usual colanders, knives and the like, as well as two frames for spits and ten spits of assorted kinds to go with them.

The opulence in Kebell's household is even more noticeable in the matter of clothing. Kebell possessed no fewer than thirteen gowns of different sorts. Some were professional dress – the gowns of blue and green ray which were the uniform of the serjeant, several now 'sore worn', and the red gown and hood which Kebell wore as assize commissioner and judge at Lancaster – it too showing signs of age. His best gown and hood was of murray, dyed in the wool, and there were also one crimson and two violet gowns with hoods.[9] The officials

9. Dr J. H. Baker has pointed out to me that all these gowns with hoods must be professional dress, since hoods were no longer worn by laymen at this date. Cf. the

did not, unfortunately, list shirts, hose and the like, so that there is no mention of the coif, that most distinctive feature of a serjeant's attire. Other gowns display the dignified country gentleman – two brown tawny gowns with fur, and his night gown of musterdevillers, furred with black lamb and valued at twelve shillings. His cloak and mantle were badly worn, as one would expect in a constant traveller, and his journeyings account also for a special riding gown lined with black cotton. Kebell's doublets were of black velvet and tawny satin, while the most costly of all his garments was a black velvet jacket, trimmed with marten fur. The remnants of this velvet are listed separately in the inventory at twelve shillings a yard, and the cloth was specifically bequeathed to Lady Hungerford in Kebell's will.[10] Nor had advancing years diminished Kebell's love of ostentation. His chests were stuffed with doublet cloths of tawny satin and black stamyn and four new gown cloths, of green ray, of blue ray and mustard, of blue ray and tawny and of green ray and violet. Smaller items of dress that were noticed included an old harness girdle, ornamented with bars – even a lawyer might need to go armed – and a velvet purse with a silver and gilt ring. Two necklaces are mentioned, one of large amber beads, of little value, and a more splendid one, of jasper and chalcedony stones, decorated with gold and, presumably, worn by Kebell's wife. The lawyer himself wore a gold chain which had originally belonged to his father, and later to his brother John, but this is not in the inventory; it was possibly a Beauchamp livery collar, shorn now of its original feudal significance.[11] It could have been left at Serjeant's Inn, but Kebell's will does not suggest that he had any personal property outside Humberstone. The inventory also fails to mention either the gold cross which the serjeant had bought, or his gold tablets.[12]

In common with other men of standing, Thomas Kebell made private provisions for religious observances. He had close relationships with Sir John Hamon, the vicar of Humberstone, who witnessed his will, but the serjeant also had a private chaplain, 'my curat Maister Philipp Morgan'.[13] Morgan obviously served the private chapel, and presumably he resided at the house. Kebell also needed a priest to sing mass in Humberstone church for the soul of Richard

description of Thomas Yonge in his first year as a serjeant 'arrayed yn a long blue gown ungurd with a scarlet hode vnrolled and j standyng roon cap of scarlet as the custom is of sergeantes to go' – a description which does not fully tally with the Inner Temple miniatures: *Trans. Bristol and Gloucestershire Arch. Soc.* 15. 175.

10. See below, Appendix A, p. 427.

11. See below, Appendix A, p. 426.

12. See below, Appendix A, p. 426.

13. See below, Appendix A, p. 431.

Hotoft, and as no third cleric is named it seems probable that this was either Hamon or Morgan. The chapel at Humberstone which Philip Morgan served probably occupied the whole ground floor of the projecting wing, but the chambers above show that it did not have the magnificent two-storey window found in several houses of the period.[14] There were curtains around the altar, two sets of altar furnishings, one more ornate than the other, and the crucifix was of wood, gilded. Two statues encouraged devotion, the one of the Virgin, the other of St John, and there were sacramental vessels of latten for daily use, together with a vestment and a corporas for the priest. The better chapel furnishings were stored elsewhere. In Kebell's own room was a valuable altar cloth of arras, valued at £4, and among his wardrobe, at least two complete sets of vestments in green board-alexander, an altar cloth to match, and an altar frontal of green silk, presumably to deck the chapel on festal days. Plate for the altar comprised a silver paxbread, cruets, a small bowl and a partially gilt sacring bell, plus a chalice and paten, with a cover, in silver, partly gilded. No candlesticks are listed, but even without them, the household chapel at Humberstone was eloquent both of the piety and of the substance of its owner.

The glory of Humberstone, as of other manor houses of the age, was its plate. No less than one third of Kebell's wealth consisted in gold and silver, in all forty-nine items, not counting forty-seven spoons and the vessels for the chapel. The collection weighed, in the prosaic way plate was then evaluated, 1,339 ounces troy, equivalent to over three-quarters of a hundredweight avoirdupois. Given their relative standing, the serjeant here does not compare unfavourably with Henry VIII's illegitimate son, the duke of Richmond, who, at his death, possessed 4,800 ounces of domestic plate; neither, however, were in the same category as Sir John Fastolf with his 1,175 troy pounds.[15] To Kebell and his contemporaries, plate was the best way to store wealth and the best way to display wealth; the man who could load his table was a man of substance, with assets readily realisable. Pride of place at Humberstone belonged to a pair of basins with matching ewers, partly gilt, weighing 183 ounces and worth over

14. Wood, *The Medieval House*, 237.

15. *Inventories of the Wardrobes of Henry, Duke of Richmond*, ed. J. G. Nichols, Camden Miscellany 3 (1855), 4–11; *Paston Letters*, i. 468–75; cf. the marginally different figures in *Paston Letters and Papers*, i. 107–8. William Paston J. had much the same amount of plate as Kebell – 1405 oz.: Bennett, *The Pastons*, 3 n.3.

£30. Originally purchased from the Hastings family, these may have had some connection with William, the first peer, or Thomas may have bought them in 1483 to assist his widow and son in that difficult year.[16] Other items were nearly as impressive – six great bowls, six pieces, or plates, each chased and partly gilded, and two more sets of basin and ewer; less magnificent than the first, these latter were still, at 117 ounces, fit to wash the hands of a prominent gentleman and his guests.[17] Strangely enough, Kebell had only two of the great salt-cellars prized and so important in the social distinctions of the day, perhaps for the mundane reason that such pieces were not so easy to sacrifice to the melting pot when cash was required. Those he had, however, were chased and gilt and weighed fifty-two ounces, and there were five smaller salts as well. By comparison, Sir John Fastolf owned nine salts, eight of them 'great'.[18] As for drinking vessels, Humberstone could boast thirteen covered goblets, all gilt, two partly gilt and four others pounced, with three standing cups, one of them plain and the others chased, each with its cover, and two mazers; two of the standing cups were especially notable – Kebell mentioned them in his will – but the mazers were less valuable.[19] Among pots, the inventory noted particularly a pair weighing together 94 ounces and double gilt, that is gilded inside as well as out.

The art of the English silversmith was renowned throughout Europe, and some of the descriptions of Kebell's plate give tantalising hints of artistic quality – twelve great spoons with 'wrethyn' knobs, or a cover for a small salt cellar 'wrethyn and enamelyd'. Another of the salts, whether 'great' or 'litell' is not clear, was cast in the form of a woman, while the cover of one of the standing cups was embellished with an eagle.[20] Although most of Kebell's plate was of silver, gilt wholly or in part, he had a few items of solid gold, a little spoon of 'working', or impure metal, a little salt, and his signet ring, together with his tablets and chain.[21] The salt was very small, but it had a cover decorated with oak leaves and was important enough to be specially bequeathed to Lady Hungerford.[22] What the 'signet of fyne gold of the Splayed egle' was like can be told from the impressions of it which

16. Kebell bought them from Lady Katharine and Lord Edward, and so probably shortly after the death of Lord William; they were a residual legacy to Lady Hungerford: see Appendix A, p. 428.
17. The bowls were also a residual legacy to Lady Hungerford.
18. *Paston Letters*, i. 468–75.
19. See below, Appendix A, p. 428.
20. See below, Appendix A, p. 428.
21. See above, p. 359.
22. See below, Appendix A, p. 427.

survive.[23] An odd omission is any reference to ready money. According to his widow, he had a considerable amount of cash, and his will supports this, but, together with his chain and tablets, it was not recorded in the inventory.[24] Such a collection of plate speaks more eloquently than any other of Kebell's possessions of the status and wealth which he enjoyed – a man with neither family connections nor favour. It is small wonder that the lawyers earned the opprobrium and envy of so many.

Kebell's contemporaries would have been principally impressed with his display of plate. But for readers of his inventory today his most impressive possession is his library. This was considerable by contemporary standards and indicates the level of education which the layman could reach without the help of a university training. Kebell possessed thirty-three different works, in all thirty-six volumes. The most ready comparisons can be drawn with the clergy, the book users *par excellence.* In at least twenty extant inventories of clerics made before 1530, detailed lists of books are given; the average was only forty-eight, and that figure is swollen by three very substantial holdings of over a hundred volumes each.[25] If the eleven inventories which belong to Oxford University members are considered separately, the average is even lower, thirty-four. Comparison with laymen is more difficult. Sir John Fastolf had twenty-nine volumes at Caister, but six were service books as against two in Kebell's collection.[26] Of men nearer to Kebell's own status, Lady Margaret Beaufort's clerk of works, who died a few years after the serjeant, had twenty-two English books.[27] Even someone so conscious of literature as Chaucer only had sixty, although before the days of printing such a collection represented a good deal more, in effort and expense, than in Kebell's time.[28] Lawyers might be expected to own a few more books because of the professional tomes they cherished, but even so, Kebell's collection seems large. The Pastons had by 1480 forty or more books, but these were the result of three generations of collecting, and especially of the courtly taste of Sir John Paston who, an exception to the family tradition, had not been bred to the law.[29] A list

23. Leicestershire Record Office, 26D53/315.
24. See below, p. 369.
25. Sears Jayne, *Library Catalogues of the English Renaissance* (Berkeley, 1956), 93–7.
26. Bennett, *The Pastons*, 111.
27. Jayne, *Catalogues*, 93.
28. J. W. Thompson, *The Medieval Library* (Chicago, 1939), 408.
29. Bennett, *The Pastons*, 261–2. Cf. *Paston Letters and Papers*, i. 517–18.

is extant of the books owned by the Townshend family in 1500, collected largely by Kebell's near contemporary Roger Townshend J.C.P.[30] These number twenty-one, a good collection by lay standards, but considerably fewer than Kebell possessed. Further evidence is not easy to assemble, but it does seem that Kebell's book collection was considerable for a layman, even a lawyer, and would not have disgraced an academic. Perhaps he may be credited with an unusual literary interest; certainly the picture of the lawyer as a limited pedant does not apply.[31]

Kebell's books were almost evenly divided between manuscript and print, sixteen of each with one in doubt, and illustrate well the impact of the introduction of printing. Manuscripts were expensive; even though the laborious copier did not grow fat on the proceeds, a penny or twopence a sheet could make a large volume very costly. One half of Kebell's manuscripts were valued at twenty shillings or more, and one in four at two pounds ten shillings or above. By contrast, no printed book cost more than ten shillings, two out of three cost four shillings, and one in three two shillings or less. Occasional manuscripts did sink to that level – Kebell had two 'old' Latin manuscripts each worth two shillings and eight pence, and a 'litell old boke of englisshe in parchement' worth twenty pence, but these were clearly of slight importance.[32] Among printed books, however, a shilling provided Sir John Mandeville's *Travels*, and one shilling and four pence, Caxton's 1481 Cicero or his 1478 Boethius.[33]

The advantage of print was, moreover, not simply price. Just as important was supply. It was not that many books were produced – with the small impressions of the early presses, this was not so – but books were obtainable where few or none had been obtainable before. A lawyer with London connections could go out and purchase the latest products of the city presses or recent imports from abroad, where previously he would have had to find a text to borrow and then a scrivener to copy it. Manuscripts were not ousted by the press – they retained their social precedence until the seventeenth century – but books were available where before there were none. Mundane considerations of price and supply, to say nothing of business caution,

30. B.L. Add. Ms. 41,139 f. 23v.
31. Cf. Ives, in *Profession, Vocation etc.*, 181–5.
32. St Ambrose, *De Officiis Ministrorum* and Isidore of Seville, *Etymologies*; the English work is not named.
33. For a full description of the contents of Kebell's library, see below, Appendix B, pp. 445–7, and Ives, *L.Q.R.* 85. 104–16.

explain also the unadventurous nature of early English publishing. The safe market was for recognised standard works and texts, and Caxton and his followers produced no revolution in reading tastes. All this is reflected in Thomas Kebell's library. The manuscript retains pride of place, but the humbler books in print represent a considerable collection of standard medieval scholarship, hitherto hard to find outside the learned library.

Although some of Kebell's printed books came from English presses, seventy-five per cent were from abroad. Of those printed in England, two, and perhaps a third were produced by Caxton, while the remaining item was a law book, almost certainly published by Pynson. With three of the continental books it is possible to specify the exact edition Kebell owned, thanks to the mention in the inventory of the opening words of a particular folio. Each came from Strassburg. The earliest is a copy of Johannes Balbus' *Catholicon* of 1482, the second is the *De Proprietatibus Rerum* of Bartholomeus Anglicus (1485) and the third is the *Vocabularius Breviloquius* of Johannes Reuchlin, issued in 1488. Each is a fine example of Renaissance printing, and the *Catholicon* is also an enormous folio, but the finest of the three is undoubtedly *De Proprietatibus Rerum*, clearly intended to be decorated by hand. The opening capital letter of the surviving British Library copy is coloured blue and filled in with gold leaf, the whole surrounded by a rectangle, half red and half green. The initial letters of succeeding chapters and the chapter headings are alternately red and blue, sometimes edged with silver, and underlining in the text is in red. Kebell's books were evidently objects of pride as well as study. Considering that English publishing was in its infancy, the dominance of continental volumes in Kebell's inventory is not surprising. It does, however, indicate how vulnerable the country and the educated class were to foreign influence, a fact which was to have enormous importance.

Kebell's library falls readily into four sections, but the obvious category, law books, is, in fact, surprisingly small – at most five volumes. Kebell may have had books elsewhere, but there is no evidence of this, and what comparison is possible with other lawyers suggests that half-a-dozen was a perfectly respectable total.[34] This throws into relief the importance of the inn libraries, but even more confirms earlier conclusions about legal skill in Kebell's day.[35] '*Nos*

34. Cf. the Townshend inventory: see above, p. 363; Putnam, *Early Treatises*, 177 n.2, 182 nn.1,5; Ives, in *Profession, Vocation etc.*, 193–6.

35. See above, p. 160.

livres' were useful, but of far more value was imagination and mental agility. Kebell's attitude to printed law books bears this out. Although quite a number were available, the serjeant owned only one.[36]

It is unfortunate that few of Kebell's law books can be firmly identified, especially the one which he kept with him as a *vade mecum*.[37] 'A boke of lawe enfrenche of yeres and termes', is clearly one of the first year-book printings. Assuming that the volume was made up of a run of years, it must either be Machlinia's edition of 33 to 37 Henry VI, or Pynson's 1496 printing of 3 to 8 Edward IV, and if made up of miscellaneous items, still no part could be older than 33 Henry VI, 1454/5, just before Kebell began to read for the bar. This again indicates how much late fifteenth-century law was a living science; the demand of the lawyers was for collections of cases from the period just before they began their own working notes.[38] Another volume was either a year book or else one of the collections of miscellaneous cases which are now often found in year books. The finest was a treatise, beautifully bound and the most expensive item in the whole library. Firm identification is difficult. Kebell was in a good position to obtain a copy of Thomas Littleton's *Tenures*, but he certainly had access to Bracton, and the size of the volume suggests the latter.[39]

The largest category amongst Kebell's books was religious, over a third of the total. Two were service books – an expensive psalter with a gloss, and a mass book. Several were directly biblical. Pride of place went to a four-volumed edition of the bible and the commentary of Nicholas of Lyra; copies of at least the 1486 Nuremberg edition circulated in England, and continental printings were common. Nicholas was the most popular of late medieval commentators, and at the forefront of the move in biblical scholarship away from allegorical interpretation to concern for the plain and literal meaning of the text. Dean Colet was much influenced by him. Kebell, however, also had time for the older fashion, for his books included the allegorical but highly popular *St Gregory on the Song of Solomon*. The prominence of scripture in the serjeant's library contrasts with the accepted picture of the English on the eve of the Reformation as a people deprived of the bible. Whereas biblical translations no less than Latin editions were common abroad, there was not one sentence of the Vulgate in

36. Other lawyers seem to have been similarly unexcited about the arrival of printed law books: see above, p. 160. Cf. the 65 copies of *Nova Statuta* unsold in 1483: E13/170 m.vi.

37. See below Appendix B, p. 444.

38. See above, p. 160.

39. See above, p. 271, but no French translation of Bracton is extant.

print in England, and nothing in translation. But Kebell's languages made this no problem for him, and other educated and monied laymen may have been equally unaffected.

The religious books also included three devotional items, the most notable being a continental edition of Ludwig of Saxony's *De Vita Christi*. This was no mere biography, but a book of spiritual exercises, and since Kebell kept it in his own room, it is reasonable to assume that it meant something in his spiritual life and was by him in his last hours.[40] The lawyer also had two volumes of sermons and one of the moral treatises of St Ambrose. What are suprisingly absent from Kebell's list are the works of pious mythology and hagiography which formed such a staple of the English printing houses.[41] As with his taste for scripture, this argues a distinctive attitude, even perhaps an impatience with current religious preoccupations. Other Englishmen may have been subsisting on a diet of the *Golden Legend* and the *Hours of the Virgin*, but not so Thomas Kebell.

The serjeant was, on the other hand, entirely conventional in his taste for encyclopaedia. No fewer than five books fall into this category, including the fine volumes from Strassburg. As did others of his day, Kebell admired the polymath. The earliest collection was that of the seventh-century Isidore of Seville which ranges from theology and classical philosophy to furniture. He also owned the digest of biblical history made by Peter Comestor and circulating under the title *Historia Scholastica*; this dated from the twelfth century. Bartholomeus Anglicus' *De Proprietatibus Rerum* was the most common of late medieval collections on science, dealing with everything from the angelic orders to inanimate matter. The late thirteenth-century *Catholicon* provided the basis of grammar and rhetoric and also served as a Latin dictionary, while the *Vocabularius Breviloquius* was also a dictionary prefaced by linguistic matter. Altogether, Kebell had a remarkably complete collection of standard authorities.

Classical authors were, however, less well represented in Kebell's library. He had two copies of Boethius' *De Consolatione Philosophiae*, one of them the Chaucer translation printed by Caxton. Cicero appeared twice: Caxton's edition of the Tiptoft translation of *De Senectute*, *de Amicitia*, *de Nobilitate*, and *De Officiis*, in Latin with a commentary. Thus the serjeant owned the standard treatments of

40. See below Appendix B, p. 436.
41. A. G. Dickens, *The English Reformation* (1964), 5–9.

faith and reason, obligation, friendship, old age and virtue, but little of special interest. The exception was Nicholas Trevet's commentary on the elder Seneca's *Controversiae*. The original consists of subtly argued legal niceties, and Trevet built on to these a superstructure of moralising, making the whole a valuable handbook for the preacher. It was a book whose legal disputations might ring a special bell in a lawyer's mind.

Far more revealing are the remaining books in the collection, those concerning travel and the imagination. Most notable of all was a fine French manuscript of Boccaccio's *Decameron*. It was covered with black satin and had silver and gilt clasps. Equally valuable was a manuscript of Froissart's *Chronicle*, which the serjeant selected as another bequest for Lady Hungerford.[42] French literature clearly appealed to Kebell, for he also had a copy of René of Anjou's allegorical poem, *L'Abuse en Court*.[43] Two other items were books of travel. One was almost new, the 1499 edition of Sir John Mandeville's *Travels*; the other was a guide book to Venice.

If the plate in Humberstone Manor is evidence of the wealth of Thomas Kebell, the books kept there are eloquent of his mind and tastes. He quite clearly loved them and took the trouble to accumulate a larger than average library, often securing the products of foreign presses. Together, the value of his books exceeded that of the whole of the furniture of the house, outside Kebell's own room. Generally his tastes were conventional; both titles and topics were those popular with his contemporaries. Only in religion does he seem at all distinctive. He was also a man of imagination. In his last days the books which were out of the book-press, in addition to the *De Vita Christi* and his law notes, were Froissart and René of Anjou.[44] He sums up his attitude in his will where, anxious that his son Walter should be properly brought up, he bequeathed to him[45]

> all my bookes of scripture, of Lawe, of Cronicles or stories, and alle other my bookes in latyn frenssh or English to thentent that he shall the Rather applye him to vertue and konnyng.

'Cunning' – intellectual ability, knowledge – this was the thing to prize, and books the way to attain it.

42. See below, Appendix A, p. 427 and Appendix B, p. 436.
43. See below, Appendix B, p. 436.
44. See below, Appendix B, p. 436.
45. See below, Appendix A, p. 426.

17

SOCIAL MOBILITY: THE KEBELLS OF HUMBERSTONE

Contrasts between societies are often most complete when it comes to marriage and the family. In twentieth-century Britain, mutual attraction and dependence of husband and wife are primary, children are of consequential importance (and that for a relatively brief period), and the economic advantage of the union and the need to secure the succession rarely of any importance. The conventions of Kebell's day reversed this order.

I

Thomas Kebell of Humberstone, serjeant-at-law, married three times. 'Margerie and Anne my wifes', as he describes them in his will, were buried at Humberstone Church, while Margaret survived him, to marry again and live until 1534.[1] About the identity of Margery there is some confusion, but the second wife is clearly known and considerable documentation exists for the third. Agnes, or, as Kebell referred to his second wife, 'Anne', was the daughter and heiress of Peter Saltbie and the widow of Thomas Flore of Oakham, son of Roger Flore, speaker of the house of commons in 1416, 1417, 1419 and 1422, chief steward in the north parts of the duchy of Lancaster.[2] Thomas Flore died in 1483 and Kebell married his widow within months.[3] Since Agnes already had two sons, Roger and Austin Flore, both of whom were remembered in the serjeant's will, she could bring no promise of any permanent increment to the Kebell estate. However she brought to Kebell her own life interest in her inheritance and whatever Flore property she was entitled to, depending on the terms of her first marriage settlement. Agnes had a son by Kebell, Walter,

1. For Thomas Kebell's genealogical connections, see Figure 1 at p. 27. For references to Kebell's will, see below, Appendix A, pp. 425–31; cf. Ives, *Bull. John Rylands Lib.* 52. 348–9; Ives, in *Wealth and Power*, 33, 43.
2. Wedgwood, *Biographies*; Somerville, *Duchy of Lancaster*, i. 419–20.
3. Farnham, *Village Notes*, iv. 335.

born late in 1486, who lived to carry on the Kebell line, but she was dead by 1498.[4] Kebell's will shows that there was another son, Edward, who died before his father, but whether by Margery or Anne is not known, although the former is more likely.[5]

Kebell's third wife, Margaret, was about twenty or twenty-two when she married him in 1498.[6] She was the daughter of Ralph Basset of Blore in Staffordshire, and a considerable heiress.[7] The Bassets were a powerful clan; William, her grandfather, was a prominent figure in the north midlands and, with Kebell, a client of William, Lord Hastings.[8] Margaret's father, Ralph, had died during William's lifetime, leaving her uncle, William Basset, junior, as the male heir, so that Margaret's expectations had been reduced. Nevertheless, she remained a matrimonial prize of some importance; as she herself later claimed, she was 'enhabitable to landes and tenementes of gret yerly valew', as well as possessing 'certayn sumes of mony'.[9]

Margaret Basset's marriage with Thomas Kebell was arranged shortly after the death of her grandfather by his widow, Joan, and William Basset the younger.[10] The settlement provided that in return for the land and cash she brought with her, the lawyer should make her a jointure of £40 per annum for life, free of all charges. By contemporary assessment, this was a notable match: Margaret's inheritance linked with the wealth and status earned by Kebell at the law. Whether it was successful in human terms it is impossible to say. His will makes only one bequest to a wife forty years his junior: 'I wol that Margaret my wife haue all suche thinges as the lawe will that she shuld haue', and this in a document 120 lines long. But the foolishness over Shakespeare's second-best bed is a warning not to place too much on a single phrase; the instruction was probably included simply to preserve to Margaret the normal widow's portion, while more substantial provision had been promised outside the will. Kebell also relied on her enough to appoint her one of his executors. But Margaret Basset was not the grand passion of the serjeant's life; he remembered the relatives of both his previous wives among his bequests, but he left no token at all to his third.

The interest of Kebell's second and third marriages lies in one of the wives being a widow and both being heiresses. Marriage had for

4. Walter was fourteen *et amplius* in June 1500. *Cal. inquisitions post mortem*, ii. 497.
5. Edward Hastings his name-sake was born 1466: G.E.C., *Peerage*, vi. 374.
6. C142/56/51.
7. Ives, *Bull. John Rylands Lib.* 52. 348.
8. Dunham, 'Indentured retainers', 118.
9. C1/329/51.
10. C142/56/51.

long been a way to wealth and would remain so for generations; it had been so for Walter Kebell, while in the seventeenth century there would be the citizen of the Isle of Wight who 'by God's blessing and the loss of five wives grew very rich'.[11] In the competition for wealthy wives, lawyers were very well placed. As against the small portion of the ordinary younger son, the lawyer could offer the wealth his practice had brought him. Perhaps, too, as against an established gentleman, a lawyer had a greater freedom to consider marriages from different areas of the country, at least until he himself had bought land and settled down in one locality. The lawyer, too, probably had better access to information. With contacts from a wide area, a confidential position in the service of possibly a number of landed families and a web of connection with other informed members of the profession, a lawyer should have had accurate and complete knowledge of the marriage market. The sort of discussion which we know took place in the late summer of 1454 between Serjeant Thomas Billing and Lord Grey of Ruthin about Elizabeth Paston must often have occurred.[12]

Measuring the success of lawyers in securing advantageous marriages is an impossibility. That they were successful can, however, be readily demonstrated, for example in the regularity with which lawyers married widows or heiresses. This test is a rough and ready one, for an heiress or widow was not necessarily wealthier than another woman, and makers of pedigrees have, in any case, had a propensity for labelling brides 'heiresses'. Nevertheless the incidence of lawyers marrying with these two groups of women where at least some wealth can be presumed is impressive. Ten of the leading apprentices of Kebell's last years were called to the coif in 1503. Between them they made fifteen marriages, and something is known of all but one of the brides. Eight had been married before, including one who was also an heiress, another was a spinster heiress, and two more clearly could dispose of considerable property. Robert Brudenell's first marriage, to the widow of William Wyville of Stonton Wyville, put him in the position eventually to buy out the Wyville estate.[13] Guy Palmes, the younger of two Yorkshire brothers at the Middle Temple, secured the great prize of Joan More, widow of Nicholas More of Allington in Hampshire and daughter of a Bristol

11. J. E. C. Hill, *Century of Revolution* (1961), 16.
12. *Paston Letters and Papers*, i. 155.
13. J. Wake, *The Brudenells of Deene* (1953), 18–19.

merchant.[14] She brought him two infant children but also the manor of Allington which More had settled on her for life, and probably the custody of the rest of More's substantial lands until his daughters took livery of his lands in 1512. Thomas Marowe married Isabel, the elder daughter and co-heiress of Nicholas Brome of Baddesley Clinton in Warwickshire, and received the manor of Kingswood, town property in Warwick and several hundred acres of land in the villages round as his wife's jointure.[15]

Any call of serjeants yields similar evidence. Of the 1486 serjeants, in addition to Kebell and his marriages, seven men took eight wives. No details can be discovered of one of these, but four were heiresses, one was a widow and the remaining two each had wealth. John Fineux, chief justice of the king's bench, took, as his second wife, Elizabeth, daughter of Sir John Paston and widow of William, eldest son of Sir Robert Clere. In 1498 Sir Robert had settled 100 marks a year on Elizabeth as her jointure, and in 1507 when she married Fineux, not only did Clere ratify the grant, but he improved the security for payment.[16] Richard Jay, a Hampshire man and a member of Gray's Inn, married Joan the daughter of John Wakefield and so became possessed of ten properties in London, in and around Lombard Street, including 'le Bell' in Birchin Lane.[17] Richard and Joan had had a son who died, and so on his wife's death in 1488, Richard was entitled by curtesy to retain the estate for the rest of his life; as it happened this was only a matter of five-and-a-half years, but even at the nominal inquisition *post mortem* value of £20 a year, 'the curtesy of England' had brought no small profit to Richard.[18] But none of the serjeants of 1486, or indeed of any call in Kebell's day, were more successful in matrimony than his junior at the Inner Temple, Humphrey Coningsby, called to the coif in 1495. His first wife was an heiress, his second, already widowed twice, was heiress to six of her relations, his third, again a widow, was heiress to an important northern family, and he enjoyed her estates for nineteen years.[19]

Numerous examples also demonstrate the success of lawyers in securing advantageous marriages for their children, although here the

14. *Minutes of Parliament*, i. 3, 6, 7; *Cal. inquisitions post mortem*, i. 1196; iii. 729; *Testamenta Eboracensia*, v. 80.
15. Putnam, *Early Treatises*, 138–40; *Cal. inquisitions post mortem*, iii. 141.
16. *Cal. Ancient Deeds*, iv. A7773.
17. *Cal. Patent Rolls, 1485–94*, 469; Wedgwood, *Biographies*.
18. *Cal. Fine Rolls, 1485–1509*, 498; *Cal. inquisitions post mortem*, iii. 689.
19. Ives, *Trans. Royal Hist. Soc.*, 5 ser., 18. 158.

problem of isolating the specific influence of legal wealth is more complex. The professional gains of the father were only one factor in pricing a marriage – whether the child was an heir, what were the wealth and connections of the mother, what was the current tariff for marriages in the particular part of the country concerned, all these had their effect and must be allowed for. Even more, there is the problem of making a hypothetical estimate of the sort of marriage which might have been made in other circumstances. Most children marry somebody: the question is, did being a lawyer's child significantly improve the chances of marrying well? In the case of Kebell's only surviving child, Walter, the answer is clearly, yes. The serjeant's will required of his executors to find for his heir 'sum Conuenyent mariage of an heritour yf they can', and although they did not secure an heiress, they did find a well-endowed girl for Walter – Jane, the daughter of Sir John Villiers, a wealthy Leicestershire landowner.[20] In 1519, after Jane's death, Walter married the daughter of Thomas Haselrig of Noseley, and she brought him Haselrigge's manor in Humberstone, thus uniting the whole of the village under the Kebells.[21] Even granted that Thomas Kebell was a grandson of the Folvilles, even granted that he had been endowed by Richard Hotoft, Walter would have made neither marriage if he had been only the owner of miscellaneous property about Great Stretton, a cadet of the declining Kebells of Rearsby. Thomas Frowyk, chief justice of the common pleas, came from an established family of London and Middlesex aldermen and members of parliament, and his relations married within the city oligarchy or with known country families like the Throckmortons or the Lewkenors.[22] Frideswide Frowyk, the chief justice's heiress, was secured by Thomas Cheney, the future treasurer of Henry VIII's household and lord warden of the Cinque Ports.[23] Guy Fairfax, by blood the third son of a moderate Yorkshire family but by profession justice of the king's bench, married two of his sons to sisters of the future Lord Roos.[24] In all these cases and in many others, the wealth of the lawyer transferred his children to a higher division of the matrimonial league.

The impact of the legal profession on the marriage market can also

20. Leicestershire Record Office, DE73 – Register 1, f. 185.
21. C142/39/99.
22. Putnam, *Early Treatises*, 127–38; Wedgwood, *Biographies*; Thrupp, *Merchant Class*, 342–3.
23. *D.N.B.*, Supplement, i. 421.
24. William Dugdale, *Visitation of Yorkshire*, ed. J. W. Clay (Exeter, 1899–1917), ii. 186.

be measured by the marriage portions enjoyed by younger children. Roger Townshend J.C.P. bequeathed his daughters £200 each; Guy Palmes, despite the fact that he had five sons, bought one daughter a marriage worth, apparently, £250, and left his other daughter a portion of 225 marks.[25] The numerous granddaughters of Humphrey Coningsby received between £45 and 40 marks from his estate for their marriages, in addition to whatever their parents provided.[26] Robert Constable bequeathed his younger son 200 marks and his two daughters £100 each.[27] Less prominent men had less to dispose of, but still the sums were not insignificant. Walter Grene, keeper of parts of the palace of Westminster and a clerk in exchequer, married his two daughters with at least 50 marks apiece.[28] The younger took as a second husband John Holgrave, baron of the exchequer, and his wealth enabled their younger son and daughter each to have £100.[29] In the case of the Pastons the matrimonial fortunes of a family of lawyers can be followed. Elizabeth, daughter of Judge Paston, had to wait a long time for a suitable husband, or so she, and her mother with whom she lived, both felt, but the problem was not her dowry of 400 marks but the determination of her brother John to exploit a sellers' market. Eventually she married, first, a son of Lord Poynings and grandson of Lord Grey of Ruthin, and second, Sir George Browne, one of the principal Yorkists of Surrey.[30] William Paston, the judge's third son, did even better; he married the third daughter of the duke of Somerset and so became by marriage the cousin of Lady Margaret Beaufort, Henry VII's mother.[31] Clement Paston, grandfather of Elizabeth and William, had been of doubtful gentility, but his grandchildren moved in court circles and the elevator was the wealth of William Paston J.K.B. An informative comparison is with the next generation, the children of John Paston, Judge William's heir. Like his father, John was a lawyer, but a less successful one, whose entanglement in the affairs of Sir John Fastolf led, in his wife's view, to 'his distruccion'; despite his own marriage with an heiress, John's children found marriages only within the county of Norfolk.[32] There was no magic in the name 'legis-peritus'; advantage was directly proportionate to how successful a lawyer you were.

25. PROB11/18 ff. 194–195v. 26. PROB11/25 ff. 217v–219v.
27. *Testamenta Eboracensia*, iv. 195–7.
28. PROB11/4 f. 116v. 29. PROB11/4 ff. 29A, 29AV.
30. *Paston Letters and Papers*, i. lvi, lvii. 31. *ibid.*, i. lvii.
32. *ibid.*, i. lx–lxiii, 361. John Paston, his second son and eventual heir, did make a second marriage with a widow from Sussex.

II

The role of the lawyer and his wealth in the marriage market raises the question of the wider impact of the legal profession upon English society. The intake of new stocks by marriage is not the only way for a society to recruit itself. For example, the man who did not marry into society could buy himself in. In some ways this had and has always been true in England; blue blood is an illusion produced by observing the red corpuscles of economic success through the glass of time and tradition. But late medieval and Tudor society was particularly fluid. For reasons which varied from generation to generation, the two centuries between the Black Death and the English Civil War were a time when many people changed their standing decisively. Status was ultimately an expression of wealth, and the man who got wealth would get status, especially if he invested in its supreme demonstration, land. Perhaps, for a few years, the rawness of the transition would gall established neighbours, but soreness would be healed by time, assisted by such well-established emollients as a bogus pedigree or a conveniently discovered coat of arms. An acute description which has been applied to the late middle ages applies to the whole of this period: it was 'an age of ambition'. And to such ambition the profession of lawyer offered, as we have seen, more than either the church or the city. The childless William Callow J.C.P. expressed it well in his will when he left his plate and books to his clerks and friends 'suche as entende to encrease theimself in the lawe'.[33] This explains why the profession was not principally the refuge of the younger son that it became later, but a career for the heir of a small or moderate family with some land.[34] Nor was expectation falsified. In many a family tree the earliest name is that of a successful lawyer's father, remembered not as the first important member of the house, but as the shadowy parent of the real founder.

What success in the law could achieve is exemplified by the two chief justices before whom Thomas Kebell made most of his court appearances, William Hussey, C.J.K.B. from 1481 to 1495, and Thomas Bryan, C.J.C.P. from 1471 to 1500. Hussey, who served as king's attorney for seven years before becoming a serjeant, came from a Lincolnshire family below the rank of justice of the peace.[35] His close connections with Edward IV brought him an early grant of the

33. PROB 11/8 ff. 57–58v. 34. See above, p. 33. 35. Wedgwood, *Biographies*.

manor of Burton Pedwardine in Lincolnshire, which had been forfeited by the attainted Thomas Danyell, and in 1475 he converted this notoriously risky title into secure ownership by a nice exercise of his influence. He arranged to get the attainder annulled and to secure for Danyell a grant of lands in Ireland in return for a surrender of all claim to Burton; Danyell managed to retain a rent of ten marks, but this Hussey extinguished by getting him two more Irish manors.[36] He was also granted two wardships by the Yorkists, and life tenancy of the manor of Frieston by Henry VII.[37] But far more important were his purchases, which gave him a sizeable estate scattered over a number of counties.[38]

William Hussey's own marriage was not notable, but he married his eldest son, John, to one of his wards, Margaret Blount, who inherited from her grandfather property in Wiltshire, Somerset, Gloucester and the March of Wales.[39] His youngest son, Robert, married one of the heiresses of Thomas Say.[40] Sir William placed both his heir, John, and his second son William at court, where the latter went on to become a gentleman usher and eventually to be knighted at Tournai; Robert, too, may have been knighted.[41] John, in the meantime, was successively squire of the body to Henry VII, knight of the body, comptroller of the household and master of the wards.[42] After narrowly escaping the fate of Empson and Dudley, Sir John won the favour of Henry VIII, continued as master of the wards, became a banneret at the 1513 campaign and in 1529 was raised to the peerage as Baron Hussey of Sleaford. In the Pilgrimage of Grace he played, so the king thought, an equivocal role, and John Hussey was executed in 1537 at the age of seventy. It is ironic that this classic example of the Tudor 'new man' should be known in many histories as a northern feudal magnate.

Setting aside the final aberration, John Hussey was enormously successful; he was the only one of Henry VII's close administrators to be made a peer, indeed, until Thomas Cromwell, the only royal official to be ennobled by the Tudors. Much of this success must be

36. *Cal. Close Rolls, 1468–76*, 1437, 1474; *Cal. Patent Rolls, 1461–67*, 182; in 1465 the manor was granted to a John Harley: *ibid., 1461–67*, 479.
37. *ibid., 1476–85*, 391; *ibid., 1485–94*, 111; *Cal. inquisitions post mortem*, i. 869.
38. *ibid.*, i. 1166, 1209; ii. 207.
39. *ibid.*, i. 869; *Cal. Patent Rolls, 1494–1509*, 279; *Cal. Close Rolls, 1485–1500*, 620.
40. *L. and P.*, i. 438 (4 m.14).
41. *ibid.*, i. 20 (p. 15), 2301; *Lincolnshire Pedigrees*, ii. 526.
42. G.E.C., *Peerage*, vii. 15–18.

put to John's own credit, or perhaps discredit, if the stripping of the debt-ridden earl of Kent was typical.[43] Something must be allowed to luck: generally, in being younger than Lovell and his other colleagues and so able to become part of the new reign, not a legacy from Henry VII; particularly, in escaping the debacle of 1509 which had the added benefit of removing several important rivals. But something must also be allowed to the legal eminence of William Hussey. Thanks to his father, John had substantial estates, a wealthy wife, the entrée to the court and, very probably, considerable reserves of cash. In 1503, some months before he became master of the wards and a year before he joined the king's fiscal extortioners, John was paid 1,000 marks for the wardship and marriage of his son and heir, William, by no less a person than Sir Thomas Lovell, and most of this must have been paid for Sir William's fortune.[44]

If William Hussey, coming from a minor gentry family, raised his son to the royal court, his colleague in the common pleas, Thomas Bryan, had further to go, for nothing about Bryan's ancestry is certain. Although his home as an established lawyer was at Ashridge in Buckinghamshire, as a young man his connections were almost always with Londoners, and it is highly probable that he belonged to the city.[45] His most plausible relative is a Robert Bryan, tailor, who appears fleetingly in the city's plea and memoranda rolls in 1460.[46] A Gray's Inn man, like Hussey, Bryan differed from his younger colleague in having fewer links with the crown and so fewer grants in reward, but his career among the city corporations, as common serjeant, and finally at the head of the most lucrative of the courts, may have given him the greater fortune.[47] Bryan's inquisition *post mortem* has not survived, but he seems to have acquired property steadily, first in Sussex and then in Hertfordshire, London and

43. *Cal. Ancient Deeds*, iii. D1194; *Cal. Close Rolls, 1500–9*, 473, 554, 702, 724, 740, 757, 763.
44. *ibid.*, *1500–9*, 305, 338.
45. *ibid.*, *1447–54*, 359, 429; *ibid.*, *1454–61*, 121, 201, 213, 493; *Cal. Fine Rolls, 1452–61*, 251; *Cal. Patent Rolls, 1422–9*, 550; *ibid.*, *1461–7*, 141; London, *Plea and Memoranda Rolls*, v. 145, 177, 182; vi. 23, 149, 156, 159.
46. *ibid.*, vi. 156; *Cal. Ancient Deeds*, i. C472; iii. C3580; v. A11501. He also had links with Katharine, widow of Thomas Oteleye, and her second husband, Bartholomew Seman (d. 1431): PROB11/12 f. 105v; *Cal. Wills proved and enrolled in the Court of Hustings, London, 1258–1688*, ed. R. R. Sharpe (1889–90), i. 362, 456, 459.
47. *Acts of the Court of the Mercers' Company, 1453–1527*, ed. L. Lyell and F. D. Watney (1936), 59; John Stowe, *Survey of London*, ed. John Strype (1720), ii. 161.

Buckinghamshire.[48] He married the widow of Thomas Blount, customer of Hull, in or before 1474, although an unknown earlier marriage seems very probable.[49] Isabel Bryan's dower from the Blount lands was assigned at common law, so that Thomas enjoyed a third of the Blount estate for the term of his wife's life.[50]

Chief Justice Bryan had one son, also named Thomas, who was placed in Henry VII's household. He progressed to become a knight of the body, and later vice-chamberlain to Catherine of Aragon.[51] Thomas Bryan C.J. secured an exceptional marriage for this son; the bride was Margaret, daughter of Elizabeth, countess of Surrey, by her first husband, Humphrey Bourchier, and widow of John, son of Sir William Sandes.[52] The match cost Bryan a minimum of 1,040 marks, but it made Thomas the younger the step-son by marriage of Thomas Howard, earl of Surrey and later duke of Norfolk.[53] Margaret Bryan, the chief justice's daughter-in-law, had successive charge of Henry VIII's infant children; his two grand-daughters married Sir Henry Guildford, master of the revels and later comptroller of the household, and Nicholas Carew, the future master of the horse, while his grandson, Sir Frances Bryan, the poet, was among Henry VIII's closest companions.[54] The father of Chief Justice Bryan has so far escaped detection; there is no missing his grandson, swimming sinuously and with profit in the murky but treasure-filled waters of Henry VIII's privy chamber. As with the Husseys, the wealth and professional status of the elder Bryan gave the son a flying start at court and the opportunities to exploit his own talents. Without Chief Justice William and Chief Justice Thomas, who would have bothered with John Hussey of Sleaford and Thomas Bryan the younger of who-knows-where?

48. *Cal. Close Rolls, 1461–8*, 315–16; *ibid., 1485–1500*, 1205; *Cal. Ancient Deeds*, i. C47; Williams, *Early Holborn*, 152, 842, 854, 865; *L. and P.*, Addenda i. 276; C1/38/104; *Cal. Patent Rolls, 1477–85*, 514; V.C.H., *Buckinghamshire*, iii. 364, 393.
49. *Cal. Patent Rolls, 1467–77*, 477; *Cal. Close Rolls, 1468–76*, 1232; Wedgwood, *Biographies*.
50. *Visitations of Essex, 1552 etc.*, i. 3 gives a second marriage, to Margaret, widow of Lord Barnes, *recte* Berners, probably a confusion with the marriage of his son, whose wife was *sister* to John, Lord Berners: G.E.C. *Peerage*, ii. 153.
51. *L. and P.*, i. 438 (3 m. 32); ii. 1850.
52. C1/84/74; C1/186/88; G.E.C., *Peerage*, ix. 614.
53. PROB11/12 ff. 105v, 106.
54. J. G. Nichols, *Literary Remains of King Edward VI*, Roxburghe Club (1857), i. xxxii; *Cal. Ancient Deeds*, iii. D 1094; *L. and P.*, i. 3419; ii. 1850; *D.N.B.*

III

Since there is no way to 'quantify' the impact of the common lawyers upon English society, the historian has to use examples. But the problem with an impressionistic technique is that the examples may be unrepresentative. Of all the lawyers Kebell knew, only seven were raised to the rank of chief justice, and Hussey at least was also outstanding as an individual; a contemporary wrote of Sir William:

> The king hath not another such man to do him service in attendance about him for the Chief Justice is *homo universalis*.[55]

Lawyers' children did not habitually rise to the royal court or the peerage. John Mordaunt's son was made a peer, so was Robert Brudenell's grandson and William Fairfax's great-grandson, while Edmund Dudley married the daughter of Viscount Lisle and put his son John on the road to the dukedom of Northumberland, but the point remains: these were not typical.[56] Yet the difference between their success and the success of others lay in degree, not kind. At every level of the profession, the successful lawyer would command social advancement. Of fifty-three serjeants-at-law created between 1463 and 1510, no fewer than thirty-four left families which figure in the heraldic visitations later in the sixteenth century or can be described as gentry on other grounds, and virtually all the remainder can be accounted for by accidents of mortality and descent. For the rank below the serjeants, it is possible to show that twenty-seven of the forty-nine barristers practising in 1518 had descendants among the country gentry, while the rest seem to have been similarly victims of genetics.

As with Hussey and Bryan, not all this advancement must be attributed exclusively to the law. Where William Danvers of Thatcham, despite being the second son by a second marriage, inherited property bequeathed by his father and the estates of his maternal grandfather, his ability to establish three sons as landed gentlemen was not entirely the consequence of lucrative legal practice and his own marriage with an heiress.[57] But although perhaps a majority of lawyers enjoyed some patrimony, only a few were as fortunate as Danvers, and for them it was the law which provided the great opportunity. Thomas Pigot,

55. MacNamara, *Danvers Family*, 162–3.
56. G.E.C., *Peerage*, iii. 13; v. 228; viii. 63; ix. 193.
57. MacNamara, *Danvers Family*, 178–90.

apparently the heir to a younger son who had married an heiress, owed his home to his mother's family, but this alone could not have enabled him to bequeath substantial property to each of his five sons and five hundred marks to each of his two daughters.[58] Thomas Pope was the son of the warden of the Holy Trinity Guild of Deddington in Oxfordshire, but he went to Gray's Inn and became, apparently at the age of only twenty-eight, treasurer of the court of augmentations; he was knighted and in the last years of his life served as one of Mary Tudor's privy council. Sir Thomas died childless, but although he had founded Trinity College, Oxford, he was able to leave very considerable estates to his brother, including Wroxton Abbey, and it was Sir Thomas' fortune which enabled his nephew to build the present house and to take on new dignity as the first earl of Downe.[59] Gregory Adgore, perhaps from even humbler circumstances, rose at the Inner Temple to become a serjeant, only to die within months of appointment, but even his estates, left to his wife for life, excited the cupidity of Humphrey Wingfield, fellow lawyer and the wealthiest commoner in his locality.[60] Again and again, a small landowner secured a substantial increment in social status by following, or putting his son to, the law.

Nowhere are the career objectives of the common lawyers more obvious than in the widespread refusal of families to forge continuing links with the profession. The law was a means to an end, and if that end were satisfactorily achieved, the means could be discarded. Thomas Kebell's will is redolent of his concern for his young son, Walter; nevertheless, there is no hint that Walter should follow him at the Inner Temple. The serjeant, as we have seen, did bequeath to his son all his books, including the books of law, but this was primarily for the boy's general education. His instructions to his executors are clear:

> I humbly and hertely pray and beseche theim to take the payne vppon theym to se him brough vp in vertue and good maners and to haue connyng Whereby vertue and Wisedom growith and is norisshed.

Walter was to be 'cunning', not necessarily 'learned'. Equally impor-

58. PROB11/19 ff. 207–8.
59. *L. and P.*, i. 438 (2 m. 34); *Cal. inquisitions post mortem*, i. 1146, 1251; *D.N.B.*; G.E.C., *Peerage*, iv. 449.
60. PROB11/14 f. 159v; *L. and P.*, i. 1221 (56); *Visitations of Suffolk, 1561 etc.*, 176. Wingfield bought some Adgore land and, in 1537, wrote that he had lost half his living by his wife's death: *L. and P.*, xii(2). 1342; see above, pp. 15–16.

tant in launching his son was the connection with the Hastings family and the proper provision of farm land and stock at Walter's majority. Nor did the serjeant's executors feel that training at the inns was a necessary way to discharge their obligations. Both they and the father saw Walter's future as a Leicestershire country gentleman.

In this, Thomas Kebell was once again representative. Twenty-seven of those serjeants-at-law created between 1463 and 1510 who were first-generation lawyers left sons who grew to be adults, and only just over one-third followed their father into the law; for two families in three, one generation provided all that was needed. Among apprentices there was a great tendency for sons to follow fathers, or so the 1518 list would suggest; three-quarters of those, themselves new to the law, were followed in the profession by their sons.[61] But where both serjeants and apprentices seem to have been at one was in the rarity of a family's connection with the law persisting beyond two generations. There were, of course, famous exceptions. The Ropers held the post of clerk of the crown in the king's bench until the office seemed hereditary in the family.[62] The Jenneys were prominent at Lincoln's Inn from the start of the fifteenth century to the close of the sixteenth.[63] The connection of the Townshends with the law lasted from Roger, who joined the profession in 1454, to Henry, who died a justice of Chester in 1621.[64] But connections of such duration were unusual, and where they did occur the tradition was often passed from father to younger son, as it was with the Townshends. Even where the tradition did pass by primogeniture, the third and later generations rarely reached the top of the profession; the distractions of a landed inheritance prevented concentration on a professional career. Such would certainly seem to explain the effective retirement from Lincoln's Inn of Edmund Jenney in 1480, son though he was of a judge and grandson of a governor of the inn.[65] In the England of Kebell's day the common lawyers were not a caste; the common law was a lucrative career for individual gentlemen.

61. For this list, see Appendix C.
62. Easter 1498 to Michaelmas 1616. Blatcher, 'Working of king's bench', 12.
63. *Admission Book*, i. 6, 166.
64. *ibid.*, i. 12; P. Williams, *The Council in the Marches of Wales under Elizabeth I* (Cardiff, 1958), 358–9.
65. *Black Books*, i. 71; he retained his chambers until 1498–9 at least, possibly to after 1503: *ibid.*, i. 112, 116, 119, 130.

IV

Among the classic antitheses of French social history is the dichotomy between the *noblesse d'épée* and the *noblesse de robe*, and it is equally a fundamental of English history that a similar division was absent from English society. The gentleman who entered the law remained in connections and attitudes a member of the landowning society of his area. Nevertheless, to enter the law was inevitably to acquire new acquaintances and new interests; a lawyer's horizon stretched beyond the county or region to which he belonged. The old organic connections of family and locality were not supplanted, but the recruit added to them membership of the artificial society of the profession.

Some sort of social relationship among lawyers would have been guaranteed by continued appearances in the same courts, and by the habit of judges and clients of treating them as a distinct group. The integration of the profession was, however, accentuated by the organisation of the 'men of court' considered in an earlier chapter. Training for the law was based on corporate exercises; lawyers shared the administrative offices and chores of their inn, and so too its cramped living accommodation.[66] The initial requirement for membership was not academic, but attendance at Christmas festivities; and as others besides would-be career lawyers grew more interested in the inns, so this social emphasis increased. In such a situation it would have been very odd if mutual ties of friendship had not sprung up. How close these could be is as well illustrated by the frivolous letter which John Paston received one December from his colleagues at the Inner Temple, summoning him to come to the Christmas celebrations, as by the many instances of fellows of an inn helping each other in business.[67] A warm affection also grew towards the society as a whole. Thomas Billing reinforced unpalatable (and overtly disingenuous) advice to a client in 1454 by saying 'I wylde ye schull do wyll be cause ye ar a felaw in Grays In wer I was a felaw', and he evidently expected this motive to be accepted.[68] On occasion lawyers turned their affection into benefactions and bequests to their inn; Lincoln's Inn library enjoyed a building largely donated by John Nethersole, a Canterbury attorney and fellow of the house.[69]

66. See above, pp. 37–40.
67. *Paston Letters and Papers*, ii. 316–18; see above, pp. 104–7. 68. *ibid.*, i. 154.
69. PROB11/14 ff. 195–196v; *Black Books*, i. 136. William Ayloffe bequeathed a year book *1–13 Edward III* and a *Book of Assizes* to Lincoln's Inn library: PROB11/19 f. 1v; Richard Eliot left furniture to the Middle Temple: PROB11/20 ff. 189–190v.

A sense of community existed also between the inns. There was little internecine ragging and fighting; the general hostility of the outside world and the specific dislike of Londoners for 'the men of court' was enough to make the inns stand together. Judicial orders played a part too, laying down rules common to all the societies, and the houses themselves attempted to keep in line on important issues, while personal and professional ties spilled over from inn to inn, binding the senior members of the various societies together.[70] This corporate feeling, characteristically for the period, was expressed in religious devotion, and although no religious fraternities of lawyers are so far known, it is quite clear that certain of the London churches were 'lawyers' churches'. Thomas Kebell attended the Whitefriars, as did Humphrey Coningsby, William Copley and a number of others, mostly members of one of the Temples.[71] Gray's Inn men seem to have had a close connection with the Greyfriars, and many were buried there.[72] Yet these churches were not so identified with one inn as to exclude members of another. Justice Thomas Yonge of the Middle Temple was interred at the Greyfriars and so too John Grenefield of Clifford's Inn, an inn of chancery linked to the Inner Temple.[73] The judges and serjeants likewise had a tradition of worshipping at St Dunstan's in the West where an aisle was reserved for them, but Chief Justice Bryan preferred to worship at the Temple and at St Andrew's, Holborn.[74] What determined the particular church which a lawyer would use might thus be convenience and preference as much as a connection with an inn, but that certain churches had been annexed by the profession is clear. The same was probably true of taverns. When Thomas Tropenell, the Wiltshire squire, came to London in the spring of 1482 to see his lawyers, he was taken to

> the taverne callid the Cardynal's Hatte withoute Newgate wich is a place accustomed for lerned men in the lawe to comen maters concernyng the lawe for thassurans of mens titles,

70. See above, pp. 16–17.
71. PROB11/25 f. 217v; John Stowe, *Survey of London*, ed. C. L. Kingsford (Oxford, 1908), ii. 46–7. William Copley is probably William Copley junior, of the Middle Temple, clerk of assize, nephew to the prothonotary: *Testamenta Eboracensia*, iv. 48–9; *Cal. Patent Rolls, 1485–94*, 283. Note also the role of the Temple Church; Richard Wye, I.T., asked to be buried 'in the Temple Church in the place where gentilmen of our company walke': PROB11/19 f. 264.
72. C. L. Kingsford, 'The Grey Friars of London', in *British Society of Franciscan Studies* 6 (1915), 86, 93, 102, 106, 109, 116, 120, 121, 125, 236.
73. *ibid.*, 6. 9, 93.
74. See John Caryll, below, p. 456; PROB11/12 f. 105v.

and other consultations there are known.[75] Accounts make it clear that much of a lawyer's work took place in taverns: another used was the Pannier in Paternoster Row, a third, the Dolphin at Bishopsgate, and if Tropenell was entirely correct in his report, particular taverns were associated with particular types of business; the analogy with the coffee-houses and the rise of London's commercial structure in the eighteenth century is pressing.[76]

All in all, therefore, the common lawyers, although not a caste, were more than a mere occupational group. Perhaps the plainest demonstration of this is the impressive pattern of matrimonial alliances between members of the profession. Lawyers marrying the relatives or widows of other lawyers, betrothing their sons to the daughters and nieces of colleagues and arranging matches for their own daughters within the profession, bound themselves together in a thick web of connection. Thomas Kebell's first wife has not, so far, been considered. She is a shadowy figure and her identity is not absolutely established, but in all probability she was one of the Palmers of Carlton, a noted family of Northamptonshire lawyers.[77] If so, by his marriage to Margery, Thomas Kebell, a newcomer to the profession, became linked with, not only her younger brother Thomas, but a more distant relative, also a lawyer, Thomas Palmer of Holt; this second Thomas married the aunt of the William Catesby who was to serve Richard III and whose own uncle was John Catesby J.C.P.[78] After Kebell had been in practice for some years, his aunt Mary Folville married (for the third time) and her husband was Thomas Billing, chief justice of the king's bench.[79] Billing's granddaughter, Joan, married John Haugh of Lincoln's Inn, who was called to the coif with Kebell in 1486 and became a judge in 1487.[80] Nor were these relationships a mere genealogical curiosity. Kebell lent to Thomas Palmer a grey horse and £20, and his will converted the horse and ten

75. *Tropenell Cartulary*, ii. 348; *Paston Letters and Papers*, ii. 594–5.
76. H.M.C., *Ninth Report*, i. 138–9; Magdalen College, Fastolf Ms. 71.
77. V.C.H., *Northamptonshire*, Genealogical Volume, 240–3; cf. the heraldry on Kebell's tomb: Nichols, *Leicestershire*, iii. plate XXXIV, figs. 17–20; see below, p. 387.
78. For the Palmer family, see Figure 4 at p. 385. Thomas Palmer, Kebell's brother-in-law, was clerk of the peace for Leicestershire and clerk of assize for the western circuit: B.L. Lansd. 127 f. 32; *Cal. Patent Rolls, 1494–1509*, 290. For Palmer of Holt, see Wedgwood, *Biographies*; *Cal. Patent Rolls*, *1452–61*, 551; PROB11/7 f. 114v; see above, p. 133.
79. Wedgwood, *Biographies*, 76; Weever, *Funeral Monuments*, 269.
80. *Visitation of Northants., 1564*, 34; *Testamenta Vetusta*, ed. N.H. Nicholas (1826), i. 410; *Cal. inquisitions post mortem*, i. 753; Foss, *Judges*, v. 54.

marks of the money into a bequest to 'my brother Palmer'. Kebell was, as we have seen, a friend of William Catesby at the Inner Temple and a feoffee for his estates, and he was a feoffee for Billing and Billing's daughter too.[81]

The ramifications of some connections among the lawyers put Kebell's into the shade. The Catesbys had links with half-a-dozen other families in addition to the Palmers.[82] Justice John Catesby married the daughter of the Walter Grene, clerk in the exchequer, whose second daughter, as we have seen, married John Holgrave, baron of the exchequer, after an earlier marriage to John Arderne, almost certainly related to Peter Arderne, chief baron.[83] Catesby's son, Humphrey, married the daughter of Richard Maryot of the Inner Temple and had a son, Antony, who married the daughter of Serjeant Thomas Pigot.[84] Another of the judge's grandchildren was married, first to the son of a prothonotary and, second, to a judge of the common pleas; the prothonotary's brother and nephew were also officers of the common pleas.[85] On William Catesby's attainder, his heir was secured by Richard Empson of the Middle Temple and this linked in also Empson's son, the recorder of Coventry, and the descendants of Edward IV's attorney-general, Henry Sotehill. Others who can be fitted in are Richard Nele J.C.P. and Thomas Nevill, an apprentice in the 1518 list.[86]

A better-known group centred on the Roper family.[87] John Roper, Henry VIII's attorney, married a daughter of Chief Justice Fineux; her sisters were married to the grandson of James Hobart A.G. and to the grandson of Reynold Sonde of the king's bench (who was also a

81. See above, pp. 108–11; Leicestershire Record Office, 26D53/653; *Cal. inquisitions post mortem*, i. 749, 753.

82. See Figure 4 opposite.

83. PROB11/4 f. 116 v; 11/8 f. 29; see above, p. 373.

84. *Visitation of Buckinghamshire, 1634*, 100; *Visitation of the County of Northampton, 1681*, ed. H.I. Longden, Harleian Soc. 87 (1935), 43; *Visitation of Northants, 1564*, 172.

85. Wyborough Catesby married Richard, son of John Jenour, prothonotary, and (2nd) Richard Weston J.C.P.; Jenour's brother, Robert, and his nephew, Richard Lone, were officers of the common pleas: Somerville, *Duchy of Lancaster*, i. 403; *Visitations of Essex, 1552 etc.*, i. 221; P. Morant, *History and Antiquities of Essex* (1768), ii. 426; PROB11/29 f. 81; cf. Spelman, *Reports*, ii. *378*.

86. Nele's son married the granddaughter, and Nevill was the grandson, of Thomas Palmer the elder.

87. See Figure 5 at p. 386; *Visitation of Kent, 1619–21, passim*; *Visitations of Kent, 1530 etc.*, ii. 26, 128; *Genealogist*, new ser., 33 (1917), 266; Chambers, *More*, 58; *Visitation of Buckinghamshire, 1634*, 185; *Visitations of Essex, 1552 etc.*, i. 5, 254; *Lincolnshire Pedigrees*, ii. 526; Thorne, *Readings and Moots*, i. xxxi; Spelman, *Reports*, ii. *55–7*; Blatcher, *Court of King's Bench*, 149–50.

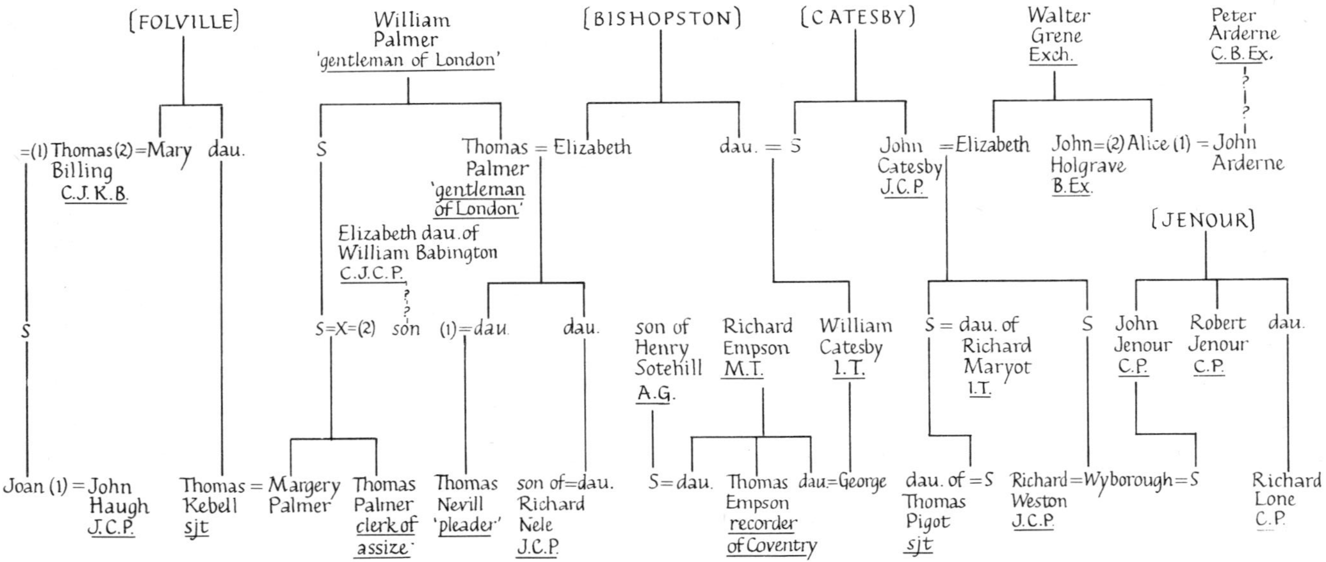

Fig. 4. Connections of the Palmer and Catesby families

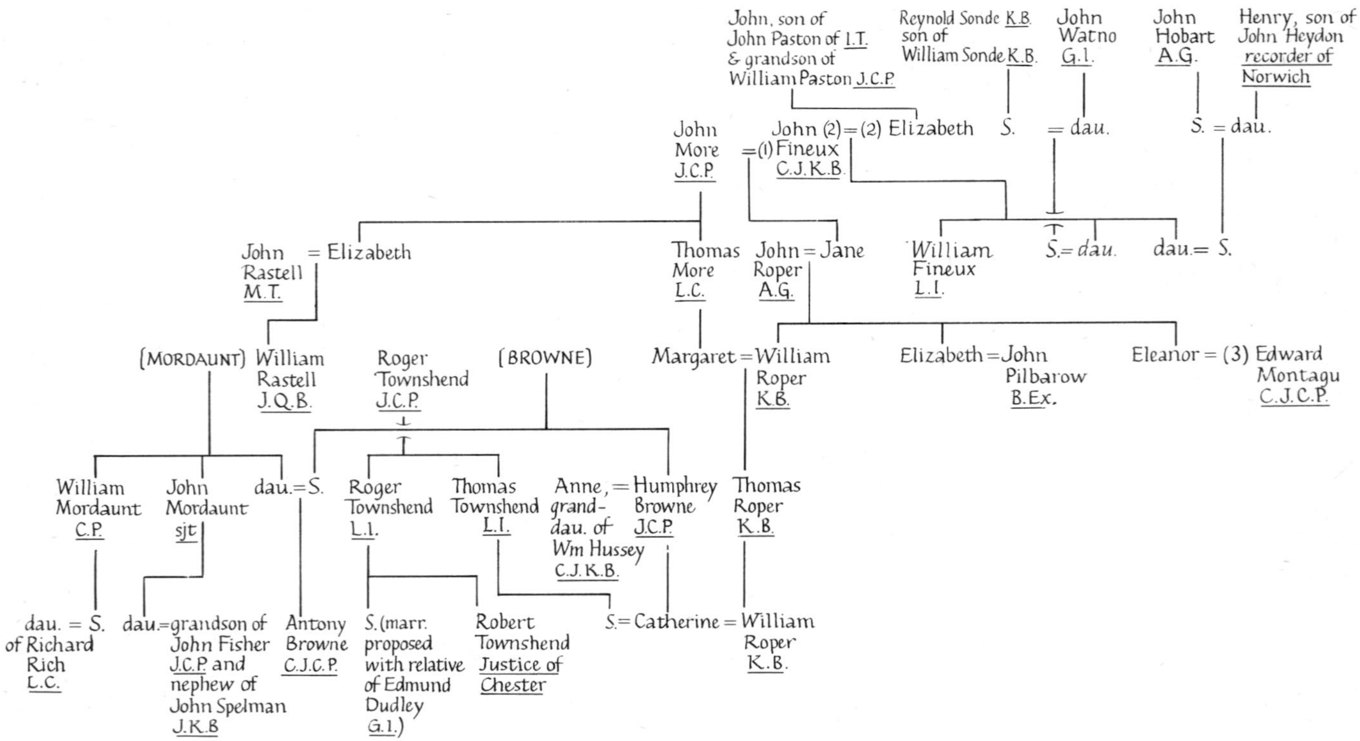

Fig. 5. Connections of the Roper and Fineux families

grandson of John Watno of Gray's Inn). One of Roper's daughters married John Pilbarow, baron of the exchequer, another became the third wife of Edward Montagu, later chief justice, while his heir, William, was chief clerk of the king's bench and married Margaret, daughter of Sir Thomas More and granddaughter of Justice John More. Through the More connection there were links with John Rastell of the Middle Temple and his son William Rastell J.Q.B. William Roper's son and grandson both followed him in the king's bench and the latter married the daughter of Humphrey Browne J.C.P. after her first husband, one of the Townshend clan, had died. Browne's wife had been the granddaughter of Chief Justice Hussey, his brother had married the sister of Serjeant John Mordaunt and William Mordaunt of the common pleas, his nephew, Antony, was to become chief justice of the common pleas and other connections bring in Richard Rich, Justice Fisher and Justice Spelman and, but for his disgrace, would have brought in Edmund Dudley. Genealogical networks of this sort can be multiplied.

Kebell's second and third marriages outside the legal clans do, of course, suggest caution in interpreting this wholesale intermarriage. Since the legal profession was primarily a projection of the landed gentry, are not these connections merely evidence that gentry tended to marry gentry? If Margery, Thomas Kebell's first wife, was the daughter of William Palmer, the connection could have been forged through the retinue of William, Lord Hastings, since William Palmer was a retainer of the lord chamberlain.[88] Significantly, perhaps, Kebell's third wife can also be linked with the retinue, for Margaret Basset's grandfather, who probably began the negotiations for her marriage with the serjeant, had been sworn to Lord William.[89] Thus, if the groupings of bastard feudalism represent the social relationships of a community as much as the drawing power of an over-mighty subject, two at least of Kebell's matches may be explained by clientage patterns in the midlands. Analogous comments could be made about the evident interrelation between the lawyers who came from East Anglia or those who came from the West Riding, or the Roper connections which cluster in London and the home counties.

Justified caution has, nevertheless, no reason to turn into scepticism. In many instances the law seems the only connection upon which a marriage could have been made. The Ropers of Swalecliffe on

88. Dunham. 'Indentured retainers', 118; see above, pp. 100–3. 89. *ibid.*, 118.

the north coast of Kent might well marry into the Fineux family from Herne, the next township, but hardly, without the help of the law, with the Mores of Chelsea. Similarly, in Loddon Church, between Norwich and Yarmouth, there is a memorial to Chief Justice Fineux's daughter Anne, the wife of Henry Hobart of Hales, grandson of Sir James Hobart, Henry VII's attorney, and this connection must have come through the law.[90] Is it more likely that Robert Packington from Gloucestershire should have married Anne, daughter of John Baldwin, of Aylesbury, C.J., as a consequence of chance acquaintance, than as a result of his elder brother, John Packington, being a contemporary of Baldwin at the Inner Temple?[91] And there is the cumulative weight of the evidence. So many lawyers can be linked by ties of marriage that it is stretching doubt beyond reason to attribute the connections to the normal inter-communication of the landed gentry.

V

What were the consequences of all this interrelation? The social cohesion of the common lawyers was a fact of considerable importance in the development of the common law. It helped to guarantee common-law methods; it encouraged stability, and it is hard to see how the sixteenth-century profession could have reformed the law as it did without having this cohesion. It had, too, or so critics averred, disadvantages in the tendency of the profession to engage in a collective fraud against the public. And it was hard for the disenchanted litigant to watch the lawyer he had feed fraternising with the enemy in the way Stephen Gardiner described:

> Here was an experience of the learned men in the Kynges lawe att this assyse whiles I was a wrytyng theis letters, who in courte pleading their matters were very earnest with prety quicke sayenges one to another as the matter served wisely wittely and learnedly; and after at my boorde mer[r]ely, without private grudge rehersed some part of their doing, howe eche had changed othir and travailed one another with this and that feat, and so departed very frendes.[92]

Yet the cohesion of the legal profession probably had its greatest

90. Stephenson, *Brasses*, 344; *Visitation of Norfolk*, ed. Dashwood, ii. 115; *Visitation of Norfolk, 1563*, ed. W. Rye, Harleian Soc. 32 (1891), 165.
91. *Visitation of Worcestershire, 1569*, ed. W.P.W. Phillimore, Harleian Soc. 27 (1888), 101–3; *Inner Temple Records*, i. *passim*.
92. Stephen Gardiner, *Letters*, ed. J.A. Muller (Cambridge, 1933), 349.

impact upon society, rather than the law. In the first place, it reinforced the role which the legal profession played in providing an avenue for ambition. The law gave the new entrant the opportunity to make money and to buy social status. The community of the common lawyers meant that he did so in the company of others. The legal profession was not a collection of individuals creating wealth, but a community which traded in the wealth its members made. Many an outsider would have liked to marry a lawyer's fortune, but time after time these were disposed of within the profession. The second effect upon society was that a coherent body of lawyers helped to make the landowners a more coherent entity. It is now nearly fifty years since A. F. Pollard pointed out that the Reformation Parliament was a 'matrimonial agency', and the significance of this for the self-awareness of the Commons. The matrimonial agency which was the legal profession had a parallel impact on the gentry. Social mobility did occur among landowning families not represented in the profession, but for many, any link with, even awareness of, gentry outside the confines of their immediate geographical hinterland must have come through the legal communities off Holborn, Chancery Lane and Fleet Street. It would be an exaggeration to say that the lawyers made the English gentry into an integrated estate in the kingdom, but their influence pressed in that direction. 'Think you', asked the Edwardian pamphleteer, 'that the lawyers could be such purchasers if their pleas were short and all their judgements, justice and conscience?'[93] Perhaps not, but the moralist muddies the issue; it was the demand for legal services which created the demand for the lawyers. But given that demand, then the lawyers became purchasers indeed. The legal profession was a principal agent in social change. It is worthwhile noting again the conclusion which Erasmus drew from his stay with Thomas More: 'In England, those who succeed in [the law] are hightly thought of, and there is no better way to eminence there, for the nobility are mostly recruited from the law.'[94]

VI

When Thomas Kebell died at Humberstone on 26 June 1500, successful, wealthy, with just that increment in social status which so many men desired, contemporaries may well have envied the lot of the

93. See above, p. 321. 94. Chambers, *More*, 85.

heir.[95] The elder branch of the family was now eclipsed; the 1524 subsidy assessed the Humberstone Kebells at more than double their Rearsby cousins. An immediate set-back, it is true, was the crown's claim to wardship of the fourteen-year-old heir, despite Thomas Kebell's conviction that 'to my knowlige my said sonne owith not to be in warde to any persone'. The wardship was, however, bought by Thomas' patroness and executor, Lady Mary Hastings, and whether she did so as an investment or to fulfil the serjeant's wish that if a claimant to the wardship appeared the executors should buy 'the warde and mariage' hardly matters; the guardianship of Lady Hastings was worth a good deal in Leicestershire.[96] Walter reached his majority in 1508; by 1514 he was a J.P. and in 1519–20 he became a freeman of Leicester.[97] His connection with the Hastings persisted after his godmother's daughter-in-law died, and Walter named his heir Francis, after Lady Mary's grandson, the future second earl of Huntingdon.[98] His marriages into two families of note secured some profit, at the least the second manor at Humberstone, but Walter Kebell was never as prominent as his father, not only at a national level but in Leicestershire as well.[99] The probable explanation is simple. Walter died when he was not yet thirty-six, in 1522, and his will makes it clear that he was then still under the dominance of Sir John Villiers, the father of his first wife, and of Thomas Kebell of Rearsby, his cousin and a man ten years his elder. Walter had neither the time, the independence nor, perhaps, the character to make his mark.

But even Walter Kebell's standing in Leicestershire was beyond the reach of his descendants, and from his death, the Kebells of Humberstone begin to look very much like a family in decline. Francis, Walter's son, was two years old at his father's death, according to the inquisition *post mortem*, and custody of the child seems to have gone to the Sacheverell family; Walter had been friendly with the Sacheverells, a connection probably springing from his dependence on the Hastings family.[100] Francis married the daughter of Ralph

95. *Cal. inquisitions post mortem*, ii. 497.
96. *Cal. Patent Rolls, 1494–1509*, 279, 597; C1/329/51.
97. *L. and P.*, ii. 1213; *Register of the Freemen of Leicester, 1196–1930*, ed. H. Hartopp (Leicester, 1927–33), i. 65.
98. Lady Katharine's daughter-in-law Mary died in 1511, leaving Kebell's will partially unexecuted: *Hastings Mss.*, i. 307.
99. Leicestershire Record Office, DE73 – Register 1, f. 185; C1/142/39/99.
100. G.F. Farnham 'Prestwold and its hamlets in medieval times', in *Trans. Leicester-*

Sacheverell, but Kebell of Humberstone is not included among the list of 'gentilmen of Leyrcestershir that be there most of reputation' which John Leland drew up in the 1540s.[101] Soon after, the signs of decline became obvious as Francis began to sell land, and in 1549, if not before, direct farming of the Stretton pastures was abandoned in favour of leases yielding less than the nominal values of the serjeant's day.[102] Francis died even younger than his father, leaving the estate to a minor for the third time in succession, and Francis, earl of Huntingdon, secured the wardship of Henry Kebell, a son who once more bore the name of the Hastings' heir.[103] That the Kebell estates were still worth having is clear by the marriage of Henry to Jane Griffin, the daughter of Mary Tudor's attorney-general, but even this alliance was a mixed blessing.[104] It strengthened, if it did not initiate, a commitment at Humberstone to the Catholic church.[105] In the 1560s this did not mean heavy monetary loss, but, rather, estrangement from the establishment, and it may be that at this point the Hastings connection was broken. But Henry Kebell, in any case, was as short-lived as his father and died in 1571, leaving two young daughters whose wardship and marriage was one of the shower of benefactions Elizabeth I was then pouring on her favourite, Christopher Hatton.[106] Elizabeth, the elder, married Antony Colley of Glaston in Rutland, while Margaret, the younger daughter, married Richard Bowes of Elford in Staffordshire.[107] Elizabeth Colley and her husband sold their portion of the Kebell lands in the 1580s and 1590s, and passed out of Leicestershire history.[108] Margaret's share included the Humberstone estate and it was while her mother and she occupied the manor that its name for recusancy was established. Eventually Margaret disposed of the property to Sir Henry Hastings. And so Burton could write his epitaph on Thomas Kebell's great estate 'all sold, dispersed, gone'.

shire Archaeological Soc. 17 (1931–3), 47, 78; *Hastings Mss.*, i. 26; Nichols, *Leicestershire*, iii. 574.

101. Farnham, *Medieval Pedigrees*, 79; John Leland, *Itinerary*, ed. L.T. Smith (1906–8), i. 21.
102. *Hastings Mss.*, i. 55; Farnham, *Quorndon Records*, 223; Farnham, *Village Notes*, iv. 171; v. 353.
103. *Cal. Patent Rolls, 1555–7*, 14.
104. Farnham, *Medieval Pedigrees*, 79.
105. V.C.H., *Leicestershire*, ii. 58n; iv. 440.
106. *ibid.*, v. 290; *Cal. Patent Rolls, 1569–72*, 3282.
107. *Visitation of the County of Rutland, 1618–19*, ed. G.J. Armytage, Harleian Soc. 3 (1870), 25–6.
108. V.C.H., *Leicestershire*, v. 439–42.

The extinction of the Kebells of Humberstone after the enormous success of Serjeant Thomas may seem harder to explain than the disappearance of the Rearsby line founded by his father. The cadet branch was much wealthier, it was more prominent, it was, even in decline, consistently patronised by the house of Hastings, which was steadily rising in wealth and royal favour. But, in fact, the principal causes of the decline would seem to be the same as for the elder line, with genetic and actuarial factors the most important.[109] Not even the most successful of founding fathers could provide against an inability to rear large families and a recurrent pattern of early death. While four Rearsby marriages produced only three sons and two daughters, in the Humberstone family, seven marriages yielded no more than eight adult children in all. Continuity almost always depended on a single life, and far too often there was no adult to represent the family and watch over the heir. As for a poor life expectancy, Humberstone had a worse record than Rearsby; there the serjeant's godson, Thomas, did inherit when an adult, but at Humberstone every Kebell succeeded under age; the estates suffered four minorities in succession, one lengthy, and for more than half the period from the death of the serjeant to the death of his great-grandson Henry, the family property was in wardship. It looks very much as though the Kebells were dogged with low fertility and poor physique.

Continual minorities not only meant less efficient estate management but also that the family was continually being drained of money. Instead of the family reaping the profits from the heir's marriage, these profits went elsewhere. Executors probably did what they could, and the Hastings family may have forgone its profit when possessed of the wardship, but there was nothing to substitute for the hard-headed calculation of advantage in, for example, the Paston family. But the greatest burden which arose from the vital statistics of the Kebell family was the continual need to provide for children and young widows; the estate was endlessly encumbered with widows' dowers and children's portions. Ironically enough, the serjeant's own last marriage did the greatest harm. After his death, Margaret Basset returned to her family home at Blore in Staffordshire, and in 1502 she was the victim of a notorious abduction which was to echo through nearly every court of the land over the next five years.[110] But Margaret still had her claims on the Kebell estate, and, in 1508, having escaped

109. See above, pp. 34–5. 110. Ives, in *Wealth and Power*, 31–43.

finally from her abductor, she sued in chancery for her jointure of £40 a year.[111] She won, and Walter and Lady Mary Hastings had to make over a large portion of the estate; she occupied it until 1534. Fortunately for Walter, there were no portions for younger children, but there was his father's will and testament to perform with its requirement to maintain the Hotoft chantry priest in perpetuity. When Walter died the burdens became worse. He charged Humberstone, Hamilton and Congerstone with raising 600 marks for his two daughters and this probably led to the sale of the Barrow on Soar property.[112] He also left his wife, Milicent Haselrig, a life tenancy of lands worth £20 per annum net, plus the Haselrig land he had acquired, plus her dower, and confirmed the £40 a year due to his step-mother, now Lady Margaret Egerton; and to make matters worse Milicent (with her second husband, Eustace Braham), and Walter's executors and heir (and Lady Egerton) fell out and went to law.[113] Even the death of Lady Egerton in 1534 hardly relieved the pressure since Milicent at once seized the dower lands, and in any case the heir with his estates was still in wardship to the Sacheverells.[114] Some respite followed with Francis' majority and his selling of land to meet obligations, but from 1552 dower was again being charged against the estate, and after Henry Kebell's death in 1571, yet another Kebell widow went to law for her rights.[115]

And so the Kebells of Humberstone disappeared, defeated in the end by the ultimate realities of birth and death, marriage and widowhood. With no resident squire, all knowledge of Kebell's house disappeared; with no family, however distant, to protect it, the serjeant's memorial tomb was smashed. Only in a field of the deserted village of Stretton was the name preserved, 'Keble's Close', and some two hundred years ago even that died out. '*Sic dii voluere*.'

111. C1/329/51. 112. Leicestershire Record Office, DE73 – Register 1, f. 185.
113. C1/501/4; CP40/1043 m. 326. 114. C142/56/51. 115. C3/108/3.

18

THOMAS KEBELL AND THE PRE-REFORMATION LEGAL PROFESSION

For Francis Bacon, 'just and parfitte historie' had three forms – the chronicle of a 'time', the 'life' of a person and the narrative of an 'action', and this book is none of them, particularly it is not a 'life' of Thomas Kebell.[1] But it is impossible to investigate over more than two decades the career of a single individual, so that any index automatically falls open at the letter 'K', without wanting to know something of the man himself. And here is temptation. It is all too easy to disguise ignorance with probability – 'some others were, therefore Kebell was' – or to invest the known with plausible imaginative colour – 'In June 1484 Kebell rode to Kirby Muxloe with a heavy heart' – or to exaggerate a supporting role – 'Kebell was present, therefore Kebell did'. Much of our evidence must come from the year books, and J.H. Baker has warned that reports and the like

> are not materials on which to assess character or ability – a judicial biography of that kind is only appropriate for those very few judges . . . whose contributions are marked and remarkable.[2]

The caution is just, and even more true of counsel, so that discretion would leave the character and abilities of Kebell in that historical limbo of things we shall never know. But indiscretion is sometimes irresistible, and, for what they are worth, some speculative conclusions about Kebell's ideas, attitudes and personality can be offered.

I

When the antiquary William Burton wrote that Kebell was 'a man of sound judgement, quick and sharp conceit, great reading and very eloquent' he expressed the reaction of anyone scrutinising the later

1. Francis Bacon, *Of the Proficience and Advancement of Learning* (1605), quoted in L. B. Campbell, *Shakespeare's Histories* (San Marino, 1947), 52.
2. Spelman, *Reports*, i. xv, xvii.

year books.[3] Granted their textual complexity, the advantageous position Kebell enjoyed over several terms, and the pressure to produce the challenging and the novel, it remains true that, on the evidence, Thomas Kebell had few equals in perception, imagination, energy and invention. By the nature of things it is his clashes with the bench which make the most interesting reading, but even when hostile, the courts were often stretched by his submissions. On numerous less dramatic occasions it was the justice who agreed with the serjeant:

> *Kebell*, who was of counsel with the other party: 'The contrary seems to me to be the case.' As to [X] . . . he said . . . , which was agreed by Fineux, chief justice, and Rede his colleague. And further, Kebell said that . . . , and so it seemed to Fineux and Rede.[4]

Those who reported cases were quick to record where he stood. An example from Hilary 1487 ends, 'but note the opinion of Kebell'; a year later we find the comment 'all the justices held this view, Kebell being of the contrary opinion'.[5] The reporter of a case dated Michaelmas 1489 added this gloss, 'I think that Kebell's argument is not answered' and the year book for 14 Henry VII includes the remark, 'query this, because Kebell denied it'.[6] His opinion gives weight to a court decision – 'It was said by all the justices of the common pleas and by Kebell' – while his absence is worth noting and his opposition can suggest that a matter is still unsettled – 'which Bryan denied and Kebell was of the contrary, therefore query this case'.[7] His *dicta* circulated for years. In *Savage's (Sir John) Case*, heard nearly twenty years after Kebell's death, a casual comment at the bar ended 'this was always Kebell's opinion, whom God absolve'.[8]

Thomas Kebell's most forthright statement about the philosophy of law occurred in a discussion of a device to secure more effective execution of a judgement for damages obtained at assizes; the record had been transferred to common pleas where, since the original action had alleged violence, the crown was able to arrest the defendant, so allowing the plaintiff to extort the damages against an adversary in

3. Burton, *Leicestershire*, 128.
4. Keilwey, *Reports* f. 31v; cf. *Y.B.* Hil. 3 Hen. VII, p. 14 f. 4; Mich. 6 Hen. VII, p. 4 f. 8; Hil. 10 Hen. VII, p. 16 f. 17.
5. *ibid.*, Hil. 2 Hen. VII, p. 8 f. 11; Hil. 3 Hen. VII, p. 5 f. 2.
6. *ibid.*, Mich. 5 Hen. VII, p. 13 f. 7; Mich. 14 Hen VII, p. 20 f. 10.
7. *ibid.*, Hil. 6 Hen. VII, p. 6 f. 15; Trin. 14 Hen. VII, p. 2 f. 28; Trin. 16 Hen. VII, p. 2 f. 9.
8. Keilwey, *Reports*, ff. 86, 196v.

custody.[9] The defence, however, argued that no advantage could be taken of process from common pleas because this was not the court which had originally awarded judgement; the plaintiff must, it was suggested, proceed by *scire facias*, a much slower remedy than had been open at assizes, and one which would allow the defendant to argue yet again before the bench. Kebell tried to demolish this by a direct appeal to the judges:

> The king has sent the record into this court [of common pleas] with the intention of doing right to the parties, and he has made you justices for the purpose of ministering right to each person according to the law.
>
> You have no reason to set the defendant at liberty now, and to oblige the plaintiff to sue a *scire facias* in order to secure execution [of the judgement in his favour], other than that you yourselves are not the justices before whom judgement was given. This, as I hold, is of little substance, since you are yourselves in the identical position that they were in, that is justices who have before them the same record which they had in front of them, a record which is agreed to be sound, and your office is to do right.

These sentiments are hardly original, but it is this which makes them interesting. Kebell thought it worthwhile to justify a departure from tradition by appealing to the ultimate duty of a court to see that right prevails, and at least one reporter thought his return to first principles was worth recording.

Something of the same thinking appears in a king's bench case of 1481, one of the earliest where Kebell's opinions are known. The issue was an adjournment wrongly entered in the record. Kebell, however, argued that judicial error should not affect the parties, since, 'as commonly understood, the justices have a perfect knowledge of the law so it will not be presumed that they would adjourn without reasonable cause'.[10] An even closer parallel is in *Rex* v. *the Steelyard* in exchequer chamber. As we have seen, the merchants found themselves being dunned on an earlier judgement in exchequer for customs evasion, a judgement which they were trying to challenge for error under an act of 1357, but without success, since when they appeared the chancellor and the treasurer were always missing, and without these officials the writ could not be heard.[11] Thomas Kebell declared:

> Sir, the defendant is not obliged to make the justices come to the exchequer chamber for the king is under an obligation to do right to the parties.[12] Nor is

9. *Y.B.* Hil. 14 Hen. VII, p. 5 f. 16; cf. Pas. 13 Hen. VII, p. 7 f. 21, Pas. 14 Hen. VII, p. 2 f. 20, Pas. 15 Hen. VII, p. 1 f. 5.
10. *ibid.*, Mich. 21 Edw. IV, p. 42 ff. 65–6.
11. *31 Edward III, Stat. I* c. 12.
12. The exchequer chamber referred to by Kebell is not the court in which he was arguing but the special court set up in 1357 for errors in the exchequer.

the judge obliged to come at the request of the plaintiff in the writ of error. Nor are they obliged to give them a fee or money [in hand]. But they are appointed judges in this matter by Act of Parliament, and so their non-appearance will not be put down to the [party's] default. [Indeed] in no case will non-appearance of the justices be blamed on failure by the litigants.[13]

Year books also preserve other comments on the law which Kebell ventured in the course of his arguments, comments which may reflect his personal views, or the common stock of legal assumption, or both. Twentieth-century readers will warm most readily to his humanity. He was horrified at the suggestion that J.P.s might proceed to trial despite a *certiorari* removing an indictment to king's bench if the accused did not specifically claim benefit of the writ:

This Kebell expressly denied, and said that he would not for anything take execution against a prisoner after such a *certiorari* for it could be that the judgement in that case was for felony.[14]

He appeared for an alleged villein and persuaded the court that 'it is a good exercise of [judicial] discretion to favour liberty, so long as it is [justifiable] by reason'.[15] What argument 'by reason' could lead to (and a warning not to credit Kebell with anachronistic liberal ideas) is seen in another case alleging villein status.[16] There he argued that although the defendant had been judged free in an earlier trespass case, this was no proof of freedom because the purpose of that case was only to sue for damages and not to try the right of villeinage.

In making this appeal to reason, Kebell was touching on one of the central concepts of his profession. Reason was constantly invoked, by judges and counsel alike. Sometimes, as in both villein cases, the word implied a line of reasoning or simply rational argument.[17] At others the stress was on consistency. When an abbot, on the ground of his new rank, tried to evade a bond entered into when a prior, Kebell remarked 'I think it contrary to reason that the abbot by his own action should defeat his own obligation.'[18] In an opposite situation Kebell had used the term 'repugnant': 'it is repugnant if I make on one occasion a discharge of a bond and later charge it again'.[19] Yet again the appeal could be to common sense. When a jury fled in face of

13. *Y.B.* Hil. 6 Hen. VII, p. 9 f. 16.
14. *ibid.*, Hil. 6 Hen. VII, p. 6 ff. 15–16.
15. *ibid.*, Hil. 13 Hen. VII, p. 20 f. 17.
16. *ibid.*, Mich. 14 Hen. VII, p. 12 f. 6.
17. Cf. *ibid.*, Hil. 4 Hen VII, p. 7 f. 4: '*le construction par reason issera a ceo point . . .*'; Mich. 5 Hen. VII, p. 13 f. 6: '*tout est un, ley et raison ou . . .*'.
18. *ibid.*, Pas. 5 Hen. VII, p. 7 f. 25.
19. *ibid.*, Pas. 1 Hen. VII, p. 2 f. 15; cf. Hil. 13 Hen. VII, p. 23 f. 18.

torrential rain while viewing disputed property, Kebell described that conduct as 'reasonable'.[20] But beyond this, reason had a deeper meaning for Kebell and his colleagues; it was the ordering principle of the law. Thomas Eliot remarked:

it may nat be denyed but that al lawes be founded on the depest parte of raison, and I suppose, no one lawe so moche as our owne,

and the conviction echoed the language of the courts as well as Fortescue and St German.[21] The *eruditions* which the profession took as axioms were expressions of this essential reason, and St German was inclined to class them under that head.[22] It was a concern to show the rational basis and structure of the law which inspired Littleton to write his *Tenures* for his son Richard, Kebell's friend at the Inner Temple; 'the law is more honoured when its reasons are approved'.[23] Used in this philosophic sense, the reason of English law was, as St German pointed out, the natural law of European legal analysis.[24] It was an assertion that the common law stood on all fours with the great law of Rome and the continental codes which had sprung from it. William Yelverton J. was quite explicit in a case from the 1460s.

We must act in this case as the canonists and civilians do when faced with a new case for which they have no existing law. Then they resort to the law of nature which is the ground of all laws and according to whatever is decided to be most beneficial to the commonweal, so they act and so must we.[25]

The consequences of this attitude can be seen in Kebell's sensitivity to the implications of arguments and decisions. Sometimes he was concerned with 'inconvenience' in law which would result. Arguing in 1484 for the power of the courts to redress error in a judgement of error already awarded (as against recourse to parliament), Kebell said, 'Sir, as it seems to me, it is no inconvenience in law [for the justices] to reverse the judgement themselves.'[26] Similarly, in an action to enforce a legacy against three executors, Kebell claimed that they were all

20. *ibid.*, Hil. 15 Hen. VII, p. 2 f. 1; cf. Hil. 3 Hen. VII, p. 1 f. 1: '*par common ley et comon reason, nienobstant le Stat. de Westm. 1° et Westm. 2°*'.
21. Eliot, *The Gouernour*, i. 133–4; Chrimes, *Constitutional Ideas*, 200; St German, *Doctor and Student*, 31. For comments by the courts on the role of 'reason' in the law, see Ives, in *Profession, Vocation etc.*, 191–3.
22. St German, *Doctor and Student*, 67.
23. Thomas Littleton, *Tenures* (Richard Tottell, 1583), f. 142(2r).
24. St German, *Doctor and Student*, 31, 33.
25. *Y.B.* Mich. 9 Edw. IV, p. 9 ff. 12–13.
26. *ibid.*, Mich. 2 Ric. III, p. 49 f. 21.

liable on a judgement obtained against only one.[27] If not, a subsequent action against the other two could lead to their handing over the deceased's property, so defeating the earlier judgement – '*ne fuit reason*'. It was this same awareness which led him, more than once, to contrast the technicalities of the law and what the layman could be expected to know. In *Broke* v. *Latimer* he argued that failure by the crown to enrol (as it should have done) a deed of gift to the king, did not invalidate a plea based on that deed:

because although it would be risky to plead the general issue, that is not obvious to a layman . . . And a plea has been similarly allowed in many instances where to do [otherwise] would cause doubt and confusion among the jurors.[28]

On other occasions Kebell was more concerned with Yelverton's test of benefit to the community. Sometimes this was implicit. When an arbitration over the value of a bale of woad collapsed because no equivalent was available in the warehouse specified, Kebell appealed to general principle; the debtor should have obtained a bale from elsewhere: 'since he has bound himself to perform the [terms of the] arbitration, he must perform it if he can, if at all possible'.[29] In exchequer chamber he enunciated basic principle again, this time that 'the judgement given in the court of the king must [remain] in force and be of effect, and will not be voided'.[30] In other cases, the point of public interest is made explicitly. At a murder case, dated 1481, Kebell told the judges, 'because you are conservators of the common profit, you can [yourselves] put [the accused] to execution [after conviction]'.[31] A *nota* in Keilwey's *Reports* has Kebell making the argument of public interest in respect of ownership:

Where my animals of their own error, without my will and knowledge, break into someone else's close, I will be punished, since I am a trespasser along with my animals. This was also agreed [by the court] to be the law because the law requires me to guard my animals without doing wrong to anyone.[32]

Concern for the public good could, perhaps, be a factor in even Kebell's most technical pleas. When the prior of Dunstable refused to pay a London fishmonger for fish supplied on the order of his

27. Keilwey, *Reports*, ff. 22–5; cf. Kebell at Hall's reading, 'it is the most convenient judgement to save the rights of both . . .': Thorne, *Readings and Moots*, i. 168.
28. Keilwey, *Reports*, ff. 9v, 10; cf. *Y.B.* Pas. 11 Hen. VII, p. 1 f. 17: '*leys ne pouvent av conisance de tiel mannere de voidance*'.
29. *Y.B.* Hil. 9 Hen. VII, p. 7 ff. 15–16.
30. *ibid.*, Hil. 4 Hen. VII, p. 4 f. 3.
31. *ibid.*, Mich. 21 Edw. IV, p. 57 f. 73.
32. Keilwey, *Reports*, f. 3v.

predecessor, the merchant (who had no written contract) could bring only an action of debt, and on this the prior could claim the right to 'wage his law', that is, to clear himself on oath.[33] Kebell, representing the merchant, attempted a distinction between the position of the new prior and that of his predecessor: 'it is contrary to reason that he should wage his law, for the contract was entered into by another person [the previous prior], and he was not party to it'. The right of the former prior to wager of law was beyond question, but if Kebell had been successful in denying it to the successor (and Chief Justice Bryan agreed with him), the consequence would have been a modest but nevertheless significant defiance of one of the most stultifying of common-law rules.

The reason of the law was, thus, concerned with the general good. Alongside this, we find in Kebell an awareness of Littleton's point, that there was a shape or logic in the common law, a logic which required even that a murder suspect, now free from suspicion, should not be discharged except by due legal process.[34] As we have seen, this logic persisted despite statutory enactment.[35] It included a concept of the law as the king's law which, as again we have seen, led Kebell and his colleagues to important professional attitudes and interpretations.[36] The law, also, was first and foremost a property law, with a hierarchy of interests to which Kebell referred in *Rede* v. *Capel* – that the freehold takes precedence over the chattel (and 'chattel' included such commercial titles as the lease); other lawyers made similar remarks.[37] Another emphasis was on the feudal element in the law, something stressed by Sir John Fortescue.[38] 'The guardians [of a ward]', Kebell told the common pleas in *Rex* v. *the Bishop of Chester*, 'are favoured by the law', a point amplified in another report, in which a connection is made with the preference in the common law for title by freehold.[39] It was the logic of the common law also to prevent hindrance to litigation. In the slander case brought by Lord Beauchamp against Sir Richard Croft, Kebell commented:

Notwithstanding that the action [alleging forgery] was false and found against the plaintiff . . . no remedy is given and provided [in law] against those who sue such false actions, and the reason is the favour [given to] plaintiffs and demandants so that they should not be held back from suing their actions

33. *Y.B.* Mich. 13 Hen. VII, p. 2 ff. 2–3; cf. Pas. 1 Hen. VII, p. 18 f. 25.
34. Keilwey, *Reports*, f. 34v.
35. See above, p. 164. 36. See above, pp. 222–3. 37. See above, p. 218.
38. Fortescue, *De Laudibus*, 107–11.
39. *Y. B.* Pas. 14 Hen. VII, p. 4 f. 26; Pas. 15 Hen. VII, p. 2 f. 7.

according to the cases [they have], etc. For it might be found against them even though they did have a good cause of action.[40]

Similar attitudes underlie Kebell's frequent stress on the rights of plaintiffs in general and the need for haste to remedy their wrongs. Delay was sometimes necessary to preserve the rights of the defendant. In *Broke* v. *Latimer*, one of the defendant's attorneys had made default but another had entered an essoin, or excuse for absence.[41] Kebell argued:

When one made default and the other [entered] an essoin, it is right that [the essoin] should excuse his master's default because the law takes it that he had legal matter to plead . . . and could not come for illness or other such reasonable excuse as he has made by his essoin.

Generally, however, the law should be urgent to meet the plaintiff's claim; 'all laws favour the plaintiff because the law presumes he has suffered a wrong'.[42] In an argument about pleading new matter in a case, Kebell said:

I hold that when a man has once pleaded a plea [alleging new matter] he cannot on another day leave his plea and have another plea [alleging new matter]because [that will] delay the plaintiff indefinitely.[43]

Thomas Kebell, after all, well appreciated that the law was often a matter of balance, one interest against another. In a replevin case he persuaded the court that two proposed 'issues' were worthless to the plaintiff and that to reject them would do the defendant no harm:

If these issues were found in favour of the plaintiff, . . . yet he will by these issues be in no better position than he is now; . . . therefore it is not right to delay him by such an issue of which he can, in no way, take advantage.[44]

In *John Duplage* v. *Sir Gilbert Debenham* he argued that although the land pledged under a statute staple (possibly fraudulently) could no longer be occupied to recoup the debt, the debtor should still be arrested and held in gaol, 'for the law presumes that he will [in consequence] make greater haste to satisfy the [creditor]'.[45] One of his earliest reported cases has Kebell throwing the responsibility for the balance of hardship on the judges directly. The plaintiff had brought a writ of trespass alleging the wrongful pasturing of animals on his

40. Keilwey, *Reports*, f. 26v.
41. *Y.B.* Mich. 12 Hen. VII, p. 5 f. 9.
42. *ibid.*, Pas. 14 Hen. VII, p. 2 f. 20.
43. *ibid.*, Trin. 16 Hen. VII, p. 5 f. 11.
44. *ibid.*, Trin. 13 Hen. VII, p. 7 f. 28.
45. *ibid.*, Mich. 15 Hen. VII, p. 6 ff. 14–16.

land on 10 May by the lessee of the land from a life tenant whose death the day before had had the effect of terminating the lease.

> [The lessee] must show [the date at which] he removed his animals, and if it appears to the court a reasonable time . . . after the death, so the plea will be good, and this will be in the discretion of the judges on his own showing, whether he drove off his beasts within a reasonable time after the decease [of the life tenant].[46]

On occasion Kebell even applied 'profit and loss' to technicalities of pleading. In *John Donne* v. *E[dmund] Cornwall et feme*, a suit for £10 owed on a bond, the defendant argued that he had discharged the debt but that Donne had repossessed the document by force.[47] Kebell denied that this was an inadmissible 'double' plea because it alleged both payment and repossession. That was so:

> only where the court would be misled in giving judgement or when one part of the plea is found in favour of the plaintiff and the other for the defendant or [where there is] the mischief that [the respondent] would reply to one [part] and the party which pleaded the plea would stand on the other, but in this case there are no such factors.

Kebell was also aware of relativity in relation to time. He noticed historical differences:

> In ancient times the law was that everybody could kill an attainted felon;

he had some sense of historical explanation:

> The origin of the disclaimers was . . . and it was the consideration of skilled lawyers in the past *(anciens sages del' ley)* that . . .;

he was aware of change in the law: 'It seems to me that the older opinion was the better'; 'the case has not been in use in recent days'.[48]

None of this must be taken to mean that Thomas Kebell was a major, still less an original legal thinker, but it does suggest that ordinary lawyers were aware of more than technique. The common law had nothing to rival the weight of civil-law philosophy, and it is easy to contrast the few who wrote reflectively – Fortescue, Dudley, More, Eliot, St German – with the many who collected reports. But Kebell's ideas, although glimpsed only occasionally, show that men

46. *ibid.*, Mich. 22 Edw. IV, p. 7 f. 27.
47. *ibid.*, Pas. 1 Hen. VII, p. 2 ff. 14–17.
48. *ibid.*, Mich. 21 Edw. IV, p. 57 f. 73; Trin. 13 Hen VII, p. 6 ff. 27–8; Hil. 11 Hen.VII, p. 11 f. 15; Trin. 13 Hen. VII, p. 6 f. 28; cf. Kebell's reading: '*L'oppinion du ancientes q'il . . . mez ore l'oppinion est . . .*'. B. L. Hargrave Ms. 87 f. 303v.

who were steeped in, and never considered writing anything other than, year-book reports, nevertheless worked within and took for granted a wide framework of jurisprudence.

II

Since the year books do not in the main deal directly in terms of substantive propositions it is not possible to ask what Kebell's opinions were on the development of English law. That lawyers did have distinctive views on certain issues is clear, though these were usually points of pleading. Kebell remembered Grantham by his *dicta*, and others were to remember Kebell in the same way.[49] From time to time a reporter will note that such and such an proposal is always opposed by a particular judge.[50] But we cannot go beyond this.

Where the year books do have something to tell us, is about Kebell's character and personality. The first impression is of his self-confidence. 'Kebell denied utterly'; 'Kebell said that the cases were clear'; 'He said for clear law'; 'If what I say is law, as I have always understood it is, then . . .'.[51] This was certainly an expression of professional expertise, but it also seems to be a trait of personality. On more than one occasion he insisted on arguing when the bench had told him that his point was already accepted or else too far-fetched to bother with.[52] He clearly enjoyed the sound of his own voice – indulging in lectures on this or that point of law; and in a case dated 1493 he announced 'I will only put one case, which has been judged' and then proceeded at some length.[53] Another dimension of this was his readiness to criticise opponents. He opened his defence of Sir Thomas Grene's servants by dismissing the plaintiff's arguments as 'conceits', which may not imply 'far-fetched' but certainly means no better than 'hypotheses'.[54] Kebell was also capable of a good deal of impudence. In a case concerning uses, Kebell opposed the ruling of the court. Bryan replied:

49. *Y.B.* Trin. 13 Hen. VII, p. 6 f. 28; Keilwey, *Reports*, f. 86: '*issint fuit lestatute . . . construe quant Kebell fuit serjiant del' roy*, ut dictum fuit per Rudhall et Pigot qui interfuerunt *arguonts*'.
50. See above, p. 172.
51. *Y.B.* Hil. 2 Hen. VII, p. 19 f. 14; Pas. 16 Hen. VII, p. 4 f. 6; Trin. 16 Hen. VII, p. 12 f. 15; Pas. 1 Hen. VII, p. 2 f. 16; Mich. 14 Hen. VII, p. 9 f. 4.
52. *ibid.*, Pas. 8 Hen. VII, p. 1 f. 11; Trin. 10 Hen. VII, p. 1 f. 24; Pas. 13 Hen. VII, p. 9 f. 23.
53. *ibid.*, Mich. 9 Hen. VII, p. 6 f. 10.
54. *ibid.*, Mich. 14 Hen. VII, p. 19 f. 8.

Yes, truly. And you have a matter pending [before this court] on the very same ground, something you don't mention even though it has passed in your favour![55]

Kebell's style was aggressive as well as assertive. In *Pind* v. *Eriche* Kebell appeared for the plaintiff against Robert Rede.[56] Rede tried to 'confess and avoid' the plaintiff's claim, that is, he admitted that it was true in the form stated but argued that it did not have the consequences that were claimed. Kebell objected that he must enter a traverse, that is, stand on the facts he had alleged.

Vavasour: Put the case to us, for we do not see that he has not [successfully] confessed this and avoided it.
Kebell: When [*etc.*] . . .
Vavasour: I deny that. And there is a distinction [*viz.*] . . .
Kebell: You say truly if [X] . . . but when [Y] . . .
Vavasour: This [point] has been judged . . .
Kebell: There the discontinuance is defeated by the recovery . . . but if this condition is in suspense during the life tenancy, then in our case the discontinuance remains in full force.
Bryan to Kebell: It seems to you that the condition is in suspense . . . but this does not seem so to us . . .

Rede then, contrary to the opinion of the court, accepted the traverse.

Kebell: Still the plea is not good for he has now 'avoided' us by two alternative routes . . .
Danvers: Nothing satisfies you, because first you wanted to have him take a traverse and now when he has taken a traverse you are [still] not content.
Kebell: I want him to leave the condition out . . .
Bryan to *Rede*: Take his papers from him and take careful consideration against tomorrow, whether he will traverse him or not.

This is the most revealing instance, but there are others. On one occasion Thomas Wode said to Kebell 'You need not be as hasty as you are'; on another, Kebell said to Bryan, 'Saving your correction, you are denying me the law.'[57] There are also the times when Kebell asserted his knowledge of *nos livres* against both bench and the rest of the bar.[58]

One of the most frequent characteristics of Kebell's pleading was the personal example. This was common practice in the profession. Usually the examples are hypothetical – 'if I am obliged . . .', 'if I

55. *ibid.*, Trin. 10 Hen. VII, p. 24 f. 29.
56. *ibid.*, Pas. 11 Hen. VII, p. 10 ff. 21–22.
57. *ibid.*, Pas. 11 Hen. VII, p. 2 f. 19; Trin. 11 Hen. VII, p. 15 f. 29.
58. See above, pp. 157–8.

avow . . .', 'if I make a man my executor . . .', 'if I grant a rent . . .'.[59] Sometimes we have reflected the concerns of the time: 'if I am bound to make a payment in Westminster Hall'; 'if a man takes my horse'; 'if a stranger distrains my animals'; 'if a lord grants me hunting rights'; 'if a man makes an obligation to me and then enters a religious order . . .'.[60] Very occasionally we have a first-hand illustration:

> If a bill should be brought against me [consigning me] to the custody of the Marshalsea under the name of Thomas Kebell, gentleman, and the sheriff arrests Thomas Kebell, yeoman, the said Thomas Kebell, yeoman, will have a good action for false imprisonment against the sheriff.[61]

This was in 1481, but some ten years later we find that the titles have risen:

> If I am obliged to you by the name of Thomas Kebell, gentleman, and then I am made a knight . . .[62]

Whether this was said with humour is not clear: the case did warrant the example, but it is hard not to imagine some smile when, in appearing for Robert Sheffield, Kebell had to argue against the claim that a verdict that defendants had taken 2,000 roach from a fishery did not necessarily imply that they had fished there![63] Sometimes the personal example crosses the court: 'if I am obliged to stand to the arbitration of my Lord Bryan . . .'.[64] Sometimes the allusion gets out of Westminster Hall entirely. In the suit against William Say's bailiff Kebell remarked:

> If I grant a man [permission] to take each year a deer, a hare or a rabbit . . . and if I grant my parker the shoulders and the umbles of every deer which will be killed, this grant is valid.[65]

Arguing that a sheriff could take armed men with him when executing a replevin, Kebell said:

59. *Y.B.* Pas. 13 Hen. VII, p. 1 f. 19; Hil. 10 Hen. VII, p. 12 f. 15; Pas. 10 Hen. VII, p. 1 f. 18; Trin. 12 Hen. VII, p. 5 f. 25.
60. *ibid.*, Hil. 10 Hen. VII, p. 4 f. 13; Hil. 12 Hen. VII, p. 2 f. 15; Trin. 16 Hen. VII, p. 11 f. 15; Mich. 11 Hen. VII, p. 30 f. 8; Pas. 5 Hen. VII, p. 7 f. 25.
61. *ibid.*, Mich. 21 Edw. IV, p. 56 f. 71.
62. *ibid.*, Trin. 11 Hen. VII, p. 4 f. 25.
63. *ibid.*, Pas. 11 Hen. VII, p. 4 ff. 19–20; see above, pp. 179–80. Cf. Kebell's comment that the only difference between a boat and a boot is the letter 'o': Spelman, *Reports*, ii. 212.
64. *Y.B.* Trin. 4 Hen. VII, p. 8 f. 12.
65. *ibid.*, Trin. 10 Hen. VII, p. 28 f. 30.

The use of armour [and weapons] is not invariably punishable, as on Midsummer Night in London where [they go in harness] for sport, and it is not prohibited.[66]

We come closest to Thomas Kebell as a person when we note a further characteristic in his pleadings, his interest in words. There are forty or more reports where the serjeant makes some verbal or grammatical point, often at length. The criticism of documents is, of course, part of a lawyer's trade, and a number of instances fall under this head. In *King's College, Cambridge* v. *the Vicar of C.* he attacked the patent on which the college sought to rely:

It is by exemplification and says '*Datum per manum nostram tali die*' and does not say '*in cuius rei testimonia has litteras nostras patentes fieri fecimus*'.[67]

A case arising from the rights of a manorial lord finds Kebell saying:

The *capias* is conditional because of these words – '*Ita quod habeas* [in order to have] . . .', but in a *habere facias seisinam* the writ instructs the sheriff to put the party in possession, without [using] such conditional words.[68]

In *Lord Greystoke's Case* Kebell enunciated a principle for the construction of ambiguous pleas, that the sense least advantageous to the party pleading should be the one taken, but not where the alternative meaning is expressly given.[69]

But over and above these and other instances of legal construction are those in which Kebell shows some acquaintance with the vocabulary of grammar and rhetoric. Early in Henry VII's reign, John Butler tried to argue that a claim to land 'as son and heir' did not amount to a claim to be the 'son and heir'.[70] Kebell rejected this:

These words *come* or *ut* [as] will only be understood as a similitude [in apposition], and, in any case, as a statement of fact, since if anyone says 'J.S. as my father' it is nothing but a similitude and not the thing itself [i.e. something separate]. And in any case, it will be taken as a statement of fact according to normal speech where one cannot do otherwise – as to say that X is seised in his demesne as of fee, there this is taken as a statement of fact, and the words are in the form of a similitude, for it cannot otherwise be taken, and so here.

Commenting on *De Haeretico Comburendo* he said: 'the statute is conditional – "that the bishop should . . ." . . . the statute is in the

66. *ibid.*, Hil. 3 Hen. VII, p. 1 f. 1.
67. *ibid.*, Trin. 7 Hen. VII, p. 1 f. 14
68. *ibid.*, Trin. 16 Hen. VII, p. 9 f. 14.
69. *ibid.*, Hil. 3 Hen. VII, p. 10 f. 3
70. *ibid.*, Mich. 5 Hen. VII, p. 3 f. 2.

disjunctive – "or if . . ." '.[71] He frequently had to argue whether a plea should be general or special, in the affirmative or in the negative, and he was perfectly familiar with the 'pregnant negative', the negative which, as Kebell said, 'implies an affirmative'.[72] In the *Case of the Vicars of Salisbury*, Vavasour had argued that a defendant who claimed that he had not been asked to pay for bread delivered was obliged to be more specific.[73] Kebell disagreed:

He has spoken in the negative and so he does not [need to] show any certainty . . . But if the reply must be in the affirmative, then he must show [the] certainty . . . And in this case the issue is not *negativa praegnans*, because it agrees with the wording of the [original] condition [of the contract].

Other lawyers, notably Thomas Bryan, shared Kebell's facility in grammar, but that this was not universal is shown by the reports of the case which arose from an agreement to make over an estate 'as counsel learned in the law would advise'.[74] Kebell, for the plaintiff, raised several objections to the defence plea that no advice had been forthcoming and then he drew the court's attention to the wording of the plea:

Sir, it is a point which I am doubtful about, whether the plea should be this – 'that no counsel (*nullum consilium*) gave advice', or [else] – 'that counsel gave no advice (*consilium nullum*)'. But to say [as the defendant had] – 'that counsel did not give advice', seems to be far too general.
Bryan: It seems to me (as you have said) that it is not [a proper] plea, for if you are a good sophister the universal negative and the particular negative are not the same thing. For the sophister's tag is *prae contradictio, post contrarietas per postque subalternitas*. And this tag proves that a universal negative and a particular negative are in different places of the figure [sequence]. 'No counsel gave advice' is a universal negative which proves that no advice was given, but 'counsel did not advise' [would still allow advice to have been given, e.g. by certain counsel where others did not advise]. And so it seems to me that the plea is not good, but he must say '*Nullum consilium* . . .' or '*Consilium nullum* . . .' and not say 'Counsel did not give advice.'
Townshend: I think the opposite. And I am not a good sophister, but I can see that the issue is perfectly good [in law] . . .

71. *ibid.*, Hil. 10 Hen. VII, p. 17 f. 18. Cf. *ibid.*, Mich. 14 Hen. VII, p. 19 f. 8: 'it seems to me that *adtune et ibidem* will be understood as . . .'.
72. *ibid.*, Mich. 9 Hen. VII, p. 8 f. 13; cf. Pas. 21 Edw. IV, p. 22 ff. 7–10; Trin. 22 Edw. IV, p. 41 ff. 15–17; Mich. 5 Hen. VII, p. 18 f. 8; Pas. 16 Hen. VII, p. 10 f. 7; Trin. 16 Hen. VII, p. 3 f. 11.
73. *ibid.*, Trin. 4 Hen. VII, p. 8 f. 12.
74. *ibid.*, Trin. 6 Hen. VII, p. 3 f. 4; Trin. 11 Hen. VII, p. 1 f. 23; see above, pp. 144, 170, 172–3.

Even after five hundred years, Roger Townshend's distrust of Kebell and Bryan rings out clearly.

Not only had Thomas Kebell some formal grasp of English grammar but he was fluent in Latin. Apart from the books in his library and his frequent Latin tags – '*per particula illa*', '*gratia argumenti*', '*nec e converso*' and others more familiar – he suggested himself that ability in all three languages of the common law was to be expected of a lawyer.[75]

If I order a man to make a deed of feoffment in my name according to a copy shown him in Latin, if he makes a deed of feoffment according to the effect of the words but in English or French, the feoffment is without warrant for he has not followed his authorisation.[76]

Kebell was well able to debate meanings. He asserted that '*approbamus, ratificamus et confirmamus ac etiam damus et concedimus*' was self-evidently contradictory since to 'ratify' and to 'grant' are different operations in time.[77] On another occasion he pointed out that an ambiguity in English would have been perfectly clear in Latin.[78] A grant read:

I grant to John a Stile the keeping of my park of Dale for term of life, and all the windfall wood within the same during the said term

and the question was, whether the grantee had to account for the wood. Kebell thought that he did:

For the plaintiff granted him only the custody of the park and the trees, which is a copulative. Thus if the grant were in Latin the matter would be plain. For if I make a grant in these words '*Sciatis me concessisse Johanni Stile custodiam parci mei Oxoniae &c arborum vento prostratorum*', he will account for both. But if the grant should be in the accusative case, '*Concessi custodiam* parci mei *&c arbores vento prostratos*', the grantee will not [have to] account [for the wood].

Where Kebell had learned his languages we do not know, but he had certainly learned them.

75. *ibid.*, Pas. 15 Hen. VII, p. 2 f. 8; Trin. 5 Hen. VII, p. 4 f. 39; Pas. 10 Hen. VII, p. 5 f. 19.
76. *ibid.*, Mich. 10 Hen. VII, p. 20 f. 9.
77. *ibid.*, Trin. 7 Hen. VII, p. 1 f. 14.
78. *ibid.*, Mich. 10 Hen. VII, p. 16 f. 8.

III

The year books thus show us a Thomas Kebell who is a reflective, educated man with a distinct personality and idiosyncrasies. The only other personal glimpses we have are those to be found in his single extant private letter (to the corporation of Coventry), and in his last will and testament.[79] The letter is substantially concerned with professional matters, but it does contain one phrase of interest, 'I, unworthy, am named to be sergeaunt at the lawe.' The phrase is found elsewhere, and raises the whole question of the attitude of the lawyers to their profession. William Paston referred to himself as a serjeant 'thow he be vnworthy'.[80] Thomas Bryan said in his will that 'though unworthy' he was chief justice, and his successor, Thomas Wode, described himself as 'Simple Justice of the Commene place'.[81] Humphrey Coningsby was more elaborate and described himself as justice of the common pleas though 'unwurthye to haue any suche office or degree'.[82] What significance should be attached to such self-deprecation is not clear. A convention may be all that is involved, but beyond this, the overt modesty probably disguises pride in achievement. If so it parallels the directions of various testators, Kebell included, to be buried:

in suche fourme as myn executours think convenient for the degre that it hath pleasid God to calle me to in this world.[83]

That 'degree' refers specifically to the rank of serjeant is, however, unlikely; it probably has the sense of 'general status'. Miles Metcalfe, recorder of York, and, like Kebell, a justice at Lancaster, could ask to:

be doone fore at my beryall . . . conveniently and according to my degree and the office the which I had in the citee.[84]

Other evidence supports the suggestion that lawyers were conscious of achievement and status. Two of Baron Clerk's daughters died in his lifetime. For each there is a monumental brass and in each case there is a reference to the rank of John Clerk.[85] When the serjeants of 1486

79. *Coventry Leet Book*, i. 526–8; PROB11/12 ff. 22v–23v; see Appendix A.
80. *Paston Letters and Papers*, i. 11.
81. PROB11/12 ff. 105v, 106; 11/13 f.161v; cf. Spelman, *Reports*, i. plate 10.
82. PROB11/25 f. 217v.
83. For the following, see Appendix A, pp. 425–31 below.
84. *Testamenta Eboracensia*, iv. 9.
85. Stephenson, *Brasses*, 204, 244.

gave the customary rings to mark their elevation, some at least were engraved with suitable tags; John Fineux chose as his motto, 'everyone is the maker of his own fortune'.[86]

The pride of lawyers in their success was certainly shared by their families and friends. Thomas Kebell specified only 'a conuenyent tome for me and my wifes' but his executors took this to mean a full-length alabaster effigy in the scarlet robes Kebell had worn on assize and at Lancaster.[87] The serjeant's figure was flanked by his first two wives, and the personal element in his success was unintentionally emphasised by the sparse heraldic display on the tomb – the Folville arms of his mother which he used as his own, and shields showing his marriages. Most funeral monuments to lawyers were equally as anxious to draw attention to the professional standing of the deceased. Many tomb effigies have been destroyed – Kebell's disappeared between 1638 and 1795 – but at least nine have survived for serjeants for the years to 1531 and of these six show the deceased in legal robes.[88] Lawyers were also commemorated in stained glass. Kebell's own shield of arms was in the windows of St Dunstan's, Fleet Street.[89] At Long Melford in Suffolk are late fifteenth-century lights commemorating William Howard, one of Edward I's judges, and two more recent lawyers, Serjeant Richard Pigot (d. 1483) and John Haugh J.C.P. (d. 1489); all three are in legal dress.[90] Brasses were more common. Royal judges are known to have been depicted on brasses from the mid-fourteenth century, and the earliest extant brass for a serjeant is that of John Rede (d. 1404).[91] In a few instances, it is true, there is a hint that contemporaries saw a tension between the social status achieved by the lawyer and the profession he had followed. Sir John Mordaunt, serjeant-at-law, lies on his tomb in full armour – justified, perhaps, by his service at the battle of Stoke – but there had been nothing martial about the similarly portrayed Thomas

86. Foss, *Judges*, v. 16.

87. Nichols, *Leicestershire*, iii. 270.

88. Between the 1638 edition of Burton, *Leicestershire* and Nichols, *Leicestershire* (1795–1815). Tombs survive for Robert Brudenell (d. 1531), John Fortescue (d. *c.* 1479), William Gascoigne (d. 1419), John Mordaunt (d. 1504), Richard Newton (d. 1449), John Portington (d. 1462), William Rickhill (d. 1407), William Rudhale (d. 1530), Richard Willoughby (d. 1362): F. H. Crossley, *English Church Monuments, 1150–1550* (1921), 86–103; see also Ives, in *Profession, Vocation etc.*, 188–9.

89. Nichols, *Leicestershire*, iii. 270.

90. W. N. Hargreaves-Mawdsley, *History of Legal Dress in Europe* (Oxford, 1963), plate 10B.

91. Stephenson, *Brasses*, 404, 445–6.

Playter, Fastolf's law agent.[92] The brass of Sir William Yelverton J.K.B. is incongruous to a degree – coif and judicial robes over full armour – as Norfolk latten workers tried to portray a knight who was at the same time a judge; the effigy of Sir John Portington at Eastrington in the East Riding is similarly hermaphrodite.[93] But the more usual emotion was open pride. Robert Baynard's brass refers to him as *vir egregius et legis peritus*; the inscription on the tomb of John Edward describes him as *famosus apprenticius in lege peritus*.[94] In the case of Robert Skern, learned in the law, there is even the tag, 'living by the regimen of the law promotes men to honour'.[95]

Consciousness of status informs Kebell's will and testament throughout. He is to be conveyed to his burial as his executors think:

> convenyent for the honeste of me and my frendes, all veyne glory and pompe of the world sett apart;

Alms are to be given as 'most convenyent for my degre and to the pleasur of God'. Kebell would have seen no incongruity here. He took completely for granted the religious essence of social order and the alleged discovery of later Calvinists that success is evidence of divine approval. His degree is what 'it hath pleasid God to calle me to in this world'; he disposes of 'suche goodes as God hath suffered me to have here in erth'; he acknowledges 'the manyfold benefittes and goodnes that He hath sent to me in erth'. And Kebell recognised not only the ultimate goodness of God but a proximate debt to other people. He lists among those 'I am bounden to prey for' not only 'my good lorde William, late Lord Hastinges and other' and 'my good cousin Richard Hotoft' but also:

> the soules of theym of whome I haue had any manner of benefittes and specially for the soulis whos benefittes I haue not deserued.

Similar considerations explain the comments and provisions relating to his son. Walter is to capitalise on the connection with the Hastings family:

> [I charge him] that he kepe treuly his legiaunce and always be kinde, loving and do his feithfull seruice to his power to my singular good lady, my Lady

92. John Mordaunt, Turvey, Beds.: Polydore Vergil, *Historia Anglia*, ed. D. Hay, Camden Soc., 3 ser., 74 (1950), 23; Thomas Playter, Sotterley, Suff.
93. William Yelverton, Rougham, Norf.: H. W. Macklin, *Brasses of England* (1907), 177.
94. Stephenson, *Brasses*, 155, 532.
95. *ibid.*, 489: '*regalis juris vivens promovit honores*'.

Hastinges his godmother, to my lord hir sonne, and my moost singuler good lady, my Lady Hungreford his wife, and ther children.

Lady Hungerford was an executor and received a handsome bequest. One of the obligations which she shared with the widow Margaret and the other two executors, Canon Robert Mome and Kebell's cousin, Thomas Cotton, was the consolidation of the Kebell fortunes in the wardship and marriage of the heir. The father is quite specific about the posthumous daughter-in-law he wants:

I beseche and pray myn executours that with suche goodes and money as I shall leve to theim they will helpe to prouide for my said sonne sum conuenyent mariage of an heritour yf they can.

With the patronage of the Hastings family and an heiress for a wife, the position of Walter Kebell would be secure.

In an equally conventional way, Thomas Kebell's will shows evidence of strong family piety. He left cash to three nieces and three cousins, two of whom were his godsons, to his brother-in-law Thomas Palmer and to his two step-sons. His nephew George Villiers was granted an annuity 'to prey for me and to be loving to his cousyn my sonne'; another niece received his deceased wife's best bonnet and a gown and the rest of her clothes were to be divided between 'my necis, cousins and frendis'. The family emphasis is even stronger in the contingent arrangements to cover the death of Walter or Walter's heir under the age of twenty-four. Half of the 'stuf and houshold henginges and bedding' would then be divided between 'my nevieus, necis and cosyn Thomas Cotton the elder'. His nephew Thomas Kebell of Rearsby would get some plate, and Thomas Cotton the elder other items, while Cotton's son, Thomas, would receive 'a potell pot of siluer'. As for the land, the Kebells of Rearsby would get Humberstone and other property to the total value of £12 13s. 4d. a year; George Villiers would get the reversion of Billesdon and four marks of land elsewhere, and the Cottons estates worth £10 annually. The family motif is also seen in the remainder upon a remainder which Kebell laid down for Humberstone. If the Kebells of Rearsby died out, the estate would then revert to his aunt (*recte* the heirs of his aunt) Mary Billing, thus vesting the property of his cousin Richard Hotoft in the Cottons and the Lacys, the surviving descendants of Kebell's Folville grandfather. Kebell evidently shared the conventional feeling that 'livelihood' or family property ought, in morality if not in law, to be passed on to the heirs, however distant.

Yet it would be unfair to dismiss Thomas Kebell as a stereotype of contemporary attitudes and values. The Hastings connection was personal as well as calculated. If Kebell's direct heirs were to die out, Lady Hungerford was to have the pick of his plate and the widow of William, Lord Hastings, 'my speciall good lady', £20 in money. He might charge Walter to be 'kinde and loving to my kynnesfolk and his and to my seruantes and frendes and lovers' and grant the annuity to George Villiers or a bequest to William Smith, 'preying him to be loving to my sowle and to my sonne', but his concern extended to his deceased nephew's widow, Rose, who was not to be forgotten when the clothes were shared out. As for his son, Kebell wanted more than dynastic immortality. The interest in Walter's education which led to the bequest of all the serjeant's books, led also to careful provisions for his minority, which was to extend until the age of twenty-four.[96] The power that Kebell gave the executors to withhold or even refuse Walter his father's chattels if he failed to 'dispose him to vertue and goodnesse' was not unusual, but their positive obligations were expressed with feeling.[97] And Walter's material interests were to be protected also. When he came of age the executors were to see to it that the Hamilton and Stretton pastures were being actively farmed and carrying a full complement of animals.

There is no less reason to accept Kebell's religious sentiments as genuine, and deeply felt. The religious provisions of his will are certainly conventional. He left a total of £42 3s. 4d. in specified amounts, plus 'suche mortuarys as accordith with the lawe' to his curate, and 'convenyent' costs 'for my conueyng to Humberstone' and a number of religious purchases. He remembered his childhood parish of Rearsby, the church at Humberstone, the beadhouse and the friaries in Leicester, the Whitefriars in London and various religious houses where he had connections.[98] The full office for the dead was to be said a thousand times immediately after his death and daily services held for seven years at an annual cost of eight marks. But the personal motto engraved on Kebell's signet ring was 'God me gide' and there are sufficient touches in the will to confirm that his religion was not the last-minute prompting of the parson at the death-bed. The daily celebration was not to be merely a mass but matins, commendations and vespers, with the seven penitential psalms and the litany alternating with the rosary on weekdays and the psalms of

96. See above, p. 367. 97. See below, pp. 426–7. 98. See above, p. 135.

the passion every Sunday. In addition to forty shillings for 'tithes forgotin' and five marks 'to the relief of the chirch' at Humberstone, he ordered the purchase of a chalice (unpriced), vestments for a deacon and sub-deacon of 'bawdekin', shot silk or silk and gold thread, and a matching cope for the celebrant at high mass. For the Hotoft chantry chapel in the church, he provided two sets of vestments and altar cloths, one for everyday and one for festivals, a chalice, price £4, and his own mass book, 'coverid with white' – either the 'litell old masse boke . . . of freres vse' worth 13s. 4d. or a 'sawter in parchment glosed' valued at 30s.[99] To add to this, we have the evidence of Kebell's own domestic religious arrangements at Humberstone Manor and his anxiety for the soul of Richard Hotoft.[100] In the serjeant's lifetime prayers had been a personal obligation, but others might feel less committed. Kebell therefore instructed his executors to erect a suitable rent-charge on his estates, and to build a house in Humberstone for the chantry priest. In the event of the family dying without heirs a second chantry was to be set up to pray:

> for me, my lady Hungerford and the soule of my cousin Hotofte and for the soules afore in this my wil or in my testament rehersid,

and both were to be formally amortised by royal licence.

The more personal our insights become, the less Kebell remains a representative of the profession at large: we simply do not know if his religious devotion was typical. His attitudes can be paralleled. William Copley, prothonotary of the common pleas, annotated his rotulets with the motto, 'Think and thank God', and provided, for a month after his burial, a daily mass and a procession to the grave for the recitation of the *De Profundis*.[101] Humphrey Coningsby declared that he died 'in stedfast truth and in perfite beleve in Almighty God and holy churche'.[102] If he died near either Aldenham (Herts.) or Rock (Worcs.) his main properties outside London, he was to be buried in the appropriate parish church, in the 'high chauncell' 'where as the sepulture of our Lord Jesu Christ is vsed to be sett and stande on Good Fryday'. His principal benefactions were, that:

> the south ile of the church of Aldenham shalbe made owt in length and brede in almaner of worke in stone, tymbre, lede, glasse and all other thinges

99. See Appendix B, pp. 445–6.

100. See above, 359–60.

101. Hastings, *Common Pleas*, 116, 266; *Testamenta Eboracensia*, iv. 46–50.

102. PROB11/25 f. 217v. John Catesby prayed that his sons would be 'nothing if not Catholic, strong and vigorous in doing good, and Godfearing', *ibid.*, 8 f. 4.

conueinent and necessaire vnto the est ende of the high chauncell . . . [and] a goodly table to be made for an aulter in the same ile and cause the same and also the tabernacle of Saint Mary Magdaleyn standing in the same ile to be goodly paynted and gilte in goodly wise,

and the repainting and gilding of the statues in the Lady Chapel at Rock, together with a new altar there.[103] Other lawyers who erected churches include Nicholas Ashton J.C.P. and, most strikingly, Brian Roucliffe, baron of the exchequer, who rebuilt Cowthorpe church in the West Riding, and while building was going on had the parish services held in his private chapel.[104] His memorial brass showed Brian and his wife holding the new church between them.[105]

Yet not all lawyers display such personal religious interest. Many wills were too much a matter of desperate urgency to permit elaboration. Others go to the heart of the matter, the distribution of wealth, with a perfunctory gesture to the religious conventions. In the case of the surly Yorkshire judge, John Vavasour, a certain calculation marks the religious instructions, and the principal personal impression left is of his unhappy marriage and the desire to be revenged on his wife.[106] It is quite impossible to generalise about 'the religious attitude of the legal profession'. That all performed the required religious duties can be assumed; it does not follow that all shared the devotion of Kebell, Copley, Coningsby or Roucliffe.

Historians have sometimes suggested that bequests for religious purposes were characteristic of pre-Reformation society, and concern for the alleviation of poverty a later phenomenon. In Kebell's case this neat distinction is blurred. He left £20 to be distributed to the poor on the day of his burial, more than he paid for the 1,000 masses, and instructions that:

Johan Nichol and Emmitt Lyez which were old seruauntes to my fader and moder and nowe be old and pooer have yerely conuenyent Releif and help by myn executours Whilis they lief, to pray for me and the soules aforerehersid.

Should the family die out, the executors were not only to set up a chantry but also to establish almshouses for twelve poor men to pray for Kebell. The serjeant did not, as many lawyers did, leave money or doles for the prisoners in London and Westminster – Coningsby arranged for Newgate, Ludgate, the king's bench and Marshalsea

103. *ibid.*, 25 f. 218.
104. Stephenson, *Brasses*, 71; *Testamenta Eboracensia*, iv. 103n.
105. Stephenson, *Brasses*, 546.
106. PROB11/15 ff. 128, 128v; *Testamenta Eboracensia*, iv. 89–92.

each to receive in the first week of Lent a cade (five gross) of red herrings and thirteen pence worth of brown bread.[107] Kebell did, however, ask his executors, if Walter died without heirs, to dispose of his chattels:

in dedis of almes and pitte by there discrecion, hertely praying theim to haue in remembraunce my poore kynnesfolk and my neighborous and suche places of religion of this cuntre as be poore.

He was also generous to those who owed him money. Thomas Palmer was allowed ten marks of the £20 he owed. The vicar of Thrussington was given 40s. from his debt. His accountant, Thomas Turner, was forgiven all his arrears and debts except £20, a gift worth at least £13 6s. 8d., and even in collecting what was left the executors were to:

shewe him conuenient favour by ther discrecion in the payment ther of, so that he may [pay] it and not to his vndoyng.[108]

This same favour was to be given to relatives wishing to buy any land the executors sold. Kebell's concern for his son's education was also matched more generally. Twenty marks a year for twenty years were to go 'to the fynding of scolers at Oxford and Cambrigge in art and diuinite', in addition to the annuity of 40s. he had given to a John Lokton, evidently already a student, who was also to receive a gown and 20s. Again we must not be anachronistic or read into Kebell's will more than is justified. Nor must we forget that Kebell's motives were probably quite traditional. But in a concern for the poor and for education the charitable aspirations of later generations had little to teach him.

IV

By nature the historian always wants to know more than the sources reveal; by nature also, the most complete source can never reveal more than part of the experience of the past. Given the fragmentary material, it is inevitable that we shall see Thomas Kebell, if at all, through a glass darkly. But we can see enough to perceive a man there behind the black letter, the indenture, the enrolment. A man of learning, intellectual power, vigour of expression, interested in books and languages, deeply attached to his home territory but travelled, proud of his success, conscious of his standing, enjoying his pro-

107. PROB11/25 f. 218v. 108. See above, p. 346.

sperity but generous and concerned more to see his son inherit 'vertue and konnyng' than mere material advantages, a man who is quite conventional but in a way which modifies our own conventional assumptions – the narrowness of the lawyers, the barrenness of religion, the necessity for Renaissance and reform. It was only because men like Kebell were in English public life that Renaissance and reform had their way.

RETROSPECT

At the outset of this study three areas were identified where a legal profession may have significance – impact upon the law, a role as a managerial group, and influence upon society. Each can be demonstrated to an abundant degree in the England of the Yorkist and early Tudor kings.

Of the three, it is the last which catches the eye. The law precipitated social mobility. It was the safest and most convenient way for a family to acquire free capital for investment in land or on the marriage market. Entry into the law also brought membership of a group which was socially advantageous, thanks to its internal cohesion and its wide connections. That this did not lead to the English profession following the *noblesse de robe* is explained by the continuing ties which a lawyer had with his home or adopted community, and by the openness of English society, which enabled a family to abandon the law after one or two generations and become indistinguishable from less aspiring or less adventurous representatives of the gentry. A profession in terms of both status and organisation, and with the added characteristics of much intermarriage and business co-operation, the lawyers nevertheless did not become a caste.

Principal importance, however, must belong to the first of the areas identified, the relations between the profession and the law. The lawyers of Kebell's time were in at the start of a reform which enabled the law to meet the new problems of the day and so, unwittingly, they saved for the world the distinctive procedures and doctrines of the English common law. What has been difficult to particularise in this is the weight to give to the initiative of the profession. Were the lawyers simply brokers, approached by clients with problems and seeking possible ways to have these problems solved? In some cases this was certainly true; in most cases it must have been true in part. But it is not the whole story. Equally vital was the ability and the willingness of the lawyers and the law to respond. Without this, reluctance to litigate would not have been merely a statistically detectable current, it would have been a flood-tide. In Kebell's day the law was the collective wisdom of the profession, thrashed out in an atmosphere of close-knit co-operation and competition and a shared jurisprudence. It is hard to read debates in court and in the inns without concluding that it was the legal argument which counted. This is not to ignore the element of calculation, either the immediate interest in winning the case for a client or ulterior considerations – willingness to accommodate the greatest employer, the crown, is as obvious as the hostility of certain men to the rival jurisdiction of the canon law. But interest was not all. The law was fluid; certain procedures were flexible. Novel claims could thus be put forward with some chance of success and, in the absence of much fixed precedent, similar claims could be tested again and again, and all this in a forum where reason and public interest as well as legal erudition and private opinion could have full rein.

The remaining influence – that of the profession as a managerial group – is writ large in the history of the period. The difficulty, however, is to assess the precise importance to give to professionalism. Were lawyers responding to a genuine need for their special skills and knowledge, were they, instead, a convenient body of men for hire and familiar with business, or had a stereotype evolved of what a manager or agent was expected to be; did lawyers, even, spread legalism as the norm in administration, so creating, consciously or unconsciously, an exclusive market for their skills? Or was it all of these together?

There is no doubt that the profession found management an occasion for profit, and it would only have been natural for lawyers to emphasise the distinct need for their skills. There certainly was an undercurrent of popular irritation at their influence, a current which eventually burst to the surface in the agitation for Interregnum law reform. As Thomas Starkey wrote, they 'which were first institute for the maintenance and setting forward of true justice and equity now [are] the destruction of the same with all injury'.[1] Particularly important here was the uniform assumption that administration and law were identified, a reflection of the age-old reality that a court was both the place where the lord exercised authority over his men and the place where they came to him for justice. Administration therefore began in the context of law, and it was automatic for lawyers to carry over professional attitudes and assumptions. The

1. Starkey, *Dialogue*, 113.

same result followed from the monopoly position the lawyers held as the one trained managerial group in the community. This could not but expand the ambience of the law.

Nevertheless, opportunity was there, in the end, because the system demanded law. As Gerrard Winstanley, one of the sternest seventeenth-century critics recognised, 'The Law is the great Idol that men dote on.'[2] The thought-patterns of the day positively called for legal services. It was the responsibility of the king to do justice, and doing justice required lawyers. Society was divinely ordered so that men had fixed rights and obligations, and it was the lawyers who existed to preserve these. As the prayer for the profession, published in 1553, said:

> We know, O Lord, that the law is good, if a man use it lawfully, given of Thee as a singular gift unto the children of men for maintenance of godly orders, for putting away of iniquity and wrong, for restoring of men unto their right, for the advancement of virtue and punishment of vice.[3]

Nor was this mere piety. The only alternative to a society regulated by law was a society regulated by power.

That lawyers were responding primarily to demand rather than creating an artificial monopoly is certainly suggested by what appears to have happened as the sixteenth century progressed. The new assumptions of humanism came to dominate education, and efforts to introduce these to the inns of court came to nothing. It is true that there was a massive expansion in student admissions to the inns of court, especially in the reign of Elizabeth, but most of the additional students were interested marginally, if at all, in learning law. What is more, the particular management areas where lawyers had been supreme were opened to laymen by the guide-books and technical literature which now began to pour from the printing press. The lawyers lost their automatic position as the managers of the nation once law ceased to be the only non-manual and non-commercial opening for the layman. Changes in government also had an effect, notably the increasing distinction between policy-making and executive action, symbolised by the development of the state paper and the emergence of the privy council. It thus became less possible to move from executive duties to political influence, and in the later part of the century there was nothing to parallel the gaggle of lawyers who,

2. Gerrard Winstanley, *Works*, ed. G.H. Sabine (New York, 1941), 361.
3. Becon, *Prayers*, 25.

between 1460 and 1540, effectively were the government. The pattern becomes, instead, that of the university-trained administrator who makes his way through patronage and service at court – men like Cecil, Mildmay and Walsingham, whose time at the inns was more a formality than formative. When Kebell died, the greatest generation of lawyer-servants to the Tudor monarchy was already in prospect; some men were already in practice. But More, Cromwell and the others had no successors of equivalent standing. The law had begun its long and slow retreat to the courts.

Pre-Reformation England is impossible to conceive of without its common lawyers and the influences they exerted. Sir John Fortescue closed his treatise on the law of England by putting into the mouth of the young prince of Wales the promise that:

> to me this law will always be exceptional among all other laws of the earth, among which I see it shine like Venus among the stars.[4]

Although today the observer may not share this opinion, he can have no doubt of the brilliance of the men who served that law. It would be hard to find a brighter galaxy anywhere.

4. Fortescue, *De Laudibus*, 139.

APPENDICES

APPENDIX A

THE WILL OF THOMAS KEBELL

25 JUNE 1500 PROB/12 FF. 22V–23V

[Abbreviations have been extended without indication, proper nouns uniformly capitalised and punctuation modernised.]

[f.22v] IN THE NAME OF GOD AMEN. I, Thomas Kebell, the kynges Seriaunt at Lawe, being hoole of mynde, thankid be God, considering the vnstablenesse of the world, the certentie and necessite of deth to the which I and euery creatur leving is bounden, willyng to prouide and ordeyne for the disposicion of suche goodes as God hath suffered me to haue here in erth, Ordeygne and make my testament and last wil of my goodes and cataillis in fourme Articulerly folowyng: FIRST I BEQUETH my sowle to Almyghti God my maker, my Redemer, my preseruer from many perilles of sowle and body, and my singuler Relief comfort and helpe in necessite, aduersite, infirmite pouerte and all diseasis, humbely beching him to accept it to his mercy and grace. And my simple body to be buried at Humberston in the Chapell where bothe Margerie and Anne my Wifes and my kynde cousyn Richard Hotoft and my sonne Edward lyen buried, in suche fourme as myn Executours thinke convenient for the degre that it hath pleasid God to calle me to in this world, and ther for to haue a conuenyent tombe for me and my wifes. Also I wil that suche coostes be doon for my conueyng to Humberston as by myn Executours shalbe thought convenyent for the honeste of me and my frendes, all veyne glory and pompe of the world sett apart. Also I wil that ther be distributed for me to poor folkes the day of my buryng, or at other tymes as shalbe thought to myn Executours most convenyent for my degre and to the pleasur of God, xxli. Also I bequeth to my Curate suche mortuarys as accordith with the lawe; Also to the parson of Rerisbury for tithes forgotin xxs.; Also to the vicar of Humberston for the same xls.; Also to the Relief of the Chirch of Rerisburye xxs.; Also to the Relief of the Chirch of Humberston v marc. Also I bequeth to the Abbey of Leycester to pray for me v marc; Also to the College of Newe Werk to pray for me v marc; Also to the beadhous to pray for me xxs.; Also to euery hous of Freres at Leycestre to pray for me xiijs. iiijd. Also I bequeth to the White Freres at London to pray for me xxs.; Also to the Prioresse and covent of Clerkinwell to pray for me xls.; Also to the prioresse and covent of Langley to pray for me xls. Also I wol that a thousand masses and as many tymes placebo and dirige be said for me Immediatly aftre my decesse and euery preste to haue iiijd., the somme Whereof Amounteth to xvjli. xiijs. iiijd., or els so many Trentalles as a M[l] masses cometh to, by the discrecion of myn Executours. Also I wol that a preste be founden for me at Humberston vij yeres aftre my decesse, to say daily for me and for the soules of my said wifes, cousyn, child, fader and moder and all Cristin soules, placebo, dirige, comendacion and masse, and thris in the weke on severall daies wekely vij psalmes and letayne, And in other iij dayes oure lady Sawter and euery Sonday the psalmes of the passion, and shalhaue by the yer viij marc. Also I wol that Johan Nichol and Emmitt Lyez, which were old seruauntes to my fader and moder and nowe be old and pooer, haue yerely conuenyent Releif and help by myn executours Whilis they lief, to pray for me and the soules aforerehersid. Also I hertely praye myn Executours to content and treuly pay my dettes to euery body that I am indettid to. Also I pray them to Recompense alle suche persones as I haue doon Wrong vnto in any Wise. Also I bequeth to my sonne Water Kebell goddis blissing and myne, and hertely require and pray him and on my blissing charge him to be good and vertuous and eschewe all vices and misserule, and treuly serue God and duly thank him for the manyfold benefittes and goodnes that he hath sent to me in erth, and that he kepe treuly his legiaunce and alway be kinde loving and do his feithfull seruice to his power to my singuler good lady my lady Hastinges, his godmoder, to my lord hir sonne, and my moost singuler good lady my lady Hungreford his wife and there children. And that he be loving to my soule, his moders soule, the sowlis of my fader and moder and my cousin Hotoft, And cause vs to be praied for; and that he truly help to the perfourmyng of this my Will, And that he be kinde and loving to my kynnesfolk and his, and to my seruantes and frendes and lovers. Also I bequeth and gif to my said sonne alle my stuf of household, henginges, bedding and Napery, Except suche as by this my Wil is or shall be gevin to any persone. Also I bequeth to my said sonne all my bookes of Scripture, of Lawe, of Cronicles or stories, and alle other my bookes in latyn, Frenssh or Englissh to thentent that he shall the Rather applye him to vertue and konnyng. Also I geve to my said son a Cheyne of goold that was my faders and aftre that my brothers, and a crosse that I bought, and also my signet Ringe and Tablettes. Also I wol that my sonne haue alle my plate and Juels, Except as by this my Will is or shalbe appoynted to any persone or persones. Also I wol that at suche tyme as my sonne comith to suche age as he, aftre this my Wil, shalhaue the pasturis of Hamuldon and Stretton in his owen handis, that the same pastures be stuffid by myne executours with suche Cataillis as I shall leve therin or With other, And my said sonne to haue alle that store and cataillis as his owen. And I wol that alle thise goodes, juels and Cataillis befor appoynted to my said sonne be kept by myne executours vnto my said sonne come to the age of xxiiij yeris, to thentent that they may see his disposicion and towarlynesse. And if he dispose him to vertue and goodnesse, thenne to haue deliuery of hit, or els to kepe it tyll he so dispose him, And if he Wilnot amende and applie him to vertue truth and goodnesse, thenne he shalhaue noo part thereof but the same to be appleied in purchase of livelod and the same to be disposid as in my Wil of my livelood among other thinges shalbe conteyned. Also I wol that my said sonne be in the gouernaunce of myn executours. And I humbly and hertely pray and beseche theim to take the payne vppon theym to se him brough vp in vertue and good maner, and to haue connyng, whereby Vertue and Wisedom growith and is norisshed. And for asmoche as to my knowlige my said sonne owith not to be in warde to any persone, I hartly pray theim yf any persone can prove him to be intitelid to haue the warde and mariage of him, that they bye the Warde and mariage of him with suche goodes as shall remayne ouer my Wil perfourmed. Also I beseche and pray myn Executours that, with suche goodes and money as I shall leve to theim, they will helpe to prouide for my said sonne sum Conuenyent mariage of an heritour yf they can. Also I Woll that vnto suche tyme as my sonne shall com to the Age of xxiiij yeris, myn Executours haue and occupie my ferme at Stretton toward the perfourmyng of my Will. And Whenne my sonne comith to his saide age of xxiiij yeris, thenne he to haue the said ferme vnto the ende of suche yeris as I haue in the same. Also I bequeth vnto my Goddoughter and Nece Joies Kebell toward her mariage xli, over and aboue x li of money which I have of hirs in keping for hir part of hir fader goodes. Also to hir [f. 23] Suster Elizabeth which is content and paied of hir xli. which I had of her faders goodes by the handis of hir brother and other, I bequeth x marc to pray for me; Also to my Nece Mary Willers toward hir mariage x marc; Also to my godson and cousin Thomas Cotton x marc; Also to my godson and cousin, the sonne of my cousin Thomas Lacy, x marc; Also to my cousin Thomas Broughton of London to pray for me xls. Also I bequeth to my singuler good Lady, my Lady Hungreford, my salt of goold and the booke of Frosard and also ij peces of blak veluet either of theim conteynyng xix yardes or ther aboutes beseching hir to haue me in hir Remembraunce and praieers amonges hir other seruantes, and to take this poor bequest in grace. Also I wol that suche dublet clothes of veluet and other silkes as I haue, be made in vestimentes and disposid for my soule. Also I bequeth to Maistress Elizabeth Ferrers to pray for me ij kene, xx Weders and v marc in money. Also to my brother Palmer the gray hors Which he nowe hath and x marc of the xxli. of money which he owith to me to be abated and relesid to him; Also to William Smith on of my hors by the disposicion of myn executours and v marc in money, preyng him to be loving to my sowle and to my sonne; Also to Richard Eyre xls., Also to William Reynold xls., Also to Robert Brett xxvjs. viijd., Also to Robert Gaddisby xxvjs. viijd., Also to Elton xls., Also to Richard Chamberleyn xxs., Also to Richard Prudlose xxs., Also to James xxs. Also where Thomas Turnour owith me by obligacion certeyn money and also vppon a Rereagis of a nother accompt xvli or more Whiche in the hoole amontith to more then L marc, I bequeth and release to him alle the said dettes except xxli., Which xxli I woll that myne executours haue of him toward the performyng of my Will and that they shewe him conuenient favour by ther discrecion in the payement ther of, So that he may[1] it and not to his vndoyng; Also to Thomas Butteler xxs.; Also to John Cook xiijs. iiijd.; Also to Oliuer vjs. viijd.; Also to Margery vjs. viijd.; Also to Sir John Hamond xls. to prey for me, Also I bequeth to the vicar of Thursington xls. of the money that he owith me by obligacon. Also I wol that the foresaid bequestes and paiementes of my dettes be made and perfourmed With alle my cornes and cataill and with my dettes that be dewe to me for catailles soold, And yf they suffice not to perfourme the same, thenne the Residue to be had of the profittes of my landes tenementes and fermes; Also that my Nevieu Georg Wyllers haue yerely during his life of the profittes of my landis xls. to prey for me and to be loving to his cousyn my sonne. Also I wol that with the profittes of the said landis tenementes and fermes therebe yeven yerely, during the time of xx[ti] yeris next aftre my decesse, xx[ti] marc to the fynding of Scolers at Oxford and Cambrigge in Art

1. 'pay' omitted.

and Diuinite by the discrecion and appoyntment of myn Executours. Also I wol that John Lokton haue yerely his Annuyte of xls. Which I haue gevin him by patent And oone of my gownes and xxs. in money. Also I wil that ther be purveied a chalice price vj marc for my cousin Hotoftes chauntry Which with a masse boke that I haue coverid with white be appointed to the same Chauntrye; And also ij soortes of vestimentes and Awter clothis for the same chauntre, oon for euery day the other for halidaies. Also I wol that myne Executours purvey a Chalis and also a soort of vestimentes for /dekin and subdekin/[2] of bawdekin and a Cope of the same sute to be gevin to the church of Humberston to pray for me and for the sowlis afore Rehersid. Also I bequeth to Austyn Flore the portnos that was his moders cloth to make him a gowne and an hoode and v marc in money to prey for me. Also I bequeth to Roger Flore his brother oon of my hors by the discrecion of myne executours and v marc in money. Also I bequeth to my Nece Motton my last wifes best bonett of velvett, hir best frontelet and a gowne of hirs by the discrecion of myn Executours. Also I wol that the Remenauntes of my said wifes bonettes, Frontelettes, gownes and kirtelittes be disposid among my Necis, Cousins and frendis by the discrecion of myne Executours, And I wol that my Nece Roose Kebell haue part of theim. Also I wol that yf my sonne Water deceasse a fore he come to the age of xxiiij yeris as is abouesaid, and haue Issue of his body, the same Issue that is heire of his body haue the stufe, plate, Juels and alle other thinges to the said Water bequethid and appoynted whenne the same heire commyth to theage of xxiiij^{ti} yere. And if that heire dye afore that age, thenne his brother or suster heire of the body of the same Water shall at there like age haue the same stuf, plate, Jueles and other premissis. And if the said Water afore his saide age deceasse withoute Issue, or yf his said Issue dye afore there said ages, Thenne I wol that the oon half of the said stuf and houshold henginges and bedding before bequethid to the said Water to be devidid among my Nevieus, Necis and Cosyn Thomas Cotton theelder by the discrecion of myn Executours, And the other part to be sold And the money therefore had to be disposid for the perfourmyng of this my Will. And of the said plate and Jueles bequethed to the said Water, I will that my good Lady Hungreford, yf she be thenne on live, haue ij basins and ij Ewris of siluer parcelle gilt that I bought of my lady Hastinges and my lord Hastinges, the Woman bering a salt,[3] /vj bollis gilt/[4] my Tabelettes of goold; And my Nevieu Thomas Kebell, if he be thenne on liue, a stonding cup of siluer and gilt that was my lady Lanams and xij spones; Master Robert Mome, yf he be thenne alive, a stonding cup with a kouer gilt with an Egle in the keuer; My cousin Thomas Cotton theeldre, yf he be thenne on live, a flat cup siluer and a potell pot; Thomas Cotton my Godson, yf he be thenne onn live, a potell pot of siluer. And yf any of thise persones aboue rehersid be thenne deceassid, the plate to theym appoynted goo to the performyng of my wil. Also I wil that of

2. / – /: passage omitted and inserted above.
3. There is an omission here, probably by the registry-office scribe. Kebell is apparently indicating one of his salts, but there is no mention in the inventory of any piece carrying or decorated with a female figure.
4. / – /: passage omitted and inserted above.

the money afore pointed to the said Water, my speciall good lady, my lady Hastinges, haue xx^ti li.; the Residue[5] and of the dettes Jueles and other thinges to him appointed before the decesse of hym and his Issue as is aforesaid, to be disposed for the soules of me, my wifes, oure childern, oure Auncestres, my cousin Otofte and other cousins, And for the soules of my good lorde, William late Lord Hastinges and other that I am bounden to prey fore, And for the Welefare of my good Lady Hastinges and my lord Hastinges and my lady Hungreford and myne Executours and for there sowlis Whenne they be disceasid, in dedis of Almes and pitte by there discrecion, hertely preying theim to haue in Remembraunce my poore kynnesfolk and my Neghborous and suche places of Religion of this Cuntre as be poore or els as I haue had fee of. Also I wol that myne Executours for the perfourmyng of my Will in the goodes appoynted to the said Water haue aftre his deceasse, as is aforsaid, like sommes of money as I shall appoynt theim for there labour and performyng of my Will. Also I wol that myne Executours haue there Resonable costes abowte the performyng of my Will. Also I wol that there be an house bildid at Humberston in sum convenyent ground of myn for the Chauntry preste that shall serue my cousin Hotoftes Chauntrie perpetually. Also I wol that Margaret my wife haue all suche thinges as the lawe will that she shuld haue.

THIS IS THE LAST WILL of me Thomas Kebell the kinges seriaunt att the Lawe of all my landes tenementes [*Vltima voluntas eiusdem*][6] [f. 23v] and inheritaunces as here aftre Articulerly folowith. First I wol that myn Executours haue, perceyve and take thissues, profittes and Revenuez of alle my landes, tenementes, inheritaunces and fermes duryng the tyme that they haue perfourmed my testament and last will according to theffect of the same. Also I wol that myne Executours haue, perceive and take thissues, profittes and Revenues of alle my landes, tenementes, inheritaunces and fermes vnto the tyme that Water Kebell my sonne, or who so euer shall happe to be the heire of my body, come to the full age of xxiiij yeris; And therewith, ouer my will and testament perfourmed, to finde my said sonne or myn other heire of my body conueniently by ther discrecion; And the Residue thereof to employe in perchase of Lyvelode to the vse of myn heires of my body comyng; And for Lak of suche Issue of my body, to be disposid for the sowlis of me, my wifes, childern, fader and moder, Cousin Hotoft and other myn Auncestres and cousyns, and for the soules and Welfares of suche as by my testament be ordeyned to be praied fore and for all Cristin sowlis, Also I wol that whenne my said sonne or other heire of my body commith to his said Age of xxiiij yeris astate be made of the said landes, tenementes and inheritaunces to the same heire and to the heiris of his or her body commyng, the Remaynder ouer for lak of suche Issue to the heiris of my body commyng. And for lak of Issue, I woll that Thomas Kebell haue all my landes and tenementes in Humberston and other of my landes and tenementes by the discrecion of myne executours, to the yerely value of xli., to be had to the same Thomas and to the heires of his body commyng, And for lak of suche issue the Remaynder to the right heiris of my moders body commyng, And for lak of such Issue the Remaynder to dame Marye Billyng myn Aunt and to the heiris of hir body commyng;

5. 'of the money' must be understood. 6. Side heading.

Prouided alway that there be ground Reserued in Humberston to bilde vppon for my Cousin Hotoftes Chauntrie and for the Chauntrye and Almeshows hereaftre specified, by the discrecion of myn Executours, Which grounde I wilbe exceptid in the said gift. Also I will that for lak of Issue of my body,[7] Thomas Kebell my Nevieu and godson haue my Maner, landes and tenementes in Congestone and other landes and tenementes of myne by the discrecion of myne Executours to the yerely value of xliijs. iiijd., to haue and to hold the said maner, londes, and tenementes to the said Thomas and to the heiris of his body commyng. Also I wol that for lak of heiris of my body George Willers my Nevieu haue to him and to the heiris of his body commyng alle my landes and tenementes in Bilston, Wherein certeyn persones be infeoffid to the vse of Nicholas Temple and of his wife during there lives And aftre there deceasse to the vse of me and myne heiris. And ouer that I wol that the same George haue to him and to his heiris, londes and tenementes to the yerely value of iiij marc by the discrecion and assigment of myn Executours. Also I wol that for lak of Issue of my body, my Cousin and godson Thomas Cotton haue to him and to heiris of his body Landis and tenementes in Demesnie and Reuersion to the yerely value of xli. ouer alle charges, by the assignement and discrecion of myn Executours, And for lak of Issue of the same Thomas Cotton to Remayne to my Cousin Thomas Cottons Fader and to the heiris of his body commyng. MORE OUER, my good cousin Richard Hotoft gave to me and to myne heires his landes and tenementes in moche Stretton and Lytill Stretton and diuers other places to thentent that I shuld for euer kepe his Obit yerely, and also fynde a preste yerely and perpetually to say diuine seruice daily for his soule in the Chirch of Humberston at the Auter in the Chapell where he lieth buried, And that I shuld bynde the said lond as straitly and suerly or[8] cough or myght,[9] not Amortasying it, for the suerte of the treue continuaunce of the said Seruice and preiers. I hartly beseche and prey myn Executours, yf this be not put in suertie by me in my life, that they for the wele of my said Cousins soule and the discharge and Wele of my soule Will cause this to be put in suertie and to appointe a Resonable some oute of the said landes in Stretton and Stretton for the fynding of the said preste and keping of the said obite. Furthermore, Wher as I haue purchasid diuers landes and tenementes in Stretton and Stretton aforesaid and also haue made there inclosurs and approumentes, I will that yf I dye Without Issue of my body that a nother prest be founde perpetually to prey for me, my lady Hungreford and the soule of my Cousyn Hotofte and for the soules afore in this my wil or in my testament Rehersid, And also for the soules of theym of whome I haue had any manner of benefittes and specially for the soulis whos benefittes I haue not deserued; And xij poore men to be founden at Humberston perpetually to prey daily for me and alle other before Reherced. And thees both Chauntries and Almes menne to be Amortaizid founded and establissid by Licence of the kinge and sufficiently endowed of alle the said landes in Stretton and Stretton and of alle my Landes in Evington, Burkeley,[10] Thorp Barkby, Quenebourgh, Scraptopt and Sitheston in the Countie of Leicestre And yf that suffise not for

7. This line is marked with a cross in the left-hand margin.
8. 'or' = 'as'.
9. 'be' must be understood.
10. Scribal error for Barkebey.

there finding, thenne to geve theim of my[11] other landes, so that they may haue sufficient finding by the discrecion of myn Executours. Also I wol that the Residue of my landes and tenementes, ouer the said Amortesment and ouer the said Landes so appoynted and yevin in taill, And also the Remaynders of the same landes so appoynted be sold by myne Executours or feoffers, or the lenger lyver of theim, And the money therof had to be disposid part for the said Amortesment and bilding and the residue thereof in dedes of Almes by the discrecion of myn Executours. Also I wol that myne heire or my cousyn Cotton be preferrid in the bying of any of my livelood that they wilhaue, and haue Resonable favour in the paiement thereof, So that it let not the spedy performyng of this my Will And specially for the said Amortesment and bildinges of the Chauntries and Almes hows. AND OF THIS my testament and last will I name make ordeyne and constitute my said good Lady my lady Marie Hastynges[12] Hungreford and Margaret my wife aforesaid and my Right Welbeloued frendes Maister Robert Mome, Chanon of the cathedrall chirch of Lincoln, and Thomas Cotton esquier myn Executours and performers of the same, hertely requiryng theim to fulfill it as it is aboue Rehercid. YEVIN and datid at Humberston the xxv^{ti} day of Juine the yere of our lord god M^{l} ccccc and xv yere of the reigne of king Henry the vijth, Thenne being present Syr John Hamon vicar of Humberston a foresaid my Curat Maister Philipp Morgan William Raynold Joys Kebell and Marie Willers and other moo.

PROBATUM [blank]

11. This line is marked with a cross in the left-hand margin.
12. 'and' omitted.

APPENDIX B

THE INVENTORY OF THOMAS KEBELL

6 July 1500 Wiltshire Record Office 88:5/17a

[Abbreviations have been extended without indication and punctuation inserted as necessary.]

[m. 1] This is the Inuentary/indented/[1]of all the goodes Cataillys Plate Redy money and dettes that were Thomas Kebeell Seriaunt of lawe praysed by Valentyne Mason Generall Appraysour vnto the most Reuerent Fader in god my lord Cardynall and Archbisshopp of Caunterbury the vjth day of Jule the xvth yere of Kyng Henry the vijth

IN THE HALLE

ffirst iij Costrynges of Reed Say sore worn, price	iijs iiijd
Item A longe fourme, price	iiijd
Item A cupbord, price	viijd
	Summa – iiijs iiijd

IN THE CHAMBRE OUER THE BOTRY

Item A complete hangyng of olde Rede Say, price	vs
Item A Seler, A Tester and iij curtens of bordeAlexaundre, price	xs
Item A Federbed with a Bolster, price	xijs
Item j peyre Blankettes, price	ijs
Item j olde materas and j old couerlet, price	xxd
Item A Counterpoynt of BordeAlexaunder, price	ijs viijd
Item A materas of Flokkes, price	iijs iiijd
Item j Palette stuffyd with strawe, price	viijd
Item ij olde Blankettys, price	xijd
Items iij pillowes stuffed with feders, price	ijs
Item j lityll brokyn carpet, price	viijd
	Summa – xljs

1. / – / word omitted and inserted above.

IN THE LITELL CHAMBRE NEXTE

Item j complete hangyng with a Seler and a testour of olde Reed say, price	ijs
Item a litell Fetherbed with a bolster, price	viijs
Item ij couerlettys of Englissh makyng, price	iijs
Item j payre of Blankettys, price	xxd
Item ij pillowes of Fethers, price	xijd
Item j materas, price	xvjd
Summa – xvijs	

IN THE CHAMBRE NEXTE Y^e WYDDRAWGH

Item ij White hangyng beddes Withoute curteyns, price	iijs iiijd
Item iij materasses and ij bolsters and j pillowe, price	viijs
Item ij peyre blankettys, price	ijs
Item ij Couerlettys of englisshe makynge, price	ijs viijd
Summa – xvjs	

IN THE CHAMBRE OUER THE CHAPELL

Item A complete hangyng of borde Alexandre conteynyng in lengthe xxj yerdys and in breedth iij yerdes *Summa* in yerdes lxiij, At ijd le yerde *Summa*	xs vjd
Item j Sperver of bord Alexaunder, price	xiijs iiijd
Item j peyre of Fustians, price	xs
Item an olde Counterpoynt of Counterfette Arras, price	xijs
Item A Fetherbed and a bolster, price	xs
Item an olde materas, price	xxd
Item a litell Fetherbed with a bolster, price	iijs iiijd
Item j peyre of Blankettys, price	ijs
Item j couerlette of englisshe makynge, price	xijd
Item A litell materas, price	xvjd
Item j old broken Carpet, price	vjd
Item A Shipcheste, price	ijs viijd
Item j Table j Cheyre and iiij ioyned stoles, price	ijs
Item x broken Cusshyns of Tapestry Worke, price	iijs iiijd
Summa – iij li xiijs viijd	

IN THE CHAMBRE NEXTE

Item j hangyng of old grene say, price	xijd
Item j litell sperver of bord Alizaunder, price	vs

Item j Counterpoynt of Verders[2], price	vs
Item A Fetherbed and a bolster, price	viijs
Item j peyre blankettys, price	ijs
Item j old Couerlette, price	xd
Item j peyre course shetys, price	xxd
Item A materasse, price	xvjd
Item iij pillowes of downe, price	vjs
Item j litell Fetherbed and j bolster, price	vjs viijd
Item A materasse, price	ijs
Item j peyre blankettes, price	xxd
Item j peyre shetys, price	xviijd
Item ij old Couerlettys, price	ijs
Item j Table, ij Tresstellys, j Cupbord j Fourme, and ij ioyned stoles, price	xvjd
	Summa – xlvjs

IN THE CLERKYS CHAMBRE

Item an olde brokyn Fetherbed with a bolster, price	iijs iiijd
Item A materasse, price	ijs
Item ij peyre shetys, price	iijs iiijd
Item ij payre blankettys, price	ijs viijd
Item ij Couerlettys, price	ijs
Item an olde paynted cloth, price	xd
Item j Chayre	iiijd
	Summa – xiiijs vjd

IN THE INNER GARRET CHAMBRE

Item j Seler and a Testour of white sore brokyn, price	xd
Item a Fetherbed and a bolster, price	vjs viijd
Item j peyre of Shetys, price	ijs
Item j Couerlette and ij olde blankettys, price	ijs
Item ij pillowes of Fethers, price	xd
	Summa – xijs iiijd

IN THE PARLER

Item A Complete hangyng of borde Alexander conteynyng in length lx yerdes and in breed iij. *Summa* in yerdes vj^xx, at ijd le yerde *Summa*	xxs
Item j dosen cusshyns of verders stuffed with fethers, price	xxxiijs iiijd

2. Design based on leaves and flowers.

Item A Sperver of bord Alexaunder, price	xiijs iiijd
Item j Fetherbed and a bolster, price	xxs
Item j peyre of old Fustians, price	viijs
Item j peyre of blankettes, price	ijs
Item A peyre of Flexan shetys of iij breedes conteynyng xxj [m.2] yerdes, at vjd le yerde *Summa*	xs vjd
Item A Counterpoynt of Tapestry Work soręworne, price	vs
Item a Tabyll, ij Trestyllys, ij Fourmes, ij Chayres, and A Cuppebord to gydder, price	ijs
Item an old Cupbordeclothe of grene say, price	vjd
Summa v li xiiijs viijd	

IN THE CHAMBER OUER THE PARLOUR

Item A Complete hangyng of grene say, price	vjs viijd
Item ij Carpettys, price	xs
Item A Sperver of borde Alexander, price	xs
Item an old Fetherbed and a bolster, price	viijs
Item j old Counterpoynt of Tapestry Work, price	iijs iiijd
Item A Counterpoynt of Imagery Work, price	xs
Item A Counterpoynt of verders with byrdes, price	xls
Item A Cuppebord, price	ijs
Item A Counterpoynt of Rede damaske sore Worn conteynyng in all xxiiij yerdes, price	cs
Item a Sperver of Rede Damaske with curtens of rede course sarcenet, price	iij li vjs viij
Item j pillowe and ij cusshyns couered with Ray saten Abrigges[3] stuffed with fethers, price	xiijs iiijd
Item j peyre of newe fustians, price	xiijs iiijd
Item vj hangynges of Tapestry Worke conteynyng in all iiij^{xx} x yerdes, at xijd le yerde *Summa*	iiij li xs
Item j Remenaunt of blak dobyll saten conteynyng iij yerdes, at viijs le yerde *Summa*	xxiiijs
Item iij doublet clothes of Tawny satyn conteynyng in all viij yerdes and a half, at viijs le yerde *Summa*	lxviijs
Item a Remenaunt of tawny damaske conteynyng ij yerdes and a half, at vjs le yerde *Summa*	xvs
Item a Remenaunt of blak stamyn conteynyng ij yerdes *dimidium*, at ijs *Summa*	vs
Item a peyr of grete olde Amber bedys of xij stonys, price	xs
Item a peyre of bedys of x stones Cassidens and Jasper parcell couered with gold, price	iiij li

3. i.e. Bruges satin.

Item A boke wretyn in Frenche in parchement called *Labuse encourte*,[4] price	xs
Item an olde harneys girdell with dyuerse litell barres, price	xxvjs viijd
Item an Awtercloth of Arras conteignyng in lengthe iij yerdes and in brede j yerde, at xxvjs viijd le yerde *Summa*	iiij li
Item ij remenauntes of black velwet conteynyng x yerdes at xijs le yerde *Summa*	vj li
Item a pece of Tawny veluet conteynyng iij yerdes, at xijs le yerde *Summa*	xxvjs
[Item a sperver of [ ][5] of old Rede Damaske with curteyns of rede Tartron, price]	*quia prius*[6]
Item viij pecys and *dimidium* of newe borde Alexandre, at viijs le pece *Summa*	lxviijs
Item v chestys of dyuerse sortys	xs
Item ij Remenauntes of blak veluet conteignyng iiij yerdes *dimidium*, at xijs le yerde *Summa*	liiijs
Item a boke in Frenche of the Coronycles[7] in parchement, price	liijs iiijd
Item a boke enprynted called Lodowicus *de vita Christi*,[8] price	xs
Item a doblet cloth of blak stamen conteynyng iij yerdys, at ijs viijd le yerde *Summa*	viijs
Item a litell veluet pouche with a sengle Rynge siluer and gilte, *price*	xxs
Item a litell Sperver of Ray silke with curtens of grene Tartron, price	iiij li
	Summa lvij li xjs iiijd

IN THE MAYDENS CHAMBRE

Item j materasse and j bolster, price	ijs
Item j pellowe of Fethers	vjd
Item j peyre of blankettes	xvjd
Item ij olde Couerlettys, price	xvjd
	Summa vs ijd

NAPERY

Item viij peyre cours shetes for yomen and laborers, at xxd le peyre *Summa*	xiijs iiijd
Item v peyre *dimidium* of course flaxen shetys euery peyre conteignyng x yerdys, at vd le yerde *Summa*	xxjs ixd

4. René of Anjou, *L'Abuse en Court*.
5. Illegible.
6. lines 40, 41 deleted; *quia prius* written over the amount erased. See above for the earlier entry.
7. Froissart, *Chronicle*; see above, p. 367.
8. Ludwig of Saxony, *De Vita Christi*. Editions are known from 1474 at Strassburg and Nuremberg. No English printing.

Item j peyre of fyne newe shetys of iij breedes conteynyng xix yerdes, at xijd le yerde *Summa*	xixs
Item ij fyne [ ][9] hedshetes conteynyng x yerdes, at xijd le yerde *Summa*	xs
Item iiij peyre of shetys of iij breedes euery payre conteignyng xviij yerdys, at ixd le yerde *Summa*	liiijs
Item vj fyne Napkyns of Diaper, at vd le napkyn *Summa*	ijs vjd
Item xij courser napkyns of Diaper, at iiijd *Summa*	iiijs
Item ij Diaper towellys, price	vs
Item j peyre fyne shetes of iij breedes conteyning xxvij yerdes, at xviijd *Summa*	xls vjd
Item j peyre of Fyne Shetys of iij bredes conteynyng xxiiij yerdes, at xvjd *Summa*	xxxijs
Item a peyre fyne shetes of iij bredes conteynyng xviij yerdes, at xvjd *Summa*	xxiiijs
Item j peyre fyne shetys of iij bredes conteynyng xxj yerdes, At ijs le yerde *Summa*	xlijs.
Item A shete of iij bredes sore worne conteynyng xij yerdes, at ixd *Summa*	ixs.
Item ij diaper Table clothes, at vjs viijd le pece *Summa*	[xiijs iiijd.][10]
[Item vj towellys of diaper, at iijs iiijd. *Summa*	xxs][11]
Item ij olde Diaper Cupbordclothes, price	vs
Item ij pleyne old course Cupbordclothes, price	iijs
Item j peyre of Fustians conteynyng xxviij yerdys, at vd le yerde *Summa*	xjs viijd
	Summa – xv li xs jd

IN THE BOTERY AND PANTRY

[m. 3] Item ij Diaper bordclothes oone of iiij yerdes in lengthe And a yerde and *dimidium* in brede And an other conteignyng in lengthe v yerdes and in brede j yerde, price	vs
Item ij Tableclothes playne either of them conteynyng in length vj yerdes and in brede j yerde, At iiijd le yerde *Summa*	iiijs
Item iij Tabulclothes playne euery of theym conteynyng v yerdes in lengthe and in brede j yerde, At iijd *Summa*	iijs ixd
Item ij bordeclothes oon of iiij yerdes *dimidium* and an other of v yerdes in lengthe and in brede j [yerde][12] elle, at vjd le yerde *Summa*	iiijs ixd
Item iij olde broken Cuppordclothes of Diaper, price	ixd
Item ij Diaper towelles either of them conteynyng vj yerdes *dimidium* in lengthe And in brede *dimidium* a yerde, at iiijd le yerde *Summa*	iiijs iiijd

9. Erasure. 10. Written over erasure. 11. line deleted. 12. Deleted.

Item iij Diaper towellys euery of theym conteynyng iij yerdes *dimidium*, at vd le yerde *Summa*	iiijs ob
Item iij litell wasshing towelles sore worne, price	xijd
Item ij playne worne Cupbordclothes, price	vjd
[Item xxvj diaper Napkyns, at iijd ob le pece *Summa*]	*quia prius*[13]
Item viij belle Candilstikkes, At ixd le pece *Summa*	vjs
Item iij litell belle Candelstyckes and iij playne, at vjd le pece *Summa*	iijs
Item vj other litell old Candelstykkys, price	xijd
Item j pype, iij hoggeshedes, ij litell Ronlettes for Wyne, empty, price	iijs vjd
Item an hoggeshede of rede wyne fulle, price	xxvjs viijd
Item iij brode carvyng knyves, A trencher knyfe, And a Fork for grene gynger parcell gilte with blak haftys, price	iiijs
Summa iij li xijs iijd. ob.	

IN THE KECHYN

Item iij Garnysshe of Pewter vessell litell occupied, at xxjs le garnysshe *Summa*	lxiijs.
Item iij dosen platers v great Chargers ij dosen And iij potyngers And ij dozen and iij Sawsers, price to geddir	xlvjs viijd
Item a great brasse potte, price	xijs
Item ij brasse Pottys of iij galons euery potte, price	viijs
Item iij brasse pottys of ij galons *dimidium*, at iijs iiijd le pece [price][12] *Summa*	xs
Item iiij litell posnettys, at xijd le posnet *Summa*	vs
Item iij great Pannes of v galons euery panne, price	xvs
Item iij other litell pannes, price	vjs
Item a litell morter of brasse and a pestell, price	iiijs
Item ij peyre of Rakkys, price	vjs viijd
Item A litell payre of Rakkys, price	ijs
Item ij great rownde broches,[14] price	vjs
Item iiij square broches, price	xjs iiijd
Item ij litell Rounde broches, price	xxd
Item ij birde broches, price	xijd
Item ij Chaffyng disshes	ijs
Item j great water Chaffour some What broken	ijs viijd
Item iij peyre of Pottehokys And iij hangyng Irons, price	xd
Item j Friyng Panne, price	vjd
Item ij Colenders, price	iiijd
Items ij Skemers ij ladelles and j Gredyron, price	xxd

13. line deleted; *quia prius* written over the amount erased. There is no exact alternative reference.
14. i.e. spits.

Item j great ketyll, price	ijs
Item j Clevyng knyffe, And iij Slisyng knyves	viijd
Item in lumber and Trasshe	vjd
	Summa xli ixs vjd

IN THE YOMENS CHAMBRE

Item v materasses, at xviij le materasse *Summa*	vijs vjd
Items vj peyre blankettys, at xvjd le paire *Summa*	viijs
Item ix Couerlettys, at xijd le couerlet *Summa*	ixs
Item iiij Bolsters, price	iiijs
	Summa xxviijs vjd

THE CHAMBRE OUER THE NEWE STABLE

Item A materasse and j bolster, price	ijs
Item A peyre of blankettys, price	xvjd
Item iij Couerlettys good and badde, price	iijs
	Summa vjs iiijd

IN THE BAKHOUSE

Item j materasse and a bolster price	ijs
Item ij Couerlettees and ij blankettys price	iijs iiijd
	Summa vs iiijd

IN THE WEYNE MANS CHAMBER

Item a materasse and j bolster	ijs
Item a Blanket and j Couerlet price	xvjd
	Summa iijs iiijd

CORNE IN THE FELDE

Item xviij Acres barley at xxd le Acre *Summa*	xxxs
	Summa patet

WOLLE REDY CLIPPED

Item lx^{c} vj Flees of wolle after vj^{xx} le c at iiijd le Fles *Summa*	xviij li ijs
Item ij mille stones for a wyndmylle, of englisshemakyng	xviijs
	Summa xix li

A RYKE OF PEAS

Item A Ryke of pease conteynyng by estymacion xv quarter at ijs le quarter *Summa*	xxxs
	Summa patet

IN THE BARNE

Item a litell Stakke of Whete conteignyng by estymacion iiij quarter at iijs iiijd le quarter *Summa*	xiijs iiijd
	Summa patet

IN THE GARDENER

Item l quarter malte, At iijs iiijd le quarter *Summa*	viij li vjs viijd
	Summa patet

TYMBER HEWEN

Item lxxx lode Tymber, at iiijs le lode *Summa*	xvj li
	Summa patet

WEYNES AND PLOWES

Item iij Weynes shoed, at xiijs iiijd *Summa*	xls
Item ij plowes with the harneys, price	vjs viijd
Item j Foder of ledde, price	v *marcas*
	Summa v li xiijs iiijd

CATAILL AT LUBBENHAM

Item xij^xx Weders vnclipped, at xxd le pece *Summa*	xx li
Item viij^xx Ewes vnclipped, At xiijd le pece *Summa*	viij li xiijs iiijd
Item viij^xx Lambes, at vjd le pece *Summa*	iiij li
Item xxviij Bullokkys, at vijs le pece *Summa*	ix li xvjs
	Summa xlij li ixs iiijd

AT HUMBERSTON

Item iij Swannes, price	xs
Item iij Cranes, price	vs
Item ij Geete,[15] price	iijs iiijd
	Summa xviijs iiijd

15. *Sic.* Possibly geese rather than goat is intended.

CATAILL AND SHEPE AT POTTER MERSTON

[m. 4] Item j copull oxen, price	xxiijs iiijd
Item liij Steres and heiffers, at ixs *Summa*	xxiij li xvijs
Item ccccxxix weders of yonge and olde after vj^{xx} le c shorne, at ix li le c *Summa*	xxxviij li iijs vjd
Item ccclxxix Flese of wollee, at iiijd le Flese *Summa*	vj li xixs viijd
	Summa lxx li iijs vjd

SHEPE AT BRISTALE[16]

Item lx Ewes vnclipped, at xiijd *Summa*	lxvs
Item lx lambes, at vjd le pece *Summa*	xxxs
	Summa iiij li xvs

CATAILL AND SHEPE AT THURSYNGTON

Item cccv^{xx}xv hoggys clypped after vj^{xx} le c, at xijd le pece *Summa*	xxiij li xvs
Item xl sterys, at viijs le pece *Summa*	xvj li
	Summa xxxix li xvs

SHEPE AT RERESBY

Item ccxx^{ti} Ewes after vj^{xx} to the c vnclipped, at xijd le pece *Summa*	xiij li
Item viij^{xx} lambes, at vjd le pece *Summa*	iiij li
	Summa xvij li

SHEPE AT BARESBY

Item v^{xx} hoggys clipped, at xijd *Summa*	cs
	Summa patet

CATELL AND SHEPE AT HAMULDON

Item xj^{xx} Ewes and hogges clypped, At xijd le pece *Summa*	xj li
Item [x] ix[17] score lambes, at vijd le pece *Summa*	cxvjs viijd
Item x copull of Wurkyng Oxen, at xxvjs viijd le copull *Summa*	xx^{ti} *marcas*
Item vij workyng Steres, at xs le pece *Summa*	lxxs
Item xviij keyne, at viijs le pece *Summa*	vij li iiijs

16. i.e. Birstall.
17. 'x' damaged and 'ix' written, both over an erasure; the correct figure should be 'xx'.

Item j grey geldyng Trottyng price	xxs
	Summa [x]lj[18] li xvijs iiijd

CATELL AND SHEPE AT HUMBERSTON

Item xix kene, heiffers and steres, at viijs le pece *Summa*	vij li xijs
Item ccxl Ewes clipped at vj^{xx} le c, at xijd le pece *Summa*	xiiij li
Item [viij][19] score lambes, at vjd le pece *Summa*	iiij li [ ]s[20]
Item j blakke Amblyng hoby, price	xxvjs viijd
Item A Grey Amblyng Geldyng, price	[lxxiijs iiijd][21]
Item A great blak geldyng trottyng, price	xls
Item A litell Donne Amblyng horse, price	xxs
Item an old grete grey Geldyng, price	xs
Item A Grey Trottyng geldyng, price	xxvjs viijd
	Summa xxxv li viijs viijd

SHEPE AT STRETTON

Item cccxx^{ti} Wedders vnclipped after vj^{xx} [s][22] to the c at xj li le c *Summa*	xxxiiij li xvs
Item vj^{xx} Ewes vnclipped, at xiijd le pece *Summa*	vj li xs
	Summa xlj li vs

SHEPE AT COLE OVERTON

Item vj^{xx} hogges clypped, at xijd le pece *Summa*	vj li
	Summa patet

PLATE

First ij Basyns And ij Ewers of siluer parcell gilte *ponderis* cxvij vnces, at iijs iiijd le vnce *Summa*	xix li xs
Item iij standyng Cuppys with Couers ij Chased and j playne j Goblet with a Couer And ij litell saltys with a cover playne all gilte *ponderis* iiij^{xx} xvj vnces, at iijs vjd le vnce *Summa*	xvj li xvjs
Item vj great bollys with a couer gilte And ij litell Saltes with a Couer Wrethyn and enamelyd *ponderis* ccviij vnces, at iijs viijd le vnce *Summa*	xxxviij li ijs viijd
Item ij litell Goblettys with ij Couers parcell gilte, iiij old Goblettys pounsed, ij pecys chased, xxij spones, and j Flatte pece *ponderis* c vnces, at iijs le vnce *Summa*	xv li

18. Figures damaged.
19. Written over erasure.
20. Figure erased.
21. Written over erasure.
22. Deleted.

Item vj pecys chased with a Couer parcell gilte within the peces *ponderis* viij^{xx}v vnces, at iijs iiijd le vnce *Summa*	xxvij li xs
Item ij Pottys of Siluer dobill gilte *ponderis* iiij^{xx} xiiij vnces, at iiijs iiijd le vnce *Summa*	xx li vijs iiijd
Item ij great basyns with ij Ewers of syluer parcell gilte *ponderis* ix score iij vnces, at iijs iiijd le vnce *Summa*	xxx li xs
Item vj Goblettys gilte with ij Couers *ponderis* cx vnces, at iiijs le vnce *Summa*	xxij li
Item vj Goblettys with ij Couers parcell gilte *ponderis* c vnces, at iijs iiijd le vnce *Summa*	xvj li xiijs iiijd
Item ij great saltys with a Couer chased gilte *ponderis* lij vnces, at iiijs le vnce *Summa*	x li viijs
It*e*m xij great spones gilte with Wrethyn knoppys *ponderis* xxiiij vnces, at iiijs le vnce *Summa*	iiij li xvjs
Item j dozen spones White *ponderis* xiiij vnces, at iijs ijd le vnce *Summa*	xliiijs iiijd
Item A litell spone of Workyng golde *ponderis* j vnce *dimidium* and quarter, At xxvjs viijd le vnce *Summa*	xljs viijd
Item a Signet of Fyne golde of the Splayed egle *ponderis* ij vnces except xxx^{ti} peny Weight, at xls le vnce *Summa*	lxxvijs vjd
Item a litell pece with a Couer gilte *ponderis* xij vnces *dimidium*, at iiijs le vnce *Summa*	xlviijs
Item a litell potte White, j paxbred, ij Cruettes, And a litell sacryng belle parcell gilte *ponderis* xxv vnces, at iijs ijd le vnce *Summa*	lxxixs ijd
Item ij potell pottys White *ponderis* lxiij vnces *dimidium*, at iijs le vnce *Summa*	ix li xs vjd
Item A maser with a Boos brokyn, price	xxs
Item a litell salte of golde with a couer with okyn leves of fyne golde *ponderis* ij vnces *dimidem*, at xls le vnce *Summa*	cs
Item a Standyng maser with a Cover gilte, price	xxxs
Item A Chalys with a paten And a Coueryng of a pece with a rounde knoppe parcell gilte *ponderis* xvj vnces, At iijs iiijd le vnce *Summa*	liijs iiijd

Summa cclv li xvijs xd

WERYNG GERE

Item A Sengill gowne of Scarlet sore worne with a hode of ye same, price	xs
Item a Crymesyn gowne sengle with an hode of the same, price	xxs
Item a nyght gowne of Muster the villers furred with course blak lambe, price	xijs

Item A sengle gowne of violet with an hode of the same, price	xiijs iiijd
Item iij sengle Ray gownys of blewe Ray with ij hoodes soreworne, at viijs le pece *Summa*	xxiiijs
Item ij sengle gownys of grene Ray with ij hoodys, at viijs le pece *Summa*	xvjs
[m. 5] Item a gowne clothe of newe blewe Ray and Muster, price	xiijs iiijd
Item a newe gowne cloth of blewe Ray and tawny, price	xiijs iiijd
Item a gowne clothe of grene ray and violet, price	xiijs iiijd
Item an olde cloke of violet, price	vs
Item a Reed Mantell sore worne, price	iijs iiijd
Item A browne tawny gowne furred with foxe Wombes, price	xiijs iiijd
Item a browne Tawny gowne furred with blak lambe, price	xxs
Item a shorte Rydyng gowne lyned with blak Coton, price	xs
Item a Cours sengle gowne of Muster, price	viijs
Item j sengle gowne with j hode of Murray engrayned, price	xxiijs iiijd
Item a violet gowne sengle with j hode, price	xxijs
Item A doublet of blak veluet, price	xxs
Item j doublet of tawny saten sore worne, price	xijs
Item A Jaket of blak veluet furred with Martrons, price	xxvjs viijd
Item a Boke in Frenche wreten in parchement, price	xxs
Item an olde scarlet gowne of his first Wiffes vnfurred with an old purfull quarter depe of White letyce, price	xxvjs viijd
Item a Womans gowne of violet en grayne vnfurred with a purfull of Mynkes quarter depe, price	xls
Item an old gowne of his firste wifes vnfurred with a purfull of White letyce quarter depe, price	xxvjs viijd
Item A kyrtell of Russet Chamelet, price	xiijs iiijd
Item a gowne clothe of newe grene Ray, price	xiijs iiijd
Item ij Complete Vestymentes of grene bord Alexandre, price	xls
Item A Frontell for an Awter of grene silke frenged, price	xiijs iiijd
Item an Awterclothe of grene bord Alexandre, price	vs
Summa xxiiij li xvijs iiijd	

IN THE CHAPELL

Item ij Awter clothes oon Diaper an other playne, price	iijs
Item a Crucifixe of Wodde gilte, price	xxd
Item ij ymages, oon of oure lady an other of seynt John, price	ijs viijd
Item ij Curteyns for the Awter of changeable Tartron	vjs viijd
Item A vestyment sore Worne, price	xiijs iiijd
Item A Corporas And the case of old blak veluet, price	xijd

Item j pax, j sacryngbell And ij Cruettes of latyn	viijd
	Summa xxixs

BOKES

Item j olde boke of lawe in Frenche Wreten in parchement Wele lymmed at the begynnyng with the Crucifixe, price	xxs
Item a boke enprynted *de Tullius*[23] en englisshe, price	xvjd
Item j boke enprynted of Dyuerse Contres,[24] price	xijd
Item j litell old boke of englisshe in parchement, price	xxd
Item j boke of lawe enfrenche of yeres and termes emprynted,[25] price	iiijs
Item a litell old masse boke[26] in parchement wryten of Freres vse, price	xiijs iiijd
Item A great Boke of lawe[27] wreton in velom and couered with blak veluet with ij great Rounde claspes of latyn fo. *primo*, *Le premiez Chappitre*, price	x *marcas*
Item j Bible and lire[28] in iiij partes price to gidder	lxs
Item j boke of the Maister[29] of thistories in parchement Wreton fo. *secundo*, *Et pro sui Concameracione*, price	xxxs
Item j booke enprynted *de sermonibus quadragesimalibus*[30] fo. *tercio Promittit aliquos cadere in peccatum*, price	xs
Item A Boke in parchement wreton of the psalmes of the Commendacions[31] fo. iiij[to] *Non eum qui operantur/iniquitatem/*[32] price	xxs

23. Marcus Tullius Cicero, *De Senectute, de Amicitia, de Nobilitate*, folio (Caxton, 1481).
24. Either John Trevisa, *Description of Britain* (Caxton, 1480), which has no title page but begins with a sentence about 'divers chronicles'. Or (more probably) John Mandeville, *Travels* (Wynkyn de Worde, 1499) where the first paragraph of the text (f. 5a) refers to 'other dyuerse countrees'.
25. Either *Y.B. 33–37 Henry VI* (Machlinia, n.d.). Or *Y.B. 3–8 Edward IV* (Pynson, 1496).
26. 'Coverid with white', see above, p. 414.
27. Possibly Bracton, see above, p. 365.
28. Nicholas of Lyra, *Postillae Perpetuae in Universam Sanctam Scripturam*. The price suggests a printed work. A number of continental editions are known, e.g. the Nuremberg 1486 edition owned by Syon monastery: *Catalogue of the Library of Syon Monastery*, ed. M. Bateson (1898), 52, 61–62.
29. Peter Comestor, *Historia Scholastica*.
30. Possibly Robert Caracciolus, *Quadragesimale de Poenitentia* (but not Strassburg, 1473, Cologne, 1473, Basle, 1475) or *Quadragesimale de Peccatis* (but not Lyons, 1488, Strassburg, 1490). Alternatively Jean de Voragine, *Quadragesimales* (but not Augsburg, 1485, Pavia, 1499).
31. *Commendationes Animarum*, i.e. Psalms 118, 138, prayers to be said at the bedside of the dying; in England a regular element in books of hours.
32. / – / word omitted and inserted above.

Item an old boke in parchement wreton *de exposicione declamacionum Senece*[33] fo. v^to^ *Potui illud ingenium*, price	vjs viijd
Item A Boke enprynted de Tullius *de officiis cum Commento*[34] fo. vj^to^ *Tua eum hirundo*, price	vs
Item j boke enprynted *de proprietatibus Rerum*[35] fo. vij^mo^ *Faciendes et pedes velare*, price	iijs iiijd
Item j olde boke in parchement *de Tabula super librum Isodori etheriloquii*[36] fo. viij^o^ *Ostia mare iis*, price	ijs viijd
Item j boke enprynted called *vocabularius breuiloquiis*[37] fo. x^mo^ *Post expressionem proijciuntur*, price	iijs iiijd
Item A Boke emprynted called Catholicon[38] fo. x^mo^ *Si fiat consideracio*, price	viijs
Item a boke enprynted *de Commento sancti Gregorii super Cantica canticorum*[39] fo xj^mo^ *Et dicit postea*, price	vs
Item j boke enprynted couered with a Forell of parchement fo. xij^mo^ *Tu sis quia mundas*, price	ijs
Item a Feyre booke of Frenche wrton in parchement *de Jehan Boccace*[40] couered with blacke saten and claspys siluer and gilte, price	liijs iiijd
Item A Sawter in parchment glosed, price	xxxs
Item a booke enprynted *de Collacione genus hominem*[41] fo. xiij^o^ *Distinguit Phillipus in littera*, price	ijs viijd
Item A boke enprynted de Boicius *de consolacione philosofie*[42] couered with parchement, price	iijs
Item A Boke *de Boicius de consolacione philosophie* en englisshe,[43] price	xvjd
Item a litell prynted boke called *Cursus mundi*, [44] price	ijs
Item A litell booke in parchement called *Tractus super vetus testamentum*, price	iiijs

33. Nicholas Trevet, *De Exposicionem Declamationes Senecae* (i.e., Seneca's *Controversiae*).
34. Marcus Tullius Cicero, *De Officiis* (with commentary). Numerous editions known, from Cologne, 1465.
35. Bartolomaeus Anglicus, *De Proprietatibus Rerum* (Strassburg, 1485).
36. Isidore of Seville, *Etymologiae*.
37. Johannes Reuchlin, *Vocabularius Breviloquius* (Strassburg, 1488).
38. Johannes Balbus, *Catholicon* (Strassburg, 1482).
39. Gregory the Great, *De Commento Super Cantica Canticorum*. Printed abroad (but not Cologne 1473; Basle, 1496; Paris, 1498).
40. Boccaccio, *Decameron*.
41. *Collaciones ad omne genus hominium*. Apparently a collection of sermons.
42. Boethius, *De Consolatione Philosophie*. Many continental editions from 1470.
43. Boethius, *De Consolatione Philosophie*, trans. Chaucer. The price indicates a printed work, i.e. Caxton, before 1479.
44. Unidentified. Not the fourteenth-century poem, *Cursus Mundi*.

Item a litell Booke of paper in Frenche wreton with dyuerse cases of the lawe, price	iijs iiijd
[m. 6] Item A litell booke *de venicijs*[45] enprynted, price	xvjd
Item an olde[46] in parchement called *Ambrosius de officijs*,[47] price	ijs viijd
Summa xxj li xiiijs iiijd.	

Computatio ccccccclxxxxvj li xvs ijd. ob.

45. *De Veniciis*. Possibly Bernard von Breydenbach, *Viazo de Venesia al Sancto Iherusalem* (Bologna, 1500).
46. 'book' omitted.
47. St Ambrose, *De Officiis*.

APPENDIX C

LIST OF PLEADERS *c.* 1518

CHANCERY WARRANTS 10 HENRY VIII (MONTHS UNCERTAIN): C82/474/36

This list, now in a class to which it clearly does not belong, is written in a single column on a narrow piece of paper which once (as marks of sewing show) formed part of a book. There is no indication of provenance but since it is signed by Wolsey and Skewys, a member of his staff, the list was clearly prepared for the cardinal.

The document cannot be precisely dated. John Erneley surrendered as A.G. on 26 Jan. 1519, early in Hilary term. It is probable, therefore, that the document is not later than Michaelmas term 1518. The *terminus a quo* is, *prima facie*, the creation of Wolsey as cardinal in the autumn and, probably, his appointment as chancellor, 24 Dec. 1515. Since all those named are known to have been alive in Hilary 1519 and obvious names are missing, e.g. William Ayloffe of Lincoln's Inn (d. Jul./Sept. 1517) and Sir Robert Sheffield (in the Tower from Feb., died autumn 1518), the P.R.O. dating seems probable.

The purpose of the list has yet to be established, so too the significance of the crosses and marginal comment on Richard Covert (in a different hand). One possible association is with Wolsey's order to the judges and serjeants on 14 Oct. 1518 to report obstructors of justice; the chancellor might well have exacted an oath of good behaviour from the profession below the coif (whose members were already sworn): Guy, *Cardinal's Court*, 30–3, 76–8; Hastings, *Common Pleas*, 60, 73 n. 80.

THE NAMES OF THE PLEYDERS OR PRENTYSE OF T[HE] KYNGES COURTES SUPPOSED TO BE PRESENT AT THIS TERME

Sir Thomas Nevell Knyght
John Ernley the Kynges Attornay
William Rudhale
John FitzJamys
John Porte
William Ellys
John Stoke
William Wadham
Thomas More
Edwarde Halys
John Rooper
John Portmanne
Richard Haskyth
Water Luke

Richard Lister
John Goryng
John Skyllyng
John Wodde
Humphrey Browne
Humphrey Wynkefyld
Baldwyn Malyt
William Marshall
Bartholomew Huse
Thomas Willoughby
John Baldwyn
Robert Norwyche

+ Richard Couert +
qui noluit iurare
William Shelley
Richard Clark
William Conyngsby
Edmunde Knyghtley
John Pakyngton
John Baker
[John] Hynde
Richard Wye
John Petyt
John Halys

THE NAMES OF THE PLEYDERS OR PRENTYSE OF THE KYNGES COURTES SUPPOSED NOWE TO BE ABSENT FROM THIS TERME

Thomas Jubbes
Thomas Matston
Thomas Inglefyld
William Wotton
Thomas More
Rauf Rokeby
William Vowell

Thomas Thatcher
Thomas Fairfaxe
John Spilman

Johannes Skewes*
Franciscus Momford*

T[homas] *Cardinalis Eboracensis**

IDENTIFICATIONS:

John Baker	I.T., read 1522; of Sissinghurst, Kent; speaker & P.C.
John Baldwyn	I.T., read 1516; of Aylesbury, Bucks.; C.J.K.B.
Humphrey Browne	M.T., read 1516; of Terling, Essex; J.C.P.
Richard Clark	L.I., read 1515; of Lincoln; recorder of Lincoln.
William Conyngsby	I.T., read 1518; of Lynn, Norf.; J.K.B.
Richard Couert	G.I.; of Slaugham, Sussex.
William Ellys	L.I., read 1502; of Attlebridge, Norf.; B.Ex.
John Ernley A.G.	G.I., of Sidlesham, Sussex; C.J.C.P.
Thomas Fairfaxe	G.I., of Finningley, Notts.; Sjt.
John FitzJamys	M.T., read 1504; of Redlynch, Soms.; C.J.K.B.
John Goryng	G.I., of Burton, Sussex.
Edward Halys	I.T., read 1512;† of Shoreditch, London.
John Halys	G.I., read 1514; of Canterbury; B.Ex.
Richard Haskyth	G.I., read 1515; of Rufford, Lancs.

* Signatures † Second reading

Bartholomew Huse	M.T., read 1518; of Knighton, Wilts.
John Hynde	G.I., read 1518; of Madingley, Cambs.; J.C.P.
Thomas Inglefyld	M.T., read 1520; of Englefield, Berks.; J.C.P.
Thomas Jubbes	M.T., read 1505; of Bristol; recorder of Bristol.
Edmund Knyghtley	M.T., read 1523; of Fawsley, Northants.; Sjt.
Richard Lister	M.T., read 1516; of Southampton; C.J.K.B.
Walter Luke	M.T., read 1514; of Cople, Beds.; J.K.B.
Baldwin Malyt	I.T., read 1512; of West Quantoxhead, Soms.; S.G.
William Marshall	L.I., read 1512; of Dunstable, Beds.
Thomas Matston	M.T., read 1519; of Wotton-under-Edge, Glos.
Francis Momford [Mountford]	I.T., read 1519; of Feltwell, Norf.
Thomas More	M.T., read 1507; of Sherfield-upon-Loddon, Hants.
Thomas More	L.I., read 1511; of Chelsea, Middx.; L.Chanc.
Thomas Nevell, Kt	G.I., speaker & royal councillor.
Robert Norwyche	L.I., read 1518; of South Ockendon, Essex; C.J.C.P.
John Pakyngton	I.T., read 1520; of Hampton Lovett. Worcs.; Chirographer of the C.P.
John Petyt	G.I., read 1518; B.Ex.
John Porte	I.T., read 1507; of Chester, and Etwall, Derbs.; J.K.B.
John Portmanne	M.T., read 1509; of Orchard Portman, Soms.
Ralph Rokeby	L.I., read 1511; of Yafforth, Yorks.
John Rooper	L.I., read 1504; of Swalecliffe, Kent; Chief Clerk K.B. and A.G.
William Rudhale	I.T., read 1494; of Rudhall, Heref., Sjt.
William Shelley	I.T., read 1518; of Michelgrove, Sussex; J.C.P.
John Skewes	L.I., read 1505; of St Kew, Cornw.
John Skyllyng	I.T., read 1507; of Rollestone, Wilts.
John Spilman	G.I., read 1514; of Narborough, Norf.; J.K.B.
John Stoke	[no information].
Thomas Thatcher	of Westham and Pevensey, Sussex.
William Vowell	M.T., read 1517; of Wells, Soms.
William Wadham	L.I., read 1501; of Catherstone, Dorset.
Thomas Willoughby	L.I., read 1517; of Chiddingstone, Kent; J.C.P.
John Wodde	L.I., read 1496; of Fulbourn, Cambs.
William Wotton	L.I., read 1509; of North Tuddenham, Norf.; B.Ex.
Richard Wye	I.T.; of Rodmarton, Glos.
Humphrey Wynkefyld	G.I., read 1517;† of Brantham Suff.; speaker and royal councillor.

APPENDIX D

SERJEANTS-AT-LAW CREATED 1463 TO 1510

Part I of this appendix lists all serjeants created in these years, and indicates the inn they belonged to and whether they reached judicial rank.

Part II gives brief biographical notes on each serjeant. For dates of official appointments and death/retirement before 31 Dec. 1510, see Appendix E; for 1511 onwards Spelman, *Reports*, ii. *357–96*. Appointments as J.P. connected with service as justice of assize are omitted. For elections as M.P., see Wedgwood, *Biographies*. A.R., L.R. = autumn, Lent reader.

PART I CALLS TO THE COIF, 1463 TO 1510 (ALPHABETICAL ORDER)

1463	Thomas Bryan	G*	j	William Jenney	L	j
	John Catesby	I	j	Richard Nele	G	j
	Guy Fairfax	G	j	Richard Pigot	M	j
	John Grenefield	I		Thomas Yonge	M	j
1478	Thomas Brugge	G	j	John Sulyard	L	j
	William Callow	M	j	Robert Townshend	L	j
	William Hussey	G	j	Thomas Tremayle	M	j
	Thomas Rogers	G		John Vavasour	I	j
	Humphrey Starky	I	j			
1486	William Danvers	I	j	Richard Jay	G	
	John Fineux	G	j	Thomas Kebell	I	a
	John Fisher	M	j	Robert Rede	L	j
	John Haugh	L	j	Thomas Wode	M	j
1495	John Butler	L	j	John Kingsmill	M	j
	Humphrey Coningsby	I	j	John Mordaunt	M	a
	Robert Constable	L	a	Thomas Oxenbridge	G	a
	Thomas Frowyk	I	j	John Yaxley	G	
	Richard Heigham	L				

1503	Gregory Adgore	I		William Grevill	I	j
	Robert Brudenell	I	j	Thomas Marowe	I	a
	William Cutlerd	L	a	John More	L	j
	Richard Eliot	M	j	Guy Palmes	M	a
	William Fairfax	G	j	Lewis Pollard	M	j
1510	John Brook	M	a	John Newport	L	a
	Richard Brook	G	j	Brian Palmes	M	a
	John Caryll	I	a	Thomas Pigot	I	a
	Antony Fitzherbert	G	j	John Rowe	G	
	John Newdigate	L				

* The initial indicates the inn of which the serjeant had been a member.
j = subsequently became a judge.
a = served as a justice of assize but not raised to J.K.B. or J.C.P.

PART II BIOGRAPHIES OF SERJEANTS-AT-LAW CREATED 1463 TO 1510

ADGORE, *Gregory* alias *Edgore 1503*

of London and Brantham, Suff., gent., 1493; son and heir of Robert of Brantham; J.P. Suff., from 1499; marr. Anne, dau. Simon Wiseman, of Gt Thornham, Norf., esq. (J.P., M.P.) – she remarr. Humphrey Wingfield of Gray's Inn who claimed to have lost 'half his living' at her death; daus. Ella, and Dorothy, who marr. William Calybut (prob. son of Francis Calybut of L.I. and Castle Acre, Norf.) and sold inheritance to Wingfield; inherited 'Brigge place' and other lands in Brantham and was bequeathed 'Wodwardes' in Brantham by William Wodward (possibly his maternal grandfather); purchased lands in Capel and Brantham, Suff. and in Norfolk; other land in Suffolk and Essex; will and testament 24 Aug. 1504 – to be buried at Brantham, much activity as mortgagor and money-lender, executors: wife and Sir Philip Tilney; supervisors include M.R. and A.G. – probate 15 Nov. 1504; *i.p.m.* Suffolk only.

Cal. Patent Rolls, 1485–94, 429; *ibid. 1494–1500*, 660; *Cal. Close Rolls, 1500–9*, 106, 216; *Cal. Fine Rolls, 1485–1509*, 805; *L. and P.*, i. 438 (1 m.1), 1221 (56); xii(2). 1342. *Cal. inquisitions post mortem*, iii. 357; *Admission Book*, i.20; *Black Books*, i. *passim*; PROB 11/11 f. 97v, 11/14 f. 159v; 11/18 ff. 122–128v; Wedgwood, *Biographies*, 961; B.L. Add. Ms. 19114/52.

BROOK, *John 1510*

of Redcliffe St, Bristol, Long Ashton, Ashton Philip and Clifton, Soms. 1509; related to Lord Cobnam; treasurer M.T. 1501–3, A.R. 1510 on promotion to coif; gauger of Bristol, 1486; J.P. Soms. from 1494; king's serjeant 1520; justice of assize, western circuit from 1520; wife Joan, dau. & co-heiress of Richard Ameryck, sheriff of Bristol; son and heir Thomas; younger son David: of I.T., recorder of Bristol and C.B.Ex., grandson John Welsh: recorder of Bristol and J.C.P.; lands in Clifton and Ashton in right of his wife and by purchase; other land in Glos., Soms., and Northants.; chief steward of Glastonbury Abbey; employed by the duke of Buckingham; no will, brass in St Mary Redcliffe, Bristol; *i.p.m.* Soms. and Glos., died 25 or 26 Dec. 1522.

Cal. Patent Rolls, 1484–94, 159, 499; *ibid., 1494–1509*, 657; *Cal. Close Rolls, 1485–1500*, 958; *ibid., 1500–9*, 91, 92, 398, 504, 1501; *L. and P.*, i. 438 (2 m. 6); iii. 933, 3695; *Cal. inquisitions post mortem,* iii. 379; *Minutes of Parliament*, i. 1, 3, 6, 30; H. Druitt, *Manual of Costume as Illustrated by Monumental Brasses* (1906), 230; Rawcliffe, *The Staffords*, 227; *Trans. Bristol and Gloucestershire Arch. Soc.* 3 (1878–9), 222–31; C142/40/60, 85 (*i.p.m.* of his wife, *ibid.*, 59/1, 60/111, 61/37); Spelman, *Reports*, ii. *388*; *Bristol Wills*, 166; W. H. Hamilton Rogers, 'The Brook Family', in *Pro. Somerset Arch. Soc.*, 46 (1900), 111.

BROOK, *Richard 1510*

gent., 1505; of Sutton at Hone, Kent, 1528; probably originated from Sussex; cousin of William Stafford of Kent, probably customer of London and keeper of the Mint; J.P. Sussex 1498–1509, Suffolk and Surrey from 1520, Middx from 1522; justice of assize, East Anglian circuit, 1519; M.P. London, 1512, 1515; kt; marr. Anne, dau. Joan Ledys; 3 sons, 5 daus., of whom Margaret marr. William Whorwood of M.T., later A.G.; reversionary interest in lands in Sutton at Hone and elsewhere in Kent; obtained by mortgage Sussex lands of (apparently) his wife's relations; land in Kent, Norf., Suff., Sussex, Surrey; died in debt to Westminster Abbey, of which he was a brother; sold land in Kent; associate of Robert Blagge, B.Ex., William Marshall, L.I. (his clerk), and John Gardiner, I.T.; patent of exemption from the coif 1510; under-sheriff of London, recorder from 1511; J.C.P. 1520, C.B.Ex. 1526; employed by duke of Buckingham, by earl of Northumberland from whom had London house rent free; executor of: earl of Worcester, John Roper A.G., Sir Thomas Lovell, Sir William Compton; founder of Broke family of Nacton, Suff.; will and testament 1 May, will 5

May 1529 – overseers William Shelley J.C.P. and John Baker, recorder of London – probate 2 Jul. 1529; no *i.p.m.*; died 6/12 May, 1529.

Cal Patent Rolls, 1485–94, 83; *ibid., 1494–1509*, 662; *Cal. Close Rolls, 1500–9*, 63; *Cal. Ancient Deeds*, iii. D475; *L. and P.*, i. 546 (48), 876; ii. 359; iii. 347, 1081, 2993; iv. 72, 366, 1298, 1518, 4442(1), App. 133; Rawcliffe, *The Staffords*, 227–8; PROB11/23 ff. 23–5; Stephenson, *Brasses*, 494; Spelman, *Reports*, ii. *372, 383*; *Visitations of Suffolk, 1561 etc.*, 118.

BRUDENELL, *Robert 1503*

of Burnham, Bucks., 1502; of Stonton Wyville, Leics., and Deene, Northants.; younger son of Edmund Brudenell the younger, of Amersham, Bucks., gent., J.P.; A.R. at I.T., 1491 on *Westminster II*; J.P. Bucks. from 1489, Leics. from 1496; kt; marr. twice: 1st Margaret, sist. and co-heiress of Thomas Entwysell, esq., wid. of William Wyville of Stonton Wyville, esq. (d. 1494) – she died 1502; 2nd Philippa Power of Beachampton, Bucks., wid. Thomas Rufford of Edlesborough, Bucks., esq.; 4 sons (2 attended I.T., of whom Robert became clerk of assize to his father); inherited estate in Stoke Mandeville, Bucks., life estate in Burnham, Bucks., possibly also land in Middx; bought out heirs of his elder bro.; secured reversion of the Wyville estate; bought heavily in the midlands, esp. Leics.; settled at Deene; C.J.C.P. 1520; will and testament 25 Apr. 1530 'by the consent of Dame Phelipp my wife' – to be buried at Deene – probate 14 Feb. 1531; *i.p.m.* Bucks., Leics., Lincs., Northants., Rutland, Warws.; died 30 Jan. 1531.
Cal. Patent Rolls, 1485–94, 482; *ibid., 1494–1509*, 646; *Cal. Close Rolls, 1500–9*, 165; *L. and P.*, i. 438 (1 m. 18), 709 (34); *Cal. inquisitions post mortem*, i. 1049; *Inner Temple Records*, i. 71, 458; PROB11/24 f. 11; C142/52/33, 46, 64, 68, 111, 118; Thorne, *Readings and Moots*, i. xvi; Spelman, *Reports*, ii. *372*; J. Wake, *The Brudenells of Deene* (1953), 9–27.

BRUGGE, *Thomas* alias *a Brigg 1478*

of Hereford, gent., 1457; of Ross, 1461; of London, gent., 1466; J.P. Herefs. from 1461, possibly escheator 1465 and M.P. 1472–5; justice of assize, western circuit from 1481; steward of Elmley Castle, Worcs., 1478; wife Jane; son and heir John; secured the manor of Wick by Pershore by lending money to William Vampage; restored under the terms of Brugge's will. Not of Cubberley and Fownhope, escheator of Glos., since the latter died in 1493; not of Dymock, Glos., since the latter's wife was Alice; not of Evington, since the latter's heir was William; not of Wington in Leominster, since the latter was alive in 1486. No will, no *i.p.m.*

Cal. Patent Rolls, 1461–67, 61, 565; *ibid., 1476–86*, 76, 124; *Cal. Close Rolls, 1454–61*, 222; *ibid., 1461–68*, 363; *ibid., 1476–85*, 51, 648; *Cal. Fine Rolls, 1461–71*, 169; *Cal. Ancient Deeds*, i. C1765, iii. C3239, 3279, 3581, 3700; vi. C4196, 4539; *L. and P.*, i. 438 (2 m. 8); *Cal. inquisitions post mortem*, i. 857, 858; Thorne, *Readings and Moots,* i. xxxviii–xxxix; Wedgwood, *Biographies*; V.C.H., *Worcestershire*, iv. 116 n.81, 170.

BRYAN, *Thomas 1463*

see above, pp. 376–7; resident in St Andrew's, Holborn, before 1447; 'gentleman', 1452; 'apprentice-at-law', 1459; J.P. Bucks., 1470 and from 1471; kt; marr. *c.* 1474 Isabel widow Thomas Blount, esq.; 1 son, 1 dau., 1 bastard dau.; land in Lincs. in right of wife's dower; purchased Thavies Inn, 1475, and land in Bucks.; leased Hailsham rectory, Sussex, and St George's Inn, 1475; substantial grant of forfeited land, 1484; other land in London, Bucks., possibly Notts.; steward of St Bartholomew's Priory, Smithfield; will and testament 7 Feb. 1495 – to be buried at Ashridge, executors: his son Thomas and latter's wife, Margaret – probate 11 Dec. 1500; no *i.p.m.*

Cal. Patent Rolls, 1467–77, 477, 608; *ibid., 1476–85*, 514; *Cal. Close Rolls. 1447–54*, 359; *ibid., 1461–68*, 315–16; *ibid., 1468–76*, 1232; *Cal. Ancient Deeds*, i. C47; Williams, *Early Holborn*, 15, 152, 166, 842, 866; V.C.H., *Buckinghamshire*, iii. 364, 393; *Records of St Bartholomew's Smithfield*, ed. E.A. Webb (Oxford, 1921), ii. 258; H.M.C., *Mss. of Lord De L'Isle and Dudley* (1925–42), i. 211.

BUTLER, *John 1495*

of West Malling, Kent, 1493; of St Mary of Bredyn, Canterbury and Silver St and Serjeants' Inn, London, 1517; adm. L.I. 1468 after serving as butler, A.R. 1482, L.R. 1488; J.P. Kent from 1487; kt; wife Anne, co-heiress of father William and cousin Walter Elys of Sheppey; cf. Butler's quarrel with William Elys at L.I.; s.p.; lands in Sheppey and Canterbury in right of his wife; purchased land in Sheppey and Canterbury; will and testament, 20 Nov., 2 Dec. 1517 – to be buried in St Augustine's, Canterbury, all his law books to L.I., wife Anne exix – probate 14 Oct. 1519; *i.p.m.* Kent; died 15 Dec. 1517.

Cal. Patent Rolls, 1485–94, 490; *Cal. Close Rolls, 1476–85*, 1428; *ibid., 1485–1500*, 222; *Black Books*, i. 48, 63, 75, 87; PROB11/19 ff. 172, 172v.; E150/475/16.

CALLOW, *William* alias *Collow 1478*

born at Reveshale, Norf.; possibly of Holbeach. Lincs., esq., 1460; J.P. Kent from 1485; wife buried at Clerkenwell; brother-in-law William Hert the elder, gent. (M.P., attorney, related to Thomas Hert, grocer of London); s.p.; purchased Shafford's Court, Canterbury, 1476–80; other lands in Westgate Canterbury and Gillingham; heir, Leonard, son of his brother John; will and testament, 26 Apr. 1483, 5 Oct. 1485 – to be buried in the Whitefriars, London, much activity as a money-lender [see above, p. 120], executors include William Hert and Edmund Coksegge his clerk – probate 4 Feb. 1486: *i.p.m.* Kent.

Cal. Patent Rolls, 1452–61, 619; *ibid., 1485–94*, 489; *Cal. Close Rolls, 1468–76*, 413, 1309; *ibid., 1476–85*, 545, 606; *ibid., 1485–1500*, 857; *Cal. inquisitions post mortem*, i. 433; PROB11/8 ff. 57–58v; Wedgwood, *Biographies* 430; C1/108/70–1.

CARYLL, *John 1510*

'gent'., 1503; of Warnham, Sussex, gent., 1510; no certain information as to parentage; treasurer I.T., 1507–8, A.R. 1510 on election to coif, on statute of Marlborough; J.P. Sussex from 1496; clerk of assize western circuit 1495–1509; justice of assize East Anglian circuit 1518, midland 1519; marr. three times: 1st Griseld, dau. Henry Belknap (cousin and heir of Sir Ralph Boteler, Lord Sudeley) – s.p.; 2nd Margaret, sister of Thomas Elyngbrigge (Elmbridge) of Merstham, Surrey, esq. (J.P.) – 2 sons; 3rd Jane, dau. and co-heiress of Robert Rede C.J. – 4 sons, 2 daus. (John, the heir, was of I.T., attorney-general of the duchy); 3rd prothonotary C.P., 1493–1510; associate of Edmund Dudley; K.S., 1514; major law reporter; will and testament 12 May 1523 – to be buried at Warnham beside his wife Margaret, directions for John's education at the Temple, executors include Antony Fitzherbert J.C.P. and Richard Covert of G.I. – probate 25 June 1523; actually buried St Dunstan's, Fleet St, 'in the isle whereas the Judges and Sergeants dooe vsuallie sett'; no *i.p.m.*; died 17 June 1523.

Cal. Patent Rolls, *1485–94*, 502; *ibid.*, *1494–1509*, 29, 661, 662; *Cal. Close Rolls*, *1500–9*, 143, 617, 629, 633, 762, 972, 977; *L. and P.*, i. 94 (50), 438 (4 m. 27), 3049 (2); ii. 4317; iii. 347; *Cal. inquisitions post mortem*, ii. 723; iii. 467, 1039; *Inner Temple Records*, i. 10, 12, 70; Stephenson, *Brasses*, 506; PROB11/21 ff. 75–6; Somerville, *Duchy of Lancaster*, i. 408–9; Hastings, *Common Pleas*, 257; Spelman, *Reports*, ii, *348*, *378*, *388*; Simpson, *L.Q.R.* 73. 95–100; R. G. Rice, 'Warnham, its Register and Vicars', in *Sussex Archaeological Collections* 33 (1883), 170–4.

CATESBY, *John 1463*

of Whiston, Northants., senior, 1486; called 'uncle' by William Catesby, junior (speaker 1484, executed 1485), hence possibly brother of Sir William of Ashby St Legers (J.P., M.P., squire of the body) but perhaps son of Hugh Catesby of Arthingworth, Northants.; J.P. Surrey, 1466 and 1469–85, Northants., from 1467; kt; married Elizabeth, dau. William Grene of Hayes (clerk in the exchequer, keeper of parts of the palace of Westminster, J.P., M.P.) with a portion in excess of 50 marks and by this marriage related to John Arderne (probably the son of Peter Arderne, C.B.Ex.) and John Holgrave, B.Ex.; 8 sons, 2 daus. – his heir was J.P. and kt; lands in Northants., Bucks., Beds., and Warws., and in right of his wife in Middx, Kent and Westminster; retained by the duchy of Lancaster, 1478–82; will and testament 6 May, 23 Aug. 1485 – to be buried in St James, Northampton, executors include William Catesby, junior, and Serjeant Richard Pigot; probate 24 Jun. 1486; *i.p.m.* Beds., Bucks., Warws. – Leics. no lands.

Cal. Patent Rolls, 1461–7, 573; *ibid., 1467–77*, 623, 631; *ibid., 1485–94*, 22, 495; *Cal. Close Rolls, 1461–8*, 64, 237, 303, 310; *Cal. inquisitions post mortem*, i. 355, 356, 374, 375; *ibid.*, iii. 889; *Cal. Ancient Deeds*, iv. 297; vi. C5157; Williams, *Early Holborn*, 1208–12; Somerville, *Duchy of Lancaster*, i. 452; Wedgwood, *Biographies*, 163–5, 394–4; PROB11/7 ff. 114v, 115; 11/8 ff. 3v, 4.

CONINGSBY, *Humphrey 1495*

born at Rock, Worcs.; gent., 1487; of Rock, Worcs., 1510; related to the Coningsbys of Neen Sollars, Shrops. (possibly grandson of Thomas); J.P. Herts. from 1493, Lincs. Kesteven and Lindsey from 1501, Worcs. from 1504, Middx from 1505, Rutland from 1506, Shrops. from 1510; kt; marr. three times: 1st Isabel, allegedly heiress of the Fereby family of Lincs., more probably of Strood, Kent, and related to Ralph Penne of Aldenham, Herts., esq.; 2nd (in 1498–9) Alice, dau. (born *c.* 1450) and co-heiress of her father John Franceys, kt, and his sister, and of her mother Isabel (dau. and heiress of John Plessington, his nephew, and his brother, Sir Henry) – she had previously married: 1st (prior to 1463) John Worsley, and 2nd William Staveley of Bignell, Oxon., esq. (d. 1498) – she died 1500; 3rd (1504) Anne, dau. (born *c.* 1470) and heiress of Christopher Moresby, kt (of Highhead and Scaleby, Cumb., J.P. and sheriff, d. 1499), widow of James Pickering, esq. of Killington, Westm. (d. 1497) – she died 1523; 3 sons, 4 daus. – he arranged for his grandson and heir to marry the dau. of Thomas Englefield J.C.P., his second son William became 3rd prothonotary of C.P. and J.K.B., his third son John was receiver-general of the duchy, his dau. Elizabeth marr. (2nd) John

Fitzjames C.J.K.B.; in right of 2nd wife, lands in Oxon., Berks., Yorks. and interests in Lincs. and Rutland; in right of 3rd wife enjoyed Moresby family estate; bought land in Herts. and Worcs.; executor, and secured lands of Ralph Penne at Aldenham; other land Shrops., Heref., Worcs., Middx and London; 3rd prothonotary of C.P., 1480–93; retained by duchy, 1505–9, 2nd justice at Lancaster 1504, chief justice 1509–31; secured for his dau. Amphelice the marriage and lands of John, son of William Tyndale, esq., possibly after lending William money; built chantry chapel at Copthorne Hill, Aldenham and chantry in Rock parish church (licensed 1521); will and testament, 16 Nov. 1531, codicil 2 June 1535 (but also refers to his 'last will of my manors, londes and tenementes') – to be bur. at the Whitefriars, London, by his wife Isabel, or at Aldenham or at Rock; chantry to be established in Aldenham parish church; executors: his two sons, supervisors John Fitzjames and Antony Fitzherbert J.J. – probate 26 Nov. 1535; *i.p.m.* Worcs.; retired Mich. 1533, died 2 June 1535.

Cal. Patent Rolls, 1485–94, 489; *ibid., 1494–1509*, 50, 116, 209, 365, 648–50, 655, 666; *Cal. Close Rolls, 1485–1500*, 282, 847; *ibid., 1500–9*, 627; *L. and P.*, i. 438 (2 m. 11, 3 m. 28), p. 1542; ii. 3395; iii. 2055 (51, 53); *Cal. inquisitions post mortem*, i. 171, 393, 418, 1062, 1172, 1257; ii. 88, 90, 292, 294, 388, 572; iii. 105, 604; PROB 11/25 ff. 217v–219v; C1/293/27; C82/393; C142/57/1,82/1; V.C.H., *Hertfordshire*, ii. 152–3, 157, 271; Somerville, *Duchy of Lancaster*, i. 403, 470, 473; *Visitation of the County of Worcester, 1569*, ed. W.P.W. Phillimore, Harleian Soc. 27 (1888), 43; *The Genealogist*, n.s., 26 (1909–10), 212; Hastings, *Common Pleas*, 47; Spelman, *Reports*, ii, *359–60, 377–8*.

CONSTABLE, *Robert 1495*

of North Cliffe, E.R. Yorks., 1501; 2nd son Sir Robert of Flamborough, E.R. Yorks. (J.P., M.P.); adm. L.I. 1477, A.R. 1489, L.R. 1494, A.R. 1495 on *De Prerogativa Regis*, on promotion to coif; J.P., E.R. Yorks. from 1491; marr. 1490 Beatrice Hatcliffe, wid. Ralph, Lord Greystoke (d. 1487) – she took the veil in 1502; 2 sons (heir Marmaduke, a minor), 3 daus.; life interest in 7 messuages etc. in Felkirthorp and Reighton, E.R. Yorks. by gift of father; purchased manor of North Cliffe and other land in E.R. Yorks.; will and testament, 2 Sept. 1501 – exix wife and John Constable, clerk – probate 13 Jan. 1502; *i.p.m.* Yorks.

Cal. Patent Rolls, 1485–94, 315, 506; *ibid., 1494–1509*, 256; *Cal. Close Rolls, 1485–1500*, 556; *ibid., 1500–9*, 12; *Cal. inquisitions post mortem*, i. 363, ii. 567; *Admission Book*, i. 20; *Black Books*, i. 89, 99, 103; *Testamenta Eboracensia*, iii. 363; iv. 195–7, 236–9; *A Visitation of the North of England, circa*

1480–1500, ed. C.H. Hunter Blair, Surtees Soc. 144 (1930), 160 n. 7; Constable, *Prerogativa Regis*, xlvi–xlviii; Wedgwood, *Biographies*, 213.

CUTLERD, *William* alias *Robinson 1503*

of Boston, gent., 1499; related to John Robinson, baliff and customer of Boston and his son, John of Boston, merchant of the staple, possibly also to William Randson *alias* Cotler, of London and Wainfleet, Lincs. (d. 1472); associated with John Cutler, clerk, treasurer of Lincoln Cathedral; adm. L.I. 1482, A.R. 1493, L.R. 1498, A.R. 1503 on promotion to coif; J.P. Northants. 1486–90 and from 1500, Lincs. Holland from 1491, Leics. and Lincs. Lindsey from 1500, Kent and Rutland from 1501, Bucks from 1504; marr. twice: 1st wife Katharine dec. by 1498; 2nd Elyn dau. (born 1479) and co-heiress of John Iwardby, esq., of Gt. Missenden, Bucks., wid. William Knight (cf. Thomas Pigot); she survived him; son and heir, George, a minor, dau. Elizabeth; lands at Burgh le Marsh and elsewhere in Lincs.; testament 9 Oct. 1505 – to be buried at Sempringham, executors: prior of Sempringham, Robert Brudenell sjt, [blank] Thornborough of London, gent. (either John or his son Edward or Robert, all of L.I.) and wife – probate 10 Dec. 1505; *i.p.m.* Lincs.

Cal. Patent Rolls, 1476–85, 272–3, 329–30; *ibid., 1485–94*, 491, 495; *ibid., 1494–1509*, 309–10, 632, 646, 648, 655; *Cal. Close Rolls 1484–1500*, 575, 647, 1154; *ibid., 1500–9*, 413, 427, 444, 451, 539, 583, 586; *Cal. Fine Rolls, 1485–1509*, 619; *L. and P.*, i. 438 (3 m. 14), 1803 (1 m. 4); *Cal inquisitions post mortem*, ii. 208; iii. 275, 311; *Admission Book*, i. 17, 22, 26, 27; *Black Books*, i. 96, 112, 128, PROB11/6 f. 46, 14 f. 333; Wedgwood, *Biographies*, 392; V.C.H., *Buckinghamshire*, ii. 32.

DANVERS, *William 1486*

gent., 1464; of London, 1477; of Chamberhouse, Thatcham, Berks.; second son of John Danvers the elder of Banbury by his second wife Joan Bruley, grand-dau. and heiress of William Bruley of Waterstoke, Oxon., (M.P. for Oxon.); his elder bro. was Sir Thomas Danvers, apprentice-at-law, M.P., and his half-brother Sir Robert Danvers J.C.P. (d. 1467); J.P. Berks. 1458–70, Oxon. 1456–8, 1474–83 and from 1485, Oxford City spasmodically; M.P. Taunton, 1467–8, 1472–5, Hindon, 1478; kt; marr. Anne, dau. and heiress of John Pury of Chamberhouse, Thatcham – she died 1531; 4 sons (one died young), 4 daus.; on the death of Thomas, inherited his brother's estates but Waterhouse was retained by the widow for life; Chamberhouse in right of his wife; bought land in Warws., Bucks., Oxon., Berks., Hants.; endowed both his younger sons; servant of William Waynflete, bishop of Winchester, overseer of will of his brother Thomas; will and testament 18 Apr. 1504 – to be buried at Thatcham – probate 8 May 1504; writs of *diem clausit extremum* for Oxon., Berks., Bucks., Warws.; *i.p.m.* Bucks., Worcs.; *i.p.m.* of his son and heir, John: Bucks., Oxon., Worcs.

Cal. Patent Rolls, 1441–6, 344–5; *ibid., 1452–61*, 660, 675; *ibid., 1461–7*, 559; *ibid. 1467–77*, 626; *ibid., 1476–85*, 569; *ibid., 1485–94*, 497; *ibid., 1494–1509*, 371; *Cal. Close Rolls, 1461–8*, 255; *ibid., 1476–85*, 369; *Cal. Fine Rolls, 1485–1509*, 788; *L. and P.*, i. 438 (1 m. 15); PROB11/14, ff. 36–7, 11/24, ff. 27v; C142/24/18, 62(2), 63, 82, 95, 100; C1/53/254, 66/358; H.M.C., *Mss. of the Marquess of Lothian* (1905), 55; MacNamara, *Danvers Family*, *passim*.

ELIOT, *Richard 1503*

gent., 1480; of Chalk and Winterslow, Wilts.; of East Shefford, Berks., 1520; son of Simon Eliot, possibly mayor of Shaftesbury, Dors., grandson of Michael Eliot, probably of Coker, Soms.; A.R. at M.T. 1503 on call to coif; J.P. Wilts. from 1494, Oxon. from 1509, Berks. from 1514 (curiously also Essex 1501–8); M.P. Salisbury, 1495; kt; marr. twice: 1st (after 1485) Alice, dau. Sir Thomas Delamere, cousin and eventual heiress of Sir William Finderne of Carlton, Cambs., and widow of Thomas Daubridgecourt of Stratfieldsaye, Hants., esq.; 2nd (after 1503) Elizabeth, dau. and heiress of William Bessels of Besselsleigh, Berks., J.P., widow of Richard Fetiplace of East Shefford, Berks., esq., J.P.; son Thomas, later clerk of assize and humanist writer, inherited Finderne property; bought land in Oxon.; attorney-general to Elizabeth of York; J.C.P. 1513; will and testament 9 Oct. 1520 – to be buried Salisbury cathedral in tomb prepared – probate 26 May 1522; no *i.p.m.*; died Feb./May 1522.

Cal. Patent Rolls, 1476–85, 554; *ibid., 1494–1509*, 630, 639, 655, 665; *L. and P.*, i. 1836 (14) p. 1533; *Cal. inquisitions post mortem*, i. 95, 1140; ii. 918; Nicolas, *Privy Purse Expenses*, 100; PROB11/20 ff. 189–190v. Lehmberg, *Sir Thomas Elyot*, 8–9, 188 *sqq.*; Wedgwood, *Biographies*; Spelman, *Reports*, ii. *372*; *Minutes of Parliament*, i. 5.

FAIRFAX, *Guy 1463*

3rd son Richard Fairfax of Walton, W.R. Yorks.; J.P. W.R. Yorks. from 1456; kt; marr. Isabel, dau. Sir William Ryther of Ryther; son and heir William J.C.P. 1510, younger son Thomas, Sjt 1521; inherited manor of Steeton, W.R. Yorks.; granted life interest in West Walton by Henry Percy, earl of Northumberland (before 1455) and in Carlton, N.R. Yorks. by

Thomas Lord Roos (before 1461); retained by duchy of Lancaster from 1460, justice at Lancaster 1471, chief justice 1480; recorder of York, resigned 1477; executor of Henry Percy, earl of Northumberland (d. 1489) and John, Lord Scrope (d. 1498), settled estate of Anne, daughter-in-law of John Martin J.C.P.; no will, no *i.p.m.*

Cal. Patent Rolls, 1452–61, 683; *ibid., 1461–7*, 455, 521; *ibid., 1467–77*, 458, 530; *Cal. Close Rolls, 1500–9*, 12, 410, 771; *Cal. Ancient Deeds*, i. C311, 696, 725, 747, 762, 868; *Testamenta Eboracensia*, iii. 218n., 309; iv. 96; *Rot. Parl.*, iv. 164; *York Civic Records*, i. 12, 19; Somerville, *Duchy of Lancaster*, i. 452, 454, 469, 473; *Materials for the Reign of Henry VII*, ii. 554; *D.N.B.*, vi. 997; *Heraldic Visitations of the Northern Counties, 1530*, ed. W.H.D. Longstaffe, Surtees Soc. 41 (1863) 57–8; *Visitation of Yorkshire, 1563–4*, ed. C.B. Norcliffe, Harleian Soc. 16 (1881), 117–20.

FAIRFAX, *William 1503*

son and heir of Guy Fairfax J.K.B.; J.P., W.R. Yorks. 1496; marr. Elizabeth, dau. of Sir Robert Manners (his brother Thomas (Sjt 1521.) marr. Cecily, another daughter); ancestor of Thomas, Lord Fairfax (1612–71); 1 son; dau. Elizabeth married son and heir of Henry Ughtred, esq., of Kexby, E.R. Yorks., with portion of 400 marks; bought marriage of William, son and heir of Thomas Pickering, esq., of Oswaldkirk, N.R. Yorks., for dau. Ellen; inherited manor of Steeton, W.R. Yorks; recorder of York, 1490–6; second justice at Lancaster, 1509; no will, *i.p.m.*, Yorks.; died 11 May 1514.

Cal. Patent Rolls, 1494–1509, 668; *L. and P.*, i. 438 (3 m. 13), (4 m. 1), 2787; *Testamenta Eboracensia*, iii. 217n., vi. 188; *North Country Wills, 1383–1558*, ed. J. W. Clay, Surtees Soc. 116 (1908), 82; *York Civic Records*, ii. 55, 118, 128; *Yorkshire Deeds*, ii. ed. W. Brown, Surtees Soc. 50 (1914), 123; *ibid*. iii, Surtees Soc. 63 (1922), 81 Somerville, *Duchy of Lancaster*, i. 473; William Dugdale, *Visitation of Yorkshire*, ed. J. W. Clay (Exeter, 1899–1917), ii. 186; C142/29/1, 61; Spelman, *Reports*, ii. *371*.

FINEUX, *John 1486*

born at Canterbury; of Faversham and London, 1484; of Herne, kt, 1509; of the manor place of Hawe, 1525 (i.e. Hawe Farm, near Herne); according to heraldic visitations, son of William Fineux esq. of Swingfield, Kent (near Folkstone); an earlier ancestor could be the John Fineux of Sandwich, esq., pardoned 1450; J.P. Kent from 1475; M.P. Bodmin, 1478; marr. twice: 1st Mildred, dau. and heiress William Appuldrefeld of Teynham, Kent, gent. deputy chamberlain of the exchequer – one dau. marr. John Roper, chief clerk K.B. and A.G. (grandson William, later chief clerk K.B., marr. (1521) Margaret, dau. Thomas More); 2nd (probably 1507) Elizabeth, dau. John Paston kt, widow William, son of Robert Clere, kt – son William of L.I., dau. Anne marr. grandson of James Hobart, A.G., dau. Jane marr. grandson of Reynold Sonde, chief clerk K.B.; land in Kent in right of 1st wife, 2nd wife brought jointure of 100 marks p.a.; bought land in Kent and London; steward of Christ Church, Canterbury; royal grant £53 6s. 8d. p.a. during pleasure, 1484; will and testament, 11 Aug. 1525 – to be buried Canterbury Cathedral, executors include John Hales, B.Ex; *i.p.m.* Dors., Kent; died 17 Nov. 1525

Cal. Patent Rolls, 1446–52, 353; *ibid., 1467–77*, 302, 618; *ibid., 1476–85*, 513; *Cal. Ancient Deeds*, i. B178, 879, 880; ii. B2135; iv. A7773; *L. and P.*, i. 438 (4 m. 2); *Admission Book*, i. 20; PROB11/22 ff. 5–6; C142/45/2, 46/65; C1/93/7; E405/58 m. 4; Wedgwood, *Biographies*; *Christ Church Letters, passim*; *Visitation of Kent, 1619–21, passim*; *Visitations of Kent, 1530 etc., passim; Visitation of Norfolk*, ed. Dashwood, ii. 115, 267; Spelman, *Reports*, ii. *56–7, 358*.

FISHER, *John 1486*

of London, gent., 1480; of Clifton, Beds., kt, 1509; allegedly younger son of John Fisher of Hadlow, Kent, but cf. William Fisher of the Temple and Beds. (*fl.* 1470s); brother John; J.P. Beds. from 1476; wife Agnes; son and heir Michael, kt, married Margaret Frowyk, niece of Thomas, C.J.; bought Clifton and other land in Beds., also Clopton, Cambs.; other lands in Hunts.; encloser; as gent. litigating in 1475 over £200 lent on security of *The Trinity* of Calais; will and testament 17 Apr. 1510 – to be buried at Warden, Beds., where tomb is prepared, executors include Walter Luke (later J.K.B) – probate 14 Jun. 1510; memorial window in Clifton church; *i.p.m.* Beds. and Cambs.

Cal. Patent Rolls 1467–77, 489, 495, 607; *ibid., 1494–1509*, 556, 618; *Cal. Close Rolls, 1485–1500*, 498; *L. and P.*, i. 438 (1 m. 6), (2 m. 31); *Cal. inquisitions post mortem*, iii. 427; *Cal. Ancient Deeds*, iv. A8409; V.C.H., *Bedfordshire*, ii. 276–8, 280, 323; iii. 194, 257; PROB11/16 ff. 224v, 225; C142/25/57; C1/54/255; *Bedfordshire Notes and Queries*, i. 65; *Visitations of Essex, 1552 etc.*, ii. 568; C1/124/45.

FITZHERBERT, *Antony 1510*

gent., 1494; of Hamstall Ridware, Staffs. and, later, Norbury, Derbs.; younger son of Ralph Fitzherbert of Norbury, J.P. (d. 1483); cousin of John

Fitzherbert, king's remembrancer; brother-in-law Thomas Babington, recorder of Nottingham; 'at Court', i.e. Gray's Inn, in 1490; J.P. Leics. and Warws. 1509, Staffs. 1511 but Derbs. only 1530, probably reflecting earlier estrangement from his elder brother John, author of the *boke of husbandry*; kt; marr. twice: 1st Dorothy, dau. Sir Henry Willoughby; 2nd (by 1517) Maud, dau. and heiress of Thomas (Richard) Cotton, esq., of Hamstall Ridware; 4 sons, 1 dau.; inherited Norbury on death of brother John without heirs, heir to John after reconciliation; leased land in Derbs. and Staffs.; purchased lands in Staffs., Northants. and Warws.; recorder of Coventry K.S. 1516, justice of assize northern circuit, 1518; J.C.P. from 1522; C.J. Lancaster from 1531; author of legal texts, notably *La Graunde Abridgement* (1516); will and testament 12 Oct. 1537; probate 26 Aug. 1538; *i.p.m.* Derbs., Staffs.; died 27 May, 1538.

L. and P., i. 438 (4 m. 2), 1539, 1543, 1545; ii. 2592, 3949; iv. 6803(8); *Cal. inquisitions post mortem*, ii. 631, iii. 390; Somerville, *Duchy of Lancaster*, i. 470, 551; S. M. Wright, 'A gentry society of the fifteenth century: Derbyshire *c.* 1430–1509', unpublished Ph.D., University of Birmingham (1978), 390; L. J. Bowyer, *The Ancient Parish of Norbury* (1953), 92; PROB11/27 ff. 159v–160v; C142/60/30, 61/15; Staffs. R.O. D641/5/T(S) 14(2); Lichfield Joint R.O., B/A/1/141 ff. 106v – 111v; Spelman, *Reports*, ii. *373*; Ives, in *Profession, Vocation etc.*, 210 n.12.

FROWYK, *Thomas 1495*

of London, gent., 1485; of Finchley, 1501; son of Thomas Frowyk, gentleman *alias* mercer, later kt, by 2nd wife, Joan, dau. of Richard Sturgeon, gent.; grandson of Henry Frowyk, mercer, alderman and mayor of London; A.R. 1492 at I.T. on *Westminster II*, cc. 6–11, A.R. 1495 on promotion to the coif, on *Prerogativa Regis*; J.P. Middx from 1493; kt; marr. Elizabeth, dau. and heiress of William Carnevyle of Tockington, Glos.; she remarried Thomas Jakes of I.T., clerk of hell; dau. and heiress Frideswide born 1499, marr. Thomas Cheney, later K.G.; inherited land in Herts. and Middx; land in Wembley, Middx in right of his wife; purchased heavily in Middx; other lands Herts., Berks., London, Wilts.; common serjeant of London, 1486; will and testament 13 Aug. 1505, codicil 6 Oct. 1506 – to be buried at Friars Preachers, London, executors: wife, John Kingsmill, J.C.P., Thomas Jakes and Thomas Roberts, coroner of London – probate n.d.; *i.p.m.* London, Middx, Berks., Herts., Wilts. His niece married John Spelman J.K.B.

Cal. Patent Rolls, 1485–94, 493; *L. and P.*, i. 438 (1 m. 7); *Cal. inquisitions post mortem*, i. 51, 58, 159; iii. 195, 243, 279, 294, 309, 463; PROB11/15 ff. 116v–118; Putnam, *Early Treatises*, 121, 127, 129, 137 n. 6; Thrupp,

Merchant Class, 342–3; Thorne, *Readings and Moots*, i. xvi; Spelman, *Reports*, i. xiii; E315/276 f. 29v.

GRENEFIELD, *John 1463*

of Barnbow [Hall, in Barwick in Elmet], W.R. Yorks., sen., esq., 1457; son of John and grandson of William Grenefield, franklin, both of Barnbow; J.P., W.R. Yorks from 1460; marr. Margaret, dau. Sir William Ryther; she remarr. William Copley of Doncaster, prothonotary C.P.; younger son marr. Copley's dau.; son and heir John was duchy receiver at Pontefract; senior male line extinct 1541; inherited Barnbow which was later occupied by Copley in right of his wife; land in Altofts, W.R. Yorks; retained by duchy of Lancaster, 1461–3; will and testament 18 Oct. 1464 – to be buried in Barwick church, exix wife – probate 19 Mar. 1465; tomb in Barwick Church; no *i.p.m.*

Cal. Patent Rolls, 1452–61, 684; *ibid., 1467–77*, 316; *Cal. Close Rolls, 1454–61*, 274; *Testamenta Eboracensia* iv. 48; F.S. Colman, *History of the Parish of Barwick in Elmet*, Thoresby Soc. 17 (1908), 29, 43, 60, 187–96; *Wills, Registers and Monumental Inscriptions of the Parish of Barwick in Elmet*, ed. G. D. Lumb (1908), 3; Somerville, *Duchy of Lancaster*, i. 454, 516; Hastings, *Common Pleas*, 125, 263, 266; Spelman, *Reports*, ii. *375*; C1/43/161; *Y.B.* 9 Edw. IV, p. 6 f. 49; Borthwick Institute, Probate Register iii f. 301.

GREVILL, *William 1503*

of Arle and Over Lemington, Glos., 1509; son and heir of Richard Grevill of Lemington (commissioner 1486, possibly esq.); L.R. 1492 at I.T. on *Westminster II*, cc. 3–5; L.R. 1502 on *Gloucester*, c. 1; J.P. Glos. from 1486; marr. Margery; brass shows 3 sons, 7 daus., but heirs were only 3 daus.; land in Glos. and Worcs.; recorder of Bristol, 1498, 1505; will and testament 19 Oct. 1512 – houses at Arle, Cheltenham, Lemington, chief executor 'my broder Brudenell . . . the which I trust and am well assured woll take a vpon hym for the olde acqueyntaunce and love that hath longe endured betwene hym and me', codicil, 23 Mar. 1513, added wife as exix – probate 28 Apr. 1513; brass in Cheltenham Church; *i.p.m.* Glos.; died 9 Mar. 1513.

Cal. Patent Rolls, 1485–94, 103, 487; *ibid. 1494–1509*, 155; *Cal. Close Rolls, 1500–9*, 174, 637; *L. and P.*, i. 438 (4 m. 3); *Cal. inquisitions post mortem*, i. 13; *Trans. Bristol and Gloucestershire Arch. Soc.* 54 (1932), 157–8; B. H. Blacker, *Monumental Inscriptions in the Church of Cheltenham* (1900), 15; Putnam, *Early Treatises*, 181; Thorne, *Readings and Moots*, i. xvi, xxii;

Visitation of the County of Warwick, 1619, ed. J. Fetherston, Harleian Soc. 12 (1877), 143; PROB11/17 ff. 96–97v; C142/28/73.

HAUGH, *John 1486*

gent. of London, 1469; allegedly belonged to family of Walsham le Willows, Suff. and portrait exists in Long Melford Church, but few connections with Suffolk; active London; adm. L.I. 1460, A.R. 1469, L.R. 1474; J.P. only Suffolk 9 Mar. 1489; marr. Joan, dau. and co-heiress of Thomas, son and heir of Thomas Billing C.J.K.B.; son and heir, Stephen; she remarr. (as second wife) Thomas Lovet, esq. (J.P. Northants.); widow purchased lands in Kent; no will, no *i.p.m.*

Cal. Patent Rolls, 1485–94, 495, 501; *Cal. Close Rolls, 1468–76*, 370, 877; *ibid, 1476–85*, 1366; *ibid., 1485–1500*, 444, 446; *ibid., 1500–9*, 683; *Cal. inquisitions post mortem*, i. 7, 753, 1208; London, *Plea and Memoranda Rolls, 1458–82*, 65, 100 n.1, 166, 167, 173; *Admission Book*, i. 14; *Black Books*, i. 48, 56; *Miscellanea Genealogica et Heraldica*, 5 ser., 5 (1923–5), 208 *sqq.*; *Testamenta Vetusta*, ed. N. H. Nicolas (1826), i. 410; *Visitation of Northants., 1564*, 34.

HEIGHAM, *Richard 1495*

of St Thomas the Apostle, London, 1500; allegedly 4th son of Thomas Heigham of Higham, Suffolk; certainly brother of William Heigham D.D. and associated with Thomas Heigham the younger, esq., of Bury St Edmunds, Suff. (J.P.); adm. L.I. 1469, A.R. 1483, L.R. 1489; J.P. Essex 1483; marr. Emma, dau. and ultimately co-heiress of Humphrey Starky, C.B.Ex., and widow of Henry Torell, esq., of Shellow Torells, Essex, died 1492; marr. 2nd Elizabeth – certainly a widow since she has a son Hugh, probably the Elizabeth Hygham, widow, with a life interest in land in Corringham, Essex, by gift of Robert Tyrell, kt (d. 1508), possibly her step-son; son Richard, possibly filacer C.P. (assessed at £100 in the 1523 subsidy, clerk of assize, midland circuit, 1535–37, chirographer of C.P.); 2 daus.; purchased land in Ilford and Barking, Essex; other land in Upchurch, Kent, and Melton, Suff.; common serjeant of London; will and testament – prayers for Richard Starky, executors include Robert Sherborne, dean of St Paul's – probate 22 May, 1500 *recte* 1501; no. *i.p.m.*

Cal. Patent Rolls, 1452–61, 678; *ibid., 1461–7*, 573; *ibid., 1476–85*, 266, 560; *Cal. Close Rolls, 1476–85*, 1477, 1485; *ibid., 1485–1500*, 329; *Cal. Ancient Deeds*, i. C1105 (cf. C1297); ii. A3570, 3713, 3758; iii. A5365; *L. and P.*, i.

1662 (5); *Cal. inquisitions post mortem*, i. 859, 1165; iii. 531; *Admission Book*, i. 17; *Black Books*, i. 32, 77, 89; *Inner Temple Records*, i. 462; *Visitations of Essex, 1552 etc.*, i. 216; PROB11/12 ff. 181, 181v; Spelman, *Reports*, ii. *379*; Putnam, *Early Treatises*, 129.

HUSSEY, *William 1478*

see above, pp. 374–6; of Sleaford, Lincs., gent. 1454; of London, gent. 1462; son of John Hussey and Elizabeth Sheffield; J.P. Lincs. Kesteven from 1460; M.P. Bramber 1460, and Grantham 1478; kt; marr. Elizabeth, dau. Thomas Berkeley of Wymondham, Leics. (J.P.); 3 sons, 1 dau. married, unmarried dau. had portion of 600 marks; granted advowson of Oundle, 1473, wardship of Blount estates, 1476; surveyorship of Clarence's Lincs. lands, 1478; bought land in Rutland and Essex; estates in at least Lincs., Essex, Rutland; A.G. 1471–8; deputy steward of duchy (south), 1474; took pupils on apprenticeship; will and testament 15 Dec. 1494 – to be buried in the Charterhouse or, if dies 'at home', in Sempringham or Peterborough, executors include son John, surveyor, Reynold Bray – probate 4 Jul. 1496 but by comparison with *i.p.m.* the will seems defective; *i.p.m.* Essex, Rutland.

Cal. Patent Rolls, 1452–61, 669, 670; *ibid.*, *1467–77*, 292, 418; *ibid.*, *1476–85*, 37, 71; *ibid.*, *1494–1509*, 502; *Cal. Ancient Deeds*, vi. c6972; *Cal. inquisitions post mortem*, i 1166, 1209, ii. 207; G.E.C., *Peerage*, vii. 15; Somerville, *Duchy of Lancaster*, i. 431; PROB11/10 ff. 256A, 256AV, 11/14 f. 173v; Wedgwood, *Biographies*.

JAY, *Richard 1486*

gent. of London, 1476 (possibly 1455); of Birchin Lane, London 1488; son and heir of Thomas Jay and Joan his wife, possibly of South Clackford, Hants. (possibly Thomas Gay, customer of Southampton, but Richard active in London); J.P. Hants. from 1470; M.P. Portsmouth 1467, and Dowton 1472, 1478; marr. twice: 1st Joan, dau. John and Joan Wakefield (by 1454 if also wid. and exix John Beverley of London, skinner) – she died 1488; son William died s.p.; 2nd Margaret; s.p.; held the Bell in Birchin Lane and other London property in right of 1st wife and by curtesy; other lands in Middx and Hants.; not of Allington and Pymore, Dorset – he held these by the collusive enfeoffment of John Rogers, the father-in-law of his nephew (and eventual heir) John Jay; will 17 Dec., testament 7 Nov. 1493 – no executors named – date of probate not known; *i.p.m.* only for curtesy title, London, although writs issued for London and Hants.

Cal Patent Rolls, 1452–61, 133; *ibid.*, *1461–7*, 345; *ibid.*, *1467–77*, 629; *ibid.*,

1485–94, 469; *ibid., 1494–1509*, 302; *Cal. Close Rolls, 1454–61*, 104; *ibid., 1461–8*, 462; *ibid., 1476–85*, 27, 92, 169; *Cal. Fine Rolls, 1485–1509*, 475, 498, 501; *Cal. inquisitions post mortem*, i. 117, 339, 340; iii. 626, 627, 689, 1112; C1/31/329; Wedgwood, *Biographies*; PROB11/1 f. 142; 11/10 ff. 52v–4; C66/591 m. 7; Thorne, *Readings and Moots*, i. xli–xlii.

JENNEY, *William 1463*

late of Theberton, Suff. and London, gent., 1471; son and heir of John Jenney the elder, esq., of Knoddishall, Suff. (of L.I., attorney in the Guildhall, Lond., J.P. Norf., sheriff of Norf. and Suff.); adm. L.I. 1430; J.P. Norwich 1441–2, Suffolk 1445 and from 1450; M.P. Horsham 1449–50, Dunwich 1450–1, Suff. 1455–6; marr. twice according to genealogical pedigrees: 1st Elizabeth, dau. Thomas Caus; 2nd Eleanor, dau. of John Sampson of Harkstead, Suff., esq., wid. of Robert Ingleys (Inglose) of Gunton, Norf.; 2 sons, 2 daus.; inherited Knoddishall; purchased land in Norf.; counsel to John Fastolf, kt, servant to duke of Norfolk, executor of Duchess Katherine; figured frequently in affairs of Paston family – two autograph letters; no will, no *i.p.m.*

Cal. Patent Rolls, 1441–6, 475, 479; *ibid., 1446–52*, 301, 314, 595; *Cal. Close Rolls, 1447–54*, 228, 287; *ibid., 1454–61*, 432–3; *ibid., 1461–8*, 327; *Cal. Ancient Deeds*, v. A11669, 12973; *L. and P.*, i. 438 (4 m. 18); *Admission Book*, i. 6; Black Books, i. 6; *Paston Letters and Papers*, ii. 23, 154, 182, 225–6, 268, 510 and *passim*; Magdalen College, Fastolf Ms. 42; Stephenson, *Brasses*, 462; Wedgwood, *Biographies*, 498–501; *Visitation of Norfolk, 1563 etc.*, ed. W. Rye, Harleian Soc. 32 (1891), 169 *sqq.*; *Visitation of Norfolk*, ed. Dashwood, i, 132.

KEBELL, *Thomas 1486*

KINGSMILL, *John 1495*

of Freefolk, Hants., gent., 1508; son and heir apparent of Richard Kingsmill of Barkham, Berks. (gent., M.P.) and Alice, dau. Robert Inkpenne of Longparish, Hants.; possibly grandson of William Kingsmill of Barkham, scrivener of Oxford; Winchester and New College, Oxford, vacated fellowship 1479; J. P. Hants. from 1493; M.P. Heytesbury 1491; marr. Jane, allegedly daughter of Sir John Gifford of Ishill, Hants.; no mention of property but died in the lifetime of his father of whom John Newport Sjt was executor; steward of Winchester College; retained by Magdalen College, Oxford; C.J. Lancaster 1507; executor of Frowyk and Marowe; will and testament 12 Mar. 1508 –

bequest to Dean Colet; wife exix and residuary legatee – probate 20 May 1509; no *i.p.m.*; died 11 May 1509.

Cal. Patent Rolls, 1485–94, 500; Emden, *Biographical Register of Oxford to 1500*, ii. 1074–5; Wedgwood, *Biographies*; Somerville, *Duchy of Lancaster*, i. 469; PROB11/16 f. 128v, 11/17 f. 5v; Spelman, *Reports*, ii. *371*.

MAROWE, *Thomas 1503*

of Queenhithe, London, 1505; b. 1461–4, the younger son of William Marowe, grocer and mayor of London, and 2nd wife Katherine, dau. Richard Ryche, mercer, sister-in-law Thomas Urswick, C.B.Ex.; L.R. 1503 at I.T. on promotion to coif, on *Westminster I*, c. 1; J.P. Warws. from 1497, Middx from 1501; marr. Isabel, dau. and co-heiress of Nicholas Brome of Baddersley Clinton, Warws., one daughter; planned to marry as second wife, Anne dau. Sir Thomas Grene of Greens Norton, Northants., J.P. [see above pp. 237–8]; inherited £400 and London property including Marowe Wharf; lands in Kingswood etc., Warws. in right of wife; bought land in Essex; other land in Kent, Surrey, Oxon., Derbs.; common serjeant of London, 1491, under-sheriff, 1495; servant of William Warham, archbishop of Canterbury; will and testament, 31 Mar. 1505 – to be buried in St Botolph's without Bishopgate 'within the vault under the tombe where William Marowe my father lies buried', executors include Thomas Frowyk C.J.C.P. and John Kingsmill J.C.P.; *i.p.m.* Warws. and Oxon., writs also to Essex, Surrey, Middx, London.

Cal. Patent Rolls, *1494–1509*, 550, 650, 652, 663; *Cal. Fine Rolls*, *1485–1509*, 806; *Cal. inquisitions post mortem*, iii. 141, 247, 259, 807, 825; *Cal. Ancient Deeds*, i. A804; Putnam, *Early Treatises*, 115 *sqq.*; PROB11/14 ff. 221v–222v.

MORDAUNT, *John 1495*

of Turvey, Beds., kt 1504; son and heir of William Mordaunt of Turvey, esq. and Margaret, dau. John Peeke of Cople, Beds., gent., escheator; J.P. Beds. from 1483; M.P. 1485, speaker 1487, 1489, Grantham 1491 and Beds. 1495; marr. Edith, dau. and co-heiress of Nicholas Latimer, kt, of Duntish, Dors., M.P. (she remarr., supposedly, Sir 'Thomas' Carew, k. in battle 1512–13); 2 sons, 1 dau.; land in Dorset in right of wife, although problems over royal claims; inherited land in Beds. and Bucks. from both parents; bought land Beds., Bucks.; other land Cambs., Beds., Bucks., Northants., Essex, Surrey, Northumb.; Anne, countess of Warwick, a benefactor; servant of Richard Neville, earl of Warwick (d. 1471); attorney to Prince Arthur;

councillor to Margaret Beaufort, countess of Richmond; royal councillor associated with 'council learned'; chancellor of the duchy; C.J. at Chester; high steward of Cambridge Univ.; will and testament, 5 Sept. 1504 – to be buried at Turvey, executors include his brother, William Mordaunt (of Hempsted and M.T., prothonotary of C.P.), mentions interest in 'Grenes landes' and 'Veeres landes', i.e. his purchase of the wardship of three of co-heiresses of Edward, earl of Wilts., Henry Grene and their common ancestor, John Grene (two married his sons, one of whom remarried Humphrey Browne of M.T., brother-in-law of Mordaunt's sister) – probate 6 Dec. 1504; *i.p.m.* Bucks.; possibly fought for Lancastrians at Barnet; called to army in 1485 by Richard III; fought at Stoke; altar tomb at Turvey.

Cal. Patent Rolls, 1476–85, 527; *ibid., 1494–1509*, 419, 430; *Cal. Close Rolls, 1461–8*, 74, 111; *ibid., 1476–85*, 1379; *ibid., 1485–1500*, 471, 900, 1057–8, *ibid., 1500–9*, 380; *L. and P.*, i. 1803 (2 m. 1); *Cal. inquisitions post mortem*, iii. 757, 875; Somerville, *Duchy of Lancaster*, i. 392; V.C.H., *Bedfordshire*, iii. 97, 110, 111, 116, 183, 333; R. Somerville, 'Henry VII's "Council learned in the law" ', in *E.H.R.* 54 (1939), 428; CP40/905 mm. 114 d, 310; 915 m. 320; 928 mm. 297, 297d; Polydore Vergil, *Anglica Historia*, ed. D. Hay, Camden Soc., 4 ser., 74 (1950), 23; Spelman, *Reports*, ii. *375*; R. Halstead (pseud. Henry Mordaunt, 2nd earl of Peterborough), *Succinct Genealogies* (1685), 41, 67–71, 398, 493–4, 494, 501, 512–13; Wedgwood, *Biographies*; PROB11/14 ff. 172–3, 11/19 ff. 57–8.

MORE, *John 1503*

born *c.* 1451; gent., 1479; of St Lawrence, Old Jewry, London, and the manor of Gobions, North Mimms, Herts.; kt; son and heir of William More, citizen and baker of London, and Joanna Joye granddau. and heiress of John Leycester, gent. (of London, chancery clerk) dau. and heiress of John Joye, citizen and brewer of London; either steward of L.I., 1464, adm. L.I. 1470, or adm. 1475; A.R. 1490, L.R. 1495; J.P. Herts. from 1488; marr. four times: 1st (1474) Agnes, dau. Thomas Granger, alderman of London – 3 sons (the eldest Thomas More, L.C.), 3 daus. (youngest marr. John Rastell of M.T.); 2nd the wid. of John Marchall; 3rd Joan, wid. Thos. Bowes, citizen and mercer of London; 4th Alice More, sister of Christopher More of Loseley, Surrey, and wid. of John Clerk; inherited Gobions from his mother; land in London and Herts.; justice of assize from 1509; J.C.P., 1518–20; J.K.B., 1520–30; will 26 Feb. 1526 – to be buried in St Lawrence, Old Jewry, executors include son Thomas – probate 5 Dec. 1530; no *i.p.m.*; died probably 5 Nov. 1530.

Cal. Patent Rolls, 1485–94, 488; *L. and P.*, i. 132 (48); PROB11/23 f. 185;

C1/140/19; *Admission Book*, i. 19; *Black Books*, i. 39, 51, 90, 102; Spelman, *Reports*, ii. *358, 372*; M. Hastings, 'The ancestry of Sir Thomas More', in *Guildhall Miscellany* 2 (1961), 47–62; London, *Plea and Memoranda Rolls, 1458–82*, 176; Nicholas Harpsfield, *The life and death of Sir Thomas Moore*, ed. E. V. Hitchcock and R. W. Chambers, Early English Text Soc., o.s., 186 (1932), 299, 304–5.

NELE, *Richard 1463*

of Shepshed, Leics., 1444; probably son of Gervase Nele of Shepshed; J.P. Leics. from 1448; kt; marr. twice: 1st Isabel, dau. and co-heiress of William Ryddynges of Prestwold (d. 1476); 2nd Agnes, dau. and heiress of John Seyton of Martinsthorpe, Rutl., widow of William Fielding of Lutterworth (d. 1471); son and heir Christopher marr. dau. and heir of Joan Palmer, dau. and co-heiress of Thomas Palmer of Holt and wife of Thomas Rokes; son J.P. Leics. 1486 in succession to father – line died out 1559; inherited Prestwold from mother; granted royal annuity of £40, 1461; employed by Nottingham as senior counsel, 1463–4; steward of Burbage, Leics. for the earl of Kent; no will, no *i.p.m.*; tomb in Prestwold Church.

Cal. Patent Rolls, 1461–7, 96; *ibid., 1485–94*, 491; *Cal. Close Rolls, 1461–8*, 20; G. F. Farnham, 'Prestwold and its hamlets in medieval times', in *Trans. Leics. Arch. Soc.* 17 (1931), 5, 7, 43, 45, 96; G. F. Farnham, *Quorndon Records*, *Supplement* (1922), 25, 95; *Calendar of Charters Belonging to the Hospital of William Wyggeston at Leicester*, ed. A. H. Thompson (Leicester, 1933), 265; *Records of the Borough of Nottingham*, i. 374–7; *Grey of Ruthin Valor*, 64; F. A. Greenhill, *Incised Slabs of Leicestershire* (1958), 140.

NEWDIGATE, *John 1510*

of Harefield, Middx., esq., 1499, gent., 1504; son and heir of John Newdigate, esq., of Harefield and Crawley, Sussex, and Elizabeth, dau. Thomas Yonge, J.C.P.; adm. L.I. 1483, A.R. 1499, L.R. probably 1504, A.R. 1510, on call to the coif; J.P. Middx from 1498; betrothed as a minor, 1471, to Cecily, dau. Sir Robert Grene, granddau. Walter Grene, (see above, pp. 373, 384), and niece to Elizabeth, wife of John Catesby J.C.P., but marr. Amphillis, dau. of John Nevill, esq., of Sutton, Lincs; 10 sons, 7 daus. (John, son and heir, called to bar 1518; 3rd son Sebastian, Catholic martyr; two sons knights hospitaller; 4 grandsons M.P.); lands in London, Bucks., Middx; will and testament 23 June, probate 25 Aug. 1528; no. *i.p.m.*; died 16 Aug 1528.

Cal. Patent Rolls, 1494–1509, 650; *Cal. Close Rolls, 1468–76*, 881; *ibid., 1476–85*, 805; *ibid., 1485–1500*, 1133; *ibid., 1500–9*, 776(i); *Cal. inquisitions post mortem*, iii. 170; *Admission Book*, i. 22; *Black Books*, i. 116, 131, 160, 188; Stephenson, *Brasses*, 301; J. G. Nichols, 'Origin and early history of the family of Newdigate', in *Surrey Archaeological Coll.* 6 (1874), 236; PROB11/12 f. 289; *Visitation of Warwick, 1619*, ed. J. Fetherston, Harleian Soc. 12 (1877), 39; *Middlesex Pedigrees*, ed. G. J. Armytage, Harleian Soc. 65 (1914), 67.

NEWPORT, *John 1510*

gent., 1498; of Soberton, Hants., gent. *alias* esquire, 1509; probably younger son, but heir of Richard Newport, *alias* Spycer, of Soberton, esq., M.P. (d. 1477); adm. L.I. 1479, A.R. 1494, L.R. 1499; J.P. Hants. from 1486, Wilts. from 1510; justice of assize, Oxford circuit, from 1513; marr. Elizabeth; probably no surviving offspring; will and testament, 8 Aug. 1521 – witnessed by Arthur Plantagenet, kt – probate 24 Mar. 1522; no *i.p.m.*; replaced as justice of assize before death; died 1521–2.

Cal. Patent Rolls, 1485–94, 500; *Cal. Close Rolls, 1485–1500*, 1104; *L. and P.*, i. 438 (2 m. 27), 2787, p. 1546; iii. 1451(11); PROB11/20 f. 177; the *i.p.m.* for Essex and Herts., C142/42/96, 125 refer to a John Newport who died 26 May 1523 whose wife's name was Mary; *Admission Book*, i. 21; *Black Books*, i. 99, 116; Wedgwood, *Biographies*, 631.

OXENBRIDGE, *Thomas 1495*

of London, gent., 1478; of [the Ford] Brede, 1491; son and heir of Robert Oxenbridge, esq., and Anne, dau. Adam Lyvelode of Rye, M.P.; a younger son was mayor of Rye and Baron of the Cinque Ports; J.P. Sussex from 1479; married Anne, dau. and co-heiress of William Blount, son of Lord Mountjoy; s.p.; she remarr. David Owen, kt, carver to Henry VIII; inherited estates at Brede; bought land in Brede and Winchelsea, Sussex; other land in Lambeth and Southwark; feoffee of the Fiennes family, godfather to Francis, son of Lord Fiennes; will and testament 12 Nov. 1496 – executors include his brothers Godard (his heir) and Robert – probate 8 Feb. 1497; no *i.p.m.*

Cal. Patent Rolls, 1452–61, 489; *ibid., 1476–85*, 122, 378, 575; *ibid. 1485–94*, 294, 344; *L. and P.*, i. 1803 (2 m. 1); *Sussex Archaeological Collections*, 8. 213–33; 12. 203; 58. 53, 76, 90; V.C.H., *Sussex*, ix. 169; *Visitations of Sussex, 1530, 1633–4*, ed. W. B. Bannerman, Harleian Soc. 53 (1905), 122; PROB11/11 ff. 43v–44v; Wedgwood, *Biographies*.

PALMES, *Brian 1510*

of Naburn, Ripley and Hutton, Yorks., esq., 1509; son of William Palmes of Naburn and Ellen, dau. Guy Roucliffe, recorder of York; hence nephew of Brian Roucliffe of Cowthorpe, B.Ex., of whose will he was supervisor, receiving a legacy including a covered silver and gilt bowl which had been owned by Peter Arderne, C.B.Ex.; L.R. 1504 at M.T.; J.P. E.R. Yorks. from 1494; justice of assize northern circuit 1514, midland circuit 1516; marr. three times: 1st Anastasia, probably sister of Thomas Heslerton of West Heslerton, E.R.Yorks.; 2nd (1493) Ellen Acclom of Stillingfleet, at the [Acclom] manor house of Moreby, E.R.Yorks.; 3rd Anne, dau. and exix of Sir Thomas Markynfield of Markingfield, widow of Christopher Conyers, esq., of Sockburn (d. by 1497); 5 sons, 6 daus.; inherited lands in Naburn; bought heavily in Yorks.; 2nd justice at Lancaster, 1514; duchy under-steward at Pontefract and Knaresborough; retained by York 1489, recorder 1496, M.P. 1510; executor of his bro. Guy Palmes, Sjt; will and testament 31 Oct. 1519 – to be buried in St George's York – probate 11 Jan. 1520; *i.p.m.* Hants., Yorks.; died Dec. 1519.

Cal. Patent Rolls, *1485–94*, 506; *L. and P.*, i. 438 (1 m. 22), 3049 (35); ii. 1474; *Minutes of Parliament*, i. 7; Somerville, *Duchy of Lancaster*, i. 473, 514; *Testamenta Eboracensia*, ii. 30, 238; iii. 352, 358; iv. 106–7, 125; v. 103–9; *York Civic Records*, ii. 43 and 128–94 *passim*; iii. 2–70 *passim*; C142/35/7; E150/973/4.

PALMES, *Guy 1503*

younger brother of Brian Palmes, Sjt 1510 (q.v.); sponsored at M.T. under the will of his uncle Brian Roucliffe, B.Ex. (1495), A.R. 1502; summoned to take coif 1 Nov. 1503 on withdrawal of Edmund Dudley; J.P. Hants. from 1500; king's serjeant 9 May 1513; marr. Joan, dau. and probably heiress of John Drues of Bristol, merchant, widow of Nicholas More of Allington, Hants.; 6 sons, 2 daus.; held manor of Allington, Hants., in right of his wife, and plate jointly as legacy from her father; purchased lands in Hants., Berks.; other land in Lincs., Rutl., Wilts., Hants., Kingston on Hull; retained by duchy of Lancaster; nuncupative will taken at Serjeants' Inn, Fleet St, 13 Nov. 1516 – to be buried in the Whitefriars, London, two daughters shared £400, executors include brother Brian, Richard [Fox] bishop of Winchester 'my most singuler good lorde at my poure instance and desire is contented to take the payn vpon his good lordshipp to be surveyor of this my testament and last will' – probate 4 Dec. 1516; *i.p.m.* Hants., Lincs., Rutland, Wilts., Kingston on Hull; died 13 Nov. 1516.

Cal. Patent Rolls, 1494–1509, 658; *L. and P.*, i. 2787 (11); *Cal. inquisitions post mortem*, i. 1196; iii. 729; Somerville, *Duchy of Lancaster*, i. 452; *Minutes of Parliament*, i. 3, 7; Putnam, *Early Treatises*, 135 n. 1; *Testamenta Eboracensia*, iv. 105; v. 80–1; PROB11/18 ff. 194–195v; C142/31/7, 22, 32/24; E150/551/16, 682/6; cf. *i.p.m.* of brother Brian E150/973/4; C1/219/76.

PIGOT, *Richard 1463*

younger son of John Pigot of Ripon, possibly a lawyer; grandson of Sir Randolph Pigot of Clotherholme, W.R.Yorks.; J.P. N.R.Yorks. from 1460; justice of assize, East Anglian circuit, 1467; marr. Joan, dau. and heiress of William Romondbye of Romanby, N.R.Yorks.; she remarr. Richard Hastings, kt, Lord Wells and Willoughby; son, Richard Pigot, d.s.p.; inherited 40 marks and eventually parental lands on d. of elder brother; purchased land in Yorks., leased land in Northants.; under-steward of duchy manor of Knaresborough; retained by duchy 1476–82; 2nd justice at Lancaster, 1480; executor of Thomas Witham of Cornbrough, chancellor of the exchequer; will and testament 15 Apr. 1483 – to be buried at Clerkenwell or St Mary's Abbey, York – probate Lambeth 21 Jun., York 3 Aug. 1483; *i.p.m.* Essex, Herts., Yorks.

Cal. Patent Rolls, 1452–61, 683; *ibid., 1467–77*, 607–9, 617, 622, 631; *Cal. Close Rolls, 1468–76*, 857; *L. and P.*, i. 438, (1 m. 5); *Cal. inquisitions post mortem*, ii. 839; *Testamenta Eboracensia*, i. 331, 416; iii. 268, 285–6; Somerville, *Duchy of Lancaster*, i. 452, 473, 524; C140/1/38.

PIGOT, *Thomas 1510*

of Little Horwood, Bucks., gent., 1488; of Whaddon, gent., 1510; son and heir of Robert Pigot and Margaret, dau. and heiress of John Gifford, keeper of Whaddon Chase (J.P. Bucks. 1471–83); grandfather Richard Pigot (J.P. Bucks. 1468–83), probably brother of Randolph Pigot of Clotherholme, Yorks., and cousin to Richard Pigot, K.S.; L.R. at I.T., 1510; J.P. Bucks. from 1496; K.S. 1513; justice of assize midland circuit, 1517; marr. twice: 1st Agnes (possibly dau. and heiress of [ ] Forster of Writtle), 2 sons, 3 daus.; 2nd Elizabeth, dau. and co-heiress of John Iwardby, esq., of Gt Missenden, widow of William Elmes, gent., of Woolfox, Rutland, and I.T. (died 1503), 3 sons, 2 daus.; inherited and bought lands in Bucks. and Beds.; retained by the duchy 1509–20; will and testament, 25 Feb. 1520 – to be buried at Whaddon, supervisors include Brudenell – probate 15 May 1520; tomb and brass at Whaddon; *i.p.m.* Beds., Bucks.; died 25 Feb. 1520.

Cal. Patent Rolls, 1467–77, 608; *ibid. 1476–85*, 554; *ibid., 1494–1509*, 631;

Cal. Close Rolls, 1485–1500, 273; *L. and P.*, i. 54 (47), 438 (1 m. 5), 1948 (44); ii. 2919; *Cal. inquisitions post mortem*, i. 6, 8, 1080, 1125; iii. 1008; *Inner Temple Records*, i. 17; PROB11/19 ff. 207–8; C142/35/1, 107; Somerville, *Duchy of Lancaster*, i. 452; V.C.H., *Buckinghamshire*, ii. 138–9; iv. 439; G. Lipscomb, *History of the County of Buckingham* (1831–47), i. 255, 405; iii. 501; iv. 340; *Testamenta Eboracensia*, iii. 156; Stephenson, *Brasses*, 53; *Visitation of Buckinghamshire, 1634*, 100.

POLLARD, *Lewis 1503*

son of Robert Pollard (according to Moore 'of Roborough near Torrington, Devon') by Jane, dau. and co-heiress of Elizabeth Squyer and hence nephew of Walter Pollard, esq., sworn with the county elite to keep the peace, 1434; nephew (probably godson) of Lewis Pollard, clerk, rector of Bidford etc.; L.R. at M.T., 1503; J.P. Devon from 1492; M.P. Totnes 1491; kt; marr. Agnes, supposedly dau. Thomas Hext of Kingston by Totnes, Devon; 6 sons, 1 dau.; inherited estates in Devon; purchased land in Devon; other estates Somerset; recorder of Barnstaple and Exeter; J.C.P. 1514; testament 4 Nov. 1525, probate 2 Nov. 1526; part of his will is repeated in the *i.p.m.*; *i.p.m.* Devon and Soms.; died 21 Oct. 1526; the alleged inscription on the former memorial window at King's Nympton, Devon, referred to the erector as his wife Elizabeth, but the transcription must be in error.

Cal. Patent Rolls, 1485–94, 485; *Cal. Close Rolls, 1500–9*, 841, 940; *L. and P.*, i. 2964 (78); *Minutes of Parliament*, i. 4; *Barnstaple Records*, ed. J.R. Chanter and T. Wainwright (Barnstaple, 1900), ii. lxxxiii; PROB11/10 f. 122, 11/28 f. 88; C142/46/17; E150/915/14; Thomas Moore, *History of Devon* (1829), ii. 120; J.J. Alexander, 'Leading civic officials of Exeter', in *Report and Trans. Devonshire Association* 70 (1938), 421, and 'Devon magnates in 1434', in *Report and Trans. Devonshire Association* 72 (1940), 285; Wedgwood, *Biographies*; Emden, *Biographical Register of Oxford*, iii. 1492; A.F. Pollard, 'Sir Lewis Pollard', in *D.N.B.*

REDE, *Robert 1486*

gent., 1481; of London, 1483; of the king's court, 1484; of Chiddingstone, Kent, and London, kt, 1509; of Bloors Place, Kent, 1518; son of William Rede, burgess of Calais, *alias* of Wrangle, Lincs., gent., and his wife Joan; cousin of Richard Rede, merchant of the staple; adm. L.I. 1467, A.R. 1481, L.R. 1486; J.P. Kent from 1483; married by 1476, Margaret, dau. and co-heiress of John Alfegh of Chiddingstone, esq. (J.P.); 5 daus.; land in Hoo, Kent, settled on Rede and Margaret by Alfegh, also the wardship of the manor of Well etc., Kent; Chiddingstone in right of his wife on Alfegh's death, 1489 (Rede his executor); purchased land in Orpington and elsewhere in Kent, took over Bryan's house in St Sepulchre without Newgate; lands also in Surrey, Sussex, Canterbury; founded two chantries; endowed lectureship at Cambridge and was a brother of King's College but probably not a student of the university; numerous letters of confraternity; testament 29, will and partition of lands 31 Dec. 1518 – to be buried in the Charterhouse; executors include Brudenell J.K.B., his son-in-law Thomas Willoughby (later J.C.P.) but not another son-in-law, Serjeant John Caryll; supervisor Archbishop Warham – probate 24 Jan. 1519; *i.p.m.* Kent, Canterbury; died 7/8 Jan., 1519.

Cal. Patent Rolls, 1467–77, 618; *ibid., 1476–85*, 563; *ibid., 1494–1509*, 448; *Cal. Close Rolls, 1461–8*, 314; *ibid., 1476–85*, 794, 1122, 1187, 1323; *Cal. Ancient Deeds*, i. C42, 270, 353, 403, 511, 604, 1156–7, 1160–1, 1197, 1334; ii. B2170–2, C2799, 2847; vi. 3941, 5157; *L. and P.*, i. 438 (2 mm. 6, 15, 19), 3408 (29); *Cal. inquisitions post mortem*, i. 530, ii. 170; *Admission Book*, i. 16; *Black Books*, i. 71, 83; PROB11/19 ff. 97–100; C142/34/4, 70; A.B. Emden, *Biographical Register of the University of Cambridge to 1500* (Cambridge, 1963), 475, but cf. Spelman, *Reports*, ii. *125–6*; H.M.C., *Manuscripts of Lord Middleton* (1911), 466–73.

ROGERS, *Thomas 1478*

of London, gent., 1470; of Bradford-upon-Avon, 1478; supposedly son of Thomas Rogers, mayor of Bristol but at best his younger grandson, son of William Rogers of Bristol, died 1471 (but William's sons were at that date still minors); J.P. Wilts. from 1461, possibly M.P. Marlborough 1472–5; marr. twice: 1st (allegedly) Cecily, dau. and heiress of William Bessills of Bradford (hence possession of Bradford); 2nd Katharine, identified in heraldic visitations as dau. of William Courtenay of Powderham, kt, widow of Thomas Pomeroy kt; she remarr. before 12 Oct. 1479 William Huddersfield of Shillingford, Devon, A.G. 1478–83; son and heir William; son George, by Katharine, later of Shillingford, esq.; bought manor and lands in Collingbourne, Wilts.; no will; *i.p.m.* Wilts., Soms.

Cal. Patent Rolls, 1461–7, 575; *ibid. 1467–77*, 177; *ibid., 1476–85*, 169; *Cal. Close Rolls, 1468–76*, 562; *L. and P.*, i. 438 (3 m. 18); PROB11/11 f. 299 (Huddersfield); *Visitation of the County of Somerset, 1623*, ed. F.T. Colby, Harleian Soc. 11 (1876), 128; Wedgwood, *Biographies*; *Bristol Wills*, 140, 148; C140/62/7.

ROWE, *John 1510*

of Totnes, supposedly son of William Rowe; J.P. Devon from 1504; commissioner of oyer and terminer, western counties, 1540–4; marr. Agnes, supposedly dau. and heiress of William Barnhouse of Kingston, Devon; 1 son, 5 daus.; land in Devon in right of wife; other estates in Devon; recorder of Totnes; steward of the Devon bullion mines, 1520; involved (with Thomas Cromwell) in 50-year lease of the mines, 1533 (a John Rowe of Berydon, possibly related, was jurate of stannary court of Chagford, 1532); permanent member of the council of the west from 1539; offended Wolsey with a play at Gray's Inn, 1527, later associated with Cromwell; no will; *i.p.m.* Devon; died 8 Oct. 1544.

Cal. Patent Rolls, 1494–1509, 636; *L. and P.*, iii 644(17); iv. 1768, 2854; vi. 1176, 1457; xiv(1). 686, 743; xv. 942(75); xviii. 623; C142/70/43; Spelman, *Reports*, ii. *395*; *Visitation of the County of Devon, 1620*, ed. F.T. Colby, Harleian Soc. 6 (1872), 247; Stephenson, *Brasses*, 95; Thomas Moore, *History of Devon* (1829), ii. 348; W.B. Faraday, 'The recorders of Totnes', in *Report and Trans. Devonshire Association* 56 (1924), 221; E.L. Radford, 'The tinners of Devon and their laws', *Report and Trans. Devonshire Association* 62 (1930), 240.

STARKY, *Humphrey 1478*

of (Wood St) London, gent., 1457; son of Richard Starky and his wife Margaret; associated with the Starky family of Inworth, Essex and with the Starky family of Northwich, Ches.; J.P. Kent, 1471–5, Middx from 1481; kt; marr. Isabel, allegedly dau. and co-heiress of Alexander Walden of Kent (but Alexander Walden, kt, was of Matching, Essex and fl. *c.* 1396 and Isabel's jointure was in Essex) – she died 1496; 1 son (died 1493) 4 daus., one married Richard Heigham, serjeant 1495; bought land in Northwich, possibly Middx; salthouses in Ches. and Shrops.; lands in Kent, London and Middx – Essex lands settled on wife; recorder of London, 1471–83; will 20 Jul., testament 28 Jul. 1486 – to be buried St Leonard's, Shoreditch, Thomas Marowe to oversee upbringing of his heir, Richard Starky; executors include Richard Heigham – probate 2 Sept. 1486; as executor of Katherine, widow of William Marowe, had custody of 725 marks bequeathed by them to their son Thomas Marowe; *i.p.m.* Middx and Essex (*i.p.m.* of wife – Middx and Essex., of son and heir, Richard – Kent); monument formerly in St Leonard's.

Cal. Patent Rolls, 1467–77, 618; *ibid., 1476–85*, 566; *Cal. Close Rolls, 1461–8*, 397–8; *ibid., 1468–76*, 144, 766; *ibid., 1476–85*, 667; *ibid., 1500–9*, 445; *Cal. Fine Rolls*, *1452–61*, 206; *Cal. Ancient Deeds*, vi. C6021; *Cal. inquisitions post mortem*, i. 195, 279, 1165; iii. 956, 958; London, *Plea and Memoranda Rolls, 1458–82*, 85–6, 146; PROB11/7 ff. 195–6, 203v–204v; H.M.C., *Various Collections* (1901–14), ii. 1; *D.N.B.* 18. 995; Ormerod, *History of Chester*, ii. 104, 161; John Stow, *Survey of London*, ed. John Strype (1720), ii. 50–2; London County Council, *Survey of London 8: the Parish of St Leonard's Shoreditch*, ed. J. Bird (1922), 72, 97.

SULYARD, *John 1478*

gent., 1465, of London, 1469; of Wetherden, gent., late of Eye, Suff., 1472; son of John Sulyard and Alice, allegedly dau. of John Barrington, kt; adm. L.I. 1451, L.R. 1466, 1470, 1478; J.P. Suffolk from 1461, Essex from 1473; M.P. Dunwich, 1459, Hindon, 1472–5; kt; marr. twice: 1st Agnes, dau. and heiress of Richard Hungate, of Herts., J.P.; 2nd Anne, dau. and co-heiress of John Andrews of Baylham, Suff. gent. – she remarr. Thomas Bourchier, kt, sen., of Leeds Castle, Kent (she is called Elizabeth by her cousin Alice Wyche, widow of Hugh Wyche, kt, alderman of London); 3 sons, 4 daus.; lands in Suffolk, Norfolk and Essex; appointed to the council of the prince of Wales, 1473; will and testament 8 Oct. 1487 – to be buried at Wetherden – probate 11 June 1488; *i.p.m.* Essex and Suffolk; tomb at Wetherden.

Cal. Patent Rolls, 1452–61, 289; *ibid., 1461–7*, 366, 573; *ibid., 1467–77*, 614; *Cal. Close Rolls, 1454–61*, 349; *ibid., 1461–8*, 302; *ibid., 1468–76*, 505; *Cal. Ancient Deeds*, vi. C4768; *Cal. inquisitions post mortem*, i. 415, 439; *Admission Book*, i. 11; *Black Books*, i. 40, 50, 63; PROB11/8 ff. 168v – 170v; *Testamenta Vetusta*, ed. N.H. Nicolas (1826), i. 331; London, *Plea and Memoranda Rolls*, vi. 103; Weever, *Funeral Monuments*, 510; *Visitation of Suffolk, 1561 etc.*, 69; Wedgwood, *Biographies*; C1/115/94.

TOWNSHEND, *Roger 1478*

gent., 1469; son of John Townshend of Rainham, Norf.; adm. L.I., 1454, L.R. 1468, 1475; J.P. Norf. from 1466; kt; marr. Eleanor, possibly dau. and heiress of John Barrington, perhaps of Hatfield, Essex – she died 1499; 2 sons, 3 daus. – his heir Roger marr. Anne, dau. and heiress of William Brewes of Stinton, Norf., esq. (frequently described in error as his own first wife); inherited Rainham; held land in Norf. in right of Anne Brewes; secured manor of East Beckham, Norf., from Sir John Paston by mortgage; purchased land in Norf. and Beds.; land in Norf. and Suff.; retained by the duchy, 1481–4; made substantial loans to the Paston family; allegedly involved in evasion of feudal dues; will and testament 14 Aug. 1492 – to be buried at Rainham or the Whitefriars, London, wife sole exix and principal legatee (she was also bequeathed a life interest in almost all his lands) – probate not recorded; *i.p.m.* Beds., Norf., Suff.

Cal. Patent Rolls, 1452–61, 146; *ibid., 1461–7*, 338, 568; *ibid., 1485–94*, 303; *Cal. Close Rolls, 1468–76*, 1485; *ibid., 1476–85*, 154, 297; *ibid., 1485–1500*, 303; *L. and P.*, i. 438 (4 m.5); *Cal. inquisitions post mortem*, i. 479, 648, 1025, 1028, 1136, 1143; ii. 493; iii. 758; *Admission Book*, i. 12; *Black Books*, i. 45, 57; PROB11/10 ff. 11–12; Somerville, *Duchy of Lancaster*, i. 452; *Paston Letters and Papers*, i. 377, 410–11, 413, 440, 451, 455, 476–8, 484, 502, 515, 582, 584, 642; ii. 612–13; *Visitation of Norfolk*, ed. Dashwood, i. 306; F. Blomefield and C. Parkin, *Topographical History of the County of Norfolk* (1805–10), v. 406; vi. 242.

TREMAYLE, *Thomas 1478*

of London, gent., 1464; houses in St Bride's, Fleet St, Sand, Blackmoor and (principally) Cannington, Soms.; probably son of John Tremayle the elder, gent., of Sidbury, Devon; J.P. Soms. 1470–4 and from 1479; M.P. Bridport 1467–8, Bridgwater 1472–5, Lyme 1478; kt; marr. Margaret, supposedly of the Rivers family of Dunster, Soms.; 2 sons, 4 daus.; purchased land in Soms., sold land in Devon; lands in Dunster, etc., Soms. and Sidbury, Devon; A.G. of the duchy, 1472–8, retained 1479–83; recorder of Bristol; prominent in Bridgwater; associated with (possibly residuary executor of) William Dodesham (gent. of Cannington and mercer of Bridgwater, M.P.); co-founder of gild of St Mary in St Bride's church, Fleet St; testament 14 Aug. 1508 – to be buried St Bride's, Fleet St, beside his wife Margaret – probate 19 Sept. 1508; *i.p.m.* Soms. and Devon.

Cal. Patent Rolls, 1452–61, 189; *ibid., 1467–77*, 81, 628; *ibid., 1476–85*, 553, 571; *ibid., 1494–1509*, 130; *Cal. Close Rolls, 1461–8*, 230; *ibid., 1485–1500*, 45; *Cal inquisitions post mortem*, iii. 527, 541; PROB11/16 f. 32; Somerville, *Duchy of Lancaster*, i. 409; Wedgwood, *Biographies*, 276, 867–8; *Bridgwater Borough Archives*, v. 1008, 1038; *Feet of Fines for the county of Somerset* 4, Somerset Rec. Soc. 22 (1906), 136, 150; F.W. Weaver, *Visitation of Somerset, 1531* (Exeter, 1855), 82

VAVASOUR, *John 1478*

of Spaldington, E.R.Yorks., 1494; 'junior' 1468; son of John Vavasour senior, esq. (J.P., E.R.Yorks., M.P. Lincoln borough, probably clerk of estreats in C.P.), and Isabel, dau. and heiress of Thomas de la Hay of Spaldington; J.P., E.R.Yorks. from 1477; M.P. Bridport 1472; kt; marr. Elizabeth, dau. Robert Talboys (of Kyme, Lincs., kt, M.P. Lincs.) and widow of unnamed member of Greystoke family; s.p. and the couple separated *c.* 1494–*c.* 1502; inherited Spaldington from mother; bought land in Yorks.; other land in Middx, Lincs., Derbs.; 2nd justice at Lancaster, 1485; C.J. Lancaster 1495; retained by York, recorder 1486; will and testament 11 Jan. 1494 – to be buried in Austin Friars, London, or Ellerton, Yorks. – probate, Lambeth 21 Dec. 1506, York 3 Mar. 1507; *i.p.m.* Yorks., Lincs., Derbs.

Cal. Patent Rolls, 1452–61, 682; *ibid., 1467–77*, 636–7; *Cal. Close Rolls, 1468–76*, 790, 1250; *Cal. Ancient Deeds*, v. C7073; *Cal. inquisitions post mortem*, iii. 275, 276, 849; *Testamenta Eboracensia*, i. 155, iv. 89–92, 167; v. 3–4; Wedgwood, *Biographies*; Spelman, *Reports*, ii. *379*; Somerville, *Duchy of Lancaster*, i. 469, 473; *York Civic Records*, i. 29, 106, 153–78 *passim*; ii. 1–55 *passim*.

WODE, *Thomas 1486*

of London, gent., 1473; perhaps son of Thomas Wode the elder (on Berks. commission 1473); possibly related to Walter Wode, citizen and fishmonger of London; J.P. Berks. from 1478; M.P. Wallingford, 1478; kt; marr. Margaret, widow of Robert Lenham of Tidmarsh, esq. (died 1491) – she died 1498; possibly an earlier wife Isabel; probably one dau. who predeceased her father having marr. his ward, Thomas, son and heir of Nicholas Stukeley, esq., of Afton, Devon; an estate at Childrey, Berks., by 1478; will and testament 28 Aug. 1502 – to be buried Reading Abbey, Frowyk to advise executors, executors include 'my broder Richard Eliot the quenys attourney' and 'my son Thomas Stwley', supervisor the abbot of Reading – probate 6 Nov. 1502; buried as requested, wife Margaret buried at Tidmarsh; no *i.p.m.* but writs of *diem clausit extremum* for Berks. and Devon.

Cal. Patent Rolls, 1467–77, 406; *ibid., 1476–85*, 124, 554; *Cal. Close Rolls, 1468–76*, 1151; *Cal. Fine Rolls, 1485–1509*, 749–50, 819; *L. and P.*, i. 438 (2 m. 31); *Cal. inquisitions post mortem*, i. 712; ii. 374; PROB11/13 ff. 161v, 162; V.C.H., *Berkshire*, iii. 436; iv. 272 *sqq.*; G. Lipscomb, *History of the County of Buckingham* (1831–47) i. 300; *The Four Visitations of Berkshire*, ed. W.H. Rylands, Harleian Soc. 56–7 (1907–8), i. 1; Wedgwood, *Biographies*.

YAXLEY *John* alias *Herberd 1495*

'legisperitus', 1495; gent. *alias* esq.; of Pounteney Hall, Mellis, Suff.; son and heir of Richard Yaxley (*alias* Herberd) the elder, of Yaxley, Suff. (J.P. 1466–70); J.P. Suff. from 1485, Norf. from 1496; M.P. Ipswich, 1491; marr. Elizabeth, possibly dau. Richard (John) Brome of Suff., esq.; 4 sons, 3 daus. – disinherited his 'unkind' eldest son; inherited entailed lands in Mellis;

purchased land in Suff. and Norf.; burgess of Ipswich; will (actually will and testament) 12 May 1505 – to be buried at Mellis – probate 8 Nov. 1505; *i.p.m.* Suff. and Norf.

Cal. Patent Rolls, 1461–7, 52, 573; *ibid., 1467–77*, 631; *ibid., 1485–94*, 501; *ibid., 1494–1509*, 651; *Cal. Ancient Deeds*, iii. D625; v. A13156; vi. C4956; *L. and P.*, i. 438 (1 m. 10); *Cal. inquisitions post mortem*, i. 384; ii. 496; iii. 3; PROB11/14 ff. 309–10; C1/235/11–13; *Visitation of Suffolk, 1561 etc.*, 82; Wedgwood, *Biographies*.

YONGE, *Thomas 1463*

of London, gent., 1442; recorder of Bristol, 1442; of Shirehampton, nr Bristol, gent., 1452; son and heir of Thomas Yonge, merchant and mayor of Bristol (died 1427), and Joan, widow of John Canynges (merchant and mayor of Bristol) and so half-brother to William Canynges (mayor of Bristol, M.P.); his brother was John Yonge, grocer, alderman and mayor of London (died 1481); J.P. Glos., 1451–73 and from 1475; M.P. Bristol, 1435–56, Glos. 1460–1; marr. Isabel, dau. and heiress of John Burton, mayor of Bristol (for whom he was executor); 2 sons, 3 daus. including Elizabeth, mother of John Newdigate, serjeant 1510; inherited most of his father's property in Bristol; bought Shirehampton; lands in Soms., Bristol and Wilts.; active in litigation from 1436; deputy chief steward of the duchy (south), 1442; retained by the duchy 1442–66; attorney to the duke of York; imprisoned for support of York in the 1451 parliament; in the Tower again 1460 accused of treason, bailed March, case dropped November (following Yorkist revival); curious legal career; exempted from taking the coif, 1442; K.S. immediately on call to the coif, 1463; justice of assize 1466, J.C.P. 1467, but dropped on return of Edward IV to power, April 1471, nevertheless in royal favour April 1473, J.K.B. from 1475 but apparently not justice of assize – probably explicable by assuming birth *c.* 1405 and recall from retirement in 1475 to provide experience in K.B. during Edward's foreign journey, possibly following the illness of Laken; will no longer extant; *i.p.m.* Soms., Wilts.; buried Greyfriars, London.

Cal. Patent Rolls, 1436–41, 7; *ibid., 1441–6*, 127; *ibid., 1446–52*, 245, 589; *ibid., 1467–77*, 614; *Cal. Close Rolls, 1441–7*, 47, 50; *ibid., 1454–61*, 105, 420–1; *ibid., 1461–8*, 367; *ibid., 1476–85*, 332; *Cal. inquisitions post mortem*, iii. 168–71; Somerville, *Duchy of Lancaster*, i. 430–1; Wedgwood, *Biographies*, 980–2; C140/61/26; *Bristol Wills*, 115–16, 134–6; Thrupp, *Merchant Class*, 376–7; J. Maclean, 'Notes on the family of Yonge of Bristol', in *Trans. Bristol and Gloucestershire Arch. Soc.* 15 (1890–1), 227 *sqq.*; John Stowe, *Survey of London*, ed. C.L. Kingsford (Oxford, 1908), i. 321.

APPENDIX E

SENIOR MEMBERS OF THE LEGAL PROFESSION, 1461–1510

The following tables show the changes in the personnel of the upper ranks of the common-law profession for the period 1461 to 1510, year by year. All judges, barons of the exchequer, king's serjeants, serjeants and law officers are listed in order of seniority, with dates of appointment, death etc.; the seniority of serjeants is normally that of the close roll.

Names printed in roman type are of men in post on 1 Jan. of each year; additions in the year are given in italic type. Reappointments on the change of monarch are placed in square brackets.

The principal source for appointments is the patent roll. This has been augmented by the record of payments from the exchequer which were charged, by statute, on a variety of accountants – the clerk of the hanaper, the customers of London (generally, though not always, the customers of the petty custom), the customers of Bristol and Hull and the merchant staplers of Calais. Material is principally located in PRO classes E159 (K.R. Memoranda Rolls), E356 (Customs Accounts), E364 (Foreign Accounts: Pipe Office) and E405 (Tellers' Rolls), but not in E101 (Accounts Various: Hanaper). I am indebted to Miss Margaret Condon for help in tracing this material. For some of the later information I have followed the work of Dr J.H. Baker, whose tables list the senior members of the profession from (usually) 1485 to at least 1547, and also include schedules of court officers for the fifteenth and sixteenth centuries: Spelman, *Reports*, ii. *351–96*.

		1 Jan. 1461		1 Jan. 1462	
C.J.K.B.		Fortescue[1]		Markham	
		Markham J.K.B. 13.5.61[2]			
C.J.C.P.		Prisot[3]		Danby	
		Danby J.C.P. 11.5.61.[4]			
C.B.Ex.		Arderne	[8.4.61][5]	Arderne	
				Illingworth 10.8.62[26]	
J.K.B.		Yelverton	[8.4.61][6]	Yelverton	
		Markham	C.J.K.B. 13.5.61	Bingham	
		Bingham	[8.4.61][7]		
J.C.P.		Ashton	[8.4.61][8]	Ashton	
		Arderne	[8.4.61][9]	Arderne	
		Danby	[8.4.61][10]	Danvers	
			C.J.C.P. 11.4.61	Moyle	
		Danvers	[8.4.61][11]	Nedeham	
		Moyle	[8.4.61][12]	Choke	
		Nedeham	[8.4.61][13]		
		Choke K.S. 5.9.61[14]			
B.Ex.	II	Clerk	[8.4.61][15]	Clerk	
	III	Roucliffe	[8.4.61][16]	Roucliffe	
	IV	Holme	[8.4.61][17]	Holme	replaced[27]
				Ingoldesby 4.11.62[27]	
	V	Durem	[8.4.61][18]	Durem	
K.S.		Choke	[8.4.61][19]	Littleton	
			J.C.P. 5.9.61	Billing	
		Littleton	[8.4.61][20]		
		Billing	[8.4.61][21]		
Sjt.		Laken[22]		Laken	
A.G.		Nottingham	[8.4.61][23]	Sotehill	
			replaced[24]		
		Sotehill 20.4.61[24]			
S.G.		*Fowler 13.3.61*[25]		Fowler	

1. Jan. 1463		1. Jan. 1464	
Markham		Markham	
Danby		Danby	
Illingworth		Illingworth	
Yelverton		Yelverton	
Bingham		Bingham	
		Billing K.S. 9.8.64[30]	
Ashton		Ashton	
Arderne		Arderne	
Danvers		Danvers	
Moyle		Moyle	
Nedeham		Nedeham	
Choke		Choke	
Clerk		Clerk	
Roucliffe		Roucliffe	
Ingoldesby		Ingoldesby	
Durem		Durem	
Littleton		Littleton	
Billing		Billing	J.K.B. 9.8.64
Yonge 8.11.63[28]		Yonge	
		Nele 12.8.64[31]	
		Laken by 23.11.64[32]	
Laken		Laken	K.S. by 23.11.64
Yonge 7.11.63[29]		Nele	K.S. 12.8.64
	K.S. 8.11.63	Jenney	
Nele 7.11.63[29]		Fairfax	
Jenney 7.11.63[29]		Bryan	
Fairfax 7.11.63[29]		Grenefield	d. 23.10.64[33]
Bryan 7.11.63[29]		Catesby	
Grenefield 7.11.63[29]		Pigot	
Catesby 7.11.63[29]			
Pigot 7.11.63[29]			
Sotehill		Sotehill	
Fowler		Fowler	

	1 Jan. 1465		1 Jan. 1466	
C.J.K.B.	Markham		Markham	
C.J.C.P.	Danby		Danby	
C.B.Ex	Illingworth		Illingworth	
J.K.B.	Yelverton		Yelverton	
	Bingham		Bingham	
	Billing		Billing	
	Laken K.S. 4.6.65[34]		Laken	
J.C.P.	Ashton		Ashton	d. 12.3.66[35]
	Arderne		Arderne	
	Danvers		Danvers	
	Moyle		Moyle	
	Nedeham		Nedeham	
	Choke		Choke	
			Littleton K.S. 27.4.66[36]	
B.Ex. II	Clerk		Clerk	
III	Roucliffe		Roucliffe	
IV	Ingoldesby		Ingoldesby	
V	Durem		Durem	
K.S.	Littleton		Littleton	J.C.P. 27.4.66
	Yonge		Yonge	
	Nele		Nele	
	Laken	J.K.B. 4.6.65		
Sjt	Jenney		Jenney	
	Fairfax		Fairfax	
	Bryan		Bryan	
	Catesby		Catesby	
	Pigot		Pigot	
A.G.	Sotehill		Sotehill	
S.G.	Fowler		Fowler	

1 Jan. 1467		1 Jan. 1468
Markham		Markham
Danby		Danby
Illingworth		Illingworth
Yelverton		Yelverton
Bingham		Bingham
Billing		Billing
Laken		Laken
Arderne	d. 2.6.67[37]	Moyle
Danvers	d. 17.4.67[38]	Nedeham
Moyle		Choke
Nedeham		Littleton
Choke		Yonge
Littleton		
Yonge K.S. 4.11.67[39]		
Clerk		Clerk
Roucliffe		Roucliffe
Ingoldesby	replaced[40]	Wolseley
Wolseley 29.7.67[40]		
Durem		Durem
Yonge	J.C.P. 4.11.67	Nele
Nele		Fairfax
Fairfax 28.4.67[41]		Pigot
Pigot 4.11.67[42]		
Jenney		Jenney
Fairfax	K.S. 28.4.67	Bryan
Bryan		Catesby
Catesby		
Pigot	K.S. 4.11.67	
Sotehill		Sotehill
Fowler		Fowler

		1 Jan. 1469		1. Jan. 1470	
C.J.K.B.		Markham	removed[43]	Billing	[9.10.70][46]
		Billing J.K.B. 23.1.69[43]			
C.J.C.P.		Danby		Danby	[9.10.70][46]
C.B.Ex.		Illingworth		Illingworth	[9.10.70][46] replaced[47]
				Clerk II B.Ex. 14.10.70[47]	
J.K.B.		Yelverton		Yelverton	[9.10.70][46]
		Bingham		Bingham	[9.10.70][46]
		Billing	C.J.K.B. 23.1.69	Laken	[9.10.70][46]
		Laken		Nele	[9.10.70][46]
		Nele K.S. 18.4.69[44]			
J.C.P.		Moyle		Moyle	[9.10.70][46]
		Nedeham		Nedeham	[9.10.70][46]
		Choke		Choke	[9.10.70][46]
		Littleton		Littleton	[9.10.70][46]
		Yonge		Yonge	[9.10.70][46]
B.Ex.	II	Clerk		Clerk	[9.10.70][46] C.B.Ex. 14.10.70
				Roucliffe III B.Ex. 14.10.70[47]	
	III	Roucliffe		Roucliffe	[9.10.70][46] II B.Ex. 14.10.70
				Durem V B.Ex. 14.10.70[47]	
	IV	Wolseley		Wolseley	replaced
				Ingoldesby 14.6.70[48]	replaced
				Wolseley 14.10.70[47]	
	V	Durem		Durem	[9.10.70][46] III B.Ex. 14.10.70
K.S.		Nele	J.K.B. 18.4.69	Fairfax[49]	
		Fairfax		Pigot[49]	
		Pigot		Catesby[49]	
		Catesby 18.4.69[45]		*Bryan by 6.4.70*[50]	
Sjt.		Jenney		Jenney	
		Bryan		Bryan	K.S. by 6.4.70
		Catesby	K.S. 18.4.69		
A.G.		Sotehill		Sotehill	
S.G.		Fowler		Fowler	surr. 31.1.70[51]
				Page 31.1.70	

1 Jan. 1471		1 Jan. 1472	1 Jan. 1473
Billing	[17.6.71][52]	Billing	Billing
Danby	removed[53]	Bryan	Bryan
Bryan K.S. 29.5.71[53]			
Clerk	II B.Ex. 22.4.71	Urswick	Urswick
Urswick 22.5.71[54]			
Yelverton	retired[55]	Laken	Laken
Bingham	retired[56]	Nedeham	Nedeham
Laken	[17.6.71][52]		
Nele	J.C.P. 17.6.71		
Nedeham J.C.P. 17.6.71[52]			
Moyle	retired[57]	Choke	Choke
Nedeham	J.K.B. 17.6.71	Littleton	Littleton
Choke	[17.6.71][52]	Nele	Nele
Littleton	[17.6.71][52]		
Yonge	retired[58]		
Nele J.K.B. 17.6.71[52]			
Roucliffe	III B.Ex. 22.4.71	Clerk	Clerk
Clerk C.B.Ex. 22.4.71[52]			
Durem	retired[52]	Roucliffe	Roucliffe
Roucliffe III B.Ex. 22.4.71[52]			
Wolseley	not re-appointed[59]	[vacant]	[vacant]
[discontinued][60]			
Fairfax	resumed 11.4.71	Fairfax	Fairfax
Pigot	resumed 11.4.71	Pigot	Pigot
Catesby	resumed 11.4.71	Catesby	Catesby
Bryan	C.J.C.P. 29.5.71		
Jenney[61]		Yonge	Yonge
Yonge J.C.P. 5.4.71		Jenney	Jenney
Sotehill	surr. 11.7.71[62]	Hussey	Hussey
Hussey 16.6.71[63]			
Page	resumed 11.4.71	Page	Page

	1 Jan. 1474	1 Jan. 1475	
C.J.K.B.	Billing	Billing	
C.J.C.P.	Bryan	Bryan	
C.B.Ex.	Urswick	Urswick	
J.K.B.	Laken	Laken	d.6.10.75[64]
	Nedeham	Nedeham	
		Yonge S. 29.4.75[65]	
J.C.P.	Choke	Choke	
	Littleton	Littleton	
	Nele	Nele	
B.Ex. II	Clerk	Clerk	
III	Roucliffe	Roucliffe	
IV	[vacant]	[vacant]	
K.S.	Fairfax	Fairfax	
	Pigot	Pigot	
	Catesby	Catesby	
Sjt.	Yonge	Yonge	J.K.B. 29.4.75
	Jenney	Jenney	
A.G.	Hussey	Hussey	
S.G.	Page	Page	

1 Jan. 1476	1 Jan. 1477		1 Jan. 1478
Billing	Billing		Billing
Bryan	Bryan		Bryan
Urswick	Urswick		Urswick
Nedeham	Nedeham		Nedeham
Yonge	Yonge	d. 3.3.77[66]	Fairfax
	Fairfax K.S. 8.10.77[67]		
Choke	Choke		Choke
Littleton	Littleton		Littleton
Nele	Nele		Nele
Clerk	Clerk		Clerk
Roucliffe	Roucliffe		Roucliffe
[vacant]	[vacant]		*Wolseley 8.3.78*[68]
Fairfax	Fairfax	J.K.B. 8.10.77	Pigot
Pigot	Pigot		Catesby
Catesby	Catesby		*Hussey by Mich.1478*[69]
Jenney	Jenney		Jenney
			Hussey A.G. 9.6.78[70]
			K.S. by Mich. 1478
			Starky 9.6.78[70]
			Tremayle 9.6.78[70]
			Sulyard 9.6.78[70]
			Callow 9.6.78[70]
			Vavasour 9.6.78[70]
			Townshend 9.6.78[70]
			Brugge 9.6.78[70]
			Rogers 9.6.78[70]
			d. 5.10.78[71]
Hussey	Hussey		Hussey
			surr. May/June 1478[72]
			Huddersfield 17.7.78[72]
Page	Page		Page

		1 Jan. 1479		1 Jan. 1480	
C.J.K.B.		Billing		Billing	
C.J.C.P.		Bryan		Bryan	
C.B.Ex.		Urswick	d. 19.3.79[73]	Nottingham	
		Nottingham 3.4.79[73]			
J.K.B.		Nedeham		Nedeham	d. 25.5.80[74]
		Fairfax		Fairfax	
J.C.P.		Choke		Choke	
		Littleton		Littleton	
		Nele		Nele	
B.Ex.	II	Clerk		Clerk	
	III	Roucliffe		Roucliffe	
	IV	Wolseley		Wolseley	
K.S.		Pigot		Pigot	
		Catesby		Catesby	
		Hussey		Hussey	
Sjt.		Jenney		Jenney[75]	
		Starky		Starky	
		Tremayle		Tremayle	
		Sulyard		Sulyard[75]	
		Callow		Callow	
		Vavasour		Vavasour	
		Townshend		Townshend	
		Brugge		Brugge	
A.G.		Huddersfield		Huddersfield	
S.G.		Page		Page	

1 Jan. 1481		1. Jan. 1482
Billing	d. 5.5.81[76]	Hussey
Hussey K.S. 7.5.81[77]		
Bryan		Bryan
Nottingham		Nottingham
Fairfax		Fairfax
Jenney S. 14.5.81[78]		Jenney
Choke		Choke
Littleton	d. 23.8.81[79]	Nele
Nele		Catesby
Catesby K.S. 20.11.81[80]		
Clerk	deceased[81]	Whittington
Whittington 3.2.81[81]		
Roucliffe		Roucliffe
Wolseley		Wolseley
Pigot		Pigot
Catesby	J.C.P. 20.11.81	Townshend
Hussey	C.J.K.B. 7.5.81	Tremayle
Townshend 11.5.81[78]		
Tremayle 26.11.81[82]		
Jenney	J.K.B. 14.5.81	Starky
Starky		Sulyard
Tremayle	K.S. 26.11.81	Callow
Sulyard		Vavasour
Callow		Brugge
Vavasour		
Townshend	K.S. 11.5.81	
Brugge		
Huddersfield		Huddersfield
Page		Page

		1 Jan. 1483		1 Jan. 1484	
C.J.K.B		Hussey	[21.4.83][83] [26.6.83]	Hussey	
C.J.C.P.		Bryan	[26.6.83][84]	Bryan	
C.B.Ex.		Nottingham	[22.4.83][85] surr. 12.6.83[86]	Starky	
		Starky S. 15.6.83[87]	[26.6.83]		
J.K.B.		Fairfax	[21.4.83][87] [26.6.83]	Fairfax	
				Sulyard S. 22.10.84[94]	
		Jenney	[21.4.83][87] [26.6.83] d. 12.12.83[88]		
J.C.P.		Choke	[21.4.83][83] [26.6.83] d. 28.6.83[88]	Nele	
				Catesby	
		Nele	[21.4.83][83] [26.6.83]	Starky	
		Catesby	[21.4.83][83] [26.6.83]		
		Starky S. [26.8.83][89]			
B.Ex.	II	Whittington	[22.4.83][85] replaced[84]	Roucliffe	
		Roucliffe III B.Ex. 26.6.83[84]			
	III	Roucliffe	[22.4.83][85] II B.Ex. 26.6.83	Goldesborough	
		Goldesborough 26.6.83[84]			
	IV	Wolseley	[22.4.83][85] [26.6.83][84]	Wolseley	replaced[95]
				Holgrave 24.9.84[95]	
K.S.		Pigot	d. 13.6.83[88]	Townshend	
		Townshend	[27.6.83][84]	Tremayle	
		Tremayle	[14.6.83][87] [27.6.83]	Vavasour	
		Vavasour 15.6.83[87]	[27.6.83]		
Sjt.		Starky	C.B.Ex. 15.6.83 J.C.P. 26.6.83	Sulyard	J.K.B. 22.10.84
				Callow	
		Sulyard			
		Vavasour	K.S. 15.6.83		
		Brugge	d. June 1483[90]		
A.G.		Huddersfield	replaced[91]	Kidwelly	
		Kidwelly 28.5.83[92]			
S.G.		Page	replaced	Lynom	
		Lynom 26.8.83[93]			

1 Jan. 1485		1 Jan. 1486	
Hussey	[20.9.85][96]	Hussey	
Bryan	[20.9.85][97]	Bryan	
Starky	[20.9.85][98]	Starky	d. 27.7.86[109]
		Hody A.G. 29.10.86[110]	
Fairfax	[20.9.85][99]	Fairfax	
Sulyard	[20.9.85][96]	Sulyard	
Nele	[13.10.85][100]	Nele	d. 11.6.86[111]
Catesby	[20.9.85][101]	Catesby	
Starky	[20.9.85][98]	Starky	d. 27.7.86
Townshend K.S. 20.9.85[102]		Townshend	
		Haugh S. 10.12.86[112]	
Roucliffe	[24.9.85][103]	Roucliffe	
Goldesborough	[24.9.85][104]	Goldesborough	
Holgrave	[24.9.85][104]	Holgrave	
Townshend	J.C.P. 20.9.85[105]	Tremayle	
Tremayle	[12.11.85][106]	Vavasour	
Vavasour	[13.10.85][100]	*Fisher 30.6.86*[113]	
Callow		Callow	
		Danvers 4.7.86[114]	
		Jay 4.7.86[114]	
		Fisher 4.7.86[114]	
			K.S. 30.6.86
		Fineux 4.7.86[114]	
		Kebell 4.7.86[114]	
		Rede 4.7.86[114]	
		Haugh 4.7.86[114]	
			J.C.P. 10.12.86
		Wode 4.7.86[114]	
Kidwelly	replaced[107]	Hody	C.B.Ex. 29.10.86
Hody 20.9.85[100]		*Hobart 3.11.86*[115]	
Lynom	replaced	Dymmock	
Dymmock 15.11.85[108]			

		1 Jan. 1487		1 Jan. 1488	
C.J.K.B.		Hussey		Hussey	
C.J.C.P.		Bryan		Bryan	
C.B.Ex.		Hody		Hody	
J.K.B.		Fairfax		Fairfax	
		Sulyard		Sulyard	d. 18.3.88[119]
				Tremayle K.S. 16.6.88[120]	
J.C.P.		Catesby	d. 23.1.87[116]	Townshend	
		Townshend		Haugh	
		Haugh		*Danvers S. 5.2.88*[121]	
		Callow S. 31.1.87[117]	d. 29.7.87		
B.Ex.	II	Roucliffe		Roucliffe	retired[122]
				Goldesborough III B.Ex. 5.12.88[123]	
	III	Goldesborough		Goldesborough	II B.Ex. 5.12.88[123]
				Lathell 5.12.88[123]	
	IV	Holgrave	deceased[118]	[vacant]	
				Roche 5.12.88[123]	
K.S.		Tremayle		Tremayle	J.K.B. 16.7.88
		Vavasour		Vavasour	
				Fisher	
				Wode 16.6.88[124]	
Sjt.		Callow	J.C.P. 31.1.87	Danvers	J.C.P. 5.2.88
		Danvers		Jay	
				Fineux	
		Jay		Kebell	
		Fineux		Rede	
		Kebell		Wode	K.S. 16.6.88
		Rede			
		Wode			
A.G.		Hobart		Hobart	
S.G.		Dymmock		Dymmock	

1 Jan. 1489		1 Jan. 1490
Hussey		Hussey
Bryan		Bryan
Hody		Hody
Fairfax		Fairfax
Tremayle		Tremayle
Townshend		Townshend
Haugh	d. 14.3.89[125]	Danvers
Danvers		Vavasour
Vavasour K.S. 17.10.89[126]		
Goldesborough		Goldesborough
Lathell		Lathell
Roche		Roche
Vavasour	J.C.P. 17.10.89	Fisher
Fisher		Wode
Wode		Fineux
Fineux 14.8.89[127]		
Jay		Jay
Fineux	K.S. 14.8.89	Kebell
Kebell		Rede
Rede		
Hobart		Hobart
Dymmock		Dymmock

		1 Jan. 1491	1 Jan. 1492	1 Jan. 1493
C.J.K.B.		Hussey	Hussey	Hussey
C.J.C.P.		Bryan	Bryan	Bryan
C.B.Ex.		Hody	Hody	Hody
J.K.B.		Fairfax	Fairfax	Fairfax
		Tremayle	Tremayle	Tremayle
J.C.P		Townshend	Townshend	Townshend d. 9.11.93[128]
		Danvers	Danvers	Danvers
		Vavasour	Vavasour	Vavasour
B.Ex.	II	Goldesborough	Goldesborough	Goldesborough
	III	Lathell	Lathell	Lathell
	IV	Roche	Roche	Roche
K.S.		Fisher	Fisher	Fisher
		Wode	Wode	Wode
		Fineux	Fineux	Fineux
Sjt.		Jay	Jay	Jay
		Kebell	Kebell	Kebell
		Rede	Rede	Rede
A.G.		Hobart	Hobart	Hobart
S.G.		Dymmock	Dymmock	Dymmock

1 Jan. 1494		1 Jan. 1495	
Hussey		Hussey	d. 8.9.95[132]
		Fineux J.C.P.24.11..95[133]	
Bryan		Bryan	
Hody		Hody	
Fairfax		Fairfax	d. Mich.1495[134]
Tremayle		Tremayle	
		Rede K.S. 24.11.95[135]	
Danvers		Danvers	
Vavasour		Vavasour	
Fineux K.S. 11.2.94[129]		Fineux	C.J.K.B. 24.11.95
		Wode K.S. 24.11.95[136]	
Goldesborough		Goldesborough	
Lathell		Lathell	
Roche		Roche	
Fisher		Fisher	
Wode		Wode	J.C.P. 24.11.95
Fineux	J.C.P. 11.2.94	Rede	J.K.B. 24.11.95
Rede 8.4.94[130]		*Kebell 25.11.95*[137]	
		Mordaunt 25.11.95[138]	
Jay	d. 8.1.94[131]	Kebell	K.S. 25.11.95
Kebell		*Mordaunt 25.11.95*[139]	
Rede	K.S. 8.4.94		K.S. 25.11.95
		Oxenbridge 25.11.95[139]	
		Heigham 25.11.95[139]	
		Frowyk 25.11.95[139]	
		Constable 25.11.95[139]	
		Yaxley 25.11.95[139]	
		Coningsby 25.11.95[139]	
		Kingsmill 25.11.95[139]	
		Butler 25.11.95[139]	
Hobart		Hobart	
Dymmock		Dymmock	

	1 Jan. 1496	1 Jan. 1497
C.J.K.B.	Fineux	Fineux
C.J.C.P.	Bryan	Bryan
C.B.Ex.	Hody	Hody
J.K.B.	Tremayle Rede	Tremayle Rede
J.C.P.	Danvers Vavasour Wode	Danvers Vavasour Wode
B.Ex. II	Goldesborough	Goldesborough replaced[141] *Dymmock S.G. 2.5.97*[141]
III	Lathell	Lathell
IV	Roche	Roche
K.S.	Fisher Kebell Mordaunt	Fisher Kebell Mordaunt
Sjt.	Oxenbridge d.Nov./Dec.1496[140] Heigham Frowyk Constable Yaxley Coningsby Kingsmill Butler	Heigham Frowyk Constable Yaxley Coningsby Kingsmill Butler
A.G.	Hobart	Hobart
S.G.	Dymmock	Dymmock II B.Ex. 2.5.97 *Lucas*[142]

1 Jan. 1498	1 Jan. 1499	1 Jan. 1500	
Fineux	Fineux	Fineux	
Bryan	Bryan	Bryan	d. 31.8.00[143]
		Wode J.C.P.28.10.00[144]	
Hody	Hody	Hody	
Tremayle	Tremayle	Tremayle	
Rede	Rede	Rede	
Danvers	Danvers	Danvers	
Vavasour	Vavasour	Vavasour	
Wode	Wode	Wode	C.J.C.P. 28.10.00
Dymmock	Dymmock	Dymmock	
Lathell	Lathell	Lathell	
Roche	Roche	Roche	
Fisher	Fisher	Fisher	
Kebell	Kebell	Kebell	d.26.6.00[145]
Mordaunt	Mordaunt	Mordaunt	
		Coningsby 30.10.00[146]	
Heigham	Heigham	Heigham	d. 21.10.00[147]
Frowyk	Frowyk	Frowyk	
Constable	Constable	Constable	
Yaxley	Yaxley	Yaxley	
Coningsby	Coningsby	Coningsby	K.S. 30.10.00
Kingsmill	Kingsmill	Kingsmill	
Butler	Butler	Butler	
Hobart	Hobart	Hobart	
Lucas	Lucas	Lucas	

	1 Jan. 1501	1 Jan. 1502
C.J.K.B.	Fineux	Fineux
C.J.C.P.	Wode	Wode d. 31.8.02[153] *Frowyk K.S. 30.9.02*[154]
C.B.Ex.	Hody	Hody
J.K.B.	Tremayle Rede	Tremayle Rede
J.C.P.	Danvers Vavasour *Fisher K.S. 3.11.01*[148]	Danvers Vavasour Fisher
B.Ex. II	Dymmock deceased[149] *Westby 12.5.01*[149]	Westby
III	Lathell deceased[150] *Bolling 11.10.01*[150]	Bolling
IV	Roche	Roche
K.S.	Fisher J.C.P. 3.11.01 Mordaunt Coningsby *Frowyk by Mich. 1501*[151]	Mordaunt Coningsby Frowyk C.J.C.P. 30.9.02 *Kingsmill 7.11.02*[155]
Sjt.	Frowyk K.S. by Mich. 1501 Constable d. 22.11.01[152] Yaxley Kingsmill Butler	Yaxley Kingsmill K.S. 7.11.02 Butler
A.G.	Hobart	Hobart
S.G.	Lucas	Lucas

1 Jan. 1503	1 Jan. 1504	
Fineux	Fineux	
Frowyk	Frowyk	
Hody	Hody	
Tremayle	Tremayle	
Rede	Rede	
Danvers	Danvers	d. 19.4.04[157]
Vavasour	Vavasour	
Fisher	Fisher	
	Kingsmill K.S. 2.7.04[158]	
Westby	Westby	
Bolling	Bolling	
Roche	Roche	deceased[159]
	Allen 8.2.04[159]	
Mordaunt	Mordaunt	d.11.9.04[160]
Coningsby	Coningsby	
Kingsmill	Kingsmill	J.C.P. 2.7.04
	Brudenell 25.10.04[161]	
Yaxley	Yaxley	
Butler	Butler	
Brudenell 13.11.03[156]	Brudenell	K.S. 25.10.04
Grevill 13.11.03[156]	Grevill	
Marowe 13.11.03[156]	Marowe	
Adgore 13.11.03[156]	Adgore	d. 24/31.8.04[162]
More 13.11.03[156]	More	
Cutlerd 13.11.03[156]	Cutlerd	
Eliot 13.11.03[156]	Eliot	
Pollard 13.11.03[156]	Pollard	
Fairfax W. 13.11.03[156]	Fairfax W.	
Palmes G. 13.11.03[156]	Palmes G.	
Hobart	Hobart	
Lucas	Lucas	

		1 Jan. 1505		1 Jan. 1506	
C.J.K.B.		Fineux		Fineux	
C.J.C.P.		Frowyk		Frowyk	d. 7.10.06[166]
				Rede J.K.B. 26.11.06[167]	
C.B.Ex		Hody		Hody	
J.K.B.		Tremayle		Tremayle	
		Rede		Rede	C.J.C.P. 26.11.06
J.C.P.		Vavasour		Vavasour	d. 26.11.06[168]
		Fisher		Fisher	
		Kingsmill		Kingsmill	
B.Ex.	II	Westby		Westby	
	III	Bolling		Bolling	
	IV	Allen		Allen	
K.S.		Coningsby		Coningsby	
		Brudenell		Brudenell	
Sjt.		Yaxley	d. 20.7.05[163]	Butler	
		Butler		Grevill	
		Grevill		More	
		Marowe	d. 5.4.05[164]	Eliot	
		More		Pollard	
		Cutlerd	d. 12.10.05[165]	Fairfax W.	
		Eliot		Palmes G.	
		Pollard			
		Fairfax W.			
		Palmes G.			
A.G.		Hobart		Hobart	
S.G.		Lucas		Lucas	

1 Jan. 1507		1 Jan. 1508	
Fineux		Fineux	
Rede		Rede	
Hody		Hody	
Tremayle		Tremayle	d. 10. 9.08[172]
Brudenell K.S. 28.4.07[169]		Brudenell	
Fisher		Fisher	
Kingsmill		Kingsmill	
		Butler S. 26.4.08[173]	
Westby		Westby	
Bolling		Bolling	
Allen		Allen	
Coningsby		Coningsby	
Brudenell	J.K.B. 28.4.07	Eliot	
Eliot 9.7.07[170]		Pollard	
Pollard 9.7.07[170]			
Butler		Butler	J.C.P. 26.4.08
Grevill		Grevill	
More		More	
Eliot	K.S. 9.7.07	Fairfax W.	
Pollard	K.S. 9.7.07	Palmes G.	
Fairfax W.			
Palmes G.			
Hobart	replaced[171]	Erneley	
Erneley 12.7.07[171]			
Lucas		Lucas	

		1 Jan. 1509		1 Jan. 1510	
C.J.K.B.		Fineux	[25.4.09][174]	Fineux	
C.J.C.P.		Rede	[25.4.09][175]	Rede	
C.B.Ex.		Hody	[25.4.09][176]	Hody	
J.K.B.		Brudenell	[25.4.09][177]	Brudenell	
		Coningsby K.S. 21.5.09[178]		Coningsby	
J.C.P.		Fisher	[25.4.09][179]	Fisher	d. 2.5.10[189]
		Kingsmill	[?25.4.09][180] d. 11.5.09	Butler	
		Butler	[25.4.09][181]	Grevill	
		Grevill S. 21.5.09[182]		*Fairfax S. 26.6.10*[190]	
B.Ex.	II	Westby	[26.4.09][183]	Westby	
	III	Bolling	[26.4.09][184]	Bolling	
	IV	Allen	[25.4.09][185]	Allen	
K.S.		Coningsby	J.K.B. 21.5.09	Eliot	
		Eliot	[28.4.09][186]	Pollard	
		Pollard	[28.4.09][186]		
Sjt.		Grevill	J.C.P. 21.5.09	More	
		More		Fairfax W.	J.C.P. 26.6.10
		Fairfax W.		Palmes G.	
		Palmes G.		*Newport 18.11.10*[191]	
				Newdigate 18.11.10[191]	
				Fitzherbert 18.11.10[191]	
				Brook J. 18.11.10[191]	
				Pigot 18.11.10[191]	
				Caryll 18.11.10[191]	
				Brook R. 18.11.10[191]	
				Palmes B. 18.11.10[191]	
				Rowe 18.11.10[191]	
A.G.		Erneley	[28.4.09][187]	Erneley	
S.G.		Lucas	replaced[188]	Port	
		Port 2.6.09[188]			

NOTES TO APPENDIX E

1. Early Feb. 1461 joined the Lancastrian forces; not reappointed on Edward IV's accession, 4 Mar.; fled after the battle of Towton, 29 Mar. and was attainted 21 Dec.: Fortescue, *De Laudibus*, lxvi.
2. *Cal. Patent Rolls, 1461–7*, 14. J.K.B. since 6 Feb. 1444: *ibid., 1441–6*, 232.
3. Prisot was alive on 8 Dec. 1460 and dead by 10 Feb. 1462, and probably before patents to judges were issued by Edward IV: *ibid., 1452–61*, 653, cf. 634; *Cal. Close Rolls, 1461–8*, 96. Thomas Jakes noted that the post of C.J. was vacant for Easter term 1461: IND 17180 f. 5.
4. *Cal. Patent Rolls, 1461–7*, 7.
5. E159/238 E 1; *Cal. Patent Rolls, 1461–7*, 128; in post since 2 May 1448: *ibid., 1446–52*, 180.
6. *ibid., 1461–7*, 14; in post since 1 Jul. 1443: E356/20 m. 7.
7. *Cal. Patent Rolls, 1461–7*, 14; in post since 5 May 1445: *ibid., 1441–6*, 343.
8. *ibid., 1461–7*, 14; in post since 9 Oct. 1444: E356/20 m. 1.
9. *Cal. Patent Rolls, 1461–67*, p. 119; in post since 7 Jun. 1448, jointly with the post of C.B.Ex., but not in receipt of wages: *ibid., 1446–52*, p.184; E356/20 mm. 1–9; E364/95 m.3.
10. E364/95 m.3; in post since 4 Jul.1449: E356/20 m.1.
11. *Cal. Patent Rolls, 1461–7*, 14; in post since 14 Aug. 1450: *ibid., 1446–52*, 333.
12. *ibid., 1461–7*, 14; in post since 9 Jul. 1454: *ibid., 1452–61*, 158.
13. *ibid., 1461–7*, 14; in post since 9 May 1457: *ibid., 1452–61*, p.354.
14. *ibid., 1461–7*, 98.
15. E159/238 E 1; *Cal. Patent Rolls, 1467–77*, 51; in post since 10 Oct. 1460: *ibid., 1452–61*, 628.
16. E159/238 E 1; in post since 30 Nov. 1452: *Cal. Patent Rolls, 1452–61*, 246.
17. E159/238 E 1; in post by 20 Oct. 1459 following reversionary grant 28 Jun. 1453: *Cal. Patent Rolls, 1452–61*, 88, 556.
18. E159/238 E 1; in post by 20 Oct. 1459: *Cal. Patent Rolls, 1452–61*, 556; called fifth baron in Easter 9 Edward IV: E405/50 m. 3.
19. E364/95 m. 3v; in post since 7 Jul. 1453: E356/20 m. 10v.
20. E364/95 m. 3; in post since 13 May 1455: *Cal. Patent Rolls, 1452–61*, 235.
21. E364/95 m. 3; in post since 21 Apr. 1458: *Cal. Patent Rolls, 1452–61*, 425.
22. Created 2 Jul. 1453: *Cal. Close Rolls, 1447–54*, 381. Of the eight serjeants called on that occasion, Boeff, Hyndestone and Wangford were dead; for Billing, Choke, Littleton and Nedeham, see above.
23. *Cal. Patent Rolls, 1461–7*, 1; in post since 30 Apr. 1452: *ibid., 1446–52*, 556.
24. *ibid., 1461–7*, 6. For Nottingham subsequently, see below, n. 73.
25. *ibid., 1461–7*, 54; the first recorded appointment to the office.
26. E159/239 M1; *Cal. Patent Rolls, 1461–7*, 198; Arderne remained J.C.P. and was thereafter paid: E356/21 m. 4.
27. *Cal. Patent Rolls, 1461–7*, 214, vice John Holme.
28. *ibid., 1461–7*, 300.
29. Created 7 Nov. 1463: C54/315 m. 10 (*Cal. Close Rolls, 1461–8*, 172–3).
30. *Cal. Patent Rolls, 1461–7*, 336.
31. *ibid., 1461–7*, 387.
32. Described as K.S., 23 Nov. 1464: *ibid., 1461–7*, 389; E159/254 Communia M9, but no payment traced in E356/21 or mention in E159/253 Brevia Pas. m. 2.
33. *Wills [etc.] of Barwick in Elmet*, ed. G.D. Lumb (Leeds, 1908), 4.
34. *Cal. Patent Rolls, 1461–7*, 442.
35. E356/21 m. 9v.

36. *Cal. Patent Rolls, 1461–7*, 515.
37. Brass at Latton, Essex; paid to Easter 1467: E356/21 m. 9v.
38. E159/250 Brevia Mich.m. 12.
39. *Cal. Close Rolls, 1468–76*, 586; *Cal.Patent Rolls, 1467–77*, 59.
40. *ibid., 1467–77*, 31, vice Ingoldesby; described as 'fourth baron'.
41. *ibid., 1467–77*, 51.
42. *ibid., 1467–77*, 38.
43. *ibid., 1467–77*, 120. Markham was dismissed 'shortly before': C. Ross, *Edward IV* (1974), 100; he was paid to Michaelmas 1468: E356/21 m. 10v.
44. E356/21 m. 10v.
45. *Cal. Patent Rolls, 1467–77*, 193.
46. *ibid., 1467–77*, 229. Illingworth died 26 Apr. 1476: C140/56/38.
47. E159/247 MI.
48. *Cal. Patent Rolls, 1467–77*, 211; vice Wolseley, who was, nevertheless described as 'baron of the exchequer' on 16 Mar. 1471: *Cal. Close Rolls, 1468–76*, 666.
49. The position of the king's serjeants during the Readeption is not clear. No new patents are known and Fairfax, Pigot, Catesby and Bryan were paid by Edward IV for the year to 6 Apr. 1471, presumably on the argument that their retainer had continued: E364/105 m. For.cd.
50. E364/105 m. For.cd.; cf. E159/249 Brevia Hil. m. 15.
51. E159/248 T. 2d.; *Cal. Patent Rolls, 1467–77*, 180.
52. *ibid., 1467–77*, 258. Durem's will as 'late B.Ex.' is dated 9 Mar., proved 18 Apr. 1474: PROB11/6 f. 100.
53. *Cal. Patent Rolls, 1467–77*, 258; Jakes noted that Danby was 'removed' by Edward IV: IND 17180 f. 5.
54. *Cal. Patent Rolls, 1467–77*, 259.
55. Not reappointed by Edward IV; paid to 6 Apr. 1471: E364/107 m. For.c.d. J.P.Norfolk to 30 Jun. 1476, described on his tomb as 'late J.K.B.': *Cal. Patent Rolls, 1467–77*, 622; Weever, *Funeral Monuments*, 821.
56. Not reappointed by Edward IV; paid to 6 Apr. 1471: E364/107 m. For.cd. Died 22 May, 1476: H. Druitt, *A Manual of Costume, as Illustrated by Monumental Brasses* (1906), 228.
57. No reappointment known. He was paid to 6 Apr. 1461: E364/107 m. For.cd. but on 10 Dec. 1471 as J.C.P. quitclaimed all actions against the king, presumably for arrears to pay which frequently occur in E356/20 and 21: *Cal. Close Rolls, 1468–76*, 829. Still alive 25 Jun. 1472; will proved 31 Jul. 1480: *ibid., 1468–76*, 911; *Testamenta Vetusta*, 349.
58. Not reappointed by Edward IV; paid to 6 Apr. 1471: E364/107 m. For.cd.; called 'late J.C.P.' in 1473: *Rot. Parl.*, vi. 82; appointed J.K.B. in 1475: see below, n. 65.
59. Not reappointed; referred to as 'late B.Ex.' in 1473 and 1476: *Cal. Patent Rolls, 1467–77*, 383, 577. Apparently the post was left vacant.
60. Durem was not replaced on his promotion to third baron. Apparently the post of fifth baron was discontinued.
61. Described as K.S., 14 Feb. 1471, but not paid with the K.S.: *ibid., 1467–77*, 250; E405/58 m. 2v, 59 m. 4v, 60 m. 7v, 66 m. 3.
62. *Cal. Patent Rolls, 1461–7*, 6.
63. *ibid., 1467–77*, 292.
64. Wedgwood, *Biographies*.
65. *Cal. Patent Rolls, 1467–77*, 515.
66. C140/61/26.
67. C54/334 m.12 (*Cal. Close Rolls, 1476–85*, 875).
68. *Cal. Patent Rolls, 1476–85*, 94.

69. Probably appointed immediately on call to the coif; paid for the half-year to Mich. 1478: E405/66 m. IV.
70. C54/329 m. 3 (*Cal. Close Rolls, 1476–85*, 177).
71. C140/65/7 – the Somerset return gives the date of death as 3 Oct.
72. E159/255 T 8v, on surrender of William Hussey. Huddersfield had been appointed in reversion 22 May: *Cal. Patent Rolls, 1476–85*, 37; for new patent issued 7 Jul. 1483, see Spelman, *Reports*, ii. *390*.
73. Urswick: C140/73/75. Nottingham – *Cal. Patent Rolls, 1476–85*, 154; formerly A.G., see above, n. 23.
74. Wedgwood, *Biographies*.
75. Paid as king's serjeant from 6 Apr. 1480 in E364/115 For.cd, 364/116 For.B, but described as justice of assize only in E356/22 mm. 38, 38v, 39v.
76. Wedgwood, *Biographies*; paid for the first half of 1480–1 as 'late C.J.K.B.', so probably retired after Hilary term 1481: E356/22 m. 38.
77. E356/22 m. 38.
78. *Cal. Patent Rolls, 1476–85*, 270.
79. E356/22 m. 38.
80. *Cal. Patent Rolls, 1476–85*, 288.
81. *ibid., 1476–85*, 230. Clerk's will is dated 10 Dec. 1480, proved 10 Mar. 1481: PROB11/7 ff. 15v., 16.
82. *Cal. Patent Rolls, 1476–85*, 285.
83. *ibid., 1476–85*, 350, 360.
84. *ibid., 1476–85*, 360.
85. E159/260 E 8. Whittington died 12 – 25 April 1491: *Cal. Fine Rolls, 1485–1509*, 331; PROB11/8 f. 357v.
86. *Cal. Close Rolls, 1476–85*, 1043.
87. *ibid., 1476–85*, 351, 360.
88. E356/22 m. 40.
89. *Cal. Patent Rolls, 1476–85*, 403.
90. Paid as justice of assize to 31 Mar. 1483: E356/22 m. 39v; J.P. for western assize circuit counties until 3 Jun. 1483; replaced by Callow 26 Jun. 1483: *Cal. Patent Rolls, 1476–85*, 556, 558, 559, 571, 572.
91. Not reappointed under Edward V; died 23 Sept. 1499: *Cal. inquisitions post mortem*, ii. 264.
92. *Cal. Patent Rolls, 1476–85*, 349; E356/22 m. 40.
93. Page – no reappointment by Edward V known; possibly retired for ill-health as he made his will 22 Aug. 1483 (though makes no mention of sickness): PROB11/10 f. 92v. Alive 10 Nov. 1490: *Cal. Patent Rolls, 1494–1509*, 338; will proved 8 Oct. 1493. Lynom – *ibid., 1476–85*, 460.
94. *ibid., 1476–85*, 514.
95. *ibid., 1476–85*, 473. Wolseley lived until 25 Mar. 1504: *Cal. inquisitions post mortem*, ii. 840; cf. Wedgwood, *Biographies*.
96. *Cal. Patent Rolls, 1485–94*, 13.
97. *ibid., 1485–94*, 7.
98. *ibid., 1485–94*, 9.
99. *Materials for the Reign of Henry VII*, i. 13, 14.
100. *Cal. Patent Rolls, 1485–94*, 20.
101. *ibid., 1485–94*, 33.
102. *ibid., 1485–94*, 18, but see below, n.105.
103. *ibid., 1485–94*, 13, 19.
104. *ibid., 1485–94*, 19.
105. Townshend paid as K.S. to first half of the year Michaelmas–Michaelmas 1484–5: E356/22 m. 40.

106. *ibid.*, *1485–94*, 30.
107. Not reappointed by Henry VII; died 11 Mar. 1505: *Cal. inquisitions post mortem*, iii. 112 *etc.*
108. *Cal. Patent Rolls, 1485–94*, 35. Lynom died *c.* 1518: *L. and P.*, ii. 4349.
109. *Cal. inquisitions post mortem*, i. 415.
110. *Cal. Patent Rolls, 1485–94*, 139.
111. *Y.B.* Trin. 1 Hen.VII, p.1 f. 25.
112. E356/23 m. 42; Spelman, *Reports*, ii. *369*.
113. *Cal. Patent Rolls, 1485–94*, 118, as serjeant elect.
114. C54/346 m. 7 (*Cal. Close Rolls, 1485–1500*, 11).
115. *Cal. Patent Rolls, 1485–94*, 138.
116. *Cal. inquisitions post mortem*, i. 355.
117. *Materials for the Reign of Henry VII*, ii. 114; *Cal.inquisitions post mortem*, i. 433.
118. Died 11 Dec. 1486/7 Sept. 1487. *Cal. Patent Rolls, 1485–94*, 162, 163; PROB11/8 f. 29.
119. *Cal. inquisitions post mortem*, i. 415.
120. E356/23 m. 42v; Spelman, *Reports*, ii. *357*.
121. *Cal. Patent Rolls, 1485–94*, 224.
122. Roucliffe retired; he died in 1495: *Testamenta Eboracensia*, iv. 102.
123. *Cal. Patent Rolls, 1485–94*, 258.
124. E356/23 m. 42v; Spelman, *Reports*, ii. *386*; *Materials for the Reign of Henry VII*, i. 478, where the date is wrongly given as 30 Jun. 1486.
125. E356/23 m. 43; Spelman, *Reports*, ii. *369*.
126.. E356/23 m. 43v; Spelman, *Reports*, ii. *370*. It is probable that Vavasour was originally appointed on 14 Aug.: Dugdale, *Origines*, 74; cf. the patent of John Fineux, his replacement as K.S.
127. *Cal. Patent Rolls, 1485–94*, 291, 'surrendered because otherwise in the 4th year' [*sic*]; *Materials for the Reign of Henry VII*, ii. 475. Fineux was granted a crown annuity 19 Aug. 1486 (retrospective to Easter): E356/22 m. 40v.
128. *Cal.inquisitions post mortem*, i. 1028.
129. *Cal. Patent Rolls, 1485–94*, 459.
130. *ibid.*, *1485–94*, 461.
131. *Cal. inquisitions post mortem*, iii. 689.
132. *ibid.*, i. 1209.
133. *Cal. Patent Rolls, 1494–1509*, 80.
134. Fairfax was summoned to parliament 15 Sept. 1495, commissioned J.P. 14 Nov. 1495: *Cal. Close Rolls, 1485–1500*, 845; *Cal. Patent Rolls, 1494–1509*, 646. He was replaced by Rede 24 Nov. A tradition, recorded by the antiquary, Henry Spelman (1626), has it that he was chosen C.J. after Hussey's death but died before installation: *Analecta Eboracensia*, ed. T. Widdrington (1897), but he did not serve as justice of assize Lammas 1495.
135. Spelman, *Reports*, ii. *358*.
136. *Cal. Patent Rolls, 1494–1509*, 43.
137. See above, p. 77 n. 46.
138. *Cal. Patent Rolls, 1494–1509*, 45.
139. C54/356 m. 7 (*Cal. Close Rolls, 1485–1500*, 875).
140. Died between making his will, 12 Nov. 1496 and the next commission of the peace for Sussex, 12 Dec. 1496: PROB11/11 f. 43v; *Cal. Patent Rolls*, 1494–1500, 662.
141. *ibid.*, *1494–1509*, 106. *Cal. inquisitions post mortem*, ii. 69 implies death before 6 Nov. 1496, but cf. *ibid.*, iii. 85.
142. Lucas was in office by 1503 and probably succeeded Dymmock immediately: *Rot.Parl.*, vi. 536.
143. Spelman, *Reports*, ii. *370*.

144. *Cal. Patent Rolls, 1494–1509*, 214.
145. *Cal. inquisitions post mortem*, ii. 497.
146. *Cal. Patent Rolls, 1494–1509*, 222.
147. *Visitation of Suffolk, 1561*, ed. J.J. Howard (Lowestoft, 1866, and London, 1871), 214. The probate registry copy of Heigham's will, dated 3 Mar. 1500, gives the date of probate as 22 May 1500, but this is probably an error for 1501. Heigham was named in deeds dated 13 Apr. and 12 Jul. 1500 but he was omitted from the Essex commission of the peace on 18 Nov.: *Cal. Close Rolls, 1485–1500*, 1226; *Cal. Patent Rolls, 1494–1509*, 613, 638.
148. *ibid., 1494–1509*, 253.
149. *ibid., 1494–1509*, 237. Dymmock was alive 25 May 1500, but dead by 13 Feb. 1501 and possibly by 19 Nov. 1500 when omitted from the commission of the peace for Lindsey: *ibid., 1494–1509*, 232, 649; *Cal. Close Rolls, 1485–1500*, 1165.
150. *Cal. Patent Rolls, 1494–1509*, 269. Lathell's will is dated 12 Aug. 1500, 16 Hen.VII (*sic*], proved 5 Nov. 1501: PROB11/13 f. 112v.
151. Spelman, *Reports*, ii. *386*.
152. *Cal. inquisitions post mortem*, ii. 567.
153. Spelman, *Reports*, ii. *370*.
154. *Cal. Patent Rolls, 1494–1509*, 299.
155. Spelman, *Reports*, ii. *387*.
156. c82/252. Guy Palmes was called in place of Edmund Dudley who was excused 4 Oct. 1503: Putnam, *Early Treatises*, 135; Dudley, *Tree of Commonwealth*, 9; *Minutes of Parliament*, i. 7.
157. Spelman, *Reports*, ii. *370*; MacNamara, *Danvers Family*.
158. *Cal. Patent Rolls, 1494–1509*, 354.
159. *ibid., 494–1509*, 339. Roche's will is dated 6 Dec. 1503, proved 28 Jan. 1504: PROB11/14 f. 3v.
160. *Cal. inquisitions post mortem*, iii. 875.
161. *Cal. Patent Rolls, 1494–1509*, 399.
162. 'August': *Cal. inquisitions post mortem*, iii. 357. Will dated 24 Aug. 1504: PROB11/14 f. 159v.
163. *Cal. inquisitions post mortem*, iii. 3.
164. *ibid.*, iii. 141; *ibid.*, iii. 825 gives 2 Apr. 1505.
165. *ibid.*, iii. 311.
166. *ibid.*, iii. 195.
167. IND 17180 f. 5; Spelman, *Reports*, ii. *371*.
168. *Cal. inquisitions post mortem*, iii. 275–6; the Vavasour family, however, kept his obit on 21 Nov.: *Testamenta Eboracensia*, iv. 91.
169. Spelman, *Reports*, ii. *358*.
170. *Cal. Patent Rolls, 1494–1509*, 539.
171. *ibid., 1494–1509*, 544. Hobart died 24 Feb. 1517: Spelman, *Reports*, ii. *391*.
172. *Cal. inquisitions post mortem*, iii. 527.
173. *Cal. Patent Rolls, 1494–1509*, 563.
174. Spelman, *Reports*, ii. *358*.
175. *L. and P.*, i. 11(4).
176. Spelman, *Reports*, ii. *382*.
177. *ibid.*, ii. *358*.
178. *L. and P.*, i. 54(50).
179. Spelman, *Reports*, ii. *370*.
180 Paid to 11 May 1509: *ibid.*, ii. *371*.
181. *L. and P.*, i. 11(5).
182. *ibid.*, i. 54(50).
183. *ibid.*, i. 11(8); Spelman, *Reports*, ii. *382*.

184. *L. and P.*, i. 11(7).
185. *ibid.*, i. 11(6).
186. *ibid.*, i. 11(9); Spelman, *Reports*, ii. *387*.
187. *ibid.*, i. 11(9); Spelman, *Reports*, ii. *391*.
188. *L. and P.*, i. 94(15). Lucas died 7 July 1531: Spelman, *Reports*, ii. 392.
189. E150/6/9; E150/64/3; for alternatives of 31 Apr. and 1 May see Spelman, *Reports*, ii. *371*.
190. *L. and P.*, i. 519(55).
191. *The Great Chronicle of London*, ed. A.H. Thomas and I.D. Thornley (1938), 368.

INDEX